Your fully reengineerec

The all-new learning format of your Microsoft study guide de
tools to help prepare you for the job. Features include:

ɔ.

study

- Relevant exam objectives highlighted at the start of each chapter
- "Why This Chapter Matters" and "Real World" sidebars on how you can apply learning concepts to the job
- Case scenario exercises where you work through a multi-step, real-world solution
- Troubleshooting labs on a simulated operating system for practical field experience

Lesson 2: Creating Multiple User Objects

There occasionally situations that require you to create multiple user objects quickly, such as a new class of incoming students at a school, or a group of new hires at an organization. In these situations you need to know how to effectively facilitate or automate user object creation so that you are not approaching the task on an account-by-account basis. In Lesson 1, you learned how to create and manage user objects with Active Directory Users and Computers. This lesson will extend those concepts, skills, and tools to include user object creation through template objects, imported objects, and command line scripting of objects.

After this lesson, you will be able to

- Create and utilize user object templates
- Import user objects from comma delimited files
- Leverage new command-line tools to create and manage user objects

Estimated lesson time: 15 minutes

Creating and Using User Templates

It is common for objects to share similar properties. For example, all sales representatives may belong to the same security groups, are allowed to log on to the network during the same hours, and have home folders and roaming profiles on the same server. In such cases, it is helpful when creating a user object for that object to be prepopulated with common properties. This can be accomplished by creating a generic user object—often called a *template*—and then copying that object to create new users.

To generate a user template, create a user and populate its properties. Put the user into appropriate groups.

Security Alert Be certain to *disable* the user, since it is just a template, to ensure that the account is not used for access to network resources.

To create a new user based on the template, select the template and choose Copy from the Action menu. You will be prompted for properties similar to those when you create a new user: first and last name, initials, logon names, password, and account options. When the object is created, you will find that properties are copied from the template based on the following property-page based description:

- **General** No properties copied.
- **Address** All properties except Street address are copied.

- "Off the Record" sidebars bridge the gap between how things *should* work and how they *do* work
- Security Alerts and Planning Tips you can apply in the real world
- Exam highlights—key points and terms you should know
- Exam tips written by industry insiders

3 User Accounts

Exam Objectives in this Chapter:

- Create and manage user accounts.
  - Create and modify user accounts by using the Active Directory Users and Computers MMC snap-in.
  - Create and modify user accounts by using automation.
  - Import user accounts.
- Manage local, roaming, and mandatory user profiles.
- Troubleshoot user accounts.
  - Diagnose and resolve account lockouts.
  - Diagnose and resolve issues related to user account properties.
- Troubleshoot user authentication issues.

Why This Chapter Matters

Before individuals in your enterprise can begin to access resources they require, you must enable authentication of those individuals. Of course, the primary component of that authentication is the user's identity, maintained as an account in Active Directory. In this chapter, you will review and enhance your knowledge related to the creation, maintenance, and troubleshooting of user accounts and authentication.

Each enterprise, and each day, brings with it a unique set of challenges related to user management. The properties you configure for a standard user account are likely to be different from those you apply to the account of a Help Desk team member, which are different still from those configured on the built-in Administrator account. Skills that are effective to create or modify a single user account become clumsy and inefficient when you are working with masses of accounts, for example when managing the accounts for a number of new hires.

To effectively address a diverse sampling of account management scenarios, we will examine a variety of user management skills and tools including the Active Directory Users & Computers snap-in and powerful command-line utilities.

Note Be sure to configure share permissions allowing Everyone Full Control. The Windows Server 2003 default share permissions allow Read, which is not sufficient for a roaming profile share.

On the Profile tab of the user's Properties dialog box, type the Profile Path in the format: **\\\\<server >\\<share>\\%*username*%**. The *%username%* variable will automatically be replaced with the user's logon name.

It's that simple. The next time the user logs on to their system, the system will identify the roaming profile location.

Exam Tip Roaming user profiles are nothing more than a shared folder and a path to the user's profile folder, within that share, entered into the user object's profile path property. Roaming profiles are not, in any way, a property of a computer object.

When the user logs *off* of their system, it will upload the profile to the profile server. The user can now log on to their system, or any other system in the domain, and the documents and settings that are part of the RUP will be applied.

Note Windows Server 2003 introduces a new policy: Only allow local user profiles. This policy, linked to an OU containing computer accounts, will prevent roaming profiles from being used on those computers. Users will, instead, maintain local profiles.

When a user with an RUP logs on to a new system for the first time, the system does not copy its Default User profile. Instead, it downloads the RUP from the network location. When a user logs off, or when a user logs on to a system on which they've worked before, the system copies only files that have changed.

Real World **Roaming Profile Synchronization**

Unlike previous versions of Microsoft Windows, Windows 2000, Windows XP, and Windows Server 2003 do not upload and download the entire user profile at logoff and logon. Instead, the user profile is *synchronized*. Only files that have changed are transferred between the local system and the network RUP folder. This means that logon and logoff with RUPs are significantly faster than with earlier Windows systems. Organizations that have not implemented RUPs for fear of their impact on logon and network traffic should reevaluate their configuration in this light.

MCSA/MCSE Self-Paced Training Kit (Exam 70-299): Implementing and Administering Security in a Microsoft Windows Server 2003 Network

Objective	Pages
Implementing, Managing, and Troubleshooting Security Policies	
Plan security templates based on computer role. Computer roles include computer running Microsoft SQL Server, computer running Microsoft Exchange Server, domain controller, Internet Authentication Service (IAS) server, and Internet Information Services (IIS) server.	3-4 to 3-6, 4-15 to 4-54
Configure security templates.	3-4 to 3-17
■ Configure registry and file system permissions.	3-9 to 3-12
■ Configure account policies.	3-9 to 3-12
■ Configure .pol files.	3-9 to 3-12
■ Configure audit policies.	3-9 to 3-12
■ Configure user rights assignment.	3-9 to 3-12
■ Configure security options.	3-9 to 3-12
■ Configure system services.	3-9 to 3-12
■ Configure restricted groups.	3-9 to 3-12
■ Configure event logs.	3-9 to 3-12
Deploy security templates.	3-18 to 3-30
■ Plan the deployment of security templates.	3-18 to 3-26
■ Deploy security templates by using Active Directory-based Group Policy objects (GPOs).	3-18 to 3-24
■ Deploy security templates by using command-line tools and scripting.	3-25 to 3-26
Troubleshoot security template problems.	3-31 to 3-45
■ Troubleshoot security templates in a mixed operating system environment.	3-43 to 3-43
■ Troubleshoot security policy inheritance.	3-31 to 3-37
■ Troubleshoot removal of security template settings.	3-31 to 3-37
Configure additional security based on computer roles. Server computer roles include computer running SQL Server, computer running Exchange Server, domain controller, Internet Authentication Service (IAS) server, and Internet Information Services (IIS) server. Client computer roles include desktop, portable, and kiosk.	4-3 to 4-54
■ Plan and configure security settings.	4-3 to 4-14, 4-21 to 4-49
■ Plan network zones for computer roles.	4-16 to 4-20
■ Plan and configure software restriction policies.	4-5 to 4-6, 4-10 to 4-12
■ Plan security for infrastructure services. Services include Dynamic Host Configuration Protocol (DHCP) and Domain Name System (DNS).	4-21 to 4-28
■ Plan and configure auditing and logging for a computer role. Considerations include Microsoft Windows Events, Internet Information Services (IIS), firewall log files, Netlog, and RAS log files.	4-31 to 4-49
■ Analyze security configuration. Tools include Microsoft Baseline Security Analyzer (MBSA), the MBSA command-line tool, and Security Configuration and Analysis.	4-55 to 4-61
Implementing, Managing, and Troubleshooting Update Management Infrastructure	
Plan IPSec deployment.	8-3 to 8-23
■ Decide which IPSec mode to use.	8-3 to 8-13
■ Plan authentication methods for IPSec.	8-17 to 8-20
■ Test the functionality of existing applications and services.	8-21 to 8-22
Configure IPSec policies to secure communication between networks and hosts. Hosts include domain controllers, Internet Web servers, databases, e-mail servers, and client computers.	8-24 to 8-39
■ Configure IPSec authentication.	8-24 to 8-32
■ Configure appropriate encryption levels. Considerations include the selection of perfect forward secrecy (PFS) and key lifetimes.	8-24 to 8-32
■ Configure the appropriate IPSec protocol. Protocols include Authentication Header (AH) and Encapsulating Security Payload (ESP).	8-24 to 8-32
■ Configure IPSec inbound and outbound filters and filter actions.	8-24 to 8-27
Deploy and manage IPSec policies.	9-3 to 9-39
■ Deploy IPSec policies by using Local policy objects or Group Policy objects (GPOs).	9-3 to 9-5, 9-12 to 9-14
■ Deploy IPSec policies by using commands and scripts. Tools include IPSecPol and NetSh.	9-6 to 9-9, 9-12 to 9-14
■ Deploy IPSec certificates. Considerations include deployment of certificates and renewing certificates on managed and unmanaged client computers.	9-10 to 9-14

Objective	Pages
Implementing, Managing, and Troubleshooting Update Management Infrastructure *(continued)*	
Troubleshoot IPSec.	9-18 to 9-46
■ Monitor IPSec policies by using IP Security Monitor.	9-18 to 9-22
■ Configure IPSec logging. Considerations include Oakley logs and IPSec driver logging.	9-28 to 9-29
■ Troubleshoot IPSec across networks. Considerations include network address translation, port filters, protocol filters, firewalls, and routers.	9-43
■ Troubleshoot IPSec certificates. Considerations include enterprise trust policies and certificate revocation list (CRL) checking.	9-42
Plan and implement security for wireless networks.	10-3 to 10-43
■ Plan the authentication methods for a wireless network.	10-4 to 10-12
■ Plan the encryption methods for a wireless network.	10-4 to 10-12
■ Plan wireless access policies.	10-17 to 10-18
■ Configure wireless encryption.	10-20 to 10-33
■ Install and configure wireless support for client computers.	10-24 to 10-28
Deploy, manage, and configure Secure Sockets Layer (SSL) certificates, including uses for HTTPS, LDAPS, and wireless networks. Considerations include renewing certificates and obtaining self-issued certificates instead of publicly issued certificates.	11-3 to 11-41
■ Obtain self-issued certificates and publicly issued certificates.	11-5
■ Install certificates for SSL.	11-10 to 11-23, 11-26 to 11-34
■ Renew certificates.	11-6
■ Configure SSL to secure communication channels. Communication channels include client computer to Web server, Web server to computer running SQL Server, client computer to Active Directory domain controller, and e-mail server to client computer.	11-10 to 11-23, 11-26 to 11-34
Configure security for remote access users.	12-17 to 12-41
■ Configure authentication for secure remote access. Authentication types include Password Authentication Protocol (PAP), Challenge Handshake Authentication Protocol (CHAP), MS-CHAP, MS-CHAP v2, EAP-MD5, EAP-TLS, and multifactor authentication that combines smart cards and EAP.	12-8 to 12-14, 12-17 to 12-18
■ Configure and troubleshoot virtual private network (VPN) protocols. Considerations include Internet service provider (ISP), client operating system, network address translation devices, Routing and Remote Access servers, and firewall servers.	12-5 to 12-7, 12-24 to 12-27
■ Manage client configuration for remote access security. Tools include remote access policy and the Connection Manager Administration Kit.	12-30 to 12-40
Planning, Configuring, and Troubleshooting Authentication, Authorization, and PKI	
Plan and configure authentication.	1-4 to 1-55
■ Plan, configure, and troubleshoot trust relationships.	1-41 to 1-55
■ Plan and configure authentication protocols.	1-18 to 1-31
■ Plan and configure multifactor authentication.	1-27
■ Plan and configure authentication for Web users.	1-32 to 1-40
■ Plan and configure delegated authentication.	1-34 to 1-35
Plan group structure.	2-19 to 2-37
■ Decide which types of groups to use.	2-19, 2-24 to 2-29
■ Plan security group scope.	2-20 to 2-21
■ Plan nested group structure.	2-38 to 2-44
Plan and configure authorization.	2-3 to 2-14, 2-38 to 2-46
■ Configure access control lists (ACLs).	2-3, 2-39
■ Plan and troubleshoot the assignment of user rights.	2-38 to 2-40
■ Plan requirements for digital signatures.	7-3 to 7-12
Install, manage, and configure Certificate Services.	7-3 to 7-70
■ Install and configure root, intermediate, and issuing certification authorities (CAs). Considerations include renewals and hierarchy.	7-8 to 7-16
■ Configure certificate templates.	7-19 to 7-28
■ Configure, manage, and troubleshoot the publication of certificate revocation lists (CRLs).	7-35 to 7-38
■ Configure archival and recovery of keys.	7-46 to 7-59
■ Deploy and revoke certificates to users, computers, and CAs.	7-31 to 7-45
■ Back up and restore the CA.	7-8 to 7-12

Note Exam objectives are subject to change at anytime without prior notice and at Microsoft's sole discretion. Please visit Microsoft's Training & Certification Web site (*www.microsoft.com/traincert*) for the most current listing of exam objectives.

Microsoft®

MCSA/MCSE Self-Paced Training Kit (Exam 70-299): Implementing and Administering Security in a Microsoft® Windows Server™ 2003 Network

Tony Northrup
and
Orin Thomas

PUBLISHED BY
Microsoft Press
A Division of Microsoft Corporation
One Microsoft Way
Redmond, Washington 98052-6399

Library of Congress Cataloging-in-Publication Data pending.

Printed and bound in the United States of America.

3 4 5 6 7 8 9 QWT 8 7

Distributed in Canada by H.B. Fenn and Company Ltd.

A CIP catalogue record for this book is available from the British Library.

Microsoft Press books are available through booksellers and distributors worldwide. For further information about international editions, contact your local Microsoft Corporation office or contact Microsoft Press International directly at fax (425) 936-7329. Visit our Web site at www.microsoft.com/learning/. Send comments to *tkinput@microsoft.com.*

Acquisitions Editor: Kathy Harding
Content Development Manager: Marzena Makuta
Project Manager: Rebecca Davis (Volt)
Technical Editors: Randall Galloway and Eli Lazich
Copyeditor: Mick Alberts
Indexer: Seth Maislin

Body Part No. X10-42153

About the Authors

Tony Northrup, MCSE and CISSP, is a consultant and author living in the Boston, Massachusetts, area. During his seven years as Principal Systems Architect at BBN/Genuity, he was ultimately responsible for the reliability and security of hundreds of Windows–based servers and dozens of Windows domains—all connected directly to the Internet. Needless to say, Tony learned the hard way how to keep Windows systems safe in a hostile environment. Tony has authored and co-authored many books on Windows and networking, from *NT Network Plumbing* in 1998 to the *Windows Server 2003 Resource Kit Performance and Troubleshooting Guide*. Tony has also written several papers for Microsoft TechNet, covering firewalls, ASP.NET, and other security topics.

Orin Thomas is a writer, editor, and systems administrator who works for the certification advice Web site Certtutor.net. His work in IT has been varied: he's done everything from providing first-level networking support to acting in the role of systems administrator for one of Australia's largest companies. He was co-author of the MCSA/MCSE self-paced training kit for Exam 70-290 and co-editor of the MCSA/MCSE self-paced training kits for exams 70-292 and 70-296, both by Microsoft Press. He holds the MCSE, CCNA, CCDA, and Linux+ certifications. He holds a bachelor's degree in Science with honors from the University of Melbourne and is currently working toward the completion of a PhD in Philosophy of Science.

Contents

Acknowledgments

The author's name appears on the cover of a book, but the author is only one member of a large team. This particular book started with a call from Neil Salkind of Studio B—a respected author himself, with far more credits to his name than I ever hope to achieve. Neil, and a team at Studio B that included Jackie Coder, David Rogelberg, and Stacey Barone, worked closely with Rajni Gulati at Microsoft to put together the team that would create this book.

I have to thank Marzena Makuta, my editor, for being remarkably patient while I learned the correct style for a Microsoft Press training kit. Rebecca Davis did a great job of keeping me (and probably everyone else!) on schedule, even when the schedule needed to be adjusted. I was fortunate enough to have two technical reviewers for this book: Jim Fuchs and Randall Galloway. The technical accuracy of this book is a result of their incredible attention to detail.

Mick Alberts, my copyeditor, helped me get the terminology straight and educated me on the difference between *patches* and *updates*. The composition team, led by Dan Latimer, handled the layout of the book. Bill Teel processed the (many, many) screenshots, and Joel Panchot created the artwork from my drawings and diagrams. The proofing team, led by Sandi Resnick, helped to make this book readable by fixing many errors that I never even knew I made.

Many people helped with this book even though they weren't formally part of the team. Kurt Dillard, one of the top security experts at Microsoft and a close friend of mine, lent his expertise many times and helped to ensure that my recommendations were consistent with those of Microsoft. My friends, especially Tara Banks, Kristin Cavour, Eric and Alyssa Faulkner, Chris and Diane Geggis, Bob Hogan, Samuel Jackson, Khristina Jones, Tom Keegan, and Eric Parucki, helped me enjoy my time away from the keyboard. More than anyone, I have to thank my wife Erica for being so patient during many long days of writing. Erica's family, Mike, Michelle, Sandi, and Raymond Edson, as always, kept me in good spirits during the holidays (and by "spirits," I mean liquor).

It makes a huge difference when you consider the people you work with to be friends. Having a great team not only improves the quality of the book; it makes it a more enjoyable experience. Writing this book was my most enjoyable project yet, and I hope I get the chance to work with everyone in the future.

Tony Northrup

I would like to thank my wonderful wife Oksana for her support during the writing process. I would also like to thank our son Rooslan for making fatherhood so easy and fun. Finally, I want to thank the entire Certtutor.net tutor team, who offer great free advice to people who want to get certified.

Orin Thomas

About This Book

Welcome to *MCSE Self-Paced Training Kit (Exam 70-299): Implementing and Administering Security in a Microsoft Windows Server 2003 Network.*

Today's networks are constantly under attack by a variety of sources. Worms and viruses are the most common sources of attacks, and because they are constantly evolving, protecting your network against them requires implementing and administering an update management infrastructure. More dangerous attacks are launched by malicious, skilled individuals and require more complex countermeasures. Microsoft Windows Server 2003 provides a variety of methods to protect your network against these threats, including Active Directory directory services, Certificate Services, and IP Security (IPSec). Implementing and administering each of these requires specialized skills that will be taught in this book. The skills you acquire will also enable you to complete the exam 70-299.

Each chapter addresses an important aspect of network security management and a range of exam objectives. The goal of both the objectives and the chapter orientation is to provide a complete guide to Microsoft Windows–based network security management. The book focuses primarily on the skills necessary to implement and administer a network security infrastructure and only briefly covers concepts related to designing network security.

Note For more information about becoming a Microsoft Certified Professional, see the section titled "The Microsoft Certified Professional Program" later in this introduction.

Intended Audience

This book was developed for information technology (IT) professionals who plan to take the related Microsoft Certified Professional Exam 70-299, *Implementing and Administering Security in a Microsoft Windows Server 2003 Network,* and for IT professionals who implement and manage software solutions for Windows-based environments using Microsoft tools and technologies.

Note Exam skills are subject to change without prior notice and at the sole discretion of Microsoft.

Prerequisites

This training kit requires that students meet the following prerequisites:

- Have a solid understanding of networking fundamentals.
- Have at least one year of experience implementing and administering a Windows-based network operating system.
- For some chapters and labs, have a basic understanding of Microsoft SQL Server 2000 and Microsoft Exchange Server 2000 or later.
- Have a basic understanding of wireless technology.

About the CD-ROM

For your use, this book includes a Supplemental CD-ROM, which contains a variety of informational aids to complement the book content:

- The Readiness Review Suite powered by MeasureUp. This suite of practice tests and objective reviews contains questions of varying degrees of complexity and offers multiple testing modes. You can assess your understanding of the concepts presented in this book and use the results to develop a learning plan that meets your needs.
- An electronic version of this book (eBook). For information about using the eBook, see the section titled "The eBook" later in this introduction.
- Files required to complete the troubleshooting labs and case scenarios presented in this book.
- An eBook of the *Microsoft Encyclopedia of Networking, Second Edition* and of the *Microsoft Encyclopedia of Security*, which provide complete and up-to-date reference materials for networking and security.
- Sample chapters from several Microsoft Learning books. These chapters give you additional information about Windows Server 2003 and introduce you to other resources that are available from Microsoft Press.
- Supplemental information, including:
    - The "Microsoft Windows Server 2003 Deployment Kit," which provides detailed information about deploying network services.
    - The "Windows Server 2003 Security Guide," which provides templates and instructions for securing Windows Server 2003.
    - The "Windows XP Security Guide," which provides instructions and templates that can be used to secure Windows XP.
    - "Threats and Countermeasures: Security Settings in Windows Server 2003 and Windows XP," which details every security setting.

A second CD-ROM contains a 180-day evaluation edition of Microsoft Windows Server 2003, Enterprise Edition.

Caution The 180-day evaluation edition provided with this training kit is not the full retail product and is provided only for the purposes of training and evaluation. Microsoft Technical Support does not support this evaluation edition.

For additional support information regarding this book and the CD-ROM (including answers to commonly asked questions about installation and use), visit the Microsoft Learning Support Web site at *http://www.microsoft.com/learning/support/default.asp/*. You can also e-mail tkinput@microsoft.com or send a letter to Microsoft Learning, Attention: *MCSA/MCSE Self-Paced Training Kit (Exam 70-299): Implementing and Administering Security in a Microsoft Windows Server 2003 Network* Editor, One Microsoft Way, Redmond, WA 98052-6399.

Features of This Book

This book has two parts. Use Part 1 to learn at your own pace and practice what you've learned with practical exercises. Part 2 contains questions and answers you can use to test yourself on what you've learned.

Part 1: Learn at Your Own Pace

Each chapter identifies the exam objectives that are covered within the chapter, provides an overview of why the topics matter by identifying how the information is applied in the real world, and lists any prerequisites that must be met to complete the lessons presented in the chapter.

The chapters are divided into lessons. Lessons contain practices that include one or more hands-on exercises. These exercises give you an opportunity to use the skills being presented or explore the part of the application being described.

After the lessons, you are given an opportunity to apply what you've learned in a case scenario exercise. In this exercise, you work through a multi-step solution for a realistic case scenario. You are also given an opportunity to work through a troubleshooting lab that explores difficulties you might encounter when applying what you've learned on the job.

Each chapter ends with a short summary of key concepts and a short section listing key topics and terms you need to know before taking the exam. This section summarizes the key topics you've learned, with a focus on demonstrating that knowledge on the exam.

Real World Helpful Information

You will find sidebars like this one that contain related information you might find helpful. "Real World" sidebars contain specific information gained through the experience of IT professionals just like you.

Part 2: Prepare for the Exam

Part 2 helps to familiarize you with the types of questions you will encounter on the MCP exam. By reviewing the objectives and sample questions, you can focus on the specific skills you need to improve on before taking the exam.

See Also For a complete list of MCP exams and their related objectives, go to *http://www.microsoft.com/learning/mcpexams/default.asp.*

Part 2 is organized by the exam's objectives. Each chapter covers one of the primary groups of objectives, referred to as *Objective Domains*. Each chapter lists the tested skills you need to master to answer the exam questions, and it includes a list of further readings to help you improve your ability to perform the tasks or skills specified by the objectives.

Within each Objective Domain, you will find the related objectives that are covered on the exam. Each objective provides you with several practice exam questions. The answers are accompanied by explanations of each correct and incorrect answer.

Note These questions are also available on the companion CD as a practice test.

Informational Notes

Several types of reader aids appear throughout the training kit.

Tip Contains methods of performing a task more quickly or in a not-so-obvious way.

Important Contains information that is essential to completing a task.

Note Contains supplemental information.

Caution Contains valuable information about possible loss of data; be sure to read this information carefully.

Warning Contains critical information about possible physical injury; be sure to read this information carefully.

See Also Contains references to other sources of information.

Planning Contains hints and useful information that should help you to plan the implementation.

On the CD Points you to supplementary information or files you need that are on the companion CD.

Security Alert Highlights information you need to know to maximize security in your work environment.

Exam Tip Flags information you should know before taking the certification exam.

Off the Record Contains practical advice about the real-world implications of information presented in the lesson.

Notational Conventions

The following conventions are used throughout this book:

- Characters or commands that you type appear in **bold** type.

- *Italic* in syntax statements indicates placeholders for variable information. *Italic* is also used for book titles.
- Acronyms appear in all uppercase.
- `Monospace` type represents code samples, examples of screen text, or entries that you might type at a command prompt or in initialization files.

Keyboard Conventions

- A plus sign (+) between two key names means that you must press those keys at the same time. For example, "Press ALT+TAB" means that you hold down ALT while you press TAB.
- A comma (,) between two or more key names means that you must press each of the keys consecutively, not together. For example, "Press ALT, F, X" means that you press and release each key in sequence. "Press ALT+W, L" means that you first press ALT and W at the same time, and then release them and press L.

Getting Started

This training kit contains hands-on exercises to help you learn about deploying, managing, and troubleshooting a Windows Server 2003 security infrastructure. Use this section to prepare your self-paced training environment. Although the requirements for each of the chapters vary, obtaining the hardware and software listed in this section will allow you to complete every exercise, troubleshooting lab, and case scenario in this book.

Caution Many of these exercises require you to configure settings that will affect addressing and other features of your network. Additionally, the computers you use for these exercises will have varying levels of security for each of the exercises you are working through. For these reasons, it is not recommended that you perform these exercises on computers that are connected to a larger network.

Hardware Requirements

To complete some of the exercises in this book, you must have two networked computers and a means of connecting both computers to the Internet. Both computers must be capable of running Windows Server 2003, be on the Windows Server 2003 Hardware Compatibility List, and have the following minimum configuration:

- 550 MHz or higher processor recommended; 133 MHz minimum required; Intel Pentium/Celeron family or the AMD K6/Athlon/Duron family.
- 256 MB RAM or higher recommended; 128 MB minimum required memory.
- 1.25 to 2 GB free hard disk space.

- CD-ROM or DVD-ROM drive.
- Super VGA (800 x 600) or higher-resolution monitor recommended; VGA or hardware that supports console redirection required.
- Keyboard and Microsoft Mouse or compatible pointing device, or hardware that supports console redirection.

Additionally, one of the chapters requires you to have a wireless access point available.

Software Requirements

A 180-day evaluation edition of Windows Server 2003, Enterprise Edition is included on the CD-ROM. Additionally, some exercises require you to have Windows XP to simulate a network client operating system. For some exercises, you will also need SQL Server 2000, Exchange Server 2000 or later, and Microsoft Office Outlook 2003.

Caution The 180-day evaluation edition of Windows Server 2003, Enterprise Edition provided with this training kit is not the full retail product and is provided only for the purposes of training and evaluation. Microsoft Technical Support does not support this evaluation edition. For additional support information regarding this book and the CD-ROMs (including answers to commonly asked questions about installation and use), visit the Microsoft Learning Support Web site at *http://www.microsoft.com/learning/support/default.asp/*. You can also e-mail tkinput@microsoft.com or send a letter to Microsoft Learning, Attn: *MCSA/MCSE Self-Paced Training Kit (Exam 70-299): Implementing and Administering Security in a Microsoft Windows Server 2003 Network* Editor, One Microsoft Way, Redmond, WA 98052-6399.

Setup Instructions

Set up your computer hardware according to the manufacturer's instructions. The software requirements vary from chapter to chapter. Therefore, you should review the Before You Begin section of each chapter and configure the computers as specified.

Caution If your computers are part of a larger network, you must verify with your network administrator that the computer names, domain name, and other information used in setting up Windows Server 2003 as described in each individual chapter do not conflict with network operations. If they do conflict, ask your network administrator to provide alternative values and use those values throughout all of the exercises in this book.

The Readiness Review Suite

The CD-ROM includes a practice test made up of 300 sample exam questions and an objective-by-objective review with an additional 125 questions. Use these tools to reinforce your learning and to identify any areas in which you need to gain more experience before taking the exam.

▶ **To install the practice test and objective review**

1. Insert the Supplemental CD-ROM into your CD-ROM drive.

Note If AutoRun is disabled on your computer, refer to the Readme.txt file on the CD-ROM.

2. Click Readiness Review Suite on the user interface menu.

Lab files

The \70-299\Labs folder on the companion CD contains lab files that you need to complete the hands-on exercises. These files are organized by chapter.

The eBook

The CD-ROM includes an electronic version of this training kit. The eBook is in portable document format (PDF) and can be viewed using Adobe Acrobat Reader.

▶ **To use the eBook**

1. Insert the Supplemental CD-ROM into your CD-ROM drive.

Note If AutoRun is disabled on your computer, refer to the Readme.txt file on the CD-ROM.

2. Click Training Kit eBook on the user interface menu. You can also review any of the other eBooks that are provided for your use.

The Microsoft Certified Professional Program

The Microsoft Certified Professional (MCP) program provides the best method to prove your command of current Microsoft products and technologies. The exams and corresponding certifications are developed to validate your mastery of critical competencies as you design and develop, or implement and support, solutions with Microsoft products and technologies. Computer professionals who become Microsoft certified are recognized as experts and are sought after throughout the industry. Certification brings a variety of benefits to the individual and to employers and organizations.

See Also For a full list of MCP benefits, go to *http://www.microsoft.com/learning/itpro/default.asp*.

Certifications

The Microsoft Certified Professional program offers multiple certifications, based on specific areas of technical expertise:

- *Microsoft Certified Professional (MCP).* Demonstrated in-depth knowledge of at least one Microsoft Windows operating system or architecturally significant platform. An MCP is qualified to implement a Microsoft product or technology as part of a business solution for an organization.
- *Microsoft Certified Solution Developer (MCSD).* Professional developers qualified to analyze, design, and develop enterprise business solutions with Microsoft development tools and technologies including the Microsoft .NET Framework.
- *Microsoft Certified Application Developer (MCAD).* Professional developers qualified to develop, test, deploy, and maintain powerful applications using Microsoft tools and technologies including Microsoft Visual Studio .NET and XML Web services.
- *Microsoft Certified Systems Engineer (MCSE).* Qualified to effectively analyze the business requirements, and design and implement the infrastructure for business solutions based on the Microsoft Windows and Microsoft Windows Server 2003 operating systems.
- *Microsoft Certified Systems Administrator (MCSA).* Individuals with the skills to manage and troubleshoot existing network and system environments based on the Microsoft Windows and Microsoft Windows Server 2003 operating systems.
- *Microsoft Certified Database Administrator (MCDBA).* Individuals who design, implement, and administer Microsoft SQL Server databases.
- *Microsoft Certified Trainer (MCT).* Instructionally and technically qualified to deliver Microsoft Official Curriculum through a Microsoft Certified Technical Education Center (CTEC).

Requirements for Becoming a Microsoft Certified Professional

The certification requirements differ for each certification and are specific to the products and job functions addressed by the certification.

To become a Microsoft Certified Professional, you must pass rigorous certification exams that provide a valid and reliable measure of technical proficiency and expertise. These exams are designed to test your expertise and your ability to perform a role or task with a product. They are developed with the input of professionals in the industry. Questions in the exams reflect how Microsoft products are used in actual organizations, and thus have "real-world" relevance.

- Microsoft Certified Professionals (MCPs) are required to pass one current Microsoft certification exam. Candidates can pass additional Microsoft certification exams to further qualify their skills with other Microsoft products, development tools, or desktop applications.
- Microsoft Certified Solution Developers (MCSDs) are required to pass three core exams and one elective exam. (MCSD for Microsoft .NET candidates are required to pass four core exams and one elective.)
- Microsoft Certified Application Developers (MCADs) are required to pass two core exams and one elective exam in an area of specialization.
- Microsoft Certified Systems Engineers (MCSEs) are required to pass five core exams and two elective exams.
- Microsoft Certified Systems Administrators (MCSAs) are required to pass three core exams and one elective exam that provide a valid and reliable measure of technical proficiency and expertise.
- Microsoft Certified Database Administrators (MCDBAs) are required to pass three core exams and one elective exam that provide a valid and reliable measure of technical proficiency and expertise.
- Microsoft Certified Trainers (MCTs) are required to meet the instructional and technical requirements specific to each Microsoft Official Curriculum course they are certified to deliver. The MCT program requires ongoing training to meet the requirements for the annual renewal of certification. For more information about becoming a Microsoft Certified Trainer, visit *http://www.microsoft.com/learning/mcp/mct/default.asp/* or contact a regional service center near you.

Technical Support

Every effort has been made to ensure the accuracy of this book and the contents of the companion disc. If you have comments, questions, or ideas regarding this book or the companion disc, please send them to Microsoft Learning using either of the following methods:

E-mail:	tkinput@microsoft.com
Postal Mail:	Microsoft Learning Attn: *MCSA/MCSE Self-Paced Training Kit (Exam 70-299): Implementing and Administering Security in a Microsoft Windows Server 2003 Network* Editor One Microsoft Way Redmond, WA 98052-6399

For additional support information regarding this book and the CD-ROM (including answers to commonly asked questions about installation and use), visit the Microsoft Learning Support Web site at *http://www.microsoft.com/learning/support/default.asp/*. To connect directly to the Microsoft Press Knowledge Base and enter a query, visit *http://www.microsoft.com/mspress/support/search.asp*. For support information regarding Microsoft software, please connect to *http://support.microsoft.com/default.aspx*.

Evaluation Edition Software Support

The 180-day evaluation edition provided with this training kit is not the full retail product and is provided only for the purposes of training and evaluation. Microsoft and Microsoft Technical Support do not support this evaluation edition.

Caution The evaluation edition of Windows Server 2003, Enterprise Edition, included with this book should not be used on a primary work computer. The evaluation edition is unsupported. For online support information relating to the full version of Windows Server 2003, Enterprise Edition, that *might* also apply to the evaluation edition, you can connect to *http://support.microsoft.com/*.

Information about any issues relating to the use of this evaluation edition with this training kit is posted to the Support section of the Microsoft Learning Web site (*http://www.microsoft.com/learning/support/default.asp*). For information about ordering the full version of any Microsoft software, please call Microsoft Sales at (800) 426-9400 or visit *http://www.microsoft.com*.

Part I
Learn at Your Own Pace

1 Planning and Configuring an Authentication Strategy

Exam Objectives in this Chapter:

- Plan and configure authentication
- Plan, configure, and troubleshoot trust relationships
- Plan and configure authentication protocols
- Plan and configure multifactor authentication
- Plan and configure authentication for Web users
- Plan and configure delegated authentication

> **Note** Public key infrastructure (PKI) is covered in Chapter 7, "Installing, Configuring, and Managing Certification Services."

Why This Chapter Matters

Authentication distinguishes legitimate users from uninvited guests, and is the most visible, and fundamental, concept in security. From ATM PIN numbers to driver's licenses to user names and passwords, authentication is a part of everyone's daily life. Without authentication, it is impossible to restrict access to network resources. If an authentication strategy is too weak, uninvited guests such as worms, Trojan horses, and malicious attackers gain access to your network. Password guessing, password cracking, and man-in-the-middle attacks all attempt to exploit weaknesses in an organization's authentication strategy. If an authentication strategy is too restrictive, attackers are kept out, but legitimate users may not be able to do their jobs.

While authentication is a security concept, it can affect an organization's productivity and costs. If authentication is distributed, users will have different user names and passwords for each network resource they access. This, in turn, will increase Help desk costs when users lose track of passwords. Similarly, requiring extremely complex passwords will make it more difficult to impersonate legitimate users. However, if those users cannot remember their passwords, they will be denied access to network resources, which decreases their productivity.

This chapter introduces you to the separate but related concepts of authentication and authorization. You will learn about the various credentials that can be used to verify a user's identity and the variety of protocols that can be used to transmit credentials across a network. You will understand how to authenticate users who access your network resources by using a Web browser, in addition to users who are members of domains other than your own.

Lessons in this Chapter:

Before You Begin

- This chapter presents the skills and concepts that are required to plan and configure authentication strategies in a Microsoft Windows Server 2003 environment.

To complete the practices, examples, and lab exercises in this chapter, you must have:

- A private, non-routed network.
  - Two computers. On the first computer, perform a Windows Server 2003 installation with default settings, and assign the computer name Computer1.
  - On the second computer, configure the hard disk with two partitions. Install Windows 98 on the first partition. Then install Windows Server 2003 on the second partition so that the computer can dual-boot between the two platforms. On both Windows 98 and Windows Server 2003, assign the computer name Computer2.
- Added the domain controller role to both computers using the default settings. Computer1 should host the domain cohowinery.com. Computer2 should host the domain cohovineyard.com.
- Both computers should be configured to use themselves as their own primary DNS server and the other computer as the secondary DNS server.

After completing this module, you will be able to:

- Describe the importance of authentication.
- Distinguish between problems caused by authentication and authorization.

- Design an authentication strategy that meets an organization's security requirements without becoming too costly or cumbersome.
- Determine the authentication protocols that should be enabled on your network.
- Configure authentication for users who access network resources by using a Web browser.
- Keep anonymous Web users from accessing resources that they are not specifically allowed to access.
- Create trusts between Active Directory domains to enable authentication for resources in remote domains.

Lesson 1: Understanding the Components of an Authentication Model

In this lesson, you will learn the meaning of the term *authentication*, and how it differs from authorization. You will understand that network authentication is similar in function to the common methods of authenticating people in the physical world. You will learn how to optimize the security of authentication in Windows Server 2003 environments while ensuring compatibility with every client that will access your network resources. Finally, you will explore the tools provided for troubleshooting authentication problems.

After this lesson, you will be able to

- Select an appropriate authentication protocol.
- Explain how the NTLM authentication process works.
- Explain how the Kerberos authentication process works.
- Determine how Windows Server 2003 stores passwords and secrets to support authentication.
- Select appropriate tools to troubleshoot authentication problems.

Estimated lesson time: 30 minutes

The Difference Between Authentication and Authorization

Whether you're withdrawing money from a bank, entering a restricted building, or boarding an airplane, gaining access to a restricted resource requires both authentication and authorization. The two processes are closely related and often confused. To understand the difference between authentication and authorization, consider an example in the physical world that most people are familiar with: boarding an airplane. Before you can board a plane, you must present both your identification and your ticket. Your identification, typically a driver's license or a passport, enables the airport staff to determine who you are. Validating your identity is the *authentication* part of the boarding process. The airport staff also checks your ticket to make sure that the flight you are boarding is the correct one. Verifying that you are allowed to board the plane is the *authorization* process.

On networks, authentication is often performed by providing a user name and password. The user name identifies you, and the password offers the computer system some assurance that you really are who you claim to be. After you are authenticated, the computer agrees that you are who you claim to be. However, it doesn't yet know whether you are allowed to access the resource you are requesting. For example, Help desk support staff should have the right to reset a user's password, but members of the accounting department should be able to change only their own passwords. To authorize the user, the computer system typically checks an access control list (ACL). The ACL lists users, and groups of users, who are permitted to access a resource.

See Also Authorization is covered in Chapter 2, "Planning and Configuring an Authorization Strategy."

Network Authentication Systems

In order to authenticate a user on a network with some reasonable certainty that the user is who he or she claims to be, the user needs to provide two pieces of information: identification and proof of identity. In most networks, users identify themselves with a user name or an e-mail address. The way users prove their identity varies, however.

Traditionally, a password is used to prove a user's identity. A password is a form of a shared secret. The user knows his or her password, and the server authenticating the user either has the password stored, or has some information that can be used to validate the password.

Passwords prove your identity because they are *something you know*. Other ways to prove your identity are with *something you have* or *something you are*. Many modern computer systems authenticate users by reading information from a smart card—something you have. Other computer systems are satisfied that you are who you claim to be only when you prove it with something you are. Biometrics can do this by scanning a unique part of your body such as your fingerprint, your retina, or your facial features.

Passwords can be guessed, and smart cards can be stolen. One form of authentication alone may not meet your organization's security requirements. Multifactor authentication combines two or more authentication methods, and significantly reduces the likelihood that an attacker will be able to impersonate a user during the authentication process. The most common example of multifactor authentication is combining a smart card with a password. Typically, the password is required to retrieve a key stored on the smart card. Before you can authenticate to such a system, you must provide a password (something you know) and a smart card (something you have).

Note The examples in this book rely on using passwords alone for authentication. While this is one of the less secure ways to authenticate users, you probably don't have smart cards or fingerprint readers connected to your computer. You almost certainly have a keyboard, though.

Storing User Credentials

The server that authenticates the user must be able to determine that the user's credentials are valid. To do this, the server must store information that can be used to verify the user's credentials. How and where this information is stored are important decisions to make when designing an authentication model.

The way the user credentials are stored can determine how difficult it is for an attacker to misuse the information and whether those user credentials can be migrated to a new authentication system in the future. Naturally, it is important that this information remains confidential. Instead of simply storing a list of user passwords on a server, and directly comparing the password provided by the user against the list, it's common to store an encrypted or hashed version of the user password. If an attacker does gain access to the server's copy of the user's credentials, the attacker still needs to decrypt the contents before they can be used to impersonate a user.

Real World

Since the beginning of computer systems, some of the most widely used security attacks have changed upon the attacker gaining access to the operating system's password file. When multi-user computer systems were first created, developers didn't understand the importance of security, and password files were often created in plain text. Anyone who could gain access to the password file would easily be able to read every user's password.

Later, operating system developers used various forms of encryption and hashing to obscure user credentials. This was a huge step forward, because the casual attacker couldn't read the files without first decrypting them. However, security experts (whether wearing a white or a black hat) have always put a huge amount of energy into finding ways to uncover user credentials based on a captured password file. Over time, these security experts have found ways to unencrypt, in a reasonable amount of time, just about every encryption scheme operating system developers have created for protecting password files. This trend is bound to continue in the future, but you can reduce the risk of someone misusing access to your password file by requiring users to use strong passwords, requiring regular password changes, and using the cracking tools yourself to identify easily cracked passwords that should be changed.

Determining where user credentials are stored requires choosing between centralized and decentralized authentication models. Decentralized authentication models require each network resource to maintain a list of users and their credentials. While this provides granular control over which users can authenticate to network resources, it becomes impossible to manage on networks with more than a handful of servers. In

Windows networks, each server maintains a list of local users that can be used to implement a decentralized authentication model.

Centralized authentication models provide significantly simpler management in larger networks, which lowers Help desk costs related to password management. In a centralized model, network resources rely on a central authority to authenticate users. Centralized authentication is required in environments where users should access all network resources with a single set of credentials, an ideal situation known as *single sign-on*. In Windows networks, centralized authentication is provided by means of Active Directory domains. Larger networks might use multiple domains, with *trusts* used to enable network resources in one domain to authorize users in another domain.

Authentication Features of Windows Server 2003

Windows Server 2003 provides robust and flexible authentication methods that can be configured to meet the needs of organizations from small businesses to enterprises. Key authentication features of Windows Server 2003 include:

- *Central administration of user accounts.* The Active Directory directory service allows users to log on to computers in a multidomain or multiforest environment by using single-factor authentication or various types of multifactor authentication.
- *Single sign-on environment.* When a user is authenticated to a Windows Server 2003 domain, the user's credentials are used to access resources in the domain, thereby eliminating the need for users to authenticate to every resource that they attempt to access. When this technology is used with the Windows XP credential manager, users can access resources in other domains by providing the password one time and storing the password as part of the domain user account.
- *Computer and service accounts.* In addition to users, computer and service accounts authenticate to the domain. Collectively, users, computers, and service accounts are referred to as *security principals*.
- *Multifactor support.* Windows Server 2003 natively supports smart cards and a variety of other multifactor authentication mechanisms.
- *Auditing.* Windows Server 2003 provides the ability to audit logon attempts and access to resources.
- *Protocols.* Windows Server 2003 uses a variety of authentication protocols, including LM, NTLM, NTLMv2, and Kerberos.

Authentication Protocols in Windows Server 2003

Windows Server 2003 provides the ability to authenticate a variety of client operating systems. Because client operating systems support various levels of authentication protocols, Windows Server 2003 supports two primary authentication protocols: NTLM and Kerberos.

The NTLM authentication protocol uses a challenge-response mechanism to authenticate users and computers running Windows Me and earlier operating systems, or computers running Windows 2000 or later that are not part of a domain. A user is prompted (the challenge) to provide some private piece of information unique to the user (the response). Windows Server 2003 supports the following three methods of challenge-response authentication:

- *LAN Manager (LM).* Developed jointly by IBM and Microsoft for use in OS2 and Windows for Workgroups, Windows 95, Windows 98, and Windows Me. It is the least secure form of challenge-response authentication because it is susceptible to eavesdropping attacks, and servers that authenticate users with LM authentication must store credentials in an *LMHash*.
- *NTLM version 1.* A more secure form of challenge-response authentication than LM. It is used for connecting to servers running Windows NT with Service Pack 3 or earlier. NTLMv1 uses 56-bit encryption to secure the protocol. Servers that authenticate users with any version of NTLM authentication must store credentials in an *NT Hash*.
- *NTLM version 2.* The most secure form of challenge-response authentication available. This version includes a secure channel to protect the authentication process. It is used for connecting to servers running Windows 2000, Windows XP, and Windows NT with Service Pack 4 or higher. NTLMv2 uses 128-bit encryption to secure the protocol.

Kerberos is the default authentication protocol for Windows Server 2003, Windows 2000, and Windows XP Professional. Kerberos is designed to be more secure and scalable than NTLM across large, diverse networks. Kerberos provides the following additional benefits to those provided by NTLM:

- *Efficiency.* When a server needs to authenticate a client, the server can validate the client's credentials without having to contact a domain controller.
- *Mutual authentication.* In addition to authenticating the client to the server, Kerberos enables the server to be authenticated to the client.
- *Delegated authentication.* Allows services to impersonate clients when accessing resources on their behalf.
- *Simplified trust management.* Kerberos can use transitive trusts between domains in the same forest and domains connected with a forest trust.
- *Interoperability.* Kerberos is based on the Internet Engineering Task Force (IETF) standards and is therefore compatible with other IETF-compliant Kerberos realms.

LM Authentication

You can use LM authentication to provide compatibility with earlier operating systems, including Windows 95, Windows 98, and Windows NT 4.0 Service Pack 3 or earlier. There are also earlier applications that might rely on this authentication mechanism. For example, earlier versions of Netscape Navigator support only LM authentication. However, LM authentication is the weakest protocol, and the easiest to compromise. Do not use LM authentication in a Windows Server 2003 environment. Upgrade any computers that rely on the LM protocol to eliminate this security vulnerability.

Storing LM passwords

A major reason not to use LM protocol is that when a password is created by the user and stored for use with LM, the password is converted to an LMHash. The LMHash contains user names and hashes of the corresponding user password. A *hash* is a form of one-way encryption. When a client attempts to authenticate a user with LM authentication, the hash of the password, rather than the password itself, is transmitted across the network. The server will only be able to authenticate the user if the server has the LMHash stored.

The LMHash has several weaknesses that make it more vulnerable to attack than the NT Hash. The LMHash is stored in all uppercase, is limited to 14 characters, and is divided into two discreet components before hashing. If a knowledgeable, malicious attacker does obtain access to LMHashes for a large number of users, it is likely that the attacker would be able to identify at least one user's password. Table 1.1 shows examples of passwords and the corresponding LMHashes that would be stored.

Table 1.1 LM Passwords

Password	LMHash
tiger	C6E4266FEBEBD6A8AAD3B435B51404EE
12345	AEBD4DE384C7EC43AAD3B435B51404EE
SECTION	D5F34F69EB965B8E3AAD3B435B51404EE
SYNERGY	CE910CFA90B123F9AAD3B435B51404EE
Player24	DD4B68A4219ED226FF17365FAF1FFE89

Examine Table 1.1. Notice that passwords with fewer than eight characters all share the last sixteen characters. During the process of computing the hash, the original password is divided into two sets of seven characters. If the password is seven characters or less, the second set of seven characters is null. This results in the last sixteen characters being a well-known value that indicates to the attacker that the original password is less than eight characters. Knowing that the password is short significantly reduces the amount of work an attacker needs to perform in order to identify the original password. This method of storing passwords makes the LMHash vulnerable to attacks that can reveal the unencrypted password.

Disabling LM passwords

Windows Server 2003 allows you to disable the LMHash to remove the vulnerabilities presented by LM authentication. However, if you have clients running Windows 3.1 or the original release of Windows 95 that need to connect to a computer running Windows Server 2003, it is imperative that you do not disable the LMHash. However, you can still disable the use of the LMHash on an account-by-account basis by doing one of the following:

- Using passwords that are 15 characters or longer.
- Enabling the NoLMHash registry value locally on a computer or by using security policy.
- Using specific ALT characters in passwords. ALT characters are inserted into a password by holding down the ALT key, typing the ALT code using the number pad, and then releasing the ALT key.

Exam Tip Only specific ALT character ranges will disable the LMHash. You don't need to memorize these for the exam, but you should be aware that not all ALT keys will work. The ALT character ranges that will disable the LMHash are: 128–159, 306–307, 312, 319–320, 329–331, 383, 385–406, 408–409, 411–414, 418–424, 426, 428–429, 433–437, 439–447, 449–450, 452–460, 477, 480–483, 494–495, 497–608, 610–631, 633–696, 699, 701–707, 709, 711, 716, 718–729, 731, 733–767, 773–775, 777, 779–781, 783–806, 808–816, 819–893, 895–912, 914, 918–919, 921–927, 929–930, 933, 935–936, 938–944, 947, 950–955, 957–959, 961–962, 965, and 967–1023.

NTLM Authentication

As mentioned earlier, NTLM includes three methods of challenge-response authentication: LM, NTLMv1, and NTLMv2. The authentication process for all the methods is the same, but they differ in the level of encryption.

Authentication process

The following steps demonstrate the flow of events that occur when a client authenticates to a domain controller using any of the NTLM protocols:

1. The client and server negotiate an authentication protocol. This is accomplished through the Microsoft *negotiate* Security Support Provider (SSP).
2. The client sends the user name and domain name to the domain controller.
3. The domain controller generates a 16-byte random character string called a *nonce*.

4. The client encrypts the nonce with a hash of the user password and sends it back to the domain controller.
5. The domain controller retrieves the hash of the user password from the security account database.
6. The domain controller uses the hash value retrieved from the security account database to encrypt the nonce. The value is compared with the value received from the client. If the values match, the client is authenticated.

The Kerberos Authentication Process

The Kerberos protocol gets it name from the three-headed dog in Greek mythology. The three components of Kerberos are:

- The client requesting services or authentication.
- The server hosting the services requested by the client.
- A computer that is trusted by the client and server (in this case, a Windows Server 2003 domain controller running the Kerberos Key Distribution Center service).

Kerberos authentication is based on specially formatted data packets known as *tickets*. In Kerberos, these tickets pass through the network instead of passwords. Transmitting tickets instead of passwords makes the authentication process more resistant to attackers who can intercept the network traffic.

Key Distribution Center

The Key Distribution Center (KDC) maintains a database of account information for all security principals in the domain. The KDC stores a cryptographic key known only to the security principal and the KDC. This key is used in exchanges between the security principal and the KDC and is known as a *long term key*. The long term key is derived from a user's logon password.

Kerberos authentication process

In a Kerberos environment, the authentication process begins at logon. The following steps describe the Kerberos authentication process:

1. When a user enters a user name and password, the computer sends the user name to the KDC. The KDC contains a master database of unique long term keys for every principal in its realm.
2. The KDC looks up the user's master key (KA), which is based on the user's password. The KDC then creates two items: a session key (SA) to share with the user and a Ticket-Granting Ticket (TGT). The TGT includes a second copy of the SA, the user name, and an expiration time. The KDC encrypts this ticket by using its own master key (KKDC), which only the KDC knows.

Note Kerberos implements secret key cryptography, which is different from public key cryptography in that it does not use a public and private key pair.

3. The client computer receives the information from the KDC and runs the user's password through a one-way hashing function, which converts the password into the user's KA. The client computer now has a session key and a TGT so that it can securely communicate with the KDC. The client is now authenticated to the domain and is ready to access other resources in the domain by using the Kerberos protocol.

Important When a client receives the session key and TGT from the server, it stores that information in volatile memory and not on the hard disk. Storing the information in the volatile memory and not on the hard disk makes the information more secure, because the information would be lost if the server were physically removed.

4. When a Kerberos client needs to access resources on a server that is a member of the same domain, it contacts the KDC. The client will present its TGT and a timestamp encrypted with the session key that is already shared with the KDC. The KDC decrypts the TGT using its KKDC. The TGT contains the user name and a copy of the SA. The KDC uses the SA to decrypt the timestamp. The KDC can confirm that this request actually comes from the user because only the user can use the SA.
5. Next, the KDC creates a pair of tickets, one for the client and one for the server on which the client needs to access resources. Each ticket contains the name of the user requesting the service, the recipient of the request, a timestamp that declares when the ticket was created, and a time duration that says how long the tickets are valid. Both tickets also contain a new key (KAB) that will be shared between the client and the server so they can securely communicate.
6. The KDC takes the server's ticket and encrypts it using the server master key (KB). Then the KDC nests the server's ticket inside the client's ticket, which also contains the KAB. The KDC encrypts the whole thing using the session key that it shares with the user from the logon process. The KDC then sends all the information to the user.
7. When the user receives the ticket, the user decrypts it using the SA. This exposes the KAB to the client and also exposes the server's ticket. The user cannot read the server's ticket. The user will encrypt the timestamp by using the KAB and send the timestamp and the server's ticket to the server on which the client wants to access resources. When it receives these two items, the server first decrypts its own ticket by using its KB. This permits access to the KAB, which can then decrypt the timestamp from the client.

Now both the client and the server have the KAB. The server can be sure that the client has truthfully identified itself because the client used the KAB to encrypt the timestamp. If it is necessary for the server to respond to the user, the server will use the KAB. The client will know that the server has truthfully identified itself because the server had to use its KB to get the KAB.

Exam Tip Be sure you understand the Kerberos authentication process for the exam!

Storage of Local User Credentials

To reduce the likelihood of passwords being discovered and compromised, Windows Server 2003, Windows 2000, and Windows XP must store passwords securely. To ensure the highest level of password integrity, passwords can be stored at the domain level in Active Directory. To enable each server to authenticate users without relying on Active Directory, Windows Server 2003 locally stores a separate database of user credentials called the Local Security Authority (LSA). The LSA is responsible for:

- Managing local security policies.
- Authenticating users.
- Creating access tokens.
- Controlling audit policies.

The sensitive information stored by the LSA is known as *LSA secrets*. LSA secrets contain:

- Trust relationship passwords
- User names
- Passwords
- Service account passwords
- Service account names

LSA secrets can be extracted by any security principal with the Debug Programs right. To help protect LSA secrets, you can use the syskey.exe program, which further encrypts the contents of the LSA by using a public and a private key. Only Administrators can run the syskey.exe program.

See Also For more information about the syskey.exe program, see *http://support.microsoft.com/?kbid=310105*.

Tools for Troubleshooting Authentication Problems

Sometimes, troubleshooting an authentication problem is as simple as resetting a user's password. At other times it can be more challenging. For example, it might be difficult to detect the cause of an authentication failure if a domain controller is offline or a WAN link to a remote office has failed. Sometimes, NTLMv2 and Kerberos authentication failures can also be attributed to a clock synchronization failure. The tolerances for clocks that are out of synchronization are 30 minutes for NTLMv2 and 5 minutes for Kerberos. To assist you in determining the cause of authentication failures, Windows Server 2003 and the Resource Kit include several troubleshooting tools. Table 1.2 lists the tools that will help you troubleshoot authentication problems.

Table 1.2 Troubleshooting Tools for Authentication Problems

Tool	Description
Kerbtray.exe	This GUI tool displays Kerberos ticket information. It also allows you to view and purge the ticket cache. Included with the Windows Server 2003 Resource Kit tools.
Klist.exe	This command-line tool lets you view and delete Kerberos tickets granted to the current logon session. Included with the Windows Server 2003 Resource Kit tools.
CmdKey.exe	Creates, lists, and deletes stored user names and passwords or credentials. Included with Windows Server 2003.

See Also For all Resource Kit tools, see *http://www.microsoft.com/downloads/details.aspx?displaylang=en&familyid=9D467A69-57FF-4AE7-96EE-B18C4790CFFD*.

Lesson Review

The following questions are intended to reinforce key information presented in this lesson. If you are unable to answer a question, review the lesson materials and try the question again. You can find answers to the questions in the "Questions and Answers" section at the end of this chapter.

1. Is showing your identification to prove that you are of age to purchase a product an example of authentication or authorization?

   ____

   ____

2. Is showing your identification to a cashier to verify that the credit card you are using belongs to you an example of authentication or authorization?

   ____

   ____

3. Which of the following passwords will not be stored in an LMHash?
   a. tyia
   b. imsitrjs5itr
   c. passwordpassword
   d. l%@3tty7&

____

____

Lesson Summary

- Authentication is the process of proving your identity. In Windows networks, users frequently authenticate themselves using a user name and password pair. How the user name and password are communicated across the network has changed with different versions of Windows.
- Earlier versions of Windows use LM authentication, which is still supported by Windows Server 2003 for backward compatibility but carries with it potential security vulnerabilities. LM authentication should be disabled whenever compatibility with Windows 95 or Windows 98 is not required.
- If LM authentication cannot be disabled, the storage of the LMHash can be avoided for specific user accounts by using passwords greater than 14 characters or passwords that contain special ALT characters.
- Newer versions of Windows use NTLMv1, NTLMv2, or Kerberos authentication. The Kerberos protocol is designed to be more secure and scalable than NTLM authentication.
- Local passwords are stored and maintained by the Local Security Authority (LSA). The LSA is responsible for managing local security policies, authenticating users, creating access tokens, and controlling audit policies.
- Windows Server 2003 and the Resource Kit include the Kerbtray.exe, Klist.exe, and CmdKey.exe tools for troubleshooting Kerberos authentication problems.

Lesson 2: Planning and Implementing an Authentication Strategy

Most organizations need to support seamless access to the network for multiple types of users, such as office workers, employees who are traveling, business partners, and customers. At the same time, organizations need to protect network resources from potential intruders. A well-designed authentication strategy can help you achieve this complex balance between providing reliable access for users and strong network security for your organization.

After this lesson, you will be able to

- Evaluate the factors that influence the needs of your authorization strategy.
- Create a strong password policy.
- Configure settings to implement account lockout polices and logon restrictions on users.
- Configure settings for creating a Kerberos ticket policy.
- Select appropriate Windows authentication methods for earlier applications.
- Enable secure authentication.
- Design a strategy for supplemental authentication.
- Explain the benefits of applications that are certified for use with Windows.

Estimated lesson time: 45 minutes

Considerations for Evaluating Your Environment

When establishing an authentication strategy for your organization, you must become familiar with your current environment, including the structure of your organization; the users, computers, and services in your organization that require authentication; and the applications and services that are in use. This will help you to understand the requirements and constraints of your organization.

When evaluating your environment, identify the following:

- *The number of domain controllers in your organization.* Ensure that there are enough domain controllers to support client logon requests and authentication requests while meeting your redundancy requirements. A sufficient number of domain controllers will ensure that a large volume of authentication requests will not result in authentication failures, even if a domain controller is offline because of hardware or network failures.
- *The type of network connectivity between site locations in your organization.* Ensure that clients in remote sites are connected well enough to authenticate to

domain controllers located in main sites. If connectivity is an issue, consider installing domain controllers in sites that might have logon problems because of slow or unreliable links.

> **Planning** Everyone is always concerned about whether they have enough bandwidth, but it's latency that's more likely to cause authentication problems across wide area network links. Authentication requires very little bandwidth. However, packets must go back and forth across the link several times. If latency causes a significant delay for each round trip, authentication will seem slow.

- *The number of certification authorities (CAs) that are available in your organization and their locations.* Ensure that you have enough CAs to support the anticipated number of certificate requests.

Guidelines for Creating a Strong Password Policy

Encryption limits your vulnerability to having user credentials intercepted and misused. Specifically, password encryption is designed to be extremely difficult for unauthorized users to decrypt. Ideally, when a strong password is used, it should take an attacker months, years, or decades to identify the unencrypted password after the attacker captures the encrypted or hashed password. During that time, the password should have been changed—making the unencrypted password now useless.

In contrast, weak passwords can be identified in a matter of hours or days, even when they have been encrypted. Encryption cannot protect against passwords that are easily guessed, because weak passwords are vulnerable to *dictionary attacks*. Dictionary attacks encrypt a list of common passwords, and compare each possibility with the captured cyphertext. If the password appears in the password dictionary, the attacker will identify the password quickly. You can defend against this vulnerability by implementing a strong password policy.

> **Off the Record** The best way to understand how effective dictionary attacks are is to grab a password cracking tool from the Internet and experiment with it on a test machine. I can't point you to a specific tool, but they're not hard to find.

What is a strong password?

A strong password is one that can be remembered by the user but that is also complex enough to be difficult to guess. For example, *&_I5y#<.h may appear to be a good password, but the user might be forced to write it down in order to remember it, creating a significant security vulnerability. Fortunately, there are techniques for creating strong passwords that the human brain can remember. For example, you could take a password that is easy to remember (and easy to guess), such as *99Butterflies*, and add an easy-to-remember suffix to it to make it more secure: *99Butterflies@complexpassword.com*. You now have a password that is 33 characters long, uses uppercase, lowercase, and symbols, is easy to remember, and that, because of the length, is harder than the *&_I5y#<.h password to crack.

In the example above, an e-mail type suffix was added to the end of the password to make it complex. You can also add phone numbers, addresses, and file path locations (like c:\winnt\system32) to make a password complex.

Strong password policy

When implementing and enforcing a password policy, consider the users' inability to remember passwords that are too complex, change too often, and are too long. When passwords are too complex or too long, the eventuality that users will use other methods to remember their passwords, such as writing them down, is more likely.

> **Important** There is nothing seriously wrong with a user writing down a password to remember it, as long as the written-down copy is not easily accessible. Actually, users feel more comfortable if they can write down their passwords and are more likely to create more complex passwords.

To help implement a strong password policy, Windows Server 2003 provides a feature known as Password Complexity. Password Complexity is enforced by default in the Windows Server 2003 environment. The Password Complexity feature requires that passwords:

- Do not contain all or part of the user's account name.
- Be at least six characters in length.
- Contain characters from three of the following four categories:
  - Uppercase characters (A through Z)
  - Lowercase characters (a through z)
  - Base 10 digits (0 through 9)
  - Non-alphabetic characters (for example, !, $, #, %)

> **Note** By default, Windows Server 2003 requires that passwords are seven characters long, exceeding the requirement imposed by the Password Complexity feature.

Table 1.3 describes the security policy settings that you can use to implement a strong password policy. These policy settings are located in the Password Policy node in Account Policies.

See Also Security configuration settings such as minimum password length are configured using security policy. Security policy is covered in more detail in Chapter 3, "Deploying and Troubleshooting Security Templates."

Table 1.3 Security Policy Settings for Strong Passwords

Security policy setting	Description
Maximum password age	Determines how long passwords can be used before users are required to change them. The default value of 42 days is generally appropriate. Ideally, this value would be lower than the time it takes a commercial password cracking program to compromise the passwords in your organization. Lowering this value decreases the likelihood that a password will be cracked while it is still valid, but may increase the number of support calls relating to forgotten passwords.
Enforce password history	Stores the passwords that users have used previously and prevents reuse of those passwords. The default setting is also the maximum: 24 passwords remembered.
Minimum password age	Determines how long a user must keep a password before changing it. The default setting of one day will prevent a user from immediately changing a password to a previous one.
Minimum password length	Determines the minimum length of a password. The minimum recommended setting is the default of 7 characters.

Tip You can use the Microsoft Platform Software Development Kit (SDK) to develop custom password complexity requirements for your organization.

Although you can enforce strong passwords through security policy in Windows Server 2003 Active Directory, employee education is the only way to keep users from writing down passwords in public locations or using discoverable personal information in passwords.

Options for Account Lockout Policies

Account lockout policies exist to limit your vulnerability to password-guessing attacks. When an account lockout policy is defined, a user account is automatically locked out after a specified number of incorrect password attempts. Windows Server 2003 does not enable account lockouts by default, and for a good reason: enabling account lockouts exposes you to a denial-of-service vulnerability. A malicious attacker with access to user names can guess incorrect passwords, which will cause those accounts to become locked out, which denies legitimate users from accessing network resources.

Therefore, account lockout policies should only be enabled in environments where the threat from guessed passwords is greater than the threat of a denial-of-service attack. Account lockout policies are set and enforced at the domain level. When enabled, these policies should be set to allow for user error, but to prevent attacks on user accounts.

Security Alert Account lockout policies are not necessary in environments where an intrusion detection system exists. An intrusion detection system will detect that an attacker is repeatedly guessing passwords and notify a system administrator. The system administrator can then track down the malicious attacker and stop the attack before the password is successfully guessed.

Account lockout settings

Table 1.4 describes the various account lockout settings that you can use to secure your network. These policy settings are located in the Account Lockout Policy in Account Policies.

Table 1.4 Password and Account Lockout Settings

Security policy setting	Description
Account lockout threshold	Determines how many logon attempts can be made before the account is locked out. This setting does not apply to attempts to log on at the console of a locked workstation or to attempts to unlock a screensaver, because locked workstations cannot be forced to run password-cracking programs.
Account lockout duration	Determines how many minutes a locked-out account will remain disabled before being automatically enabled. Setting this to 0 will require an administrator to unlock the account manually.
Reset account lockout counter after	Determines the number of minutes that must elapse after a failed logon attempt before the counter is reset to 0 bad logon attempts.

Options for Creating a Kerberos Ticket Policy

You should establish reasonable lifetimes for Kerberos tickets in your organization. Reasonable Kerberos ticket lifetimes must be short enough to prevent attackers from cracking the cryptography that protects the ticket's stored credentials. Reasonable ticket lifetimes must also be long enough to ensure that requests for new tickets do not overload the KDC and network.

Default domain policies for Kerberos tickets

Table 1.5 describes the default domain policy options available for Kerberos tickets. These policy settings are located in the Kerberos Policy node in Account Policies.

Table 1.5 Security Policy Settings for Kerberos Ticket Policy

Security policy setting	Description
Enforce user logon restrictions	Determines whether the KDC validates every request for a session ticket by examining the user rights policy on the target computer. This option also serves as a means of ensuring that the requesting account is still valid and was not disabled since the Kerberos ticket was issued. This option could potentially slow down network logons.
Maximum lifetime for service ticket	Determines the amount of time a service ticket is available before it expires. This setting should be set the same as the user ticket setting, unless your users run jobs that are longer then their user tickets would allow.
Maximum lifetime for user ticket	Determines the amount of time a user ticket is available before it expires. This setting should be set according to the average amount of time a user logs on to a computer at your organization.
Maximum lifetime for user ticket renewal	Determines the number of days for which a user's TGT can be renewed. The default is seven days. Shortening this interval will increase security but put more load on the KDC.
Maximum tolerance for computer clock synchronization	Determines the maximum time difference (in minutes) between the time on the user's computer's clock and the time on the domain controller. Raising this value from the default of five minutes increases your vulnerability to replay attacks, in which encrypted credentials captured from the network are resubmitted by a malicious attacker. Lowering this value will increase the number of authentication failures caused by unsynchronized clocks.

Windows 2003 Authentication Methods for Earlier Operating Systems

Authentication protocols have improved over time and will continue to improve in the future. As a result, earlier operating systems support fewer and less secure authentication protocols than newer operating systems. By default, computers running Windows Server 2003 can accept all types of authentication protocols, including LM, NTLMv2, and Kerberos, to ensure compatibility with earlier operating systems. If your organization does not require this backward compatibility, you can you can configure security policy to support only the more secure protocols, such as NTLMv2 and Kerberos.

The Network Security LAN Manager Authentication Level policy defines which authentication protocols a computer sends and accepts. This policy is contained within the Local Policies\Security Options security policy node. Table 1.6 describes the options for this policy setting. The policy settings are listed in order from least to most secure. Increasing the security of this policy reduces compatibility with earlier clients and servers.

Table 1.6 LM Authentication Levels

Security policy setting	Description
Send LM & NTLM responses	Clients use LM and NTLM authentication and never use NTLMv2 session security; domain controllers accept LM, NTLM, and NTLMv2 authentication. This setting ensures that clients will be able to authenticate with servers using operating systems earlier than Windows NT 4.0 Service Pack 4 by forcing clients to send only LM and NTLM authentication. This setting reduces authentication security.
Send LM & NTLM responses – use NTLMv2 session security if negotiated	Clients use LM and NTLM authentication and use NTLMv2 session security if the server supports it; domain controllers accept LM, NTLM, and NTLMv2 authentication. This setting enables the more secure NTLMv2 authentication protocol to be used when possible, while providing backward compatibility.
Send NTLM response only	Clients use NTLM authentication only and use NTLMv2 session security if the server supports it; domain controllers accept LM, NTLM, and NTLMv2 authentication. This setting eliminates the possibility that LM authentication will be used; however, clients will not be able to authenticate to computers running Windows 95 or Windows 98.
Send NTLMv2 response only	Clients use NTLMv2 authentication only and use NTLMv2 session security if the server supports it; domain controllers accept LM, NTLM, and NTLMv2 authentication. This setting improves authentication security by forcing clients to refuse down-level authentication protocols required by servers using operating systems earlier than Windows NT 4.0 Service Pack 4.

Table 1.6 LM Authentication Levels

Security policy setting	Description
Send NTLMv2 response only\refuse LM	Clients use NTLMv2 authentication only and use NTLMv2 session security if the server supports it; domain controllers refuse LM (accept only NTLM and NTLMv2 authentication). This setting will cause clients running Windows 95, Windows 98, and Windows NT 4.0 Service Pack 3 (or earlier) to be unable to authenticate to domain controllers.
Send NTLMv2 response only\refuse LM & NTLM	Clients use NTLMv2 authentication only and use NTLMv2 session security if the server supports it; domain controllers refuse LM and NTLM (accept only NTLMv2 authentication). This setting will cause clients running Windows 95, Windows 98, and Windows NT 4.0 Service Pack 3 (or earlier) to be unable to authenticate to domain controllers.

Enabling anonymous authentication for earlier applications

Anonymous authentication allows users and network clients to be authenticated (but not necessarily authorized to access network resources) without providing any credentials. Unlike earlier Windows operating systems, in Windows Server 2003, anonymous users are not considered to be members of the Everyone group and therefore will not be authorized to use any network resources. However, there are some scenarios in which anonymous access needs to be granted to provide compatibility with systems prior to Windows 2000. Situations in which this access might be necessary include:

- Remote Access Server (RAS) servers on Windows NT 4.0 use anonymous access to determine dial-in permissions.
- Windows NT 4.0 might use anonymous access to enumerate shares or gather information from domain controllers.
- Anonymous access might be used to enumerate shares and users in a one-way cross-forest trust.
- Earlier operating systems might use anonymous access to change passwords in Active Directory. This is accomplished through the Pre–Windows 2000–compatible access group.

If you have earlier systems in your Windows Server 2003 domain, you will need to determine which resources need anonymous access. You can then enable anonymous access by performing one of the following tasks:

- *Add the Anonymous Logon security principal to the ACL that needs access.* This is the preferred method for enabling anonymous access to resources because it is the most granular.

- *Enable the Network Access: Share That Can Be Accessed Anonymously security policy setting.* This security policy setting contains a list of shares that can be accessed and is useful for enabling anonymous access to a specific share on multiple computers.
- *Enable the Network Access: Let Everyone Permissions Apply To Anonymous Users security policy setting.* This setting causes unauthenticated users to be considered members of the Everyone group, which might authorize users to access network resources without being authenticated as valid users. This setting should only be enabled when absolutely necessary, because it creates a significant, exploitable vulnerability.

Caution Apply the Anonymous Logon, Network Access: Share That Can Be Accessed Anonymously, Network Access: Let Everyone Permissions Apply To Anonymous Users settings only to the OU or server that needs them. Enabling these settings at the domain level will decrease network security.

Enabling secure authentication for domain controllers

Though many systems on a network may authenticate users that exist within a local user database, domain controllers provide most authentication services for network resources in Active Directory environments. Whenever possible, you should configure domain controllers to refuse LM authentication, because LM authentication is more vulnerable than other authentication protocols. To configure domain controllers to reject LM authentication:

1. On a domain controller, click Start, click Administrative Tools, and then click Domain Controller Security Policy.
2. Expand Local Policies and then select Security Options, as shown in Figure 1.1.

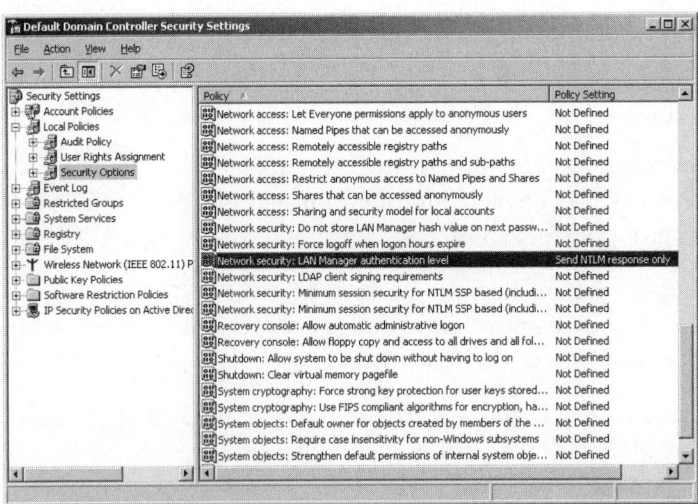

Figure 1.1 The Default Domain Controllers Security Settings console

3. Double-click Network Security: LAN Manager Authentication Level. The Network Security: LAN Manager Authentication Level Properties dialog box appears, as shown in Figure 1.2.

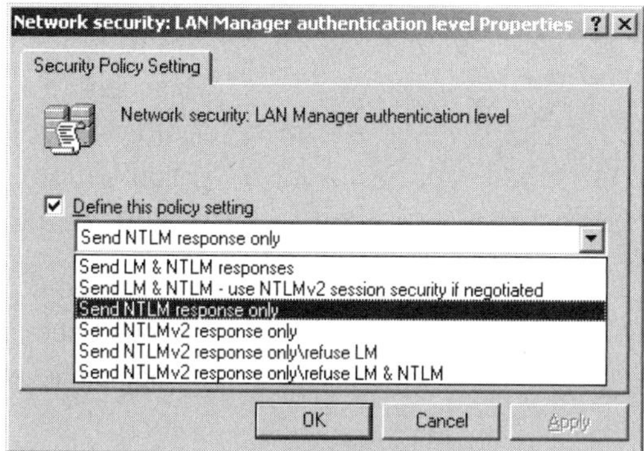

Figure 1.2 Security policy settings

4. Select the Define This Policy Setting check box, if it is not already selected.
5. Select Send NTLMv2 Response Only\Refuse LM, and then click OK.
6. Close the Default Domain Controller Security Settings console.
7. Click Start, and then click Run. Type **gpupdate.exe**, and click OK. This causes the policy to take effect on the local domain controller immediately.

Using Multifactor Authentication

As described earlier in this chapter, multifactor authentication significantly increases authentication security. Windows Server 2003 supports multifactor authentication by using smart cards and can support a variety of other authentication mechanisms using non-Microsoft hardware and software.

Smart cards can be required for all users in an organization. However, because of the additional cost, smart cards are often assigned only for specific users. Often network administrators are required to use smart cards because their privileges on the network would provide an attacker significant opportunity.

To require a smart card for interactive logon, launch the Active Directory Users And Computers console. Double-click the user account to view the properties, and click the Account tab. In the Account Options list, select Smart Card Is Required For Interactive Logon.

Requiring smart cards for authentication can cause problems with existing applications. However, if an application includes the Certified for Windows Server 2003 logo, the application has been tested to ensure that it meets Microsoft security standards for Windows Server 2003. From a security perspective, an application that is identified as

Certified for Windows Server 2003 meets the following criteria:

- *Support smart card logons.* The application should work correctly with smart card authentication and will allow smart card authentication to a terminal service.
- *Provide secure credential management.* Ensures that users will get appropriate prompting for credentials and storing credentials. Also means that the application can use Kerberos, NTLM, and Secure Sockets Layer (SSL) protocols. A user can also log on using a user principal name (UPN) format.
- *Can be run in a highly secure configuration.* Applications can perform all primary functions in a highly secure configuration. In a highly secure configuration, applications cannot use the unsafe communication protocol NTLM; strong authentication and account policies are set; and group membership is restricted. A highly secure configuration is a system with a clean installation of Windows and with the predefined security template Hisecws.inf applied.
- *Provide secure network connections.* Applications using network connections must not depend on protocols that are known to have vulnerabilities.

Practice: Adjusting Authentication Options

In this practice, you will secure authentication on a Windows 2003 Server by using security policy. You must be logged on to Computer1.cohowinery.com with an account that has administrative credentials to create and modify the default domain controller security policy.

Your company has recently updated its security policy. The new security policy specifically forbids using the LM authentication protocol to authenticate users in the cohowinery.com domain. To comply with the updated security policy, you will use the Domain Controller Security Policy console to ensure that LM authentication is not used on any cohowinery.com domain controller.

▶ Exercise 1: Disabling LM Authentication

In this exercise, you will configure the domain controllers to accept only NTLM and refuse LM default domain controllers security policy.

1. Log on to the cohowinery.com domain on Computer1 using the Administrator account.
2. Click Start, click Administrative Tools, and then click Domain Controller Security Policy.
3. Expand Local Policies, and then select Security Options.
4. In the right pane, double-click Network Security: LAN Manager Authentication Level.

5. Select the Define This Policy Setting check box if it is not already selected.
6. Select Send NTLMv2 Response Only\Refuse LM, and then click OK.
7. Click Start, and then click Run. Type **gpupdate.exe**, and click OK. This causes the policy to take effect on the local domain controller immediately. .

▶ Exercise 2: Enable Account Lockout

In this exercise, you will configure the domain controllers to accept only NTLM and refuse LM default domain controller security policy.

1. Log on to the cohowinery.com domain on Computer1 using the Administrator account.
2. Click Start, click Administrative Tools, and then click Active Directory Users And Computers.
3. Right-click the Users node, click New, and then click User.
4. In the First Name field, type **Admin1**. In the User Logon Name field, type **Admin1**.
5. In the Password and Confirm Password fields, type a complex password. Clear the User Must Change Password At Next Logon check box. Click Next, and then click Finish.
6. In Active Directory Users And Computers, double-click the Admin1 user you just created.
7. In the Admin1 Properties dialog box, click the Member Of tab. Click Add, and then specify the Administrators group. Click OK twice to return to the Active Directory Users And Computers console.
8. Click Start, click Administrative Tools, and then click Domain Security Policy.
9. Expand Account Policies, and then select Account Lockout Policy.
10. In the right pane, double-click Account Lockout Threshold.
11. In the Account Lockout Threshold Properties dialog box, select Define This Policy Setting. In the Account Will Lock Out After field, type **6**. Click OK.
12. Review the Suggested Value Changes dialog box, and then click OK.
13. Click Start, and then click Run. Type **gpupdate.exe**, and click OK. This causes the policy to take effect on the local domain controller immediately.
14. Log off from Computer1.
15. Attempt to log on as Admin1, but do not type a password. Repeatedly attempt to log on to simulate a malicious attacker attempting to guess a password. After six attempts, you will be notified that the Admin1 account is locked out, as shown in Figure 1.3.

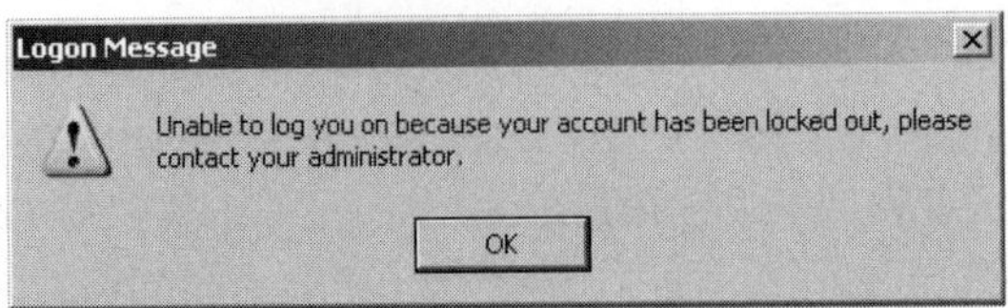

Figure 1.3 Account lockout warning

After completing this exercise, remove the Admin1 account and return the account lockout policies to their default settings.

Lesson Review

The following questions are intended to reinforce key information presented in this lesson. If you are unable to answer a question, review the lesson materials and try the question again. You can find answers to the questions in the "Questions and Answers" section at the end of this chapter.

1. Which of the following passwords is an example of a strong password?
   - **a.** tyia
   - **b.** imsitrjs5itr
   - **c.** passwordpassword
   - **d.** l%@3tty7&

   ____

   ____

   ____

2. Which of the following are valid reasons to enable LM authentication? (Choose all that apply.)
   - **a.** Users will access network resources using computers running Windows 95.
   - **b.** Users will access network resources using computers running Windows 98.
   - **c.** Users will access network resources using computers running Windows NT.
   - **d.** Users will access network resources using computers running Windows Me.
   - **e.** Users will access network resources using computers running Windows 2000.
   - **f.** Users will access network resources using computers running Windows XP.

   ____

   ____

3. Enabling account lockout accomplishes which of the following goals?
   a. Makes it impossible to steal a user's password.
   b. Reduces the likelihood that a malicious attacker will use brute force techniques to discover a user's password.
   c. Eliminates the need for strong passwords.
   d. Reduces Help desk costs.

Lesson Summary

- Use security policy settings to configure authentication requirements.
- Implement a strong password policy in your organization to reduce the likelihood that your users' credentials will be compromised.
- Although you can enforce complex passwords by using security policy in Windows Server 2003 Active Directory, employee education is the only way to keep users from writing down passwords or using discoverable personal information in passwords.
- An account lockout policy prevents malicious attackers from logging on by continually guessing passwords; however, it enables malicious attackers to perform a denial-of-service attack that denies valid users from successful authentication.
- Kerberos ticket lifetimes must be short enough to prevent attackers from cracking the cryptography that protects the ticket's stored credentials, but long enough to minimize the number of tickets that clients request.
- Use delegated authentication and constrained delegation as strategies for implementing supplemental authentication where required.
- Any application that has the Certified for Windows Server 2003 logo has been tested to ensure that it will function in environments that require multifactor authentication.

Lesson 3: Configuring Authentication for Web Users

Active Directory is a perfect way to store credentials for internal users because it can provide single sign-on authentication for a variety of network resources, including Web servers. If your organization provides an internal Web site, the Web site should authenticate users by using their existing Active Directory user accounts. If the Web site accesses information on the user's behalf, such as querying a database to retrieve confidential benefits information, the Web site should access that information by using the user's own credentials.

Active Directory is not the ideal way to store credentials for external users. Many organizations invite customers, potential customers, and partners outside the organization to access information, files, and data. Today, information is usually shared with external users by means of a Web site. If the Web site allows anyone on the Internet to access content, these Web users will be considered anonymous. However, the anonymous user's requests must still be issued in the context of a valid security principal in order to access files and data.

Configuring Anonymous Access for Web Users

Most public Web sites on the Internet allow anonymous access for at least a portion of the site. In other words, the general public can retrieve pages from the Web server without providing credentials. This does not mean that authentication is not taking place, however. Any user or process that accesses a file or other network resource must do so in the context of a security principal (a user, a computer, or a service account). When Internet Information Services (IIS) accesses files to be sent to an anonymous user, it uses a specified user account to access those files. When anonymous access is not allowed, users must provide their own credentials.

As an administrator, you can control which user account IIS uses to access files and other network resources on behalf of anonymous users. By default, this account is automatically created during the IIS installation process and is named IUSR_*computername*. To specify different user credentials for IIS to use when accessing files and resources on behalf of an anonymous user, first create a new user account, and then follow these steps:

1. Log on to the computer as an administrator.
2. Click Start, click Administrative Tools, and then click Internet Information Services Manager.
3. Expand the computer node, and then expand the Web Sites folder. Right-click the node for the Web site you are editing, and then click Properties.
4. Click the Directory Security tab. In the Authentication And Access Control grouping, click the Edit button.

5. The Authentication Methods dialog box appears. Type the user's credentials in the User Name and Password fields, and then click OK.
6. Click OK again to return to the Internet Information Services Manager.

Configuring Web Authentication

This chapter has already described three authentication protocols: LM, NTLM, and Kerberos. However, none of these protocols can be used by a Web browser to authenticate a user to a Web server because Web browsers and Web servers can use only Hypertext Transfer Protocol (HTTP) to communicate. Web browsers must authenticate to Web servers using an authentication protocol that is contained within HTTP. Administrators configuring an IIS server have several authentication options that differ in how they pass the credentials to IIS and which browsers support them:

- *Basic Authentication.* Selecting this option enables browsers to submit the user's password in an encoded format that is equivalent to clear text. If the authentication traffic is intercepted, an attacker could easily determine the user's password. While this authentication method is vulnerable to being intercepted, it is supported by a wide range of browsers. Basic authentication should be chosen only when browser compatibility is required.
- *Digest Authentication For Windows Domain Servers.* Selecting this option allows the Web browser to submit the user's password in an MD5 hash. If digest authentication traffic is intercepted, an attacker would be able to easily determine the user's password.

Security Alert Digest authentication functions only if the domain controller has a reversibly encrypted (clear text) copy of the requesting user's password stored in Active Directory. Using reversible encryption is not recommended. As a result, integrated Windows authentication is recommended over digest authentication.

- *Integrated Windows Authentication.* Selecting this option enables Kerberos v5 authentication and NTLM authentication within the Web requests. This allows the Web browser to send the user's password in the form of a hash without requiring the user's password to be stored using reversible encryption. Integrated Windows Authentication is supported by Microsoft Internet Explorer but may not be supported by other browsers.
- *.NET Passport Authentication.* Select this option if your organization is using the .NET Passport service for authentication. .NET Passport provides a central authentication service that many different organizations can use and allows users to authenticate themselves to many different, unrelated Web sites. Selecting this option will have no effect unless application developers have created a .NET Passport–enabled site.

Planning If your users will have a recent version of Internet Explorer, use Integrated Windows Authentication. If you can't mandate a particular browser, enable both Integrated Windows Authentication and Basic Authentication.

Delegated Authentication

Delegated authentication occurs when a network service accepts a request from a user and assumes that user's identity in order to initiate a new connection to a second network service. Delegated authentication occurs by default when anonymous access is disabled for IIS. A typical architecture in which delegated authentication is used is shown in Figure 1.4.

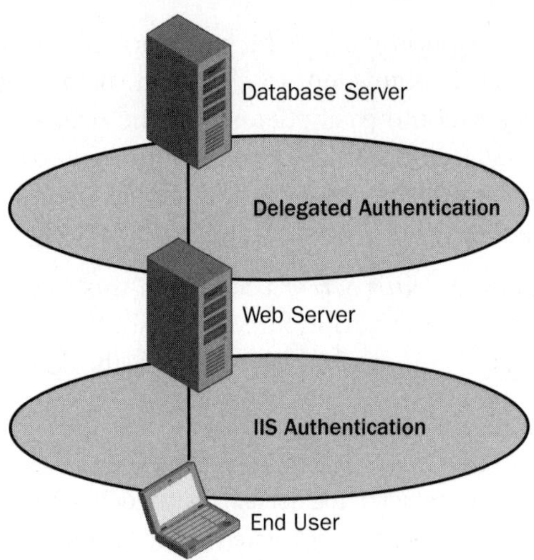

Figure 1.4 Typical delegated authentication architecture

Using delegated authentication increases the security of back-end network services. Without the use of delegated authentication, a back-end database must grant the Web server access to all data that any user would potentially need to access. In essence, without delegated authentication, the database must rely entirely on the Web server to authenticate and authorize users.

With delegated authentication, the Web server presents the end user's credentials when accessing data from the back-end database. The database can then determine whether the user should be able to access the requested piece of information. In the case of a human resources database, the database administrators could configure the database to allow employees to only view the names and locations of users. However, employees working in the human resources department could be granted access to view and update specific rows and columns in the database that should not be accessible to all users.

To delegate this right, assign the Enable Computer And User Accounts To Be Trusted For Delegation user right to the selected individuals. By default, Administrators have this right. Users who are assigned the right to enable delegated authentication can then edit the properties of computer accounts in the Active Directory Users And Computers console, select the Delegation tab, and click one of the two Trust This Computer For Delegation options. This setting should be specified for computer and service accounts that are used to provide users information that is stored on back-end servers and must be accessed securely.

Security Alert Misuse of this user right, or of the Trusted For Delegation setting, could make the network vulnerable to sophisticated attacks such as Trojan horse programs that impersonate incoming clients and use their credentials to gain access to network resources. As a result, you should set the Account Cannot Be Delegated option on accounts that are sensitive.

By enabling delegated authentication, you can prevent an attacker who gains control of a server from accessing data stored on other servers that require user credentials to access. By requiring that all data be accessed by means of credentials that are delegated to the server for use on the client's behalf, you ensure that the server cannot be compromised and then used to gain access to sensitive information on other servers. However, if the server itself was given access to information stored on other servers, an attacker who gains control of a server would be able to access the information stored on the other servers.

Important If you enable Encrypting File System (EFS) on a file server, that server must be trusted for delegation to obtain certificates on behalf of a user to encrypt and decrypt files.

When you enable delegated authentication for a computer account by selecting the Trust This Computer For Delegation To Any Service option, delegation is automatically enabled for all services on that computer. Constrained delegation allows administrators to specify particular services from which a computer that is trusted for delegation can request resources. By using constrained delegation, you can prevent attackers who compromise a server from accessing resources that are not intended to be accessed by that server. Specify constrained delegation by selecting the Trust This Computer For Delegation To Specified Services Only option, specifying the available authentication protocols, and then selecting the services, as shown in Figure 1.5.

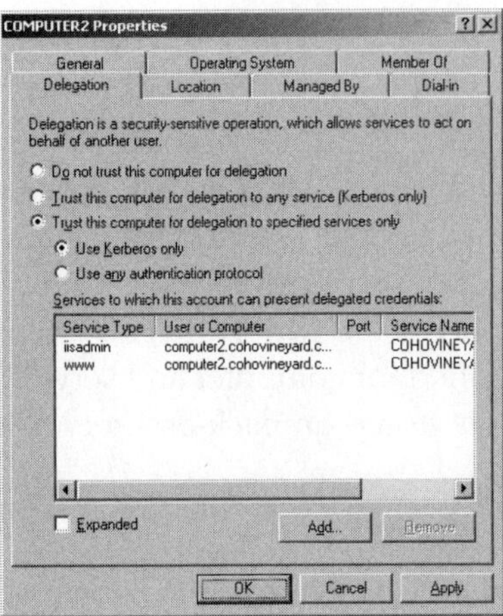

Figure 1.5 Computer account properties dialog box

Practice: Configuring Anonymous Authentication

In this practice, you will install the Application Server role on Computer1.cohowinery.com. You will then configure it so that it does not allow anonymous Web requests, and verify that it is configured correctly by issuing a request from Computer2.cohovineyard.com.

▶ Exercise 1: Installing the Application Server Role

In this exercise, you install the Application Server role. While this exercise is not directly significant to the material covered on the exam, the Application Server role must be available for future exercises that relate directly to configuring authentication for Web users.

> **Warning** It is critical that your server is not connected to a public network during this exercise. Installing the Application Server role may introduce security vulnerabilities.

1. Log on to the cohowinery.com domain on Computer1 by using the Administrator account.
2. Click Start, click Administrative Tools, and then click Manage Your Server.
3. Click Add Or Remove A Role.
4. On the Preliminary Steps page of the Configure Your Server Wizard, click Next.
5. On the Server Role page, click Application Server, and then click Next.
6. On the Application Server Options page, select Enable ASP.NET, and then click Next.

7. On the Summary Of Selections page, click Next.
8. Follow the instructions provided by the wizard. When the installation has completed, click Finish.

▶ Exercise 2: Verifying Anonymous Access

In this exercise, you verify that anonymous access to Web pages is enabled by default by issuing an anonymous request from Computer2.cohovineyard.com.

1. Log on to the cohovineyard.com domain on Computer2 by using the Administrator account.
2. Click Start, click All Programs, and then click Internet Explorer. Close any warnings that appear.
3. In the Address field of Internet Explorer, type **http://computer1.cohowinery.com**, and then click Go.

   An Under Construction page will appear. While this resembles an error page produced by Internet Explorer, the page titled Under Construction is an HTML page located at C:\Inetpub\wwwroot\iisstart.htm on Computer1. The page was successfully retrieved by Internet Explorer because anonymous access is currently enabled in IIS. IIS accessed the file using the IUSR_Computer1 user account.

▶ Exercise 3: Removing Anonymous Access

In this exercise, you remove anonymous access and verify that anonymous requests are rejected.

1. Log on to the cohowinery.com domain on Computer1 by using the Administrator account.
2. Click Start, click Administrative Tools, and then click Internet Information Services Manager.
3. Expand the Computer1 node, and then expand the Web Sites folder. Right-click Default Web Site, and then click Properties. The Default Web Site Properties dialog box appears.
4. Click the Directory Security tab. In the Authentication And Access Control grouping, click the Edit button. The Authentication Methods dialog box appears, as shown in Figure 1.6.

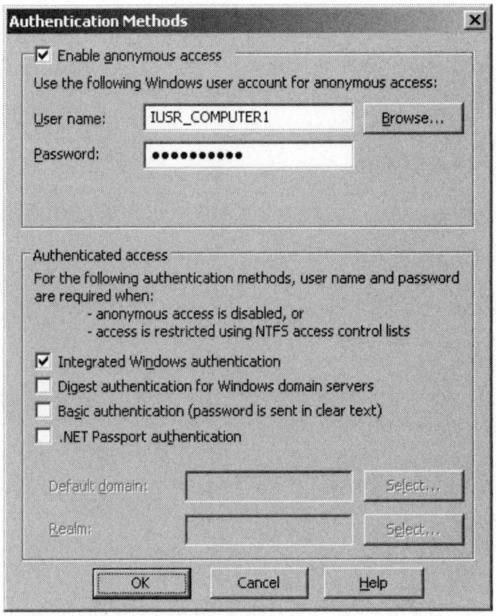

Figure 1.6 Authentication Methods dialog box

Notice that Enable Anonymous access is currently selected. IUSR_COMPUTER1 appears in the User Name field. Any resources that anonymous users attempt to access through IIS will be accessed by the IUSR_COMPUTER1 account. The IUSR_*computername* account is automatically created when the Application Server role is added to the computer.

5. Clear Enable Anonymous Access, and then click OK. Click OK again to close the Default Web Site Properties dialog box.

6. Return to Computer2. In Internet Explorer, click the View menu, and then click Refresh.

   After you click Refresh, Internet Explorer sends another anonymous request for the iisstart.htm file that it is currently displaying. However, this time IIS will not return the page. Instead, IIS will return an access denied error, also known as a Hypertext Transfer Protocol (HTTP) 401 error.

7. Because the anonymous request was denied by IIS, Internet Explorer opens the Connect To Computer1.cohowinery.com dialog to prompt you for a user name and password, as shown in Figure 1.7. Click Cancel.

Figure 1.7 Internet Explorer prompt for credentials

Internet Explorer displays a friendly description of the access denied error. This is the default error that users receive when they are either not adequately authenticated or not authorized to access content. Web application developers can customize the error message.

8. In Internet Explorer, on the View menu, click Refresh. You will again be prompted to provide credentials to access the page.

9. In the User Name field, type **Administrator**. In the Password field, type the Computer1 administrator password. Click OK.

   Internet Explorer successfully displays the Under Construction page because you provided credentials that were authorized to access the requested file. Note that you did not directly retrieve the iisstart.htm file from the file system. Instead, IIS retrieved the file on your behalf using the Administrator credentials you provided, and then returned the page to Internet Explorer.

Lesson Review

The following questions are intended to reinforce key information presented in this lesson. If you are unable to answer a question, review the lesson materials and try the question again. You can find answers to the questions in the "Questions and Answers" section at the end of this chapter.

1. Which of the following authentication methods should be chosen for a Web site on a public Internet with minimal security requirements, where administrators have no control over which browser a client uses?

   a. Basic Authentication

   b. Digest Authentication For Windows Domain Servers

c. Integrated Windows Authentication

d. .NET Passport Authentication

____

____

____

2. Which of the following authentication methods should be chosen for a high-security, internal Web site in an Active Directory environment where single sign-on is a requirement?

   a. Basic Authentication

   b. Digest Authentication For Windows Domain Servers

   c. Integrated Windows Authentication

   d. .NET Passport Authentication

____

3. Which of the following scenarios requires delegated authentication?

   a. A public Web site from which all content should be anonymously accessed.

   b. An internal Web site from which all content should be anonymously accessed.

   c. An internal Web site containing simple Hypertext Markup Language (HTML) documents that only managers should be able to access.

   d. An internal Web site that accesses a back-end server containing data that only specific users should be able to access.

____

____

Lesson Summary

- Web users have special authentication considerations. Specifically, you must choose whether anonymous access will be allowed, and what account will be used to access resources on behalf of anonymous users. If anonymous access is not allowed, you will be making use of delegated authentication.
- Web users have four choices for Web authentication methods: Basic Authentication, Digest Authentication For Windows Domain Servers, Integrated Windows Authentication, and .NET Passport Authentication.
- Use delegated authentication, and the more granular constrained delegation, when front-end servers must access back-end services on behalf of authenticated users.

Lesson 4: Creating Trusts in Windows Server 2003

You should already be familiar with the role Active Directory fulfills for authenticating users on a domain. Briefly, Active Directory stores and organizes a list of users that have access to network resources. Network resources that participate in an Active Directory domain rely on the Active Directory domain controllers to authenticate a user's credentials before the network resource determines whether the user is authorized to access the resource. Active Directory enables administrators to organize these users in a variety of ways to delegate administrative responsibilities, simplify administration, and improve security.

Many smaller organizations are able to manage their network resources by using a single Active Directory domain. In the single domain model, all user and computer accounts are contained within a single domain. Users must have an account in that domain to access network resources. While the simplicity of a single domain makes it ideal, there are many circumstances that require multiple domains that must interact with each other.

Windows Server 2003 requires that enterprises create multiple domains to apply different security policies to users or resources. Some aspects of an enterprise's security policy, such as minimum password length, can only be defined once for an entire Active Directory domain. Therefore, if an organization within the enterprise requires higher security than the rest of the enterprise, that organization might require its own domain. For more information about security policies, refer to Chapter 3, "Deploying and Troubleshooting Security Templates."

Many enterprises are using multiple domains to enable compatibility with earlier operating systems. It was common practice to create separate Windows NT 4 domains for each geographic location or to separate users from resources. While those are not valid reasons to create separate Windows 2000 Server or Windows Server 2003 domains, enterprises might choose to maintain an existing, if outdated, domain model.

Managing trusts between large numbers of domains is complicated and laborious. To simplify this task, Active Directory domains can be organized into *forests*. A forest is a hierarchical structure that begins with a *forest root domain*. When domains are added to a forest, they inherit the root domain name, schema, and other characteristics from the forest root domain. Figure 1.8 shows an example of a forest.

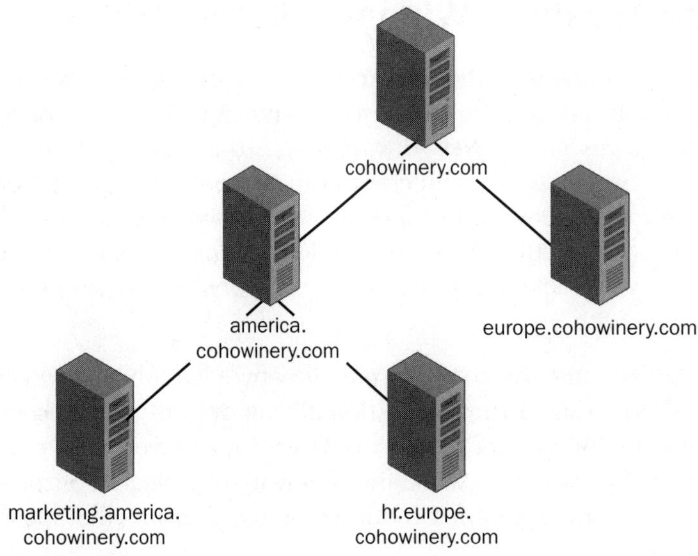

Figure 1.8 A forest

Enterprises that have multiple domains often need to allow users in one domain to access resources in another domain. Active Directory provides security across multiple domains and forests by using domain and forest trusts. Trusts are a critical part of a networking infrastructure and one of the concepts that seem to be misunderstood quite frequently.

> **See Also** This training kit focuses on implementing and managing trusts. For more information about domain and forest design, refer to *MCSE Self-Paced Training Kit (Exam 70-297): Designing a Microsoft Windows Server 2003 Active Directory and Network Infrastructure*.

In this lesson, you will learn about the various elements of trusts, types of trusts, common scenarios for creating trusts, and how to effectively manage the security of trusts.

After this lesson, you will be able to

- Decide which trust type to create in a given situation.
- Determine which authentication method to use with each trust type.
- Determine the appropriate trust type for an operating system.
- Create a cross-forest trust.

Estimated lesson time: 20 minutes

Trusts in Windows Server 2003

A *trust* is a relationship that is established between domains or forests that enables users and other security principals from one domain to be authenticated by domain controllers in another domain. Configuring a trust enables a domain to authenticate users and other security principals that exist in a remote domain. A trust does not authorize users to access resources in the remote domain, however. Network resources authorize trusted users just as they would authorize a user in the local domain: through the use of security descriptors on the resources that need to be accessed.

For example, if John has an account in domain A and attempts to print to a printer in domain B immediately after the trust has been created, he will be denied access. However, because the trust is in place, an administrator will be able to grant John's account access to print to the printer. Without the trust in place, the administrator would not be able to select John's user account when authorizing users to print.

Types of trusts

Table 1.7 describes the types of trusts supported in Windows Server 2003.

Table 1.7 Windows Server 2003 Trusts

Trust type	Description
Parent/child trust	In Windows Server 2003, this is a default trust between all domains in the forest. This two-way transitive trust allows security principals to be authenticated in any domain in the forest. These trusts are created by default and cannot be removed.
Tree/root trust	In Windows Server 2003, this is a default trust between all domain trees in the forest. This two-way transitive trust allows security principals to be authenticated in any domain in the forest. These trusts are created by default and cannot be removed.
External	This trust type is created manually between domains that are not part of the forest. These trusts can be one-way or two-way and are not transitive.
Realm	This trust type is created manually between a non-Windows-brand operating system domain (referred to as a *Kerberos realm*) and a Windows Server 2003 domain. These trusts can be one-way or two-way and can be transitive or non-transitive.
Forest	This trust type is created manually between forests that use the Windows Server 2003 domain functional level. These trusts can be one-way or two-way and can be transitive or non-transitive.
Shortcut	This trust type is created manually within a Windows Server 2003 forest to reduce logon times between domains in a forest. This one-way or two-way trust is particularly useful when traversing tree-root trusts, because the trust path to a destination domain is potentially reduced.

Tip You can create trusts by using the Active Directory Domains And Trusts console or the Netdom.exe command-line tool.

Microsoft Windows Small Business Server 2003 does not support the creation of trusts.

Authentication methods used with trusts in Windows Server 2003

Because trusts allow you to facilitate access to resources in a multidomain environment, it is important that you use the most secure authentication protocol whenever possible when creating trusts between domains and realms. You also need to understand the various authentication types associated with each trust type. For example, if you have secured your authentication in your organization to accept only Kerberos authentication, an external trust to a Windows NT 4.0 domain will fail because a Windows NT 4.0 domain cannot use Kerberos.

Table 1.8 lists the various authentication protocols that can be used with specific trust types.

Table 1.8 Authentication Protocols Used with Trusts

Trust type	Authentication protocol
Parent/child trusts	Kerberos, NTLM
Tree/root trusts	Kerberos, NTLM
External	NTLM
Realm	Kerberos
Forest	Kerberos, NTLM
Shortcut	Kerberos, NTLM

The attributes of each authentication protocol will be discussed later in this chapter.

Note By default, new external and forest trusts in Windows Server 2003 Active Directory enforce SID filtering.

Trust authentication protocols

The version of the server operating system you are running will determine which authentication protocols you can use across a trust. Additionally, certain operating systems have the capability to use only certain authentication protocols. For example, Windows 95 can use only the LanMan authentication protocol. Therefore, the types of trusts that you create between domains and forests depends on the operating systems used in each domain or forest. For example, if your security policy requires Kerberos authentication but you need to establish a trust to a Windows NT 4.0 domain, you will need to relax your authentication policy to allow for the NTLM protocol.

Authentication between Windows Server 2003 forests Forest trusts provide features that other trust types cannot support, such as Kerberos authentication, user principal name (UPN) logon, and security policy support. If a forest trust feature or forest-wide authentication is needed, you must use a forest trust. Before establishing a trust between two Windows Server 2003 forests, determine if all domains will need to authenticate users from all other domains. For example, if the trust is required only to allow users from only one domain in a forest to authenticate to a single domain in a remote forest, a forest trust would be excessive. When authentication is required between a limited number of domains, establish one-way or two-way external trusts between the domains that require authentication instead of forest trusts.

Authentication between Windows Server 2003 and Windows 2000 forests Kerberos trusts only work between Windows Server 2003 forests. You cannot create transitive Kerberos trusts between Windows Server 2003 forests and Windows 2000 forests because Windows 2000 is not able to find Kerberos Key Distribution Centers (KDCs) in other domains. To establish trusts between Windows Server 2003 and Windows 2000 forests, create one-way or two-way external trusts between forests.

Authentication between Windows Server 2003 forests and Windows NT 4.0 forests As with Windows 2000 and Windows Server 2003, you cannot create transitive Kerberos trusts between Windows Server 2003 and Windows NT 4.0 forests. To establish trusts between Windows Server 2003 and Windows NT 4.0 domains, establish one-way or two-way external trusts between domains that need access to resources.

Authentication with servers running other operating systems Unlike Windows 2000 and Windows NT 4.0, you can create trusts between Windows 2003 domains and domains that use UNIX or other operating systems that support MIT-compliant Kerberos versions. This type of trust is known as a *realm trust*. Like external trusts, realm trusts can be one-way or two-way. However, user and service accounts in the Kerberos realm do not contain group associations that are used for access control in the Windows Server 2003 environment. To make the Kerberos realm security principals aware of Active Directory, you can use account mappings in Windows Server 2003 to map accounts from the Kerberos realm to the Windows Server 2003 accounts.

See Also Although this is beyond the scope of this book, more information about realm trusts can be found in the *Distributed Services Guide* in the *Windows Server 2003 Resource Kit*, which is available at *http://www.microsoft.com/reskit*.

See Also For more information about establishing trust relationships, see *Understanding Trusts* in *Windows Server 2003 Help and Support*.

Securing trusts with SID filtering

Windows grants or denies users access to resources by using access control lists (ACLs). ACLs use security identifiers (SIDs) to uniquely identify principals and their group membership. Every SID is made up of two parts: a domain SID that is shared by all principals for that domain, and a relative ID (RID) that is unique to the principal within the domain.

When a principal's credentials are verified during authentication, a process known as the *local security authority subsystem* (lsass.exe) retrieves the principal's SID, in addition to SIDs for all the groups to which the principal belongs. For example, when a user Joe, who belongs to the Administrator group, is authenticated, the local security authority subsystem retrieves Joe's user SID and the SID for the Administrator group. When Joe requests access to a resource, his SIDs are checked by the local security authority subsystem against the ACL to determine if he is allowed to perform the action.

SID spoofing Users with the proper privileges, such as domain administrators, can manipulate the SIDs that are associated with specific accounts. *SID spoofing* occurs when a domain administrator from a trusted domain attaches a well-known security principal onto the SID of a normal user account from the trusted domain. In the SID spoofing process, a rogue or coerced administrator sniffs packets from the trusted domain to find the SID of a security principal that has full access to resources in the trusted domain. Using a variety of programs, an administrator can attach the sniffed SID to the SIDHistory attribute of a user. By doing this, administrators from trusted domains can escalate their privileges in the trusted domain to access resources that they are not authorized to access.

Therefore, if you do not have confidence in other domain administrators, do not establish trust relationships with them. However, in the real world, this is not always possible. By understanding the threat, we can mitigate the vulnerability.

Real World

A recent client of mine was creating an Active Directory structure that would incorporate five Windows NT domains from four different companies into one Windows Server 2003 forest owned by the holding company. This design was chosen to support a unified mail structure between the companies. None of the domains had previously had trusts established, and the domain administrators were apprehensive about other domains having the ability to authenticate against resources in their domains. Although the decision was not the choice of the administrators, they felt better knowing that the default SID filtering and proper resource management would minimize security vulnerabilities.

Using SID filtering to secure trusts You can use SID filtering to prevent SID spoofing. *SID filtering* enables administrators to discard credentials that use SIDs that are likely candidates for spoofing.

When security principals are created in a domain, the domain SID is included in the security principal's SID to identify the domain in which it was created. The domain SID is an important characteristic of a security principal because the Windows security subsystem uses it to verify the security principal's authenticity.

Similarly, outgoing external trusts created from the trusting domain use SID filtering to verify that incoming authentication requests made from security principals in the trusted domain contain only SIDs of security principals in the trusted domain. This is done by comparing the SIDs of the incoming security principal with the domain SID of the trusted domain. If any of the security principal SIDs include a domain SID other than the one from the trusted domain, the trust removes the offending SID.

You can use Netdom.exe to enable or disable SID filtering on any trust relationship between domains or forests.

> **Tip** If you have domains running Windows 2000 Service Pack 3 or earlier, you can use Netdom.exe to enable SID filtering on external trusts.

Disabling SID filtering Even though it is not generally recommended, in some instances you might need to turn off SID filtering by using the Netdom.exe tool. SID filtering should be disabled only in the following situations:

- You have the same level of confidence for all administrators who have physical access to domain controllers in the trusted domain as you have for the administrators in the trusting domain.
- You have a strict written security policy requirement to assign universal groups to resources in the trusting domain that were not created in the trusted domain.
- Users have been migrated to the trusted domain with their SID histories preserved, and you want to grant them access to resources in the trusting domain based on the SIDHistory attribute. For example, user accounts are migrated from domain A to domain B, but there are still resources that have not yet been migrated from domain A to domain B. To allow the migrated users in domain A to be able to access resources in domain B, you turn off SID filtering so the users can still use the old SID from domain B to access resources in domain B.

Creating trusts

You can use Active Directory Domains And Trusts to create trust relationships between forests or between domains in the same forest. You can also use it to create shortcut trusts.

Before you create a forest trust, you must ensure that the Domain Name System (DNS) name resolution is working between the two forests. You can use stub zones, conditional forwarding, secondary zones, or a shared root hints server between the two forests with proper delegation. You also need to make sure that the forest functionality level between the two forests is set to Windows Server 2003.

To create a trust, perform the following steps:

1. Open Active Directory Domains And Trusts.
2. In the console tree, right-click the domain node for the forest root domain, and then click Properties.
3. On the Trusts tab, click New Trust, and then click Next.
4. On the Welcome page of the New Trust Wizard, click Next.
5. On the Trust Name page, perform one of the following steps:
    - If you are creating a forest trust, type the DNS name of the second forest, and then click Next.
    - If you are creating a shortcut trust, type the DNS name of the domain, type and confirm the trust password, and then click Next.
    - If you are creating an external trust, type the DNS name of the domain, and then click Next.
    - If you are creating a realm trust, type the realm name for the target realm, and then click Next.
6. On the Direction Of Trust page, perform one of the following steps:
    - To create a two-way trust, click Two-way, and then click Next.
    - To create a one-way incoming trust, click One-way: Incoming, and then click Next.
    - To create a one-way outgoing trust, click One-way: Outgoing, and then click Next.
7. On the Sides Of Trust page, perform one of the following steps:
    - To create a trust in only the local domain, click This Domain Only, and then click Next.
    - To create a trust in both the local domain and the remote domain, click Both This Domain And The Specified Domain, and then click Next. On the User Name And Password page, provide Domain Admin authentication for the remote domain, and click Next.
8. The remaining pages vary depending on your previous choices. Follow the instructions in the wizard to create, and optionally verify, the trust.

Practice: Creating Trusts

In this practice, you will create a cross-forest trust. You must be logged on with an account that has permission to create a cross-forest trust.

Your company, Coho Winery, needs to create a trust with your primary partner, Coho Vineyards, to share information between your organizations. You will create a cross-forest trust between the two companies by using Active Directory Domains And Trusts.

▶ Exercise 1: Raising the Functional Level of the Windows Server 2003 Domains

When all domain controllers in a forest are using Windows Server 2003, you can raise the domain functional level to take advantage of new features that are not available in Windows 2000 Server domains. Both of the domain controllers used in the exercises in this chapter run Windows Server 2003. Therefore, in this exercise, we will raise the domain functional level to Windows Server 2003 from the default Windows 2000 Server domain functional level.

1. Log on to the cohowinery.com domain on Computer1 using the Administrator account.
2. Click Start, click Administrative Tools, and then click Active Directory Domains And Trusts.
3. In the console tree, right-click cohowinery.com, and then click Raise Domain Functional Level.
4. Select Windows Server 2003, as shown in Figure 1.9.

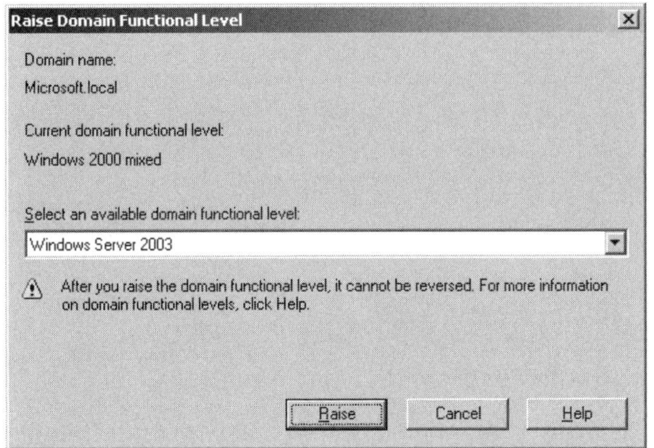

Figure 1.9 Raising the domain functional level

5. Click Raise.
6. When warned that the change cannot be reversed, click OK.

7. Click OK again when notified that the upgrade was successful.
8. Repeat steps 1 through 7 on Computer2 for the cohovineyards.com domain.

▶ Exercise 2: Creating a Cross-Forest Trust

Complete the following procedure to create a trust between cohowinery.com and cohovineyard.com.

1. Log on to the cohowinery.com domain on Computer1 using the Administrator account.
2. Click Start, click Administrative Tools, and then click Active Directory Domains And Trusts.
3. In the console tree, right-click cohowinery.com, and then click Properties.
4. Click the Trusts tab, and then click New Trust.
5. The New Trust Wizard appears. On the Welcome To The New Trust Wizard page, click Next.
6. On the Trust Name page, type **cohovinyard.com** as shown in Figure 1.10, and then click Next.

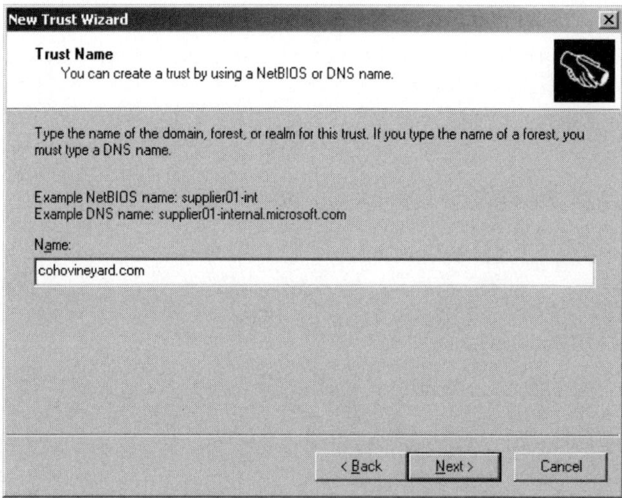

Figure 1.10 The Trust Name page of the New Trust Wizard

7. On the Direction Of Trust page, click Two-way, as shown in Figure 1.11.

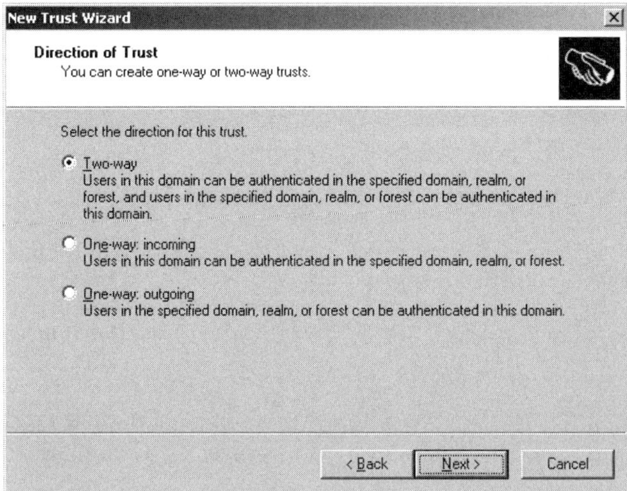

Figure 1.11 The Direction Of Trust page of the New Trust Wizard

8. On the Sides Of Trust page, select Both This Domain And The Specified Domain, and then click Next.
9. On the User Name And Password page, provide the Computer2 Administrator user name and password, as shown in Figure 1.12, and then click Next.

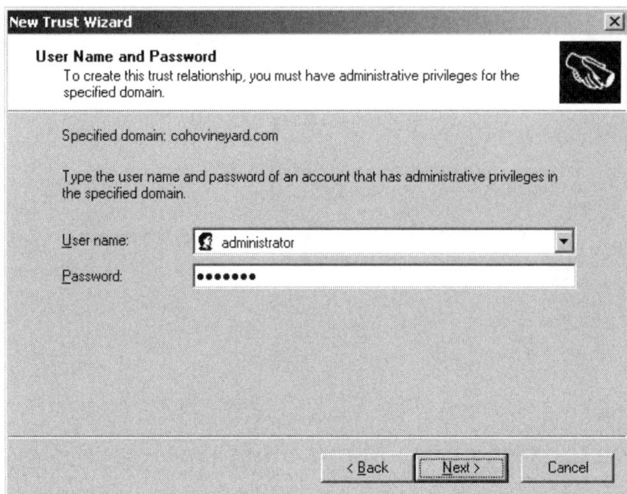

Figure 1.12 The User Name And Password page of the New Trust Wizard

10. On the Outgoing Trust Authentication Level—Local Domain page, select Domain-Wide Authentication, and then click Next.
11. On the Outgoing Trust Authentication Level—Specified Domain page, select Domain-Wide Authentication, and then click Next.

12. Review the results shown in the Trust Selections Complete page, which will resemble the following:

```
This domain: cohowinery.com
Specified domain: cohovineyard.com
Direction:
Two-way: Users in the local domain can authenticate in the specified
domain and users in the specified domain can authenticate in the local domain.
Trust type: External
Transitive: No
Outgoing trust authentication level: Domain-wide authentication in local and
specified forests.
Sides of trust: Create the trust for both this domain and the specified domain.
```

13. After reviewing the results, click Next.
14. On the Trust Creation Complete page, review the results to verify that the trust was created successfully. Click Next.
15. On the Confirm Outgoing Trust page, click No, and then click Next.
16. On the Confirm Incoming Trust page, click No, and then click Next.

Note You will manually verify the trusts after completing the wizard.

17. On the Completing The New Trust Wizard page, click Finish.
18. A dialog box will notify you that SID filtering is enabled by default, as shown in Figure 1.13. Click OK.

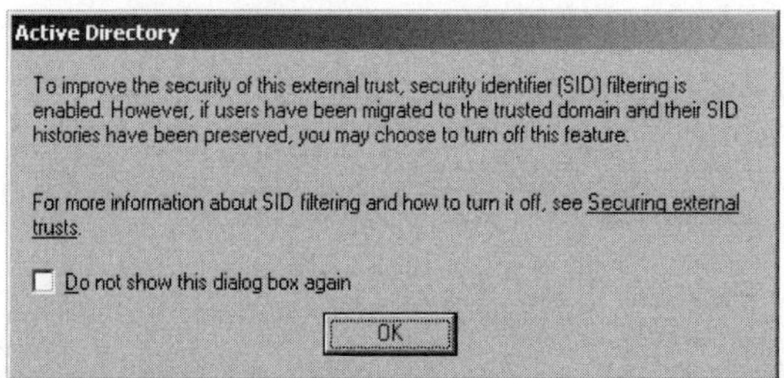

Figure 1.13 Dialog box notifying you that SID filtering is enabled by default

▶ Exercise 3: Verifying the Outgoing and Incoming Trusts

After creating a trust, you are returned to the Cohowinery.com Properties dialog box. Now that a trust has been created, you can use this dialog box to verify that the incoming and outgoing trusts were created successfully. To verify trusts, complete the following steps:

1. In the Cohowinery.com Properties dialog box, select Cohovineyard.com in the Domains Trusted By This Domain list, and then click Properties.
2. Click Validate.

3. Because this is a two-way trust, you will be automatically prompted to validate the incoming trust as well. As shown in Figure 1.14, click Yes and provide the Computer2 Administrator user name and password. Click OK.

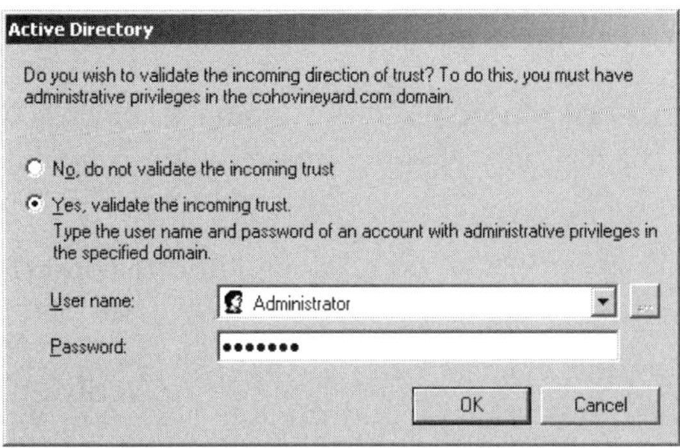

Figure 1.14 Verifying an incoming trust

4. If both directions of the trust were successfully validated, a dialog box will appear explaining that the trust is in place and active.

If you experience a problem verifying the trust, test connectivity and name resolution between the domain controllers. On Computer1, open a command prompt and issue the command `ping computer2.cohovineyard.com`. If the ping fails, verify that Computer1 has the IP address of Computer2 configured as a secondary DNS server. Next, on Computer2, ping computer1.cohowinery.com. If the ping fails, verify that Computer2 has the IP address of Computer1 configured as a secondary DNS server.

Lesson Review

The following questions are intended to reinforce key information presented in this lesson. If you are unable to answer a question, review the lesson materials and try the question again. You can find answers to the questions in the "Questions and Answers" section at the end of this chapter.

1. In which of the following situations should you use trusts? (Choose all that apply.)

   a. To enable access to an external Web site by customers from dozens of different companies.

   b. To enable access to shared folders by employees of a recently acquired company who have accounts in a different domain.

   c. To enable all employees within an enterprise that uses multiple domains to print to a printer.

   d. To enable employees of a consulting firm to send e-mail messages to internal employees with whom they are working closely.

____

____

2. In which of the following scenarios should you raise the domain functional level to Windows Server 2003? (Choose all that apply.)

   a. An environment with domain controllers running Windows NT, Windows 2000, and Windows Server 2003 that has only client computers that run Windows XP.

   b. An environment with domain controllers running Windows 2000 and Windows Server 2003 that has only client computers that run Windows NT and Windows 98.

   c. An environment with only domain controllers that run Windows Server 2003 and with only client computers that run Windows 98 and Windows XP.

   d. An environment with only domain controllers that run Windows Server 2003 and with only client computers that run Windows XP and Windows Server 2003.

____

____

3. Which type of trust should you create to enable users from a UNIX-based Kerberos realm to access resources in a Windows Server 2003 domain?

   a. Parent/child trust

   b. Tree/root trust

   c. External

   d. Realm

   e. Forest

   f. Shortcut

____

____

4. Which type of trust is automatically created when a new domain joins an existing forest?

   a. Parent/child trust

   b. Tree/root trust

   c. External

   d. Realm

   e. Forest

   f. Shortcut

____

5. Creating a two-way trust between DomainA and DomainB will have which of the following effects? (Choose all that apply.)

   a. Enable all users in DomainA to access all shared folders in DomainB.

   b. Enable members of the Domain Admins group in DomainA to access all shared folders in DomainB.

   c. Enable administrators of DomainA to grant access to shared folders to users in DomainB.

   d. Enable administrators of DomainA to view a list of users and groups in DomainB.

   ____

   ____

   ____

Lesson Summary

- A trust is a relationship that is established between domains that enables security principals from one domain to be authenticated by domain controllers in another domain.
- Use Active Directory Domains And Trusts to create trust relationships between forests or between domains in the same forest.
- When all domain controllers within a domain are running Windows Server 2003, raise the domain functional level to Windows Server 2003.
- The following are valid types of trusts:
  - Parent/child
  - Tree/root
  - External
  - Realm
  - Forest
  - Shortcut
- The following are valid authentication protocols that can be used between trusts:
  - NTLM
  - Kerberos
- You can use SID filtering to prevent SID spoofing. SID filtering enables administrators to discard credentials that use SIDs that are likely candidates for spoofing.

Case Scenario Exercise

Your chief security officer is concerned about recent news reports of a virus. After a computer on an internal network is infected, the virus spreads by scanning all the IP addresses on the subnet for open shares. It then attempts to propagate itself into those shares using the Anonymous Logon credentials. You want to reduce your exposure to this virus, as the requirements below outline.

Even though anonymous users are not members of the Everyone group in Windows Server 2003, you have some applications that require anonymous access to shares on a computer named Computer3. To allow them to access the shares, you have enabled the Network Access: Let Everyone Permissions Apply To Anonymous Users option, as shown in Figure 1.15.

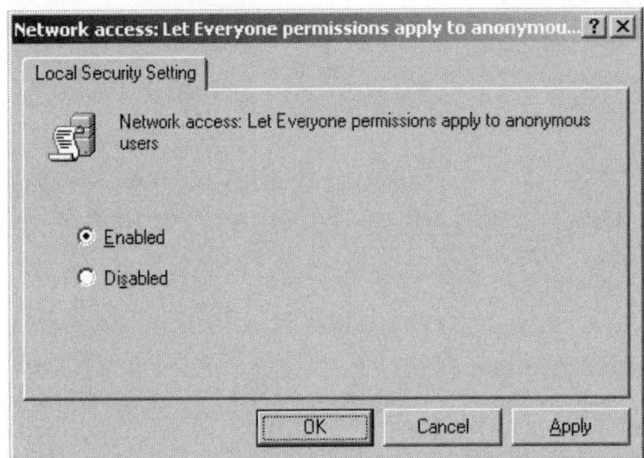

Figure 1.15 Enabling earlier applications to connect anonymously to shares

1. What should you do to improve the security of Computer3 while retaining backward compatibility? (Choose all that apply.)
   - **a.** Evaluate which shares require anonymous access, and configure those shares as hidden by appending a $ to the share name.
   - **b.** Disable the Network Access: Let Everyone Permissions Apply To Anonymous Users setting.
   - **c.** Enable the Network Access: Shares That Can Be Accessed Anonymously setting for those shares required by the legacy application.
   - **d.** Enable the Network Access: Let Everyone Permissions Apply To Anonymous Users setting for all computers in the domain.

____

____

____

____

2. The presence of one of the following security principals in the ACL of a shared folder indicates that anonymous users have access to the shared folder. Which security principal would indicate this?

    a. Everyone

    b. Anonymous

    c. Anonymous Logon

    d. Unauthenticated Users

    ____

    ____

Troubleshooting Lab

In this lab, you troubleshoot a problem related to authentication. To complete this lab, you must have completed Exercise 1 in Lesson 2 of this chapter.

1. On Computer2, start Windows 98.
2. Log on to Windows 98 by providing the user name Administrator and the Administrator password assigned to Computer1.
3. Click Start, click programs, and then click Windows Explorer.
4. On the Tools menu, click Map Network Drive.
5. In the Path field, type **computer1****c$**, and then click OK.

You will be prompted for a password. Typing the correct password will not enable you to connect to the shared folder, however. In fact, Windows 98 has already attempted to authenticate using the credentials you used to log on to Windows 98. Computer1 does not accept the LM authentication protocol, and Windows 98 interprets the rejection as the user providing invalid credentials.

1. Since you provided the correct user name and password, why was Windows 98 unable to connect to the shared folder?

    ____

    ____

2. How could you resolve the problem without reducing authentication security?

    ____

    ____

3. How could you resolve the problem without upgrading the client computer?

____

____

____

Chapter Summary

- Authentication is the process of proving your identity. In Windows networks, users frequently authenticate themselves using a user name and password pair. How the user name and password are communicated across the network has changed with different versions of Windows.
- Earlier versions of Windows use LM authentication, which is still supported by Windows Server 2003 for backward compatibility but carries with it potential security vulnerabilities. LM authentication should be disabled whenever compatibility with Windows 95 or Windows 98 is not required.
- If LM authentication cannot be disabled, the storage of the LMHash can be avoided for specific user accounts by using passwords that have more than 14 characters or passwords that contain special ALT characters.
- Newer versions of Windows use NTLMv1, NTLMv2, or Kerberos authentication. The Kerberos protocol is designed to be more secure and scalable than NTLM authentication.
- Local passwords are stored and maintained by the Local Security Authority (LSA). The LSA is responsible for managing local security policies, authenticating users, creating access tokens, and controlling audit policies.
- The Windows Server 2003 Resource Kit includes the Kerbtray.exe, Klist.exe, and CmdKey.exe tools for troubleshooting Kerberos authentication problems.
- Use security policy settings to configure authentication requirements.
- Implement a strong password policy in your organization to reduce the likelihood that your users' credentials will be compromised.
- Although you can enforce complex passwords by using security policy in Windows Server 2003 Active Directory, employee education is the only way to keep users from writing down passwords or using discoverable personal information in passwords.
- An account lockout policy prevents malicious attackers from logging on by continually guessing passwords; however, it enables malicious attackers to perform denial-of-service attacks that deny valid users from successful authentication.

- Kerberos ticket lifetimes must be short enough to prevent attackers from cracking the cryptography that protects the ticket's stored credentials but long enough to minimize the number of tickets that clients request.
- Use delegated authentication and constrained delegation as strategies for implementing supplemental authentication where required.
- Any application that has the Certified for Windows Server 2003 logo has been tested to ensure that it will function in environments that require multifactor authentication.
- Web users have special authentication considerations. Specifically, you must choose whether anonymous access will be allowed, and which account will be used to access resources on behalf of anonymous users. If anonymous access is not allowed, you will be using delegated authentication.
- Web users have four choices for Web authentication methods: Basic Authentication, Digest Authentication For Windows Domain Servers, Integrated Windows Authentication, and .NET Passport Authentication.
- Use delegated authentication, and the more granular constrained delegation, when front-end servers must access back-end services on behalf of authenticated users.
- A trust is a relationship that is established between domains that enables security principals from one domain to be authenticated by domain controllers in another domain.
- Use Active Directory Domains And Trusts to create trust relationships between forests or between domains in the same forest.
- When all domain controllers within a domain are running Windows Server 2003, raise the domain functional level to Windows Server 2003.
- The following are valid types of trusts:
  - Parent/child
  - Tree/root
  - External
  - Realm
  - Forest
  - Shortcut
- The following are valid authentication protocols that can be used between trusts:
  - NTLM
  - Kerberos

- You can use SID filtering to prevent SID spoofing. SID filtering enables administrators to discard credentials that use SIDs that are likely candidates for spoofing.

Exam Highlights

Before taking the exam, review the key topics and terms that are presented in this chapter. You need to know this information.

Key Topics

- Understand the authentication protocols supported by Windows Server 2003, the differences between the protocols, and how the authentication process works with each protocol.
- Be familiar with every security policy setting related to controlling authentication.
- Understand the differences between Web authentication protocols, and know the advantages and disadvantages of each.
- Know the user account created by default for IIS anonymous access.
- Understand the types of trusts supported by Windows Server 2003, how to configure these trusts, and in what situations each trust type should be used.

Key Terms

Authentication Authentication is the process of verifying the identity of something or someone. Authentication usually involves a user name and a password, but can include any method of demonstrating identity, such as a smart card, a retinal scan, voice recognition, or a fingerprint.

Authorization Authorization is the process of determining whether an identified user or process is permitted access to a resource and determining the appropriate level of access for the user. The owner of a resource, or someone who has been granted permission, determines whether a user is a part of a predetermined group or has a certain level of security clearance. By setting the permissions on a resource, the owner controls which users and groups on the network can access the resource.

Kerberos As the default authentication protocol for Windows 2000 and Windows XP Professional, the Kerberos protocol is designed to be more secure and scalable across large, diverse networks.

NTLM protocol This service uses a challenge-response mechanism to authenticate users and computers running Windows Me and earlier or computers running Windows 2000 and later that are not part of a domain.

Trusts Trusts are the mechanisms that ensure that users who are authenticated in their own domains can access resources in any trusted domain.

Questions and Answers

Lesson 1 Review

Page 1-16

1. Is showing your identification to prove that you are of age to purchase a product an example of authentication or authorization?

   Authorization. In this example, your identity is not being validated—only whether you are old enough to be authorized to complete the purchase.

2. Is showing your identification to a cashier to verify that the credit card you are using belongs to you an example of authentication or authorization?

   Authentication. In this example, the cashier needs to validate that you are who you claim to be—and your identification is sufficient proof of that.

3. Which of the following passwords will not be stored in an LMHash?

   a. tyia

   b. imsitrjs5itr

   c. passwordpassword

   d. l%@3tty7&

   c. While this is not a strong password, it is longer than 14 characters and therefore cannot be stored in an LMHash.

Lesson 2 Review

Page 1-30

1. Which of the following passwords is an example of a strong password?

   a. tyia

   b. imsitrjs5itr

   c. passwordpassword

   d. l%@3tty7&

   d. This is a strong password because it does not contain all or part of the user's account name, it is at least six characters in length, and it contains lowercase characters, base 10 digits, and non-alphabetic characters.

2. Which of the following are valid reasons to enable LM authentication? (Choose all that apply.)

   a. Users will access network resources using computers running Windows 95.

   b. Users will access network resources using computers running Windows 98.

   c. Users will access network resources using computers running Windows NT.

   d. Users will access network resources using computers running Windows Me.

   e. Users will access network resources using computers running Windows 2000.

   f. Users will access network resources using computers running Windows XP.

   a, b. Computers running Windows 95 and Windows 98 require LM authentication to connect to network resources.

3. Enabling account lockout accomplishes which of the following goals?

   a. Makes it impossible to steal a user's password.

   b. Reduces the likelihood that a malicious attacker will use brute force techniques to discover a user's password.

   c. Eliminates the need for strong passwords.

   d. Reduces Help desk costs.

   b. Account lockout makes it more difficult for a malicious attacker to guess a user's password.

Lesson 3 Review

Page 1-39

1. Which of the following authentication methods should be chosen for a Web site on a public Internet with minimal security requirements, where administrators have no control over which browser a client uses?

   a. Basic Authentication

   b. Digest Authentication For Windows Domain Servers

   c. Integrated Windows Authentication

   d. .NET Passport Authentication

   a. Basic Authentication is the oldest method for authenticating Web users and is supported by the widest range of clients. However, it does not encrypt the user's password before transmitting it.

2. Which of the following authentication methods should be chosen for a high-security, internal Web site in an Active Directory environment where single sign-on is a requirement?

   a. Basic Authentication

   b. Digest Authentication For Windows Domain Servers

   c. Integrated Windows Authentication

   d. .NET Passport Authentication

   c. Integrated Windows Authentication provides single sign-on with the highest security possible.

3. Which of the following scenarios requires delegated authentication?

   a. A public Web site from which all content should be anonymously accessed.

   b. An internal Web site from which all content should be anonymously accessed.

   c. An internal Web site containing simple Hypertext Markup Language (HTML) documents that only managers should be able to access.

   d. An internal Web site that accesses a back-end server containing data that only specific users should be able to access.

   d. Delegated authentication is only necessary when the Web server must use the user's credentials to access back-end information.

Lesson 4 Review

Page 1-53

1. In which of the following situations should you use trusts? (Choose all that apply.)

   a. To enable access to an external Web site by customers from dozens of different companies.

   b. To enable access to shared folders by employees of a recently acquired company who have accounts in a different domain.

   c. To enable all employees within an enterprise that uses multiple domains to print to a printer.

   d. To enable employees of a consulting firm to send e-mail messages to internal employees with whom they are working closely.

   c. Trusts should only be used to enable authentication between internal domains. Trusts should generally not be created between organizations that are not part of the same entity.

2. In which of the following scenarios should you raise the domain functional level to Windows Server 2003? (Choose all that apply.)

   a. An environment with domain controllers running Windows NT, Windows 2000, and Windows Server 2003 that has only client computers that run Windows XP.

   b. An environment with domain controllers running Windows 2000 and Windows Server 2003 that has only client computers that run Windows NT and Windows 98.

   c. An environment with only domain controllers that run Windows Server 2003 and with only client computers that run Windows 98 and Windows XP.

   d. An environment with only domain controllers that run Windows Server 2003 and with only client computers that run Windows XP and Windows Server 2003.

   c, d. You should raise the domain functional level for domains that consist entirely of computers running Windows Server 2003.

3. Which type of trust should you create to enable users from a UNIX-based Kerberos realm to access resources in a Windows Server 2003 domain?

   a. Parent/child trust

   b. Tree/root trust

   c. External

   d. Realm

   e. Forest

   f. Shortcut

   d. Realm trusts are used only for connecting non-Windows Kerberos realms to Windows domains.

4. Which type of trust is automatically created when a new domain joins an existing forest?

   a. Parent/child trust

   b. Tree/root trust

   c. External

   d. Realm

   e. Forest

   f. Shortcut

   a. The parent/child trust is created automatically when a new domain is added to a forest.

5. Creating a two-way trust between DomainA and DomainB will have which of the following effects? (Choose all that apply.)

   a. Enable all users in DomainA to access all shared folders in DomainB.

   b. Enable members of the Domain Admins group in DomainA to access all shared folders in DomainB.

   c. Enable administrators of DomainA to grant access to shared folders to users in DomainB.

   d. Enable administrators of DomainA to view a list of users and groups in DomainB.

   c, d. Trusts enable authentication between domains but do not authorize users to access resources. However, to enable administrators to authorize users of the remote domain to access network resources, administrators can retrieve a list of users from the trusted domain.

Design Activity: Case Scenario Exercise

Page 1-56

1. What should you do to improve the security of Computer3 while retaining backward compatibility? (Choose all that apply.)

   a. Evaluate which shares require anonymous access, and configure those shares as hidden by appending a $ to the share name.

   b. Disable the Network Access: Let Everyone Permissions Apply To Anonymous Users setting.

   c. Enable the Network Access: Shares That Can Be Accessed Anonymously setting for those shares required by the legacy application.

   d. Enable the Network Access: Let Everyone Permissions Apply To Anonymous Users setting for all computers in the domain.

   a, b, c. Option d is not correct, because that option would enable anonymous access to shares throughout the domain, which would allow the virus to infect every system with a shared folder. Options a, b, and c collectively ensure that only those shares required by the legacy application allow anonymous access, and that those shares are hidden.

2. The presence of one of the following security principals in the ACL of a shared folder indicates that anonymous users have access to the shared folder. Which security principal would indicate this?

   a. Everyone

   b. Anonymous

   c. Anonymous Logon

   d. Unauthenticated Users

   c. Unauthenticated users can be granted access to resources by assigning rights using the Anonymous Logon security principal.

Design Activity: Troubleshooting Lab

Page 1-57

1. Since you provided the correct user name and password, why was Windows 98 unable to connect to the shared folder?

   Earlier in this chapter, we configured Computer1 to refuse LM authentication. Windows 98 is only capable of using LM authentication.

2. How could you resolve the problem without reducing authentication security?

   Upgrading the computer running Windows 98 to a newer operating system that supports NTLM or Kerberos authentication, such as Windows XP, would resolve the problem.

3. How could you resolve the problem without upgrading the client computer?

   Setting the Network Security: LAN Manager Authentication Level security policy setting to anything other than Send NTLMv2 Response Only\Refuse LM or Send NTLMv2 Response Only\Refuse LM & NTLM would allow the Windows 98 computer to authenticate using LM.

2 Planning and Configuring an Authorization Strategy

Exam Objectives in this Chapter:

- Plan group structure
    - Decide which types of groups to use
    - Plan security group scope
    - Plan nested group structure
- Plan and configure authorization
    - Configure access control lists (ACLs)
    - Plan and troubleshoot the assignment of user rights

Why This Chapter Matters

In Chapter 1, you learned the importance of authentication: validating a user's identity. In this chapter, you will learn about authorization. Authorization is the process of determining whether a user, after they have been validated, really should have access to do what they've requested. It's authorization that distinguishes between guests, regular users, and administrators.

While Microsoft Windows Server 2003 makes it simple to assign rights to individual users, such an authorization strategy would become impossible to manage in a large enterprise. You must learn to use groups to simplify access management. Windows Server 2003 provides a flexible, but not obvious, group structure that must be studied to be used effectively.

One of the challenges of managing authorization is limiting users to the rights they need to complete their assignments, without granting them excessive privileges. The more tightly you control authorization to network resources, the more time you will spend troubleshooting user rights. For example, it is common for users to be denied access to a network resource they really should be able to use. As the administrator, you must be able to identify the cause of their access denial and determine the best way to resolve the problem.

This chapter introduces you to authorization as a concept. You will learn how Windows Server 2003 implements access control and how to effectively manage assigning rights to users and groups. When you have completed the chapter, you will know exactly how to isolate and resolve problems relating to overly restrictive privileges.

Lessons in this Chapter:

Before You Begin

This chapter presents the skills and concepts that are required to configure security templates, deploy them across your network, and troubleshoot problems related to Group Policy. If you fulfilled the requirements for previous chapters, then you already have the necessary hardware and software configured. You can use the computers in the state they were in after completing the previous chapter, or your can install the software from scratch. To do the practices, examples, and lab exercises in this chapter, you must have:

- A private non-routed network.
- One computer. On the computer, perform a Windows Server 2003 installation with default settings, and assign the computer name Computer1. Add the domain controller role to Computer1, using the default settings, and assign the domain name cohowinery.com. The computer should be configured to use itself as its own primary Domain Name System (DNS) server.

Lesson 1: Understanding Authorization

Authorization is the process of determining whether an authenticated user is allowed to perform a requested action. Each time you open a file, Windows Server 2003 verifies that you are authorized to open that file. Each time you print, Windows Server 2003 verifies that you have Print permissions to that printer. In fact, Windows Server 2003 verifies your authorization to access just about every object you can imagine: files and folders, shared folders, printers, services, Active Directory directory service objects, Terminal Services connections, Windows Management Interface objects, and registry keys and values.

Understanding how authorization works for each of these different types of objects is complicated, because each type requires unique permissions. For example, you need to control whether users can read files or write to files, but for services, your concern is whether a given user can start or stop the service. Fortunately, Windows Server 2003 simplifies authorization management by using a standard model for all types of objects. This model uses access control lists, inherited permissions, and both standard and special permissions. Even the user interface for specifying permissions for each object type is similar.

After this lesson, you will be able to

- Describe the significance of access control lists and access control entries.
- Assign permissions to a variety of objects.
- Calculate a user's effective permissions, given enough information about the user's group memberships and relevant access control entries.
- Use inherited permissions to minimize the number of permissions you need to manually assign.
- Describe the relationship between standard and special permissions.

Estimated lesson time: 45 minutes

Access Control Lists

Windows Server 2003, like all recent members of the Microsoft Windows family, keeps track of the privileges users have to resources by using a discretionary access control list (DACL). DACLs, or simply ACLs, identify the users and groups that are assigned or denied access permissions on an object. If an ACL does not explicitly identify a user, or any groups that a user is a member of, the user will be denied access to that object. By default, an ACL is controlled by the owner of an object or the person who created the object, and it contains access control entries (ACEs) that determine user access to the object. An access control entry (ACEs) is an entry in an object's ACL that grants permissions to a user or group.

Though a description of ACLs and ACEs is complex, they are very easy to manage. Figure 2.1 shows the Windows Server 2003 graphical user interface dialog box for managing permissions to a folder named Secret. The GG Boston Research security group is highlighted so that the dialog box displays the permissions assigned to that group: Read & Execute, List Folder Contents, and Read. Collectively, these permissions allow members of the GG Boston Research security group to read the contents of the folder.

Note All of the users and groups listed in the dialog box have an ACE defined for the folder, but that doesn't necessarily mean they have any access to the folder. If the Deny permission is assigned, that user or group will not be able to access the object—even if they have also been granted access through another group membership.

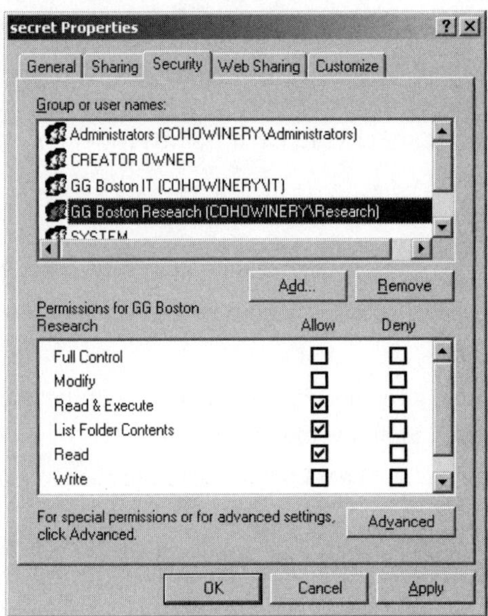

Figure 2.1 Windows Server 2003 represents ACLs by listing the permissions assigned to users and groups

Effective Permissions

Calculating a user's effective permissions requires more than simply looking up that user's name in the ACL. ACEs can assign rights directly to the user, or they can assign rights to a security group or a special group. Additionally, users can be members of multiple groups, and groups can be nested within each other. Therefore, a single user can have several different ACEs in a single ACL. To understand what a user's effective permissions will be, you must understand how permissions are calculated when multiple ACEs apply to the user.

Permissions that are granted to a user, or the groups to which the user belongs, are cumulative. If Mary is a member of both the Accounting group and the Managers group, and the ACL for a file grants Mary's user account Read privileges, the Accounting group Modify privileges, and the Managers group Full Control privileges, Mary will have Full Control privileges. There's a catch, though. ACEs that deny access always override ACEs that grant access. Therefore, if the Accounting group is explicitly denied access to the file, Mary will not be able to open the file. Even though Mary is a member of the Managers group, and the Managers group has Full Control privileges, the Deny ACE means that all members of the Managers group will be denied access to the file.

See Also Groups are described in more detail later in this chapter.

If no ACEs in an ACL apply to a user, that user will be denied access to the object. In other words, not explicitly having privileges to an object is exactly the same as being explicitly denied access.

Tip By default, the Everyone special group is assigned permissions to most objects on the system. Users automatically become members of the Everyone group when they authenticate. This process will be described in more detail later in this chapter.

Inheriting Permissions

When you assign permissions directly to an object, you create an *explicit permission*. Assigning explicit permissions to every individual folder, file, registry value, and Active Directory object would be a ponderous task. In fact, managing the massive number of ACLs that would be required would significantly impact the performance of Windows Server 2003.

To make managing permissions more efficient, Windows Server 2003 includes the concept of inheritance. When Windows Server 2003 is initially installed, most objects only have *inherited permissions*. Inherited permissions propagate to an object from its parent object. For example, the file system uses inherited permissions. Therefore, each new folder you create in the root C:\ folder will inherit the exact permissions assigned to the C:\ folder. Similarly, each subkey you create in the HKEY_LOCAL_MACHINE\SOFTWARE\ key will inherit the exact permissions assigned to the parent key.

Security Alert Explicit Allow permissions always override inherited Deny permissions.

After you set permissions on a parent object, new child objects automatically inherit these permissions. You can override this default behavior, however. Using the file system as an example, if you do not want child folders to inherit permissions, click the Advanced button on the Security tab of the folder's properties dialog box and use the Advanced Security Settings dialog box to add permissions. Then select This Folder Only in the Apply Onto list when you specify permissions for the parent folder, as shown in Figure 2.2. To specify permissions that do not apply to the parent folder, but exist only to be inherited, select Subfolders And Files Only, Subfolders Only, or Files Only. Other objects, such as the registry, provide similar functionality.

Tip If the Apply Onto list is dimmed, the permission was inherited from the parent. You can only change inheritance for explicit permissions.

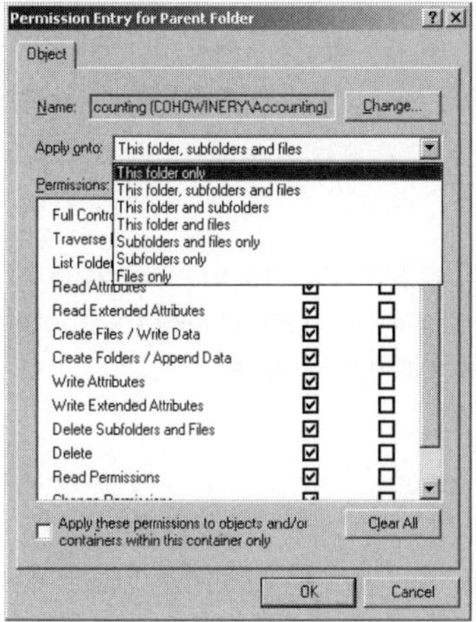

Figure 2.2 Permissions are inherited by default, but this behavior can be manually overridden

You can also control inheritance from the child objects. If you do not want a child object to inherit the parent's permissions, open the Advanced Security Settings dialog box and clear the Allow Inheritable Permissions From The Parent To Propagate To This Object And All Child Objects check box. You will be prompted to copy the inherited permissions to explicit permissions, or to simply discard the inherited permissions. If you choose not to copy the permissions, you will need to immediately assign explicit permissions so that users can access the object.

If you do disable inheritance on a child object and later want to re-enable inheritance, you can do so from the Advanced Security Settings dialog box of the parent folder. Simply select the Replace Permission Entries On All Child Objects check box, and Windows Server 2003 will remove all explicit permissions on all child objects and replace them with inherited permissions. This is an excellent way to recover files, folders, or registry values that users have made inaccessible by removing inherited permissions.

Standard and Special Permissions

Access control lists for the file system, registry, printers, services, and Active Directory can all be configured using both standard and special permissions. Special permissions are very granular and enable minute control over a user's access to an object. Standard permissions exist to make special permissions easier to manage. When you select a standard permission, Windows Server 2003 selects a set of special permissions that have been assigned to that standard permission.

> **Exam Tip** Neither standard nor special permissions map directly to access control entries. However, for the sake of the exam, it's sufficient to understand that standard permissions are used to simplify management of special permissions.

The permissions available when you view the Security tab of a file or folder's properties dialog box are standard permissions. These include the Full Control, Modify, Read & Execute, Read, and Write standard permissions. If you grant Read & Execute standard permission, Windows Server 2003 automatically grants the List Folder/Read Data, Read Attributes, Read Extended Attributes, and Read Permissions special permissions. Similarly, if you deny the Read & Execute standard permission, the same special permissions are denied. You could choose to select those special permissions manually, but selecting the standard permission is more efficient.

File and folder permissions

As you learned in Chapter 1, file and folder permissions enable users to restrict access to content stored on NTFS volumes. You can grant access to open, edit, or delete files and folders. Files and folders also have the concept of *ownership*. The user who creates a file or folder is the owner of that object and by default has the ability to specify the level of access that other users have.

The following are the standard permissions that can be applied to files and folders:

- Full Control. Users can perform any action on the file or folder, including creating and deleting files and folders, and modifying permissions.
- Modify. Users can read, edit, and delete files and folders.
- Read & Execute. Users can view files and execute applications.
- List Folder Contents. Users can browse a folder.
- Read. Users can view a file or the contents of a folder. If an executable file has Read but not Read & Execute permission, the user will not be able to start the executable.

- Write. Users can create files in a directory, but not necessarily read them. This permission is useful for creating a folder in which multiple users can deliver files, without allowing the users to access each other's files or even see what other files exist.
- Special Permissions. There are more than a dozen special permissions that can be assigned to a user or group. This permission shows as selected if the set of selected special permissions does not match a standard permission.

When any of these standard permissions are selected, Windows Server 2003 automatically selects one or more of the following special permissions:

Exam Tip You do not need to memorize special permissions for the exam. However, it is important to understand the relationship between standard permissions and special permissions.

- Traverse Folder/Execute File. Traverse Folder, which applies only to folders, allows moving through folders to reach other files or folders, even if the user has no permissions for the traversed folders. Traverse Folder takes effect only when the group or user is not granted the Bypass traverse checking user right, which Everyone has by default. Execute File, which applies only to files, allows running program files. Setting the Traverse Folder permission on a folder does not automatically set the Execute File permission on all files within that folder.

Tip Some special permissions, such as Traverse Folder/Execute File and List Folder/Read Data, have a different effect depending on the object type to which the permission is applied.

- List Folder/Read Data. List Folder, which applies only to folders, allows viewing file names and subfolder names within the folder. Read Data, which applies only to files, allows viewing the contents of a file.
- Read Attributes. Allows viewing the attributes of a file or folder, such as read-only and hidden.
- Read Extended Attributes. Allows viewing the extended attributes of a file or folder. Extended attributes are defined by programs and may vary by program.
- Create Files/Write Data. Create Files, which applies only to folders, allows creating files within the folder. Write Data, which applies only to files, allows or denies making changes to the file and overwriting existing content.
- Create Folders/Append Data. Create Folders, which applies only to folders, allows or denies creating folders within the folder. Append Data, which applies only to files, allows or denies making changes to the end of the file but not changing, deleting, or overwriting existing data.

- Write Attributes. Allows changing the attributes of a file or folder, such as read-only or hidden.
- Write Extended Attributes. Allows changing the extended attributes of a file or folder.
- Delete Subfolders and Files. Allows deleting subfolders and files, even if the Delete permission has not been granted on the subfolder or file.
- Delete. Allows deleting the file or folder. If you don't have Delete permission on a file or folder, you can still delete it if you have been granted Delete Subfolders and Files on the parent folder.
- Read Permissions. Allows reading permissions of the file or folder, such as Full Control, Read, and Write.
- Change Permissions. Allows changing permissions of the file or folder, such as Full Control, Read, and Write.
- Take Ownership. Allows taking ownership of the file or folder. The owner of a file or folder can always change permissions on it, regardless of any existing permissions that protect the file or folder.

When you are editing file and folder permissions and you specify the Full Control standard permission, every possible special permission is added to the ACE for the user or group. When you specify the Modify standard permission, every special permission is assigned except the Change Permissions and Take Ownership special permissions. Selecting the Read & Execute standard permission adds ACEs for Traverse Folder/Execute File, List Folder/Read Data, Read Attributes, Read Extended Attributes, and Read Permissions special permissions. The standard Read permission is identical to Read & Execute, except that it lacks the Traverse Folder/Execute File special permission. Finally, the friendly Write standard permission grants Create Files/Write Data, Create Folders/Append Data, Write Attributes, and Write Extended Attributes special permissions.

> **Security Alert** In the real world, you rarely have to deal with special permissions. In fact, you should avoid it whenever possible because it's more difficult to manage special permissions than standard permissions. Standard permissions are granular enough to meet all but the tightest security requirements.

To set, view, change, or remove special permissions for files and folders:

1. Open Windows Explorer, and then locate the file or folder for which you want to set special permissions.
2. Right-click the file or folder, click Properties, and then click the Security tab.

3. Click Advanced, and then do one of the following:
   - To set special permissions for a new group or user, click Add. In the Name box, type the name of the user or group using the format *domain-name\name*. When you are finished, click OK to automatically open the Permission Entry dialog box.
   - To view or change special permissions for an existing group or user, click the name of the group or user and then click View/Edit.
   - To remove a group or user and its special permissions, click the name of the group or user and then click Remove. If the Remove button is unavailable, clear the Allow Inheritable Permissions check box. The file or folder will no longer inherit permissions. Skip steps 4, 5, and 6.
4. In the Permission Entry dialog box, click where you want the permissions applied in Apply Onto, if necessary. Apply Onto is available only for folders.
5. In Permissions, click Allow or Deny for each permission.
6. If you want to prevent subfolders and files within the tree from inheriting these permissions, select the Apply These Permissions check box.

This book does not describe individual special permissions for other types of objects, nor how to edit them. However, the user interface for editing special permissions for other objects is similar to that for files and folders.

Active Directory permissions

If you are familiar with other user databases, you will probably be surprised to learn that every object within Active Directory can have unique permissions assigned. Just as each folder and file in a file system has its own permissions, each organizational unit (OU) and user in Active Directory has permissions. This isn't the case with the local user database present in Windows Server 2003 member computers. However, Active Directory is much more than a simple user database, and configuring object permissions is important not only for security reasons, but to ease management of Active Directory.

The most common permissions-related task is to delegate administrative control over portions of Active Directory. This reduces the workload placed on a single administrator because other members of the support team can manage portions of Active Directory without handing them the keys to the corporate network. The most efficient way to assign permissions to objects in Active Directory is to open the Active Directory Users And Computers console, right-click the object, and then click Delegate Control. You can also assign permissions to objects by using ADSI Edit. To use ADSI Edit, open a blank Microsoft Management Console (MMC) console and add the ADSI Edit snap-in.

Following are the standard permissions that can be applied to Active Directory objects:

- Full Control. Users can perform any action on the Active Directory object, including creating and deleting new child objects and modifying permissions.
- Read. Users can view all object properties, the object permissions, and the object's contents (if any).
- Write. Users can edit object properties.
- Create All Child Objects. If the object is a container, such as an organizational unit, users can create any type of child object in the container. You can use special permissions to limit the types of objects that a user can create. For example, special permissions can be used to allow a user to create users, but not groups or computers.
- Delete All Child Objects. If the object is a container, such as an organizational unit, users can delete any type of child object in the container. You can use special permissions to limit the types of objects that a user can delete. For example, special permissions can be used to allow a user to delete users, but not groups or computers.
- Special Permissions. There are more than twenty special permissions that can be assigned to a user or group. This permission shows as selected if the set of selected special permissions does not match a standard permission.

As with other types of objects, selecting standard permissions selects one or more special permissions. The special permissions that can be assigned to Active Directory objects are quite complex, however. While many environments require very granular control over Active Directory permissions, the details of each special permission are not likely to be covered in this exam.

It's important to understand access control on Active Directory objects. However, you should avoid changing the permissions whenever it is not absolutely required by your applications or your environment's security requirements. If you do need to modify the permissions, do so carefully. A user who intentionally or accidentally changes Active Directory objects, or the permissions assigned to those objects, can quickly affect many users and applications on the network.

Specifying too many explicit permissions on Active Directory objects can cause performance problems, particularly in environments with multiple domain controllers. Active Directory objects, and the ACEs associated with the assigned permissions, must be replicated between domain controllers. Therefore, the more permissions you assign, the longer replication will take, and the more significant impact replication will have on your network.

Registry permissions

The registry stores the bulk of configuration information for both the operating system and applications. Being able to control registry permissions is important. In some cases, you should restrict permissions to prevent users from modifying registry keys that could present a security vulnerability or cause other problems on their computers. In other cases, you may want to grant users additional permissions to parts of the registry to allow them to run applications that they could not otherwise run. You can assign permissions to the values and keys in the registry by using the registry editor. To edit permissions within the registry editor, right-click the registry key, and then select Permissions.

Following are the standard permissions that can be applied to registry keys and values:

- Full Control. Users can perform any action on the registry key or value, including creating and deleting new values and subkeys.
- Read. Users can view values and subkeys, but cannot create, delete, or edit them.
- Special Permissions. There are more than ten special permissions that can be assigned to a user or group. This permission shows as selected if the set of selected special permissions does not match a standard permission.

Service permissions

Service permissions are among the least frequently used permissions, but they can be useful in some environments. If your organization has separate groups that manage various services on a computer, you can grant the members of those groups the ability to control only the permissions that they manage. For example, you could grant the team responsible for managing your Web site access to restart the World Wide Web Publishing Service without allowing them to stop the Terminal Services service.

You might expect to modify service permissions by using the Services console. There's no user interface for modifying permissions in the Services console, however, so you have to use the System Services node in a security template. Security templates are discussed in more detail in Chapter 3, "Deploying and Troubleshooting Security Templates."

Following are the standard permissions that can be applied to services:

- Full Control. Users can perform any action on the service, including starting and stopping the service, modifying the service's permissions, and specifying whether a service starts automatically.
- Read. Users can view the status, permissions, and dependencies of a service.
- Start, Stop, And Pause. As you would expect, users can start, stop, and pause the service.

- Write. Users cannot directly start or stop a service; however, they can specify whether the service is disabled, set to start manually, or starts automatically when the server reboots.
- Delete. Users can delete the service.
- Special Permissions. There are more than ten special permissions that can be assigned to a user or group. This permission shows as selected if the set of selected special permissions does not match a standard permission.

Printer permissions

Controlling access to printers is useful for specifying users who can manage the printers and the print queue. You can assign permissions to printers by using Printers And Faxes, viewing the printer's properties, and clicking the Security tab. The following are the standard permissions that can be applied to printers:

- Print. The user can connect to a printer and send documents to the printer. By default, the Print permission is assigned to all members of the Everyone group.
- Manage Printers. The user can perform the tasks associated with the Print permission and has complete administrative control of the printer. The user can pause and restart the printer, change spooler settings, share a printer, adjust printer permissions, and change printer properties.
- Manage Documents. The user can pause, resume, restart, cancel, and rearrange the order of documents submitted by all other users. The user cannot, however, send documents to the printer or control the status of the printer. By default, the Manage Documents permission is assigned to members of the Creator Owner special group to allow users to manage their own print jobs. When a user is assigned the Manage Documents permission, the user cannot access existing documents currently waiting to print. The permission will only apply to documents sent to the printer after the permission is assigned to the user.
- Special Permissions. There are only six special permissions for printers. Besides the standard permissions, there are permissions for Read Permissions, Change Permissions, and Take Ownership.

By default, members of the Administrators and Power Users groups have full access to printers, which means that the users are assigned the Print, Manage Documents, and Manage Printers permissions.

Share permissions

Use Windows Explorer to specify permissions for shared folders. To do so, right-click the shared folder, select Sharing And Security, and then click the Permissions button. The following are the standard permissions that can be applied to shared folders:

- Full Control. Users can read, write, and change permissions on files and folders within the share if allowed to do so by file and folder permissions.
- Change. Users can read and write to files and folders within the share if allowed to do so by file and folder permissions.
- Read. Users can read files and folders within the share if allowed to do so by file and folder permissions.

Share permissions are simpler than other types of permissions, and there is no need for special share permissions. Share permissions are considered an additional layer of security above and beyond file and folder permissions. In most cases, you should rely on file and folder permissions to secure the file system, regardless of whether it will be accessed locally or across a network. Share permissions are primarily used on servers with FAT32 volumes, since FAT32 volumes lack the file system security of NTFS.

Practice: Denying Access Using Group Membership

In this practice, you will observe the method Windows Server 2003 uses to calculate effective permissions.

▶ **Exercise: Use Windows Explorer to Deny a User Access to a File**

In this exercise, you will use Windows Explorer to configure permissions on a file on Computer1.

1. Log on to the cohowinery.com domain on Computer1 using the Administrator account.
2. Use the Active Directory Users And Computers console to create global security groups named GG Boston Accounting and GG Boston Managers.
3. Use the Active Directory Users And Computers console to create a user account with the user name mgibson. Mary's full name is Mary Gibson. Assign the user account a complex password, and make Mary a member of the Administrators group.

> **Note** We're making Mary a member of the Administrators group so that Mary can log on to a domain controller interactively.

4. Start Windows Explorer by clicking Start, pointing to All Programs, pointing to Accessories, and then clicking Windows Explorer.
5. Select the root of drive C, and then create a new folder named TK70-299. Double-click the new folder.
6. On the File menu, click New, and then select Text Document to create a new file in the C:\TK70-299 folder. Name the file ACLTest.txt.

7. Right-click the ACLTest.txt file, and then click Properties.
8. Click the Security tab, and then click the Add button.

   The Select Users, Computers, Or Groups dialog box appears.
9. Type **Mary** in the Enter The Object Names To Select field, and then click Check Names.

   Mary is replaced by the full user name, as shown in Figure 2.3.

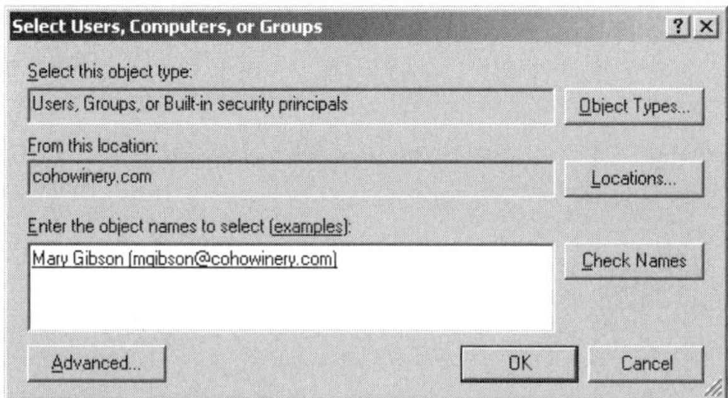

Figure 2.3 The ACEs assigned to Mary's account, and her group memberships, will determine the effective permissions

10. Click OK.

    At the ACLText.txt Properties dialog box, notice that Mary Gibson has only Read and Read & Execute permissions.
11. Click the Add button, and then add the Accounting group.
12. Click the Accounting group, and then select the Modify check box in the Allow column.
13. Click the Add button again, and then add the Managers group.
14. Click the Managers group, and then select the Full Control check box in the Allow column.
15. Click OK to return to Windows Explorer.
16. Log off, and then log on to Computer1 again using the user name mgibson.
17. Start Windows Explorer and navigate to the C:\TK70-299\ folder.
18. In the right pane, double-click ACLTest.txt. The file should open in Notepad. Type **Mary can edit this file**. Save and close the file.
19. Log off, and then log on to Computer1 again using the Administrator account.
20. Start Windows Explorer. Right-click the ACLTest.txt file and click Properties.
21. Click the Security tab, and then click Accounting. Select the Full Control check box in the Deny column, as shown in Figure 2.4.

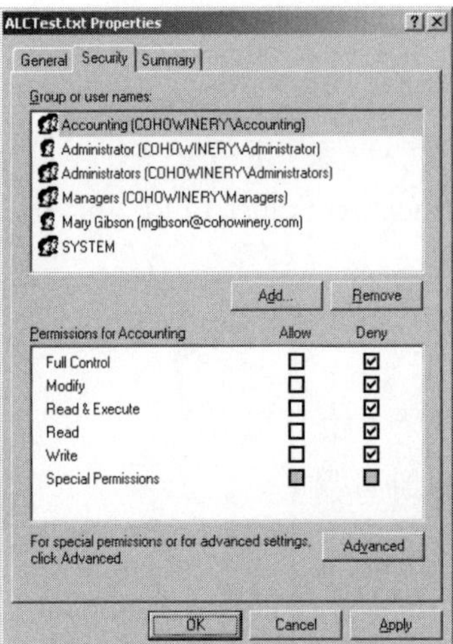

Figure 2.4 Deny ACEs override all ACEs that grant permissions

22. Click OK.

    You are warned that you are setting a deny permissions entry that will override grant entries.

23. Click Yes to return to Windows Explorer.
24. Log off, and then log on again using the user name mgibson.
25. Launch Windows Explorer and navigate to the C:\TK70-299\ folder.
26. In the right pane, double-click ACLTest.txt.

    Notepad will open, but the contents of the file will not be displayed. Instead, you will see an Access Is Denied message.

27. Click OK, and log off from the computer.

Lesson Review

The following questions are intended to reinforce key information presented in this lesson. If you are unable to answer a question, review the lesson materials and try the question again. You can find answers to the questions in the "Questions and Answers" section at the end of this chapter.

1. Sam is a member of both the IT group and the Administrators group. Sam is attempting to access a file with the following permissions:

    - Administrators: Grant Full Control
    - IT: Grant Modify

What are Sam's effective privileges to the file?

a. Full Control
b. Modify
c. Read & Execute
d. Read
e. Write
f. None

2. Sam is a member of both the IT group and the Administrators group. Sam is attempting to access a file with the following permissions:

- Administrators: Grant Full Control
- IT: Deny Full Control

What are Sam's effective privileges to the file?

a. Full Control
b. Modify
c. Read & Execute
d. Read
e. Write
f. None

3. Which of the following is a standard permission for a file or folder?

a. Read Attributes
b. Delete
c. Read & Execute
d. Take Ownership

Lesson Summary

- Files and folders, shared folders, printers, services, Active Directory objects, Terminal Services connections, Windows Management Interface objects, and registry keys and values have similar, but not identical, authorization methods.
- An access control list (ACL) defines who can access an object and what actions the users can take with the object. An ACL consists of multiple access control entries (ACEs). An ACE defines how a specific user or group is allowed to access an object.
- ACEs can either grant or deny access. If a user, through group membership, has both Grant and Deny ACEs for a single object, the Deny ACE always takes precedence.
- Explicit permissions are assigned directly to an object, while inherited permissions propagate to an object from its parent object. Using inherited permissions greatly simplifies managing permissions.
- When editing permissions for most types of objects, Windows Server 2003 presents standard permissions. Standard permissions consist of one or more special permissions and serve to simplify permission management. Standard permissions are usually sufficient to provide the level of control you need over access to an object. Special permissions should only be assigned when you have extremely granular access control requirements.

Lesson 2: Managing Groups in Windows Server 2003

A *group* is a collection of user accounts. You can use groups to efficiently manage access to domain resources, which helps simplify network maintenance and administration. For example, if all employees in the research department should have access to a file server, you could grant each individual the right to read the files. However, each time an employee joined or left the research department, you would need to manually add or remove the employee from the file share's access control list. If you had hundreds of such network resources, this would be impossible to manage. A better way to organize this is to place all members of the research department into a group named Research, and then assign privileges to the Research group. When employees change departments, you only need to modify the Research group membership.

You can use groups separately, or you can place one group within another to further reduce the amount of administration involved in managing groups. For example, if you have created separate groups for the research departments on the East and West coasts, you could place both groups into a national Research group. This simplifies administration in the same way as putting user accounts into groups.

Before you can use groups effectively, you must understand the types of groups available in a Windows Server 2003 environment, and the function of those groups.

This lesson describes the types of groups that you can create in Windows Server 2003. The lesson also describes the behavior of global, domain local, and universal groups and the strategies to use when implementing groups.

After this lesson, you will be able to

- Determine the type of group to create in Windows Server 2003 to meet the security requirements of your organization.
- Determine the domain functionality–level impact on group nesting and universal groups.
- Select an appropriate built-in group for controlling access to resources.
- Select an appropriate special group for controlling access to resources.
- Select appropriate tools for administering groups in Windows Server 2003.
- Create a Restricted Group Policy.

Estimated lesson time: 30 minutes

Types of Groups in Windows Server 2003

You use groups to organize user accounts, computer accounts, and other group accounts into manageable units. While the local user databases on member servers and standalone servers only support security groups, there are two types of groups in Active Directory: distribution groups and security groups.

Distribution groups are primarily used for sending e-mail to multiple users. You can use distribution groups with Active Directory–aware applications and e-mail applications, such as Microsoft Exchange Server and Microsoft Outlook, to send messages to users that are contained in the distribution group. Distribution groups are not security-enabled, and cannot be listed in ACLs. In other words, if you have created a distribution group for the human resources department, you cannot use the group to grant the members of that group access to a printer. You can, however, send the group an e-mail message telling them that they'll have access to their new printer as soon as you create a security group.

Security groups can be used to grant (or deny) access to network resources, because security groups can be listed in ACLs. For example, granting the Research security group Read access to a shared folder will enable the members of that group to access the files. Security groups can also be used for e-mail distribution. So you could use the Research security group to grant access to a shared folder, and then send an e-mail message to the group letting them know that they now have access to their files.

Tip Security groups do everything distribution groups do, and more. However, distribution groups should be used whenever possible because they do not become part of a user's security token. This makes the authentication process quicker than if a security group were used.

You can use *nesting* to place one or more groups into another group. For example, if you need two separate groups named Accounts Payable and Accounts Receivable for users in the Accounting group, you could nest them into another group called All Accounting. You can then use the All Accounting group when assigning permissions for resources that all members of the accounting department should access. When you use nested groups, a group inherits the permissions of the group of which it is a member, which simplifies the process of assigning permissions to several groups at one time.

Warning In a mixed-mode domain, you cannot nest groups that have the same group scope. For example, if my domain was at Windows 2000 Mixed-Mode, you would not be able to nest global groups inside of other global groups. You can nest global groups only when the domain functional level is set to Windows 2000 native or higher. Group scope is described in the next section.

Group Scopes

Each group in Windows Server 2003 has a scope attribute, which determines which security principals can be members of the group and where you can use that group in a multidomain or multiforest environment. Windows Server 2003 supports the following group scopes:

- Local Groups. Local groups reside on member servers and client computers. Use a local group to grant access to local resources on the computer where they reside.

Note Local groups are the only group type available in a non-domain environment.

- Global Groups. Global groups reside in Active Directory at the domain level. Use a global group to organize users who share the same job tasks and need similar network access requirements, such as all accountants in an organization's accounting department. Global groups can be members of other global groups, universal groups, and domain local groups.
- Domain Local Groups. Domain local groups reside in Active Directory at the domain level. Use a domain local group when you want to assign access permissions to resources that are located in the same domain in which you create the domain local group. You can add all global groups that need to share the same resources to the appropriate domain local group.
- Universal Groups. Universal groups reside in Active Directory at the forest level. Use universal groups when you want to nest global groups so that you can assign permissions to related resources in multiple domains. Universal groups can be members of other universal groups, global groups, and domain local groups. The Windows Server 2003 domain functional level must be at Windows 2000 native mode or higher to use universal security groups. You can use universal distribution groups in a Windows Server 2003 domain that is in Windows 2000 mixed mode and higher.

Figure 2.5 shows the relationship between the group scopes, with arrows used to indicate which group types can be nested within other group types.

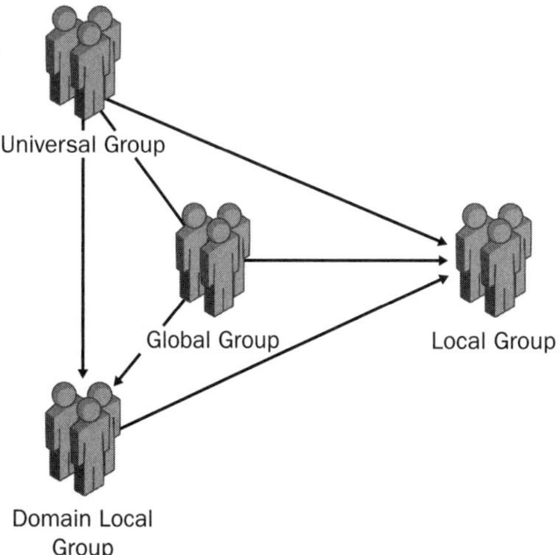

Figure 2.5 Some group types can be nested within other group types

Note The domain functional level determines the type of group that you can create. For example, not all group types are available until the domain functional level has been raised. You will learn more about domain functional levels in later topics.

Domain and Forest Functional Levels

In Windows Server 2003, the forest or domain functional level defines which advanced features are available to domain controllers in the organization. The functional level of a domain or forest will also define which versions of operating systems can run on domain controllers. For example, if all domain controllers in your domain or forest are running Windows Server 2003 and the forest functional level is set to Windows Server 2003, all domain- and forest-wide features are available. When Microsoft Windows NT 4.0 or Windows 2000 domain controllers are included in your domain or forest with domain controllers running Windows Server 2003, Active Directory features are limited. The domain and forest functional levels for a domain determine which group types will be available in Windows Server 2003.

Caution Raising a functional level has the potential to alienate older operating systems. For example, if you raise the domain functional level to Windows 2000 native mode and Windows NT 4.0 domain controllers are present, they will no longer participate in replication.

Table 2.1 lists the four domain functional levels and a list of features relevant to security associated with each level.

Table 2.1 Domain Functional Levels and Their Features

Domain functional level	Features
Windows 2000 mixed	Universal groups (distribution only) Groups nesting (distribution only)
Windows 2000 native	Universal groups Nesting groups Converting groups SID history
Windows Server 2003 interim	Renaming domain controllers Update logon timestamp User password on InetOrgPerson object Universal groups Nesting groups Converting groups SID history

Table 2.1 Domain Functional Levels and Their Features

Domain functional level	Features
Windows Server 2003	Renaming domain controllers Update logon timestamp User password on InetOrgPerson object Universal groups Nesting groups Converting groups SID history

See Also For more information about the features available for each domain functional level, see Windows Server 2003 Help and Support or Microsoft Technet at *http://www.microsoft.com/technet/prodtechnol/windowsserver2003/proddocs/standard/sag_levels.asp.*

Note When you first install Windows Server 2003, the default domain functional level is Windows 2000 mixed. When you raise the domain functional level to Windows 2000 native, Windows Server 2003 interim, or Windows Server 2003, the applicable features for that domain are enabled.

Table 2.2 lists the forest functional levels and a list of relevant features associated with each level.

Table 2.2 Forest Functional Levels and Their Features

Forest functional level	Features
Windows 2000	Global catalog Partial Attribute Set (PAS) replication improvements (Windows Server 2003 global catalogs only)
Windows 2003 Interim	Global catalog PAS replication improvements
Windows Server 2003	Global catalog PAS replication improvements

See Also For more information about the features available for each forest functional level, see Windows Server 2003 Help and Support or Microsoft Technet at *http://www.microsoft.com/technet/prodtechnol/windowsserver2003/proddocs/standard/sag_levels.asp.*

A detailed discussion of the features of Windows Server 2003 for each functional level is beyond the scope of this book.

Built-In Groups

Windows Server 2003 provides many built-in groups. Built-in groups are automatically created when you create an Active Directory domain. You can use built-in groups to manage access to shared resources and to delegate specific domain-wide administrative roles. For example, you could put the user account of a junior administrator into the Account Operators group to allow the junior administrator to create user accounts and groups.

Many built-in groups are automatically assigned a set of user rights that determine what each group and their members can do within the scope of a domain or forest. User rights authorize members of a group to perform specific actions, such as logging on to a local system or backing up files and folders. For example, a member of the Backup Operators group has the right to perform backup operations for all domain controllers in the domain. Therefore, to create an effective security strategy for a network, it is important that you understand the default rights associated with each built-in group. This section describes each built-in group and the rights and capabilities associated with each.

Account Operators

Members of the Account Operators group can create, modify, and delete accounts for users, groups, and computers located in the Users or Computers containers and organizational units in the domain, except the Domain Controllers organizational unit. Members of this group do not have permission to modify the Administrators or the Domain Admins groups, nor do they have permission to modify the accounts for members of those groups. Members of this group can log on locally to domain controllers in the domain and shut them down. Because this group has significant power in the domain, add users with caution. Members of this group have the following default user rights:

- Allow logon locally.
- Shut down the system.

Warning Do not change the default user right assignments on a production computer unless you really know what you are doing. If you do get into a position where you need to restore the default user right assignments, use the setup security.inf security template provided with Windows Server 2003. Security templates are covered in more detail in Chapter 3, "Deploying and Troubleshooting Security Templates."

Administrators

Members of the Administrators group have full control of the server and can assign user rights and access control permissions to users as necessary. Add users with caution. When joined to a domain, the Domain Admins group is automatically added to this group. The default Administrator user account is made a member of the Administrators group. Members of this group have almost every user right available on a system.

Backup Operators

Members can back up and restore all files on domain controllers in the domain, regardless of their own individual permissions on those files. Backup Operators can also log on to domain controllers and shut them down. This group has no default members. Because this group has significant power on domain controllers, add users with caution. Members of this group have the following default user rights:

- Back up files and directories.
- Allow logon locally.
- Restore files and directories.
- Shut down the system.

Incoming Forest Trust Builders

This group only appears in the forest root domain. Members of this group can create one-way, incoming forest trusts to the forest root domain. For example, members of this group residing in Forest A can create a one-way, incoming forest trust from Forest B. This one-way, incoming forest trust allows users in Forest A to access resources located in Forest B. Members of this group are granted the Create Inbound Forest Trust permission on the forest root domain. This group has no default members and no default user rights.

Network Configuration Operators

This group is intended to be used for staff responsible for managing the network configuration of servers and workstations in a domain. Members of this group can make changes to Transmission Control Protocol/Internet Protocol (TCP/IP) settings and renew and release TCP/IP addresses on domain controllers in the domain. This group has no default members and no default user rights.

Performance Log Users

Members of this group can manage performance counters, logs, and alerts on domain controllers in the domain, locally and from remote clients, without being a member of the Administrators group. Members of this group have no default user rights.

Performance Monitor Users

Members of this group can monitor performance counters on domain controllers in the domain, locally and from remote clients, without being a member of the Administrators or Performance Log Users groups. This group has no default members and no default user rights.

Pre–Windows 2000 Compatible Access

Members of this group have read access on all users and groups in the domain. This group is provided for backward compatibility with computers running Windows NT 4.0 and earlier. By default, the special identity Authenticated Users is a member of this group. Members of this group have the following default user rights:

- Access this computer from the network.
- Bypass traverse checking.

Print Operators

Members of this group can manage, create, share, and delete printers connected to domain controllers in the domain. They can also manage Active Directory printer objects in the domain. Because members of this group can load and unload device drivers on all domain controllers in the domain, add users with caution. A member of the Print Operators group with malicious intent could take control of a domain controller. This group has no default members. Members of this group have the following default user rights:

- Allow logon locally.
- Shut down the system.

Remote Desktop Users

Members of this group can remotely log on to domain controllers in the domain. This group has no default members and no default user rights.

Replicator

This group supports directory replication functions and is used by the File Replication service on domain controllers in the domain. This group has no default members and no default user rights. Because this group is owned by the operating system, adding users to this group can cause problems with the File Replication Service.

Server Operators

On domain controllers, members of this group can log on interactively, create and delete shared resources, start and stop some services, back up and restore files, format the hard disk, and shut down the computer. This group has no default members. Members of this group have the following default user rights:

- Back up files and directories.
- Change the system time.

- Force shutdown from a remote system.
- Allow logon locally.
- Restore files and directories.
- Shut down the system.

Terminal Server License Servers

Members of this group have access to Terminal Server License Servers on the system. This group has no default members and no default user rights.

Users

Members of this group can perform most common tasks, such as running applications, using local and network printers, and locking the server. By default, the Domain Users group, the Authenticated Users group, and the Interactive group are members of this group. All user accounts in the domain are members of this group. Members of this group have no default user rights.

Windows Authorization Access Group

This group exists to simplify granting accounts permission to query a user's group information. Members of this group have access to the computed tokenGroupsGlobal-AndUniversal attribute on User objects. Add members to this group only when specifically required by an application. By default, only the Enterprise Domain Controllers group is a member of this group.

See Also For more information about built-in groups see *http://www.microsoft.com/technet/prodtechnol/windowsserver2003/proddocs/entserver/sag_ADgroups_9builtin_intro.asp.*

Real World The Principle of Least Privilege

In the real world, the built-in groups are often misused. It's a common practice to add users to the Power Users group so that an application that won't run with regular User privileges will work as expected. While this is better than adding the user to the Administrators group, there is a risk associated with this practice—the risk that the user will be granted unnecessary rights that will later be misused. Even if the user would never intentionally misuse the elevated privileges of the Power Users group, a virus or Trojan horse might take advantage of the additional privileges without the user being aware.

Special Groups and Accounts

Servers running Windows Server 2003 include several special identities in addition to the groups in the Users and Builtin containers. These identities are generally referred to as *special groups*. Special groups, also called *special identities*, are designed to provide access to resources without administrative or user interaction.

> **Tip** You can recognize most special groups because their names are in all capital letters. There are a few exceptions to this, however, such as the Authenticated Users special group.

Users become members of special groups by simply interacting with the operating system. For example, when users log on locally to a computer, they become members of the Interactive group. You can grant user rights and permissions to these special groups, but you cannot modify or view their memberships. In addition, group scopes do not apply to special groups.

It is important to understand the purpose of special groups because you can use them for security administration, as they allow you to create more granular access policies and control access to resources. To understand how special groups help provide secure access, consider blocking access for dial-up users to a folder containing confidential documents. As shown in Figure 2.6, denying access to a folder is as simple as adding the Dialup special group to the folder's ACL.

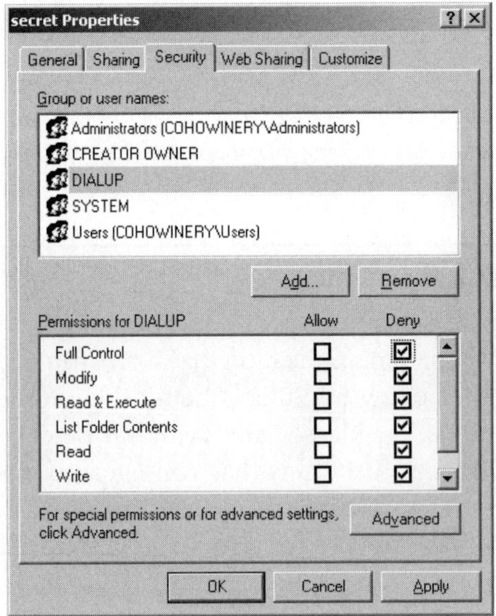

Figure 2.6 You can assign permissions to special groups that apply to users based on how they connect to the network

Following are the special groups included in Windows Server 2003 that can be used to control access to resources in an organization.

Exam Tip Digest Authentication, Schannel Authentication, NTLM Authentication, Proxy, Remote Interactive Logon, and Restricted are special groups and accounts that appear when browsing accounts. However, they are rarely used and are not likely to be covered on the exam.

Anonymous Logon

The Anonymous Logon special group represents users and services that access a computer and its resources through the network without using an account name, password, or domain name. On computers running Windows NT and earlier, the Anonymous Logon special group is a member of the Everyone group by default. On computers running a member of the Windows Server 2003 family, the Anonymous Logon special group is not a member of the Everyone group by default. If you want to create a file share for an anonymous user, grant permissions to the Anonymous Logon special group.

Authenticated Users

The Authenticated Users special group represents all users and computers whose identities have been authenticated. Authenticated Users does not include Guest even if the Guest account has a password. Membership in the Authenticated Users special group is mutually exclusive to membership in the Anonymous Logons special group.

Batch

The Batch special group includes all users and services that access a computer and its resources through the network by using a batch queue facility, for example, task scheduler jobs.

Creator Group

The Creator Group special group includes the user account for the user who created the resource. The Creator Group special group is a placeholder in an inheritable ACE. When the ACE is inherited, the system replaces this security identifier (SID) with the SID for the primary group of the object's current owner.

Creator Owner

The Creator Owner special group includes the user account for the user who created or took ownership of a resource. If a member of the Administrators group creates a resource, the Administrators group is the owner of the resource. The Creator Owner special group is a placeholder in an inheritable ACE. When the ACE is inherited, the system replaces this SID with the SID for the object's current owner.

Dialup

The Dialup special group includes all users who are logged on to the system through a dial-up connection.

Everyone

The Everyone special group represents all current network users, including guests and users from other domains. Whenever a user logs on to the network, the user is automatically added to the Everyone special group. The Anonymous Logon special group is no longer contained in the Everyone special group, as in previous versions of Windows Server.

Interactive

The Interactive special group represents all users currently logged on to a particular computer and accessing a given resource located on that computer, as opposed to users who access the resource over the network. Whenever a user accesses a resource on the computer to which they are currently logged on, the user is automatically added to the Interactive special group.

Local Service

The Local Service account is a special built-in account that is similar to an authenticated user account. The Local Service account has the same level of access to resources and objects as members of the Users group. This limited access helps safeguard your system if individual services or processes are compromised. Services that run as the Local Service account access network resources as a null session with no credentials.

Network

The Network special group represents users currently accessing a given resource over the network, as opposed to users who access the resource by logging on locally at the computer on which the resource is located. Whenever a user accesses a given resource over the network, the user is automatically added to the Network special group.

Network Service

The Network Service account is a special built-in account that is similar to an authenticated user account. The Network Service account has the same level of access to resources and objects as members of the Users group. This limited access helps safeguard your system if individual services or processes are compromised. Services that run as the Network Service account access network resources using the credentials of the computer account.

Other Organization

This special group contains users who authenticated from another domain. Adding this special group to an ACL causes a check to ensure that a user from another forest or domain that is trusted is allowed to authenticate to a particular service in the trusted domain.

Self

The Self special group is a placeholder group in an ACE on a user, group, or computer object in Active Directory. When you grant permissions to Principal Self, you grant them to the security principal represented by the object. During an access check, the operating system replaces the SID for Principal Self with the SID for the security principal represented by the object.

Service

The Service special group is a group that includes all security principals that have logged on as a service. Membership is controlled by the operating system.

System

The System special group is used by the operating system and by services that run under Windows. It has privileges that are similar to those of the Administrators group. The System account is an internal account, does not show up in User Manager, cannot be added to any groups, and cannot have user rights assigned to it. The System account does show up when assigning file permissions, however.

Terminal Server Users

The Terminal Server Users special group includes all users who have logged on to a Terminal Services server that is in Terminal Services version 4.0 application compatibility mode.

This Organization

When there are trusted domains for forests, the This Organization special group is added by the authentication server to the authentication data of a user to identify the user's organization, provided the Other Organization SID is not already present.

Tools for Administering Security Groups

Windows Server 2003 supports a number of tools that make it easy for you to troubleshoot and enumerate groups and their members. Table 2.3 outlines the tools related to administering security groups and their functions:

Table 2.3 Windows Server 2003 Tools for Administering Security Groups

Tool	Description
Active Directory Users and Computers	Graphical tool used to administer users and groups in Active Directory. This tool can be started from the Administrative Tools program group.
Dsadd	Command-line tool for creating groups and manipulating group membership.
Getsid	Command-line tool for comparing the SIDs of two user accounts.
Ifmember	Command-line tool for enumerating all groups that the current member belongs to. Commonly used in logon scripts. This tool is one of the Windows Server 2003 Resource Kit tools.
Local Users and Groups	MMC snap-in that enables the creation and editing of users and groups in the local user database. This snap-in is often accessed from the Computer Management console. This tool is not available on domain controllers.
Whoami	Command-line tool capable of displaying the complete contents of the access token. It can display the user name and SID, the groups and their SIDs, the privileges and their status (for example, enabled or disabled), and the logon ID. For usage information, execute **whoami /?** at a command prompt.

See Also For more information about the parameters for the security group administration tools, see *A-Z Command Line Reference* in Windows Server 2003 Help and Support.

Creating Restricted Groups Policy

Earlier in this chapter, you learned that you can assign rights to computers by using both the groups stored on individual computers and groups stored in Active Directory. It would be difficult, however, to manually add a new IT group that you created in Active Directory as a member of the Administrators local group on every computer in an enterprise. Fortunately, you can use security policies to control local group memberships on domain member computers.

Windows Server 2003 includes a security policy setting called Restricted Groups that allows you to control group membership. By using the Restricted Groups policy, you can specify the membership of a group anywhere in your Active Directory domain. For example, you can create a Restricted Groups policy to limit the access on an OU that contains computers containing sensitive data. The Restricted Groups policy would remove domain users from the local users group and thereby limit the number of users who can log on to the computer. Group members that are not specified in the policy are removed when the Group Policy setting is applied or refreshed to the computer or OU. The Restricted Groups policy settings include two properties: Members and Member Of. The Members property defines who belongs and who does not belong to the restricted group. The Member Of property specifies the other groups to which the restricted group can belong.

When a Restricted Groups policy is enforced, any current member of a restricted group that is not on the Members list is removed. Members who can be removed include Administrators. Any user on the Members list who is not currently a member of the restricted group is added. In addition, each restricted group is a member of only those groups that are specified in the Member Of column.

Figure 2.7 shows Restricted Groups being used to add the IT security group from the cohowinery.com domain to the local Administrators group on all domain member computers.

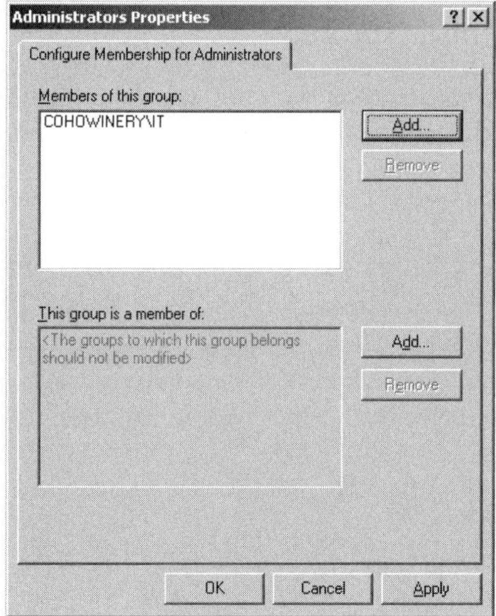

Figure 2.7 Use Restricted Groups to control group membership on domain members

Note The security setting is located in a security policy object in the Restricted Groups node.

You can apply a Restricted Groups policy in the following ways:

- Define the policy in a security template, which will be applied during configuration on your local computer.
- Define the setting directly on a Group Policy object (GPO). Defining the setting in this way will ensure that the operating system continually enforces the restricted groups.

▶ **To create a Restricted Groups policy:**

1. Open a security policy tool, such as the Domain Security Policy console.
2. In the console tree, right-click Restricted Groups, and then click Add Group.
3. In the Group field, type the name of the group to which you want to restrict membership, and then click OK.
4. On the properties dialog box, click Add beside the This Group Is A Member Of field.
5. Under Group Membership, type the name of the group you want to add to this group, and then click OK.
6. Click OK again.

Practice: Creating Groups and Assigning Rights

In this practice, you will create a restricted group and assign appropriate rights to the members of the group. To complete this practice, you must be logged in with an account that has permission to create and manage groups and GPOs in Active Directory. Complete this task from Computer1.cohowinery.com.

You are the security administrator for the Coho Winery organization. Your organization recently hired several new staff members to support desktop computers. These staff members should have administrative rights to all member computers in the domain, but they should not have rights to domain controllers. You decide to create a group for the new staff members and to add that group to the local Administrators group on all non-domain controller computers in your domain.

▶ **Exercise 1: Create a New Security Group**

Create a new security group called Desktop Support.

1. Open Active Directory Users And Computers.
2. In the console tree, right-click the Users container, point to New, and then click Group.

3. In the New Object – Group dialog box, in the Group Name field, type **Desktop Support**.
4. Click OK.

▶ **Exercise 2: Configure the Domain Security Policy**

1. Open the Domain Security Policy console.
2. In the console tree, right-click Restricted Groups, and then click Add Group.
3. Click the Browse button to select the Desktop Support group. Click OK.
4. On the Desktop Support Properties page, click Add beside the This Group Is A Member Of field.
5. Under Group Membership, type **Administrators**, and then click OK.

▶ **Exercise 3: Populate the Group**

Finally, populate the Desktop Support security group with the following users:

- Jo Berry
- Ken Sanchez
- Nancy Buchanan

1. Open a command prompt.
2. Type the following text, and then provide a complex password when prompted: **dsadd user "cn=Jo Berry,cn=Users,dc=cohowinery,dc=com" –disabled no –memberof "cn=Desktop Support,cn=Users,dc=cohowinery,dc=com" –pwd ***
3. Type the following text, and then provide a complex password when prompted: **dsadd user "cn=Ken Sanchez,cn=Users,dc=cohowinery,dc=com" –disabled no –memberof "cn=Desktop Support,cn=Users,dc=cohowinery,dc=com" –pwd ***
4. Type the following text, and then provide a complex password when prompted: **dsadd user "cn=Nancy Buchanan,cn=Users,dc=cohowinery,dc=com" –disabled no –memberof "cn=Desktop Support,cn=Users,dc=cohowinery,dc=com" –pwd ***

Lesson Review

The following questions are intended to reinforce key information presented in this lesson. If you are unable to answer a question, review the lesson materials and try the question again. You can find answers to the questions in the "Questions and Answers" section at the end of this chapter.

1. Which of the following built-in groups is present on a domain controller?

   a. Administrators

   b. Power Users

   c. DHCP Users

   d. Backup Operators

   ____

   ____

2. Which of the following special groups could you assign to an ACL to prevent access from unauthenticated users?

   a. Everyone

   b. Anonymous Logon

   c. Authenticated Users

   d. Interactive

   ____

   ____

3. Which of the following are not available at the Windows 2000 native domain functional level?

   a. Universal groups

   b. Nesting groups

   c. Converting groups

   d. Renaming domain controllers

   e. SID history

   ____

   ____

4. Which of the following group types could be nested within a universal group?

   a. Local group

   b. Domain local group

   c. Global group

   d. Distribution group

   ____

Lesson Summary

- You can use groups to efficiently manage access to domain resources, which helps simplify administration.
- There are two types of groups in Active Directory: distribution groups and security groups.
- Groups are characterized by a scope that identifies the extent to which the group is applied in the domain tree or forest. The group scope determines whether the group spans multiple domains or is limited to a single domain. Windows Server 2003 supports the following group scopes:
  - Local
  - Global
  - Domain Local
  - Universal
- Depending on the functional level, certain features are enabled or disabled in Active Directory.
- The default domain functional level is Windows 2000 mixed. When you raise the domain functional level to Windows 2000 native, Windows Server 2003 interim, or Windows Server 2003, the applicable features for that domain are enabled.
- You can use built-in groups to manage shared resources and delegate specific domain-wide administrative roles.
- Special groups, also called *special identities*, are designed to provide access to resources without administrative or user interaction.
- You can use Restricted Groups policy to control group membership.

Lesson 3: Planning, Implementing, and Maintaining an Authorization Strategy

Groups play an important role in making network administration easier. To ensure that the convenience of using groups does not compromise network security, you need to come up with a well-designed plan for creating and managing groups in your organization. This lesson will provide you with guidelines and best practices for effectively planning, creating, and managing groups in an enterprise environment.

After this lesson, you will be able to

- Describe the User/ACL access method of controlling access to resources.
- Describe the Account Group/ACL access method of controlling access to resources.
- Describe the Account Group/Resource Group access method of controlling access to resources.
- Determine the strategies for naming a group in a multidomain and multiforest organization.
- Determine which users are allowed to create groups in an organization.
- Describe the impact and benefits of nesting groups inside other groups.
- Determine when to retire groups.

Estimated lesson time: 30 minutes

Authentication, Authorization, and the Principle of Least Privilege

To review, *authentication* is the process of verifying the identity of something or someone. Authentication usually involves a user name and a password, but can include any method of demonstrating identity, such as a smart card, a retinal scan, voice recognition, or a fingerprint.

Authorization is the process of determining whether an identified user or process is permitted access to a resource and what the appropriate level of access is for that user. The owner of a resource, or someone who has been granted permission, determines whether a user is a member of a predetermined group or has a certain level of security clearance. By setting the permissions on a resource, the owner controls which users and groups on the network can access the resource. For example, users who have logged on to the domain are authenticated to the domain. However, when users try to access resources that they have not been given permission to, they are denied access.

The principle of *least privilege* states that you should provide users with the necessary level of privilege to perform their jobs—and no more. By restricting access that is not necessary to job performance, you can prevent malicious users from using extraneous privileges to circumvent network security. For example, regional managers may need permissions to modify their own human resources databases, but they may need only read access to the databases of other regions. A corporate human resources manager may require permissions to modify all databases, but a payroll manager may require only read access on the same databases. The concept of least privilege states that access controls should be used to ensure that these users only have the access they absolutely need.

User/ACL Authorization Method

When using the User/ACL method of controlling access to resources, you add the user account that needs access directly to the ACL of the resource. For example, a user John creates a file share and adds Sarah as an authorized user, giving her read-only permission to the share.

The User/ACL method works well for small organizations with less than 10 users. Generally, smaller organizations require fewer groups to manage access to resources, which reduces the complexity of the process of assigning permissions. Using the User/ACL method in large organizations has the following limitations:

- Users within the same job function might have inconsistent access to resources. Usually, users who share the same job role need uniform access to resources. For example, one engineer might have access to a laser printer, a plotter, a backup device, and many file shares. Another engineer in the same group might need access to the same resources, but might have access to only a subset of those resources. Therefore, when there is not uniform access, the network administrator will have to modify the rights for every individual who needs more access.
- Administrator overhead increases because administrators will need to control access to resources on a user-by-user basis.
- This method does not scale well for larger organizations.
- Troubleshooting and tracking which users have access to which resources can be time-consuming and result in higher administrative overhead.
- Access control lists will grow very large, which will cause performance degradation.

Warning Even small organizations will regret using the User/ACL method the first time an employee is replaced.

Account Group/ACL Authorization Method

When using the Account Group/ACL method, you place the user accounts into a global group. Instead of adding the user accounts to the ACL, you add the global group to the ACL. You then assign the group a set of access permissions. The Account Group/ACL method provides the following benefits:

- Grouping users into groups makes management easier.
- By placing users performing the same role in a common group, you provide them with the same set of permissions.
- You can add global groups to the access control lists of trusted domains.

For example, an administrator can put all accounting user accounts into a global group called GG-All Accountants and then put that global group on an ACL and assign permissions. The Account Group/ACL method also has some limitations. These include the following:

- As more account groups are added to the resource, the resource administrator will experience some of the same challenges posed by the User/ACL method.
- Determining which groups need which permissions can be complicated.
- It is not as straightforward for non-administrators to assign access as it is when using the User/ACL method.

Account Group/Resource Group Authorization Method

The Account Group/Resource Group method of controlling access to resources is similar to the Account – Global Group – Domain Local Group – Permission (A-G-DL-P) method. When using this method, you add users with similar access requirements into account groups, and then add account groups as members to a resource group that has been granted specific resource access permissions. This strategy provides the most flexibility while reducing the complexity of assigning access permissions to the network. This method is most commonly used by large organizations for controlling access to recourses.

When creating a resource group to control access to a resource, you can create a local group at the resource or create a domain local group on a domain controller. By creating a domain local group instead of a local group to control access, an administrator can configure groups for access from the Active Directory Users And Computers console. A local group would require the administrator to connect directly to the resource to administer it.

To understand how the Account Group/Resource Group authorization method can be used in an organization, consider the following example. Nwtraders.msft needs to provide its users access to a printer named ColorLaser. However, the requirements of various users differ. Some users only need to be able to print with the printer, whereas others need to be able to print and manage the printer. In such a scenario, instead of adding each user or group into the ACL for the printer, you can create resource groups for the two sets of users and then provide the resource groups with appropriate permissions.

The Account Group/Resource Group authorization method is highly scalable and provides the following benefits:

- Instead of modifying permissions for an individual group, you can add the account group into a resource group that has been configured with the appropriate permissions.
- You can place account groups on ACLs in trusted domains.
- You can provide groups with access to resources by simply placing account groups into resource groups.

The Account Group/Resource Group authorization method is not practical for small organizations. For a small organization that has fewer groups, the use of the Account Group/Resource Group authorization group method is unnecessary. With fewer groups, it is more practical to use the Account Group/ACL or even the User/ACL authorization method.

Group Naming Conventions

Designing naming standards may not seem like an important job, but a non-intuitive group naming convention can potentially lead to a security compromise. For example, if you named three global groups Group1, Group2, and Group3, a resource owner might not know which group contains the users who need access to the resource. The less intuitive the naming convention, the more likely users are to accidentally receive unnecessary permissions.

Table 2.4 lists the components of an intuitive naming convention.

Table 2.4 Components of a Naming Convention

Components	Example
Group type	GG for global group, UN for universal group, DLG for domain local group
Location of the group	Sea for Seattle
Purpose of the group	Admins for administrators

Your group naming convention can be based on geographic location, domain membership, or a resource. The main goal is to make the group name intuitive so that resource owners know the type and purpose of the group so that they can grant appropriate access to users. Windows Server 2003 does not provide any means of enforcing a group naming convention. You should enforce a group naming convention in your organization by educating users who create groups and also by monitoring group names. Additionally, someone in your organization should have the responsibility of auditing group names on a weekly or monthly basis and correcting any groups that have been misnamed.

Tip When creating a name, ensure that the important details are in the first 20 characters of the name. This placement will allow you to view the important details in most dialog boxes without resizing the window.

To design a naming convention, you must understand how your organization will assign resources. For example, the organization may or may not have resources divided by regions. If an organization has marketing departments in Boston, Austin, and San Diego, and each of these marketing departments uses separate resources, then you should include location in the group naming convention because you will be required to make separate groups for each team in each location. Following are examples of what those groups might be named:

- GG BOS Marketing
- GG SAN Marketing
- GG AUS Marketing

However, if the marketing teams from all locations work closely together and do not maintain separate resources, you do not need to include location in the group name. For example, the group name GG Marketing would be sufficiently granular. If there are resources that should only be accessed by users in a particular location regardless of the department they work in, you can create groups for each location, such as GG Austin, GG Boston, and GG San Diego.

Tip Keeping the most general information towards the left of the name string and more specific information towards the right makes sorting more logical.

If you decide to use resource groups, you must determine how to uniquely and logically name the groups so that it is obvious which resources those groups should be assigned to. For example, in a small office with a single laser jet printer and a single bubble jet printer, the following names would be acceptable for resource groups:

- DL LJ Print Only
- DL LJ Managers
- DL LJ Administrators
- DL BJ Print Only

- DL BJ Managers
- DL BJ Administrators

However, in an enterprise with hundreds of printers, that naming convention would be confusing. Larger organizations need to include a description of the location in the group name. For example, if an enterprise uses a building code and office code to describe locations, the following names would be acceptable for resources groups:

- DL 25-2003C LJ Print Only
- DL 25-2003C LJ Managers
- DL 25-2003C LJ Administrators

Defining Which Users Can Create Groups

In large organizations, the task of creating and managing groups can be time consuming for IT personnel. In such cases, you can delegate the task of creating and maintaining groups to other users in the organization. By delegating security group maintenance to the appropriate individuals, you can help to ensure that requests for changes in membership are evaluated by individuals who:

- Can judge the appropriateness of the request.
- Have the authority to make the change.
- Are motivated to keep group membership and access permissions correct and up-to-date.

However, delegating the right of managing groups to other users could also lead to security breaches because the delegated group administrators might incorrectly configure access to resources. Therefore, it is important that you carefully determine who can create and maintain groups in your organization.

When delegating users to administer and maintain groups, keep the following considerations in mind:

- Select users who are familiar with the department in which the resource is located and who have an understanding of the access needs of that department. Generally, an administrative assistant in a department has a good understanding of the access needs and requirements for those users and is a good choice for administering groups.
- After you select the appropriate users, assign them permission to create and maintain groups. Delegating permissions to these departmental administrators can be done at the OU level, or by giving them the appropriate permissions on the resources they will need to configure.

> **Caution** After you have created and delegated permissions to the departmental administrators, ensure that only the users you have selected are members of this group. Accidentally adding users to this group can result in loss of data or other security compromises. To prevent these risks, you can use restricted groups at the OU level.

Group Nesting

Group nesting is the process of placing security groups into other security groups. Group nesting is an effective way to scale the groups in an organization. For example, if you have account groups called GG Sales Managers, GG Training Managers, and GG Marketing Managers, you can nest these three account groups into another account group called All Managers. You could then apply permissions to all nested groups at one time.

> **Tip** To nest account groups inside of other account groups, the domain functional level must be set at Windows 2000 native or greater.

When nesting groups, keep the following considerations in mind:

- If you nest too many groups, access token size might become large. Group membership is limited to 120 groups.
- Just as with any group naming strategy, if you do not provide an intuitive name for the nested group, it can lead to improper access to resources when another administrator mistakenly grants access to the incorrect group.
- Make sure that you monitor the members of the groups. Not monitoring members of groups could lead to inappropriate access to resources. Monitoring nested groups is more complicated than managing regular groups because nested groups contain other groups. The membership of the nested groups will need to be exposed to determine the overall membership.

When to Retire Groups

As organizations grow and evolve, security groups can become obsolete. Obsolete security groups provide users with permissions they might no longer need, which can lead to security vulnerability. Although account groups for very small teams might not change frequently, large account groups experience almost continuous turnover in membership. If an account group's membership has not changed at all for some time, the group might be obsolete. Therefore, it is important that you constantly monitor which groups are no longer needed in your organization.

You should also develop and enforce processes to remove groups that are no longer in use. For example, you might create an account group called GG Picnic Planners for a new morale project in your organization. To facilitate the project, you provide the group access to the color laser printer to print handouts. When the project is over, if you do not retire the group, the users will still have access to the color laser printer.

Lesson Review

The following questions are intended to reinforce key information presented in this lesson. If you are unable to answer a question, review the lesson materials and try the question again. You can find answers to the questions in the "Questions and Answers" section at the end of this chapter.

1. Which of the following group names was created with an effective group naming strategy?
   - **a.** HR
   - **b.** GG BOS HR
   - **c.** Cohowinery Global Group Boston Human Resources
   - **d.** Resources Human

   ____

   ____

2. Is the User/ACL or the Account Group/ACL method more effective in large enterprises?

   ____

   ____

3. Which of the following describes the principle of least privilege?
   - **a.** Ensure that users have the minimal privileges necessary to do their jobs.
   - **b.** Ensure that users have no permissions unless they have authenticated with both a password and a smart card.
   - **c.** Create users with administrator privileges and then gradually reduce their privileges to the lowest level possible that allows applications to still function.
   - **d.** Unauthenticated users must have the lowest level of privileges on the network.

   ____

   ____

Lesson Summary

- When using the User/Access control method, you add the user account that needs access to a resource directly to the ACL of the resource.
- The User/Access control method does not scale well for larger organizations.
- When using the Account Group/Access Control List method, you place the user account into a global group, and instead of adding the user account to the ACL, you add the global group to the ACL.
- When using the Account Group/Resource Group method, you add users with similar access requirements into account groups, and then add account groups as members to a resource group that has been granted specific resource access permissions.
- Define a group naming convention that identifies the group type, its location, and the purpose of the group.
- By delegating security group maintenance to the appropriate individuals, you can ensure that requests for changes in membership are evaluated by individuals who can judge the appropriateness of the request, who have the authority to make the change, and who are motivated to keep group membership and access permissions correct and up-to-date.
- Group nesting is the process of placing security groups into other security groups. Group nesting is an effective way to scale the groups in an organization.

Lesson 4: Troubleshooting Authorization Problems

The more effort you make to tighten access control, the more likely your users are to experience authorization problems. Authorization problems occur when a legitimate user should have access to perform a particular action on an object according to your organization's management team, but overly restrictive access control prevents the user from performing that action.

The first thing to check when troubleshooting an authorization problem is the target object's ACL. The problem may be as simple as an ACE that explicitly denies access to that user. More often, the problem is caused by the user not having any permissions assigned to the object. If examining the object's ACL does not identify the problem, check the object's effective permissions.

If you cannot identify which objects the user needs access to, you can use auditing to identify which objects the user is attempting to access and how the user is accessing the file. It is common for applications to access resources that an administrator would not be able to anticipate. For example, the application might require access to Dynamic Link Libraries (DLLs) located in the system directory, or the application might attempt to write temporary files to an unusual location. Troubleshooting authorization using auditing is complex, but it can identify insufficient privileges that would otherwise be nearly impossible to find.

Tip You can quickly identify whether a particular problem is caused by authorization by performing the action while logged on as an administrator. If it works as an administrator, but not as a standard user, then authorization is almost certainly the cause of the problem.

After this lesson, you will be able to

- Identify a user's effective permissions for an object.
- Determine the source of incorrectly assigned permissions.
- Identify which objects a user or an application is attempting to access.
- Resolve problems relating to users who cannot access required resources.

Estimated lesson time: 45 minutes

Troubleshooting Simple Authorization Problems

If you are troubleshooting a simple authorization problem in which you know which objects the user cannot access, start by examining the object's access control list. The user interface varies slightly depending on what type of object you are examining, but the concepts are the same. In most circumstances, you will follow these steps to analyze effective permissions and resolve the problem:

1. View the object's permissions.
2. Click the Advanced button.
3. In the Advanced Security Settings dialog box, click Effective Permissions.
4. Click Select. In the Select User, Computer, Or Group dialog box, type the name of the user and click OK.
5. Examine the Effective Permissions list, as shown in Figure 2.8, to identify permissions that the user requires but currently lacks. Click OK to return to the object's permissions dialog box.

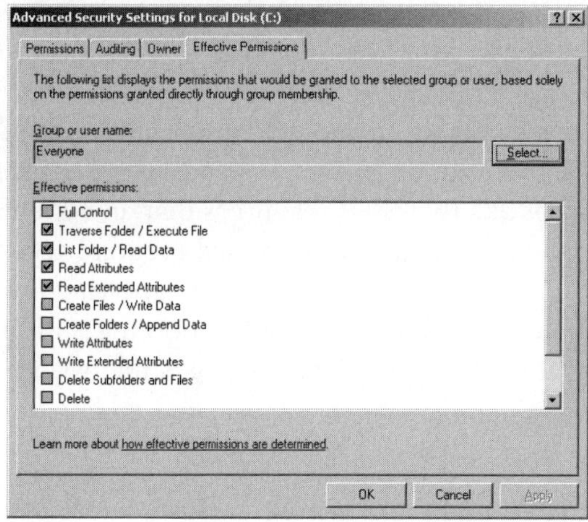

Figure 2.8 Windows Server 2003 allows you to view the effective permissions for most object types

6. Grant the user, or a group to which the user belongs, the privileges necessary to perform the action.

When correcting authorization problems, follow the same guidelines you used for initially designing the authorization strategy. Whenever possible, assign permissions to a group rather than a user. If the user should have access to all the objects in a container, assign permissions to the container itself and allow those permissions to be inherited by the child objects.

Warning Check your organization's security policy before elevating any user's permissions to an object.

Troubleshooting Complex Authorization Problems

Part of the challenge of troubleshooting authorization problems is identifying which objects the user is attempting to access. If the user is attempting to edit a file and is denied access, identifying the file is straightforward. However, if a custom application is returning an ambiguous error message because it cannot access a required object, identifying the specific object the application is attempting to access is much more complex. In fact, it may not be clear whether the application is attempting to access a file, printer, registry value, Active Directory object, or service.

Fortunately, you can use auditing to identify objects that a user or application is attempting to access. The flowchart in Figure 2.9 illustrates the authorization troubleshooting process that occurs when you use auditing.

Off the Record Most people think of auditing as solely an intrusion detection mechanism. In reality, its usefulness for intrusion detection is limited because auditing tends to generate far too many events to successfully parse. However, it is immensely useful when troubleshooting authorization problems.

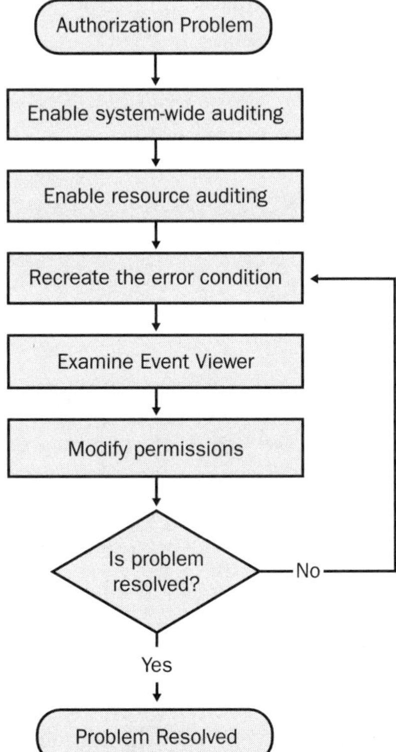

Figure 2.9 Use auditing to troubleshoot complex authorization problems

While most of the troubleshooting process is self-explanatory, enabling system auditing, enabling resource auditing, and analyzing events by using Event Viewer deserve further explanation.

Enabling system auditing

The first step in identifying resources with insufficient privileges is to enable auditing on a system-wide basis:

1. As an administrator, log on to the system with the resources you are troubleshooting. If you are troubleshooting access to Active Directory objects, log on to a domain controller.
2. Click Start, and then click Administrative Tools. If this is a domain members or a standalone computer, click Local Security Policy. If this is a domain controller, click Domain Controller Security Policy.
3. Expand Local Policies, and then click Audit Policy.
4. If you are troubleshooting access to Active Directory objects, double-click Audit Directory Service Access. If you are troubleshooting access to any other type of object, double-click Audit Object Access.
5. Make note of the current setting. You will return this setting to its original state after you have completed the troubleshooting process.
6. Select Define These Policy Settings, and then select Failure, as shown in Figure 2.10. Click OK.

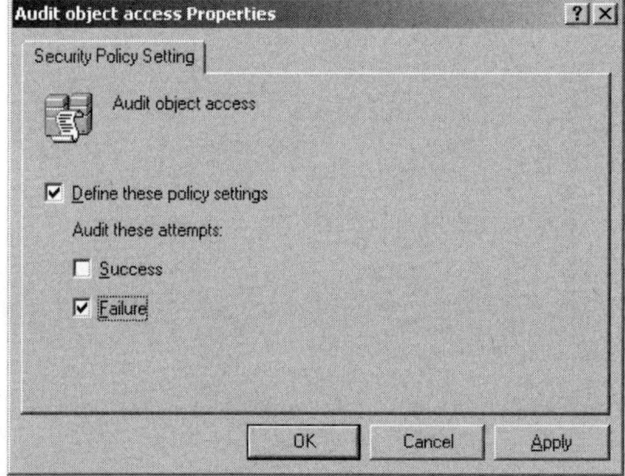

Figure 2.10 Auditing must be enabled for the system before it can be enabled for individual resources

Enabling resource auditing

After enabling failure auditing for the Audit Object Access or Audit Directory Services Access policies, you must enable auditing for the individual resources that are being accessed. The exact process varies depending on the type of object you want to audit. The following process applies to enabling auditing for folders or files, the most common source of authorization problems. The process for auditing other types of objects is very similar, although you will use a different tool for each object. For information on the specific tools to use for each object type, refer to the "Standard and Special Permissions" section in this chapter.

1. Click Start, point to All Programs, point to Accessories, and then click Windows Explorer.
2. Navigate to the file or folder you want to audit. If you are not sure which object is being accessed, you can enable auditing for entire disks.
3. Right-click the file or folder, and then click Properties.

Tip If you were auditing the registry, you would right-click the registry key and select Permissions.

4. On the Security tab, click the Advanced button.
5. In the Advanced Security Settings dialog box, click the Auditing tab. Make note of the current settings, and then click Add.
6. In the Select User Or Group dialog box, type the name of the user whose problem you are troubleshooting, and then click OK. The Auditing Entry dialog box appears.
7. Click the Failed check box for the Full Control entry, as shown in Figure 2.11. All Failed check boxes will be automatically selected.

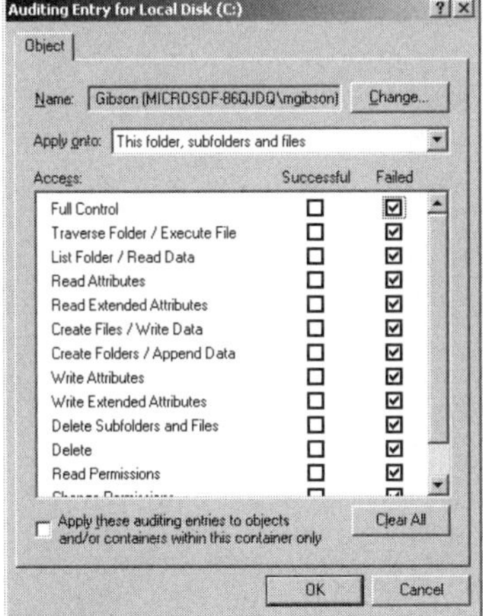

Figure 2.11 Failure auditing causes events to be added to the event log when a user is denied access to a resource

8. Click OK twice. Windows Server 2003 will apply the auditing setting to the folder, subfolder, and files automatically. If you are applying access to a large number of files, such as the entire C drive, this may take a moment.
9. Click OK to close the properties dialog box and return to Windows Explorer.

Now that failure auditing is enabled for those resources, every time the specified user is denied access to the resource, Windows Server 2003 will add an event to the Security event log.

Analyzing events in Event Viewer

After you have enabled auditing and re-created the problem condition, Windows Server 2003 will add events to the Security event log describing which resource could not be accessed and the type of operation that was attempted. To view failure audit events by using Event Viewer:

1. As an administrator, log on to the system with the resources you are troubleshooting. If you are troubleshooting access to Active Directory objects, log on to a domain controller.
2. Click Start, click Administrative Tools, and then click Event Viewer.
3. In the left pane, click Security. The Security event log will be displayed.
4. On the View menu, click Filter. The Security Properties dialog box appears.
5. Clear the Information, Warning, Error, and Success Audit check boxes. Only the Failure Audit check box should remain selected. Click OK.
6. Event Viewer will now display only failure audits in the right pane. Double-click the most recent failure audit to examine the contents of the event. The Event Properties dialog box appears, as shown in Figure 2.12.

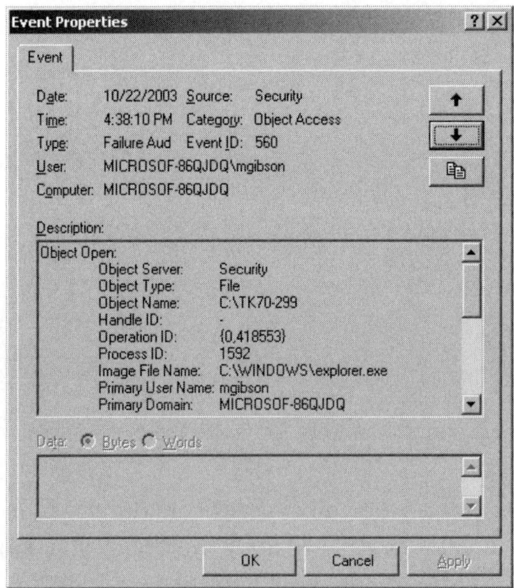

Figure 2.12 Event Viewer reveals the object that the user lacked sufficient permissions to access

7. Examine the Description field. This field shows the type of object, the object name, the process ID and image file name of the application used to access the object, and the type of operation that was performed on the object. For example, the following are the contents of the Description field for a user, mgibson, that was denied access to the C:\TK70-299 folder when she attempted to access the folder using Windows Explorer.

```
Object Open:

Object Server:    Security

Object Type:    File

Object Name:    C:\TK70-299

Handle ID:    -

Operation ID:    {0,419122}

Process ID:    1592

Image File Name:    C:\WINDOWS\explorer.exe

Primary User Name:    mgibson

Primary Domain:    MICROSOF-86QJDQ

Primary Logon ID:    (0x0,0x60641)

Client User Name:    -

Client Domain:    -

Client Logon ID:    -

Accesses:    SYNCHRONIZE

ReadData (or ListDirectory)

Privileges:    -

Restricted Sid Count:    0

Access Mask:    0x100001
```

   Notice that the Accesses line lists Synchronize and ReadData. This indicates that the user was attempting to gain read access to the C:\TK70-299 directory. To resolve this problem, you would grant the user (or a group to which the user belongs) read access to that folder.

8. Browse through other failure audit events to determine other resources to which the user might require access.

   After identifying the resources the user requires access to and assigning new permissions, repeat the troubleshooting process by re-creating the problem. If the problem is resolved, follow the procedure described in "Enabling resource auditing" and "Enabling system auditing" in this chapter to return the auditing configuration to its original state. If the problem isn't resolved, review the Security event log again to identify other permissions that are lacking, and repeat this process.

Lesson Review

The following questions are intended to reinforce key information presented in this lesson. If you are unable to answer a question, review the lesson materials and try the question again. You can find answers to the questions in the "Questions and Answers" section at the end of this chapter.

1. John is a member of both the IT and Finance groups. When John attempts to edit a file, he is denied access. Which of the following scenarios are potential causes of this problem? (Choose all that apply.)

   a. The IT group has the Deny Read & Execute file permission assigned, and the Finance Group has the Grant Modify permission assigned.

   b. The IT group has the Grant Modify permission assigned, and the Finance group has no permissions assigned.

   c. Neither the IT group, the Finance group, nor John's user account have permissions to the object explicitly assigned.

   d. The IT group has the Grant Modify permission assigned, and the Finance group has the Deny Change Permission special permissions assigned.

   ____

   ____

   ____

2. The Effective Permissions tool can be used to discover which of the following pieces of information? (Choose all that apply.)

   a. That the user John is a member of the Interactive special group

   b. That the user John is a member of the Finance security group

   c. That the Finance security group has been denied access to a folder

   d. That the user John will be denied access to a file because access is denied to a group of which John is a member

   ____

   ____

Lesson Summary

- Identify whether a particular problem is related to authorization by attempting to perform the action using an administrator account.
- If you follow the principle of least privilege carefully, you are likely to inadvertently restrict users from accessing resources they should legitimately be able to access.
- To troubleshoot authorization problems, start by identifying the objects that are required by the user. Auditing can be used to identify which objects the user is being denied access to. After auditing is enabled, Windows Server 2003 will add events to the event log describing the resource with insufficient privileges.
- If you enable auditing for the purpose of troubleshooting, return it to its original state after the problem has been resolved.
- Use the Effective Permissions tool to identify the permissions a user or group has to an object.

Case Scenario Exercise

In this exercise, you will read a scenario about a fictitious pharmaceutical company's Active Directory deployment, and then answer the questions that follow. The questions are intended to reinforce key information presented in this chapter. If you are unable to answer a question, review the lessons and try the question again. You can find answers to the questions in the "Questions and Answers" section at the end of this chapter.

Scenario

You are consulting for a pharmaceutical company named Fabrikam, Inc., that specializes in the development of drugs that fight heart disease. Fabrikam employs a staff of over 600 scientists and researchers, many of whom have worked for other companies in the pharmaceutical industry. Fabrikam's headquarters are located in Ithaca, New York. Fabrikam has remote offices in Boston, Massachusetts, and Palo Alto, California.

Fabrikam is in the planning phase of a new Active Directory deployment, and has asked you to design their group strategy. The consultant responsible for the Active Directory design informs you that Fabrikam's business groups are not limited to a single office. In other words, members of the accounts payable team in both Ithaca and Palo Alto will be granted access to the same resources. However, each location has resources, such as printers, that only users at a specific location should be allowed to access.

Questions

1. Which of the following group names is most fitting to an appropriate naming strategy?
   a. Accounts Payable
   b. Boston AP
   c. GG Accounts Payable
   d. GG Ithaca Accounts Payable
   e. GG Ithaca New York Accounts Payable

2. How will you recommend that Fabrikam enforce the group naming conventions?

3. Will you recommend the User/ACL, Account Group/ACL, or Account Group/Resource Group authorization method?

Troubleshooting Lab

In this lab, you troubleshoot a problem related to authorization. Read the following scenario and then answer the questions that follow. The questions are intended to reinforce key information presented in this chapter. If you are unable to answer a question, review the lessons and try the question again. You can find answers to the questions in the "Questions and Answers" section at the end of this chapter.

Important To complete this lab, you must have completed the exercise in Lesson 1 of this chapter.

Scenario

A user, Mary Gibson, is complaining about her inability to access the C:\TK70-299\ACLTest.txt file on Computer1. Use the troubleshooting tools described in this chapter to identify the source of the problem. Then identify the best way to resolve the problem and implement the appropriate change.

Questions

1. What is the best way to quickly determine what access Mary has to the file?

 ____

 ____

 ____

2. What permissions does Mary have to the file?

 ____

3. How can you identify the user membership that is causing Mary to be denied access to the file?

 ____

 ____

 ____

 ____

 ____

4. What access control entry is responsible for Mary's access being denied?

____

____

5. What should you do before modifying the permissions to grant Mary access?

____

____

____

____

____

____

____

____

Chapter Summary

- Files and folders, shared folders, printers, services, Active Directory objects, Terminal Services connections, Windows Management Interface objects, and registry keys and values have similar but not identical authorization methods.
- An access control list (ACL) defines who can access an object and what actions the users can take with the object. An ACL consists of multiple access control entries (ACEs). An ACE defines how a specific user or group is allowed to access an object.
- Explicit permissions are assigned directly to an object, whereas inherited permissions propagate to an object from its parent object. Using inherited permissions greatly simplifies managing permissions.
- You can use groups to efficiently manage access to domain resources, which helps simplify administration. There are two types of groups in Active Directory: distribution groups and security groups.
- Groups are characterized by a scope that identifies the extent to which the group is applied in the domain tree or forest. The group scope determines whether the group spans multiple domains or is limited to a single domain. Windows Server 2003 supports the following group scopes:
    - Local
    - Global
    - Domain Local
    - Universal

- Depending on the functional level, certain features are enabled or disabled in Active Directory. The default domain functional level is Windows 2000 mixed. When you raise the domain functional level to Windows 2000 native, Windows Server 2003 interim, or Windows Server 2003, the applicable features for that domain are enabled.
- When using the User/Access control method, you add the user account that needs access to a resource directly to the ACL of the resource. When using the Account Group/Resource Group method, you add users with similar access requirements into account groups, and then add account groups as members to a resource group that has been granted specific resource access permissions.
- By delegating security group maintenance to the appropriate individuals, you can ensure that requests for changes in membership are evaluated by individuals who can judge the appropriateness of the requests, who have the authority to make the changes, and who are motivated to keep group membership and access permissions correct and up-to-date.
- To troubleshoot authorization problems, start by identifying the objects that are required by the user. Auditing can be used to identify which objects the user is being denied access to. After auditing is enabled, Windows Server 2003 will add events to the event log describing the resource with insufficient privileges.

Exam Highlights

Before taking the exam, review the key topics and terms that are presented in this chapter. You need to know this information.

Key Topics

- Understand the difference between authorization and authentication.
- Understand the relationship between standard and special permissions.
- Know how effective permissions are calculated.
- Be able to compare the various types of groups, and to diagram how different types of groups can be nested.
- Be able to list the built-in and special groups.
- Be able to create group naming strategies to suit various types of environments.
- Be able to troubleshoot authorization problems.

Key Terms

access control entry An entry in an object's access control list that grants permissions to a user or group.

access control list A collection of access control entries that collectively defines the access that all users and groups have to the object.

authorization The process of determining whether a user, after having been validated, really should have access to do what he or she has requested.

least privilege A fundamental security principle wherein the administrator makes an effort to grant users only the minimal permissions they need to do their job.

special groups Groups created by Windows Server 2003 whose membership is dynamic and determined by the way a user interacts with the system.

Questions and Answers

Questions and Answers

Lesson 1 Review

Page 2-16

1. Sam is a member of both the IT group and the Administrators group. Sam is attempting to access a file with the following permissions:

   - Administrators: Grant Full Control
   - IT: Grant Modify

   What are Sam's effective privileges to the file?

   a. Full Control

   b. Modify

   c. Read & Execute

   d. Read

   e. Write

   f. None

   a. Sam has Full Control over the file because he is a member of the Administrators group, and nothing has overridden the ACE assigning Full Control privileges to the Administrators group.

2. Sam is a member of both the IT group and the Administrators group. Sam is attempting to access a file with the following permissions:

   - Administrators: Grant Full Control
   - IT: Deny Full Control

   What are Sam's effective privileges to the file?

   a. Full Control

   b. Modify

   c. Read & Execute

   d. Read

   e. Write

   f. None

   f. Sam will be denied access to the file because Sam is a member of the IT group. The Deny ACE assigned to the IT group overrides all ACEs that grant privileges.

3. Which of the following is a standard permission for a file or folder?

   a. Read Attributes

   b. Delete

   c. Read & Execute

   d. Take Ownership

   c. Read & Execute is a standard file and folder permission. The other options are valid special permissions.

Lesson 2 Review

Page 2-35

1. Which of the following built-in groups is present on a domain controller?

   a. Administrators

   b. Power Users

   c. DHCP Users

   d. Backup Operators

   c. DHCP Users is a domain group. All the other options exist in the local user database of standalone or member servers.

2. Which of the following special groups could you assign to an ACL to prevent access from unauthenticated users?

   a. Everyone

   b. Anonymous Logon

   c. Authenticated Users

   d. Interactive

   b. The Anonymous Logon special group contains members who have not been authenticated.

3. Which of the following are not available at the Windows 2000 native domain functional level?

   a. Universal groups

   b. Nesting groups

   c. Converting groups

   d. Renaming domain controllers

   e. SID history

   d. Renaming domain controllers is not an option when using the Windows 2000 native domain functional level.

4. Which of the following group types could be nested within a universal group?
   - **a.** Local group
   - **b.** Domain local group
   - **c.** Global group
   - **d.** Distribution group

   c. Global groups can be nested within universal groups.

The following table provides the answers.

Group Naming Exercise—Answer Key

Existing group name	Description	Recommended group name
Sales-Main	Sales global group for all sales personnel	GG Sales All
Sales-Mgr	Sales global group for sales managers	GG Sales Managers
Sales-Main Office	Sales global group for sales personnel located in the main office	GG Sales Main Office
Sales-Brn	Sales global group for personnel located in branch offices	GG Sales Branch Offices
Sales-Prnt Mngr	Domain local group of sales personnel who can manage the printer located in building 25	DL Sales Bldg25 Print Managers
Sales-Prnt User	Domain local group of sales personnel who can print to the printer located in building 25	DL Sales Bldg25 Print Users

Lesson 3 Review

Page 2-45

1. Which of the following group names was created with an effective group naming strategy?
   - **a.** HR
   - **b.** GG BOS HR
   - **c.** Cohowinery Global Group Boston Human Resources
   - **d.** Resources Human

   b. The naming strategy used to create this group name produced a short but descriptive group name.

2. Is the User/ACL or the Account Group/ACL method more effective in large enterprises?

   Account Group/ACL. This method of assigning rights scales more effectively in large enterprises.

3. Which of the following describes the principle of least privilege?

   a. Ensure that users have the minimal privileges necessary to do their jobs.

   b. Ensure that users have no permissions unless they have authenticated with both a password and a smart card.

   c. Create users with administrator privileges and then gradually reduce their privileges to the lowest level possible that allows applications to still function.

   d. Unauthenticated users must have the lowest level of privileges on the network.

   a. The principle of least privilege states that only the minimal rights required by users should be assigned.

Lesson 4 Review

Page 2-54

1. John is a member of both the IT and Finance groups. When John attempts to edit a file, he is denied access. Which of the following scenarios are potential causes of this problem? (Choose all that apply.)

   a. The IT group has the Deny Read & Execute file permission assigned, and the Finance Group has the Grant Modify permission assigned.

   b. The IT group has the Grant Modify permission assigned, and the Finance group has no permissions assigned.

   c. Neither the IT group, the Finance group, nor John's user account have permissions to the object explicitly assigned.

   d. The IT group has the Grant Modify permission assigned, and the Finance group has the Deny Change Permission special permissions assigned.

   a, c. Both of these scenarios describe situations in which John cannot edit the file, either because one of his group memberships is explicitly denied access or because he has no permissions to the file.

2. The Effective Permissions tool can be used to discover which of the following pieces of information? (Choose all that apply.)

   a. That the user John is a member of the Interactive special group

   b. That the user John is a member of the Finance security group

   c. That the Finance security group has been denied access to a folder

d. That the user John will be denied access to a file because access is denied to a group of which John is a member

c, d. The Effective Permissions tool is capable of showing what permissions a user or group has to an object. It cannot, however, enumerate group memberships.

Design Activity: Case Scenario Exercise

Page 2-55

1. Which of the following group names is most fitting to an appropriate naming strategy?

   a. Accounts Payable

   b. Boston AP

   c. GG Accounts Payable

   d. GG Ithaca Accounts Payable

   e. GG Ithaca New York Accounts Payable

   c. Given Fabrikam's requirements, an appropriate group naming strategy would include the group scope and a concise description of the group. You do not need to include the location of the group in the name. Even though some resources will only be assigned to users in specific locations, the group design does not require that business groups be divided by location. Separate groups can be created for each of the three locations, and employees in each location can be added to those groups.

2. How will you recommend that Fabrikam enforce the group naming conventions?

   Although Windows Server 2003 does not include a way to enforce group naming conventions at the time a group is created, auditing works wonders to enforce standards. Ideally, you would recommend that Fabrikam's security team audit group names on a weekly or monthly basis to ensure conformance with the naming conventions.

3. Will you recommend the User/ACL, Account Group/ACL, or Account Group/Resource Group authorization method?

   Fabrikam has 600 users, so the User/ACL authorization method would be impossible to manage. The Account Group/Resource Group authorization model is probably the most appropriate choice here, though Account Group/ACL is also a valid choice.

Design Activity: Troubleshooting Lab

Page 2-57

1. What is the best way to quickly determine what access Mary has to the file?

   You can use the Effective Permissions tool to determine Mary's user account permissions. You could also look up Mary's group memberships and manually calculate her effective permissions. However, this would be time-consuming.

2. What permissions does Mary have to the file?

   Mary has no permission to the file.

3. How can you identify the user membership that is causing Mary to be denied access to the file?

   First, view Mary's user account properties to determine the list of groups to which she belongs. Then use the Effective Permissions tool to test the permissions of each group. Using Effective Permissions is more effective than manually reviewing the list of permissions because groups can be nested, and it is not always obvious which groups a user belongs to.

4. What access control entry is responsible for Mary's access being denied?

   The Deny Accounting group access control entry is responsible, because Mary is a member of Accounting.

5. What should you do before modifying the permissions to grant Mary access?

   You should determine why the Accounting group was initially denied access to the file. There is probably a legitimate reason for denying Mary access. If not, you must decide whether the entire Accounting group should have access to the file, or just Mary. If the entire Accounting group should have access to the file, grant the Accounting group access by removing the appropriate Deny permissions for the file. If only Mary should have access, you can add an explicit permission that will override the inherited Deny permission. Additionally, you must determine what level of access the Accounting group or Mary should have to the file.

3 Deploying and Troubleshooting Security Templates

Exam Objectives in this Chapter:

- Configure security templates
  - Configure registry and file system permissions
  - Configure account policies
  - Configure .pol files
  - Configure audit policies
  - Configure user rights assignment
  - Configure security options
  - Configure system services
  - Configure restricted groups
  - Configure event logs
- Deploy security templates
  - Plan security template deployment
  - Deploy security templates by using Active Directory–based Group Policy
  - Deploy security templates by using command-line tools and scripting
- Troubleshoot security template problems
  - Troubleshoot security templates in a mixed operating system environment
  - Troubleshoot security policy inheritance
  - Troubleshoot removal of security template settings

Why This Chapter Matters

Without a strategy for configuring and maintaining security settings on all computers on your network, the security of the systems will degrade over time. Even if you are willing to manually configure the security of every system, you could not count on that security staying the same. Administrators and users troubleshooting problems, installing new applications, or applying updates might inadvertently leave important configuration settings in a different, and possibly less secure, state.

Administrators use security templates to configure security settings on computers running Microsoft Windows. By itself, a security template is a convenient way to configure the security of a single system. When combined with Group Policy or scripting, security templates make it possible to maintain the security of networks with hundreds or thousands of computers running Windows.

Lessons in this Chapter:

Before You Begin

This chapter presents the skills and concepts that are required to configure security templates, deploy them across your network, and troubleshoot problems related to Group Policy. If you fulfilled the requirements for previous chapters, then you already have the necessary hardware and software configured. You can use the computers in the state they were in after completing the previous chapter, or you can install the software from scratch. To complete the practices, examples, and lab exercises in this chapter, you must have:

- A private, non-routed network.
- One computer. On this computer, perform a Microsoft Windows Server 2003 installation with default settings, and assign the computer name Computer1.
- Add the Domain Controller role to Computer1 using the default settings, and assigned the domain name cohowinery.com. The computer should be configured to use itself as its own primary Domain Name System (DNS) server.

Real World

I used to work at a hosting provider that managed hundreds of computers running Microsoft Windows NT Server 4.0 for external customers. We took security very seriously and put a great deal of energy into hardening those servers. Unfortunately, configuring a server securely is much easier than maintaining that security—a lesson I unfortunately had to learn the hard way.

When you harden the security of a system, you're bound to break some applications that were designed to work on a system with a standard security configuration. This isn't unusual; it just means that an administrator needs to identify the security settings required by the application and set them in a manner that allows the application to function without compromising the security of the system. At one point, a customer complained that an application wouldn't work, and one of the administrators on duty began troubleshooting the problem. The administrator did manage to solve the problem—unfortunately, the administrator did so by granting Everyone Full Control permissions over a directory that was accessible from the public Internet. The customer was happy with the solution…until a month later when an attacker used those weakened permissions to take control of the system.

This scenario could more easily be avoided today, thanks to the improvements offered by Windows Server 2003. With security templates and Group Policy properly configured, the administrator on duty would have been able to identify the cause of the problem and temporarily change the permissions. However, the administrator would need to request permission from a Domain Admin to change the centralized Group Policy to allow the new permissions, which would have given the Domain Admin the opportunity to suggest something more secure that would not have presented such a significant security vulnerability.

Lesson 1: Configuring Security Templates

Early versions of Windows provided a great number of security configuration items. You could configure everything from the minimum password length to whether a logon was displayed. However, you had to use several different tools to configure these options. This made security configuration a cumbersome task and caused many administrators to overlook important security settings. Clearly, these tools needed to be simplified.

Windows NT 4.0 introduced the System Policy Editor, which provided a single user interface to manage all of the various security settings on the system. This single interface made it simple for an administrator to make critical decisions about the security of the system. Administrators managing multiple computers were especially thrilled with it, because they could easily copy configurations between systems on a network and apply various settings to different computers and users.

Windows 2000, Windows XP, and Windows Server 2003 use security templates and Group Policy to (mostly) replace System Policy. *Security templates* are files that represent a system's security configuration, and Group Policy provides an extremely flexible and robust distribution mechanism for security templates. Using these tools together, administrators can create complex security configurations and mix and match those configurations for each of the various roles computers serve in their organizations. When deployed across a network, security templates allow you to implement consistent, scalable, and reproducible security settings throughout your enterprise.

This lesson focuses on configuring security templates. In this lesson, you will explore the predefined security templates, familiarize yourself with the settings available in security templates, and learn the effects of changing key settings.

After this lesson, you will be able to

- Edit security templates.
- Use security templates to specify permissions for files, folders, services, event logs, and the registry.
- Specify account policies and security options by using security templates.
- Control group memberships by using security templates.
- Determine the best methods to configure security settings for various Microsoft operating systems.

Estimated lesson time: 45 minutes

Predefined Security Templates

Security templates are text files that describe a set of security configuration settings. You can make your own security templates from scratch. However, it is almost always easier, and more thorough, to start with one of the default security templates included with Windows Server 2003. The Windows Server 2003 family includes several predefined security templates that you can copy and modify to meet the security requirements for your organization and apply to computers in your network. By default, these predefined security templates are stored in C:\Windows\Security\Templates.

> **Warning** Do not modify the predefined security templates. These files are well known, and another administrator might attempt to use your modified file without being aware of the changes you have made. Instead, copy the predefined security templates to create a new security template that you can modify as needed.

The following list describes each of these predefined security templates:

- **Setup Security.inf and DC Security.inf.** The setup security template is the default security setting of a new install of the Windows Server 2003 family. Setup Security.inf is different for each workstation or server. For the domain controller setup, Security.inf is used with the DC Security.inf template. The DC security template defines system services settings that are appropriate for a domain controller.
- **Compatws.inf.** If you do not want your users to run as Power Users, this template makes the default permissions for the Users group less restrictive so that older applications are more likely to run correctly. This configuration is not considered a secure environment. This template will remove all members in the Power Users group on computers running Windows Server 2003 family operating systems.
- **Securews.inf and Securedc.inf.** These templates increase security for areas of the operating system that are not covered by permissions, including Account Policy, Auditing, and selected security-relevant registry keys. This template will remove all members in the Power Users group on computers running Windows XP.
- **Hisecws.inf and Hisecdc.inf.** These templates are provided for computers that operate in a network running in Windows 2000 native or the Windows Server 2003 family domain functionality native mode. In this configuration, all network communications must be digitally signed and encrypted at a level that can only be provided by Windows 2000, Windows XP, or the Windows Server 2003 family. Thus, a highly secure computer running a Windows Server 2003 family operating system can communicate only with another computer running one of those operating systems.

- **Rootsec.inf.** This template resets the default permission entries of the system root folder and propagates the permissions to all subfolders and files. The permission entries of the root folder are inherited by all files and subfolders, except those files or subfolders that have had explicit permissions set. Note that this template is new to Windows Server 2003.
- **Iesacls.inf.** This template is provided to enable auditing of registry settings that control Microsoft Internet Explorer security. Applying this template does not improve Internet Explorer security; instead, this security template should be used as a starting point for creating a template for Internet Explorer–related security.

See Also The Windows Server 2003 Security Guide includes many other useful security templates. It can be found at *http://www.microsoft.com/technet/security/prodtech/windows/win2003/w2003hg/sgch00.asp*.

Off the Record It might be tempting to simply apply the high security predefined security templates. After all, more security is better, right? Unfortunately, it's not that simple. Security is a compromise, and you almost always give something up for increased security. In general, the more tightly you secure your computers, the more help desk calls you will receive, the more applications will fail, and the more productive work time will be lost because users cannot use systems they should have access to.

Security Template Planning

The predefined security templates are designed to secure different computer roles at different security levels. Whether you create your own security templates or use the predefined templates, you should use separate security templates for each of the various roles computers serve in your organization. If different computers require different levels of security, you might be required to create multiple templates for each role to satisfy the need to provide higher and lower security for different computers.

When deciding how your security templates will be designed, think in terms of computer roles, rather than individual computers. It's simple to apply multiple security templates to a single computer, but much more complicated to separate the security settings required by each of the individual roles a computer might serve. For example, if you have a domain controller that also acts as a file server, you should create separate security templates for the domain controller role and the file server role. In the future, if you add a dedicated domain controller or file server, you can apply only the security template that is required.

In large organizations, it is likely that different divisions within the organization will have different security requirements. This is most evident in government organizations, where material classified at different levels has distinctly different security requirements. In this case, you should first determine which roles are required, and then determine the security levels required by each role. If one organization has a file server that stores only public content, and another organization has a file server that stores highly confidential files, you should create two file server security templates.

Creating and Editing Security Templates

There are three ways to create a new security template. The simplest way is to copy the predefined template that most closely matches your requirements and then change settings as needed. You can also create a new security template from scratch. If you have existing systems that you have configured to meet your security needs, you can create a new security template based on that existing configuration.

Copying a predefined template

Most of the time, when you create a new security template, you will do so by copying one of the predefined security templates. To copy a predefined security template using the Security Templates snap-in, follow these steps:

1. Create a new Microsoft Management Console (MMC) console, and add the Security Templates snap-in.
2. Expand the Security Templates node, and then expand the C:\Windows\Security\Templates node.
3. Right-click the security template you want to copy, and click Save As.
4. In the Save As dialog box, specify the file name of the new template, and then click Save.

The Security Templates snap-in will automatically refresh the display. If you saved the security template in the same folder as the predefined security templates, it will immediately appear in the snap-in.

Tip You can also create a new security template based on a predefined security template by manually copying the .inf file.

Creating a new security template

To create a new security template from scratch, follow these steps:

1. Create a new MMC console, and add the Security Templates snap-in.

2. Expand the Security Templates node.
3. If the folder you want to store your new security template in is not listed as a template search path within the Security Templates node, right-click Security Templates and then click New Template Search Path. Specify the location in which you will store the new template, and click OK.
4. Right-click the template search path that will contain your new template, and then click New Template.
5. Specify a name and description for the security template, and then click OK.

After you create a new security template, you should edit it by using the Security Templates snap-in. In the left pane of the Security Templates snap-in, you can browse the categories of security policies that can be defined. When you select a node in the left pane, the policies contained within that node will be displayed in the right pane.

If you created a new security template by copying an existing security template, all of the security settings defined in the original template will be defined for this template. If you created a blank security template, no policies will be defined. This is an important point to remember: blank security templates do not contain default settings; they simply have no policies defined. Policies that have not been defined show Not Defined in the Computer Setting column. Before a security template is useful, you must define one or more policies.

To define a policy, or to change a previously defined policy, double-click the policy in the right pane of the Security Templates snap-in. A dialog box will appear that allows you to choose whether the policy is defined and to specify the policy's definition. Select the Define This Policy Setting In The Template check box. Then specify the policy setting and click OK. Figure 3.1 shows the Security Templates snap-in being used to edit a security template with only the Minimum Password Length policy defined.

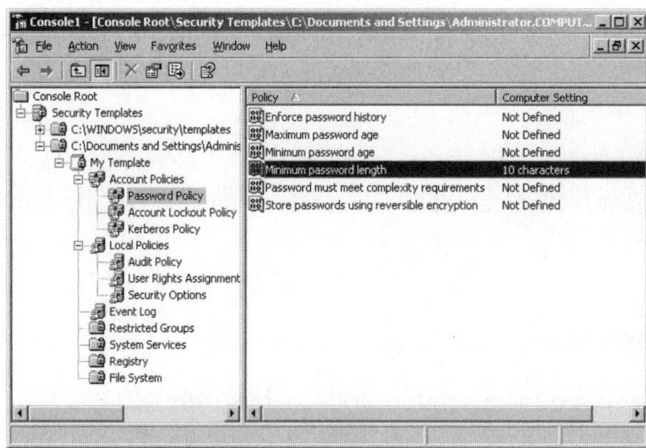

Figure 3.1 The Security Templates snap-in

Copying an existing configuration

You can use the Secedit.exe command-line tool to create a security template using the security settings currently defined on a computer. This is an excellent way to copy the settings from a system that you have already configured to meet your organization's security requirements. This is also the preferred method for migrating to using Active Directory Group Policy, rather than local security policy, to apply security settings to computers.

To create a security template based on a computer's existing security configuration, follow these steps:

1. Open a command prompt by clicking Start, pointing to All Programs, pointing to Accessories, and then clicking Command Prompt.
2. At the command prompt, type **secedit /export /cfg *filename*.inf**. For example, to export the current configuration to the C:\Windows\Security\Templates\Current Security.inf file, execute the following command:

   secedit /export /cfg "C:\Windows\Security\Templates\Current Security.inf"

Security Template Settings

In Chapter 2, you learned how to use security policies to control authorization. The structure of security policies is identical to that of security templates, so you are already familiar with many of the settings available within a security template. For example, you can use a security template to configure the permissions associated with files, folders, registry entries, and services. Security templates can have more security options than the Local Computer Policy, however, because security templates include options for both standalone computers and computers that are participating in a domain.

Understanding the types of security settings that can and cannot be configured using security templates is critical for both passing the exam and using security templates successfully. The following sections describe the various types of settings that can be defined in a security template.

Tip There are far too many security options in a security template to describe them all in detail. The best way to familiarize yourself with the options available is to browse through them, open each policy, and view the choices available.

Account policies

Account policies affect how user accounts can interact with the computer or domain. Account policies can only be defined once within a domain. The Account Policies node contains three nodes:

- **Password Policy.** Determines settings for passwords, such as whether a password history is maintained, the minimum and maximum password ages, and password complexity and length requirements.

Security Alert Set the minimum password age only if you have also defined a maximum password age and password history requirement. The minimum password age prevents users from changing their password back to the original password after being required to change it because it reached the maximum password age.

- **Account Lockout Policy.** Determines the circumstances and length of time that an account will be locked out of the system.

Security Alert Enabling account lockout doesn't necessarily increase security. In fact, it actually creates a new vulnerability. An attacker who knows valid user names can guess incorrect passwords for users and lock legitimate users out, creating a denial-of-service attack.

- **Kerberos Policy.** Determines Kerberos-related settings, such as ticket lifetimes and enforcement. Kerberos policies do not exist in Local Computer Policy.

For domain accounts, there can be only one account policy. The account policy must be defined in the Default Domain Policy, and it is enforced by the domain controllers that make up the domain. A domain controller always obtains the account policy from the Default Domain Policy Group Policy object (GPO), even if there is a different account policy applied to the organizational unit (OU) that contains the domain controller. By default, workstations and servers that are joined to a domain (such as member computers) will also receive the same account policy for their local accounts. However, local account policies can be different from the domain account policy, such as when you define an account policy specifically for the local accounts.

Local policies

The Local Policies node in a security template contains policies that control auditing, user rights, and miscellaneous security options for a computer. The Local Policies node contains three nodes:

- **Audit Policy.** The auditing policies that you choose for the event categories define your auditing policy. On member servers and workstations that are joined to a domain, auditing settings for the event categories are undefined by default. On domain controllers, auditing is turned off by default. By defining auditing settings for specific event categories, you can create an auditing policy that suits the security needs of your organization.

See Also For information on using auditing to troubleshoot authorization problems, see Chapter 2.

- **User Rights Assignment.** These policies define dozens of options that specify which users can perform various actions on a computer. You can use the policies contained in this node to control who can and cannot log on to a computer, back up files on a computer, and restart a system (among other actions). Generally, it is better to add users who need additional rights to built-in groups, such as Power Users.
- **Security Options.** The Security Options node contains policies that didn't fit well into the other policy groups. These options include whether a computer will shut itself down when the Security event log is full, whether unsigned drivers can be installed, and whether Ctrl+Alt+Del is required to log on.

Event logs

The Event Log node in a security template contains policies that define how the computer's event logs behave. These policies define the maximum size for the three main log files: the Application event log, the Security event log, and the System event log. You can also use these policies to control which users are authorized to access each of the three primary event logs. Of particular importance for environments that require retaining a history of actions performed on a computer, you can define policies that control how log files are retained. Specifically, you can require that log files are retained for a minimum number of days, and specify whether events are overridden as needed or deleted after a specific number of days.

It is common practice to define the Retain Security Log policy so that Windows Server 2003 keeps security events for 30 days. This enables you to review the Security event log after an attack has been detected to potentially uncover clues as to how an attacker accessed your system.

Group memberships

Unlike the Account Policies, Local Policies, and Event Logs nodes, the Restricted Groups node does not contain a list of policies. Instead, you can use this node to specify security groups by name and limit the memberships of those groups. For each group you specify, you can specify two properties: Members and Members Of. The Members list defines who belongs and who does not belong to the restricted group. The Members Of list specifies which other groups the restricted group belongs to.

When a Restricted Groups Policy is enforced, any current member of a restricted group that is not on the Members list is removed. Any user on the Members list who is not currently a member of the restricted group is added.

See Also For more information on using Restricted Groups, refer to Chapter 2.

Services

This node of a security template is used to define the startup type and authorization for system services on a computer. For example, if you want users to be able to start the Messenger service as needed, you can define a policy setting to set the Messenger service startup type to manual, and then configure the Messenger service authorization so that only Domain Users have permissions to start, stop, and pause the service.

Registry permissions

This node of a security template is used to define the authorization for registry keys and values. While the default registry authorization settings for Windows Server 2003 are sufficient for most environments, applications often store information that should be kept private in the registry. Applications that create their own registry keys and values might not adequately restrict the permissions associated with that information. Fortunately, you can use security templates to further restrict those permissions.

To add a registry key to a security template, right-click the Registry node and then click Add Key. Use the Select Registry Key dialog box to specify the registry key. If it does not exist on the local computer, but you will use the security template to apply permissions to other computers, you can manually type the name of the registry key in the Selected Key field.

File and folder permissions

The File System node of a security template allows you to use the security template to specify file and folder permissions. To add a file or folder to a security template, right-click the File System node and then click Add File. Use the Add A File Or Folder dialog box to specify the file system object. If it does not exist on the local computer, but you will use the security template to apply permissions to other computers, you can manually type the name of the file or folder. After specifying the file or folder, you can use the familiar graphical interface, introduced in Chapter 2, to configure standard and special permissions.

Security Configuration for Earlier Versions of Windows

Most administrators will use Group Policy to deploy security templates through a network. Windows Server 2003, Windows 2000 Server, Windows 2000 Professional, and Windows XP Professional all fully support Group Policy, making it simple to apply a security template. However, many enterprise networks will include other Windows operating systems, including Windows Millennium Edition, Windows 98, and Windows NT 4.0. You must consider the potential security vulnerabilities of earlier versions of Windows when deploying security configurations to systems on your network. After all, earlier versions of Windows are more likely to have security vulnerabilities than newer versions.

Windows NT 4.0, Windows 95, Windows 98, and Windows Millennium Edition clients use System Policy rather than Group Policy. System Policy is a policy based on registry settings specified by using the System Policy Editor, Poledit.exe. System Policy Editor can be obtained from a Windows NT 4.0 CD.

Off the Record You can use both System Policy and Group Policy together, but it makes life much more difficult for you. You'll experience more problems deploying security settings, and you'll spend more time troubleshooting them. When possible, upgrade Windows NT 4.0 domains to Windows 2000 or Windows Server 2003 domains, and upgrade older computers to an operating system that supports Group Policy.

Although System Policy Editor (Poledit.exe) is mostly replaced by Group Policy, it is still useful to create .pol files that can define security-related registry settings on a computer. .pol files contain a list of registry values and can be automatically deployed to a computer upon startup or when a user logs on. The .pol file you create varies depending on the operating system you are targeting:

- **Windows 95 or Windows 98.** System Policy Editor must be run locally on computers that run Windows 98 or Windows 95 to create Config.pol files that are compatible with the local operating system.
- **Windows NT 4.0 Workstation and Windows NT 4.0 Server.** Run System Policy Editor on a Windows NT 4.0 computer, as shown in Figure 3.2, to create a file named Ntconfig.pol.

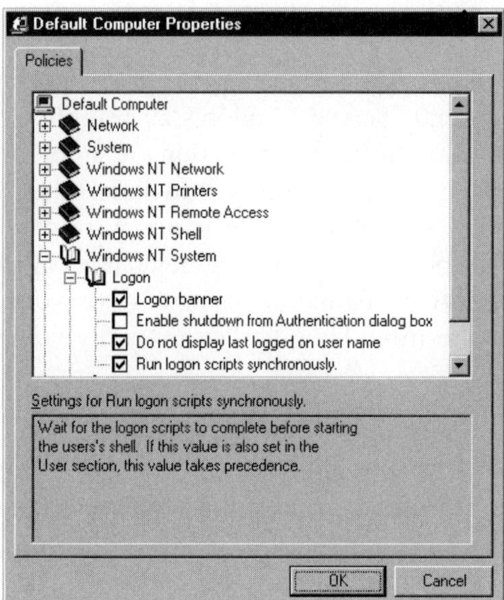

Figure 3.2 System Policy Editor on Windows NT 4.0

After creating a system policy, copy the resultant .pol file to the Netlogon share (%systemroot%\sysvol*DomainName*\scripts) of any domain controller. Client computers running Windows XP and Windows 2000 ignore System Policy settings that are put in the Netlogon share of a Windows Server 2003 domain controller. Instead, they will apply Group Policy settings. These clients will apply System Policy if they're joined to a Windows NT 4.0 domain controller, however.

> **Planning** Neither System Policy nor Group Policy apply to Windows XP Home Edition, Windows NT 3.51, Windows 3.1, and MS-DOS operating systems. In your planning, be sure to create a strategy for migrating these clients to newer platforms.

Practice: Create and Examine a New Security Template

In this practice, you will create a security template. You will apply this template in Lesson 2.

Exercise 1: Create a Security Template

In this exercise, you will create a new blank security template.

1. Log on to the cohowinery.com domain on Computer1 using the Administrator account.
2. Create a new MMC console, and add the Security Templates snap-in.
3. Expand the Security Templates node.

4. Right-click Security Templates, and then click New Template Search Path.
5. In the Browse For Folder dialog box, click My Documents, and then click Make New Folder. Type the name **Templates**, and then click OK.

> **Security Alert** It is important to store security templates used for a production environment in a secure location that only administrators responsible for implementing security can access—not because others should be unable to view the security templates, but rather to prevent unauthorized changes to security templates.

6. Right-click the newly created template search path that will contain your new template, and click New Template.
7. In the Template Name field, type **Domain Password Requirements**. In the Description field, type **Security template that defines the password requirements for domain member computers. Created by *your name* on *today's date* for learning purposes only**. Click OK.

> **Real World**
>
> Descriptions are important. A descriptive name isn't enough, because other administrators might have to analyze, edit, and apply your security template. If another administrator applies the wrong template because the name was confusing, your network's security could be reduced. For example, if you name a Web server security template "Web template," another administrator might confuse your template with the template that should be applied to desktop computers to secure Internet Explorer. Not only would your template fail to secure Internet Explorer, it might even reduce the security of the desktop computers by granting network access to files—a necessary setting for a Web server, but a dangerous setting for a desktop computer. Always provide a detailed description that includes your name, the date, and precisely what the template should be used for.

8. Expand the Domain Password Requirements node, expand Account Policies, and then click Password Policy.
9. In the right pane, double-click Minimum Password Length. Select Define This Policy Setting In The Template, and then specify 10 characters. Click OK.
10. Double-click Passwords Must Meet Complexity Requirements. Select Define This Policy Setting In The Template, and then click Enabled. Click OK.
11. Double-click Store Passwords Using Reversible Encryption. Select Define This Policy Setting In The Template, and then click Disabled. Click OK.
12. In the right pane, right-click Domain Password Requirements, and then click Save.

Exercise 2: Examine the Security Template

In this exercise, you will examine your newly created security template using a text editor.

1. Start Windows Explorer, and navigate to the My Documents\Templates\ folder.
2. Double-click the Domain Password Requirements.inf file.
3. Examine the security template. In particular, notice the [System Access] section of the file.
4. Close Notepad.

   You will use this security template in the following lesson's practice.

Lesson Review

The following questions are intended to reinforce key information presented in this lesson. If you are unable to answer a question, review the lesson materials and try the question again. You can find answers to the questions in the "Questions and Answers" section at the end of this chapter.

1. Which predefined security template can be used to improve the ability of Users to run applications without being logged on as an administrator?
   - **a.** Setup Security.inf
   - **b.** Compatws.inf
   - **c.** Securews.inf
   - **d.** Hisecws.inf

   ____

   ____

2. Which predefined security template can be used to return a system to its original security settings?
   - **a.** Setup Security.inf
   - **b.** Compatws.inf
   - **c.** Securews.inf
   - **d.** Hisecws.inf

   ____

   ____

3. Which of the following tools can be used to copy a security template? (Choose all that apply.)
   a. Active Directory Users And Computers
   b. Group Policy Object Editor
   c. Security Templates snap-in
   d. Security Configuration And Analysis
   e. Secedit
   f. Windows Explorer

____

____

Lesson Summary

- Most new security templates should be based on predefined security templates.
- Create security templates for computer roles, not for individual computers.
- The Security Templates snap-in is a graphical tool for creating and editing security templates.
- Secedit is a command-line tool that can create security templates based on an existing computer's settings.
- Security templates can be used to configure account policies, group memberships, event log settings, local policies, and permissions for folders, files, services, and the registry.

Lesson 2: Deploying Security Templates

Deploying your security templates can be a more complex, time-consuming process than creating the templates. Depending on the network environment, you can choose from several different methods of deploying security templates, including:

- Manually importing the templates into Local Group Policy on individual computers.
- Importing the templates automatically by using scripting.
- Importing the templates into Group Policy objects linked to Active Directory directory service.

Additionally, you have a great deal of flexibility in configuring which templates are applied to which computers. Understanding the various ways to link and filter Group Policy objects is important knowledge, both for administering a Windows Server 2003 network and to pass this exam.

After this lesson, you will be able to

- Add security templates to Group Policy.
- Describe how inheritance affects Group Policy.
- Deploy Group Policy to systems across your network.
- Carefully control which systems Group Policy is applied to.
- Deploy security templates in environments that do not use Active Directory.
- Deploy System Policy to Windows NT 4.0 and earlier operating systems.

Estimated lesson time: 60 minutes

Deploying Security Templates Using Active Directory

Most environments with security requirements complex enough to require the use of security templates will also deploy Active Directory to simplify the management of the computers. Active Directory makes it easy to deploy a security template to the computers in your domain by using Group Policy.

Using Group Policy

Windows XP, Windows 2000, and Windows Server 2003 use Group Policy to configure a variety of security and non-security settings. All systems have a Local Group Policy which, in the absence of a higher priority Group Policy setting, is used to define configuration settings. In a domain, Group Policy simplifies management of large numbers of computers by allowing administrators to define software configurations, install new software, deploy updates, and many other tasks for both servers and user computers.

An administrator can use Group Policy to set policies that apply across a site, a range of organizational units (OUs), or an entire domain. These network Group Policy settings take priority over the Local Group Policy when present.

Exam Tip Remember this for the exam: support for Group Policy is available on computers running Windows 2000 Server, Windows 2000 Professional, Windows XP Professional, and Windows Server 2003. Earlier operating systems do not support Group Policy.

A GPO is a collection of Group Policy settings. GPOs are essentially the documents created by the Group Policy Object Editor. GPOs are stored at the domain level, and they affect users and computers that are contained in sites, domains, and organizational units.

While a complete discussion of Group Policy is outside the scope of the exam and this book, it is important to understand how Group Policy can be used to deploy security templates to computers in a domain. In a nutshell, one or more security templates can be imported into a Group Policy object. When the Group Policy object is deployed to client systems, those systems will automatically apply the settings contained within the imported security templates.

Important If you make an update to a security template, be sure to re-import it into the Group Policy object.

Importing templates into Group Policy objects

To import a security template into a GPO:

1. Open Active Directory Users And Computers.
2. In the console tree, right-click the domain, site, or OU you want to set Group Policy for.
3. Click Properties, and then click the Group Policy tab.
4. If you are editing an existing GPO, click the GPO you want to import the security template into. If you need to create a new GPO, click New and then type a name for the GPO.
5. Click Edit to open the GPO.

   The Group Policy Object Editor appears.
6. Expand Computer Configuration, and then expand Windows Settings.
7. Right-click Security Settings, and then click Import Policy.

8. Browse for the security template you want to import. If you want to remove security settings that already exist in the GPO, select the Clear This Database Before Importing check box. Click Open.
9. Close the Group Policy Object Editor.

At this point, the GPO has the settings you defined in your security template. However, systems might not have the latest version of the GPO. You can use the Gpupdate.exe tool to immediately apply the template to an individual system, or you can wait until the updated GPO is automatically applied. By default, the security settings are refreshed every 90 minutes on a workstation or server and every 5 minutes on a domain controller. You will see this event if any changes have occurred during these intervals. In addition, the settings are also refreshed every 16 hours, regardless of whether new changes have taken place.

If multiple Group Policy objects are linked to a single domain, site, or OU, verify that the order the policies are applied is correct. If there are conflicting settings in different policies, the higher policy in the list has higher precedence and will overwrite conflicting settings from other policies. As shown in Figure 3.3, you can use the Up and Down buttons on the Group Policy tab of the domain, site, or OU properties to set the precedence.

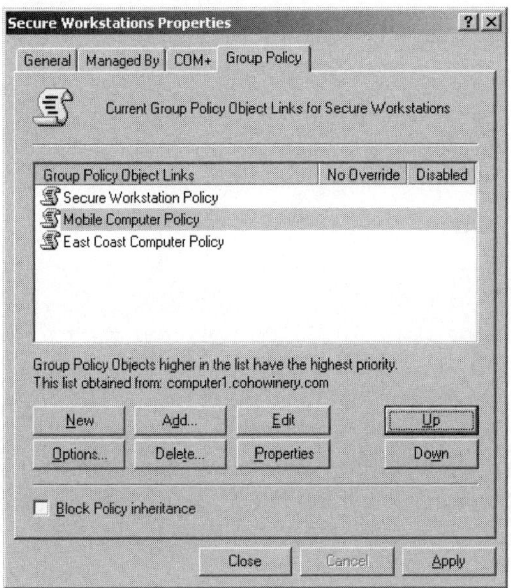

Figure 3.3 Modifying Group Policy precedence

Standard Group Policy inheritance

In general, Group Policy is passed down from parent to child containers within a domain. Group Policy is not inherited from parent to child domains. For example,

Group Policy is not inherited from cohowinery.com to accounting.cohowinery.com. However, if you assign a specific Group Policy setting to a high-level parent container, that Group Policy setting applies to all containers beneath the parent container, including the user and computer objects in each container. If a policy setting is defined for a parent organizational unit and the same policy setting is not defined for a child organizational unit, the child inherits the parent's enabled or disabled policy setting. If you explicitly specify a Group Policy setting for a child container, the child container's Group Policy setting overrides the parent container's setting. When multiple GPOs apply, and they do not have a parent/child relationship, the policies are processed in this order: local, site, domain, organizational unit.

If a policy setting that is applied to a parent organizational unit and a policy setting that is applied to a child organizational unit are compatible, the child organizational unit inherits the parent policy setting, and the child's setting is also applied. If a policy setting that is configured for a parent organizational unit is incompatible with the same policy setting that is configured for a child organizational unit (because the setting is enabled in one case and disabled in the other), the child does not inherit the policy setting from the parent. The policy setting in the child is applied.

You can block policy inheritance at the domain or OU level by opening the properties dialog box for the domain or organizational unit and selecting the **Block Policy Inheritance** check box. You can enforce policy inheritance by setting the No Override option on a GPO link. When you select the No Override check box, you force all child policy containers to inherit the parent's policy, even if that policy conflicts with the child's policy and even if Block Inheritance has been set for the child. You can set No Override on a GPO link by opening the properties dialog box for the site, domain, or organizational unit and making sure that the No Override check box is selected.

Exam Tip Policies that are set to No Override cannot be blocked—know this for the exam!

Group Policy inheritance with security groups

You cannot link Group Policy objects directly to a security group. You can, however, use security group membership to allow or disallow members of the group from applying a Group Policy object. In this way, you can control which users receive a Group Policy object by placing them into specific groups.

By default, all Authenticated Users are authorized to apply a Group Policy object. Therefore, to allow only specific groups to apply a GPO, you must first remove the default permissions for Authenticated Users, and then grant permissions for the specific groups to apply the GPO. The most common ways to edit the properties and permissions for a GPO are:

- Using Active Directory Users And Computers
  a. Click Start, click Administrative Tools, and then click Active Directory Users And Computers.
  b. Right-click the domain or OU, and then click Properties.
  c. Click the Group Policy tab.
  d. Click the GPO you want to edit, and then click Properties.
  e. Click the Security tab.
- Using Active Directory Sites And Services
  a. Click Start, click Administrative Tools, and then click Active Directory Sites And Services.
  b. Expand Sites, right-click the site to which the GPO is linked, and then click Properties.
  c. Click the Group Policy tab.
  d. Click the GPO you want to edit, and then click Properties.
  e. Click the Security tab.
- Using the Group Policy Object Editor
  a. Use the Group Policy Object Editor to open the GPO whose scope you want to control by using security groups.
  b. In the console tree, right-click the GPO node, and then click Properties.
  c. Click the Security tab.

Note Additionally, you can edit GPOs by using the Group Policy Management Console (GPMC). For more information about GPMC, visit *http://www.microsoft.com/windowsserver2003 /gpmc/*.

After you have opened the properties dialog box for a GPO, enable only a specified group to apply a Group Policy object by following these steps:

1. Click the Authenticated Users group. In the Permissions box, select the Deny Apply Group Policy check box.
2. Click the Add button to add the security group to the Group Or User Names list.
3. Click the new security group. In the Permissions box for the selected security group, select the Grant Apply Group Policy check box, as shown in Figure 3.4, to explicitly allow the selected security group to apply the Group Policy object.

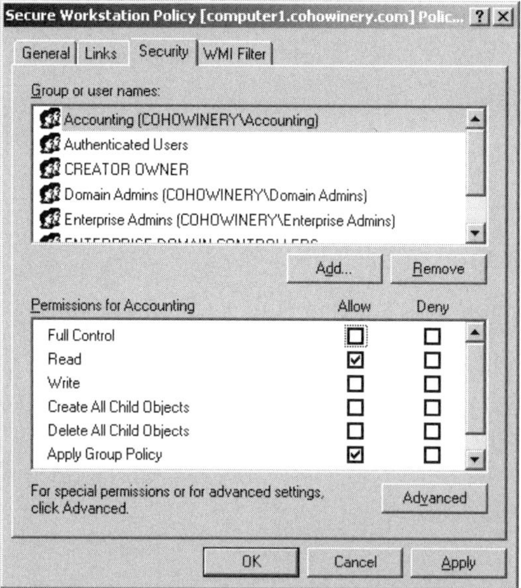

Figure 3.4 Denying a security group access to a Group Policy object

Modifying Group Policy inheritance using WMI filtering

When you need to restrict the application of GPOs based on a property of the user or computer, rather than security group memberships, you can use Windows Management Instrumentation (WMI) filters. Each GPO can be linked to one WMI filter; however, the same WMI filter can be linked to multiple GPOs. Before you can link a WMI filter to a GPO, you must create the filter. The WMI filter is evaluated on the destination computer (running either Windows XP or Windows Server 2003) during processing of Group Policy.

A WMI filter consists of one or more WMI Query Language (WQL) queries. The WMI filter applies to every setting in the GPO, so administrators must create separate GPOs if they have different filtering requirements for different settings. The WMI filters are evaluated on the destination computer after the list of potential GPOs is determined and filtered based on security group membership. Windows XP and Windows Server 2003 will only apply the GPO if the WMI filter evaluates to TRUE. Windows 2000 does not support WMI filtering, so computers running Windows 2000 ignore the WMI filter and will always apply the GPO.

Because WMI filters are ignored on computers running Windows 2000, a filtered GPO will always be applied on them. However, you can work around this by using two GPOs and giving the one with Windows 2000 settings higher precedence. Then use a WMI filter for that Windows 2000 GPO, and only apply it if the operating system is Windows 2000, not Windows XP Professional. The computer running Windows 2000 will receive the Windows 2000 GPO and will override the settings in the Windows XP

Professional GPO. The client running Windows XP Professional will receive all the settings in the Windows XP Professional GPO.

To define and apply a new WMI filter, follow these steps:

1. View the GPO properties.
2. Click the WMI Filter tab.
3. Click This Filter, and then click Browse/Manage.
4. In the Manage WMI Filters window, click Advanced, and then click New.
5. Complete the Name, Description, and Queries fields, and then click Save.

   Figure 3.5 shows the Manage WMI Filters window with a filter designed to apply the GPO only to computers running Windows XP Professional.

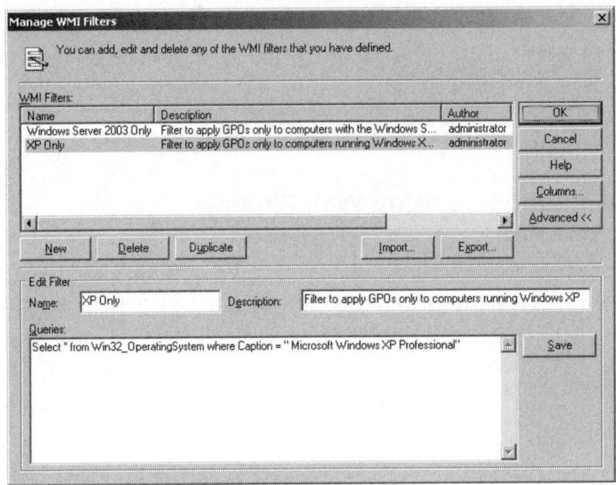

Figure 3.5 Managing WMI filters

6. Click the filter you want to apply to the GPO, and then click OK to close the GPO Properties page.

This book does not cover creating WMI filter queries. For the purposes of the exam, it is important to understand that computers running Windows 2000 and earlier do not support WMI filtering and will always apply a GPO with WMI filtering. You should also know that you can use WMI filters to apply a GPO to computers based on operating system, hardware, and other factors. When troubleshooting a problem related to a GPO not being applied to a computer running Windows XP Professional or Windows Server 2003, check to verify that WMI filtering is not the cause of the problem.

Deploying Security Templates Without Active Directory

Using Active Directory makes managing a large network of computers running Windows much easier. However, not all networks use Active Directory. Fortunately, you can still deploy security templates by using tools that do not rely on Active Directory, including the Group Policy Object Editor, the Security Configuration And Analysis snap-in, and Secedit.

Using Group Policy Object Editor

You can use the Group Policy Object Editor snap-in to immediately apply configuration settings to the Local Group Policy object on a computer. To do this, follow these steps:

1. Open a blank MMC console by clicking Start and then clicking Run. Type **mmc**, and then click OK.
2. On the File menu, click Add/Remove Snap-In.
3. Click Add, click Group Policy Object Editor, and then click Add.

   The Group Policy Wizard appears. The Local Computer GPO should be selected by default.
4. Click Finish.
5. Expand Local Computer Policy, Computer Configuration, and then Windows Settings.
6. Right-click Security Settings, and then click Import Policy.
7. Browse to select the security template you want to import, and then click Open.

Using Security Configuration And Analysis

You can also use the Security Configuration And Analysis snap-in to immediately apply configuration settings to a computer. To do this, follow these steps:

1. Open a blank MMC console, and add the Security Configuration And Analysis snap-in.
2. In the console tree, right-click Security Configuration And Analysis, and then click Open Database.
3. In the File Name box, type a file name and then click Open.
4. Browse for the security template you want to import. If you want to remove security settings that already exist in the GPO, select the Clear This Database Before Importing check box. Click Open.

5. If you want to apply multiple security templates to the computer, right-click Security Configuration And Analysis, and then click Import Template. Browse for the security template you want to import, and then click Open. Repeat this step for each security template you want to import.
6. In the console tree, right-click Security Configuration And Analysis, and then click Configure Computer Now.
7. Use the default error log path by clicking OK.

   The Configuring Computer Security window appears while the security template is being applied. The security settings take effect immediately.

See Also The Security Configuration And Analysis snap-in is described in more detail in Chapter 4, "Hardening Computers for Specific Roles."

Using Secedit

Secedit.exe is a command-line tool that provides similar functionality to the graphical Security Configuration And Analysis snap-in. By calling the Secedit.exe tool at a command prompt from a batch file or an automatic task scheduler, you can use it to automatically create and apply templates and analyze system security. You can also run it dynamically from a command prompt. Secedit.exe is useful when you have multiple computers on which security must be analyzed or configured, and you need to perform these tasks during off hours.

To apply a security template by using Secedit, follow these steps:

1. Open a command prompt by clicking Start, pointing to All Programs, pointing to Accessories, and then clicking Command Prompt.
2. At the command prompt, type **secedit /import /cfg *filename*.inf**. For example, to import the hisecdc.inf predefined security template, execute the following command:

   secedit /configure /db hisecws.sdb /cfg %windir%\security\templates \hisecdc.inf /overwrite /log hisecws.log
3. When prompted, type **y**.

Secedit has a unique ability not found in other tools—it can import only portions of a security template by using the /areas parameter. After the /areas parameter, list one or more of the following options to import that portion of the security template:

- **SECURITYPOLICY.** Imports account policies, audit policies, event log settings, and security options.
- **GROUP_MGMT.** Imports restricted group settings.

- **USER_RIGHTS.** Imports user rights assignment.
- **REGKEYS.** Imports registry permissions.
- **FILESTORE.** Imports file system permissions.
- **SERVICES.** Imports system service settings.

For example, the following command imports only the services and file system portions of the hisecdc.inf predefined security template:

```
secedit /configure /db hisecws.sdb /cfg %windir%\security\templates\hisecdc.inf
/overwrite /log hisecws.log /areas SERVICES FILESTORE
```

For a complete description of Secedit, execute the command **Secedit /?** at a command prompt.

Practice: Applying and Deploying Security Templates

In this practice, you will manually apply a security template and then view the effects. You will then import a security template into Group Policy.

Exercise 1: Review Current Password Policies

In this exercise, you will determine Computer1's active password policy settings. Later, you will apply a security template to modify these settings.

1. Log on to the cohowinery.com domain on Computer1 using the Administrator account.
2. Create a new MMC console, and add the Resultant Set Of Policy snap-in.
3. In the left pane, right-click Resultant Set Of Policy, and then click Generate RSoP Data.

   The Resultant Set Of Policy Wizard appears.
4. On the Welcome page, click Next.
5. On the Mode Selection page, click Logging Mode, and then click Next.
6. On the Computer Selection page, click This Computer, and then click Next.
7. On the User Selection page, click Do Not Display User Policy Settings In The Results, and then click Next.
8. On the Summary Of Selections page, click Next.

   The Resultant Set Of Policy Wizard analyzes Computer1's current configuration. This is the best way to determine what security settings are currently applied to a computer, because any one computer can receive security settings from multiple sources.

9. On the Completing The Resultant Set Of Policy Wizard page, click Finish.
10. In the left pane of the MMC console, expand COMPUTER1 – RSoP, then expand Computer Configuration, Windows Settings, Security Settings, and Account Policies.
11. Click Password Policy.

    The right pane will display Computer1's active password policies. Note the minimum password length, which should still be set to the default setting.

Exercise 2: Apply the Security Template

In this exercise, you will apply the security template you created in Lesson 1 to Computer1 by using the Domain Controller Security Policy console, and then verify that the settings were applied.

1. Open the Domain Controller Security Policy console.
2. Right-click Security Settings, and then click Import Policy.
3. In the Import Policy From dialog box, navigate to My Documents\Templates. Click Domain Password Requirements.inf, and then click Open.
4. In the left pane, expand Account Policies, and then click Password Policy. Note that the Minimum Password Length, Password Must Meet Complexity Requirements, and Store Passwords Using Reversible Encryption policies are all defined.
5. Close the Domain Controller Security Policy console.
6. Click Start, and then click Run. In the Open field, type **gpupdate /force**, and then click OK.

    The Gpupdate tool causes Windows Server 2003 to immediately refresh Group Policy settings.
7. After Gpupdate has finished, return to the console you created in Exercise 1 of this lesson. Right-click COMPUTER1 – RSoP, and then click Refresh Query.
8. In the left pane of the MMC console, expand COMPUTER1 – RSoP, and then expand Computer Configuration, Windows Settings, Security Settings, and Account Policies.
9. Click Password Policy.

    The right pane will display Computer1's active password policies. Note the minimum password length, which should be set to 10 characters—the policy defined in the custom Domain Password Requirements security template.

Exercise 3: Apply a Predefined Template Using Group Policy

In this exercise, you will apply one of the predefined security templates to an OU by using Group Policy.

1. Open the Active Directory Users And Computers console.
2. Right-click cohowinery.com, click New, and then click Organizational Unit.

   The New Object dialog box appears.
3. In the Name field, type **Secure Workstations**. Click OK.
4. Right-click Secure Workstations, and then click Properties.
5. Click the Group Policy tab, and then click the New button.
6. Name the Group Policy **Secure Workstation Policy**.
7. Click the new policy, and then click Edit.

   The Group Policy Object Editor appears.
8. Expand Computer Configuration, and then expand Windows Settings. Right-click Security Settings, and then click Import Policy.
9. In the Import Policy From dialog box, navigate to C:\Windows\Security\Templates, and click Hisecws.inf. Click Open.
10. Close the Group Policy Object Editor.
11. In the Secure Workstation Properties dialog box, click Close to return to the Active Directory Users And Computers console.

    Now any computers you add to the Secure Workstations OU will have the Hisecws.inf predefined security template applied.

Lesson Review

The following questions are intended to reinforce key information presented in this lesson. If you are unable to answer a question, review the lesson materials and try the question again. You can find answers to the questions in the "Questions and Answers" section at the end of this chapter.

1. Which is the correct tool to use to most efficiently deploy a security template to a single domain member?
   - **a.** Group Policy Object Editor snap-in
   - **b.** Security Configuration And Analysis snap-in
   - **c.** Security Templates snap-in
   - **d.** Local Security Policy console snap-in
   - **e.** Secedit command-line tool

   ____

   ____

   ____

2. Which is the correct tool to use to most efficiently deploy a security template to hundreds of computers in a domain?
   a. Group Policy Object Editor snap-in
   b. Security Configuration And Analysis snap-in
   c. Security Templates snap-in
   d. Local Security Policy console snap-in
   e. Secedit command-line tool

   ____

   ____

3. Which is the correct tool to use to most efficiently deploy a security template to dozens of standalone computers?
   a. Group Policy Object Editor snap-in
   b. Security Configuration And Analysis snap-in
   c. Security Templates snap-in
   d. Local Security Policy console snap-in
   e. Secedit command-line tool

   ____

   ____

   ____

Lesson Summary

- The easiest way to deploy security templates to multiple systems is to use Group Policy.
- Group Policy can be applied to a domain, a site, or an OU.
- You can further restrict which computers and users a Group Policy object applies to by restricting permissions to the Group Policy object, or by using WMI filtering.
- You can use Secedit to apply a security template from the command line. By using this tool, you can automatically deploy security policies to systems that are not members of a domain.
- You can manually apply a security template to a computer by using the Group Policy Object Editor or the Security Configuration And Analysis snap-in.

Lesson 3: Troubleshooting Security Templates

Applying security templates to a single computer is straightforward. However, when you apply security templates by using Group Policy, it gets much more complex, and complexity can lead to problems. To successfully deploy security templates by using Group Policy, you must understand how to isolate and resolve these problems. There are two primary types of problems you might experience when deploying security templates: Group Policy that fails to be applied to a system, and unexpected security settings.

After this lesson, you will be able to

- Manually refresh Group Policy.
- Isolate the cause of a GPO that is not successfully applied.
- Identify the source of an unexpected security policy.
- List the various tools that can be used to isolate the source of problems that can occur when applying GPOs.
- Identify which tool is best for various Group Policy troubleshooting tasks.

Estimated lesson time: 45 minutes

Troubleshooting Problems with Applying Group Policy

When Group Policy fails to be applied to a system, the problem is usually related to network connectivity, incorrect system time, a policy being blocked, or insufficient user permissions. Figure 3.6 shows a flowchart that can be followed to troubleshoot problems relating to a Group Policy object that is not successfully applied to a system.

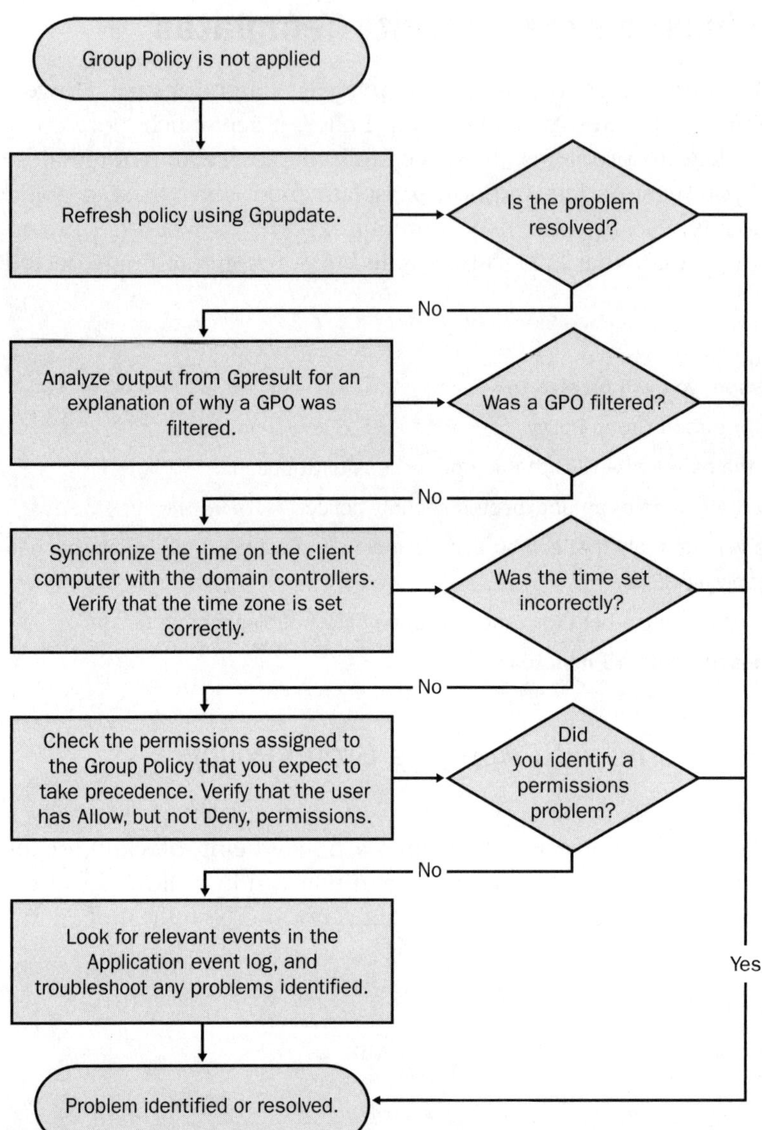

Figure 3.6 Troubleshooting problems relating to failed Group Policy

The sections that follow describe individual tasks for identifying the source of Group Policy problems.

Refreshing Group Policy

Problems with applying Group Policy can often be quickly resolved by refreshing policies. With Gpupdate, a command-line tool, you can force a computer to immediately re-apply all Group Policy. Gpupdate replaces and improves upon the Windows 2000 command secedit /refreshpolicy. To use Gpupdate to force all policies to be updated, follow these steps:

1. Open a command prompt.
2. Execute the command **Gpupdate /force**.

Tip This doesn't relate to security settings, but some policy items, such as computer-assigned software, require a reboot to take effect. User-assigned software requires the user to log on and log off.

Gpresult

Gpresult is a command-line tool that displays detailed information about user and computer policies. Though many administrators shy away from command-line tools, Gpresult is the best way to quickly determine what Group Policy objects were applied, in which order they were applied, and what security group memberships might have influenced which Group Policy objects the computer or user has permissions to access. Unlike other tools, Gpresult displays policies that were filtered, and why they were filtered. This is a common cause of problems relating to GPOs not being applied.

Note Gpresult used to be a free download from Microsoft. It's now included with Windows Server 2003.

When run with the /Z parameter, Gpresult provides several useful pieces of information that Help And Support Center does not provide. The information Gpresult provides includes the following:

- Operating system
- Computer information, including computer name and location in Active Directory
- Domain and site information
- User information, including user name, location in Active Directory, and profile details
- Group memberships for both the computer and the current user
- Time the Group Policy object was updated
- Group Policy objects that were filtered out

- The last time policy was applied and the domain controller that applied policy, for the user and computer
- The complete list of applied GPOs and their details, including a summary of the extensions that each GPO contains
- Registry settings that were applied and their details
- Folders that are redirected and their details
- Software management information detailing assigned and published applications
- The resultant set of policies
- User security privileges

The following is an excerpt from a sample output from the Gpresult tool:

```
COMPUTER SETTINGS
------------------
    CN=COMPUTER1,OU=Domain Controllers,DC=cohowinery,DC=com
    Last time Group Policy was applied: 10/29/2003 at 5:35:50 PM
    Group Policy was applied from:      computer1.cohowinery.com
    Group Policy slow link threshold:   500 kbps
    Domain Name:                        COHOWINERY
    Domain Type:                        Windows 2000

    Applied Group Policy Objects
    -----------------------------
        Default Domain Controllers Policy
        Default Domain Policy

    The following GPOs were not applied because they were filtered out
    -------------------------------------------------------------------
        Local Group Policy
            Filtering:  Not Applied (Empty)

    The computer is a part of the following security groups
    -------------------------------------------------------
        BUILTIN\Administrators
        Everyone
        BUILTIN\Pre-Windows 2000 Compatible Access
        BUILTIN\Users
        Windows Authorization Access Group
        NT AUTHORITY\NETWORK
        NT AUTHORITY\Authenticated Users
        This Organization
        COMPUTER1$
        Dial-up Accessible Computers
        Domain Controllers
        NT AUTHORITY\ENTERPRISE DOMAIN CONTROLLERS
```

To view the output of Gpresult, execute the following commands at a command prompt:

```
Gpresult /Z > Gpresult.txt
Notepad Gpresult.txt
```

The /Z parameter for Gpresult causes it to output so much information that much of it would be lost if you attempted to view the output in a command prompt.

Help And Support Center Advanced System Information

The Advanced System Information tool in Help And Support Center displays information about the result Group Policy has had on the current computer and logged-on user. It provides information that is similar to that provided by Gpresult, but it provides a friendlier, graphical interface. Generally, Gpresult is more useful because it provides more information, but you should be familiar with Help And Support Center's functionality.

The Advanced System Information tool provides the following information:

- Operating system
- Domain
- Site
- Time the Group Policy object was updated
- Group memberships for both the computer and the current user
- Startup, shutdown, logon, and logoff scripts
- Security settings applied from the Group Policy object, including restricted groups and file system and registry permissions

You can access the Advanced System Information report from Help And Support Center by following these steps:

1. Click Start, and then click Help And Support.
2. Click Support.
3. Under See Also, click Advanced System Information.
4. Under Advanced System Information, click View Group Policy Settings Applied.

   Help And Support Center displays Group Policy results, as shown in Figure 3.7.

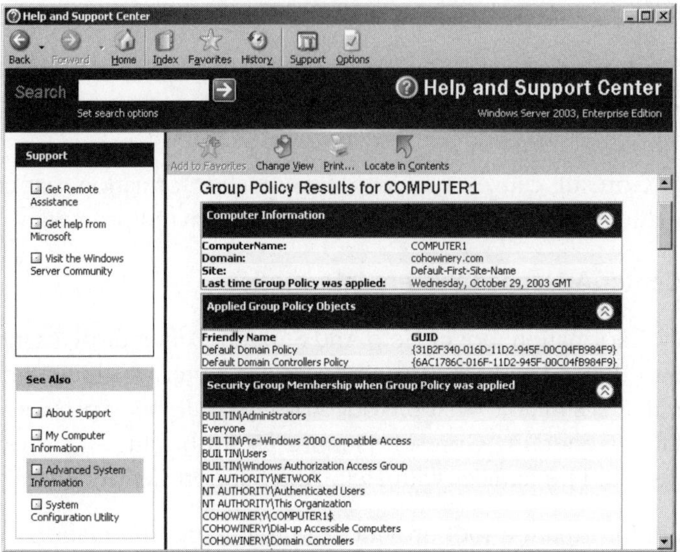

Figure 3.7 Help And Support Center Group Policy information

Analyzing permissions

As discussed earlier, a computer or user must have permission to apply a Group Policy object. By default, Group Policy objects allow the Authenticated Users special group to read and apply a Group Policy object. However, this default permission can be overridden or changed, which can lead to a complex troubleshooting situation.

When analyzing Group Policy permissions, start by identifying which security groups the computer or user is a member of. The quickest way to list these groups is to use the Gpresult command-line tool. After you have determined the group memberships, check for the presence of these in the list of permissions for the Group Policy object that you expected to be applied.

Caution If you link a Group Policy object to an OU and then create a security group in that OU, members of the security group will not inherit the Group Policy object. Group Policy is only inherited through domains, organizational units, and sites.

Analyzing WMI filtering

Another potential cause of a Group Policy object not being applied to a system is WMI filtering. You can quickly diagnose such a problem by examining the complete output of Gpresult. Specifically, look for lines in the output that include the word *filtering*. The following excerpt from a sample Gpresult output shows that the GPO named East Coast Computer Policy was not applied because of a WMI filter named XP Only:

```
COMPUTER SETTINGS
------------------
    CN=COMPUTER1,OU=Domain Controllers,DC=cohowinery,DC=com
    Last time Group Policy was applied: 10/30/2003 at 2:34:08 PM
    Group Policy was applied from:      computer1.cohowinery.com
    Group Policy slow link threshold:   500 kbps
    Domain Name:                        COHOWINERY
    Domain Type:                        Windows 2000

    Applied Group Policy Objects
    -----------------------------
        Default Domain Controllers Policy
        Default Domain Policy

    The following GPOs were not applied because they were filtered out
    -------------------------------------------------------------------
        East Coast Computer Policy
            Filtering:  Denied (WMI Filter)
            WMI Filter: XP Only
```

If you determine that Group Policy is being incorrectly filtered because of a WMI filter, edit the WMI filter by following these steps:

1. Open a blank MMC console and add the Group Policy Object Editor snap-in.
2. When the Group Policy Wizard appears, specify the GPO that you identified as being filtered because of WMI filtering.
3. After you open the Group Policy Object Editor snap-in, right-click the Group Policy node, and then click Properties.
4. Click the WMI Filter tab.
5. Click Browse/Manage. In the Manage WMI Filters window, click Advanced.
6. Click the WMI filter named in the Gpresult output.
7. Edit the Queries field as necessary to correct your problem, and then click Save.
8. Click OK twice to return to the Group Policy Object Editor snap-in.

Caution A single WMI filter can be associated with multiple GPOs. Be careful when editing them—you can affect the filtering of Group Policy objects you didn't intend to modify!

Analyzing events in Event Viewer

When a Group Policy object is applied or when a problem occurs, Windows Server 2003 adds an event to the Application event log, as shown in Figure 3.8. All events will have the source ID SceCli, which enables you to use event filtering to display only those events relating to the application of Group Policy. When troubleshooting Group

Policy problems, check the Application event log for related warning events. The informational events signify that Group Policy was applied, but they are not useful for troubleshooting because they do not provide much information about the policies.

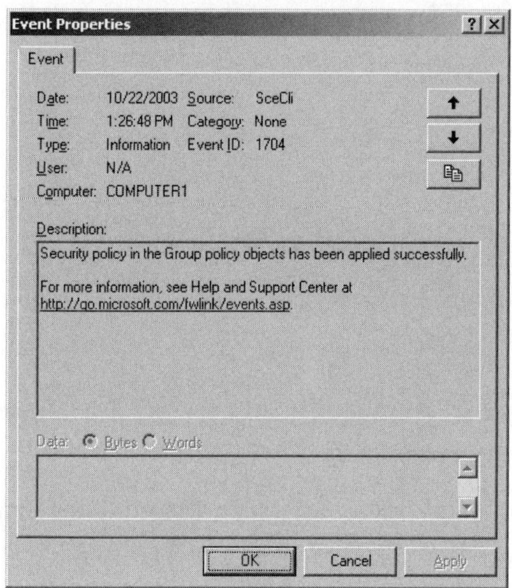

Figure 3.8 A Group Policy event

Exam Tip For the exam, be aware that you can check Event Viewer to see if Group Policy was applied. In the real world, it's easier to use tools such as Help And Support Center or Gpresult.

Troubleshooting Unexpected Security Settings

Unexpected security settings can result when multiple templates are applied to a system using multiple GPOs. In these cases, the GPOs might not be prioritized as you expect, another administrator might have caused inheritance to be blocked or overridden, or changes, such as removing a GPO, might not have reached a system yet. Figure 3.9 shows a flowchart that can be followed to troubleshoot problems relating to unexpected Group Policy inheritance.

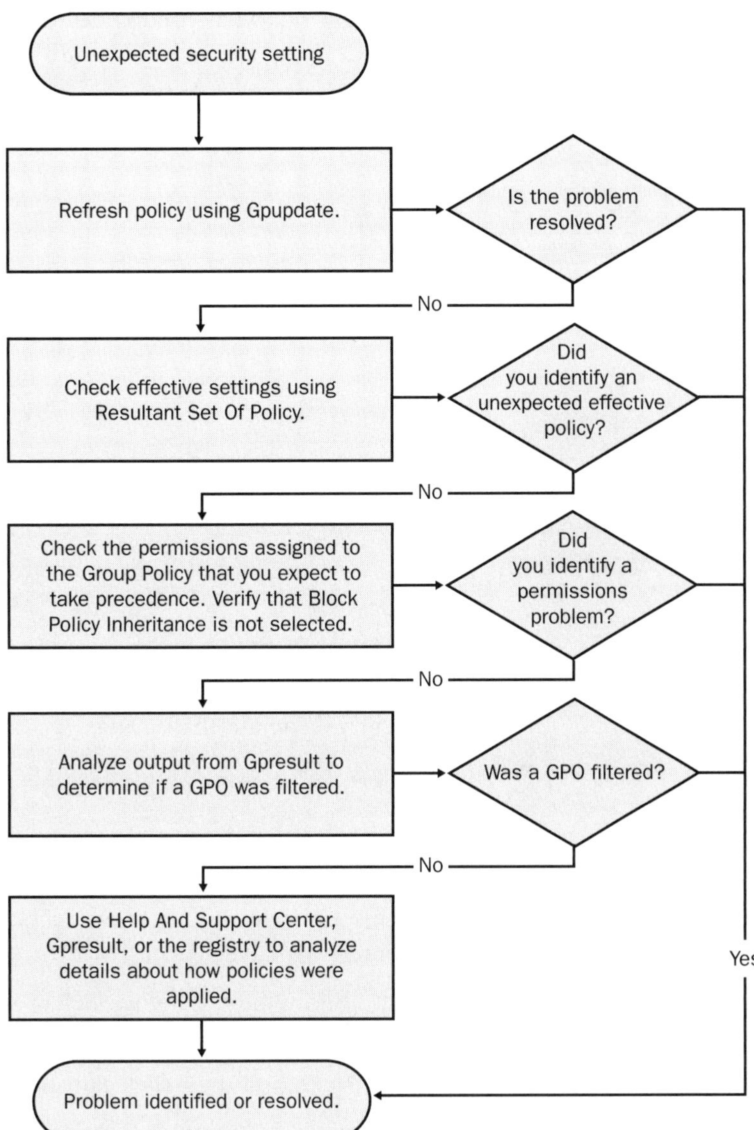

Figure 3.9 Troubleshooting problems related to unexpected inheritance

Resultant Set Of Policy snap-in

The Resultant Set Of Policy (RSoP) snap-in provides a familiar user interface that shows you the effective setting for each of the security template policies. It is an excellent way to verify that the settings you've configured in your security templates are applied to target systems as you expected. If a policy setting is not what you expected, RSoP identifies the Group Policy object responsible for defining the policy. Figure 3.10 shows RSoP displaying password policies.

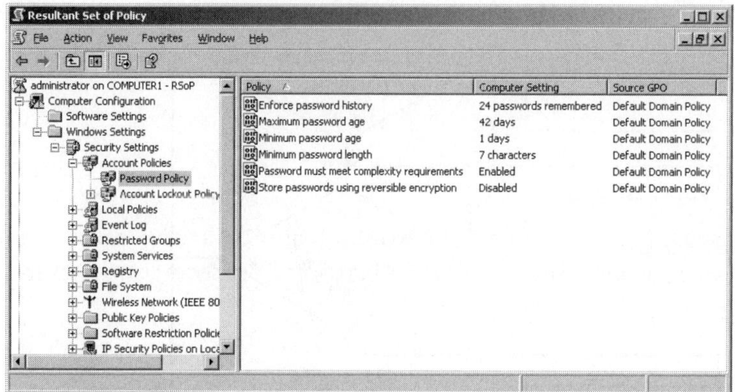

Figure 3.10 Resultant Set Of Policy

To run RSoP, follow these steps:

1. Open a blank MMC console, and add the Resultant Set Of Policy snap-in.
2. Right-click Resultant Set Of Policy, and click Generate RSoP Data.

   The Resultant Set Of Policy Wizard appears.
3. Click Next.
4. On the Mode Selection page, click Logging Mode, and then click Next.
5. To analyze the local computer, click This Computer. Otherwise, click Another Computer, and specify the remote computer to analyze. Click Next.
6. To analyze the current user, click Current User. Otherwise, click Select A Specific User, and specify the user to analyze. Click Next.
7. On the Summary Of Selections page, click Next, and then click Finish.
8. To view computer security configuration, expand Computer Configuration, Windows Settings, and then Security Settings.

Analyzing Group Policy using the registry

When Group Policy objects are applied to a computer, the computer stores important information about the Group Policy objects it is applying in the last place you'd look: the registry. Information about computer policies is stored under the HKEY_LOCAL_MACHINE\Software\Microsoft\Windows\CurrentVersion\Group Policy\History key. Information about user policies (relating to the currently logged on user) is stored under the HKEY_CURRENT_USER\Software\Microsoft\Windows\CurrentVersion\Group Policy\History key.

To view this information, follow these steps:

1. Click Start, and then click Run. Type **Regedit**, and then click OK.
2. In the Registry Editor, navigate to one of the following two keys:
    - If you are troubleshooting problems relating to a computer policy, navigate to HKEY_LOCAL_MACHINE\Software\Microsoft\Windows\CurrentVersion\Group Policy\History.
    - If you are troubleshooting problems relating to a user policy, navigate to HKEY_CURRENT_USER\Software\Microsoft\Windows\CurrentVersion\Group Policy\History.
3. Expand the History key to reveal one or more subkeys relating to Group Policy Extensions.
4. Expand each of the Group Policy Extension keys. You will find one or more subkeys, numbered starting at 0.

    The numbers indicate the order in which the policies were applied to the system. Lower numbers were applied first.
5. As shown in Figure 3.11, click each of the keys and examine the values contained within.

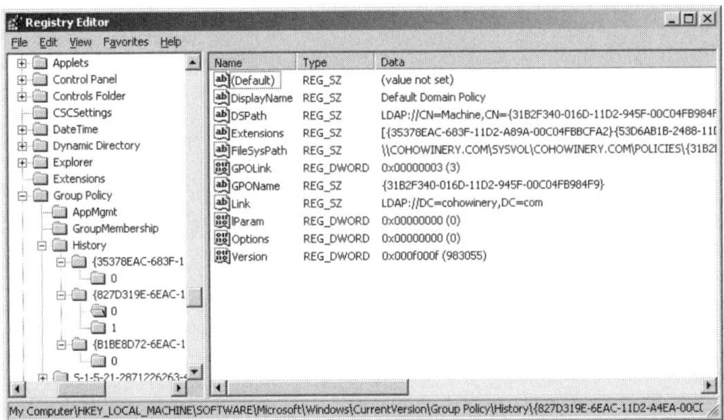

Figure 3.11 Group Policy information stored in the registry

An explanation of each of the registry values that can be used follows:

- **DisplayName.** DisplayName is the friendly name of the GPO.
- **DSPath.** DSPath is the distinguished name of the path to the GPO stored in Active Directory. This attribute will not be present for Local GPOs.

- **FileSysPath.** FileSysPath is the path to the Group Policy template, or file-based policy, contained in a Group Policy object. If this is a GPO from the domain, the path will be a Universal Naming Convention (UNC) path to the SYSVOL share on the domain controllers. If this is a Local GPO, the path will be a local path that points to the structure beginning with the path %SystemRoot%\system32\GroupPolicy.
- **GPOLink.** The GPOLink value identifies what scope the GPO was applied to, therefore affecting the computer or user. The following values are valid:
  - 0= No link information
  - 1= The GPO is linked to a machine (local)
  - 2= The GPO is linked to a site
  - 3= The GPO is linked to a domain
  - 4= The GPO is linked to an organizational unit
- **GPOName.** The GPOName value contains the name of the GPO as it is referenced. For GPOs associated with computers, this name will be the friendly name of the GPO. For GPOs stored in Active Directory, this will be the globally unique identifier (GUID) of the GPO.
- **lParam.** The lParam value is used to perform various functions on GPOs.
- **Options.** The Options value represents the options selected by the administrator when configuring the GPO link, such as whether to disable the GPO or to force the settings defined in the GPO on subcontainers.
- **Version.** The Version registry value specifies the version number of the GPO when it was applied last. The number is used to determine if the GPO has changed since it was last applied.

In the context of troubleshooting, you can use this information to trace GPOs back to their source in Active Directory. You can also determine the order in which Group Policy objects were applied. If the order is not the order you expected, use the Active Directory Users And Computers console to modify the order in which Group Policy objects are applied.

Troubleshooting checklist

Use the following checklist to identify the source of unexpected Group Policy inheritance:

- Verify that the intended policy is not being blocked.
- Verify that no overriding policy that is set at a higher level of Active Directory has been set to No Override. If Block and No Override are both used, No Override takes precedence.

- Verify that the user or computer is not a member of any security group for which the Apply Group Policy permission is set to Deny.
- Verify that the user or computer is a member of at least one security group for which the Apply Group Policy permission is set to Allow.
- Verify that the user or computer is a member of at least one security group for which the Read permission is set to Allow.

Troubleshooting System Policy

You can experience the same problems applying system policies to earlier Windows operating systems as you can experience applying Group Policy objects to Windows 2000, Windows XP, and Windows Server 2003 computers. However, you must use completely different tools and procedures to troubleshoot the problems.

If you experience a problem with a system policy that is not applied to a system successfully, first verify that the policy file is correctly named. For Windows NT 4.0 clients, the policy file must be named Ntconfig.pol. For computers running Windows 95 and Windows 98, you must name the policy file Config.pol.

Next, verify that the .pol file is located in the correct folder. It should be located in the Netlogon share on a domain controller. Technically, it must be located in the Netlogon share of the domain controller to which it authenticates; however, after you place the .pol file on one domain controller, it should automatically replicate to other domain controllers. If you copy the .pol file to the correct folder on a domain controller and it fails to replicate, troubleshoot the problem as an issue with file synchronization between domain controllers.

System policies can experience problems similar to the inheritance problems Group Policy can experience. System Policy can be associated with security groups, and if a user is a member of multiple groups, then multiple security policies will be applied. The system policy itself determines the order in which the policies associated with the various groups are applied. If the wrong security setting is being applied, reorder the group priority:

1. Start System Policy Editor.
2. On the File menu, click Open Policy.
3. Open the policy that you want. For computers running Windows Millennium Edition and Windows 98, open Config.pol. For computers running Windows NT 4.0, open Ntconfig.pol.
4. On the Options menu, click Group Priority.
5. Click a group in the Group Order list, as shown in Figure 3.12, and then click either Move Up or Move Down.

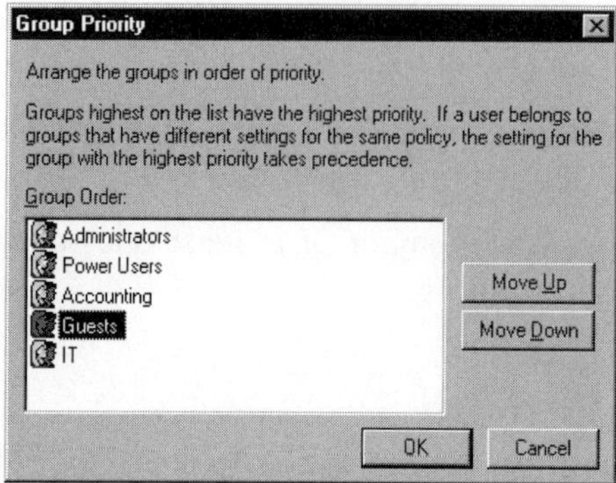

Figure 3.12 Group order for system policies

6. After you configure the groups in order of priority, click OK.
7. On the File menu, click Save.
8. Quit System Policy Editor.

Lesson Review

The following questions are intended to reinforce key information presented in this lesson. If you are unable to answer a question, review the lesson materials and try the question again. You can find answers to the questions in the "Questions and Answers" section at the end of this chapter.

1. Which of the following tools can be used to identify which GPOs were applied to a computer? (Choose all that apply.)
   - **a.** Resultant Set Of Policy
   - **b.** Help And Support Center
   - **c.** Gpresult
   - **d.** Gpupdate
   - **e.** Active Directory Users And Computers
   - **f.** Group Policy Object Editor
   - **g.** Registry Editor

   ____

   ____

2. Which of the following tools can be used to identify the current Minimum Password Length setting and the responsible GPO? (Choose all that apply.)
   - **a.** Resultant Set Of Policy
   - **b.** Help And Support Center

c. Gpresult

d. Gpupdate

e. Active Directory Users And Computers

f. Group Policy Object Editor

g. Registry Editor

____

____

3. Which of the following tools can be used to force a computer to refresh all Group Policy objects?

a. Resultant Set Of Policy

b. Help And Support Center

c. Gpresult

d. Gpupdate

e. Active Directory Users And Computers

f. Group Policy Object Editor

g. Registry Editor

____

____

Lesson Summary

- Use Gpupdate to refresh policy before you begin troubleshooting and after each change you make to Group Policy.
- The Advanced System Information tool in Help And Support Center is a graphical tool that provides a thorough description of GPOs applied to a user and computer.
- Gpresult displays the most complete set of information about GPOs applied to a user and computer.
- Windows Server 2003 records information about applied GPOs in the registry.

Case Scenario Exercise

Your manager has asked you to manage the security configurations of the 10 servers and 150 portable and desktop computers in your Active Directory domain environment. In the past, computers have been compromised because end users modified the security configurations of their computers. Your manager wants the solution you create to ensure that end users cannot reduce the security of their computers.

Most servers perform multiple tasks. In total, your 10 servers perform the following roles:

- Six file servers
- Three domain controllers
- Three mail servers
- Two external Web servers
- Two internal Web servers
- Two proxy servers
- Four database servers

Though you have been pushing management to fund upgrades for all portable and desktop systems, you still have many older operating systems in use. Of the 150 portable and desktop computers, you have:

- 120 computers running Windows XP Professional
- 10 computers running Windows NT Workstation 4.0
- 5 computers running Windows XP Home Edition
- 7 computers running Windows 2000 Professional
- 4 computers running Windows Millennium Edition
- 4 computers running Windows 95

The following questions are intended to reinforce key information presented in this lesson. If you are unable to answer a question, review the lesson materials and try the question again. You can find answers to the questions in the "Questions and Answers" section at the end of this chapter.

1. How many different security templates will you create, and what will each one be used for?

____

____

____

____

____

____

____

2. Which of the following is the right choice for deploying security templates in your environment?
   - a. Importing the security templates into Local Group Policy.
   - b. Importing the security templates by using Secedit.
   - c. Importing the security templates by using the Security Configuration And Analysis tool.
   - d. Importing the security templates by using GPOs linked to Active Directory.

3. Which of the portable and desktop computers will not be able to use Group Policy?
   - a. The computers running Windows XP Professional
   - b. The computers running Windows NT Workstation 4.0
   - c. The computers running Windows XP Home Edition
   - d. The computers running Windows 2000 Professional
   - e. The computers running Windows Millennium Edition
   - f. The computers running Windows 95

4. How will you apply security settings to those systems that do not support Group Policy?

Troubleshooting Lab

In this lab, you troubleshoot a problem related to deploying security configurations that were imported into a GPO.

During a recent audit of configuration settings, you discovered that one of your client systems does not have the security configuration you imported into the Portable Computers Policy GPO. After logging on to the computer, you open a command prompt and execute Gpresult. You notice the following output:

```
The following GPOs were not applied because they were filtered out
--------------------------------------------------------------------
    Portable Computers Policy
        Filtering:  Denied (Security)

    Local Group Policy
        Filtering:  Not Applied (Empty)

The computer is a part of the following security groups
--------------------------------------------------------
    BUILTIN\Administrators
    Everyone
    BUILTIN\Pre-Windows 2000 Compatible Access
    BUILTIN\Users
    Windows Authorization Access Group
    NT AUTHORITY\NETWORK
    NT AUTHORITY\Authenticated Users
    This Organization
    PORTACOMPUTER$
    Dial-up Accessible Computers
```

The following questions are intended to reinforce key information presented in this lesson. If you are unable to answer a question, review the lesson materials and try the question again. You can find answers to the questions in the "Questions and Answers" section at the end of this chapter.

1. Why was the Portable Computers Policy not applied?

   ____

   ____

2. How will you resolve the problem?

   ____

   ____

   ____

   ____

3. Why was the Local Group Policy not applied?

4. Which other tools could you have used to identify the source of the problem?

Chapter Summary

- Most new security templates should be based on predefined security templates.
- Create security templates for computer roles, not for individual computers.
- The Security Templates snap-in is a graphical tool for creating and editing security templates.
- Secedit is a command-line tool that can create security templates based on an existing computer's settings.
- Security templates can be used to configure account policies, group memberships, event log settings, local policies, and permissions for folders, files, services, and the registry.
- The easiest way to deploy security templates to multiple systems is to use Group Policy.
- Group Policy can be applied to a domain, a site, or an OU.
- You can further restrict which computers and users a Group Policy object applies to by restricting permissions to the Group Policy object, or by using WMI filtering.
- You can use Secedit to apply a security template from the command line. By using Secedit, you can automatically deploy security policies to computers that are not members of a domain.
- You can manually apply a security template to a computer by using the Security Configuration And Analysis snap-in.
- Use Gpupdate to refresh policy before you begin troubleshooting and after each change you make to Group Policy.
- The Advanced System Information tool in Help And Support Center is a graphical tool that provides a thorough description of GPOs applied to a user and computer.

- Gpresult displays the most complete set of information about GPOs applied to a user and computer.
- Windows Server 2003 records information about applied GPOs in the registry.

Exam Highlights

Before taking the exam, review the key topics and terms that are presented in this chapter. You need to know this information.

Key Topics

- Understand the importance of security templates and Group Policy for establishing and maintaining the security of the computers on your network.
- Be familiar with each of the tools used for configuring, deploying, and troubleshooting security templates.
- Be able to describe the purpose of every security setting available within a security template.
- Know the operating systems that can and cannot use Group Policy. Understand how to configure the security of systems that do not support Group Policy.
- Be able to determine which Group Policy objects were applied to a computer from both a graphical interface and the command line.

Key Terms

Group Policy A mechanism for storing many types of policy data, for example, file deployment, application deployment, logon/logoff scripts and startup/shutdown scripts, domain security, and Internet Protocol security. The collections of policies are referred to as Group Policy objects (GPOs).

Group Policy object The Group Policy settings that administrators create are contained in GPOs, which are in turn associated with selected Active Directory containers: sites, domains, and OUs.

security template A physical file representation of a security configuration that can be applied to a local computer or imported to a GPO in Active Directory. When you import a security template to a GPO, Group Policy processes the template and makes the corresponding changes to the members of that GPO, which can be users or computers.

System Policy Used by system administrators to control user and computer configurations for operating systems prior to Windows 2000 from a single location on a network. System policies propagate registry settings to a large number of computers without requiring the administrator to have detailed knowledge of the registry.

Questions and Answers

Lesson 1 Review

Page 3-16

1. Which predefined security template can be used to improve the ability of Users to run applications without being logged on as an administrator?
   - **a.** Setup Security.inf
   - **b.** Compatws.inf
   - **c.** Securews.inf
   - **d.** Hisecws.inf

   b. The Compatws.inf security template makes the default permissions for the Users group less restrictive so that older applications are more likely to run correctly.

2. Which predefined security template can be used to return a system to its original security settings?
   - **a.** Setup Security.inf
   - **b.** Compatws.inf
   - **c.** Securews.inf
   - **d.** Hisecws.inf

   a. The Setup Security.inf security template contains the security settings that Windows Server 2003 uses by default.

3. Which of the following tools can be used to copy a security template? (Choose all that apply.)
   - **a.** Active Directory Users And Computers
   - **b.** Group Policy Object Editor
   - **c.** Security Templates snap-in
   - **d.** Security Configuration And Analysis
   - **e.** Secedit
   - **f.** Windows Explorer

   c, f. The Security Templates snap-in and Windows Explorer can both be used to copy security templates.

Lesson 2 Review

Page 3-29

1. Which is the correct tool to use to most efficiently deploy a security template to a single domain member?

   a. Group Policy Object Editor snap-in

   b. Security Configuration And Analysis snap-in

   c. Security Templates snap-in

   d. Local Security Policy console snap-in

   e. Secedit command-line tool

   d. The Local Security Policy console snap-in is the most efficient way to apply a security template to a single system because it is graphical and allows the administrator to apply security settings with a few clicks.

2. Which is the correct tool to use to most efficiently deploy a security template to hundreds of computers in a domain?

   a. Group Policy Object Editor snap-in

   b. Security Configuration And Analysis snap-in

   c. Security Templates snap-in

   d. Local Security Policy console snap-in

   e. Secedit command-line tool

   a. Group Policy objects, configured by using the Group Policy Object Editor snap-in, are the most efficient way to apply a security template to multiple systems in a domain.

3. Which is the correct tool to use to most efficiently deploy a security template to dozens of standalone computers?

   a. Group Policy Object Editor snap-in

   b. Security Configuration And Analysis snap-in

   c. Security Templates snap-in

   d. Local Security Policy console snap-in

   e. Secedit command-line tool

   e. The Secedit command-line tool is the most efficient way to deploy a security template to multiple computers that are not in a domain, because the security policy can be applied to a system by using scripts.

Lesson 3 Review

Page 3-44

1. Which of the following tools can be used to identify which GPOs were applied to a computer? (Choose all that apply.)
   - **a.** Resultant Set Of Policy
   - **b.** Help And Support Center
   - **c.** Gpresult
   - **d.** Gpupdate
   - **e.** Active Directory Users And Computers
   - **f.** Group Policy Object Editor
   - **g.** Registry Editor

   a, b, c, g. RSoP, Help And Support Center, Gpresult, and the Registry Editor can all be used to determine which GPOs were applied to a computer.

2. Which of the following tools can be used to identify the current Minimum Password Length setting and the responsible GPO? (Choose all that apply.)
   - **a.** Resultant Set Of Policy
   - **b.** Help And Support Center
   - **c.** Gpresult
   - **d.** Gpupdate
   - **e.** Active Directory Users And Computers
   - **f.** Group Policy Object Editor
   - **g.** Registry Editor

   a, c. RSoP and Gpresult will show current policy settings and the GPO that defined them.

3. Which of the following tools can be used to force a computer to refresh all Group Policy objects?
   - **a.** Resultant Set Of Policy
   - **b.** Help And Support Center
   - **c.** Gpresult
   - **d.** Gpupdate
   - **e.** Active Directory Users And Computers
   - **f.** Group Policy Object Editor
   - **g.** Registry Editor

   d. Gpupdate is used to force the computer to immediately download and apply GPOs.

Design Activity: Case Scenario Exercise

Page 3-46

1. How many different security templates will you create, and what will each one be used for?

   Your answer will vary, but you should at a minimum create nine security templates for the following roles:

   - File server
   - Domain controller
   - Mail server
   - External Web server
   - Internal Web server
   - Proxy server
   - Database server
   - Portable computer
   - Desktop computer

2. Which of the following is the right choice for deploying security templates in your environment?

   a. Importing the security templates into Local Group Policy.

   b. Importing the security templates by using Secedit.

   c. Importing the security templates by using the Security Configuration And Analysis tool.

   d. Importing the security templates by using GPOs linked to Active Directory.

   d. The only efficient way to manage the security of such a large number of computers is to use GPOs linked to Active Directory. Applying security templates to individual computers would be time consuming and difficult to maintain.

3. Which of the portable and desktop computers will not be able to use Group Policy?

   a. The computers running Windows XP Professional

   b. The computers running Windows NT Workstation 4.0

   c. The computers running Windows XP Home Edition

   d. The computers running Windows 2000 Professional

   e. The computers running Windows Millennium Edition

   f. The computers running Windows 95

b, c, e, f. Of the desktop platforms you have deployed, only the computers running Windows XP Professional and Windows 2000 Professional will be able to use Group Policy. Fortunately, these make up the majority of your computers.

4. How will you apply security settings to those systems that do not support Group Policy?

Ideally, you can convince management to upgrade these computers to Windows XP Professional, which supports Group Policy. That is the only way to ensure that end users do not change the security settings on their computers. If this is not possible, you can use System Policy or manually configure the security settings on each computer. However, that solution does not meet management's original requirements.

Design Activity: Troubleshooting Exercise

Page 3-48

1. Why was the Portable Computers Policy not applied?

Gpresult identified the problem as Security, which indicates that the client computer did not have sufficient permissions to apply the Group Policy.

2. How will you resolve the problem?

View the properties for the GPO, and examine the security settings. Either the computer account, or one of the security groups the computer is a member of, was denied access to the Group Policy object. You must identify the group membership that is denied access and allow that group access to the Group Policy object. It is also possible that the computer was not denied access, but was also not granted access. If this is the case, modify the permissions for the Group Policy object to allow the Apply Group Policy permission to one of the groups the computer is a member of.

3. Why was the Local Group Policy not applied?

The Local Group Policy was not applied because it is empty. Since there are no settings to apply, this is the expected behavior and is not indicative of a problem.

4. Which other tools could you have used to identify the source of the problem?

There are no other tools that would reveal filtered GPOs.

4 Hardening Computers for Specific Roles

Exam Objectives in this Chapter:

- Plan security templates based on computer role. Computer roles include Microsoft SQL Server computer, Microsoft Exchange Server computer, domain controller, Internet Authentication Service (IAS) server, and Internet Information Services (IIS) server.
- Configure additional security based on computer roles. Server computer roles include SQL Server computer, Exchange Server computer, domain controller, Internet Authentication Service (IAS) server, and Internet Information Services (IIS) server. Client computer roles include desktop, portable, and kiosk.
    - Plan and configure security settings.
    - Plan network zones for computer roles.
    - Plan and configure software restriction policies.
    - Plan security for infrastructure services. Services include Dynamic Host Configuration Protocol (DHCP) and Domain Name System (DNS).
    - Plan and configure auditing and logging for a computer role. Considerations include Windows Events, IIS, firewall log files, Netlog, and Remote Access Service (RAS) log files.
    - Analyze security configuration. Tools include Microsoft Baseline Security Analyzer (MBSA), the MBSA command-line tool, and Security Configuration And Analysis.

Why This Chapter Matters

Different computers must be secured in different ways, depending on their roles. Public Web servers must allow incoming requests from browsers and should allow anonymous users on the Internet to retrieve files. Domain controllers, on the other hand, should never accept requests from anonymous users. Therefore, by tuning a server's security settings to its role, you can reduce the possibility of a security compromise. This chapter shows you how to customize and maintain both network and system security to minimize risks, while still allowing legitimate users to access the services on your network.

Similar considerations must be made for client systems. Your desktop computer should have different security settings than your CEO's laptop computer, because the CEO stores confidential documents, travels with the computer, and may need to connect to wireless networks outside of the company's intranet. Sometimes hardening a client computer involves more than restricting access from attackers; it can require ensuring limited access to legitimate users. Many organizations choose to restrict which applications a user can run and what settings a user can change. While users enjoy having the freedom to perform any task on their computers, restricting their activities makes the computers more reliable and decreases help desk costs. This chapter will show you how to configure security for common client computer roles.

After you determine how each computer role should be configured, you must deploy that configuration and then audit your computer systems to ensure that the desired settings are taking effect. Understanding the tools used for analyzing configurations is important, both for maintaining a secure environment and for passing this exam. This chapter provides detailed instructions for validating security settings and critical updates on both client and server computers.

Lessons in this Chapter:

Before You Begin

This chapter presents the skills and concepts that are required to configure and manage security settings for common client and server computer roles. If you fulfilled the requirements for previous chapters, then you already have the necessary hardware and software configured. You can use the computers in the state they were in after completing any of the previous chapters, or you can install the software from scratch. To do the practices, examples, and lab exercises in this chapter, you must have:

- A private, non-routed network.
- Two computers. On the first computer, perform a Microsoft Windows Server 2003 installation with default settings, and assign the computer name Computer1. Add the domain controller role using the default settings, and specify the domain name cohowinery.com. On the second computer, perform a Windows Server 2003 installation with default settings, and assign the computer name Computer2.

Lesson 1: Tuning Security for Client Roles

Administrators tune the security of server roles to reduce the risk of a malicious attacker compromising a server. For client computer roles, security tuning tends to focus on reducing costs by restricting the desktop environment. Many of the most time-consuming help desk calls occur after a user installs non-standard hardware and software. Fortunately, Microsoft Windows clients that participate in an Active Directory directory service domain can be centrally configured and managed to provide administrators with very granular control over what users can and cannot do.

You can specify which applications users can access and which features are available based on users' job types, services provided by the IT department, and the needs of your environment. For example, you can use Group Policy settings to prevent users from accessing various storage devices, such as floppy disk drives, hard disks, or CD-ROMs. By using security policy or access control lists (ACLs), you can also secure objects, such as system files and the registry, so that your users cannot gain access to them.

Implementing restricted client configurations can result in increased user productivity by reducing the incidence of computer-related problems. Also, because standard configurations are easier to troubleshoot or replace, using them brings about a reduction in support costs.

See Also For more information, read *Windows Server 2003 Deployment Kit: Designing a Managed Environment*.

After this lesson, you will be able to

- Use software restriction policies to limit the applications that can be run on client computers.
- Understand the various mechanisms for restricting software, and explain the advantages of each.
- Design security configurations for desktop computer systems.
- Reduce the risk of mobile computers being compromised while connected to unprotected networks, and limit the loss of confidential information if a mobile computer is stolen.
- Explain how to configure security for computers that will operate as kiosks.

Estimated lesson time: 30 minutes

Planning Managed Client Computers

When planning the requirements for managed client computers, start by identifying the baseline security level that is appropriate for users to have on their computers. The baseline user security level is specified by granting users membership to one of these groups: Users, Power Users, and Administrators. Membership in the Users group gives the most protection from a number of external threats, such as viruses, and it limits the damage that users can accidentally or intentionally cause to their computers. However, user level permissions have the most incompatibility problems with older applications. Take particular care before you give users privileged access to computers that they share with other employees.

Next, identify the types of systems users need to interoperate with. Interoperability with earlier systems, such as Microsoft Windows NT 4.0–based servers and UNIX file servers, necessitates that some of the security you might use in a pure Windows Server 2003 environment must be relaxed.

Finally, consider the level of support users provide for their own computers. Users who use portable computers and provide their own support might require administrator rights on their computers. Other high-performance users, such as developers, might also need administrative rights.

Real World

Sure, we've all been annoyed by the user who decided to free up some disk space by deleting the useless Windows folder, but the worst users to deal with are other administrators. We system administrators think we know everything about computers. The fact is, even if you know Windows Server like the back of your hand, that doesn't mean you're an expert about Windows on a desktop computer.

For example, I destroyed the modem in my laptop a few years ago by plugging it into the digital phone line at a hotel. Digital phone lines have higher voltages than analog lines, and the extra voltage will damage the modem's circuitry. It was a dumb mistake, and it's one that every desktop support guy has heard a dozen times. The IT guy I called immediately knew that I had broken my modem, but I had no idea until I talked to him. Even though I had managed a large modem bank, I had no experience with using modems on the go.

Before deploying your management solutions to a wide base, fully test your design in a lab environment. Minimally, your test environment should consist of a domain controller and one computer representative of each client computer type in your organization. These client computer types might include desktop computer, mobile computer, and highly restricted kiosk computer. If you are testing software installation through Group Policy, include one or more servers set up as software distribution points. By setting up a test-to-production environment deployment process, you can ensure that you provide a reliable and consistent configuration management solution.

Document the testing network in addition to all steps required to set it up. If new hardware, such as a new server, is being added to your organization's network, use this same hardware in your test deployment if possible. To minimize variables and to ensure that testing does not interfere with your organization's network services, keep the testing network on its own isolated local area network (LAN).

After completing tests in a controlled environment, select a group of users to pilot your configuration. Keep the users to a manageable number. A pilot can expose unexpected problems on a small scale so that you can resolve them before deploying on a large scale. Verify that the deployed technology is operating as expected. If you perform an iterated deployment, deploy and test in phases, and then emphasize the testing of the final configuration.

Software Restriction Policies

Software restriction policies are a feature in Windows XP and Windows Server 2003 that can be used to regulate unknown or untrusted software. Businesses that do not use software restriction policies put the burden of identifying safe and unsafe software on the users. Users who access the Internet must constantly make decisions about running unknown software. Malicious users intentionally disguise viruses and Trojans to trick users into running them. It is difficult for users to make safe choices about what software they should run.

With software restriction policies, you can protect your network from untrusted software by identifying and specifying the software that is allowed to run. You can define a default security level of Unrestricted or Disallowed for a Group Policy object (GPO) so that software is either allowed or not allowed to run by default. You can make exceptions to this default security level by creating software restriction policy rules for specific software. For example, if the default security level is set to Disallowed, you can create rules that allow specific software to run.

You can use four types of rules to create a software restriction policy: hash rules, certificate rules, path rules, and Internet zone rules. When a hash rule is created for a software program, software restriction policies calculate a unique hash of the executable file. When a user tries to start an application, Windows generates a hash of the application and compares it to existing hash rules for software restriction policies. The hash of a software program is always the same, regardless of where the program is located on the computer. However, if a software program is altered in any way, its hash also changes, and it no longer matches the hash in the hash rule for software restriction policies.

You can create a certificate rule that identifies software and then allows or does not allow the software to run, depending on the security level. For example, you can use certificate rules to automatically trust software from a trusted source in a domain without prompting the user. You can also use certificate rules to run files in disallowed areas of your operating system.

A path rule identifies software by its file path. For example, if you have a computer that has a default security level of Disallowed, you can still grant unrestricted access to a specific folder for each user. You can create a path rule by using the file path and setting the security level of the path rule to Unrestricted. Some common paths for this type of rule are %userprofile%, %windir%, %appdata%, %programfiles%, and %temp%. You can also create registry path rules that use the registry key of the software as the path. Because these rules are specified by the path, if a software program is moved, the path rule no longer applies.

An Internet zone rule can identify software from a zone that is specified through Microsoft Internet Explorer. Internet zone rules are useful for preventing users from running applications downloaded from the Internet, but still allowing programs stored on the local computer or other trusted computers to run. The zones you can choose from are Internet, Local Intranet, Restricted Sites, Trusted Sites, and My Computer.

The My Computer zone includes any applications installed on the local computer. The Local Intranet zone is intended to be used for computers located within your organization's internal network, but it does not include any sites by default. The Trusted Sites zone, by default, includes only Web sites used to download updates from Microsoft and to submit error messages to Microsoft. By default, the Restricted Sites zone is empty. The Internet zone includes any computers not located in any of the other zones.

To specify which computers on the network are included in the Local Intranet, Restricted Sites, and Trusted Sites zones for a single computer, start Internet Explorer, and on the Tools menu, click Internet Options, and then click the Security tab. You can then select Local Intranet, Restricted Sites, or Trusted Sites and click the Sites button to add additional locations that will be included in that zone. You can also configure zones by using a GPO: Open a GPO in the Group Policy Object Editor, expand User Configuration\Windows Settings\Internet Explorer Maintenance, and then click Security. Then, in the right pane, double-click Security Zones And Content Ratings.

Software restriction policies consist of the default security level and all the rules that apply to a GPO. Software restriction policies can be applied across a domain, to local computers, or to individual users. Software restriction policies provide a number of ways to identify software, and they provide a policy-based infrastructure to enforce decisions about whether the identified software can run. With software restriction policies, when users run software programs, they must adhere to the guidelines that are set up by administrators.

With software restriction policies, you can control the ability of software to run on your system. For example, if you are concerned about users receiving viruses through e-mail, you can apply a policy setting that does not allow certain file types to run in the e-mail attachment directory of your e-mail program. You can even restrict policies based on users, allowing certain users on a computer to run an application, but not others.

Security for Desktop Computers

When a computer manufacturer delivers a new computer to an organization, the operating system is generally configured to provide the greatest flexibility to the typical user. Many organizations have additional software installed on top of the operating system, such as Microsoft Office. This provides power users with the tools they need to do their jobs.

However, many types of employees do not require much flexibility and will actually be more productive if the software on their computers is restricted. For example, a user in the accounts payable department might only need access to an e-mail client, accounting software, and a Web browser. For this type of user, restricting the applications they can run can make them more productive (for example, by removing Solitaire). Additionally, it can reduce the risk of malicious software, such as viruses and Trojans, infecting the computer.

In a typical restricted desktop computer role, the desktop and Start menu are significantly simplified. Users cannot make extensive customizations, other than a limited number of application-specific settings. Applications are typically allocated to users based on their job roles, and users cannot add or remove applications. This type of desktop configuration is appropriate in a marketing or finance department, for example. In these areas, users require only a specific and limited set (typically three to five) of productivity and in-house applications to do their jobs.

If your environment requires secure desktops, create a security template that contains the standard desktop security settings. Base this new security template on the Hisecws.inf predefined security template, which contains the majority of the settings you would need to specify. Besides the settings already defined in the Hisecws.inf template, you should consider enabling both the Accounts: Rename Administrator Account and Accounts: Rename Guest Account policies. Also, your organization's security policy might require that you warn users as they log on by enabling the Interactive Logon: Message Text For Users Attempting To Log On and Interactive Logon: Message Title For Users Attempting To Log On policies. Consult your legal department for the exact messages used to warn users.

See Also For more information on copying and importing security templates, refer to Chapter 3, "Deploying and Troubleshooting Security Templates."

After you create the security template, create a new GPO for your secure desktops and import the security template into the GPO. There are many settings within the GPO that cannot be defined in the security template but that can be used to help secure a desktop computer. Specifically, examine each Group Policy setting contained in the User Configuration\Administrative Templates node, as shown in Figure 4.1. These settings allow you to carefully configure the desktop and remove items that may be unnecessary or undesired, such as the Run option on the Start menu.

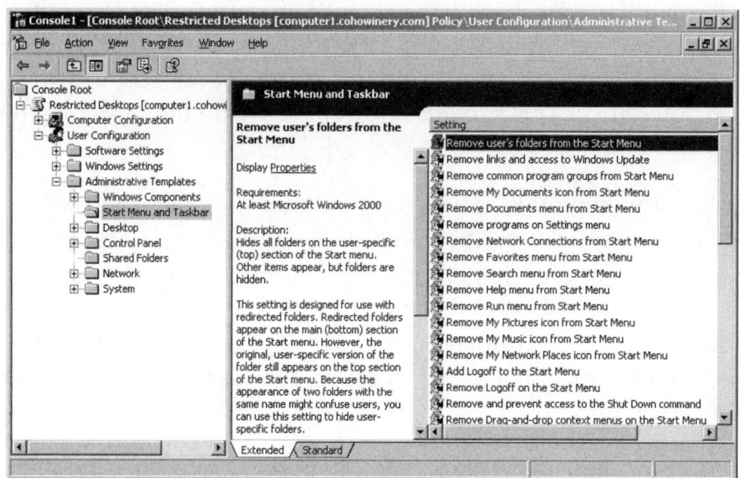

Figure 4.1 Administrative Templates GPO settings

Security for Mobile Computers

Mobile computers require that you attend to several additional security considerations beyond those of desktop computers. Mobile users might use their computers while traveling, which might require them to perform administrative tasks that a member of the IT group would normally perform. For example, a mobile user might need to print a document using a different printer than the one installed in the office, and would need to install the correct printer driver. To allow this, disable the Devices: Prevent Users From Installing Printer Drivers security option. If you anticipate that users who work away from the office will need to install or reinstall applications while working remotely, you might want to enable the Always Install With Elevated Privileges setting in the Administrative Templates\Windows Components\Windows Installer node.

Mobile users might connect to foreign networks, such as a wireless hotspot at a coffee shop. These foreign networks won't have the benefit of your organization's network security, so mobile users have an elevated risk of being attacked across the network. To mitigate this risk, enable the Internet Connection Firewall (ICF, known in Service Pack 2 as Windows Firewall) on all network interfaces for mobile computers. Unfortunately, ICF cannot be configured by using Group Policy settings. Lesson 2 in this chapter contains more information about firewalls.

It's much more likely that a mobile computer will be stolen than a desktop computer, which makes Encrypting File System (EFS) extremely important on mobile computers. To reduce the likelihood that an act of theft will compromise your business's secrets, any confidential documents should be encrypted with EFS. Though EFS cannot be enabled for specific folders using security templates, you can create a logon script that enables EFS for folders that might contain confidential data.

Mobile users might require additional flexibility to configure their systems, for example, they might need to configure virtual private network (VPN) connections. In such cases, modify the appropriate settings under the User Configuration\Administrative Templates\Network\Network Connections node of the applicable GPO.

Security for Kiosks

A kiosk is a public workstation that runs only one application, runs unattended, and uses a single user account that automatically logs on. A kiosk should be highly secure, should be simple to operate, and should not allow users to make changes to the default settings. The Start menu, and even the desktop, should be unavailable. Users should not be able to customize the computer, install applications, save any data, or access the file system directly.

Off the Record Ever pick up the quarterly hacker's magazine *2600*? It's always an interesting read, and it can be educational for those of us working on the lawful side of the information security industry. Well, if you read a couple of issues of it, you are bound to find detailed descriptions of how to hack into some kind of kiosk computer. It seems like there's always a way to make a kiosk computer do something it's not intended to do. One common trick is to press CTRL+C during startup when a script is running—this can interrupt the script and give the user a command prompt.

Kiosks usually run dedicated applications. The dedicated application could be a custom application, a Web application accessed by means of Internet Explorer, or another application, such as Microsoft PowerPoint. The default application should not be Windows Explorer, or any other shell-like application, because of the flexibility and potential for misuse that Windows Explorer provides. Be sure the command prompt is disabled and Windows Explorer cannot be accessed. Applications used for kiosk scenarios must be carefully checked to ensure they do not contain "backdoors" that allow users to circumvent system policies.

When creating a security template for a kiosk computer, start by creating a copy of the Hisecws.inf template. Assuming that you plan to make the primary kiosk user account a member of the local Users group on the computer, modify the security template so that the Users group is not granted the Shut Down The System user right, which might be granted by default.

Within the Audit Policy node of the template, you should enable restrictive password and account lockout policy settings for the local accounts. If a user does manage to get to a logon prompt, the account lockout settings will prevent the user from successfully guessing a password. Enable extensive security logging and system auditing. This can be useful for proving that a user did attempt to misuse the system and for identifying how the attacker compromised the computer.

Within the Security Options node of the security template, enable both the Accounts: Rename Administrator Account and Accounts: Rename Guest Account policies. Use file and folder permissions to prohibit changes to files or folders outside of the user's profile folder. Specifically, apply more restrictive access controls in the root directory. Restrict registry permissions to limit access to the computer registry hive, which prohibits the user from making changes.

After importing the kiosk security template into the kiosk GPO, you should specify several GPO settings that are not configurable by means of security templates. Specifically, expand User Configuration\Administrative Templates, and examine each node contained within. You should enable every setting starting with Remove in the Start Menu And Taskbar node. Also, carefully review and configure the settings contained within the Desktop, Network, System, and Control Panel nodes of the GPO.

Practice: Restricting Software

In this practice, you will restrict two applications from running on Computer1. You must complete this practice before completing the troubleshooting lab in this chapter.

Exercise: Configure software restrictions

In this exercise, you will familiarize yourself with software restriction policies by creating a new GPO.

1. Log on to the cohowinery.com domain on Computer1 using the Administrator account.
2. Create a new Microsoft Management Console (MMC) console, and add the Group Policy Object Editor snap-in.
3. When the Group Policy Wizard appears, click the Browse button.
4. In the Browse For A Group Policy Object dialog box, click the Create New Group Policy Object button.
5. Name the GPO **Test Software Restriction Policy**. Click the new GPO, and then click OK. Click Finish, click Close, and then click OK to return to the MMC console.
6. Expand Test Software Restriction Policy, Computer Configuration, Windows Settings, and Security Settings.

7. Right-click Software Restriction Policies, and then click New Software Restriction Policies.
8. In the left pane, click Software Restriction Policies.
9. In the right pane, right-click Enforcement, and then click Properties.
10. Click All Software Files.

    Dynamic Link Libraries (DLLs) are not programs in themselves. They are the building blocks of programs, and they contain libraries of functions that perform specific tasks, such as creating a new file or establishing a network connection. To have the policies apply to all software files, including DLLs, select All Software Files. Otherwise, leave All Software Files Except Libraries selected.
11. Click All Users, and then click OK.

    To have the software restrictions apply to administrators in addition to regular users, leave All Users selected. If you would rather enable administrators to more easily troubleshoot software problems by bypassing the restrictions, select All Users Except Local Administrators.
12. In the left pane, click Security Levels. The right pane shows two levels: Disallowed and Unrestricted. Leave Unrestricted specified as the default.

    Unless an administrator has changed the setting, Unrestricted is specified as the default. This allows all applications to run unless specifically denied. Although this allows administrators to name applications that should not be run, it can be easily bypassed by a user who renames an application file. Specifying Disallowed as the default ensures that no applications can run unless specified by an administrator. Using the Disallowed setting requires a great deal of configuration and testing because otherwise it will prevent end users from accessing their software.
13. In the left pane, right-click the Additional Rules node, and then click New Hash Rule.
14. Click the Browse button, and then navigate to C:\Windows\Notepad.exe. Click Open.
15. Click Security Level, and then select Disallowed.

    This prevents anyone logged on to a computer to which the GPO applies from running the Notepad executable file.
16. Click OK.
17. In the left pane, right-click the Additional Rules node, and then click New Path Rule.
18. Click the Browse button, and then navigate to C:\Windows\PcHealth\HelpCtr\Binaries. Click OK.

19. Click Security Level, and then select Disallowed.

    This prevents anyone logged on to a computer to which the GPO applies from running Msconfig, an executable file in the specified path.

20. Click OK.
21. Close the Group Policy Object Editor.
22. Start the Active Directory Users And Computers console.
23. Right-click Domain Controllers, and then click Properties.
24. Click the Group Policy tab, and then click the Add button.
25. In the Add A Group Policy Object Link dialog box, click the All tab. Click Test Software Restriction Policy, and then click OK twice.
26. Restart the computer to ensure that the updated Group Policy takes effect. After the computer restarts, log on to the cohowinery.com domain on Computer1 using the Administrator account.
27. Click Start, and then click Run. Type **Notepad**, and then click OK.

    The application will not run, because the software restriction policy does not allow it. Instead, you will see the dialog box shown in Figure 4.2.

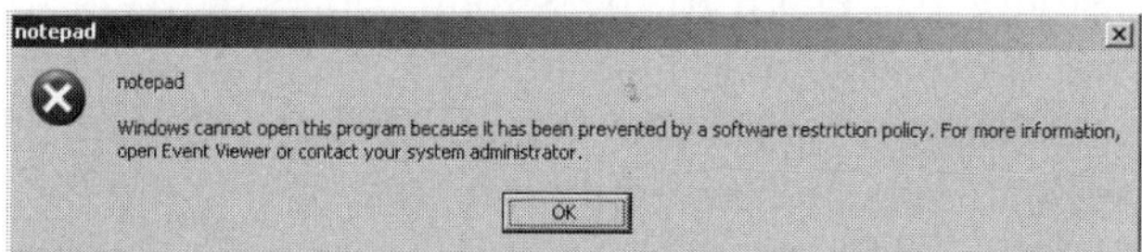

Figure 4.2 Software restrictions forbidding the execution of Notepad

28. Click Start, and then click Run. Type **Msconfig**, and then click OK.

    The application will not run, because the software restriction policy does not allow it.

29. Use Windows Explorer to browse to the C:\Windows folder. Right-click Notepad.exe, and then click Copy. Right-click the C:\Windows folder in the right pane, and then click Paste.
30. In the right pane, scroll to the bottom of the list of files, and double-click the file Copy Of Notepad.exe.

    The application will not run, because the software restriction policy does not allow files that match the hash of the Notepad.exe file to run. Therefore, even though you have renamed the file, it will still not run.

31. Use Windows Explorer to browse to the C:\Windows\PcHealth\HelpCtr\Binaries folder. Right-click Msconfig.exe, and then click Copy. Right-click the C:\Windows folder in the left pane, and then click Paste.

32. In the left pane, click the C:\Windows folder. In the right pane, double-click the file Msconfig.exe.

    The application will run, because the software restriction policy was configured to restrict the path of the file, and not the file itself. Therefore, moving the file to a different path allows the user to bypass the restriction.

Lesson Review

The following questions are intended to reinforce key information presented in this lesson. If you are unable to answer a question, review the lesson materials and try the question again. You can find answers to the questions in the "Questions and Answers" section at the end of this chapter.

1. Which of the following software restriction rules can be used to allow any application on an intranet to be run on a computer?

    a. Hash rules

    b. Certificate rules

    c. Path rules

    d. Internet zone rules

    ____

    ____

    ____

2. Which of the following software restriction rules should be used to ensure that a particular executable file cannot be run?

    a. Hash rules

    b. Certificate rules

    c. Path rules

    d. Internet zone rules

    ____

    ____

    ____

3. Which of the following rules would you not enforce on a computer to be used as a kiosk?

   a. Remove the Run menu item from the Start menu.

   b. Deny the Everyone group the right to log on locally.

   c. Require a user to log on automatically.

   d. Deny the interactive user the right to change his or her own password.

____

____

____

Lesson Summary

- Software restriction policies can be applied to a GPO to restrict the applications that can run on a target system. Software restriction policies can restrict applications based on a hash of the executable file, the path in the file system, a certificate associated with the application, or the Internet zone from which the application is running.
- You should create security templates for the various computer roles in your organizations, including desktop computers, mobile computers, and kiosks. Whenever possible, you should base these templates on a predefined security template.
- Security templates are useful for creating GPOs, but they contain only a subset of the settings available when configuring a GPO. Therefore, after importing a security template into a GPO, you might have to use the Group Policy Object Editor to specify additional settings.
- Mobile computers have different security considerations than desktop computers. Mobile computers are subject to a wider array of network attacks because they might connect to unprotected networks. Additionally, they are more likely to be stolen, so encryption of the disk's physical contents might be necessary.
- Kiosks require security settings that are tightly restricted to prevent abuse. GPOs allow an administrator to remove all major user interface elements and configure kiosk computers to log on a user and launch a single application automatically at startup.

Lesson 2: Tuning Security for Server Roles

To be effective, security settings must be fine-tuned to the role that each computer serves on a network. Database servers, such as a SQL Server, must be configured to allow authorized user accounts to issue database queries. Messaging servers, such as a computer running Exchange Server, must be configured to authenticate messaging users and must have security configured to allow the exchange of messages with other systems.

Each network service that is added to a computer system inherently exposes another potential vulnerability. Although adding the DHCP Server role does not necessarily expose you to a vulnerability, configuring that role does cause the server to listen for an additional type of request from clients. Without the DHCP Server role installed, the server would simply ignore those types of requests. At some point in the future, if a vulnerability is discovered that can exploit DHCP servers, your computer could be vulnerable.

Although each additional role increases a computer's attack surface, and thereby introduces an additional security risk, you as an administrator can do a great deal to mitigate that risk. Some of those mitigating steps, such as enabling packet filtering, are implemented by using tools provided by the operating system. Other steps can be taken by using the tools provided with the server role, such as limiting Web requests to those from specific internal networks.

This lesson describes the most common server roles used on enterprise networks and how to configure those roles to meet your organization's security requirements.

After this lesson, you will be able to

- Use firewalls and perimeter networks to provide an additional layer of security for computers running Windows Server 2003.
- Customize security settings for infrastructure servers, such as DHCP servers, DNS servers, and domain controllers.
- Configure a Web server to serve content to the public Internet while minimizing the risk that the system will provide attackers with an entry point to the internal network.
- Describe the role an Internet Authentication server provides on a network, and describe the circumstances under which the RADIUS protocol should be used.
- Understand the risks and benefits of the two different authentication modes provided by SQL Server, and describe the authorization capabilities built into the database software.
- Describe the security implications of deploying an Exchange Server computer, and configure network security to minimize the exposure of your messaging server while still allowing all necessary network communications.

Estimated lesson time: 60 minutes

Firewalls

In the physical world, businesses rely on several layers of security. First, they rely on their country's government and military forces to keep order. They also trust their local police to patrol the streets and respond to any crimes that occur. They further supplement these public security mechanisms by using locks on doors and windows, employee badges, and security systems. If all these defenses fail and a business is a victim of a crime, the business's insurance agency absorbs part of the impact by compensating the business for a portion of the loss.

Unfortunately, the state of networking today lacks these multiple levels of protection. Federal and local governments do what they can to impede network crime, but they're far less effective than police forces are at preventing physical crime. Beyond prevention, law enforcement generally responds only to the most serious network intrusions. The average Internet-connected business is attacked dozens of times per day, and no police force is equipped to handle that volume of complaints. Losses from computer crime are hard to quantify and predict, and as a result most business insurance policies do little to compensate for the losses that result from a successful attack.

The one aspect of physical security, however, that isn't missing from network security is the equivalent of door locks: firewalls. Just as you lock your car and home, you need to protect your computers and networks. Firewalls are these locks, and, just like in the physical world, they come in different shapes and sizes to suit various needs.

Security Alert Like physical locks, firewalls are not impenetrable. No firewall, whether a host-based firewall or a several-thousand-dollar enterprise firewall array, will make your computers impervious to attack. Firewalls are merely barriers to attack. By making it difficult for attackers to get into your network, by making them invest lots of time, you can make your organization less attractive. However, it's impossible to fully prevent every intrusion: As long as you must allow legitimate traffic through, the network connection can be misused for an attack. Additionally, all software has bugs, and someone might find an obscure bug in your firewall that allows them to launch an attack. In a nutshell, there's no such thing as absolute security. How much you invest in firewalls should be a function of how much you have to lose if an attack is successful.

There are two main types of firewalls: network firewalls and host-based firewalls. Network firewalls, such as the software-based Microsoft Internet Security and Acceleration (ISA) Server or the hardware-based Nortel Networks Alteon Switched Firewall System, protect the perimeter of a network by monitoring traffic that enters and leaves. Host-based firewalls, such as Internet Connection Firewall (ICF), which is included with Windows XP and Windows Server 2003, protect an individual computer regardless of the network it's connected to. Most businesses require a combination of both types of firewalls to meet their security requirements.

TCP/IP flow basics

To understand how firewalls determine whether to allow or deny traffic, you must understand how Transmission Control Protocol/Internet Protocol (TCP/IP) packages information. TCP/IP traffic is broken into packets, and firewalls must examine each packet to determine whether to drop it or forward it to the destination. Packets have three key sections: the IP header, the TCP or User Datagram Protocol (UDP) header, and the actual contents of the packet. The IP header contains the IP addresses of the source, which is the sender, and the destination, which is the receiver. The TCP or UDP header contains the source port of the sender and the destination port of the receiver to identify the applications that are sending and receiving the traffic. In addition, TCP headers contain additional information such as sequence numbers, acknowledgment numbers, and the conversation state. The destination TCP and UDP ports define the locations for delivery of the data on the server when the packet reaches its destination.

It's important to appreciate the communication flow of a TCP/IP conversation when configuring the firewall. When a browser, for example, sends a Hypertext Transfer Protocol (HTTP) request to a Web server, the request contains the identity of the client computer, the source IP address, and the source port that the request went out on. The source port of the client identifies the client application that sent the request—in this case, the browser. When the Web server sends a response, it uses the client's source port as the destination port in the response. The client operating system recognizes the port number as belonging to a session the browser application started and provides the data to the browser. The source port for a client is typically a value greater than 1024 and less than 5000.

Packet filtering

The primary purpose of a firewall is to filter traffic. Firewalls inspect packets as they pass through and, based on the criteria that the administrator has defined, allow or deny each packet.

By default, most firewalls block everything that you haven't specifically allowed. Routers with filtering capabilities are a simplified example of a firewall. Administrators often configure them to allow all outbound connections from the internal network but to block all incoming traffic. So a user on the internal network would be able to download e-mail without a problem, but an administrator would need to customize the router configuration to allow users to connect to their work computers from their homes by using Remote Desktop.

You use packet filters to instruct a firewall to drop traffic that meets certain criteria. For example, you could create a filter that would drop all ping requests. You can also configure filters with more complex exceptions to a rule. For example, a filter might assist with troubleshooting the firewall by allowing the firewall to respond to ping requests coming from a monitoring station's IP address. By default, ISA Server doesn't respond to ping queries on its external interface. You would need to create a packet filter on the ISA Server computer for it to respond to a ping request.

The following are the main TCP/IP attributes used in implementing filtering rules:

- Source IP addresses
- Destination IP addresses
- IP protocol
- Source TCP and UDP ports
- Destination TCP and UDP ports
- The interface to which the packet arrives
- The interface to which the packet is destined

If you've configured the firewall to allow all traffic by default, you can use filters to block specific traffic. If you've configured the firewall to deny all traffic, filters allow only specific traffic through. A common packet-filtering configuration is to allow inbound DNS requests from the public Internet so that a DNS service can respond.

Some types of firewalls (but not ICF) can filter traffic based on source or destination IP address. Filtering based on source or destination address is useful because it enables you to allow or deny traffic based on the computers or networks that are sending or receiving the traffic. This enables firewalls to allow or deny traffic based on the computer sending the request. This allows administrators to disable instant messaging from the computer in one organization, while allowing the same protocol from a different set of computers.

Source filtering also allows you to give greater access to users on internal networks than to those on external networks. It's common to use a firewall to block all requests sent to an internal e-mail server except for those requests from users on the internal network. You can also use source filtering to block all requests from a specific address, for example, to block traffic from an IP address identified as having attacked the network.

Advanced firewall features

Packet filtering based on IP address and port number is a fundamental feature of even the most basic firewalls. More advanced firewalls include features such as stateful packet inspection, application layer intelligence, intrusion detection, and VPN.

Stateful inspection is the process of inspecting packets as they reach the firewall and maintaining the state of the connection by allowing or disallowing packets to pass based on the access policy. Firewalls that lack support for stateful inspection simply forward any packets that are marked as participating in an existing connection. This can allow an attacker to send packets through a firewall, but it doesn't necessarily allow the attacker to establish a connection with a system on the internal network. ICF supports stateful inspection.

Note Proxy servers and firewalls that support Network Address Translation (NAT) always provide stateful inspection.

Application layer firewalls can analyze the data within the traffic flowing through them and allow or deny traffic based on the content. For example, an application layer firewall positioned in front of a Web server could check each page that a user requests and determine whether that user is allowed to request that particular page from the Web server. While this type of filtering could also be done on the Web server itself, performing the filtering in a firewall provides an additional layer of protection.

Firewalls that include intrusion detection capabilities search through traffic and look for telltale signs of an attack taking place. They can then respond in real time by notifying an administrator, blocking access from the attacker's network, or issuing a counterattack. Intrusion detection is also useful because it includes extensive logging, which might be useful when identifying or prosecuting an attacker.

Firewalls with VPN capabilities simplify remote access and can allow remote networks to connect to each other across the Internet. While VPN capabilities are built into Windows Server 2003, relying on a separate firewall for VPN functions reduces the load on your server. Additionally, combining VPN and firewall functionality allows the firewall to perform filtering and analysis on traffic contained within the encrypted VPN tunnel.

See Also For more information on VPNs, refer to Chapter 8, "Planning and Configuring IPSec," and Chapter 9, "Deploying and Troubleshooting IPSec."

Perimeter Networks

Most organizations use their Internet connection to make one or more services available to the public Internet. At a minimum, Simple Mail Transfer Protocol (SMTP) services are exposed to allow inbound e-mail. You can use filtering and port forwarding to allow this traffic through a firewall, but many organizations require a perimeter network, also known as a demilitarized zone (DMZ). The purpose of a perimeter network is to offer a layer of protection for the internal network in the event that one of the servers on the perimeter network is compromised.

To provide protection, the perimeter network is made up of:

- A firewall that protects the front-end servers from Internet traffic.
- A set of "security-hardened" servers that support the services the application provides. You set up these servers so that dangerous Internet services, such as file sharing and Telnet, are disabled.
- A firewall that separates the back-end servers from the corporate networks and enables communication between the back-end servers and a few servers within the corporate network.

Figure 4.3 shows a network with the Web, e-mail, and DNS servers placed in a single-layer perimeter network separate from the internal network.

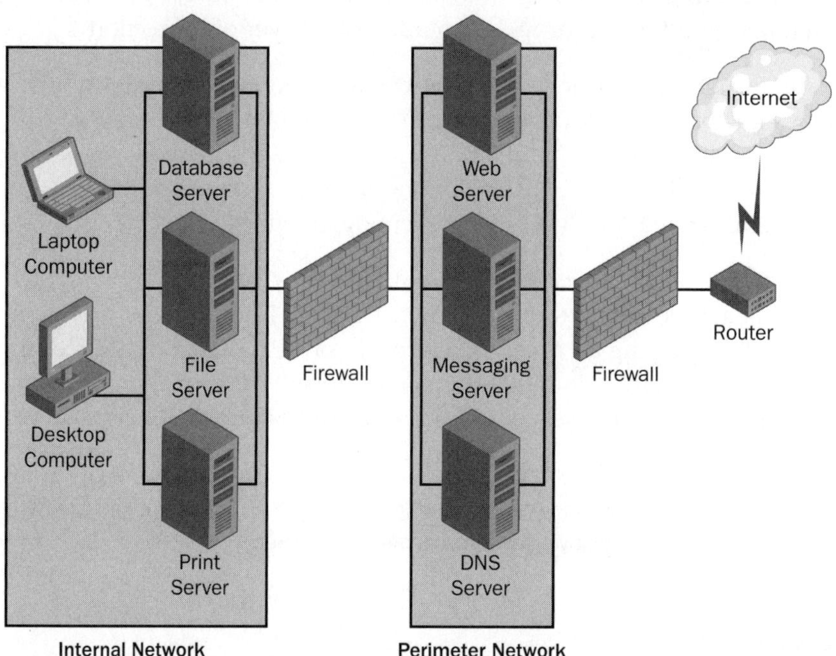

Figure 4.3 Services placed in a single-layer perimeter network

A perimeter network is an important element for securing a site. You need to take additional security measures to protect data that the back-end servers store. You can also store extremely sensitive data or data that's needed elsewhere in your enterprise outside the perimeter network, although doing so has negative performance implications and runs the risk, however small, of opening your corporate network to an attacker.

A multilayer perimeter network consists of front-end servers, back-end servers, and firewalls. The firewalls protect the front-end servers from the public network and filter traffic between the corporate network and the back-end servers. A perimeter network provides a multilayer protection system between the Internet and the internal network of an organization.

Security for DHCP Servers

Dynamic Host Configuration Protocol (DHCP) is an IP standard designed to reduce the complexity of administering address configurations. DHCP servers enable an administrator to assign TCP/IP configurations to client computers automatically upon startup. When a client computer moves between subnets, its old IP address is freed for reuse. The client reconfigures its TCP/IP settings automatically when the computer is restarted in its new location.

> **Note** Packet filtering isn't much of a concern with DHCP servers, since DHCP requests are broadcast messages and don't cross a router unless specifically configured to do so.

Configuring the DHCP Server role

You can install DHCP by clicking Add/Remove Windows Components in the Add Or Remove Programs dialog box, clicking Networking Services, clicking the Details button, and then selecting Dynamic Host Configuration Protocol. However, the simplest way to install and configure DHCP is to install the DHCP Server role by using the Manage Your Server window:

1. Click Start, and then click Manage Your Server.
2. Click Add Or Remove A Role. The Configure Your Server Wizard appears.
3. Click Next, click DHCP Server, and then click Next twice. The New Scope Wizard appears.
4. Click Next, and follow the wizard prompts to configure your DHCP scope.

Authorizing DHCP servers

Although the role of a DHCP infrastructure server might seem mundane, a DHCP server can actually be used maliciously to compromise the security of DHCP client computers. DHCP clients trust the DHCP server that assigns an IP address to provide them with information about the default gateway and DNS servers. An attacker could place a DHCP server on a network segment and replace the default gateway and DNS server information with the IP addresses of computers owned by the attacker. These computers could then intercept all traffic from the client, allowing the traffic to be analyzed for confidential information and enabling man-in-the-middle attacks.

Physical and network security is the only way to ensure that an attacker does not place a rogue DHCP server on your network. However, Windows Server 2003 can limit the risk of a user unintentionally starting a Windows-based DHCP server on your network, which could result in DHCP clients getting incorrect address information and not being able to access network resources. Active Directory contains a list of IP addresses available for the computers that you authorize to operate as DHCP servers on your network, and supports detection of unauthorized DHCP servers and prevention of their starting or running on your network.

Security Alert Microsoft Windows NT 4.0 and earlier Windows operating systems do not check for DHCP server authorization.

To authorize a computer as a DHCP server, first log on as an enterprise administrator. Then launch the DHCP console, right-click the server, and click Authorize. When a DHCP server is authorized, the server computer is added to the list of authorized DHCP servers maintained in the directory service database. You can verify that a server has been authorized by right-clicking the DHCP node in the DHCP console and clicking Manage Authorized Servers. The Manage Authorized Servers dialog box appears, as shown in Figure 4.4.

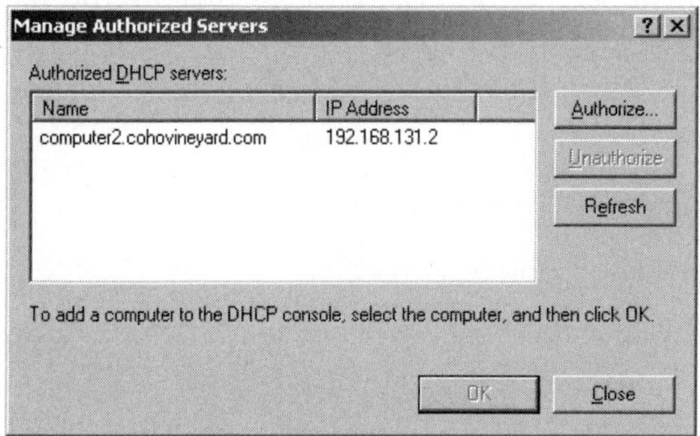

Figure 4.4 Managing authorized DHCP servers

A DHCP server running Windows Server 2003 uses the following process to determine whether Active Directory is available. If an Active Directory domain is found, the server validates its own authorization by following one of the procedures presented below, depending on whether it is a member server or a standalone server:

For member servers (a server joined to a domain that is part of an enterprise), the DHCP server queries Active Directory for the list of authorized DHCP server IP addresses. If the server finds its IP address in the authorized list, it initializes and starts providing DHCP service to clients. If it does not find itself in the authorized list, it does not initialize and stops providing DHCP services. When installed in a multiple forest environment, DHCP servers seek authorization from within their forest only. After being authorized, DHCP servers in a multiple forest environment lease IP addresses to all reachable clients. Therefore, if clients from another forest are reached using routers with DHCP/BOOTP forwarding enabled, the DHCP server leases IP addresses to them. If Active Directory is not available, the DHCP server continues to operate in its last known state.

For standalone servers (a server not joined to any domain or part of an existing enterprise), when the DHCP service starts, it sends a DHCP information message (DHCPINFORM). This message includes several vendor-specific option types that are known and supported by other DHCP servers running Windows Server 2003. When received by other DHCP servers, these option types enable the query and retrieval of information about the root domain. When queried, the other DHCP servers reply with DHCP acknowledgement messages (DHCPACK). If the standalone server receives no reply, it initializes and starts providing DHCP services to clients. If the standalone server receives a reply from a DHCP server that is authorized in Active Directory, the standalone server does not initialize and does not provide DHCP services to clients.

Authorized servers repeat the detection process at a default interval of 60 minutes. Unauthorized servers repeat the detection process at a default interval of 10 minutes. Efforts to detect unauthorized servers are noted as "Restarting rogue detection" entries in the audit log.

Dynamic DNS updates

DHCP and DNS are closely related, because you can configure the DHCP server to perform updates on behalf of its DHCP clients to any DNS servers that support dynamic updates. This is an important concept to understand for security reasons, because network services such as IIS might use DNS when authorizing requests. Additionally, network services that create usage or auditing log files might store DNS information about clients. Therefore, having DNS information for every computer on the network increases your network security by enabling you to more easily trace IP communications back to the correct computer.

The DHCP server can be used to register and update the pointer (PTR) and host (A) resource records on behalf of its DHCP-enabled clients. The PTR record resolves the client's IP address to its hostname, and the A record resolves the fully qualified domain name (FQDN) to the IP address. Although end-users rely on A records to find services on the network, PTR records are more useful for security-related tasks such as filtering incoming requests based on the client's domain name.

By default, Windows Server 2003 registers and updates client information with the authoritative DNS server of the zone in which the DHCP server is located according to the DHCP client request. In this mode, the DHCP client can request the manner in which the DHCP server performs updates of its host (A) and pointer (PTR) resource records. If possible, the DHCP server accommodates the client request for handling updates to its name and IP address information in DNS. This is the default setting, but it can lead to DHCP clients not having DNS records updated, because the client is trusted to register its own DNS records. To select this setting, view the properties of the DHCP server or a DHCP scope. Click the DNS tab, and select the Dynamically Update DNS A And PTR Records Only If Requested By The DHCP Clients check box.

To configure the DHCP server to always update the DNS records for a client, view the properties of the DHCP server or a DHCP scope, click the DNS tab, and select the Always Dynamically Update DNS A And PTR Records check box. In this mode, the DHCP server always performs updates of the client's FQDN, leased IP address information, and both its A and PTR resource records, regardless of whether the client has requested to perform its own updates. If you prefer to trust the clients to update their own DNS records, you can clear the Enable DNS Dynamic Updates According To The Settings Below check box.

Although all recent versions of Windows are capable of registering their own DNS records, including Windows 2000, Windows XP, and Windows Server 2003, earlier versions of Windows such as Windows 98 do not have this capability. Configure the DHCP server to register DNS records on behalf of these clients by selecting the Dynamically Update DNS A And PTR Records For DHCP Clients That Do Not Request Updates check box, as shown in Figure 4.5.

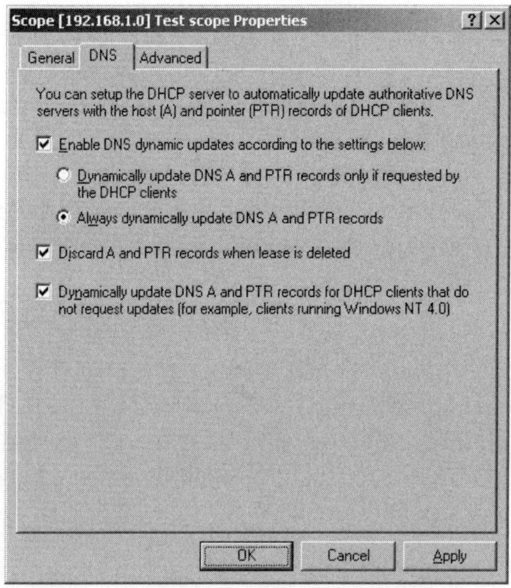

Figure 4.5 DHCP dynamic update options

Security Alert Although being able to look up the PTR record registered to a particular IP address can be useful when tracking down the source of a request, it's hardly a reliable tool when attempting to identify an attacker. An attacker would either use an IP address without registering with the DHCP server or would spoof another user's IP.

Known DHCP server security risks

The DHCP protocol itself, an open Internet standard, has several known security vulnerabilities. First, DHCP is an unauthenticated protocol. When a user connects to the network, the user is not required to provide credentials to obtain a lease. An unauthenticated user can, therefore, obtain a lease for any DHCP client whenever a DHCP server is available to provide a lease. Any option values that the DHCP server provides with the lease, such as Windows Internet Naming Service (WINS) server or DNS server IP addresses, are available to the unauthenticated user. If the DHCP client is identified as a member of a user class or vendor class, the options that are associated with the class are also available.

Malicious users with physical access to the DHCP-enabled network can instigate denial-of-service attacks on DHCP servers by requesting many leases from the server, thereby depleting the number of leases that are available to other DHCP clients. Additionally, such a denial-of-service attack can also impact the DNS server when the DHCP server is configured to perform DNS dynamic updates.

Tip When clients running Windows XP use 802.1X-enabled LAN switches or wireless access points to access a network, authentication occurs before the DHCP server assigns a lease, thereby providing greater security for DHCP.

To mitigate these risks, ensure that unauthorized persons do not have physical or wireless access to your network, and enable audit logging for every DHCP server on your network, as described in the next section. Configure DHCP servers in pairs, splitting DHCP server scopes between servers so that 80 percent of the addresses are distributed by one DHCP server and 20 percent by another to ensure that clients can continue receiving IP address configurations in the event of a server failure.

Logging considerations

Enable audit logging for every DHCP server on your network. Regularly check audit log files and monitor them when the DHCP server receives an unusually high number of lease requests from clients. Audit log files provide the information that you need to track the source of any attacks made against the DHCP server. The default location of audit log files is %systemroot%\system32\dhcp. You can also check the system event log for explanatory information about the DHCP Server service.

By default, the DHCP service only logs startup and shutdown events in the Event Viewer. A more detailed log can be enabled on the DHCP server by following these steps:

1. Start the DHCP console, right-click the DHCP server, and then click Properties.
2. Click the General tab, and then select Enable DHCP Audit Logging.

Use the DHCP audit logs to monitor DNS dynamic updates by the DHCP server. The Event ID 30 represents a dynamic update to a DNS server. Event ID 31 means that the dynamic update failed, and Event ID 32 means the update was successful. The IP address of the DHCP client is included in the DHCP audit log, providing the ability to track the source of the denial-of-service attack.

DHCP clients are often difficult to locate in log entries because the only information that is stored in most event logs is computer names, not IP addresses. The DHCP audit logs can provide one more tool for locating the sources of internal attacks or inadvertent activities. However, the information in these logs is not by any means foolproof, since both host names and media access control (MAC) addresses can be forged or spoofed. (*Spoofing* is the practice of making a transmission appear to come from a user other than the user who performed the action.) Nevertheless, the benefits of collecting this information by far exceed the costs incurred by enabling logging on a DHCP server. Having more than just an IP address and a machine name can be of great assistance in determining how a particular IP address was used on a network.

By default, Server Operators and Authenticated Users have read permissions to these log files. To best preserve the integrity of the information logged by a DHCP server, it is recommended that access to these logs be limited to server administrators. The Server Operators and Authenticated Users groups should be removed from the ACL of the %systemroot%\system32\dhcp folder.

Security for DNS Servers

DNS is the TCP/IP name resolution service that is used on the Internet. The DNS service enables client computers on your network to register and resolve user-friendly DNS names. It also allows network services to resolve IP addresses to host names, a common, but unreliable, method of filtering requests. Most network applications rely on DNS, and, as a result, a successful attack against DNS can have serious consequences.

Configuring the DNS Server role

You can install DNS by clicking Add/Remove Windows Components in the Add Or Remove Programs dialog box, clicking Networking Services, clicking the Details button, and then selecting Domain Name System. However, the simplest way to install and configure DNS is to install the DNS Server role by using the Manage Your Server window. To install the DNS Server role:

1. Click Start, and then click Manage Your Server.
2. Click Add Or Remove A Role. The Configure Your Server Wizard appears.
3. Click Next, click DNS Server, and then click Next again. Follow the prompts to configure the new role.

Securing DNS servers

If a DNS zone is not stored in Active Directory, secure the DNS zone file by modifying permissions on the DNS zone file or on the folder in which the zone files are stored. The zone file or folder permissions should be configured to allow Full Control only to the System group. By default, zone files are stored in the %systemroot%\System32\Dns folder. Also secure the DNS registry keys. The DNS registry keys can be found in the registry under HKEY_LOCAL_MACHINE\System\CurrentControlSet\Services\DNS.

On DNS servers that do not respond to DNS clients directly and are not configured with forwarders, disable recursion. A DNS server requires recursion only if it responds to recursive queries from DNS clients or is configured with a forwarder. The DNS server will use iterative queries to communicate with other DNS servers. To disable recursion:

1. Open the DNS console.
2. In the console tree, right-click the applicable DNS server, and then click Properties.
3. Click the Advanced tab.
4. Under Server Options, select the Disable Recursion check box, and then click OK.

If your DNS server will not be resolving Internet names for clients, configure the root hints to only point to the DNS servers hosting your root domain. By default, the root hints contain a list of Internet DNS servers to enable any public domain names to be resolved. To update root hints on the DNS server:

1. Open the DNS console.
2. On the Action menu, click Properties.
3. Click the Root Hints tab.
4. Modify server root hints as follows:
    - To add a root server to the list, click Add, and then specify the name and IP address of the server to be added to the list.
    - To modify a root server in the list, click Edit, and then specify the name and IP address of the server to be modified in the list.

- ❑ To remove a root server from the list, select it in the list, and then click Remove.
- ❑ To copy root hints from a DNS server, click Copy From Server, and then specify the IP address of the DNS server from which you want to copy a list of root servers to use in resolving queries. These root hints will not overwrite any existing root hints.

Security considerations for Active Directory–integrated DNS

Safeguarding DNS servers is essential to any environment with Active Directory because clients use DNS to find their Active Directory servers. When a DNS server is attacked, one possible goal of the attacker is to control the DNS information being returned in response to DNS client queries. In this way, clients can be misdirected to computers controlled by the attacker. Cache poisoning is an example of this type of attack. To use cache poisoning in an attack, an attacker inserts false information into the cache of a DNS server. This results in a legitimate DNS server returning incorrect results, thereby redirecting clients to unauthorized computers.

The Windows Server 2003 DNS client service supports Dynamic DNS updates, which allow client systems to add DNS records directly into the database. Dynamic DNS (DDNS) servers can receive malicious or unauthorized updates from an attacker using a client that supports the DDNS protocol if the server is configured to accept unsecured updates. At a minimum, an attacker can add bogus entries to the DNS database; at worst, the attacker can overwrite or delete legitimate entries in the DNS database. Using secure DDNS updates guarantees that registration requests are processed only if they are sent from valid clients in an Active Directory forest. This greatly limits the opportunity for an attacker to compromise the integrity of a DNS server.

DNS servers provide a mechanism called a *zone transfer* to replicate information about a DNS zone between servers. A DNS server that is not configured to limit who can request zone transfers will transfer the entire DNS zone to anyone who requests it. Unfortunately, this can make the entire domain's DNS dataset available, including which hosts are serving as domain controllers, Web servers, and databases.

Logging considerations

The DNS service generates logging information that is useful for determining whether an attack occurred and how it was carried out. DNS logging is enabled by default and can be modified from the Event Logging tab of the DNS server properties dialog box. To view the DNS server logs, open the DNS console, expand Event Viewer, and then click DNS Events. DNS events will appear in the right pane. Alternatively, you can view DNS events by using the standard Event Viewer console.

Protecting DNS servers with firewalls

As this section has made clear, a great deal of damage can be done to an organization if a DNS server is compromised. To mitigate this risk, limit access to your DNS server to only those clients that should be making DNS requests. Use packet filtering to block all traffic from DNS clients, except for packets transmitted by means of UDP or TCP port 53. If you plan to receive DNS requests from the public Internet, you will have to allow requests on UDP and TCP port 53 from all addresses. However, you should use packet filtering to block all other traffic destined to your DNS servers from the public Internet.

Security for Domain Controllers

Domain controllers are responsible for authenticating users on your network. In essence, they hold the keys to the kingdom. If an attacker compromises a domain controller, the attacker can use the information contained in Active Directory to map out network resources and might be able to use the information to access those resources.

See Also For information on controlling authorization for Active Directory objects, refer to Chapter 2, "Planning and Configuring an Authorization Strategy."

Configuring the Domain Controller role

The simplest way to install and configure Active Directory on a server is to install the domain controller role by using the Manage Your Server window. To install the domain controller role:

1. Click Start, and then click Manage Your Server.
2. Click Add Or Remove A Role. The Configure Your Server Wizard appears.
3. Click Next, click Domain Controller, and then click Next again. Follow the prompts to configure the new role.

The Active Directory database

Safeguarding the Active Directory database and log files is crucial to maintaining directory integrity and reliability. Moving the Ntds.dit, Edb.log, and Temp.edb files from their default locations will help to conceal them from an attacker if a domain controller is compromised. Furthermore, moving the files off the system volume to a separate physical disk will also improve domain controller performance.

If an attacker does gain access to a domain controller, it is likely that the attacker will attempt to discover user credentials by using password-cracking software. The System Key utility (Syskey) provides an extra line of defense against offline password-cracking software by using strong encryption techniques to secure account password information. By default, Syskey is enabled on all computers running Windows Server 2003 in Mode 1 (obfuscated key). There are many reasons to recommend using Syskey in Mode 2 (console password) or Mode 3 (floppy storage of Syskey password) for any domain controller that is exposed to physical security threats.

To create or update a system key:

1. Click Start, click Run, type **syskey**, and then click OK.
2. Click Encryption Enabled, and then click Update.
3. Click the desired option, and then click OK.

Logging considerations

Like DNS servers, Active Directory servers add event logs that can be viewed by using the Event Viewer console. Besides the DNS Server log, adding the Domain Controller role adds the Directory Service and File Replication Service roles. To ensure that these log files can store an adequate amount of information, consider increasing the maximum size of the log files. If you discover that you were attacked days, weeks, or months in the past, having a sufficiently large event log will allow you to review the logs from the period of the attack. Increasing the size of the Directory Service and File Replication Service log files from the 512-kilobyte (KB) default to 16 megabytes (MB) is generally sufficient.

Protecting domain controllers with firewalls

You should use a firewall to limit the opportunity an attacker has to connect to your domain controllers. Use packet filtering to block all unnecessary traffic to and from your domain controllers. Domain controllers use several different protocols for communicating with clients and peers. Whenever possible, limit the communication so that only the necessary ports are opened between a domain controller and another computer. Table 4.1 shows common domain controller communications and the port numbers used.

Table 4.1 Ports Used by Active Directory

Active Directory communication	Traffic required
A user network logon across a firewall	Microsoft-DS traffic (445/tcp, 445/udp) Kerberos authentication protocol (88/tcp, 88/udp) Lightweight Directory Access Protocol (LDAP) ping (389/udp) DNS (53/tcp, 53/udp)
A computer logon to a domain controller	Microsoft-DS traffic (445/tcp, 445/udp) Kerberos authentication protocol (88/tcp, 88/udp) LDAP ping (389/udp) DNS (53/tcp, 53/udp)

Table 4.1 Ports Used by Active Directory

Active Directory communication	Traffic required
Establishing a trust between domain controllers in different domains	Microsoft-DS traffic (445/tcp, 445/udp) LDAP (389/tcp or 686/tcp if using SSL) LDAP ping (389/udp) Kerberos authentication protocol (88/tcp, 88/udp) DNS (53/tcp, 53/udp)
Trust validation between two domain controllers	Microsoft-DS traffic (445/tcp, 445/udp) LDAP (389/tcp or 686/tcp if using SSL) LDAP ping (389/udp) Kerberos (88/tcp, 88/udp) DNS (53/tcp, 53/udp) Netlogon

Security for Internet Information Services

Internet Information Services (IIS) 6.0 is a complete Web server available in all versions of Windows Server 2003. Designed for intranets, the Internet, and extranets, IIS 6.0 makes it possible for organizations of all sizes to quickly and easily deploy powerful Web sites, applications, and Web services. In addition, IIS 6.0 provides a high-performance platform for applications built using the Microsoft .NET Framework.

> **See Also** Controlling access to Web content in IIS is done by using restrictive file permissions. For information about restricting file permissions, refer to Chapter 2, "Planning and Configuring an Authorization Strategy."

Changes since Windows 2000

Earlier versions of IIS have been popular security targets, and vulnerabilities in IIS have caused many Windows computers to be compromised. In order to reduce the Web infrastructure attack surface, IIS 6.0 is not installed by default on Windows Server 2003. You must explicitly select and install IIS 6.0 on all members of the Windows Server 2003 family, except for Windows Server 2003, Web Edition. This means that now it does not need to be uninstalled after Windows has been installed. IIS 6.0 will also be disabled when a server is being upgraded to Windows Server 2003, unless the IIS 5.0 Lockdown Tool has been installed prior to upgrade, or unless a registry key has been configured. If IIS isn't being used, you should explicitly disable it by using Group Policy settings.

IIS 6.0 is configured in a locked-down state when installed. After installation, IIS 6.0 accepts requests for only static files until configured to serve dynamic content, and all time-outs and settings are set to aggressively secure defaults. Programmatic functionality provided by Internet Server API (ISAPI) extensions or Common Gateway Interfaces (CGI) must be manually enabled by an IIS 6.0 administrator. ISAPI and CGI extend the functionality of your Web pages, and for this reason they are referred to as *Web service extensions*. For example, to run Active Server Pages (ASP) with this version of IIS 6.0, the ISAPI that implements ASP.dll must be specifically enabled as a Web service extension. Microsoft FrontPage Server extensions and Microsoft ASP.NET also have to be enabled before their functionality will work. Using the Web Service Extensions feature, Web site administrators can enable or disable IIS 6.0 functionality based on the individual needs of the organization. This functionality is globally enforced across the entire server. IIS 6.0 provides programmatic, command-line, and graphical interfaces for enabling Web service extensions.

By default, IIS 6.0 worker processes, which run Web service extensions, run as a Network Service account. The Network Service account is a new built-in account with exactly seven privileges:

- Adjust memory quotas for a process.
- Generate security audits.
- Log on as a service.
- Replace process-level token.
- Impersonate a client after authentication.
- Allow logon locally.
- Access this computer from the network.

Running as a low-privileged account is one of the most important security principles. The ability to exploit a security vulnerability can be contained effectively if the worker process has very few rights on the underlying system. Administrators can configure the application pool to run as any account (Network Service, Local System, Local Service, or a configured account) if desired.

See Also For information about IIS authentication options, refer to Chapter 1, "Planning and Configuring an Authentication Strategy."

Configuring the Application Server role

You can install IIS by using Add/Remove Windows Components and installing the Application Server component. However, the simplest way to install and configure the security settings for IIS is to install the Application Server role from the Manage Your Server window. Application Server is a new server role for Windows Server 2003 that combines IIS 6.0, the .NET Framework, ASP.NET, ASP, Universal Description Discovery and Integration (UDDI) Services, COM+, and Microsoft Message Queuing (MSMQ). To install the Application Server role:

1. Click Start, and then click Manage Your Server.
2. Click Add Or Remove A Role. The Configure Your Server Wizard appears.
3. Click Next, click Application Server, and then click Next again.
4. The Application Server Options page appears. As shown in Figure 4.6, you can choose to install the FrontPage Server Extensions and ASP.NET support. Select either option only if you have already determined that the option is required by your application. Both options carry the risk of introducing additional security vulnerabilities. You can always enable the options later if you need to. Click Next.

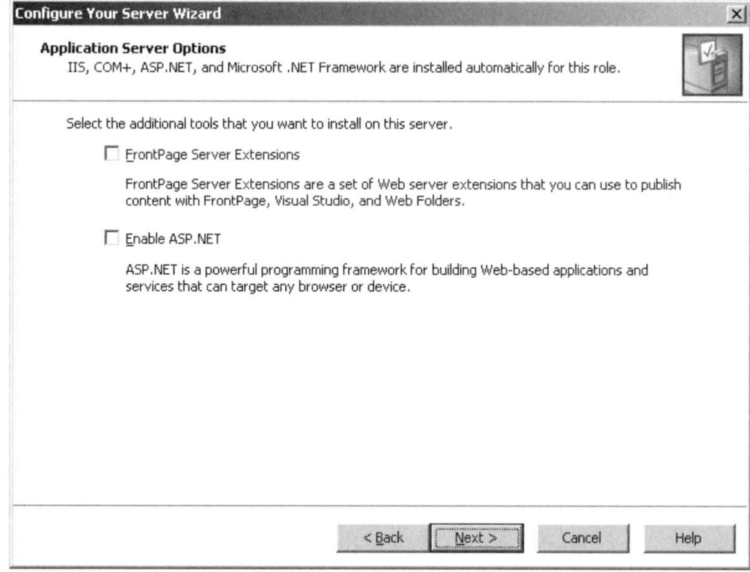

Figure 4.6 Configuring Application Server options

5. On the Summary page, click Next.
6. After Windows Server 2003 configures the Application Server role, click Finish.

IIS subcomponents

When using the Add/Remove Windows Components tool, you have a great deal of control over which IIS subcomponents will be installed. Understanding which of these components is required for your application to function is critical. Without a necessary component, parts of a Web application will simply not work. If unnecessary components are enabled, you are exposing the server to unnecessary risk. Table 4.2 describes the available IIS subcomponents and lists whether each component is automatically installed when you add the Application Server role.

Table 4.2 IIS Subcomponent Roles

Subcomponent	Description	Default setting
Background Intelligent Transfer Service (BITS) server extension	A background file transfer mechanism used by Windows Update and Automatic Update. This component is required when Windows updates or automatic updates are used to automatically apply service packs and hotfixes to an IIS server.	Disabled
Common Files	Files required by IIS. They must always be enabled on IIS servers.	Enabled
File Transfer Protocol (FTP) Service	Allows IIS servers to provide FTP services. This service is not required for dedicated IIS servers.	Disabled
FrontPage 2002 Server Extensions	Provides FrontPage support for administering and publishing Web sites. Disable on dedicated IIS servers when no Web sites use FrontPage extensions.	Disabled
Internet Information Services Manager	Administrative interface for IIS.	Enabled
Internet Printing	Provides Web-based printer management and allows printers to be shared over HTTP. This is not required on dedicated IIS servers.	Disabled
NNTP Service	Distributes, queries, retrieves, and posts Usenet news articles on the Internet. This component is not required on dedicated IIS servers.	Disabled
SMTP Service	Supports the transfer of e-mail. This component is not required on dedicated IIS servers.	Disabled
World Wide Web Service	Provides Web services and static and dynamic content to clients. This component is required on dedicated IIS servers.	Enabled

IP address and domain name restrictions

IIS can deny or allow incoming requests based on the source IP address, the network from which the request originated, or the source IP address's domain name. Although these techniques can be used for increasing the Web site's security, they are hardly impenetrable. Source IP addresses can be spoofed, and domain name lookups are only as secure as the DNS server hosting the reverse lookup domain. Nonetheless, they can be useful as part of a layered security strategy when used in conjunction with other security mechanisms.

To configure IP address and domain name restrictions for IIS:

1. Open the Internet Information Services Manager.
2. Right-click the Web site and click Properties.
3. Click the Directory Security tab.
4. Under IP Address And Domain Name Restrictions, click Edit.
5. To list IP addresses and domains that will be allowed and deny all other requests, click Denied Access. To list only those IP addresses and domains that should be ignored, click Granted Access.
6. Click the Add button.
7. Click Single Computer, Group Of Computers, or Domain Name. Provide the IP address, network ID and subnet mask, or domain name, and then click OK. Figure 4.7 demonstrates how to filter requests for the private network 192.168.1.0.

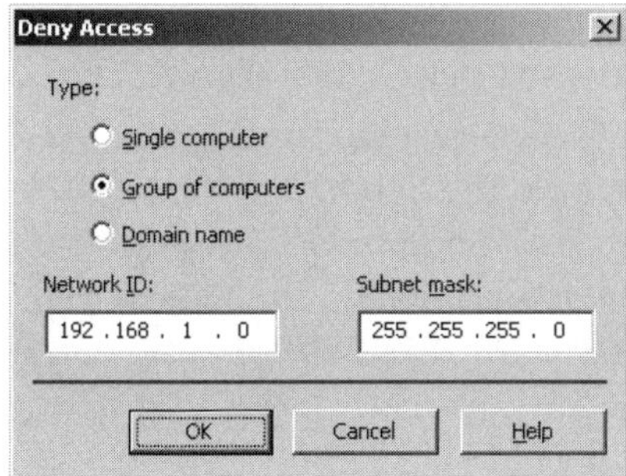

Figure 4.7 Filtering IIS requests by network

8. Repeat step 7 for each filter required.
9. Click OK twice to return to the Internet Information Services Manager.

If you restrict access by domain name, IIS has to perform a reverse DNS lookup for every new source IP address that sends a request. This slows down the responsiveness of the first page, which will probably upset your Webmaster. Additionally, if you have a busy site, all those DNS requests can really bog your DNS server.

Logging considerations

By default, IIS logs information about each incoming request to a text-based log file located within %systemroot%\System32\LogFiles\W3SVC*x*. These log files are completely separate from the logs viewable in Event Viewer. Each Web site creates a separate log file that includes information such as the source IP address, the number of bytes sent and received, the user name (if provided by the browser), and the type of browser used to make the request. Following is an example of a single log entry created when the Administrator user requested the page /autoupdate/administration/default.asp:

```
2003-07-28 13:38:34 127.0.0.1 GET /autoupdate/administration/default.asp -
 80 DOMAIN1\Administrator 127.0.0.1 Mozilla/
4.0+(compatible;+MSIE+6.0;+Windows+NT+5.2;+.NET+CLR+1.1.4322) 200 0 0
```

The information in this log file is primarily intended for nonsecurity-related analysis of Web site traffic. For example, members of the marketing team could use this information to determine which partner Web site was directing the highest number of users to the site. You should be familiar with IIS log files, however, because Web sites are a frequent point of entry for attackers, and analyzing IIS log files can reveal that you were attacked by a malicious user, the method the attacker used, and information about the attacker's identity.

Real World

If you host a public Web site, you are going to get attacked. In fact, you are probably going to get attacked dozens of times per day. There are thousands of systems infected with worms that perform automated attacks against random Web servers, and many of those worms are specifically seeking out earlier, nonupdated versions of IIS. Because of this, you should regularly review your IIS logs. If you don't have software specifically designed to analyze IIS logs and notify you about attacks, you can manually browse through the log files looking for unusual patterns. Look for requests for files that don't exist and requests that repeat on a regular basis.

If you discovered that someone had been coming to your home and trying to enter your house several times a day, you'd probably call the police. On the Internet, though, there are far too many attacks to notify the authorities about every single one. If and when you do find traces of a Web-based attack, you don't need to panic. First, examine the requests from that user's IP address to determine whether the attack originated from a worm. If it did, just make sure your system isn't vulnerable to attacks from that worm, and continue on with your day. You'll never be able to chase down every worm-infected host on the Internet.

If you determine that an attack originated from an actual attacker targeting your computer systems, such as an ex-employee or a competitor, you should follow up on the attack. If you decide that the attacker should be punished, you should report the attack to an appropriate law enforcement agency. The Department of Justice's How to Report Internet-Related Crime page is a useful reference, located at *http://www.cybercrime.gov/reporting.htm*.

If an attack is not serious enough to report to law enforcement, but you'd like to report it to the user's Internet service provider (ISP), find the user's IP address in the IIS log file and look it up at *http://whois.arin.net*. The American Registry for Internet Numbers (ARIN) site will tell you the ISP or organization that owns that IP address range, and usually provides an e-mail address and phone number for reporting abuse. It's up to the ISP whether, and how, they will deal with your complaint. They might choose to send the user a warning letter, ban the user completely, or simply do nothing.

IIS usage log information can also be sent directly to a database. This is useful if you manage multiple Web servers. Additionally, this improves the security of the log files. If an attacker compromises your Web server, the attacker will have to gain access to a second system, the database server, in order to erase traces of the attack present in the log file. Furthermore, logs can be written to a remote share over a network using a full Universal Naming Convention (UNC) path. Remote logging allows for administrators to set up centralized log file storage and backup. However, writing the log file over the network could negatively impact server performance.

Note IIS 6.0 creates a %systemroot%\System32\LogFiles\Httperr folder for log files with information about application errors. However, it is unlikely to be used for the purpose of identifying security incidents.

SSL encryption

Though IPSec can be configured to encrypt almost any type of network communication, IIS supports Hypertext Transfer Protocol Secure (HTTPS), an extension to HTTP that provides encryption by using a Secure Sockets Layer (SSL) certificate. If you host your own certification authority, you can create your own SSL certificate. However, if your certification authority is not a public authority that is trusted by your visitors' Web browsers, visitors will receive a warning message that your certificate is not from a trusted authority. To avoid this warning message, purchase an SSL certificate from a certification authority that is trusted by default by popular Web browsers.

To configure an IIS Web site with an SSL certificate:

1. Open the IIS Manager.
2. Right-click the Web site and click Properties.
3. Click the Directory Security tab.
4. Click Server Certificate.

   The Web Server Certificate Wizard appears.

5. Click Next.
6. Follow the prompts to create or import the SSL certificate for this site. When the wizard completes, click Finish.

See Also For more information about SSL certificates, refer to Chapter 11, "Deploying, Configuring, and Managing SSL Certificates."

Web site permissions

Although file permissions are used to restrict which users can access particular files, IIS uses Web site permissions to determine what HTTP actions can occur within a Web site, such as allowing script source access or directory browsing. Unlike file permissions, Web site permissions can be defined for Web sites or directories, but they cannot apply to individual files. Additionally, Web site permissions apply to all users who access the site.

Use the Internet Information Services Manager to specify Web site permissions. Valid choices are:

- **Read.** Users can view the content and properties of directories or files. This permission is selected by default.
- **Write.** Users can change content and properties of directories or files.
- **Script Source Access.** Users can access source files. If Read is also enabled, users can read source code; if Write is also enabled, users can change the source code.
- **Directory Browsing.** When a user requests a directory and a default file does not exist, IIS will generate a list of the directory contents that can be viewed in a browser.
- **Log Visits.** A log entry is created for each visit to the Web site.
- **Index This Resource.** Allows Indexing Service to index resources.
- **Execute.** The following options determine the level of script execution for users:
    - **None.** Does not allow scripts or executable files to run on the server.
    - **Scripts Only.** Allows only scripts to run on the server.
    - **Scripts And Executables.** Allows both scripts and executable files to run on the server.

Protecting IIS with firewalls

Web servers are commonly targeted by attackers, and, as a result, it is common practice to place a firewall between a Web server and end-users. If a simple port-filtering firewall is used, such as the Internet Connection Firewall, you will need to allow traffic using the port numbers you specify for each Web site in IIS Manager. By default, you should allow TCP port 80 for HTTP communications and TCP port 443 for encrypted HTTPS communications.

Application firewalls can provide greater security for IIS than that offered by simple packet-filtering firewalls. ISA and other application firewalls can examine inbound requests to your Web server, and outbound responses to Web clients, and use complex criteria to determine whether the request should be allowed or denied. For example, an application firewall could be configured to drop requests for confidential pages that originate from the public Internet. IIS can be configured similarly, but specifying the rules both within IIS and at the firewall provides a double-layered security combination that remains in place even if the security settings within IIS are changed.

Security for Internet Authentication Service

Internet Authentication Service (IAS) is a mechanism for authenticating users, not unlike Kerberos. IAS is also capable of providing user authorization and accounting for connection times, however. IAS acts as a Remote Authentication Dial-in User Service (RADIUS) server and proxy that provides compatibility with a wide variety of non-Microsoft hardware and software, including wireless routers, authenticating switches, remote access dial-up servers, and VPN connections.

IAS is often used to allow a third-party ISP to authenticate dial-in users against an organization's Active Directory database. This enables users to dial-in to an ISP by using their Active Directory user names and passwords, even if the ISP doesn't maintain the Active Directory service. RADIUS, like the Internet protocols Windows Server 2003 supports, is an Internet Engineering Task Force (IETF) standard.

Configuring IAS

IAS cannot be installed by using Manage Your Server. Instead, use Add/Remove Windows Components to install IAS:

1. Open Add Or Remove Programs in Control Panel.
2. Click Add/Remove Windows Components.
3. In the Windows Components Wizard, click Networking Services, and then click Details.

4. In the Networking Services dialog box, select Internet Authentication Service, click OK, and then click Next.
5. After IAS is installed, click Finish.

After IAS is installed, you can configure it by using the Internet Authentication Service console in the Administrative Tools program group.

RADIUS message authenticators

When you configure IAS for a RADIUS client, you configure the IP address of the client. If an incoming RADIUS Access-Request message does not originate from at least one of the IP addresses of configured clients, IAS automatically discards the message, providing protection for an IAS server. However, as discussed earlier, source IP addresses cannot be relied upon for authentication because they can be spoofed.

Shared secrets are used to verify that RADIUS messages, with the exception of Access-Request messages, are sent by a RADIUS-enabled device that is configured with the same shared secret. Shared secrets also verify that the RADIUS message has not been modified in transit (this is known as *message integrity*). Finally, the shared secret is used to encrypt some RADIUS attributes, such as User-Password and Tunnel-Password. To provide verification for messages, you can enable use of the RADIUS Message Authenticator attribute, as shown in Figure 4.8.

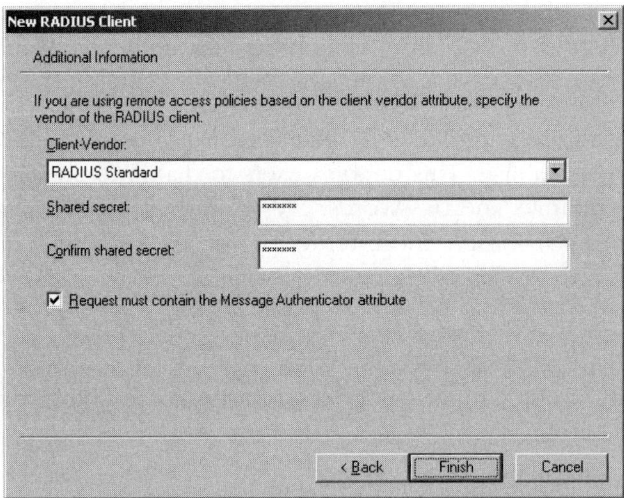

Figure 4.8 Using shared secrets and the Message Authenticator attribute

Note If you specify RADIUS clients by using an IP address range, all RADIUS clients within the address range must use the same shared secret.

Account lockout

You can use the remote access account lockout feature to specify how many times a remote access authentication can fail against a valid user account before the user is denied access. Remote access account lockout is especially important for remote access VPN connections over the Internet. An attacker on the Internet can attempt to access an organization intranet by sending credentials (valid user name, guessed password) during the VPN connection authentication process. During a dictionary attack, the attacker sends hundreds or thousands of credentials by using a list of passwords based on common words or phrases.

To enable remote access account lockout, you must set the MaxDenials value in the HKEY_LOCAL_MACHINE\SYSTEM\CurrentControlSet\Services\RemoteAccess\Parameters\AccountLockout registry key to 1 or greater. MaxDenials is the maximum number of failed attempts that can occur before the account is locked out. By default, MaxDenials is set to 0, which means that remote access account lockout is disabled.

To modify the amount of time that passes before the failed attempts counter is reset, you must set the ResetTime (mins) entry in the HKEY_LOCAL_MACHINE\SYSTEM\CurrentControlSet\Services\RemoteAccess\Parameters\AccountLockout registry key to the required number of minutes. By default, ResetTime (mins) is set to 0xb40, or 2,880 minutes (48 hours).

To manually reset a user account that has been locked out before the failed attempts counter is automatically reset, delete the HKEY_LOCAL_MACHINE\ SYSTEM\CurrentControlSet\Services\RemoteAccess\Parameters\AccountLockout\ *domain:user* registry key that corresponds to the user's account name.

Quarantine control

A remote access user provides credentials to demonstrate that he or she is a valid user, which offers some proof that the user is not an attacker. Authenticating a user does not determine whether that user's computer contains malicious software, such as a Trojan horse, a worm, or a virus. Fortunately, IAS provides quarantine control to help provide a way to determine whether a remote access user's computer is safe, which can prevent a user from unknowingly spreading worms and viruses into an otherwise secure network.

Network Access Quarantine Control, a new feature in Windows Server 2003, delays normal remote access to a private network until the configuration of the remote access computer has been examined and validated by an administrator-provided script. When a remote access computer initiates a connection to a remote access server, the user is authenticated and the remote access computer is assigned an IP address. However, the connection is placed in quarantine mode, in which network access is limited. The administrator-provided script is run on the remote access computer. When the script notifies the remote access server that it has successfully run, and the remote access computer complies with current network policies, quarantine mode is removed and the remote access computer is granted normal remote access.

The quarantine restrictions placed on individual remote access connections consist of a set of quarantine packet filters that restrict the traffic that can be sent to and from a quarantined remote access client, and a quarantine session timer that restricts the amount of time the client can remain connected in quarantine mode before being disconnected. Tools for configuring and implementing quarantine control are included with the Windows Server 2003 Resource Kit, available from *http://www.microsoft.com/windowsserver2003/techinfo/reskit/resourcekit.mspx*.

Logging considerations

IAS is capable of logging authentication requests and accounting requests. This information is vital for tracking when users attempt to connect and for identifying successful and unsuccessful attacks. To configure IAS logging:

1. Start the Internet Authentication Service console from the Administrative Tools program group.
2. Click the Remote Access Logging node in the left pane.
3. In the right pane, right-click Local File, and then click Properties.

   The Local File Properties dialog box appears.
4. Select Accounting Requests, Authentication Requests, and/or Periodic Status to enable logging for those items.

When IAS logging is enabled, log files are located by default in the %systemroot%\System32\LogFiles folder. The access control list on the LogFiles folder provides the best security for the IAS log files. The access control list is a list of users and groups that can access the folder. In addition, each user or group is assigned specific permissions that determine what actions the user or group can take with the folder. As with IIS, IAS logging can also be sent to a database server.

Protecting IAS with firewalls

If a firewall is positioned between the IAS server and a client or another IAS server, ports must be opened in the firewall. Authentication traffic uses UDP ports 1645 and 1812. Accounting traffic uses UDP ports 1813 and 1646. The notification and listener components of quarantine control use port 7250 by default. Therefore, you must allow network traffic on port 7250 through the firewall to enable the client computers to communicate with the remote access server listener.

Security for Exchange Server

Many enterprises build their messaging infrastructure on Exchange Server. Exchange provides a scaleable, reliable, Active Directory–integrated messaging platform. Exchange Server 2003 enables users to gain access to critical business communications almost whenever and wherever they need to, and it is designed to deliver greater security, availability, and reliability than other messaging platforms, and even earlier versions of Exchange.

Exam Tip Adding members to the Pre-Windows 2000 Compatible Access group always weakens security. For the exam, you should understand the implication for Exchange Server: Members of the Pre-Windows 2000 Compatible Access group can view a member list for mail-enabled groups that would otherwise be hidden.

Exam Tip This exam will not require detailed knowledge of Exchange Server. However, you should be familiar with the role Exchange Server and other messaging servers fulfill on the network, understand the potential vulnerabilities associated with this role, and be aware of the tools used to configure security for Exchange Server.

Security Alert Exchange Server is not built into Windows Server 2003. Therefore, you cannot rely on Windows Update to deliver security patches. Instead, visit *http://www.microsoft.com/exchange/downloads* to recieve the latest updates.

Exchange enables users to access their e-mail from a Web browser by connecting to an Outlook Web Access (OWA) server. OWA uses IIS; therefore, you must understand IIS to know how to configure security for OWA. After Exchange Server is installed, you manage it by using the System Manager in the Microsoft Exchange program group.

See Also For detailed information on securing Exchange, including security templates, read the Security Operations Guide for Exchange 2000 Server at *http://www.microsoft.com/technet/security/prodtech/mailexch/opsguide*.

Network encryption

Exchange uses the Transport Layer Security (TLS) protocol, which is based on and interoperable with SSL, to encrypt network communications. SSL is used by IIS and earlier versions of Exchange, including Exchange Server 5.5. To require TLS encryption:

1. Open the System Manager console.
2. Expand the Servers node, expand your server node, expand Protocols, and then expand SMTP.
3. Right-click the virtual server and then click Properties to open the Properties dialog box.
4. Click the Access tab.
5. Click Authentication. Select the Require TLS Encryption check box, as shown in Figure 4.9. Click OK.

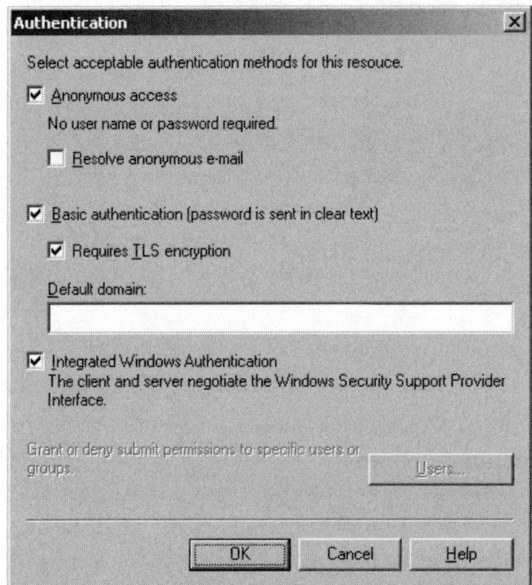

Figure 4.9 Exchange TLS encryption

6. Click the Delivery tab, and then click Outbound Security.
7. Select the TLS Encryption check box.
8. Click OK twice to return to System Manager.

Turning on TLS protects messages traveling between mail servers using SMTP but doesn't protect traffic traveling from clients to the server. To encrypt communications between Web browsers and OWA, enable the use of SSL on the Web server. Post Office Protocol version 3 (POP3) or Internet Message Access Protocol version 4 (IMAP4) users should use a client that supports the use of SSL with POP3 and IMAP4, such as

Microsoft Outlook Express. Alternatively, you can use IPSec to encrypt all traffic between clients and servers. IPSec encryption is transparent to both Exchange and the client application.

Logging considerations

Exchange is capable of logging almost every activity that occurs within the messaging server, including detailed information about messages sent to and from the server, by using the Message Tracking Center. While these logging options are essential for troubleshooting messaging problems, they are not likely to be used for security purposes (unless your server is being misused to transfer spam, which does happen).

The built-in auditing capabilities of Exchange are extremely useful for tracking use and misuse, however. Auditing in Exchange is implemented by means of the same mechanisms Windows Server 2003 uses, and auditing events will appear in the event log. To enable auditing in Exchange Server 2003:

1. Start System Manager, and expand the Servers node.
2. Right-click an auditable object, such as an address list, server, or mailbox store, and then click Properties.
3. Click the Security tab, and then click Advanced.
4. Click the Auditing tab.
5. Click the Add button, and then select users for whom you would like to audit actions.
6. The Auditing Entry dialog box appears. Select the auditing you want to enable, and then click OK.

   Notice that the Access list contains messaging-specific options such as Open Mail Send Queue, Send As, and Receive As.
7. Click OK twice to return to System Manager.

After enabling auditing, you can review auditing events in the Security event log by using the Event Viewer console.

Protecting Exchange Server with firewalls

You should use a firewall to stop unnecessary traffic from reaching your Exchange Server computers. Exchange Server computers can use several different protocols for communicating with clients and other mail servers. Whenever possible, limit the communication so that only the necessary ports are opened between an Exchange Server computer and another computer. Table 4.3 shows common domain controller communications and the port numbers used.

Table 4.3 Ports Used by Exchange Server

Network communication	Traffic required
Communications with domain controllers	LDAP standard protocol (389/tcp, 636/tcp if using SSL) Site Replication Service LDAP communications (379/tcp) Global Catalog LDAP communications (3268/tcp, 3269/tcp if using SSL)
Outgoing DNS queries to a DNS server	DNS (53/tcp and 53/udp)
Message transfer between servers	SMTP traffic (25/tcp, 465/tcp if using TLS) SMTP Link State Algorithm (691/tcp)
Client downloading e-mail using POP3	POP3 (110/tcp, 995/tcp if using SSL)
Client downloading e-mail using IMAP4	IMAP4 (143/tcp, 993/tcp if using SSL)
Client using newsreader	NNTP (119/tcp, 563/tcp if using SSL)
Web browsers downloading e-mail from OWA	HTTP protocol (80/tcp, 443/tcp if using SSL)
Clients using instant messaging	RVP (80/tcp and ports above 1024/tcp)
Clients using chat protocol	IRC/IRCX (6667/tcp, 994/tcp if using SSL)

Security for SQL Server

SQL Server is a popular database that acts as a back-end data store for many business applications that will run on Windows Server 2003. After SQL Server is installed, you manage it by using the Enterprise Manager in the Microsoft SQL Server program group.

Exam Tip Applications often store confidential information in a SQL Server database, and, as a result, knowing how to harden the security of a SQL Server computer is important both in the real world and for this exam. However, this exam will not require detailed knowledge of SQL Server. There are other certification exams dedicated to SQL Server. You should be familiar with the role SQL Server and other databases fulfill on the network, understand the potential vulnerabilities associated with this role, and be aware of the tools used to configure security for SQL Server.

> **Security Alert** SQL Server is not built into Windows Server 2003. Therefore, you cannot rely on Windows Update to deliver security patches. Instead, visit *http://www.microsoft.com/sql/downloads* to retrieve the latest updates.

Authentication

SQL Server supports two modes of authentication: Windows Authentication Mode and Mixed Mode. Windows Authentication Mode is the default authentication mode in SQL Server 2000. In Windows Authentication Mode, SQL Server 2000 relies solely on the Windows authentication of the user. Windows users or groups are then granted access to the SQL Server database resources.

Whenever possible, you should require Windows Authentication Mode for connections to SQL Server. This simplifies administration, provides single sign-on for users, and enables you to use Windows security enforcement mechanisms such as stronger authentication protocols and mandatory password complexity and expiration. Also, credentials delegation (the ability to bridge credentials across multiple servers) is only available in Windows Authentication Mode. On the client side, Windows Authentication Mode eliminates the need to store passwords, which is a major vulnerability in applications that use standard SQL Server logons.

In Mixed Mode, users can be authenticated by either Windows Authentication or by SQL Server Authentication. Users who are authenticated by SQL Server have their user name and password pairs maintained within SQL Server. If the client accessing the SQL Server database is unable to use a standard Windows logon, SQL Server requires a user name and password pair and compares this pair against those stored in its system tables.

To select an authentication mode by using Enterprise Manager:

1. Start Enterprise Manager.
2. Right-click a server, and then click Properties.
3. Click the Security tab, and then, under Authentication, click Windows Only or SQL Server And Windows, as shown in Figure 4.10.
4. Click OK.

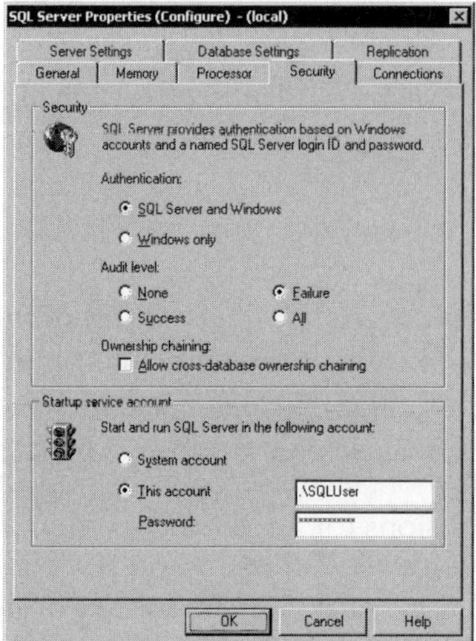

Figure 4.10 Configuring SQL Server authentication

When using Mixed Mode, you must be aware of an account named *sa*. The sa account in SQL Server is similar to the Administrator account in Windows; it is both highly privileged and built-in. Because it is built into SQL Server, it is the target of many SQL Server attacks. To decrease the risk of being exploited by such an attack, assign a strong password to the sa account. To assign the sa password:

1. Expand a server group, and then expand a server.
2. Expand Security, and then click Logins.
3. In the details pane, right-click SA, and then click Properties.
4. In the Password box, type the new password.

Authorization

SQL Server provides three authorization mechanisms: object permissions, statement permissions, and implicit permissions. Object permissions in SQL Server provide granular control over authorization to databases, tables, and even rows and columns of data contained within tables. You control access to these objects by granting, denying, or revoking the ability to run particular statements or stored procedures. For example, you can grant a user the right to SELECT information from a table, but deny the right to INSERT, UPDATE, or DELETE information in the table.

Note SELECT, INSERT, UPDATE, and DELETE are Structured Query Language (SQL) commands.

Statement permissions control administrative actions, such as creating a database or adding objects to a database. Only members of the System Administrators role and database owners can assign statement permissions. By default, normal logons aren't granted statement permissions, and you must specifically grant these permissions to logons of users that aren't administrators. For example, if a user needs to be able to create views in a database, you would assign permission to execute CREATE VIEW.

Only members of predefined system roles or database/database object owners can assign implied permissions. Implied permissions for a role can't be changed or applied to other accounts (unless these accounts are made members of the role). For example, members of the System Administrators server role can perform any activity in SQL Server. They can extend databases and kill processes. You can't revoke or assign these rights to other accounts individually.

Owners of databases and database objects also have implied permissions. These permissions allow them to perform all activities with either the databases or the objects they own, or with both. For example, a user who owns a table can view, add, change, and delete data. That user can also alter the table's definition and control the table's permissions.

Logging considerations

SQL Server includes its own authentication mechanism. To provide auditing of logon attempts for SQL Server logons, SQL Server can be configured to add events to the Application event log. This setting is set from the Security tab of the server properties dialog box. You can choose from four different auditing levels:

- **None.** No authentication logging is performed.
- **Failure.** Events are added to the Application event log when a user attempts to authenticate but fails.
- **Success.** Events are added when a user is successfully authenticated.
- **All.** Events are added with each authentication attempt, successful or unsuccessful.

Even if you enable authentication auditing to the Application log, you won't find details in the logs about certain user activities, such as which tables users access, which queries users run, and which stored procedures users invoke. To log details about these kinds of activities, use the Profiler tool, which can be started from within the SQL Server program group. Profiler can be used to create a trace of almost every activity that happens within a SQL Server database, including the exact queries submitted by users, as shown in Figure 4.11. If you believe you are being actively attacked, recording the queries submitted to SQL Server can provide you with a great deal of information about the attacker.

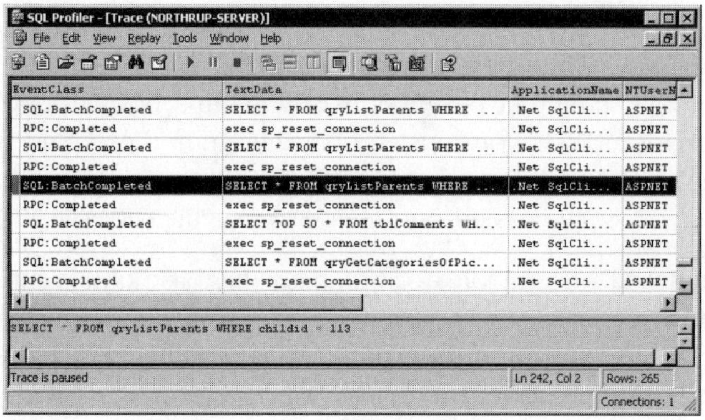

Figure 4.11 SQL Server trace data

Protecting SQL Server with firewalls

SQL Server databases should never be connected to the Internet without at least a packet-filtering firewall in place. Connecting a SQL Server database to even an internal network is risky, because other internal systems might become infected with a worm that could infect a system that accepts incoming database connections. To allow database clients to submit queries to the database server, you must allow packets with a TCP port of 1433 to be passed. However, because of the risk of worms that attempt to connect to this port, you should use a firewall to drop packets that are not from authorized database clients.

Practice: Hardening Servers and Analyzing Traffic

In this practice, you will configure packet filtering for a domain controller and analyze queries submitted to a computer running SQL Server.

Exercise 1: Configure packet filtering

In this exercise, you will configure packet filtering on Computer1 to reduce the network services that can be contacted to those required by the domain controller role.

1. Log on to the cohovineyard.com domain on Computer2 using the Administrator account.
2. Open a command prompt, and execute the command **Ping Computer1**. You should see four replies from Computer1, demonstrating that Computer1 is listening for and responding to ping requests.

3. Log on to the cohowinery.com domain on Computer1 using the Administrator account.
4. Click Start, click Control Panel, click Network Connections, right-click Local Area Connection, and then click Properties.
5. In the Local Area Connection Properties dialog box, click the Advanced tab.
6. Select the Protect My Computer And Network By Limiting Or Preventing Access To This Computer From The Internet check box.
7. Click the Settings button.
8. In the Advanced Settings dialog box, click Add. Fill in the values in the dialog box with the values in the first row of Table 4.4, and then click OK. Repeat this step for each row in Table 4.4.

Table 4.4 Active Directory Network Services

Description of service	Name or IP address	External and internal port number	TCP/UDP
DNS-TCP	127.0.0.1	53	TCP
DNS-UDP	127.0.0.1	53	UDP
Kerberos-TCP	127.0.0.1	88	TCP
Kerberos-UDP	127.0.0.1	88	UDP
LDAP-TCP	127.0.0.1	389	TCP
LDAP-UDP	127.0.0.1	389	UDP
Microsoft-DS-TCP	127.0.0.1	445	TCP
Microsoft-DS-UDP	127.0.0.1	445	UDP
LDAP-SSL-TCP	127.0.0.1	686	TCP

Note Remember, 127.0.0.1 refers to the local computer.

9. Click OK, and then click OK again to close the Advanced Settings dialog box. Click OK a third time to finalize the changes to the firewall configuration.
10. Return to the command prompt on Computer2, and repeat the **Ping Computer1** command. This time, no replies will be returned successfully. Ping uses the Internet Control Message Protocol (ICMP) protocol, which was not enabled when we configured the firewall on Computer1.
11. To ensure that future exercises work correctly on Computer1, disable the firewall. Click Start, click Control Panel, click Network Connections, right-click Local Area Connection, and then click Properties. In the Local Area Connection Properties dialog box, click the Advanced tab. Clear the Protect My Computer And Network By Limiting Or Preventing Access To This Computer From The Internet check box.

Exercise 2: Perform a trace on a SQL Server computer (optional)

In this exercise, you will perform a trace on a SQL Server computer to view the exact queries being submitted by database clients. To perform this exercise, you must have a Windows Server 2003–based computer with SQL Server 2000 installed, and active database clients. Do not perform this exercise on a production system, because performing a trace has a negative performance impact.

1. Log on to the SQL Server computer using an account that has administrator access to the database.
2. Start the SQL Profiler by clicking Start, clicking All Programs, clicking Microsoft SQL Server, and then clicking Profiler.
3. Click the File menu, click New, and then click Trace.
4. In the Connect To SQL Server dialog box, select your authentication method. If your account has administrator access to the database, click Windows Authentication, and then click OK. If you must connect using a SQL Server account, click SQL Server Authentication, provide your logon name and password, and then click OK.
5. In the Trace Properties dialog box, type **Security Audit** in the Trace Name box. Click Run.
6. Wait for a query to execute. Then, on the File menu, click Pause Trace.
7. Click each event, and examine the event details in the lower pane.
8. After you have familiarized yourself with the level of detail provided by the SQL Profiler tool, close it.

Lesson Review

The following questions are intended to reinforce key information presented in this lesson. If you are unable to answer a question, review the lesson materials and try the question again. You can find answers to the questions in the "Questions and Answers" section at the end of this chapter.

1. Which of the following types of servers should have traffic allowed on UDP port 53? (Choose all that apply.)
   a. DHCP servers
   b. DNS servers
   c. Domain controllers
   d. Web servers

e. RADIUS servers

f. Database servers

g. Messaging servers

---

2. Which of the following types of servers should have traffic allowed on TCP port 1433?

   a. DHCP servers

   b. DNS servers

   c. Domain controllers

   d. Web servers

   e. RADIUS servers

   f. Database servers

   g. Messaging servers

---

3. Which of the following types of servers create a dedicated event log that can be viewed by using Event Viewer? (Choose all that apply.)

   a. DHCP servers

   b. DNS servers

   c. Domain controllers

   d. Web servers

   e. RADIUS servers

   f. Database servers

   g. Messaging servers

---

4. Which of the following protocols can be used to encrypt traffic between a Web browser and an IIS computer?

   a. TLS

   b. EFS

   c. CHAP

   d. SSL

   e. RADIUS

Lesson Summary

- There are two major types of firewalls: host-based firewalls and network firewalls. Host-based firewalls, such as Internet Connection Firewall, protect a single system. Network firewalls, such as Microsoft Internet Security And Acceleration Server, can protect an entire network.
- Perimeter networks are used to provide multiple layers of network security for computers exposed to the public Internet. Internet-facing services such as mail servers and Web servers should be placed on a perimeter network, with a firewall protecting the systems from the Internet and a second firewall protecting the internal network from the perimeter network.
- Server roles that are often connected to the Internet, such as Web servers, DNS servers, and e-mail servers, are frequently subject to attacks. Security configuration is particularly important for these types of infrastructure servers.
- The security of DHCP and DNS servers is closely related because DHCP servers are often relied upon to register DNS names for clients. Both DHCP and DNS servers are vulnerable to denial-of-service attacks because they must accept requests from clients without authentication.
- Domain controllers store a map of the entire network and a complete set of user credentials. As a result, they are frequently the subject of attacks and must be protected at all costs. If a domain controller is compromised, the attacker might be able to gain access to many other resources on the network.
- SQL Server and Exchange Server are not built into Windows Server 2003. Nevertheless, both applications are frequently deployed on Windows Server 2003 networks, and they both often contain a great deal of confidential information. No security initiative is complete unless database and messaging systems have been protected.

Lesson 3: Analyzing Security Configurations

Over time, security configurations degrade unless they are maintained. When new vulnerabilities are discovered, updates must be applied to protect against attacks. When administrators troubleshoot problems, they might leave a computer in a less secure state than it was in when they began the troubleshooting. Fortunately, Microsoft provides tools to analyze Windows Server 2003 and other recent Windows operating systems for potential security vulnerabilities. This lesson will cover the most important tools for analyzing security configurations.

After this lesson, you will be able to

- Use the Security Configuration And Analysis tool to determine what active computer settings do not meet those specified by a security template.
- Use the Microsoft Baseline Security Analyzer (MBSA) to identify potential security vulnerabilities in Windows Server 2003 and other recent versions of Windows.
- Use the MBSA command-line interface to create an Extensible Markup Language (XML) file containing detailed information about a computer's potential security vulnerabilities.

Estimated lesson time: 30 minutes

Security Configuration And Analysis

The Security Configuration And Analysis snap-in gives you an immediate, detailed list of security settings on a computer that do not meet your security requirements. Recommendations are presented alongside current system settings, and icons or remarks are used to highlight any areas where the current settings do not match the proposed level of security. Security Configuration And Analysis uses a database to perform analysis and configuration functions. Using a database gives you the ability to compare the current security settings against custom databases that are created by importing one or more security templates.

To analyze a computer's security settings by comparing it to a security template:

1. Create a new Microsoft Management Console (MMC) console, and add the Security Configuration And Analysis snap-in.
2. Right-click Security Configuration And Analysis, and then click Open Database.
3. In the Open Database dialog box, type a name for the new database, and then click Open.
4. In the Import Template dialog box, select a security template to import. Click Open.

5. If you want to import more than one security template, right-click Security Configuration And Analysis, and then click Import Template. Select the template to import, and then click Open. Repeat this process for each security template you want to import.
6. Right-click Security Configuration And Analysis, and then click Analyze Computer Now.
7. In the Perform Analysis dialog box, click OK.

After the analysis is complete, examine the results by expanding the nodes contained within the Security Configuration And Analysis node.

You can also apply security settings by using the Security Configuration And Analysis tool, though it is generally more effective to apply security settings by using GPOs. To apply settings from one or more security templates to a computer:

1. Create a new MMC console, and add the Security Configuration And Analysis snap-in.
2. Right-click Security Configuration And Analysis, and then click Open Database.
3. In the Open Database dialog box, type a name for the new database, and then click Open.
4. In the Import Template dialog box, select a security template to import. Click Open.
5. If you want to import more than one security template, right-click Security Configuration And Analysis, and then click Import Template. Select the template to import, and then click Open. Repeat this process for each security template you want to import.
6. Right-click Security Configuration And Analysis, and then click Configure Computer Now.
7. In the Configure System dialog box, click OK.

The best way to familiarize yourself with what the Security Configuration And Analysis snap-in can do is to use the tool. Exercise 2 in this lesson guides you through the process of analyzing a test computer's security configuration.

Microsoft Baseline Security Analyzer—Graphical Interface

MBSA includes graphical and command-line interfaces that can perform local or remote scans of Windows systems. MBSA runs on computers running Windows 2000, Windows XP, and Windows Server 2003 and will scan for common system misconfigurations in Microsoft Windows NT 4.0, Windows 2000, Windows XP, Windows Server 2003, IIS 4.0 and 5.0, SQL Server 7.0 and SQL Server 2000, Internet Explorer 5.01 and later, and Office 2000 and Office XP. MBSA will also scan for missing security updates for the following products: Windows NT 4.0, Windows 2000, Windows XP, Windows Server 2003, IIS 4.0 and 5.0, SQL Server 7.0 and SQL Server 2000, Internet Explorer 5.01 and later, Exchange Server 5.5 and Exchange 2000 Server, and Microsoft Windows Media Player 6.4 and later.

MBSA can determine which critical security updates are applied to a system by referring to an XML file that is continuously updated by Microsoft. The XML file contains information about which security updates are available for particular Microsoft products. This file contains security bulletin names and titles, and detailed data about product-specific security updates, including the files in each update package and their versions and checksums, registry keys that were applied by the update installation package, information about which updates supersede others, related Microsoft Knowledge Base article numbers, and much more.

When you run MBSA for the first time, it will automatically download a copy of this XML file so that the tool can find the security updates that are available for each product. However, you must be connected to the Internet for this download to be successful. MBSA downloads the XML file in a compressed, digitally signed .cab file, verifies the signature, and then decompresses the file to the local computer on which MBSA is running. After you run MBSA, it displays a detailed list of potential vulnerabilities, as shown in Figure 4.12.

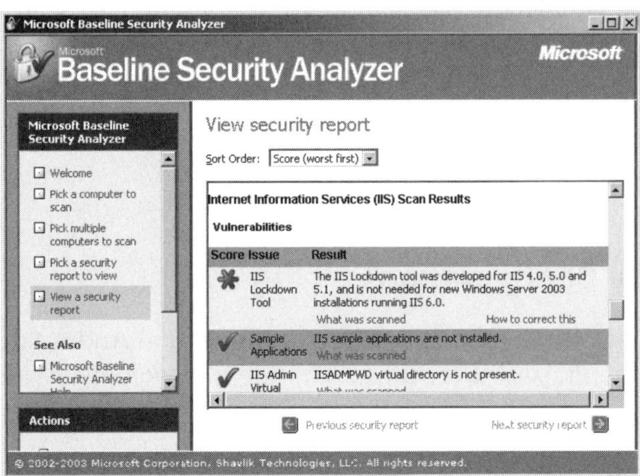

Figure 4.12 Microsoft Baseline Security Analyzer IIS results

See Also To download MBSA and read more about it, visit *http://www.microsoft.com/technet/security/tools/mbsahome.asp*.

Microsoft Baseline Security Analyzer—Command-Line Interface

Always use the MBSA graphical interface when manually scanning a system. However, if you administer more than a handful of systems, you will want to be able to automate security analysis by using scripts. Fortunately, MBSA provides a command-line interface named Mbsacli that is specifically designed to be used within a script.

Mbsacli is automatically installed with MBSA, but it is not added to the default path. To run the program, you must open a command prompt and switch to the directory into which you installed MBSA. By default, this path is C:\Program Files\Microsoft Baseline Security Analyzer.

One of the most useful features of Mbsacli is to create an XML file containing the results of an MBSA scan. Although you can use a recent Web browser to view the XML file, they are rather difficult for a human to read. They are more useful when a developer, or an administrator with scripting skills, creates a program that parses and analyzes them. You can use this functionality to integrate MBSA data into your organization's custom management tools.

To scan all computers in the 192.168.1.0 network, run the following command from the C:\Program Files\Microsoft Baseline Security Analyzer directory:

Mbsacli –r 192.168.1.1-192.168.1.254

For a complete description of Mbsacli command-line options, run Mbsacli /? from a command line.

> **Note** Mbsacli is a replacement for Hfnetchk. Mbsacli supports an Hfnetchk mode when used with the /hf parameter.

Practice: Analyzing Security Configurations

In this practice, you will use MBSA and the Security Configuration And Analysis snap-in to analyze the security settings of a computer and identify potentially insufficient policies.

Exercise 1: Scan a computer with MBSA

In this exercise, you will use MBSA to scan a computer. You should have Internet connectivity to take advantage of all of the features of MBSA, but, for security reasons, do not connect the test systems running Windows Server 2003 to the Internet. Instead, download and install MBSA on an existing Internet-connected computer with Windows 2000, Windows XP, or Windows Server 2003.

1. Start the Microsoft Baseline Security Analyzer tool.
2. Click Scan More Than One Computer.
3. On the Pick Multiple Computers To Scan page, examine the settings. Note that you can choose to scan an entire domain, or you can scan by using an IP address range.
4. In the left pane, click Welcome.
5. Click Scan A Computer.
6. On the Pick A Computer To Scan page, select the local Internet-connected computer.

   Note the scanning options that you can select, including checking for known vulnerabilities in Windows, IIS, or SQL Server, checking for weak passwords, and checking for security updates that haven't been applied. By default, the Use SUS option is not selected. When selected, you can use a Software Update Server (SUS) to determine which security updates need to be applied to the computer.

See Also For more information on SUS, refer to Chapter 5, "Planning an Update Management Infrastructure," and Chapter 6, "Assessing and Deploying an Update Management Infrastructure."

7. Click Start Scan.
8. MBSA might take several minutes to scan your computer.
9. The View Security Report page appears. Examine the results for your computer.

If you haven't scanned this computer with MBSA previously, you almost certainly have failed some critical checks, which will be marked with a red X. For each of these line items, click Result Details to identify exactly what was missing and to read more information on how to resolve the problem.

Exercise 2: Analyze a computer with Security Configuration and Analysis

In this exercise, you will analyze Computer1's security settings by using the Security Configuration And Analysis snap-in.

1. Log on to the cohowinery.com domain on Computer1 using the Administrator account.
2. Create a new MMC console, and add the Security Configuration And Analysis snap-in.
3. Right-click Security Configuration And Analysis, and then click Open Database.
4. In the Open Database dialog box, type **newdb**, and then click Open.

5. In the Import Template dialog box, select C:\Windows\Security\Templates\Hisecdc.inf. Click Open.
6. Right-click Security Configuration And Analysis, and then click Analyze Computer Now.
7. In the Perform Analysis dialog box, click OK.
8. Expand Security Configuration And Analysis, and then expand Account Policies.
9. Click Password Policy.
10. Notice the policies listed in the right pane. The policies that do not meet or exceed the settings specified in the Hisecdc.inf security template are marked with a red X, as shown in Figure 4.13.

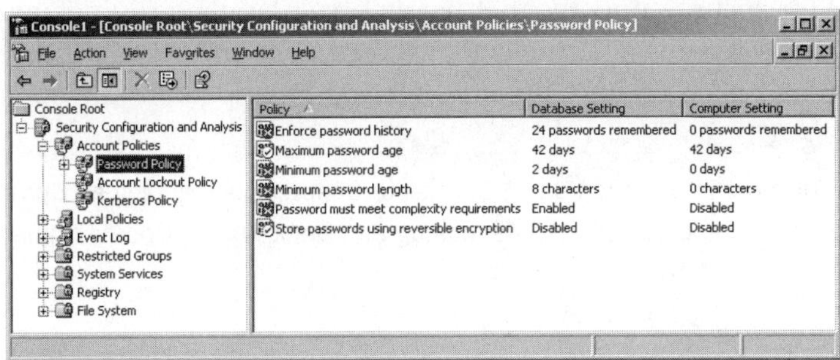

Figure 4.13 Security Configuration And Analysis identifying deficient settings

Lesson Review

The following questions are intended to reinforce key information presented in this lesson. If you are unable to answer a question, review the lesson materials and try the question again. You can find answers to the questions in the "Questions and Answers" section at the end of this chapter.

1. Which command would cause Mbsacli to analyze all computers on the network 10.236.122.0/24 subnet?
   a. mbsacli /r 10.236.122.1-10.236.122.254
   b. mbsacli /i 10.236.122.0/24
   c. mbsacli /r 10.236.122.0
   d. mbsacli /i 10.236.122.0 255.255.255.0

2. Which of the following functions can be performed with the Security Configuration And Analysis console? (Choose all that apply.)
   a. Create an XML file containing a summary of a computer's security settings.
   b. Compare the current configuration settings against a security template.
   c. Identify which GPO is responsible for a specific policy setting.
   d. Apply a security template to the local computer.

____

____

Lesson Summary

- The Security Configuration And Analysis console can be used to apply settings from a security template. However, it is more commonly used to determine which active security settings do not match those specified in a security template.
- MBSA identifies potential security vulnerabilities, including critical updates that have not been applied, on one or more systems.
- Mbsacli provides a command-line interface with functionality that is similar to that of MBSA. Mbsacli can be used to create XML files that summarize security vulnerabilities on one or more systems.

Case Scenario Exercise

The Chief Security Officer (CSO) of your organization has asked you to create a network design for the three new servers that you will be deploying: one Exchange Server computer, one IIS computer, and one DNS server. Currently, these services are provided by your ISP, but the Chief Information Officer (CIO) wants to reduce costs by bringing these services in-house. All three computers must be accessible to users on both the public Internet and the internal network. Unfortunately, your CIO has no budget for additional servers. You do, however, have an existing Internet connection with a firewall. You only have a single firewall with a total of four network interfaces.

Your CSO stresses that security is extremely important. The employees of your organization frequently send confidential information through e-mail, and if your Exchange Server computer were compromised, the losses could be huge. Your Web server hosts your company's Web site. The Web site is your company's online identity, and if an attacker were to modify the content on the site, it would hurt the image of the company. Your DNS server holds records for every system on your internal network, and if compromised, it would provide an attacker with a roadmap for future attacks against your intranet. Worse yet, a savvy attacker could modify your DNS records to get internal computers to communicate confidential information to computers controlled by the attacker.

The following questions are intended to reinforce key information presented in this lesson. If you are unable to answer a question, review the lesson materials and try the question again. You can find answers to the questions in the "Questions and Answers" section at the end of this chapter.

1. How would you design the network?

2. To which of the following ports will you have to configure the firewall to forward to the perimeter network?
   - **a.** 53/udp
   - **b.** 53/tcp
   - **c.** 80/udp
   - **d.** 80/tcp
   - **e.** 25/udp
   - **f.** 25/tcp
   - **g.** 110/udp
   - **h.** 110/tcp
   - **i.** 1433/udp
   - **j.** 1433/tcp

3. How many security templates would you use to configure and analyze the security settings on this network?

____
____
____
____
____
____
____
____

4. Besides configuring the initial security settings on the Web, messaging, and DNS servers, what security-related tasks should be performed on an ongoing basis?

____
____
____
____

Troubleshooting Lab

In this lab, you troubleshoot a problem related to a user not being able to run an application that is required for the user's job. To complete this lab, you must have completed the exercise in Lesson 1 of this chapter.

A user is experiencing frequent Stop errors on his desktop computer, which runs Windows XP. To troubleshoot the problem, you decide to selectively disable services by using the Startup tab of the System Configuration Utility (Msconfig.exe). However, when you log on to his computer as an Administrator, you are unable to run the Msconfig.exe file. Instead, you receive a message that says, "Windows cannot open this program because it has been prevented by a software restriction policy. For more information, open Event Viewer or contact your system administrator." You are the system administrator, so it's up to you to fix it.

The following questions are intended to reinforce key information presented in this lesson. If you are unable to answer a question, review the lesson materials and try the question again. You can find answers to the questions in the "Questions and Answers" section at the end of this chapter.

1. Which of the following tools can you use to identify the source of the problem? (Choose all that apply.)

   a. Event Viewer

   b. Gpresult

   c. Resultant Set Of Policy

   d. Security Templates

2. After identifying the source of the problem, list three ways to resolve or work around the problem by allowing yourself to run Msconfig.

Chapter Summary

- Software restriction policies can be applied to a GPO to restrict the applications that can run on a target system. Software restriction policies can restrict applications based on a hash of the executable file, the path in the file system, a certificate associated with the application, or the Internet zone from which the application is running.
- You should create security templates for the various computer roles in your organizations, including desktop computers, mobile computers, and kiosks. Whenever possible, base these on predefined security templates.
- Security templates are useful for creating GPOs, but they contain only a subset of the settings available when configuring a GPO. Therefore, after importing a security template into a GPO, you might have to use the Group Policy Object Editor to specify additional settings.
- Mobile computers do not have the same security considerations as desktop computers. Mobile computers are subject to a wider array of network attacks because they might connect to unprotected networks. Additionally, they are more likely to be stolen, so encryption of the disk's physical contents might be necessary.
- Kiosks require tightly restricted security settings to prevent abuse. GPOs allow an administrator to remove all major user interface elements and to configure kiosk computers to log on a user and start a single application automatically at startup.
- There are two major types of firewalls: host-based firewalls and network firewalls. Host-based firewalls, such as Internet Connection Firewall, protect a single system. Network firewalls, such as Internet Security And Acceleration Server, can protect an entire network.
- Perimeter networks are used to provide multiple layers of network security for computers exposed to the public Internet. Internet-facing services such as mail servers and Web servers should be placed on a perimeter network, with a firewall protecting the systems from the Internet and a second firewall protecting the internal network from the perimeter network.
- Server roles that are often connected to the Internet, such as Web servers, DNS servers, and e-mail servers, are frequently subject to attacks. Security configuration is particularly important for these types of infrastructure servers.
- The security of DHCP and DNS servers is closely related because DHCP servers are often relied upon to register DNS names for clients. Both DHCP and DNS servers are vulnerable to denial-of-service attacks because they must accept requests from clients without authentication.

- Domain controllers store a map of the entire network and a complete set of user credentials. As a result, they are frequently the subject of attacks and must be protected at all costs. If a domain controller is compromised, the attacker might be able to gain access to many other resources on the network.
- SQL Server and Exchange Server are not built into Windows Server 2003. Nevertheless, both applications are frequently deployed on Windows Server 2003 networks, and both applications often contain a great deal of confidential information. No security initiative is complete unless database and messaging systems have been protected.
- The Security Configuration And Analysis console can be used to apply settings from a security template. However, it is more commonly used to determine which active security settings do not match those specified in a security template.
- MBSA identifies potential security vulnerabilities, including critical updates that have not been applied, on one or more systems.
- Mbsacli provides a command-line interface with functionality that is similar to that of MBSA. Mbsacli can be used to create XML files that summarize security vulnerabilities on one or more systems.

Exam Highlights

Before taking the exam, review the key topics and terms that are presented in this chapter. You need to know this information.

Key Topics

- Understand the various roles that client computers play on the network and how each role should be configured separately.
- Be familiar with the tools you can use to control client systems, including how to configure and deploy software restrictions, how to limit a user's access to the graphical interface, and how to protect the data on a computer in the event of theft.
- Know the major roles that server computers fulfill on a network, and know how security should be configured for each. Understand how firewalls and perimeter networks should be used to create barriers between public and private networks.
- Be able to configure packet filters to allow legitimate traffic to and from various server roles.
- Understand the role that logging plays in identifying successful and unsuccessful attacks. Be able to configure logging for common server roles.
- Be able to use several different tools to analyze a computer's security configuration and the status of critical updates on the computer.

Key Terms

denial-of-service attack An attack that prevents users from using network resources.

firewall A system that creates a boundary between a public and private network.

man-in-the-middle attack A security attack in which an attacker intercepts and possibly modifies data that is transmitted between two users. To each user, the attacker pretends to be the other user. During a successful man-in-the-middle attack, the users are unaware that there is an attacker between them who is intercepting and modifying their data. Also referred to as a *bucket brigade attack*.

packet filter A basic function of firewalls that examines incoming and outgoing packets and drops packets based on predefined criteria, such as port numbers, source IP address, and destination IP address.

perimeter network A small network that is set up separately from an organization's private network and the Internet. A perimeter network provides a layer of protection for internal systems in the event that a system offering services to the Internet is compromised. Also known as a *demilitarized zone (DMZ)* or a *screened subnet*.

Questions and Answers

Lesson 1 Review

Page 4-13

1. Which of the following software restriction rules can be used to allow any application on an intranet to be run on a computer?
   - **a.** Hash rules
   - **b.** Certificate rules
   - **c.** Path rules
   - **d.** Internet zone rules

   d. Internet zone rules restrict or allow applications to run based on the zone configurations in Internet Explorer, which can be used to specify networks that are part of the intranet.

2. Which of the following software restriction rules should be used to ensure that a particular executable file cannot be run?
   - **a.** Hash rules
   - **b.** Certificate rules
   - **c.** Path rules
   - **d.** Internet zone rules

   a. Hash rules can prevent an application from running, regardless of where the executable file is located or what it is named. However, if a new version of the executable file is released, the hash rule must be updated to remain effective.

3. Which of the following rules would you not enforce on a computer to be used as a kiosk?
   - **a.** Remove the Run menu item from the Start menu.
   - **b.** Deny the Everyone group the right to log on locally.
   - **c.** Require a user to log on automatically.
   - **d.** Deny the interactive user the right to change his or her own password.

   b. A user should be configured to log on automatically; however, denying the Everyone group the right to log on interactively would not allow any user to log on, whether manually or automatically.

Lesson 2 Review

Page 4-52

1. Which of the following types of servers should have traffic allowed on UDP port 53?
   - **a.** DHCP servers
   - **b.** DNS servers
   - **c.** Domain controllers
   - **d.** Web servers
   - **e.** RADIUS servers
   - **f.** Database servers
   - **g.** Messaging servers

   b and c. UDP port 53 is used for DNS requests. DNS servers must be able to receive DNS requests. Domain controllers often, but not always, act as DNS servers.

2. Which of the following types of servers should have traffic allowed on TCP port 1433?
   - **a.** DHCP servers
   - **b.** DNS servers
   - **c.** Domain controllers
   - **d.** Web servers
   - **e.** RADIUS servers
   - **f.** Database servers
   - **g.** Messaging servers

   f. SQL Server uses TCP port 1433 to accept database queries.

3. Which of the following types of servers creates a dedicated event log that can be viewed by using Event Viewer?
   - **a.** DHCP servers
   - **b.** DNS servers
   - **c.** Domain controllers
   - **d.** Web servers
   - **e.** RADIUS servers
   - **f.** Database servers
   - **g.** Messaging servers

b and c. The DNS server role creates the DNS Server event log, and the domain controller role creates the Directory Service and File Replication Service event logs.

4. Which of the following protocols can be used to encrypt traffic between a Web browser and an IIS computer?

   a. TLS

   b. EFS

   c. Challenge Handshake Authentication Protocol (CHAP)

   d. SSL

   e. RADIUS

d. SSL is a standard method for encrypting traffic between Web browsers and servers.

Lesson 3 Review

Page 4-60

1. Which command would cause Mbsacli to analyze all computers on the network 10.236.122.0/24 subnet?

   a. mbsacli /r 10.236.122.1-10.236.122.254

   b. mbsacli /i 10.236.122.0/24

   c. mbsacli /r 10.236.122.0

   d. mbsacli /i 10.236.122.0 255.255.255.0

a. The /r option causes Mbsacli to scan a range of IP addresses.

2. Which of the following functions can be performed with the Security Configuration And Analysis console? (Choose all that apply.)

   a. Create an XML file containing a summary of a computer's security settings.

   b. Compare the current configuration settings against a security template.

   c. Identify which GPO is responsible for a specific policy setting.

   d. Apply a security template to the local computer.

b and d. The Security Configuration And Analysis console can be used to apply security templates and to compare existing settings against a security template.

Design Activity: Case Scenario Exercise

Page 4-62

1. How would you design the network?

   Given that you only have a single firewall to work with, you would probably design the network as shown in Figure 4.14. This design creates separate networks for the intranet and for the servers providing services to the public Internet, and it ensures that all traffic is protected by a firewall. Using a single firewall represents an acceptable security risk for your organization—if an attacker manages to compromise the firewall, the attacker will be able to access both the perimeter network and your internal network. Given your budget limitations, this is the best you can do.

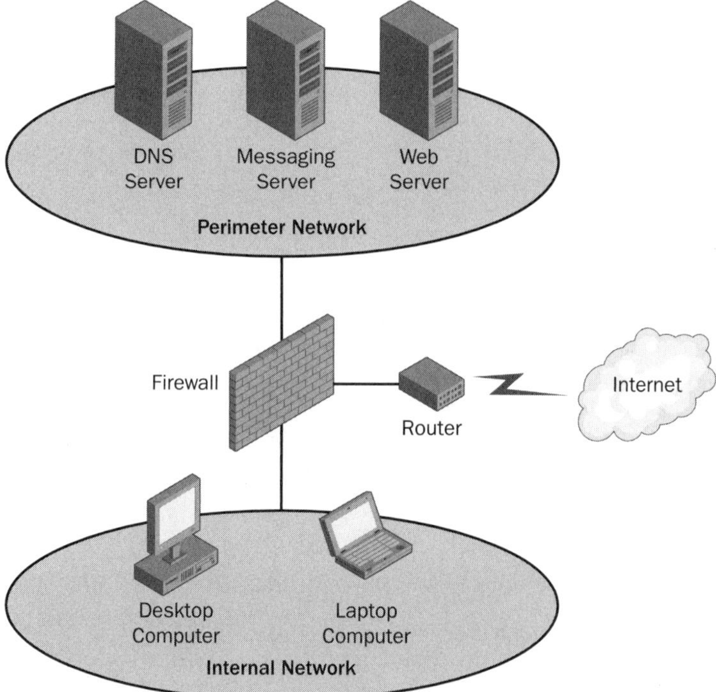

Figure 4.14 Suggested perimeter network architecture

2. To which of the following ports will you have to configure the firewall to forward to the perimeter network?

   a. 53/udp

   b. 53/tcp

   c. 80/udp

d. 80/tcp

e. 25/udp

f. 25/tcp

g. 110/udp

h. 110/tcp

i. 1433/udp

j. 1433/tcp

a, b, d, and f. 53/udp and 53/tcp are used for DNS requests, which you must accept from the public Internet. 80/tcp is used for Web requests, but 80/udp is not. 25/tcp is used for SMTP, which mail servers use to communicate with each other. 110/tcp is used for clients downloading e-mail and would have to be allowed between the internal network and the perimeter network. However, there was no mention of clients retrieving e-mail from the public network, so there is no reason to allow that traffic from the Internet connection. 1433/tcp is used for SQL Server requests, but there is no SQL Server on this network.

3. How many security templates would you use to configure and analyze the security settings on this network?

   You would definitely create separate security templates for the Web, messaging, and DNS server roles. If the firewall is based on a computer running Windows, you should create a security template for that as well. However, the scenario doesn't mention the platform used for the firewall, and most firewalls are dedicated devices that are not compatible with security templates. You would also have at least one security template for the computers on the internal network. If you have multiple computer types on the internal network, such as desktop and mobile computers, each type requires a separate security template.

4. Besides configuring the initial security settings on the Web, messaging, and DNS servers, what security-related tasks should be performed on an ongoing basis?

   On a regular basis, you should analyze the security settings on the servers by using MBSA. MBSA will also reveal whether any security updates have been released but not applied. Additionally, you should configure logging for each of the systems and review the logs on a regular basis for signs of attacks and security compromises.

Design Activity: Troubleshooting Lab

Page 4-64

1. Which of the following tools can you use to identify the source of the problem? (Choose all that apply.)

   a. Event Viewer

   b. Gpresult

   c. Resultant Set Of Policy

   d. Security Templates

   a, b, and c. The System log in Event Viewer will show events with a source of Software Restriction Policy that indicate that a software restriction policy prevented an application from running. In this case, the event has an Event ID of 866, which indicates that the restriction was placed on a specific path. The Gpresult /Z command lists all the computer and user GPOs that were applied, including details about software restriction policies. Finally, Resultant Set Of Policy is the most efficient way to identify the source of the problem.

2. After identifying the source of the problem, list three ways to resolve or work around the problem by allowing yourself to run Msconfig.

   Valid answers include:

   a. Copy the Msconfig.exe folder to a folder that is not included in a software restriction policy.

   b. Restart the computer in safe mode.

   c. Unlink the GPO from Active Directory, and then refresh Group Policy.

   d. Modify the GPO so that the software restriction policy does not apply to administrators, and then refresh Group Policy.

   e. Link a second GPO that overrides the software restriction policies of the existing GPO, and then refresh Group Policy.

5 Planning an Update Management Infrastructure

Exam Objectives in this Chapter:

- Plan the deployment of service packs and hotfixes.
  - Evaluate the applicability of service packs and hotfixes.
  - Test the compatibility of service packs and hotfixes for existing applications.
  - Plan update deployment environments for both the pilot and production phases.
  - Plan the batch deployment of multiple hotfixes.
  - Plan rollback strategy.

Why This Chapter Matters

Organizations depend on information technology resources and expect them to be trustworthy: a few hours of downtime is expensive, and a publicized security compromise can be disastrous. Viruses and worms such as Klez, Nimda, and SQL Slammer exploit known fixable security vulnerabilities in software to attack computers, and then use those compromised computing resources to launch new attacks. After a computer is infected, the virus or worm often opens new security vulnerabilities that enable an attacker to explore your internal network, shut down network resources, and gather confidential files.

Update management is a process that gives you control over the deployment and maintenance of software updates on your production computers. An effective update management process could have prevented a majority of the security compromises that have occurred on Microsoft Windows networks in the past few years. While update management might seem like a time-consuming, costly process, it is far more efficient to proactively update computers than it is to repair them after a known vulnerability is exploited.

Lessons in this Chapter:

Before You Begin

This chapter presents the skills and concepts that are required to plan an update management infrastructure to maintain an entire network of Windows-based computers. Because this chapter focuses on planning, it does not require any hardware or software.

Lesson 1: Updating Fundamentals

Microsoft continually works to improve its software. As part of this effort, Microsoft develops updates to solve problems that are discovered in software after the software is released. These problems often constitute security vulnerabilities.

There are, however, many different types of security vulnerabilities. Some have known exploits that are propagating quickly, and it is critical that these vulnerabilities are quickly fixed. *Exploits* are worms, viruses, Trojan horses, or other tools that can be used by an attacker to compromise a vulnerable computer. Others are less critical, and the risk of them being exploited isn't high enough to justify the cost of rapidly deploying an update. Vulnerabilities might only apply to a handful of computers on your network, or they might affect every system. To address the wide variety of vulnerabilities, Microsoft provides several different types of updates throughout the lifecycle of a supported product.

This lesson describes the different types of updates released by Microsoft. It will also describe the Microsoft product lifecycle, which affects update management because Microsoft stops releasing security updates for products at the end of the lifecycle.

After this lesson, you will be able to

- Describe the differences between the types of updates that Microsoft might release.
- Understand the reasons to apply each type of update, and the reasons not to apply them.
- Plan around the lifecycles of Microsoft products to ensure that software used in your production environment is supported.

Estimated lesson time: 30 minutes

Introduction to Updates

An update, also known as a *patch*, is a file or a collection of files that you can apply to a Windows-based computer to correct a specific problem. Microsoft packages updates in a single self-contained, self-installing executable file with an .exe extension. By default, all updates automatically back up files that they replace so that you have the option of removing the update later if you want to.

Updates for the Microsoft Windows Server 2003 family and Windows XP 64-Bit Edition Version 2003 are named according to specific conventions. For updates you install on 32-bit versions of the Windows Server 2003 family, the convention is WindowsServer2003-KB######-x86-*LLL*.exe. For updates you install on 64-bit versions of the Windows Server 2003 family or Windows XP 64-Bit Edition Version 2003, the convention is WindowsServer2003-KB######-ia64-*LLL*.exe.

Updates for other operating systems and applications use a similar naming scheme. Windows XP updates, logically, use the convention WindowsXP-KB######-x86-*LLL*.exe, while Windows 2000 updates use the Windows2000-KB######-x86-*LLL*.exe convention. In all cases, *######* represents the Microsoft Knowledge Base article number, and *LLL* represents the three-letter language code. For example, the 32-bit English version of the update associated with Knowledge Base article 824105 is named WindowsServer2003-KB824105-x86-ENU.exe. The 64-bit French version of the update is named WindowsServer2003-KB824105-ia64-FRA.exe.

Updates are applied only to software that is already installed when you apply the update. For instance, if you uninstall Internet Information Services (IIS) and then later reinstall it, you must also reinstall any IIS updates. The exception to this, however, is service packs. After you install a service pack, fixes are applied to all components you add or reinstall without you having to reinstall the service pack.

Types of Updates

There are many different types of problems that might need to be fixed in any piece of software, and various types of problems must be dealt with differently. When a security vulnerability is discovered in Windows, Microsoft must provide an update to customers quickly so that the vulnerability can be removed before the vulnerability is exploited on a large scale.

Though most recent updates are security related, other types of updates address reliability problems. Over time, customers might find problems related to the compatibility or reliability of a piece of software. Updates that resolve these problems are less critical to customers not actively experiencing the problem, because, although they improve the software, the cost associated with not applying the update quickly is much lower.

To address the various types of problems that might need to be fixed, Microsoft provides several different kinds of software updates: recommended updates, driver updates, security updates, critical updates, hotfixes, security rollup packages, feature packs, and service packs.

Recommended updates

A recommended update addresses a non-critical, non-security-related problem. For example, the "Update for Jet 4.0 Service Pack 8" recommended update, associated with Knowledge Base article 829558, makes a handful of improvements to a commonly used database engine included with Windows. It does not remove any security vulnerabilities, however, so it is not considered a critical update or a security update.

Recommended updates might also add new features. For example, the "Microsoft Windows Journal Viewer" recommended update for Windows XP Professional and Windows XP Home Edition allows users to view files created with an application included only with tablet computers. In this example, the recommended update is not resolving a problem; it is adding new functionality to the operating system.

Driver updates

All versions of Windows come with a large number of drivers that enable support for a wide variety of hardware. The hardware vendors are generally responsible for the support of drivers, but Microsoft occasionally releases updated versions of drivers.

> **Security Alert** Updated drivers often resolve security problems, so keep an eye out for driver updates.

The fact that Microsoft occasionally releases updated versions of drivers does not relieve you of the responsibility of working with your hardware vendors to retrieve updated drivers. Microsoft does not release updated drivers until they have been officially signed by Microsoft, a process that delays the release of the software by days or weeks. Hardware vendors often release unsigned drivers to customers before they are officially released by Microsoft.

Security updates

Just about everyone who uses any variety of Windows is familiar with security updates. A security update is an update that the Microsoft Security Response Center (MSRC) releases to resolve a security vulnerability. Microsoft security updates are available for customers to download and are accompanied by two documents: a security bulletin and a Microsoft Knowledge Base article.

A Microsoft security bulletin notifies administrators of critical security issues and vulnerabilities. Usually, but not always, the security bulletin is associated with a security update that can be used to patch the vulnerability. Security bulletins generally provide detailed information about who the bulletin concerns, the impact of the vulnerability, the severity of the vulnerability, and a recommended course of action for affected customers.

Security bulletins are written for administrations, and therefore assume that the reader is technically trained and intimately familiar with Windows and security terminology. However, security vulnerabilities also affect many end users. Therefore, Microsoft also releases end-user versions of many security bulletins. These versions use a friendlier, more accessible language to describe the risks and the best ways to resolve the vulnerabilities. If available, the end-user version of the security bulletin will be referenced in the original security bulletin.

> **Tip** End-user versions of security bulletins are useful if you need to send an e-mail to users whose computers you manage to explain why they need to apply an update.

Security bulletins usually include the following pieces of information:

- **Title.** The title of the security bulletin, in the format MS*yy-###*, where *yy* is the last two digits of the year and *###* is the bulletin number for that year.
- **Summary.** Information about who should read the bulletin, the impact of the vulnerability and the software affected, the security rating, and the MSRC's recommendation for how to respond to the bulletin.
- **Technical description.** A detailed description of the vulnerability, and the circumstances under which the vulnerability could be exploited.
- **Mitigating factors.** Technical factors that reduce the likelihood of a vulnerable system being exploited.
- **Severity rating.** A rating of None, Low, Moderate, Important, and Critical for each type of software that the vulnerability might affect.
- **Vulnerability identifier.** Links to organizations external to Microsoft that classify the security vulnerability.
- **Tested versions.** A list of software that Microsoft has tested for the vulnerability.
- **Frequently asked questions.** Answers to questions that Microsoft anticipates about the specific security bulletin.
- **Update availability.** Locations from which to download the update.
- **Additional information.** Information about installation platforms, whether a reboot is needed, whether the update can be uninstalled, and how to verify that the update was successfully installed.

The severity level of a bulletin gauges the risk posed by the vulnerability that the update fixes. This severity level can be None, Low, Moderate, Important, or Critical. The MSRC judges the severity of a vulnerability on behalf of the entire Microsoft customer base. The impact a vulnerability has on your organization might be more, or less, serious.

Security Bulletin Sample

The following is an excerpt from an actual security bulletin released for Windows Server 2003 and other Windows operating systems on July 23, 2003. This version has been edited to save space. You can find the original bulletin at *http://www.microsoft.com/technet/security/bulletin/MS03-030.asp*.

Unchecked Buffer in DirectX Could Enable System Compromise (819696)

Originally posted: July 23, 2003

Updated: August 20, 2003

Summary:

Who should read this bulletin: Customers using Microsoft Windows

Impact of vulnerability: Allow an attacker to execute code on a user's system

Maximum Severity Rating: Critical

Recommendation: Customers should apply the security patch immediately

Affected Software:

DirectX 5.2 on Windows 98

DirectX 8.1 on Windows XP or Windows Server 2003

An End User version of the bulletin is available at: *http://www.microsoft.com/security/security_bulletins/ms03-030.asp.*

Technical description:

There are two buffer overruns with identical effects in the function used by DirectShow to check parameters in a Musical Instrument Digital Interface (MIDI) file. A security vulnerability results because it could be possible for a malicious user to attempt to exploit these flaws and execute code in the security context of the logged-on user.

An attacker could seek to exploit this vulnerability by creating a specially crafted MIDI file designed to exploit this vulnerability and then host it on a Web site or on a network share, or send it by using an HTML-based e-mail. A successful attack could cause DirectShow, or an application making use of DirectShow, to fail. A successful attack could also cause an attacker's code to run on the user's computer in the security context of the user.

Mitigating factors:

By default, Microsoft Internet Explorer on Windows Server 2003 runs in Enhanced Security Configuration. This default configuration of Internet Explorer blocks the e-mail-based vector of this attack because Microsoft Outlook Express running on Windows Server 2003 by default reads e-mail in plain text. If Internet Explorer Enhanced Security Configuration were disabled, the protections put in place that prevent this vulnerability from being exploited would be removed.

Severity Rating:

DirectX 9.0a	Critical
DirectX 9.0a when installed on Windows Server 2003	Important

Vulnerability identifier: CAN-2003-0346

Tested Versions: Microsoft tested DirectX 9.0a, DirectX 8.1, DirectX 7.0.

Download locations for this patch:

DirectX 5.2, DirectX 6.1 and DirectX 7.1 on Windows 98, Windows 98 SE and Windows Millennium Edition respectively

DirectX 7.0 on Windows 2000

In addition to security bulletins, Microsoft also creates Knowledge Base articles about security vulnerabilities. However, Knowledge Base articles undergo more review than security bulletins, and they are not released until after the bulletin. Knowledge Base articles generally include more detailed information about the vulnerability, and step-by-step instructions for updating affected computers.

Critical updates

A critical update is released quickly to all customers, like a security update. However, critical updates are not related to security problems, and they do not have associated bulletins. A critical update will be associated with one or more Knowledge Base articles that describe the problem and the update in detail.

Because critical updates, like security updates, are released to customers as quickly as possible, they do not undergo extensive testing from Microsoft. Critical updates should be handled differently from security updates, however. You do not need to apply a critical update unless you are actively experiencing the problem resolved by the update. Instead, you should wait for the next service pack to be released, because the service pack will include the update and will have gone through testing to ensure compatibility. Security updates, on the other hand, should be applied proactively to prevent vulnerabilities from being exploited.

Hotfixes

A hotfix is a package that includes one or more files to address a problem for a specific customer. Generally, you receive a hotfix only when you have been working with Microsoft Product Support Services (PSS) and they determine that the problem you're experiencing is caused by a bug in Microsoft software. They will probably release an update to the bug to the general customer population, but that might take several months. In the meantime, PSS provides you a hotfix to resolve the problem.

Hotfixes developed for the current shipping service pack will not be automatically created for the immediately preceding service pack. Customers who want a hotfix on the immediately preceding service pack should contact Microsoft and request the hotfix. Security patches released with bulletins from the Microsoft Security Response Center will be reviewed and built for the immediately preceding service pack whenever commercially viable.

Note It's not technically correct, but many people use the term hotfix to refer generically to critical updates and security updates.

Security rollup packages

There have been times when Microsoft has released a significant number of security and critical updates between service packs. It is cumbersome to install a large number of updates separately, so Microsoft releases a security rollup package (SRP) to reduce the labor involved in applying updates. An SRP is a cumulative set of hotfixes, security updates, critical updates, and other updates that are packaged together for easy deployment. An update rollup generally targets a specific area of a product, such as security, or a component of a product, such as IIS. SRPs are always released with a Knowledge Base article that describes the rollup in detail.

Feature packs

Feature packs are not released to fix problems with existing software, but to add new features. In the past, Microsoft included new features with service packs, but customers were wary of installing updates that added new features that could potentially introduce new bugs. Now, service packs contain only updates to existing software, and Microsoft releases feature packs to add functionality. Feature packs are typically included with the next release of the product.

Service packs

A service pack is a cumulative set of all the hotfixes, security updates, critical updates, and other updates that have been created for a Microsoft product. A service pack also includes fixes for other problems that have been found by Microsoft since the release of the product. Service packs might also contain a limited number of customer-requested design changes or features. Like critical updates, service packs are available for download and are accompanied by Knowledge Base articles.

The chief difference between service packs and other types of updates is that service packs are strategic deliveries, where updates are tactical. That is, service packs are carefully planned and managed, and the goal is to deliver a well-tested, comprehensive set of fixes that is suitable for use on any computer. In contrast, security updates and critical updates are developed on an as-needed basis to combat specific problems that require an immediate response.

> **Exam Tip** Service packs undergo extensive regression testing that Microsoft does not perform for other types of updates.

Microsoft does not release a service pack until it meets the same quality standards as the product itself. Service packs are constantly tested as they are built, undergo weeks of rigorous final testing that includes testing in conjunction with hundreds or thousands of non-Microsoft products, and undergo a beta phase during which customers participate in the testing. If the testing reveals bugs, Microsoft will delay the release of the service pack.

Product Lifecycles

Updates might seem like a nuisance, but keeping software updated is critical for keeping your computers protected against vulnerabilities that are constantly being discovered. But there does come a point when Microsoft stops releasing updates for a particular product. Every product has a lifecycle, and at the end of the lifecycle, Microsoft stops providing updates. This doesn't mean that no new vulnerabilities will be discovered in the product, however. To keep your system protected from the latest vulnerabilities, you will need to upgrade to the latest operating system.

Microsoft offers a minimum of five years of mainstream support from the date of a product's general availability. When mainstream support ends, businesses have the option to purchase two years of extended support. Additionally, online self-help support, such as the Knowledge Base, will still be available.

Security updates will be available through the end of the extended support phase—seven years after the date of the product's general availability—at no additional cost for most products. You do not have to have an extended support contract to receive security fixes during the extended support phase. This means that Microsoft will release security updates for Windows Server 2003 until at least 2010, as shown in Figure 5.1. In all likelihood, your organization will have upgraded its Windows Server 2003–based computers to a newer operating system by then. However, you must keep the product life cycle, and particularly the period during which security updates will be released, in mind when planning future operating system upgrades.

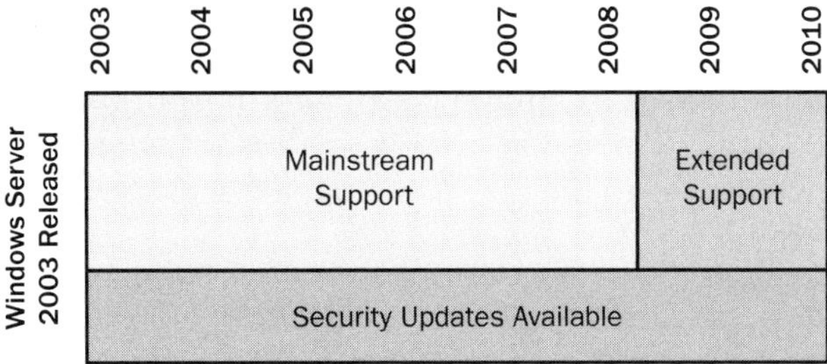

Figure 5.1 The Windows Server 2003 product lifecycle

You have to keep reasonably up-to-date on updates to continue to receive Microsoft support, because Microsoft only provides support for the current and immediately preceding service pack. This support policy allows you to receive existing hotfixes, or to request new hotfixes, for the currently shipping service pack, the immediately preceding service pack, or both during the mainstream phase.

Chaining Updates

In the past, installing multiple updates on a computer required restarting the computer between each update. If an administrator was installing several updates, the downtime on the server could be significant. Microsoft introduced the QChain tool to allow administrators to install multiple updates on computers running Microsoft Windows NT, Windows 2000, and Windows XP without restarting the computer after each update is installed. QChain handled the complexities that arose when applying multiple updates, such as ensuring that the correct version of a file is retained if it is included in multiple updates. Using QChain required creating a script to install the multiple updates and then starting QChain from the script.

Windows Server 2003 does not require the use of QChain, because QChain functionality is built into all new updates, including every update released for Windows Server 2003. To install multiple updates, you only need to launch each update's executable file using the /Z and /M parameters, and then restart the computer if necessary. The following is a sample batch file that could be used to install three updates located in the Z:\updates\ folder:

```
Z:\updates\WindowsServer2003-KB999997-x86-ENU.exe /Z /M
Z:\updates\WindowsServer2003-KB999998-x86-ENU.exe /Z /M
Z:\updates\WindowsServer2003-KB999999-x86-ENU.exe /Z /M
```

If you use Automatic Updates with the Windows Update Service or Software Update Services (SUS), updates are automatically chained without requiring administrator intervention. Some updates, such as service packs, cannot be chained with other updates.

Lesson Review

The following questions are intended to reinforce key information presented in this lesson. If you are unable to answer a question, review the lesson materials and try the question again. You can find answers to the questions in the "Questions and Answers" section at the end of this chapter.

1. Which of the following types of updates is/are cumulative? (Choose all that apply.)
   a. Updates
   b. Security updates
   c. Critical updates
   d. Hotfixes
   e. Security rollup packages
   f. Feature packs
   g. Service packs

   ____

   ____

   ____

2. Which of the following types of updates can reduce the number of vulnerabilities on a computer? (Choose all that apply.)
   a. Updates
   b. Security updates
   c. Critical updates
   d. Hotfixes
   e. Security rollup packages
   f. Feature packs
   g. Service packs

   ____

   ____

3. Which of the following types of updates have not been fully tested for compatibility by Microsoft? (Choose all that apply.)

   a. Updates
   b. Security updates
   c. Critical updates
   d. Hotfixes
   e. Security rollup packages
   f. Feature packs
   g. Service packs

   ____

   ____

   ____

4. Which of the following pieces of information are not contained in a security bulletin? (Choose all that apply.)

   a. Software affected by the vulnerability
   b. Location from which to download update
   c. Location from which to download programs that exploit vulnerabilities
   d. Severity rating

   ____

   ____

   ____

Lesson Summary

- Microsoft releases many different types of updates, including critical updates, security updates, service packs, and hotfixes.
- A security bulletin announces a new security update and contains detailed information about protecting your computers against the vulnerability.
- Chaining allows multiple updates to be applied with a single reboot.

Lesson 2: Updating Infrastructure

Deploying updates to all the computers in an enterprise is a daunting task. Even if you manage only a dozen computers, you need to put some thought into the updating infrastructure that you use to store, test, and deploy updates. Depending on the configuration, your updating infrastructure might require the addition of several new computers, or you might be able to add the additional load to existing resources.

This lesson describes the various components that make up an enterprise updating infrastructure, and provides you information with which to design an updating infrastructure for an enterprise.

After this lesson, you will be able to

- Assemble a team of individuals to manage updating responsibilities for an enterprise.
- Asses the updating needs of your organization.
- Identify the components of an updating infrastructure.
- Describe the various methods that can be used to deploy updates in an enterprise.
- Explain the importance of having a lab environment with which to test updates.

Estimated lesson time: 40 minutes

The Updating Team

Identifying individuals with the right mix of technical and project management skills for deploying updates is one of the first decisions that you, and your management, will make. Even before staffing can begin, however, you need to identify the team roles, or areas of expertise, required for update management. Microsoft suggests using the Microsoft Solutions Framework (MSF) team model, which is based on six interdependent multidisciplinary roles: product management, program management, development, testing, user experience, and release management.

- **Product management.** Product management is responsible for identifying the organization's business needs and the needs of the end users, and for making sure those needs are supported by the updating process.
- **Program management.** The program management team's goal is to deliver updates within project constraints. Program management is responsible for managing the updating schedule and budget, and for reporting status, managing project-related risk factors (such as staff illnesses), and managing the design of the updating process.

- **Development.** The development team builds the updating infrastructure according to specification. The team's responsibilities include specifying the features of the updating infrastructure, estimating the time and effort required to deploy the updating infrastructure, and preparing the infrastructure for deployment.
- **Testing.** The testing team ensures that updates are released into the production environment only after all quality issues have been identified and resolved. The team's responsibilities include developing the testing strategy, designing and building the updating lab, developing the test plan, and conducting tests.
- **User experience.** The user experience team ensures that the updating process meets the users' needs. The team gathers, analyzes, and prioritizes user requirements and complaints.
- **Release management.** The release management team is responsible for deploying the updates. In large environments, the release management team also designs and manages a pilot deployment of an update to ensure that the update is sufficiently stable for deployment into the production environment.

The MSF team roles are flexible; they can be adapted to your organization's own processes and management philosophy. In a small organization or a limited deployment, one individual might play multiple roles. In larger organizations, a team might be required to perform all of the tasks assigned to each role.

For more information about the MSF team model, see the MSF Team Model white paper at *http://www.microsoft.com/technet/itsolutions/tandp/innsol/msfrl/MSFTM31.asp.*

Assessing Your Environment

The first step in planning your strategy to deploy updates is to assess your current environment. Specifically, you need to know what operating systems and applications you have installed in order to identify updates that need to be deployed. You also need to understand the security requirements for each computer system, including which computers store highly confidential information, which are connected to the public Internet, and which will connect to exterior networks.

For each computer in your environment, gather the following information:

- **Operating system.** Document the operating system version and update level. Also document which optional components, such as IIS, are installed.
- **Applications.** Document every application installed on the computer, including versions and updates.
- **Network connectivity.** Document which networks the computer connects to, including whether the computer is connected to the public Internet, whether it connects to other networks across a VPN or dial-up connection, and whether it is a mobile computer that might connect to networks at other locations.

- **Vulnerability-limiting factors.** Firewalls and virus checkers might protect a computer against a known vulnerability, making the update unnecessary. For firewalls, document which ports are open.
- **Site.** If your organization has multiple sites, you can choose to deploy updates to computers from a server located at each site to optimize bandwidth usage. Knowing which site a computer is located in allows you to efficiently deploy the updates.
- **Bandwidth.** Computers connected across low-bandwidth links have special requirements. You can choose to transfer large updates during nonbusiness hours. For dial-up users, it might be more efficient to bypass the network link and transfer updates on removable media, such as CD-ROMs.
- **Administrator responsibility.** You must understand who is responsible for deploying the updates, and who will fix a problem if a computer fails during the updating process. If others are responsible for individual applications or services, make note of that as well.
- **Uptime requirements.** Understand any service level agreements or service level guarantees that apply to a particular computer, and whether scheduled downtime counts against the total uptime. This will enable you to prioritize computers when troubleshooting and testing updates.
- **Scheduling dependencies.** Applying updates requires planning systems to be offline. This can be a disruption for users, even if the computer only requires a quick reboot. Understand who depends on a particular computer so that you can clear downtime with them ahead of time.

Deploying Updates

To meet the needs of various types of organizations, Microsoft provides several different methods for applying updates. The preferred method for deploying updates is Software Update Services (SUS). Large organizations currently using Group Policy objects to distribute software might prefer to use Group Policy objects for deploying updates as well, because it allows them to deploy the update to many systems simultaneously. Group Policy objects can be used to automatically install updates on computers, or to make them available to users through the Add/Remove Programs tool. Finally, enterprises that use Microsoft Systems Management Server (SMS) can use SMS to deploy updates. You can even avoid manually installing updates on new systems by integrating the update directly into the Windows Server 2003 setup files.

Smaller organizations that cannot allocate computing resources to an updating infrastructure can choose to deploy updates manually by using the express or network installations. Small organizations can take advantage of automated update deployment without adding any infrastructure servers by using the Automatic Update client and the Windows Update server.

Table 5.1 lists the advantages and disadvantages of each of the update distribution methods described here.

Table 5.1 Comparison of Update Distribution Methods

Update distribution method	Advantages	Disadvantages
Windows Update	Does not require that any infrastructure be deployed.	Does not allow administrators to test or approve updates. Wastes Internet bandwidth in large organizations.
Software Update Services	Allows administrators to test, approve, and schedule updates. Reduces Internet bandwidth usage.	Requires an infrastructure server.
Group Policy	Provide granular control over which clients receive updates. Can be used to distribute other types of software.	Requires Active Directory. Other than service packs, updates must be manually added to a Windows Installer package.
Add/Remove Programs	Gives end users control over which updates are applied, and when. Can be used to distribute other types of software.	Requires Active Directory, and requires end users to choose to install updates.
Systems Management Server	Provides highly customizable, centralized control over update deployment, with the ability to audit and inventory client systems. Can be used to distribute other types of software.	Requires infrastructure servers and additional licenses.

Automatic Update client

Both Windows Update and Software Update Services use the same client to download and install updates: the Automatic Update client. The Automatic Update client can automatically notify users of critical updates and security updates available either at Windows Update or at a specified Software Update Services server.

Available in Windows 2000 Service Pack 3, Windows XP Home Edition, and Windows XP Professional, the Automatic Update client is a proactive "pull" service that allows for automatic detection, notification, download, and optionally the installation of important updates. The Automatic Update client will even reboot a computer at a scheduled time to ensure that updates take effect immediately.

The Automatic Update client provides for a great deal of control over its behavior. You can configure individual computers by using the System Control Panel utility. Networks that use Active Directory directory service can specify the configuration of each Automatic Update client by using Group Policy settings. In non-Active Directory environments, you can configure computers by changing a set of registry values.

IT administrators can configure Automatic Updates to automatically download updates and schedule their installation for a specified time. If the computer is turned off at that time, the updates can be installed as soon as the computer is turned on. Downloading updates won't affect a user's network performance either, because the client downloads the updates by using the Background Intelligent Transfer Service (BITS), an innovative bandwidth-throttling technology that uses only idle bandwidth.

Tip This book won't cover BITS in detail, but you can administer it by using the bitsadmin.exe support tool. You can install the support tools by running \Support\Tools\Suptools.MSI from the Windows Server 2003 CD-ROM.

If complete automation is not acceptable, you can also give users control over when updates are downloaded and installed. As shown in Figure 5.2, the Automatic Update client can be configured by using Group Policy settings to only notify the user that updates are available. The updates are not downloaded or applied until the user clicks the notification balloon and selects the desired updates.

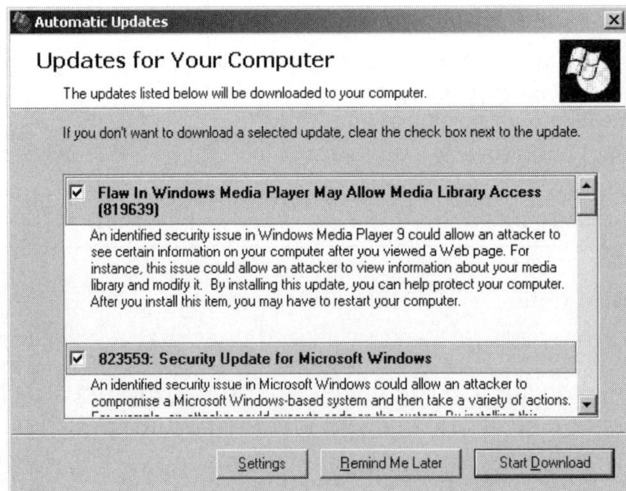

Figure 5.2 The Automatic Update client configured to prompt the user to download

After the Automatic Update client downloads updates, the client checks the digital signature on the updates before applying them to prevent an attacker from sneaking in a Trojan horse. To verify that updates were installed, you can specify the address of a Web server to which the Automatic Update client should send statistics about updates that have been downloaded, and whether the updates have been installed. These statistics appear in the IIS usage log file of the Web server.

See Also To learn more about the Automatic Update client, and to download the software, visit *http://www.microsoft.com/windowsserversystem/sus/*.

Windows Update

Windows Update is a free Microsoft service for keeping computers running Windows up-to-date with the latest software updates. Windows Update is made up of three components: the Windows Update Web site, the Automatic Update client, and the Windows Update Catalog. Millions of people use the Windows Update Web site each week as a way to keep their Windows-based systems current. When a user connects to the Windows Update site, Windows Update evaluates the user's computer to check which software updates and updated device drivers should be applied to keep the system secure and reliable.

The Windows Update Web site includes a catalog of all software update installation packages for downloading by administrators. These software update installation packages can then be stored on CD, distributed, and installed through other means, such as SMS or non-Microsoft software distribution tools, or they can be used when installing new computers.

Software Update Services

SUS is like a copy of Windows Update inside your corporate firewall for critical updates and security updates. SUS connects to the Windows Update site, downloads critical updates, security updates, and service packs, and adds them to a pipeline for administrator approval. SUS will then notify administrators by e-mail that new updates are available. After an administrator has approved and prioritized these updates, as illustrated in Figure 5.3, SUS will automatically make them available to all computers running Windows 2000 Server, Windows 2000 Professional, Windows XP, or Windows Server 2003. The client-side components on these computers will then check the SUS server and automatically download and install updates as configured by the administrators.

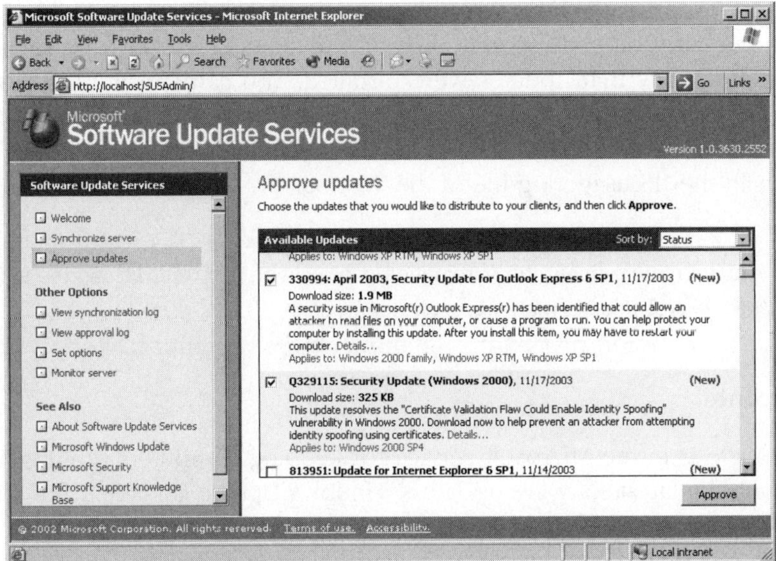

Figure 5.3 Approval of updates using Software Update Services

SUS is designed to be used in large organizations. Almost every aspect of the behavior can be customized. For example, the SUS server can download updates from Microsoft automatically, manually, or on a schedule specified by an administrator. SUS servers can be tiered as shown in Figure 5.4, with multiple SUS servers synchronizing updates between each other. This optimizes the use of your Internet connection by only requiring each update to be downloaded once for the entire organization. It also optimizes traffic on your wide area networks by allowing clients to download updates from a local SUS server.

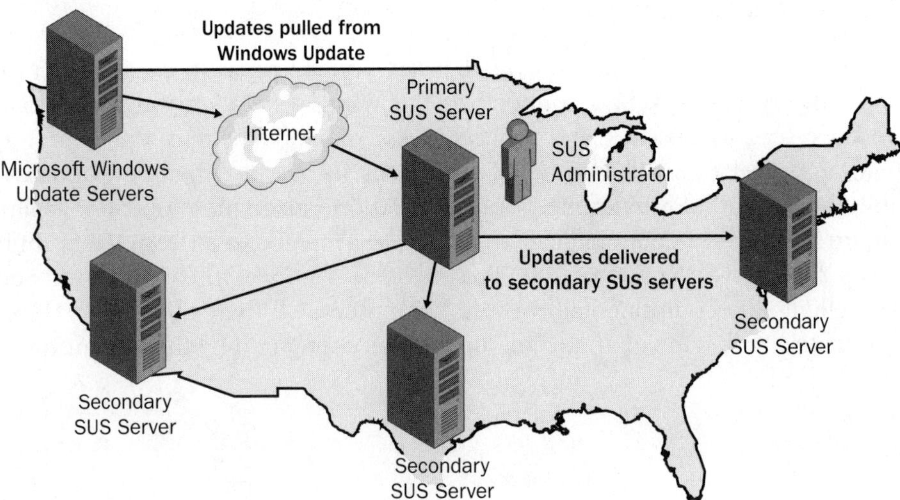

Figure 5.4 Tiered Software Update Services architecture

You can take advantage of the ability to approve updates for internal users without storing updates locally. Administrators can configure SUS to direct the Automatic Update client to retrieve approved downloads directly from Microsoft. This reduces the storage requirements on the SUS server, and can be more efficient for large networks spread over geographically disparate sites.

To install Software Update Services on a server, that computer must already have IIS 5.0 (for Windows 2000 Servers) or IIS 6.0 (for Windows Server 2003 computers) installed, because the Automatic Update client retrieves updates by using Web requests. Because this is a service that only clients on the internal network or across a VPN should be connecting to, you should protect this computer from the public Internet by using a firewall.

See Also To learn more about SUS, and to download the software, visit *http://www.microsoft.com/windowsserversystem/sus/*.

Group Policy

Any software contained in a Windows Installer package can be delivered to computers by using the Software Installation node of a Group Policy object. Windows Installer is a Windows component that standardizes and simplifies the way you install and manage software programs such as updates. You can use Windows Installer to manage the installation, modification, repair, and removal of software programs. Windows Installer facilitates consistent deployment, which enables you to manage shared resources, customize installation processes, and solve configuration problems.

Typically, the only updates Microsoft releases with Windows Installer packages are service packs. But it is possible to package other updates within an .msi file if you determine that Group Policy software installation is the best way to deploy updates in your organization. Because service packs are applied across organizations to computers rather than to specific users, you should deliver the package by using a computer-level Group Policy deployment.

To deploy a service pack or other update by using a Windows Installer file, first identify one or more shared folders in which to locate the files. Service packs, in particular, can be very large. To optimize network utilization in enterprises with multiple locales, identify shared folders at each location. Then apply separate Group Policy objects (GPOs) to each location by linking GPOs to location-based organizational units, by linking the GPOs to Active Directory sites, or by using security to allow only the computers in a specific location to apply that location's GPO. Use Windows Management Instrumentation (WMI) filtering to ensure that the update is applied only to computers with software that requires the update.

See Also For more information about using security and WMI filtering to filter GPOs, refer to Chapter 3, "Deploying and Troubleshooting Security Templates."

If you have to troubleshoot a problem with an update, or any other Windows Installer package, you might need to move the affected computers out of the scope of the Group Policy object and then back into the scope. Therefore, you should use the Uninstall This Application When It Falls Out Of The Scope Of Management option when deploying updates by using a Group Policy object, as shown in Figure 5.5. Using this option causes the update to be removed if you move a computer out of the scope of the Group Policy object.

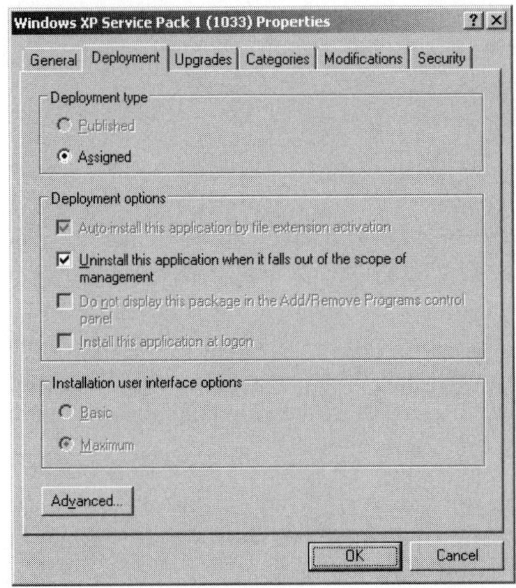

Figure 5.5 Selecting Uninstall This Application When It Falls Out Of The Scope Of Management

Add/Remove Programs

In some circumstances, you might want to make an update available to users without actually requiring them to apply the update. This is an ideal way to encourage other administrators, developers, and power users to update their own machines, without forcing them to apply an update. Development and lab environments often require that the administrators manually apply updates to avoid conflicts with other work that the administrator or developer is using the system for. Additionally, users who access the network across a dial-up link might want to choose to manually apply updates when they are not going to be using the network connection for several minutes.

If you want to advertise an update by using the Add/Remove Programs tools instead of forcibly installing the update, you can use a .zap file to allow the update to be published. Updates don't include .zap files, but they can be easily created. Installations that use .zap files require the user to be logged on as the local administrator because the update process will run under the current user's context.

See Also For more information about using .zap files, refer to Microsoft Knowledge Base article 231747 at *http://support.microsoft.com/?kbid=231747*.

If low disk space causes the service pack installation to fail, the update might appear as installed in the Add/Remove Programs tool but not appear as installed with Winver.exe. If this occurs on a portion of the deployment, move the affected computers out from under the scope of the managed program (for example, you might move them to another organizational unit). Create enough free space for the service pack to be installed, and then return the computers to the organizational unit with the service pack deployment. You must reboot the computers to accomplish both the removal and the reinstallation of the service pack.

Tip Winver.exe is more accurate than the Add/Remove Programs tool, so always use Winver.exe to verify that an update has successfully installed.

Systems Management Server

Though simply applying updates is not reason enough to deploy Systems Management Server (SMS), if you already use SMS, it is an excellent way to keep your network's computers up-to-date. SMS provides a variety of tools to help you deploy updates in your organization. With the software distribution feature of SMS, you can automatically update all of the SMS client computers in your organization with the new update. You can allow your users to run the update installation whenever they like, or you can schedule the update installation to run at a specific time. You can also schedule it to run on SMS client computers at a time when your users are not logged on.

If you are still using SMS 2.0, you should evaluate the SUS Feature Pack. With SMS 2.0 and the SUS Feature Pack, administrators are able to easily manage security updates throughout the enterprise. SMS has always been able to distribute any type of software, but the SUS Feature Pack adds functionality that streamlines the security patch management process. The SUS Feature Pack for SMS 2.0 is designed to quickly and effectively assess and deploy security patches for Windows, Microsoft Office, and other products scanned by the Microsoft Baseline Security Analyzer (MBSA). The Feature Pack provides the following new tools for SMS:

- **Security Update Inventory Tool.** This adds MBSA-style updating inventory capabilities to the existing hardware inventory capabilities of SMS.
- **Microsoft Office Inventory Tool for Updates.** This provides inventory capabilities for Office updates.
- **Distribute Software Updates Wizard.** This component provides a tool that reliably installs updates on end-user computers without forcing the computer to restart before the user is ready.
- **Web Reports Add-in for Software Updates.** This provides administrators with reports describing the current status of deployed updates in the enterprise.

The Update Test Environment

There are two primary ways you can test an update: in a test environment and in a pilot deployment. A test environment consists of a test lab or labs and includes test plans that detail what you will test and test cases that describe how you will test each component. Organizations that have the resources to test updates in a test environment should always do so, because it will reduce the number of problems caused by update incompatibility with applications. Even if your organization does not have the resources to test critical updates and security updates, you should always test service packs before deploying them to production computers.

The test lab can be made up of a single lab or of several labs, each of which supports testing without presenting risk to your production environment. In the test lab, members of the testing team can verify their deployment design assumptions, discover deployment problems, and improve their understanding of the changes implemented by specific updates. Such activities reduce the risk of errors occurring during deployment and allow the members of the test team to rapidly resolve problems that might occur while deploying an update or after applying an update.

Many organizations divide their testing teams into two subteams: the design team and the deployment team. The design team collects information that is vital to the deployment process, identifies immediate and long-term testing needs, and proposes a test lab design (or recommends improvements to the existing test lab). The deployment team completes the process by implementing the design team's decisions and then testing new updates on an ongoing basis.

During the beginning of the lifetime of the updating test environment, the deployment team will test the update deployment process to validate that the design is functional. Later, after your organization has identified an update to be deployed, the deployment will test the individual updates to ensure that all the updates are compatible with the applications used in your environment.

An updating test environment should have computers that represent each of the major computer roles in your organization, including desktop computers, mobile computers, and servers. If computers within each role have different operating systems, you should have each operating system available either on a dedicated computer or in a multi-boot configuration.

Planning It can be tough to convince management to allocate budget for a lab. To help justify that cost, calculate the potential cost of an update that causes widespread problems and the likelihood of that problem occurring, and determine how long it will take to recoup the investment.

After you have a set of computers that represent each of the various types of computers in your organization, connect them to a private network. You will also need to connect test versions of your updating infrastructure computers. For example, if you plan to deploy updates by using Software Update Services, you should connect an SUS server to the lab network.

Load every application that users will use onto the lab computers, and develop a procedure to test the functionality of each application. For example, to test the functionality of Internet Explorer, you could visit both the Microsoft Web site and an intranet Web site. Later, when testing updates, you will repeat this test. If one of the applications fails the test, it is possible that a problem was caused by the update you are currently testing.

Tip If you will be testing a large number of applications, you should identify ways to automate the testing of updates by using scripting.

The server update testing process is not complete unless the test servers are tested under a heavy load. To facilitate this, Microsoft provides several tools for testing applications under an artificial load. For testing updates to IIS, use the Web Application Stress (WAS) tool to simulate load on the server. For testing Exchange Server computers, use the Exchange Stress And Performance Tool. For Microsoft SQL Server computers, use the SQLIOStress Utility. Each of these tools can be downloaded from *http://www.microsoft.com/downloads/*.

Practice: Evaluating Your Updating Infrastructure

In this practice, you will think about the updating infrastructure that your current work environment is, and should be, using. Use the following questions to guide your thoughts.

1. How does your current organization deploy updates to computers on the network?

____

2. How long does it take for updates to be delivered to computers on your network? Is the current delay acceptable, or does it leave your network vulnerable to attack?

____

3. Who decides on whether an update should be deployed? In retrospect, have updates been deployed unnecessarily, or have important updates been skipped? Is the same group responsible for both identifying and deploying updates, and, if so, is this a conflict of interest?

____

4. If you had the opportunity to perform an overhaul of your organization's updating infrastructure, which deployment method would you use?

____

____

____

Lesson Review

The following questions are intended to reinforce key information presented in this lesson. If you are unable to answer a question, review the lesson materials and try the question again. You can find answers to the questions in the "Questions and Answers" section at the end of this chapter.

1. Which of the following deployment methods gives administrators the opportunity to approve updates before releasing them to clients? (Choose all that apply.)
   - **a.** Windows Update
   - **b.** Software Update Services
   - **c.** Group Policy
   - **d.** Add/Remove Programs
   - **e.** Systems Management Server

____

____

2. Which of the following deployment methods can be used to automatically deploy all security updates that Microsoft releases to client computers, without administrator intervention? (Choose all that apply.)
   a. Windows Update
   b. Software Update Services
   c. Group Policy
   d. Add/Remove Programs
   e. Systems Management Server

____

____

____

____

Lesson Summary

- The Automatic Update client connects to either the public Windows Update server or a private SUS server to download, and optionally install, updates.
- Systems Management Server is capable of working closely with SUS to deliver updates to an enterprise.
- Group Policy can be used to deliver updates, though it is not the preferred method.
- A lab environment is required for detailed testing of updates. The more testing you perform on an update, the fewer problems you will experience when you deploy that update to the production computers on your network.

Lesson 3: Updating Process

Deploying updates involves more than just choosing a technology to install the updates. An effective updating process involves planning, discussion, and testing. Though you should use your organization's existing change management process, if one exists, this section will describe the fundamental components of an update process. Figure 5.6 illustrates an effective updating process.

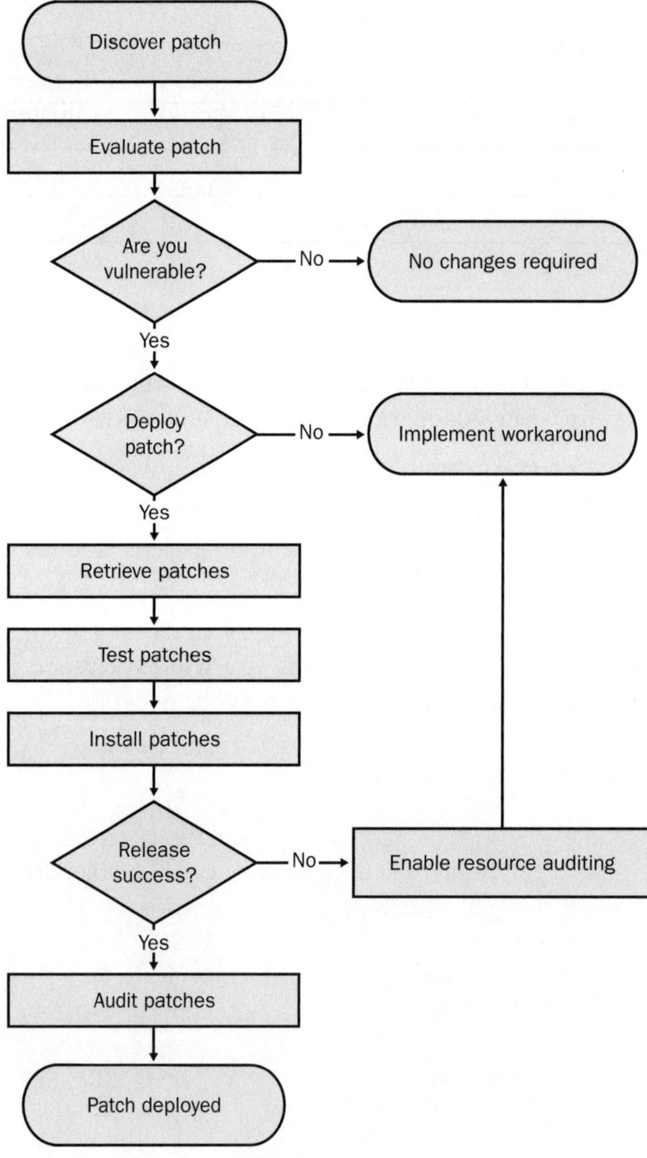

Figure 5.6 The core updating process

After this lesson, you will be able to

- Describe the various steps in an effective updating process.
- Evaluate updates to determine whether they should be applied, and evaluate their priority.
- Identify the most efficient way to identify and retrieve updates.

Estimated lesson time: 30 minutes

Discovering Updates

The security updating process starts when Microsoft releases or updates a security bulletin. Reissued bulletins that have a higher severity rating should be evaluated again to determine if an already scheduled security release should be reprioritized and accelerated. You might also initiate the security updating process when a new service pack is released.

You can be notified of Microsoft-related security issues and fixes by subscribing to the Microsoft Security Notification Services. You can register for this service from the following Web site: *http://www.microsoft.com/technet/security/bulletin/notify.asp*. If you subscribe to this service, you will receive automatic notification of security issues by e-mail. Note that you won't ever receive the update as an attachment from Microsoft. E-mail is easy to spoof, so Microsoft includes a digital signature that can be verified. However, it's generally easier to simply check the Microsoft Web site to ensure that the bulletin is officially listed.

Although many organizations start the updating process immediately when Microsoft releases an update, others choose to check for updates on a regular basis. For example, some organizations have a person assigned to check for updates every Thursday, and then initiate the updating process if required. You can retrieve a list of updates available for a product by visiting the Microsoft HotFix & Security Bulletin Service at *http://www.microsoft.com/technet/security/current.asp*. On this Web site, you can search for updates by product and service pack level.

You can also discover updates by using Automatic Updates. If the service determines that a critical update is applicable, it can notify you that the update is available, download the update and notify you that it is ready to install, or automatically download and install the updates on a schedule you define, as illustrated in Figure 5.7. Using Automatic Updates to discover and/or apply updates is great for organizations with only a handful of servers, but the approach does not scale well enough to be used by enterprises.

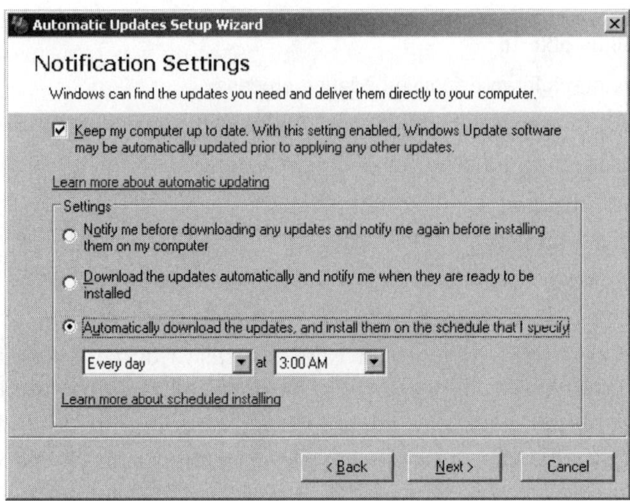

Figure 5.7 Notification settings for Automatic Updates

The Microsoft Baseline Security Analyzer (MBSA) is an excellent way to determine whether a specific system is missing updates. MBSA scans for missing security updates and vulnerabilities, reports on a computer's adherence to common security best practices, and identifies any configuration options that leave the computer open to potential security vulnerabilities. By default, MBSA contacts the Windows Update service to determine what security updates and critical updates Microsoft has released that have not been applied to the system.

Evaluating Updates

After you learn of a security update, you need to evaluate the update to determine which computers at your organization, if any, should have the update applied. Read the information that accompanies the security bulletin, and refer to the associated Knowledge Base article after it is released.

Next, look at the various parts of your environment to determine whether the vulnerability affects the computers on your network. You might not be using the software component that the update affects, or you might be protected from the vulnerability by other means, such as a firewall. For example, if Microsoft releases a security update for SQL Server and your company doesn't use SQL Server, you don't need to act. If Microsoft releases a security update for the Windows Messenger service, but you have blocked the vulnerable ports by using Internet Connection Firewall, you don't necessarily need to apply the update. Alternatively, you might decide that applying the update is not the best countermeasure for a security vulnerability. Instead, you might choose to add a firewall or adjust firewall filtering rules to limit the vulnerability's exposure.

Determining whether an update should be applied is not as straightforward as you might think. You could simply apply all critical updates and security updates, but applying an update does have a cost. You will need to dedicate time to testing, packaging, and deploying the update. In larger organizations, applying a software update to a server requires that many hours be dedicated to justifying the update and scheduling the update with the groups who use the server.

Any type of update also carries the risk of something going wrong when the update is applied. In fact, any time you restart a computer, there is a small risk that the server won't start up successfully. There's also the very real risk that the update will break existing applications. Fortunately, this risk can be offset by extensively testing the update before applying it. Naturally, there's a cost to deciding not to apply a security update too: an increased risk of a security vulnerability being exploited.

Besides testing, you can offset the risk associated with an update causing problems by having a plan to roll back the update. When evaluating an update, determine whether the release can be easily uninstalled if it causes a problem that isn't identified during testing. Functionality for uninstalling updates can vary from fully automated uninstall support, to manual uninstall procedures, to no uninstall. If an update cannot be uninstalled, your only option might be to restore the computer from a recent backup. Regardless of the uninstall method required for an update, ensure that there is a defined rollback plan in case the deployment doesn't match the success encountered in the test environment.

To be prepared for the worst, verify that you have recent backups of all computers that will be updated, and that you are prepared to restore those systems if the update cannot be successfully removed. It's not likely that an update will cause your systems to fail completely and require them to be restored from backup, but it is a circumstance you must be prepared to handle.

Off the Record Updates really can break applications. Sometimes, after you restart a computer, one of your applications will simply refuse to start. In this case, you can immediately uninstall the update and have the application up-and-running within a few minutes. Other times, the update causes more subtle problems. For example, the update might cause your application to run slightly slower—a performance decrease small enough that nobody would notice. However, a month later when many users are trying to access the application simultaneously, it might crash under a user load that it would have been able to handle before the update was applied. The problem was caused by the update you applied, but identifying the connection between the crash and an update you applied a month ago can be difficult, if not impossible.

Choosing whether to apply an update is such a complicated, yet critical, decision that larger organizations should create a security committee that collectively determines which updates should be applied. The committee should consist of employees that are familiar with the updating requirements of each different type of computer on your network. For example, if you have separate organizations that manage desktop and client computers, both organizations should have a representative in the committee. If separate individuals manage each of the Web, messaging, and infrastructure servers on your network, each should have input into whether a particular update is applied. Ask members from your UNIX, database, and networking groups, and from your internal audit teams, to play an active role—their experience and expertise can be an asset in determining risk. Depending on your needs, the committee can discuss each update as it is released, or it can meet on a weekly or biweekly basis.

If the committee determines that an update needs to be deployed, you then need to determine the urgency. If there is an active attack, you must make every effort to apply the update immediately before your system is infected. If the attack is severe enough, it might even warrant removing vulnerable computers from the network until the update can be applied.

For example, assume that you have an IIS computer connected to the public Internet when a security bulletin is announced. If the vulnerability enables an attacker to take complete control of a computer and an exploit is already known to be spreading outside of your network, your system could be infected at any moment. Alternatively, if a vulnerability only allows an attacker to perform a denial-of-service attack by restarting the computer, your risk is much lower. You can safely choose to delay the update until the update is tested and downtime can be scheduled. If you discover that an attacker is exploiting the vulnerability to restart your IIS computer, you could apply the update immediately without risking the loss of confidential data.

Retrieving Updates

Once you have decided to test and/or deploy an update, you must retrieve it from Microsoft. If you are using Windows Update or SUS as your deployment mechanism, retrieving the update is taken care of by the Automatic Update client. If you are deploying updates by using another mechanism, you should download the update from a trusted Microsoft server.

When manually installing a service pack on a computer, you can choose between a network install and an express install. If you are deploying the service pack to more than one computer in the same location, you should always use the network install. This self-extracting package contains all of the files that are required for any computer running the operating system the service pack was released for. This option is designed for administrators who want to set up a shared network folder for deploying the service pack on multiple computers.

The express install for a service pack is more efficient when installing the update on a single computer or when manually installing the update on multiple computers in various locations. Express installation is available for service packs, but not for other types of updates. This type of installation is generally intended for manually installing a service pack on a single computer; it is not optimal for organizations with more than two or three computers. The express install optimizes Internet bandwidth by detecting the service pack files that are already installed on the computer and installing only those files that must be updated. The installation package includes only the files required to start the installation and connect to a download server: the information (.inf) file, the version (.ver) file, and a URL that points to the Microsoft download server. The remaining files that you need are identified and downloaded when you link to the download server.

Testing Updates

After applying a testing update or group of updates to your test computers, you should test all applications and functionality as described in Lesson 2. In addition to testing within the update test environment, large organizations should conduct at least one pilot deployment before deploying the update or updates into the production environment. When conducting a pilot, you deploy a limited number of computers in a controlled environment, evaluate the results, and fix problems. Deploy successive pilots until you determine that the update is ready for full deployment. Be sure to include a representative cross-section of the computers in your pilot group.

Tip The more significant the update, the more important it is to use a pilot program. Service packs, in particular, require extensive testing both in and out of the lab.

In addition to testing your implementation of an update, conducting a pilot provides an opportunity to test your deployment plan and the deployment processes. It helps you to determine how much time is required to install the update, and the personnel and tools needed to do so. It also provides an opportunity to train support staff and to gauge user reaction to the updating process. For example, if a particular update takes an hour for a dial-in user to download, you might have to identify an alternative method for delivering the update to the user.

Installing Updates

After you are comfortable that you have sufficiently tested an update, you can deploy it to your production environment. During the installation process, be sure to have sufficient support staff to handle problems that might arise. Have a method in place to monitor the progress of the updates, and have an engineer ready to resolve any problems that occur in the update deployment mechanism. Notify network staff that an update deployment is taking place, so that they are aware of the cause of the increased network utilization.

For more information about how to deploy updates, refer to Lesson 2.

Removing Updates

Despite following proper planning and testing procedures, problems can arise when you deploy an update to production systems. Before deploying updates, you should have a plan in place to roll back updates from one, many, or all of the target computers. Removing an update from a single computer can often be easily done by using Add/Remove Programs, as shown in Figure 5.8.

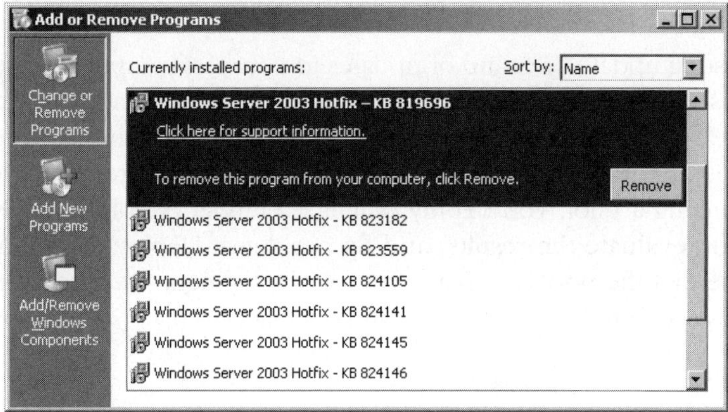

Figure 5.8 Using Add/Remove Programs for updates

Though you can remove updates from individual computers by using Add/Remove Programs, you should be prepared to remove the updates by using the same method you used to distribute the updates. For example, if you deploy a service pack by using a Group Policy object, plan to explicitly remove that service pack by using the same Group Policy object. Every Microsoft update can also be removed from the command line, allowing you to remove multiple updates with a batch file.

As part of every update deployment, you will need to define a rollback plan, in case the deployment doesn't succeed as it did in the test environment. The following are the main steps for the rollback and redeployment of updates:

- **Stop the current deployment.** Identify any steps necessary for deactivating release mechanisms used in your environment.
- **Identify and resolve any update deployment issues.** Determine what is causing an update deployment to fail. The order in which updates are applied, the release mechanism used, and flaws in the update itself are all possible causes for a failed deployment.

- **Uninstall updates if necessary.** Updates that introduce instabilities to your production environment should be removed, if possible.
- **Reactivate release mechanisms.** After resolving update issues, reactivate the appropriate release mechanism to redeploy updates. Security bulletins issued by Microsoft will always indicate whether an update can be uninstalled. Because reverting computers to a previous state is not always possible, pay close attention to this detail before deploying an update that cannot be uninstalled.

When a simple uninstall process is not available for a security update, ensure that the necessary provisions are in place for reverting your critical computers back to their original state in the unlikely event that a security patch deployment causes a computer to fail. These provisions might include having spare computers and data backup mechanisms in place so a failed computer can be rebuilt quickly.

Auditing Updates

After you have deployed an update, it is important to audit your work. Ideally, someone not responsible for deploying the update will perform the actual auditing. This reduces the possibility that the person or group responsible for deploying the update would unintentionally overlook the same set of computers during both update deployment and auditing, in addition to reducing the likelihood of someone covering up oversights or mistakes.

Auditing an update that resolves a security vulnerability can be done in one of two ways. The simplest way to audit is to use a tool such as MBSA to check for the presence of the update. This can also be done by checking the version of files that have been updated by an update, and verifying that the version matches the version of the file included with the update.

Real World

Although the staff responsible for deploying an update should be represented on the security committee, they cannot be solely responsible for deciding which updates are deployed, and their work should be audited by an objective individual or group. I was part of a committee that identified security updates that should be deployed to hundreds of Windows-based servers. Unfortunately, the group responsible for deploying the updates was too busy supporting customers to install the updates—for several months. We on the committee realized that the updates weren't being deployed only after dozens of computers were infected by a worm. I realized the importance of auditing that day, but only after it cost my company hundreds of thousands of dollars.

A more complicated, but thorough, method of auditing is to scan the computers on your network for the actual security vulnerability. This requires a non-Microsoft network scanning and auditing tool, however. To adequately test that the vulnerability has been removed, the tool must be designed specifically to exploit the security vulnerability. Although no such tool exists for every security vulnerability, various companies might release scanners to check for widely exploited vulnerabilities. For example, eEye Digital Security has released a scanner to check for the vulnerability exploited by the Nimda worm. The scanner can be downloaded from *http://www.eeye.com.*

Practice: Evaluating Your Updating Process

In this practice, you will evaluate the updating process that your current work environment is using. Use the following questions to guide your thoughts.

1. Has your organization formally identified and documented an updating process? If so, what is that process?

   ____

2. Has your organization ever had to remove an update after deploying it? If not, are you prepared to quickly remove an update from all computers on your network?

   ____

Lesson Review

The following questions are intended to reinforce key information presented in this lesson. If you are unable to answer a question, review the lesson materials and try the question again. You can find answers to the questions in the "Questions and Answers" section at the end of this chapter.

1. How can you validate that an update is genuine?

   ____

   ____

   ____

   ____

   ____

   ____

2. Which requires more testing, a service pack or a security update?

   ____

   ____

Lesson Summary

- Every organization should develop an updating process catered to its specific needs. However, every updating process should include steps for discovering, evaluating, retrieving, testing, installing, removing (if necessary), and auditing updates.
- When evaluating security updates, factor in both the cost of deploying the update and the risk associated with not deploying the update. Consider alternative ways to mitigate the vulnerability.
- Always be prepared for the worst when deploying an update. Be sure that all systems receiving the update have a recent backup available.

Case Scenario Exercise

In this exercise, you will read a scenario about identifying updates that must be deployed to a Windows Server 2003 network, and then answer the questions that follow. The questions are intended to reinforce key information presented in this chapter. If you are unable to answer a question, review the lessons and try the question again. You can find answers to the questions in the "Questions and Answers" section at the end of this chapter.

Scenario

You receive an e-mail from a friend who works as an administrator for another company. The e-mail describes four new vulnerabilities that might affect the computers on your network. Your friend describes the vulnerabilities as follows:

- **Buffer Overrun in the HTML Converter Could Allow Code Execution (KB823559).** There is a flaw in the way the Hypertext Markup Language (HTML) converter for Microsoft Windows handles a conversion request during a cut-and-paste operation. A vulnerability exists because a specially crafted request to the HTML converter could cause the converter to fail in such a way that it could run code in the context of the currently logged-on user. Because Internet Explorer uses this functionality, an attacker could craft a specially formed Web page or HTML e-mail that would cause the HTML converter to run arbitrary code on a user's computer. When a user visits an attacker's Web site, the attacker could exploit the vulnerability without any other user action.
- **A Buffer Overrun in RPCSS Could Allow an Attacker to Run Malicious Programs (KB824146).** There are three identified vulnerabilities in the part of the Windows RPC service (RPCSS) that deals with remote procedure call (RPC) messages for Distributed Component Object Model (DCOM) activation. Two of the

vulnerabilities could allow an attacker to run malicious programs; one of the vulnerabilities might result in a denial of service. The flaws result from incorrect handling of malformed messages. These vulnerabilities affect the DCOM interface in RPCSS. This interface handles DCOM object activation requests that are sent by client computers to the server. An attacker who successfully exploits these vulnerabilities might be able to run code with Local System rights on an affected computer, or cause RPCSS to stop working. The attacker could then take any action on the computer, including installing programs, viewing, changing, or deleting data, or creating new accounts with full rights.

- **Buffer Overrun in Windows Help and Support Center Could Lead to System Compromise (KB825119).** A security vulnerability exists in the Help and Support Center function that ships with Windows XP and Windows Server 2003. The affected code is also included in all other supported Windows operating systems, although no known attack vector has been identified at this time because the vulnerable protocol is not supported on those platforms. The vulnerability results because a file associated with the Help and Support Center contains an unchecked buffer. An attacker could exploit the vulnerability by constructing a URL that, when clicked by a user, could run code of the attacker's choice in the Local Computer security context. The URL could be hosted on a Web page or sent directly to the user in e-mail. In the Web-based scenario, if a user clicked the URL hosted on the Web site, an attacker could have the ability to read or launch files already present on the local machine.
- **Update for Windows Media Player Script Command Behavior (KB828026).** This update contains a change to the behavior of the ability of Microsoft Windows Media Player to launch URLs in the local computer zone from other zones. When a content owner creates an audio or a video stream, that content owner can add script commands (such as URL script commands and custom script commands) that are embedded in the stream. When the stream is played back, the script commands can trigger events in an embedded player program, or they can start a Web browser and then connect to a particular Web page. Logic was added so that when Windows Media Player does run URL script commands, the script cannot take the user from a less-trusted security zone to a more-trusted security zone.

Your small network consists of a firewall, a router, a printer, several desktop and mobile clients running Windows XP, several desktop clients running Windows 98, a computer running Windows 2000 Server, and a computer running Windows Server 2003, as shown in Figure 5.9.

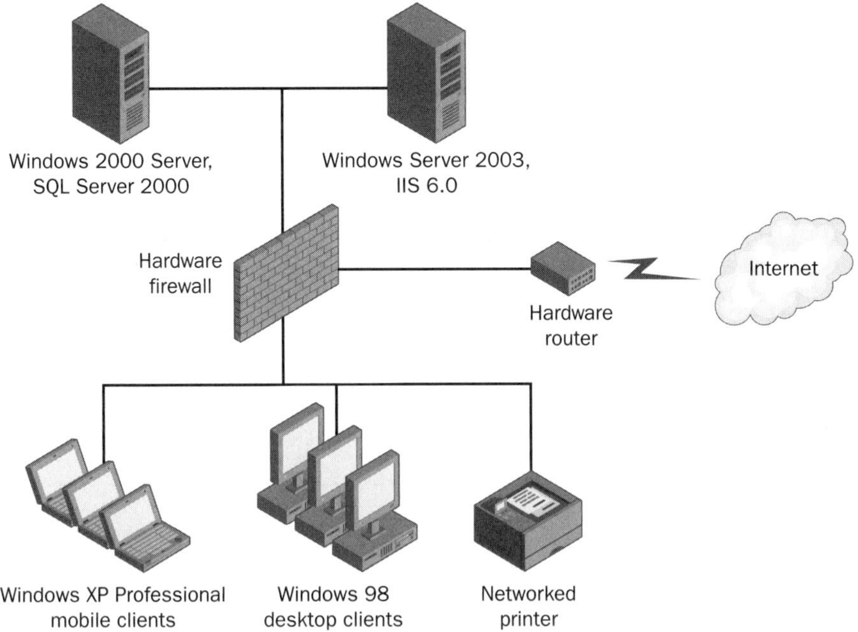

Figure 5.9 Your company's network architecture

Evaluate each of the four updates to determine their priority, and identify the computers that should receive the updates. Also consider ways to protect the computers in addition to applying updates.

Questions

1. How should you validate the updates your friend described to be sure that they really were released by Microsoft?

____

____

____

____

____

____

____

2. Which of the computers should receive the update titled Buffer Overrun in the HTML Converter Could Allow Code Execution (KB823559)? (Choose all that apply.)
   a. The computer running Windows 2000 Server
   b. The computer running Windows Server 2003
   c. The computers running Windows XP Professional
   d. The computers running Windows 98
   e. The networked printer
   f. The hardware firewall
   g. The hardware router

____

____

3. Besides applying the update, how can you protect your network from the vulnerability resolved by the update titled Buffer Overrun in the HTML Converter Could Allow Code Execution (KB823559)?

____

____

4. Which of the computers should receive the update titled A Buffer Overrun in RPCSS Could Allow an Attacker to Run Malicious Programs (KB824146)? (Choose all that apply.)
   a. The computer running Windows 2000 Server
   b. The computer running Windows Server 2003
   c. The computers running Windows XP Professional
   d. The computers running Windows 98
   e. The networked printer
   f. The hardware firewall
   g. The hardware router

____

____

____

____

____

____

5. Which of the computers should receive the update titled Buffer Overrun in Windows Help and Support Center Could Lead to System Compromise (KB825119)? (Choose all that apply.)

   a. The computer running Windows 2000 Server

   b. The computer running Windows Server 2003

   c. The computers running Windows XP Professional

   d. The computers running Windows 98

   e. The networked printer

   f. The hardware firewall

   g. The hardware router

6. Which of the computers should receive the update titled Update for Windows Media Player Script Command Behavior (KB828026)? (Choose all that apply.)

   a. The computer running Windows 2000 Server

   b. The computer running Windows Server 2003

   c. The computers running Windows XP Professional

   d. The computers running Windows 98

   e. The networked printer

   f. The hardware firewall

   g. The hardware router

7. How should you handle updates for the printer, firewall, and router?

Troubleshooting Lab

In this lab, you troubleshoot a problem related to an organization's inefficient updating process. You can find sample answers to the questions in the "Questions and Answers" section at the end of this chapter.

You are consulting for an enterprise with approximately 5,000 client computers and 200 servers. The enterprise hired you after a worm infected a large number of computers on its internal network. Use the knowledge gained by reading this chapter to answer the questions from the company's CIO. Then recommend the best way for the enterprise to resolve the problem.

1. "Our Operations group decided not to deploy an update that would have prevented this worm infection. Their reasoning was that an attack against the vulnerability would have to connect to the computers across the network, and we have a firewall blocking that traffic on our Internet connection. How could we have gotten infected?"

2. "What can we do to prevent this from happening in the future?"

3. "We simply don't have time to apply all these updates to our computers. How can we possibly keep up?"

Chapter Summary

- Microsoft releases many different types of updates, including critical updates, security updates, service packs, and hotfixes.
- A security bulletin announces a new security update and contains detailed information about protecting your computers against the vulnerability.
- Chaining allows multiple updates to be applied with a single reboot.
- The Automatic Update client connects to either the public Windows Update server or a private SUS server to download, and optionally install, updates.
- Systems Management Server is capable of working closely with SUS to deliver updates to an enterprise.
- Group Policy can be used to deliver updates, though it is not the preferred method.
- A lab environment is required for the detailed testing of updates. The more testing you perform on an update, the fewer problems you will experience when you deploy that update to the production computers on your network.
- Every organization should develop an updating process catered to its specific needs. However, every updating process should include steps for discovering, evaluating, retrieving, testing, installing, removing (if necessary), and auditing updates.
- When evaluating security updates, factor in both the cost of deploying the update and the risk associated with not deploying the update. Consider alternative ways to mitigate the vulnerability.
- Always be prepared for the worst when deploying an update. Be sure that all systems receiving the update have a recent backup available.

Exam Highlights

Before taking the exam, review the key topics and terms that are presented in this chapter. You need to know this information.

Key Topics

- Understand the need for an effective updating process.
- Be able to evaluate an update to determine whether it should be deployed to a computer.
- Be able to list the Microsoft-supported mechanisms for deploying updates to computers.
- Know the steps in an effective updating process, and understand the importance of each step.
- Understand how to remove an update from a single computer and an entire network.
- Know when to use chaining to deploy multiple updates together.
- Know the importance of each type of update released by Microsoft.

Key Terms

critical update A broadly released fix addressing a critical non-security-related bug for a specific problem.

exploit A worm, virus, Trojan horse, or other tool that can be used by an attacker to compromise a vulnerable computer.

hotfix A single package composed of one or more files used to address a problem in a product. Hotfixes address a specific customer situation, are only available through a support relationship with Microsoft, and cannot be distributed outside the customer organization without written legal consent from Microsoft. The terms *QFE* (Quick Fix Engineering update), *patch*, and *update* have been used in the past as synonyms for *hotfix*.

security rollup package A collection of security patches, critical updates, other updates, and hotfixes released as a cumulative offering or targeted at a single product component, such as IIS or Internet Explorer. Allows for easier deployment of multiple software updates.

service pack A cumulative set of hotfixes, security patches, critical updates, and other updates that have been released since the release of the product, including many resolved problems that have not been made available through any other software updates. Service packs might also contain a limited number of customer-requested design changes or features. Service packs are broadly distributed and are more thoroughly tested by Microsoft than any other software updates.

security update A broadly released fix that addresses a security vulnerability for a specific product. A security patch is often described as having a *severity*, which actually refers to the MSRC severity rating of the vulnerability that the security patch addresses.

update A broadly released fix for a specific problem. Addresses a non-critical, non-security-related bug.

Questions and Answers

Lesson 1 Review

Page 5-12

1. Which of the following types of updates is/are cumulative? (Choose all that apply.)
   - **a.** Updates
   - **b.** Security updates
   - **c.** Critical updates
   - **d.** Hotfixes
   - **e.** Security rollup packages
   - **f.** Feature packs
   - **g.** Service packs

   g. Only service packs are cumulative, meaning that they include all previous service packs. Security rollup packages include multiple security updates, but they do not necessarily include every previous update.

2. Which of the following types of updates can reduce the number of vulnerabilities on a computer? (Choose all that apply.)
   - **a.** Updates
   - **b.** Security updates
   - **c.** Critical updates
   - **d.** Hotfixes
   - **e.** Security rollup packages
   - **f.** Feature packs
   - **g.** Service packs

   b, d, e, and g. Security updates, security rollup packages, and service packs all include updates that remove known vulnerabilities. Hotfixes might or might not be security related.

3. Which of the following types of updates have not been fully tested for compatibility by Microsoft? (Choose all that apply.)
   - **a.** Updates
   - **b.** Security updates
   - **c.** Critical updates
   - **d.** Hotfixes
   - **e.** Security rollup packages

f. Feature packs

g. Service packs

a, b, c, d, and e. Only service packs and feature packs undergo a complete set of testing by Microsoft to ensure the highest level of compatibility with non-Microsoft applications. Other types of updates must bypass thorough testing in order to be released to customers quickly.

1. Which of the following pieces of information are not contained in a security bulletin?

   a. Software affected by the vulnerability

   b. Location from which to download update

   c. Location from which to download programs that exploit vulnerabilities

   d. Severity rating

c. Security bulletins do not include a location from which to download programs that exploit the vulnerability. Other companies will frequently release tools to exploit a vulnerability, either to test your computers for the presence of the vulnerability, or to be used maliciously.

Practice: Evaluating Your Updating Infrastructure

Page 5-25

1. How does your current organization deploy updates to computers on the network?

   Answers will vary based on your own experience.

2. How long does it take for updates to be delivered to computers on your network? Is the current delay acceptable, or does it leave your network vulnerable to attack?

   Answers will vary based on your own experience.

3. Who decides on whether an update should be deployed? In retrospect, have updates been deployed unnecessarily, or have important updates been skipped? Is the same group responsible for both identifying and deploying updates, and, if so, is this a conflict of interest?

   Answers will vary based on your own experience.

4. If you had the opportunity to perform an overhaul of your organization's updating infrastructure, which deployment method would you use?

   Answers will vary based on your own experience. However, Software Update Services is the ideal method for deploying updates for most organizations that do not use Systems Management Server.

Lesson 2 Review

Page 5-26

1. Which of the following deployment methods gives administrators the opportunity to approve updates before releasing them to clients? (Choose all that apply.)

   a. Windows Update

   b. Software Update Services

c. Group Policy

d. Add/Remove Programs

e. Systems Management Server

b, c, d, and e. Only Windows Update, which users use to manually apply updates to their own computers, denies the administrator the opportunity to choose which updates to deploy.

2. Which of the following deployment methods can be used to automatically deploy all security updates that Microsoft releases to client computers, without administrator intervention? (Choose all that apply.)

a. Windows Update

b. Software Update Services

c. Group Policy

d. Add/Remove Programs

e. Systems Management Server

a, b, and e. Windows Update, Software Update Services, and Systems Management Server can all be configured to automatically deploy updates to clients. Windows Update and Software Update Services rely on the Automatic Update client being correctly configured to download and install updates.

Practice: Evaluating Your Updating Process

Page 5-36

1. Has your organization formally identified and documented an updating process? If so, what is that process?

Answers will vary based on your own experience.

2. Has your organization ever had to remove an update after deploying it? If not, are you prepared to quickly remove an update from all computers on your network?

Answers will vary based on your own experience.

Lesson 3 Review

Page 5-36

1. How can you validate that an update is genuine?

Security bulletins released by Microsoft are Pretty Good Privacy (PGP) signed. You can verify the PGP signature of the message by using a PGP tools application, which is available from various software companies. You can also retrieve the security bulletin directly from the Microsoft Web site. If you retrieve the bulletin by using Hypertext Transfer Protocol Secure (HTTPS), you can verify the certificate of the server. Finally, you can verify the actual update itself by right-clicking the file, clicking Properties, and then clicking the Digital Signatures tab.

2. Which requires more testing, a service pack or a security update?

Generally, a service pack requires more testing than a security update because a service pack implements many more changes than a security update.

Design Activity: Case Scenario Exercise

Page 5-39

1. How should you validate the updates your friend described to be sure that they really were released by Microsoft?

   Though your friend is being honest, there have been several viruses and worms that masqueraded as updates from Microsoft. You should visit the Microsoft Web site and look up each of the Knowledge Base (KB) articles referenced. You can use the URL *http://support.microsoft.com/?kbid=######* (where *###### is the number of the particular article)* to access a KB article directly. For example, to read KB article 823559, you can visit *http://support.microsoft.com/?kbid=823559*. You should only retrieve the updates directly from Microsoft.

2. Which of the computers should receive the update titled Buffer Overrun in the HTML Converter Could Allow Code Execution (KB823559)? (Choose all that apply.)

   a. The computer running Windows 2000 Server

   b. The computer running Windows Server 2003

   c. The computers running Windows XP Professional

   d. The computers running Windows 98

   e. The networked printer

   f. The hardware firewall

   g. The hardware router

   a, b, c, and d. The update applies to all Windows-based computers on your network, so all computers should eventually receive the update.

3. Besides applying the update, how can you protect your network from the vulnerability resolved by the update titled Buffer Overrun in the HTML Converter Could Allow Code Execution (KB823559)?

   The vulnerability can only be exploited if a computer visits a malicious Web page. Therefore, you can remove the vulnerability without applying the update in several different ways:

   - Configure the firewall to block all outgoing Web requests.
   - Use Group Policy objects to restrict computers from visiting untrusted Web sites.
   - Use Group Policy objects to remove user access to Internet Explorer.

4. Which of the computers should receive the update titled A Buffer Overrun in RPCSS Could Allow an Attacker to Run Malicious Programs (KB824146)? (Choose all that apply.)

   a. The computer running Windows 2000 Server

   b. The computer running Windows Server 2003

   c. The computers running Windows XP Professional

   d. The computers running Windows 98

e. The networked printer

f. The hardware firewall

g. The hardware router

a, b, and c. All computers on your network should eventually receive this update, except for the computers running Windows 98, which do not require the update. (Complete information about which systems the update applies to is located in the Knowledge Base article.) Note that the firewall will protect all computers from an attack originating from the public Internet. However, you have mobile computers behind your firewall. If one of these mobile computers connects to another network, such as the user's home network or a network at an airport or coffee shop, the computer could be infected by an attack to that vulnerability. When the infected computer connects to your network, the malicious program can propagate to the other computers behind your firewall because the firewall is only blocking requests originating from the public Internet.

5. Which of the computers should receive the update titled Buffer Overrun in Windows Help and Support Center Could Lead to System Compromise (KB825119)? (Choose all that apply.)

   a. The computer running Windows 2000 Server

   b. The computer running Windows Server 2003

   c. The computers running Windows XP Professional

   d. The computers running Windows 98

   e. The networked printer

   f. The hardware firewall

   g. The hardware router

   b and c. This particular vulnerability is considered critical only for computers running Windows Server 2003 and Windows XP. Although computers running Windows 2000 are technically vulnerable, they cannot be exploited, and you can safely wait until the next service pack is released to update these computers.

6. Which of the computers should receive the update titled Update for Windows Media Player Script Command Behavior (KB828026)? (Choose all that apply.)

   a. The computer running Windows 2000 Server

   b. The computer running Windows Server 2003

   c. The computers running Windows XP Professional

   d. The computers running Windows 98

   e. The networked printer

   f. The hardware firewall

   g. The hardware router

c. Only the computers running Windows XP need to receive this update, because they are the only computers likely to be using Windows Media Player. Server computers should not be using Windows Media Player, and they should have that component of Windows removed to protect against the vulnerability.

7. How should you handle updates for the printer, firewall, and router?

Almost every networked device requires occasional updates. However, Microsoft is only responsible for releasing updates for Microsoft software. You should regularly visit the Web sites of the vendors you purchased the printer, firewall, and router from to learn about security updates that have been released for the devices.

Design Activity: Troubleshooting Lab

Page 5-42

You are consulting for an enterprise with approximately 5,000 client computers and 200 servers. The enterprise hired you after a worm infected a large number of computers on its internal network. Use the knowledge gained by reading this chapter to answer the questions from the company's CIO. Then recommend the best way for the enterprise to resolve the problem.

1. "Our Operations group decided not to deploy an update that would have prevented this worm infection. Their reasoning was that an attack against the vulnerability would have to connect to the computers across the network, and we have a firewall blocking that traffic on our Internet connection. How could we have gotten infected?"

   Perimeter security is insufficient to protect modern networks because mobile clients might become infected while connected to different networks, and then introduce worms and viruses behind the firewall. After it is introduced, a worm or virus can spread quickly on the unprotected internal network.

2. "What can we do to prevent this from happening in the future?"

   First, you need to separate the roles of evaluating and deploying updates. Currently, your Operations group is performing both roles. They cannot objectively identify updates to be deployed because each update they identify requires them to perform additional work. They might be inclined not to deploy an update when they are already occupied with more interesting assignments.

   Second, you need to acknowledge that perimeter security is insufficient to protect against network-borne attacks. You must apply updates to clients on the internal network. In addition to updating internal computers, using host-based firewalls in addition to a perimeter firewall will significantly reduce the likelihood that a worm or virus will spread within your internal network.

3. "We simply don't have time to apply all these updates to our computers. How can we possibly keep up?"

   Choose an automated update deployment mechanism, such as Software Update Services and the Automatic Update client. The effort required to deploy updates, even to a large organization, is minimal. It's certainly less than the effort required to clean up an entire network of computers that have become infected because a vulnerability was not updated.

6 Assessing and Deploying a Patch Management Infrastructure

Exam Objectives in this Chapter:

- Assess the current status of service packs and hotfixes. Tools include MBSA and MBSACLI.
  - Assess current patch levels by using MBSA.
  - Assess current patch levels by using MBSACLI scripted solutions.
- Deploy service packs and hotfixes.
  - Deploy service packs and hotfixes on new client and server computers. Considerations include slipstreaming, custom scripts, and isolated installation or test networks.
  - Deploy service packs and hotfixes to existing client and server computers.

Why This Chapter Matters

Deploying updates is one of the most daunting and complicated tasks faced by Information Technology today. Even the most carefully planned patch infrastructures will experience problems, whether caused by Internet connection issues, mobile clients disconnected from the network, or computers that users have reconfigured. Unless you are prepared for these problems, they can undermine all your other security measures.

Problems might occur when you are deploying updates to a large number of computers, and you must be prepared to handle these problems. Understanding how to deploy updates and troubleshoot these problems is a key part of securing your network, and this chapter will provide you with detailed information about the most common methods used to deploy updates. You will also need to catch those computers that miss update deployments by assessing, or auditing, the current patch levels of computers in your network. This chapter will describe how to use the Microsoft Baseline Security Analyzer (MBSA) to manually and automatically scan your network for computers that are not up to date on updates.

Lessons in this Chapter:

Before You Begin

If you fulfilled the requirements for the previous chapters, you already have the necessary hardware and software configured. You can use the computers in the state they were in after completing the previous chapters, or you can install the software from scratch. To do the practices, examples, and lab exercises in this chapter, you must have:

- A private network that is connected to the Internet and protected by a firewall. This network should not have any production computers connected to it.
- One computer. Perform a Windows Server 2003 installation with default settings, and assign the computer name Computer1. This computer must be able to resolve Internet host names.
- Add the domain controller role to Computer1, using the default settings, and specify the domain name cohowinery.com. Configure the computer to use itself as its own primary Domain Name System (DNS) server, and to use your organization's or Internet service provider's DNS server as the secondary DNS server.

Lesson 1: Assessing Patch Levels

Auditing is one of security's core concepts. Without auditing, security degrades over time. Updating is certainly no exception to this; even if you configure an airtight updating infrastructure, at some point a computer on your network will go unpatched. This can happen when a mobile computer is disconnected from the network for an extended period, when a user changes a computer's configuration settings, and when the installation process of an update is interrupted.

MBSA is a powerful tool that you can use to assess the patch levels on your network. If and when a computer fails to install an update, MBSA can detect it. If there are rogue computers on your network that are not participating in your patching infrastructure, MBSA can find them. You can even schedule MBSA to scan your network for unpatched computers at night, so you can review the reports in the morning without waiting for the scan to occur.

After this lesson, you will be able to

- Use the graphical MBSA console to identify unpatched computers on your network.
- Use the command-line MBSACLI tool to identify unpatched computers on your network.
- Schedule automatic scanning for unpatched computers.

Estimated lesson time: 60 minutes

The MBSA Console

Microsoft Baseline Security Analyzer (MBSA), which was also discussed in Chapter 4, is used to analyze one or more computers for vulnerabilities in two categories: weak security configurations and missing security updates. This section focuses on using MBSA to scan for updates that should have been installed but have not been.

After installing MBSA, you can use it to scan all computers on your network or domain for which you have administrator access. To scan all computers on a specific subnet using your current user credentials:

1. Start MBSA by clicking Start, pointing to All Programs, and then clicking Microsoft Baseline Security Advisor.
2. On the Welcome To The Microsoft Baseline Security Analyzer page, click Scan More Than One Computer.
3. On the Pick Multiple Computers To Scan page, type the IP address range you want to scan. To speed up the scanning process, clear all check boxes except for Check For Security Updates. If you have a Software Update Services (SUS) server on your network, you can further speed up the process by selecting Use SUS and specify-

ing the server. Figure 6.1 shows MBSA configured to scan the 192.168.1.0 subnet for security updates.

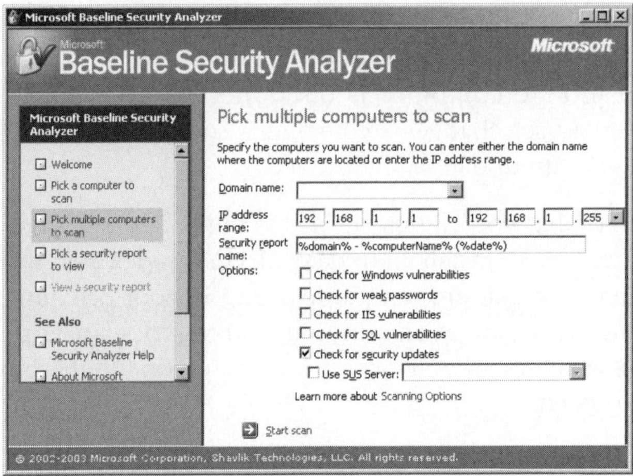

Figure 6.1 MBSA configured to scan a subnet

4. Click Start Scan.

   As MBSA performs the scan, it will keep you updated on the progress, as shown in Figure 6.2.

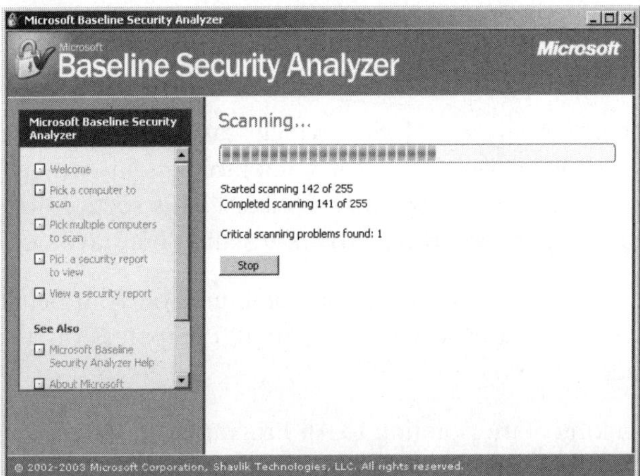

Figure 6.2 MBSA scanning a subnet

5. After the scan is completed, the View Security Report page appears, listing the computers that were scanned.

> **Note** If you do not have sufficient credentials on a computer, MBSA will display the Internet Protocol (IP) address of the computer and the message, "User Is Not An Administrator On The Scanned Machine."

Missing updates are marked by a red X, and out-of-date updates are marked with a yellow X. A green checkmark denotes a scan that was completed successfully with no missing updates found. Scan reports are stored on the computer from which you ran MBSA in the %userprofile%\SecurityScans folder. An individual security report is created for each computer that is scanned.

During the scanning process, MBSA uses NetBIOS over Transmission Control Protocol/Internet Protocol (TCP/IP) and Common Internet File System (CIFS) protocols to connect to computers, which requires TCP ports 139 and 445. If there is a firewall blocking these ports between you and the target computers, or if the computers have Internet Connection Firewall enabled and these ports have not been opened, you will not be able to scan the computers.

At the beginning of the scan, MBSA must retrieve an XML file that provides information about updates and security vulnerabilities. By default, this file is retrieved from the Microsoft Web site at *http://go.microsoft.com/fwlink/?LinkId=16932* and includes every current update available from Microsoft. If you use SUS to approve specific updates, select the Use SUS check box and provide your SUS server's host name. This will cause MBSA to retrieve the ApprovedItems.txt file located at the root of Internet Information Services' default Web site. Specifying this option will configure MBSA so that it does not mark updates that you deliberately choose not to deploy.

> **Real World The Benefits of Network Scanning**
>
> I spent several years at a company that had a few hundred Internet-connected servers that ran Microsoft Windows. Whenever there was a major worm or virus making the rounds, we would scan all of our computers for vulnerabilities to make sure they had all been updated. Normally, we did this by checking each of the IP addresses that we had listed for our servers.
>
> One day I was feeling lazy and decided to simply scan all the subnets in our data center instead of scanning just the IPs listed in our database of servers. What I found surprised me—we had dozens of servers that were vulnerable and that were not listed in the database! Most of these computers had passed by unnoticed, but a handful had been intentionally removed from the database. They all had one thing in common, though: they had not been updated.

There might be cases in which MBSA reports that an update is not installed, even after you complete an update or take the steps documented in a security bulletin. There are two reasons for these false reports, both of which should simply be noted and ignored for future scans:

- **Files scanned were updated by an installation that is unrelated to a security bulletin.** For example, a file shared by different versions of the same program might be updated by the newer version. MBSA is unaware of the new version and, because it does not encounter what is expected, it reports that the update is missing.
- **Some security bulletins arc addressed not by a file update but by a configuration change that cannot be verified.** These types of flags will appear as Note or Warning messages, marked with blue asterisks or yellow Xs, respectively.

MBSACLI

Scanning a large network should be done on a regular basis to find computers that have not been properly updated. However, scanning a large network is a time-consuming process. While the MBSA console is the most efficient way to interactively scan a network, the Microsoft Baseline Security Analyzer command-line interface (MBSACLI) provides a way to script an analysis. By using scripts, you can schedule scanning to occur automatically, without your intervention. In this way, you can have MBSACLI generate a report that you can refer to on demand.

Security Alert It's convenient to schedule MBSACLI scans after business hours so you don't consume network resources during working hours; however, if you do this, you won't scan computers that users take home with them. It's a good idea to schedule scans at various times during the day.

Another good reason to schedule scans by using MBSACLI is to scan from multiple points on your network. For example, if your organization has five remote offices, it is more efficient to scan each remote office by using a computer located in that office. This improves performance, reduces the bandwidth used on your wide area network, and allows you to scan computers even if a perimeter firewall blocks the ports that MBSACLI uses to scan.

MBSACLI runs in one of two modes: MBSA and HFNetChk. MBSA mode provides similar functionality to that of the graphical MBSA console. HFNetChk mode provides backward compatibility with earlier versions of the tool, and also provides additional functionality not supported in MBSA mode. Some of the additional features provided by HFNetChk mode are connecting to network resources as another user, specifying an XML data source, and scanning a set of computers specified in a text file. HFNetChk mode scans only for missing updates; it will not scan for other types of vulnerabilities, such as weak configuration settings.

As with the MBSA graphical console, you need administrative access to use MBSACLI to scan a computer. If you are scanning a remote computer and need to verify your administrative access and network connectivity from a command prompt, you can use the command **Net use *computername*\c$**. Establishing a connection to the hidden administrative C$ share uses the same network protocols that MBSACLI will use. After a connection is established, MBSA will use the existing connection and credentials. Therefore, if you need to connect to a remote computer using different credentials, and do not want to use HFNetChk mode, first establish a connection with the Net Use command. The following example scans the remote computer with the IP address 192.168.1.204 using the user name admin1 and the password je#o23$sti:

```
net use \\192.168.1.204\c$ /user:admin1 je#o23$sti
mbsacli /i 192.168.1.204
net use \\192.168.1.204\c$ /delete
```

Table 6.1 lists the parameters available in MBSACLI's MBSA mode.

Table 6.1 MBSACLI's MBSA Mode Parameters

Parameter	Description
/c *computername*	Scans the host with the specified computer name.
/i *ipaddress*	Scans the host with the specified IP address.
/r *ipaddress1-ipaddress2*	Specifies an IP address range to be scanned, beginning with *ipaddress1* and ending with *ipaddress2*, inclusive.
/d *domain_name*	Scans all computers in a specified domain. Of course, your computer must be able to identify those computers. It uses the same mechanism as Network Neighborhood, so if you can browse computers in Network Neighborhood, this switch will work.
/n *scans*	Skips specific scans. You can choose OS, SQL, IIS, Updates, and Password. If you want to suppress multiple scans, separate them with a + sign. For example, to scan only for updates, use the command `Mbsacli /n OS+SQL+IIS+Password`.
/o *"template"*	Uses a different template for the report file name. By default, the name is %domain% - %computername% (%date%). If you put one or more spaces in the template, be sure to enclose it in quotes.
/f *filename*	Redirects Mbsacli summary output to the specified file. This does not redirect all the output you would normally see on the console—just the summary of the scanned computers. Copyright and status information is still displayed on the console, but it is not recorded in the file.
/qp, /qe, /qr	Does not display the scan progress, error list, and report list, respectively.

Table 6.1 MBSACLI's MBSA Mode Parameters

Parameter	Description
/s *suppress_level*	Specifies a suppression level of 0, 1, or 2. Specifying a level of 1 suppresses security update check notes; the default level of 2 suppresses both security update check notes and warnings. Specifying a level of 0 suppresses nothing.
/baseline	Causes MBSACLI to check only for baseline security updates.
/nosum	Prevents MBSACLI from testing file checksums. This option is automatically enabled when you use the /sus option.
/sus *susserver*	Checks only for updates that have been approved at the specified SUS server. Provide the computer name or IP address with the http:// prefix. For example, to only scan for updates approved on a SUS server named Computer1, execute the command `Mbsacli /sus http://computer1`.
/e	Lists the errors from the latest scan, without actually performing a scan.
/l, /ls	Lists all available reports, or just the reports created in the latest scan, respectively.
/lr "*reportname*", /ld "*reportname*"	Displays an overview or detailed report summary, given the file, name of the report. You do not need to specify the full file name—only the name of the report. For example, the following command would show a report for Computer1: `mbsacli /ld "Cohowinery.com - Computer1 (11-11-2003 07-46 AM)"`
/v	Displays security update reason codes when you are viewing a report by using the /lr or /ld options. For example, the /ld parameter will list every update that could not be verified, and will provide the security update number and description. Add the /v parameter, and MBSACLI will add a detailed explanation for every update, such as "File C:\WINDOWS\system32\hhctrl.ocx has a file version [5.2.3735.0] greater than what is expected [5.2.3669.0]". In this example, viewing the reason code might allow you to determine that there is no cause for alarm.
/hf	Switches to HFNetChk mode. When used, this must be the first parameter. All parameters following this parameter must be HFNetChk-mode parameters.

MBSACLI does not output information about vulnerabilities directly to the console. Instead, it only displays the computers scanned and the overall assessment. The details of the scan are stored in an XML report that is saved in your %userprofile%\SecurityScans\ folder. By default, the file name for each report is set to *domain – computername (date)*.

You can view the reports by using the graphical MBSA console, however. Simply start MBSA and then click View Existing Security Reports. MBSA will show the Pick A Security Report To View page, listing all of the available reports. You can also view them from the command line by using the /ld parameter and specifying the report file name.

To use the HFNetChk mode of MBSACLI, use /hf as the first parameter. Then provide the standard HFNetChk parameters. Table 6.2 lists each of the parameters that can be used in HFNetChk mode. To call each of these parameters, execute the command **MBSACLI /hf *parameters***.

Table 6.2 MBSACLI's HFNetChk Mode Parameters

Parameter	Description
-about	Shows copyright information before performing standard scanning functions.
-h *computername*	As with MBSA mode, scans the host with the specified computer name.
-i *IP_Address*	As with MBSA mode, scans the host with the specified IP address.
-r *range*	As with MBSA mode, scans a range of IP addresses.
-d *domain_name*	As with MBSA mode, scans an entire domain.
-fh *hostfile*	Specifies a file containing a list of computer names to scan. To create the hostfile, simply create a text file and list each computer name on a separate line. The list can have up to 256 computer names.
-fip *ipfile*	Specifies a file containing a list of IP addresses to scan. To create the ipfile, simply create a text file and list each IP address on a separate line. The list can have up to 256 IP addresses.
-fq *ignorefile*	Specifies a file containing a list of Knowledge Base articles relating to updates that should be ignored. To create the ignorefile, simply create a text file and list each Knowledge Base article number on a separate line.
-n	Scans all computers in the local workgroups or domains. This switch is similar to the -d switch for a domain, but all computers from all domains in the network neighborhood are scanned.
-history *level*	Displays hotfixes that have been explicitly installed, explicitly not installed, or both. You can use any of three values with this switch: ■ 1: Displays hotfixes that have been explicitly installed. ■ 2: Displays hotfixes that have explicitly not been installed. ■ 3: Displays both hotfixes that have explicitly been installed and those that have explicitly not been installed.
-t *threads*	Displays the number of threads that are used to run the scan, which controls how many actions the scanner will perform simultaneously. Possible values are from 1 to 128. The default value is 64. Setting a value over 64 might increase the speed of the scanner, and setting the value lower than 64 might slow it down. You might want to slow the scanner down to reduce the network capacity consumed by the scanner.
-o *outputtype*	Specifies the output format. You can specify **-o tab** to generate output in a tab-delimited format that can be easily parsed, or the default **-o wrap** to generate output in a more readable format. You must use tab output when you scan more than 255 hosts. Use only the tab format when importing the output into another application, such as Microsoft Excel.

Table 6.2 MBSACLI's HFNetChk Mode Parameters

Parameter	Description

-x *datasource*	Specifies the XML data source that contains the hotfix information. The location can be an XML file name, a compressed XML .cab file, or a Uniform Resource Locator (URL). The default file is the Mssecure.cab file from the Microsoft Web site.
	When you run mbsacli /hf without the -x switch, the XML file is downloaded from the Microsoft Web site. The XML file is named Mssecure.xml and is typically located in the same folder as the Mbsacli_/hf.exe file. After you download the file, you can run future scans with the -x switch. For example:
	`mbsacli /hf -x http://computer1/hotfixes.xml`
	or
	`mbsacli /hf -x s:\security\hotfixfile.xml`

-s *suppress*	Suppresses note and warning messages. Using the **-s 1** parameter suppresses note messages only. Using **-s 2** suppresses both note and warning messages. By default, both notes and warnings are displayed.
-z *reg checks*	By default, the hotfix registry key specific to each update is examined to determine if the update is installed. If the registry key does not exist, MBSACLI reports that the update is missing. If the registry key does exist, MBSACLI examines the file versions and checksums. Under some circumstances, a registry key might not exist even if the hotfix is installed. Under these circumstances, you can use the command `mbsacli /hf -z` to perform only the file checks.
-nosum	Specifies that the tool should not perform checksum validation for the hotfix files. This switch exists primarily because earlier versions of MBSACLI did not detect non-English language versions of Windows, which use different checksums.
-b	Scans your computer only for those hotfixes that are marked as baseline critical by the Microsoft Security Response Center (MSRC). Use this parameter only if you have determined that your computers need only the baseline critical updates.
-v *verbose*	Displays the specific reason a test failed, and should almost always be used. This switch is enabled by default when the **-o tab** parameter is used.
-f *outfile*	Unlike MBSA mode, the HFNetChk mode of MBSACLI does not create an XML file containing the results of the report. Instead, you need to use the **–f** switch to specify the name of a file in which to store the results. For example, to store the results of a tab output to a file named Update-scan.txt on drive C, you would use the command `mbsacli /hf -o tab -f c:\Update-scan.txt`

Table 6.2 MBSACLI's HFNetChk Mode Parameters

Parameter	Description
-u *username* –p *password*	By default, mbsacli /hf scans computers by using the credentials of the user who is currently logged on to the computer that is performing the scan. This switch specifies the user name to use when you scan a local or a remote computer or group of computers.
-sus *susserver*	As with MBSA mode, this parameter specifies to check only for updates that have been approved at the specified SUS server. Unlike in MBSA mode, if you do not specify a server, MBSACLI in HFNetChk mode will try to obtain the list of approved security updates from the SUS server that is listed in the registry of the scanning computer.
-sum	Forces a checksum scan when you scan a non-English-language computer. Use this switch only if you have a custom XML file with language-specific checksums.
-trace	Creates a file named Hf.log in the local folder that contains debugging information to help with troubleshooting. You must specify the **-trace** switch immediately after the **/hf** parameter.

Practice: Assessing Patch Levels on the Current Network

In this practice, you will asses the patch levels on your network by using both the graphical and command-line MBSA tools.

Exercise 1: Assess Patch Levels on the Current Network Using MBSA

In this exercise, you will install MBSA and scan your local network.

1. Log on to the cohowinery.com domain on Computer1 using the Administrator account.
2. Temporarily connect Computer1 to the Internet, and download MBSA from *http://www.microsoft.com/technet/security/tools/tools/mbsahome.asp*.
3. Transfer the MBSA setup files to Computer1, and install MBSA.
4. Start MBSA by clicking Start, pointing to All Programs, and then clicking Microsoft Baseline Security Analyzer.
5. Click Scan More Than One Computer.
6. In the IP Address Range boxes, specify **192.168.1.1** to **192.168.1.255**.

Important If you used a different IP subnet for your computer, specify the start and end of that subnet instead.

7. Clear Check For Windows Vulnerabilities, Check For Weak Passwords, Check For IIS Vulnerabilities, and Check For SQL Vulnerabilities.
8. Click Start Scan.
9. After the scan completes, click the first security report.
10. Scroll to the Security Update Scan Results section. If a red X appears beside the Windows Security Updates row, click Results Details.
11. Examine the list of missing updates for that computer. Close the window.
12. If it is available, click Next Security Report at the bottom of the page. Examine the results of the Windows Security Updates assessment, as described in steps 10 and 11. Repeat this step until you have assessed the patch level on all computers in the subnet.

Exercise 2: Automating Scanning with MBSACLI

In this exercise, you will schedule your local network to be scanned every day at 3:00 A.M. To complete this exercise, you must have Computer1 connected to the Internet and MBSA installed, as described in Exercise 1.

1. Log on to the cohowinery.com domain on Computer1 using the Administrator account.
2. Create a folder named C:\Scripts.
3. In the C:\Scripts folder, create a text file named scan_network.bat. Edit the new file by using Notepad, and add the following line:

   "C:\Program Files\Microsoft Baseline Security Analyzer\mbsacli" /n OS+IIS+SQL+PASSWORD /r "192.168.1.1-192.168.1.255"

> **Important** If you used a different IP subnet for your computer, specify the start and end of that subnet instead.

4. Click Start, point to All Programs, point to Accessories, point to System Tools, and then click Scheduled Tasks.
5. Double-click Add Scheduled Tasks.

   The Scheduled Task Wizard appears.
6. Click Next.
7. Click the Browse button, and navigate to the C:\Scripts\Scan_network.bat file. Click Open.
8. Click Daily, and then click Next.

9. Set the Start Time field to 3:00 A.M., and then click Next.
10. Enter your user name and password in the appropriate fields, and then click Next.
11. Click Finish.
12. Verify that the scheduled task will run correctly by launching it immediately. Right-click the scan_network task, and then click Run.
13. After the scan has completed, start the graphical MBSA console.
14. Click Pick A Security Report To View. Note that the reports generated by the scheduled task appear in the list and can be viewed.
15. Close the MBSA console and disconnect Computer1 from the Internet.

Lesson Review

The following questions are intended to reinforce key information presented in this lesson. If you are unable to answer a question, review the lesson materials and try the question again. You can find answers to the questions in the "Questions and Answers" section at the end of this chapter.

1. By default, where do MBSA and MBSACLI store security reports?
   - **a.** C:\MBSA
   - **b.** C:\Documents and Settings*username*\
   - **c.** C:\Documents and Settings*username*\Security Scans\
   - **d.** C:\Documents and Settings*username*\My Documents\Security Scans\

---

2. Which of the following commands would scan the subnet 192.168.5.0?
   - **a.** mbsa –n 192.168.5.0
   - **b.** mbsacli –i 192.168.5.1-192.168.5.255
   - **c.** mbsacli –n 192.168.5.1-192.168.5.255
   - **d.** mbsacli –r 192.168.5.1-192.168.5.255

Lesson Summary

- The graphical MBSA console is the most efficient way to scan a single computer or multiple computers for the presence of updates.
- The graphical MBSA console can be configured to scan a single computer, a range of IP addresses, or all computers contained within a domain.
- MBSA stores reports in XML format in the C:\Documents and Settings*user-name*\SecurityScans folder by default. At any time, you can view these reports by using MBSA.
- MBSACLI provides a command-line interface to MBSA's scanning functionality. MBSACLI functions in two modes: standard MBSA mode and the backward compatible HFNetChk mode.
- Scanning a large number of computers can take several hours and consumes significant network resources. Therefore, you should schedule the scanning to occur after business hours by using the command-line tools.

Lesson 2: Deploying Updates on New Clients

The setup process is a very vulnerable time for new computers. Updates can fix the vast majority of vulnerabilities for computers running Microsoft Windows, but if you install a computer using the original distribution of Windows, those vulnerabilities will be present during the setup process. Fortunately, there are steps you can take to limit the risk of having those vulnerabilities exploited. First, you should leave new computers disconnected from the network during the setup process, or use a firewall to block traffic from potentially dangerous networks. Second, you can integrate as many of the updates as possible into the Windows setup files, so that the updates are present even during the setup process.

After this lesson, you will be able to

- Design a dedicated network for installing new computers one at a time, with minimal infrastructure.
- Design a dedicated network for installing new computers in assembly-line fashion.
- Integrate service packs into Windows setup files.
- Automatically install updates after an automated installation.

Estimated lesson time: 30 minutes

Security Considerations

Computers are under attack from the moment they connect to the Internet. Worms and viruses are constantly active, probing every IP address for vulnerabilities. Microsoft Windows Server 2003 is much more resilient to attacks that might occur during the installation process than earlier versions of Windows because it adheres to the "secure by default" ideal. However, vulnerabilities have been discovered in unpatched computers running Windows Server 2003, and these vulnerabilities might be exploited during the setup process.

Although it is possible to update and secure a computer running Windows so that it can be connected directly to the Internet without becoming infected by a worm or a virus, a computer does not have the benefit of updates or security hardening during the installation process. If you attempt to install Windows on a computer while it is connected to the Internet, there is a high probability that it will be attacked, and possibly exploited.

Security Alert Earlier versions of Windows have several widely exploited vulnerabilities, and will almost certainly be exploited during the setup process if connected to the Internet.

Security Alert Not all attacks originate from the Internet. Worms and viruses might have infected computers on the local area network, and will be scanning computers inside the firewall for vulnerabilities. Therefore, you must still take measures to protect computers while installing the operating system, even if they are only connected to a private network.

Ideally, you would eliminate the possibility of being attacked across the network by installing the computer without connecting it to a network. First, place all service packs and security updates that have been released for the operating system onto removable media, such as a CD-ROM. Then install the operating system by using the CD-ROM, and install the necessary service packs and security updates. Harden the computer's security configuration, as described in Chapter 4 of this book. Connect the computer to the network only after the computer has been updated and hardened.

If you must perform the installation of the operating system or updates by using the network, create a separate network segment dedicated to the installation process. Connect as few computers to this network segment as possible: the file server containing the operating system installation files, and a Software Update Services (SUS) server that can be used to retrieve the latest updates. After the installation has completed, connect the newly installed computer to the production network. Figure 6.3 illustrates a typical installation network used for installing multiple computers simultaneously.

Creating a separate network segment for installing new computers has benefits other than improved security. Installing an operating system across a network is extremely bandwidth intensive, and, depending on your network configuration, the bandwidth consumed while installing a computer can negatively impact the network performance of other computers on the network. Additionally, you can significantly reduce the time required to install a new computer by using a higher-speed network for installations. For example, if your production network segment is 100 megabits per second Ethernet and you can't justify the cost of upgrading all computers to gigabit Ethernet, you might be able to justify the cost of a small gigabit Ethernet network switch, and gigabit network interface cards, to be used only during the installation process.

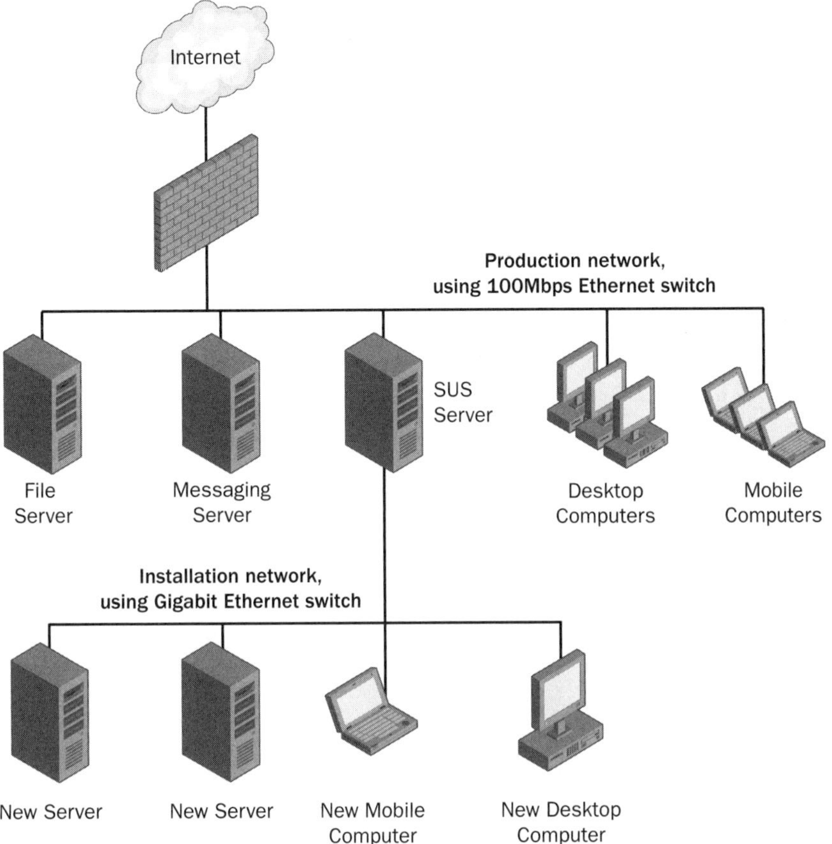

Figure 6.3 A private installation network for multiple computers

If you are installing only one computer at a time, you do not need dedicated network hardware to create a separate installation network. Simply add an additional network interface card to your SUS server, and connect the new computer directly to the SUS server by using a crossover network cable, as shown in Figure 6.4. A *crossover cable* is a special type of network cable used to connect two network interface cards directly to each other. This architecture dramatically reduces the risk of the new computer becoming infected during the installation process, because only the SUS server could possibly infect the new computer. Additionally, there is no impact on network performance, because installation traffic does not traverse the production network.

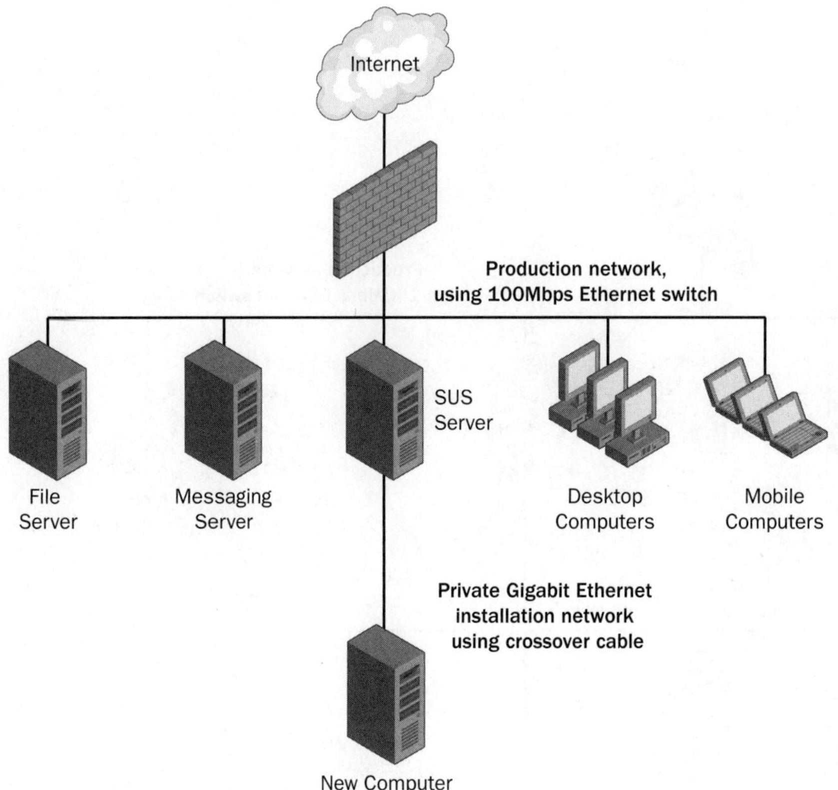

Figure 6.4 A private installation network for a single computer

If you do not maintain an SUS server, and you do not want to download updates to removable media before building a computer, you can use the Windows Update servers to update the computer. Proper network configuration can minimize the risk to which the new computer is exposed during the installation process. To allow a new computer to be installed and retrieve updates directly from Windows Update while minimizing the risk of exposing vulnerabilities, connect the computer directly to a firewall or proxy server, as shown in Figure 6.5. It is important that the new computer never have an unfiltered connection to the Internet or even to a private network.

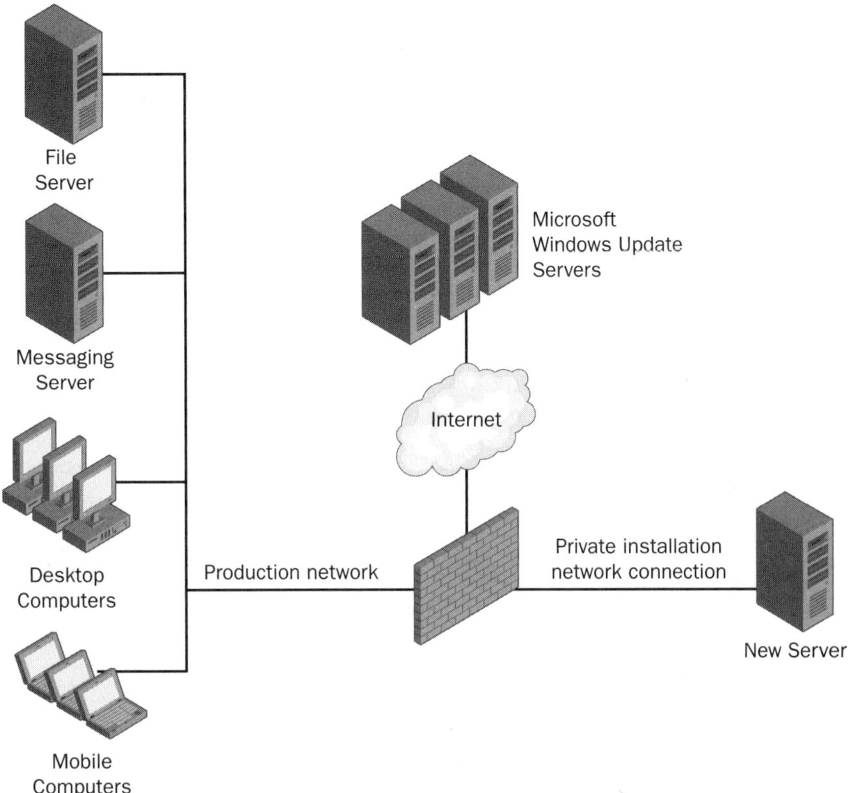

Figure 6.5 A private installation network allowing for access to Windows Update

Integrated Installation

You can apply service packs, but not necessarily other types of updates, directly to Windows 2000, Windows XP, and Windows Server 2003 installation files. The process of integrating a service pack into the original setup files for an operating system is called *slipstreaming*. Slipstreaming creates an integrated installation—including the latest service pack—that can be used when installing the operating system on new computers. Using this process improves the security of new computers, and reduces the time required to apply updates after completing the initial installation. You can either perform the installation from a shared folder or create a CD with the integrated setup files.

Because the integrated installation replaces individual files, the space requirements for this installation type are almost identical to the space requirements for the base operating system. After you slipstream a service pack into the operating system setup files, you cannot remove the service pack.

To create a shared folder containing Windows setup files with an integrated service pack:

1. Connect to the network or computer on which you want to create the distribution folder.
2. Configure the permissions on the folder so that Everyone has Read and Execute permissions, and so that only the users responsible for managing the distribution files can make changes.
3. Insert your Windows installation CD into your computer's CD-ROM drive, and then copy the entire contents of the CD to the distribution folder.
4. After the copy operation has completed, open a command prompt. Switch to the folder containing the service pack network installation executable file.
5. Slipstream the service pack into the Windows installation files by executing a command with the following syntax: *servicepack*.exe –s:*network_drive*:\. For example, if the service pack is named server2003_sp1.exe, and you have copied the Windows Server 2003 files to drive Z, you would execute the command server2003_sp1.exe –s:Z:\.

   The service pack will overwrite installation files with updated versions, as shown in Figure 6.6.

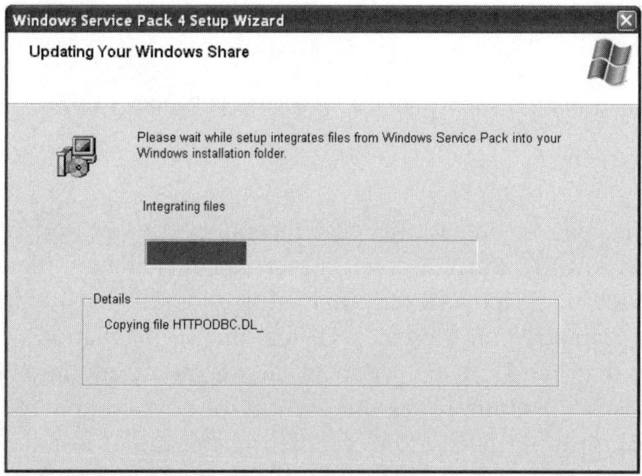

Figure 6.6 Slipstreaming a service pack

6. When prompted with a dialog box indicating that the integrated installation has successfully completed, click OK.

Note Windows Server 2003 Service Pack 1 has not been released at the time of this writing, so the actual file name will be different.

You can now install Windows directly from the shared folder. Alternatively, you can use the integrated installation to create a bootable CD-ROM. Building a new computer from an integrated installation does reduce your vulnerability to network-borne security attacks. However, it does not eliminate the risk of being attacked during the installation process. Therefore, you should still perform the installation while the computer is disconnected from the network.

Critical updates, and other types of updates other than service packs, cannot be directly integrated into installation files. Instead, you can follow these steps to automatically apply critical updates to a newly installed computer:

1. Open the \i386\dosnet.inf file, and add **svcpack** to the [OptionalSrcDirs] section. For example, this section will now contain:

   ```
   [OptionalSrcDirs]
   uniproc
   svcpack
   ```

> **Note** The Dosnet.inf file included with Windows 2000 already contains the [OptionalSrcDirs] section, but you might have to create the section for Windows XP and Windows Server 2003.

2. Create a \i386\svcpack\ folder.
3. Copy the update packages that you want to integrate, such as WindowsServer2003-KB999997-x86-ENU.exe, to the \i386\svcpack\ folder.
4. Rename the packages to fit the 8.3 naming convention using the format KB######.exe, where ###### is the Microsoft Knowledge Base article number associated with the update.
5. Open a command prompt, and extract each of the update packages to a unique temporary folder. For example, to extract the files for an update package to a folder named C:\ExtractedUpdates\KB824145\, type the following command at a command prompt:

   KB824145 /X:C:\ExtractedUpdates\KB824145

6. From the Update subfolder of the folder you extracted the update to, copy the catalog file, KB######.cat, to the \i386\svcpack\ folder.
7. Locate the binary files included with the update.

   Before Service Pack 1, security updates, critical updates, update rollups, drivers, and feature packs for Windows Server 2003 contained two copies of the same files in the RTMGDR and RTMQFE folders, which were created when you extracted the update. After Service Pack 1 is released, extracted updates might contain copies of the same files in the RTMGDR and RTMQFE folders and the SP1GDR and SP1QFE folders. Files in the *xxx*GDR folders contain only general distribution release (GDR) class fixes. Files in the *xxx*QFE folders are cumulative and contain both the GDR-class fixes and all previous hotfixes that affect the included binaries, and they should generally be used for integrated installations. Some updates include different versions of files to be applied to computers with different service pack levels. These files will be placed in a folder named after the next sequential service pack. For example, if your installation source is Windows Server 2003 Service Pack 1, you must use the files from the SP2QFE directory.

8. For each binary file (such as .exe, .dll, or .sys files) included in the folder you extracted the update to, determine whether the same file exists in the \i386 folder. The files in the \i386 folder might have an underscore for the last character in the file's extension. For example, Rpcss.dll is named Rpcss.dl_ in the \i386 folder. If there are two copies of a file, delete the original file from the \i386 folder.

9. Look in the folder into which you extracted the update for any subfolders that have the same name as a subfolder of the \i386 installation folder. If a folder contains any such subfolders, copy the updated binary files to the appropriate subfolder of \i386. For example, if the update included a subfolder named Uniproc, copy the files in the Uniproc folder to \i386\Uniproc.

10. For each file that you copied, except for KB######.cat, look in the \i386\Dosnet.inf file to determine if the file name is listed in the [Files] section. All the files that are listed in the [Files] section are preceded by "d1,". If a file is not listed, add an entry using the format **d1,*filename***. For example, if the update contains Win32k.sys, add **d1,win32k.sys** to the [Files] section of \i386\Dosnet.inf. This addition ensures that the updated versions of the files are copied during Windows setup.

11. Delete the \i386\Svcpack.in_ file.

12. Use Notepad to create a Svcpack.inf text file in the \i386 folder. To do so, use the appropriate following content, depending on whether you want to deploy a single update or multiple updates. Replace ###### with the Knowledge Base article numbers for your update .cat file:

    For Windows 2000 installations:

```
[Version]
Signature="$Windows NT$"
MajorVersion=5
MinorVersion=0
BuildNumber=2195
[SetupData]
CatalogSubDir="\i386\svcpack"
[ProductCatalogsToInstall]
KB######.cat
[SetupHotfixesToRun]
KB######.exe /Z /M
```

For Windows XP installations:

```
[Version]
Signature="$Windows NT$"
MajorVersion=5
MinorVersion=1
BuildNumber=2600
[SetupData]
CatalogSubDir="\i386\svcpack"
[ProductCatalogsToInstall]
KB######.cat
[SetupHotfixesToRun]
KB######.exe /Z /M
```

For Windows Server 2003 installations:

```
[Version] Signature="$Windows NT$"
MajorVersion=5
MinorVersion=2
BuildNumber=3790
[SetupData]
CatalogSubDir="\i386\svcpack"
[ProductCatalogsToInstall]
KB######.cat
[SetupHotfixesToRun]
KB######.exe /Z /M
```

Scripting Non-Microsoft Updates

Although updates released by Microsoft can be integrated into the operating system installation, you might have custom, non-Microsoft updates or applications that you need to automatically install after setup has completed to further improve the security of the new computer. Fortunately, it is possible to script the installation of updates, and to run this script automatically after completing an automated installation.

Exam Tip This book will not discuss every step involved in creating an automated installation of Windows. However, you should understand how to integrate the application of both Microsoft and non-Microsoft updates into a new installation.

One way to apply non-Microsoft updates is to call each of the updates that needs to be applied directly from the answer file. *Answer files* are files that provide information—without prompting the user—that all recent versions of Windows setup use to configure the system. Answer files contain a section titled [GuiRunOnce] that can include a list of commands to be run after the setup process has completed. The following is a valid section of an answer file that installs updates located in the \\server\updates shared folder:

```
[GuiRunOnce]
"\\server\updates\update1.exe /Z /M"
"\\server\updates\update2.exe /Z /M"
"\\server\updates\update3.exe /Z /M"
```

Important You can use the answer file to install updates automatically after completing the operating system installation, but you shouldn't. Instead, integrate them into the setup as described in the previous section. This ensures that the updates are applied during the setup process itself.

The applications listed in the [GuiRunOnce] section are executed in sequence, one after another. As the name indicates, the applications listed will only run once. If any of the updates called cause the computer to restart, the updates listed after that update will never be applied. Therefore, it is critical to use both the /M parameter, which causes the update to run in unattended mode, and the /Z parameter, which prevents the computer from restarting. If you use this technique to automate the application of updates, you must remember to add new updates to the answer file as they are released.

A more efficient way to install updates from the answer file is to place a batch file on a shared folder and call the updates from that batch file. If you use this technique, you can use the same answer file indefinitely. You still have to update the batch file when new updates are released, but new computers can continue to use the same answer file without modification. The following is an example of a batch file that would install three Windows Server 2003 security updates:

```
"\\server\updates\update1.exe /Z /M"
"\\server\updates\update2.exe /Z /M"
"\\server\updates\update3.exe /Z /M"
```

If you were to save this batch file as \\server\updates\post-install-updates.bat, you could automatically install those updates by using the following [GuiRunOnce] section in your answer file:

```
[GuiRunOnce]
 "\\server\updates\post-install-updates.bat"
```

Practice: Creating an Integrated Installation

In this practice, you will create an integrated installation for building new computers with a service pack already applied.

Exercise: Slipstreaming a Service Pack

In this exercise, you will create a shared folder that you can use to build new Windows 2000 Server–based computers that are pre-installed with Service Pack 4.

> **Note** This exercise uses Windows 2000 Server Service Pack 4 because a service pack has not been released for Windows Server 2003 at the time of this writing.

1. Log on to the cohowinery.com domain on Computer1 using the Administrator account.
2. Start Windows Explorer. At the root of drive C, create a new folder named Install.
3. Within the Install folder, create two new folders named Windows2000Server and Windows2000ServerSP4.
4. Right-click the C:\Install\ folder, and then click Sharing And Security.
5. Click Share This Folder. Accept the default settings by clicking OK.
6. Retrieve the English version of Service Pack 4 for Windows 2000 Server as described in Chapter 5, "Planning a Patch Management Infrastructure." Store the Service Pack 4 executable file in C:\Install\Windows2000ServerSP4\.
7. Copy the Windows 2000 Server installation files from the Windows 2000 Server CD-ROM to the C:\Install\Windows2000Server\ folder.

> **Important** You cannot use an evaluation copy of Windows 2000 Server for this exercise. If you do not have Windows 2000 Server, you can use Windows 2000 Professional, or even Windows XP and the latest Windows XP service pack.

8. Open a command prompt, and execute the following commands:

   ```
   CD \Install\Windows2000ServerSP4\
   W2ksp4_en.exe -s:C:\Install\Windows2000Server\
   ```

   Service pack 4 will extract files to a temporary directory and then slipstream the updated service pack files into the specified Windows 2000 Server installation directory.
9. After the integration installation has successfully completed, click OK.

   If you were to install a computer using the files located in C:\Install\Windows2000Server\, that computer would report Service Pack 4 being installed at the moment the installation completed.

Lesson Review

The following questions are intended to reinforce key information presented in this lesson. If you are unable to answer a question, review the lesson materials and try the question again. You can find answers to the questions in the "Questions and Answers" section at the end of this chapter.

1. Which of the following commands would slipstream a service pack named sp1.exe into an installation folder named D:\W2003\ that had been created by copying the contents of the Windows Server 2003 installation CD?

   a. sp1.exe –i:D:\W2003\

   b. sp1.exe –s:D:\W2003\

   c. sp1.exe –i:D:\W2003\i386\

   d. sp1.exe –s:D:\W2003\i386\

   ____

   ____

2. Which section of an answer file would you modify to automatically run updates after the installation completed?

   a. [Components]

   b. [RemoteInstall]

   c. [GuiRunOnce]

   d. [Shell]

   ____

   ____

Lesson Summary

- Computers should not be connected to the Internet or even to a private network with other hosts, until after the operating system and all updates have been installed.
- Computers can be built while connected to the network if you create an isolated network segment with a minimal number of trusted computers that have been scanned for worms, viruses, and other malicious software.
- You can reduce the time required to install new updates by slipstreaming a service pack into operating system installation files and configuring other updates to be automatically applied.

Lesson 3: Deploying Updates on Existing Clients

The vast majority of the energy you dedicate to updating will involve updating existing clients. Deploying updates to thousands of computers in an enterprise has always been a challenge. However, as the number of mobile computers and remote users increases, so does the challenge of keeping a large number of computers up to date.

Exam Tip This lesson describes the specific steps required to configure various methods for deploying updates. For information on choosing which methods to use for your environment, refer to Lesson 2 in Chapter 5, "Planning a Patch Management Infrastructure." In addition to the methods described in this lesson, you can deploy updates by using Add/Remove Programs in Control Panel, or Microsoft Systems Management Server. Chapter 5 includes an overview of these techniques, but you do not need to know specifically how to deploy updates by using these techniques for the exam.

After this lesson, you will be able to

- Manually install updates to a computer.
- Use the Windows Update Web site to assess a computer and apply service packs and critical updates.
- Configure SUS to make approved updates available to your organization's computers.
- Configure the Automatic Updates client to download and install updates from either Windows Update or a local SUS server.
- Distribute service packs by using a Group Policy object.

Estimated lesson time: 75 minutes

Manually Applying Updates

Microsoft distributes updates by using executable files that automatically install themselves when run. However, all Microsoft updates also support standardized command-line parameters to change the default installation behavior. Table 6.3 lists the parameters available for updates. The parameters listed in the New Parameter column can be used with updates released on or after September 17, 2003. You must use the parameters listed in the Old Parameter column for updates released prior to September 17, 2003. As of the time of this writing, new updates support the old parameters. However, backward compatibility with the old parameters might be dropped at some point, so you should always use the new parameters when possible.

Table 6.3 Update Parameters

New parameter	Old parameter	Description
/passive	/u	Performs an unattended installation while displaying a progress bar. By default, this also selects the /warnrestart switch.
/quiet	/q	Performs an unattended installation similar to that of the /u option; however, no progress bar is displayed. By default, the program restarts the computer with no prompt or warning if the update requires a restart for the changes to take effect.
/norestart	/z	Prevents the computer from automatically restarting after a service pack is applied.
/warnrestart:*seconds*	N/A	Invokes a dialog box that warns the user that a restart will occur in the specified number of seconds (it defaults to 30 seconds if no value is specified). For example, to warn that a restart will occur in 60 seconds, type **/warnrestart:60**. The dialog box contains a Cancel button and a Restart Now button. If the user clicks Cancel, the computer is not restarted.
/promptrestart	N/A	Notifies the user that the computer must be restarted for the changes to take effect. The user can choose whether to restart the computer.
/forcerestart	/f	Forces applications to close without saving files before restarting the computer.
/D *folder*	/D *folder*	Stores backed up files in the specified folder. This parameter can only be used with service packs.
/n	/n	Saves disk space by not backing up files that are replaced. You should only use this option on new computers or computers that can be quickly recovered from a backup.
/o	/o	Causes the service pack to overwrite OEM-supplied files. You should only use this option if you have tested the service pack before and determined that OEM-supplied files have been updated by Microsoft and that the update files are compatible with your hardware. This parameter can only be used with service packs.
/l	/l	Lists installed updates in a dialog box. Do not use this option from a script.
/uninstall	N/A	Uninstalls the previously installed update.
/S *folder*	/S *folder*	Slipstreams the service pack into installation files, as described in Lesson 2. This parameter can only be used with service packs.

Table 6.3 Update Parameters

New parameter	Old parameter	Description
/log	N/A	Enables the user to define the path for the local log file. This switch invokes the default logging behavior.
/extract	/x	Enables you to extract the installation files to a specified folder.
/help	/h	Displays a dialog box that shows the correct usage of the update executable file, including a list of all its command-line switches and their behaviors.

Windows Update Web Site

The quickest way to manually detect missing updates and install them on a computer is to directly access the Windows Update Web site. To update a computer with critical updates, security updates, and service packs by using Windows Update:

1. Click Start, point to All Programs, and then click Windows Update.

Note If the computer lacks an icon for Windows Update, as some older versions of Windows do, start Microsoft Internet Explorer and visit *http://windowsupdate.microsoft.com*.

2. Click Scan For Updates.
3. Click Review And Install Updates.
4. Click Install Now.

   The updates will be downloaded and installed. You might be prompted to accept a license agreement.
5. Restart the computer and return to step 1 until all critical updates and service packs have been installed.

See Also For more information on Windows Update, refer to Chapter 5, "Planning a Patch Management Infrastructure."

Software Update Services

SUS, a free download that can be installed on Windows 2000 Server–based and Windows Server 2003–based computers that have Internet Information Services (IIS) installed, provides administrators with a local alternative to the Microsoft Windows Update servers. Using the Automatic Updates client, computers on your network can automatically download and install updates from your SUS server.

The easiest way to install IIS is to use the Manage Your Server tool and add the Application Server role. For the purposes of installing Software Update Services, you can accept the default settings; neither Microsoft ASP.NET nor Microsoft FrontPage extensions are required. SUS will install itself into the Default Web Site, if it is available. Otherwise, SUS will create a new Web site.

Planning Though SUS servers are not as critical as, say, domain controllers, you might choose to deploy them redundantly to protect against long-term outages or to provide the scalability to service thousands of client computers. The easiest way to configure redundant SUS servers is to configure two or more SUS servers identically. Then create a round-robin DNS record with the IP addresses of all SUS servers. If you choose to manually approve updates, you must approve updates on both computers.

The Web site SUS is installed within must use port 80, because the Automatic Updates client cannot be configured to use a different port. SUS should only be accessible from your local network. Because you can't configure the SUS Web site to use any port other than the default of 80/tcp, you should avoid installing SUS on a publicly accessible Web server. If you must install SUS on a public Web server, create a separate Web site for SUS and configure the Web site to use a private IP address.

After installing IIS, you can download SUS from the Microsoft Web site at *http://www.microsoft.com/downloads/*. The installation is straightforward, and it provides options for specifying where both updates and Web content will be stored. When specifying the location for storing updates, keep in mind that updates will consume at least several hundreds of megabytes, and they might consume several gigabytes, depending on the options you choose when configuring SUS. Securing the updates themselves is not critical, because they are signed by Microsoft and the Automatic Updates client will refuse to install them if the file has been modified since it was originally signed.

After installation, all configuration is done by using a Web browser. SUS creates several different virtual directories within IIS's default Web site. However, you will primarily access the SUSAdmin virtual directory, which contains the SUS administration pages and configuration tools.

To configure SUS:

1. Start Internet Explorer and enter the URL **http://*computername*/SUSAdmin/**. Alternatively, you can click Start, point to Administrative Tools, and then click Microsoft Software Update Services.
2. When the administrative page appears, click Set Options in the left pane.

3. Specify the proxy server (if necessary), the server to synchronize with, whether to automatically approve updates, and where to store updates. At the bottom of the Set Options page, select only those languages you support on your network. Downloading updates for additional languages consumes unnecessary bandwidth and storage space.
4. In the left pane, click Synchronize Server.
5. Click the Synchronization Schedule button.
6. Click Synchronize Using This Schedule. The default settings cause SUS to download new updates daily at 3:00 A.M. Specify the time the SUS server will download updates, and then click OK.

You should rely on scheduled synchronization to identify new updates; however, the first time you configure SUS you should perform a manual update. To do this, click the Synchronize Now button on the Synchronize Server page. As shown in Figure 6.7, Software Update Services will synchronize with the Windows Update server. After synchronization is complete, you will be prompted to approve updates.

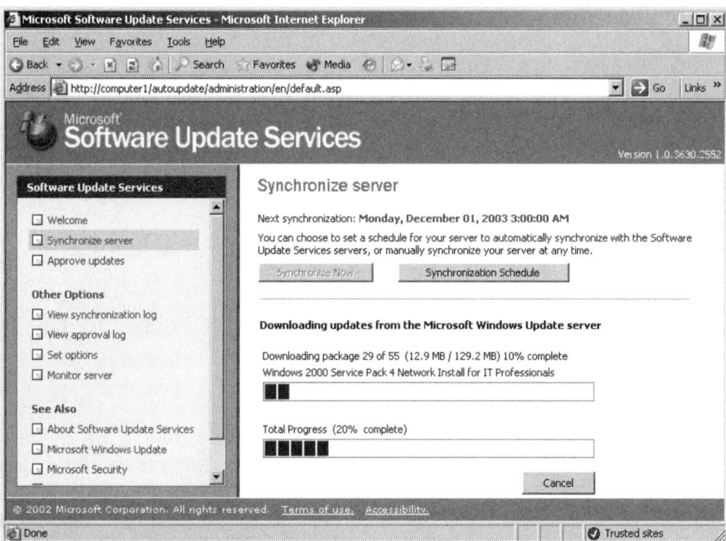

Figure 6.7 SUS synchronizing with the Windows Update server.

SUS does not provide a browser interface similar to that of Windows Updates, in which users can scan their computers and choose the updates they want to apply. Only the Automatic Updates client can access SUS.

If you experience a problem with SUS, verify that the Software Update Services Synchronization Service is configured to start automatically, and that it was able to start successfully. SUS adds events to the System event log when updates are synchronized and when problems occur. You can find these events by filtering for the source WUSyncService in the System event log. You should also check the IIS configuration, because SUS relies on IIS to communicate with the Automatic Updates client.

See Also For more information on Software Update Services, refer to Chapter 5, "Planning a Patch Management Infrastructure."

Automatic Updates Client

The Automatic Updates client retrieves updates from Windows Update or a Software Update Server and then communicates with end users to notify them that updates are available, installed, or require the computer to be restarted.

To configure the Automatic Updates client to automatically check for updates from Windows Update and, optionally, to download and install the updates:

1. Right-click My Computer, and then click Properties.
2. Click the Automatic Updates tab.
3. Select the Keep My Computer Up To Date check box.
4. Select one of the following options:
    - Notify Me Before Downloading Any Updates And Notify Me Again Before Installing Them On My Computer
    - Download The Updates Automatically And Notify Me When They Are Ready To Be Installed
    - Automatically Download The Updates, And Install Them On The Schedule I Specify
5. Click OK.

To configure the Automatic Updates client on domain members to automatically apply updates from an SUS server:

1. Create a new Group Policy object (GPO) or edit an existing GPO to which you want to add this setting.
2. Expand Computer Configuration, expand Administrative Templates, expand Windows Components, and then click Windows Update.
3. On the Windows Update template, double-click Configure Automatic Updates.
4. Click Enabled.

5. Select one of the following options:

   - 2-Notify For Download And Notify For Install. Use this option for users with limited bandwidth who must both control the updates installed on their computers and control when the updates are downloaded.
   - 3-Auto Download And Notify For Install. Use this option for users who need control over when updates are installed but do not need to control when updates are downloaded.
   - 4-Auto Download And Schedule The Install. Use this option to maximize security by minimizing the risk of exposing vulnerabilities that have been fixed by updates. This option automatically installs updates on the schedule you specify.

6. If you select Auto Download And Schedule The Install, choose the day of week and time of day that the updates should be installed, as shown in Figure 6.8.

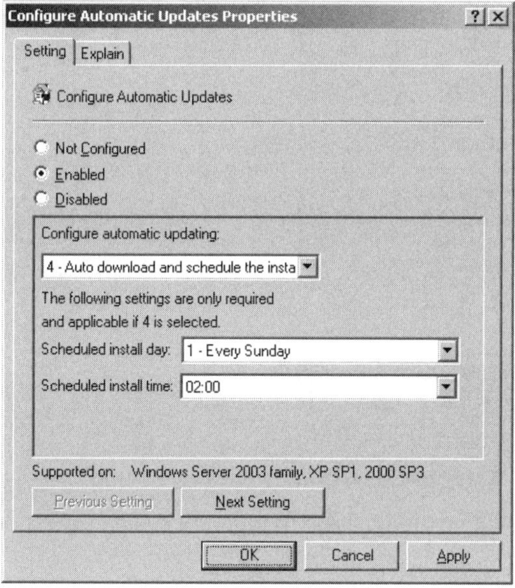

Figure 6.8 Automatic Updates configured using a Group Policy object

7. Click Next Setting.

   The Specify Intranet Microsoft Update Service Location Properties dialog box appears.

8. If you want clients to retrieve updates directly from Windows Update, select Disabled. Otherwise, select Enabled, and specify the URL to the local SUS server.

9. Click Next Setting.

   The Reschedule Automatic Updates Scheduled Installations Properties dialog box appears.

10. Most environments that specify the Auto Download And Schedule The Install setting should click Enabled for this setting. The Reschedule Automatic Updates Scheduled Installations setting is used by the Automatic Updates client to determine when it should apply a scheduled update that was skipped because the computer was turned off or in standby mode. When you enable this option, you can specify the number of minutes after startup for the Automatic Updates client to apply an update, as shown in Figure 6.9. If you don't enable this option, a computer that is turned off each night might never have updates installed.

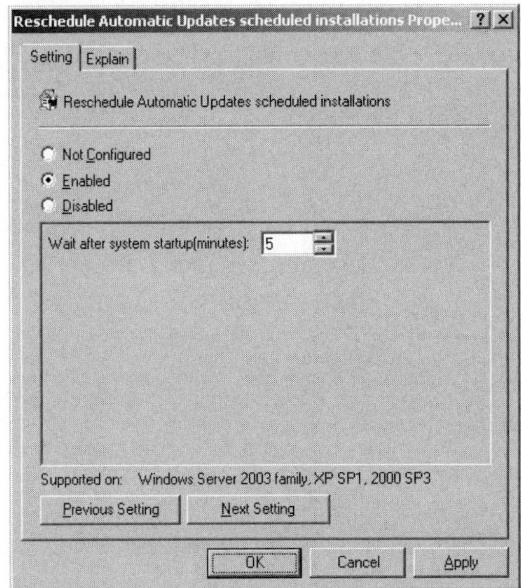

Figure 6.9 Scheduling updates that were skipped

11. Click Next Setting.

    The last Automatic Updates client properties dialog box, No Auto-Restart For Schedule Automatic Updates Installations Properties, appears.

12. To force a computer to restart automatically after applying an update, click Disabled. Users will be warned that the computer will restart in five minutes, and that they should save their work. To only notify users that they need to restart the computer, click Enabled.

13. Click OK.

If your network does not rely on Active Directory, you can configure the Automatic Updates client by using registry values. There are a total of nine registry values that control the Automatic Updates client. Seven of these registry values are contained in the HKEY_LOCAL_MACHINE\Software\Policies\Microsoft\Windows\WindowsUpdate\AU registry key:

- **NoAutoUpdate** Set this value to 0 to enable automatic updates, or to 1 to disable automatic updates.
- **AUOptions** Set this value to 2 to notify the user that updates are available for download and installation, 3 to automatically download the updates and then notify the user that the update is available for installation, or 4 to automatically download and schedule the installation.
- **ScheduledInstallTime** The hour of the day to install a new update. Use 0 for midnight, and 23 for 11:00 P.M.
- **UseWUServer** Set this to 1 to enable Automatic Updates to use the Windows Update server as specified in WUServer.
- **ScheduledInstallDay** A value between 0 and 7. Use 1 for Sunday and 7 for Saturday. Set this value to 0 to schedule updates any day of the week.
- **RescheduleWaitTime** The number of minutes the Automatic Updates client waits before installing a new update after a computer starts, if the computer was offline during the scheduled time.
- **NoAutoRebootWithLoggedOnUsers** Set this value to 0 to cause the Automatic Updates client to restart the computer 5 minutes after applying an update. Set this value to 1 to cause the Automatic Updates client to prompt the user to restart the computer.

The final two registry values are contained in the HKEY_LOCAL_MACHINE\Software\Policies\Microsoft\Windows\WindowsUpdate registry key:

- **WUServer** The URL for the SUS server that the Automatic Updates client will retrieve updates from, for example http://computer1/.
- **WUStatusServer** The URL for the IIS server that the Automatic Updates client will report usage information to, for example http://computer1/. This is generally set to the same computer as the SUS server.

After changing registry values, you must either restart the client computer or restart the Automatic Updates service.

If you experience problems with retrieving updates, verify that the Automatic Updates service is configured to start automatically, and that it has successfully started. In a domain environment, the Automatic Updates client usually receives its configuration settings from one or more Group Policy objects. Verify the configuration by using the Resultant Set Of Policy (RSoP) snap-in.

See Also For more information about RSoP, refer to Chapter 3, "Deploying and Troubleshooting Security Templates."

The Automatic Updates client adds events to the System event log when updates are downloaded or installed. Additionally, the Automatic Updates client adds an event whenever it prompts a user—for example, when the computer must be restarted, or when an error occurs. You can find these events by filtering for the source Automatic Updates in the System event log.

See Also For more information on the Automatic Updates client, refer to Chapter 5, "Planning a Patch Management Infrastructure."

Group Policy

Group Policy objects can be configured to automatically install Windows Installer packages on computers. Service packs include a Windows Installer package, making it simple to use a Group Policy object to deploy a service pack.

Service packs, more than any other type of update, require extensive testing and pilot deployments because of the extensive changes they make. Although SUS is an excellent way to distribute frequently released security updates to a large number of client computers, you cannot use a single SUS server to stage a pilot deployment to a small number of computers in your organization. Fortunately, you can use Group Policy objects to distribute service packs directly.

Off the Record As of the time of this writing, the current version of SUS does not provide any ability to control which clients receive updates. However, you could create separate SUS servers for pilot and production deployments, and approve updates on the production SUS server only after they have been proven on the pilot SUS server. You could then use Group Policy objects to point different clients at the production and pilot SUS servers.

There are some distinct advantages to using a Group Policy object rather than the Automatic Updates client to distribute service packs. Specifically, by using Group Policy objects, you can deploy a service pack only to computers in specific sites, domains, and organizational units. Additionally, you can use permissions and Windows Management Instrumentation (WMI) filtering to control which computers can apply a GPO on an even more granular level.

After you assign the service pack package, Windows Installer installs the service pack automatically when users start their computers. Users are not presented with a choice to install the service pack. Only a network administrator or someone who is logged on to a local computer as a member of the Administrators group on that computer can remove the assigned software.

To distribute a service pack by using a Group Policy object:

1. Download the network install version of the service pack to a file server.
2. Extract the service pack files using the /x parameter. For example, to extract Service Pack 4 for Windows 2000, execute the command `W2ksp4_en /x`. Extract the files to a shared folder that both client computers and domain controllers can access. After the extraction completes, click OK.

Warning Remember, new service packs have different command-line parameters and would use the /extract parameter instead of /x.

3. Connect to the shared folder just as a client would. For example, if you extracted the files to the \\server\updates shared folder, map a network drive to \\server\updates. This will ensure that clients can locate the package after the GPO instructs the client to install it.
4. Create a new GPO or edit an existing GPO that you will use to distribute the service pack.
5. Using the Group Policy Object Editor snap-in, expand Computer Configuration, expand Software Settings, and then click Software Installation.
6. Right-click Software Installation, click New, and then click Package.
7. Navigate to the folder to which you extracted the service pack, and locate the Update.msi file. Though future service packs might place this file in a different location, recent service packs have stored it in the i386\update\ directory. Click the Update.msi file, and then click Open.
8. In the Deploy Software dialog box, click Assigned, and then click OK.

After a package has been added to the Software Installation node of a GPO, you can choose to remove or deploy it for troubleshooting purposes. If a service pack installation fails to deploy successfully, you can redeploy it by right-clicking the package, clicking All Tasks, and then clicking Redeploy Application.

You can remove the package from the GPO by right-clicking the package, clicking All Tasks, and then clicking Remove. The Remove Software dialog box will appear. To uninstall the service pack, click Immediately Uninstall The Software From Users And

Computers. To leave the service pack installed on computers that have already received it, click Allow Users To Continue To Use The Software, But Prevent New Installations.

See Also For more information on using Group Policy objects to distribute service packs, refer to Chapter 5, "Planning a Patch Management Infrastructure."

Practice: Configuring Software Update Services and the Automatic Updates Client

In this practice, you will install and configure Software Update Services on Computer1. Then, you will configure all computers in the domain to retrieve updates from the SUS server.

Exercise 1: Configuring Software Update Services

In this exercise, you will add the Application Server role and then install and configure Software Update Services. Software Update Services requires IIS, so start by adding the Application Server role.

1. Log on to the cohowinery.com domain on Computer1 using the Administrator account.
2. Click Start, and then click Manage Your Server.
3. Click Add Or Remove A Role.
4. Click Next, and then click Application Server. Click Next again.
5. Click Next on the Application Server Options page. Click Next again.
6. On the final page, click Finish.

   Now that IIS is installed, download and install SUS.
7. Temporarily connect Computer1 to the Internet.
8. Start Internet Explorer, and enter the URL *http://www.microsoft.com/downloads/*. Locate the latest version of Software Update Services. Download and open the setup file.
9. If prompted to install and run the file, click Yes.
10. When the Microsoft Software Update Services Setup Wizard appears, follow the prompts to install SUS.
11. Start the SUS administration page by clicking Start, pointing to Administrative Tools, and then clicking Microsoft Software Update Services.

12. Provide your Administrator credentials, and then click OK. If you are notified that the content is untrusted, add Computer1 to the list of trusted sites.

13. When the administrative page appears, click Set Options in the left pane.

    The default settings are correct for the purposes of this exercise. However, you should examine the settings to familiarize yourself with the defaults. In particular, notice that only the English-language versions of updates will be updated. By selecting Synchronize From A Local Software Update Services Server, you can integrate this computer into a larger SUS infrastructure. Also notice that you can choose to automatically approve updates. Additionally, you can choose to reduce storage requirements by choosing to maintain the updates on the Windows Update server.

14. In the left pane, click Synchronize Server.

15. Click the Synchronization Schedule button.

16. Click Synchronize Using This Schedule. The default settings cause SUS to download new updates daily at 3:00 A.M. Click OK.

17. Click the Synchronize Now button.

    SUS will download the Microsoft Catalog and any English-language updates. After downloading completes, these updates must be approved before Automatic Updates clients will apply them. Downloading the updates will take several minutes. You can use this time to complete Exercise 2 before approving the updates.

Exercise 2: Configuring the Automatic Updates Client

In this exercise, you will configure the Automatic Updates client on Computer1 to retrieve updates from the newly installed SUS server.

1. Log on to the cohowinery.com domain on Computer1 using the Administrator account.

2. Start the Active Directory Users And Computers console.

3. Right-click Cohowinery.com, and then click Properties.

4. Click the Group Policy tab.

5. Click Default Domain Policy, and then click Edit.

   The Group Policy Object Editor appears.

6. Expand Computer Configuration, expand Administrative Templates, expand Windows Components, and then click Windows Update.

7. On the Windows Update template, double-click Configure Automatic Updates.

8. Click Enabled.

9. Click the Configure Automatic Updating list, and then click 2-Notify For Download And Notify For Install.
10. Click Next Setting.
11. Click Enabled.
12. In both the Set The Intranet Update Service For Detecting Updates box and the Set The Intranet Statistics Server box, type **http://computer1**.
13. Click OK.
14. Close the Group Policy Object Editor console. Click OK in the Cohowinery.com Properties dialog box, and then close the Active Directory Users And Computers console.

Exercise 3: Approving SUS Updates

In this exercise, you will approve updates to be installed by the Automatic Updates client.

1. Open the SUS administration page by clicking Start, pointing to Administrative Tools, and then clicking Microsoft Software Update Services.
2. Provide your Administrator credentials, and then click OK.
3. In the left pane, click Synchronize Server.

   If updates are still being synchronized, wait until the download completes.
4. If a dialog box appears indicating that the updates were synchronized, click OK. Otherwise, in the left pane, click Approve Updates.
5. Click the Sort By field, and then click Date.
6. From the Available Updates list, select each of the 823559: Security Update For Microsoft Windows check boxes.

> **Tip** If you need to approve a large quantity of updates, select the first check box, then press TAB twice, press SPACE, press TAB twice, press SPACE, and repeat.

7. Click the Approve button. Click Yes, and then click Accept. When prompted, click OK.
8. Restart Computer1 to ensure that the latest Automatic Updates policies are applied.
9. After Computer1 has started again, log on to the cohowinery.com domain on Computer1 using the Administrator account.
10. Wait several minutes for the Update Notification to appear.

    At this point, you can proceed through the update installation process to expose yourself to the experience that end users have when new updates are detected.

Lesson Review

The following questions are intended to reinforce key information presented in this lesson. If you are unable to answer a question, review the lesson materials and try the question again. You can find answers to the questions in the "Questions and Answers" section at the end of this chapter.

1. Which command-line parameter would configure an update so that it won't store copies of files that it replaces?
   a. /n
   b. /passive
   c. /o
   d. /extract

---

2. Which of the following tools can be used to identify the Automatic Updates client's configuration, in addition to the GPO that defined that configuration? (Choose all that apply.)
   a. Resultant Set Of Policy
   b. Help And Support Center
   c. Gpresult
   d. Gpupdate
   e. Active Directory Users And Computers
   f. Group Policy Object Editor

---

3. Which registry key would you edit to configure the local computer's Automatic Updates client settings?
   a. HKEY_LOCAL_MACHINE\Software\Microsoft\Windows\CurrentVersion\WindowsUpdate
   b. HKEY_LOCAL_MACHINE\Software\Policies\Microsoft\Windows\WindowsUpdate
   c. HKEY_CURRENT_USER\Software\Microsoft\Windows\CurrentVersion\WindowsUpdate
   d. HKEY_CURRENT_USER\Software\Policies\Microsoft\Windows\WindowsUpdate

---

---

4. Which of the following might provide you with useful information about a problem you are experiencing with downloading updates from an SUS server?
   - **a.** The Security event log on the SUS server
   - **b.** The System event log on the SUS server
   - **c.** The Application event log on the SUS server
   - **d.** The Security event log on the client computer
   - **e.** The System event log on the client computer
   - **f.** The Application event log on the client computer
   - **g.** The IIS usage log

   ____

   ____

   ____

Lesson Summary

- Microsoft updates support a standard set of command-line parameters to simplify the deployment of updates by using scripts. Use the /quiet (formerly /q) parameter to install an update silently. When chaining updates, use the /norestart (formerly /z) parameter to prevent the computer from automatically restarting.
- The Automatic Updates client can be configured by using GPOs linked to Active Directory, to the local GPO, or to the registry.
- SUS requires that IIS be installed on the local computer, and that the Web site be configured to use the default port 80.
- Both SUS and the Automatic Updates client store event information in the System event log.
- Service packs include a Windows Installer package that can be used to deploy the service pack by using a GPO. This provides a simple way to install the service pack on a limited number of computers during a pilot deployment.

Case Scenario Exercise

In this exercise, you will read a scenario about a company's patch management challenge and then answer the questions that follow. The questions are intended to reinforce key information presented in this chapter. If you are unable to answer a question, review the lessons and try the question again. You can find answers to the questions in the "Questions and Answers" section at the end of this chapter.

Scenario

You were recently hired by the chief security officer (CSO) of Wide World Importers to improve the overall security of their Windows network. Up until about two years ago, World Wide Importers had a large staff of systems engineers responsible for maintaining the security on the network. Unfortunately, budget cutbacks caused World Wide Importers to lay off most of the staff. With fewer staff, the engineers were forced to focus on troubleshooting problems. Security became a secondary priority, especially auditing and maintaining patch levels.

During the past two years, several worms and viruses have infected large numbers of both desktop and server computers. The CSO wants you to first implement an effective update deployment and maintenance infrastructure. Currently, Wide World Importers has one Active Directory domain, 30 servers, and about a thousand desktop and mobile computers at seven locations around the world. All computers are running Windows 2000, Windows XP, or Windows Server 2003.

Questions

1. What method will you implement to deploy updates?

   a. Provide detailed instructions to end users on how to download and install updates from the Microsoft Web site as they become available.

   b. Configure the Automatic Updates client to download and install updates from Windows Update when they become available.

   c. Deploy an SUS server at each location, and configure the Automatic Updates client to download and install updates from the local SUS server.

   d. Deploy updates using the Software Installation functionality built into GPOs.

---

2. How will you configure the Automatic Updates client?

   a. Provide detailed instructions to end users, instructing them to right-click My Computer, click Properties, click the Automatic Updates tab, and then specify the configuration settings.

b. Provide detailed instructions to end users, instructing them to use the registry editor to modify the registry values to configure the Automatic Updates client.

c. Use GPOs to deploy a .reg file containing registry values to configure the Automatic Updates client.

d. Use GPOs to configure the Windows Update administrative template to configure the Automatic Updates client.

____

3. How will you ensure that newly installed computers are updated?

____

____

____

____

____

____

____

____

____

4. How will you determine whether clients are being successfully updated?

a. Provide detailed instructions to end users, instructing them to use Add/Remove Programs to identify updates that have been installed and compare that list against the list of available updates on Windows Update.

b. Visit random computers, and view the version numbers of system files to verify that updates have been applied.

c. Use the graphical MBSA console to scan when you have free time available. Configure MBSA to check only the updates that have been approved on SUS servers.

d. Schedule the command-line MBSACLI utility to scan all of Wide World Importers subnets once per week, and examine the reports the following morning. Use the /sus command-line parameter to force MBSACLI to check only those updates approved on your SUS servers.

____

____

____

____

Troubleshooting Lab

In this lab, you troubleshoot a problem related to an Automatic Updates client that is not installing updates correctly. Read the following scenario and then answer the questions that follow. The questions are intended to reinforce key information presented in this chapter. If you are unable to answer a question, review the lessons and try the question again. You can find answers to the questions in the "Questions and Answers" section at the end of this chapter.

Scenario

After performing an MBSA scan, you notice that one of the computers has not had updates installed, as shown in Figure 6.10. You use the Resultant Set Of Policy console to verify that the computer's Automatic Updates client is correctly configured. Then you check the System event log on the client computer, but you do not find an event that indicates Automatic Updates is having problems.

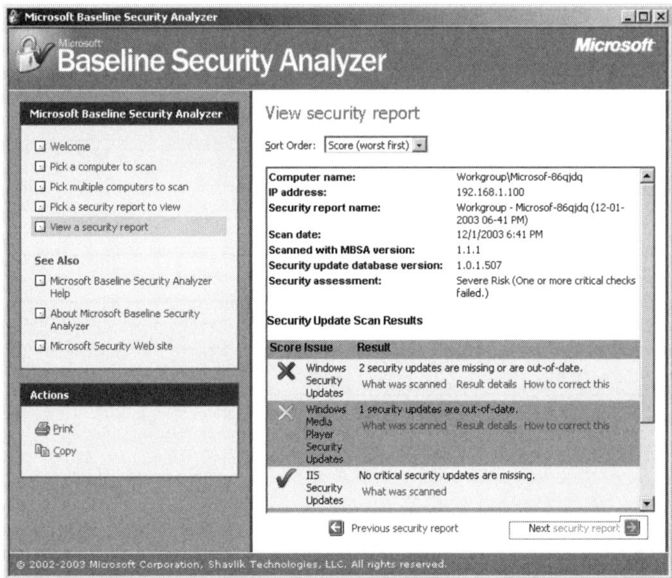

Figure 6.10 MBSA identifies an unpatched computer

You decide to check the IIS usage log in C:\Windows\System32\LogFiles\W3Svc\ to identify the last time the client computer contacted the SUS server. You search for the client's IP address, 192.168.1.100, and identify the following lines, which were created at the time of the event log error:

```
#Software: Microsoft Internet Information Services 6.0
#Version: 1.0
#Date: 2003-12-01 19:28:22
```

```
#Fields: date time s-ip cs-method cs-uri-stem cs-uri-query s-port cs-username
c-ip cs(User-Agent) sc-status sc-substatus sc-win32-status
2003-12-01 19:28:22 192.168.1.100 HEAD /iuident.cab 0312011928 80 -
 192.168.1.131 Industry+Update+Control 401 3 5
2003-12-01 19:28:22 192.168.1.100 GET /iuident.cab 0312011928 80 -
 192.168.1.131 Industry+Update+Control 401 3 5
2003-12-01 19:28:22 192.168.1.100 GET /
wutrack.bin V=1&U=42adc102bd4d664dad2564eb4de950f1&C=au&A=s&I=&D=&P=5.2.ece.2.112.2.0&
L=en-US&S=f&E=80190191&M=ver%3D5.4.3790.0&X=031201192821882 80 -
 192.168.1.131 Industry+Update+Control 401 3 5
```

Questions

1. What is the source of the problem?

2. How would you troubleshoot the problem?

Chapter Summary

- The graphical MBSA console is the most efficient way to scan a single computer or multiple computers for the presence of updates. It can be configured to scan a single computer, a range of IP addresses, or all computers contained within a domain.
- MBSA stores reports in XML format in the C:\Documents and Settings*username*\SecurityScans folder by default. At any time, you can view these reports by using MBSA.

- MBSACLI provides a scriptable, schedulable, command-line interface to MBSA's scanning functionality. MBSACLI functions in two modes: standard MBSA mode and the backward compatible HFNetChk mode.
- Computers should not be connected to the Internet or even to a private network with other hosts, until after the operating system and all updates have been installed. Computers can be built while connected to the network if you create an isolated network segment with a minimal number of trusted computers that have been scanned for worms, viruses, and other malicious software.
- You can reduce the time required to install new updates by slipstreaming a service pack into operating system installation files and configuring other updates to be automatically applied.
- Microsoft updates support a standard set of command-line parameters to simplify the deployment of updates by using scripts. Use the /quiet (formerly /q) parameter to install an update silently. When chaining updates, use the /norestart (formerly /z) parameter to prevent the computer from automatically restarting.
- The Automatic Updates client can be configured by using GPOs linked to Active Directory, to the local GPO, or to the registry.
- SUS requires that IIS be installed on the local computer, and that the Web site be configured to use the default port 80.
- Service packs include a Windows Installer package that can be used to deploy the service pack by using a GPO. This provides a simple way to install the service pack on a limited number of computers during a pilot deployment.

Exam Highlights

Before taking the exam, review the key topics and terms that are presented in this chapter. You need to know this information.

Key Topics

- Understand why it is important to assess the current patch level in your organization, and how to use the graphical and command-line versions of MBSA to perform the assessment.
- Know the various functions available in the HFNetChk mode of the MBSACLI tool.
- Know how to minimize the risk of a computer being infected by a worm, a virus, or another attacker during the installation process.

- Be able to compare the various methods for deploying updates to an organization.
- Understand how to troubleshoot clients that do not download and install updates as configured.
- Be able to describe both the strengths and the weaknesses of SUS.

Key Terms

Background Intelligent Transfer Service (BITS) A service that transfers data between from the Software Update Services or Windows Update server to the Automatic Updates client with minimal impact to other network services.

slipstreaming The process of integrating a service pack into operating system setup files so that new computers immediately have the service pack installed.

Questions and Answers

Lesson 1 Review

Page 6-13

1. By default, where do MBSA and MBSACLI store security reports?

   a. C:\MBSA

   b. C:\Documents and Settings*username*\

   c. C:\Documents and Settings*username*\Security Scans\

   d. C:\Documents and Settings*username*\My Documents\Security Scans\

   c. MBSA and MBSACLI store reports in C:\Documents and Settings*username*\Security Scans\ by default.

2. Which of the following commands would scan the subnet 192.168.5.0?

   a. mbsa –n 192.168.5.0

   b. mbsacli –i 192.168.5.1-192.168.5.255

   c. mbsacli –n 192.168.5.1-192.168.5.255

   d. mbsacli –r 192.168.5.1-192.168.5.255

   d. MBSACLI's –r parameter scans a range of IP addresses.

Lesson 2 Review

Page 6-26

1. Which of the following commands would slipstream a service pack named sp1.exe into an installation folder named D:\W2003\ that had been created by copying the contents of the Windows Server 2003 installation CD?

   a. sp1.exe –i:D:\W2003\

   b. sp1.exe –s:D:\W2003\

   c. sp1.exe –i:D:\W2003\i386\

   d. sp1.exe –s:D:\W2003\i386\

   b. The –s parameter is the correct parameter for creating an integrated installation. You should specify the folder that corresponds to the root of the setup CD; you do not need to specify the i386 directory.

2. Which section of an answer file would you modify to automatically run updates after the installation completed?

   a. [Components]

   b. [RemoteInstall]

   c. [GuiRunOnce]
   d. [Shell]

   c. The [GuiRunOnce] section of the answer file contains a list of applications to be run after setup is completed.

Lesson 3 Review

Page 6-41

1. Which command-line parameter would configure an update so that it won't store copies of files that it replaces?
   a. /n
   b. /passive
   c. /o
   d. /extract

   a. The /n parameter saves disk space by not backing up replaced files.

2. Which of the following tools can be used to identify the Automatic Updates client's configuration, in addition to the GPO that defined that configuration? (Choose all that apply.)
   a. Resultant Set Of Policy
   b. Help And Support Center
   c. Gpresult
   d. Gpupdate
   e. Active Directory Users And Computers
   f. Group Policy Object Editor

   a and c. RSoP and Gpresult will show current policy settings and the GPO that defined them.

3. Which registry key would you edit to configure the local computer's Automatic Updates client settings?
   a. HKEY_LOCAL_MACHINE\Software\Microsoft\Windows\CurrentVersion\WindowsUpdate
   b. HKEY_LOCAL_MACHINE\Software\Policies\Microsoft\Windows\WindowsUpdate
   c. HKEY_CURRENT_USER\Software\Microsoft\Windows\CurrentVersion\WindowsUpdate
   d. HKEY_CURRENT_USER\Software\Policies\Microsoft\Windows\WindowsUpdate

b. The Automatic Updates client takes its configuration information from the HKEY_LOCAL_MACHINE\Software\Policies\Microsoft\Windows\WindowsUpdate registry key and its subkeys.

4. Which of the following might provide you with useful information about a problem you are experiencing with downloading updates from an SUS server?

   a. The Security event log on the SUS server

   b. The System event log on the SUS server

   c. The Application event log on the SUS server

   d. The Security event log on the client computer

   e. The System event log on the client computer

   f. The Application event log on the client computer

   g. The IIS usage log

b, e, and g. The SUS server will add relevant events to the System event log on the SUS server. The Automatic Updates client adds events to the client's System event log. Details about individual requests to the SUS server from the Automatic Updates client are contained in the IIS usage log.

Design Activity: Case Scenario Exercise

Page 6-43

1. What method will you implement to deploy updates?

   a. Provide detailed instructions to end users on how to download and install updates from the Microsoft Web site as they become available.

   b. Configure the Automatic Updates client to download and install updates from Windows Update when they become available.

   c. Deploy an SUS server at each location, and configure the Automatic Updates client to download and install updates from the local SUS server.

   d. Deploy updates using the Software Installation functionality built into GPOs.

c. For this environment, SUS is the best way to deploy updates.

2. How will you configure the Automatic Updates client?

   a. Provide detailed instructions to end users, instructing them to right-click My Computer, click Properties, click the Automatic Updates tab, and then specify the configuration settings.

   b. Provide detailed instructions to end users, instructing them to use the registry editor to modify the registry values to configure the Automatic Updates client.

c. Use GPOs to deploy a .reg file containing registry values to configure the Automatic Updates client.

d. Use GPOs to configure the Windows Update administrative template to configure the Automatic Updates client.

d. In an Active Directory environment, GPOs are the most efficient way to configure the Automatic Updates client.

3. How will you ensure that newly installed computers are updated?

You should create an integrated installation of all operating systems that are currently being deployed to new computers. For each operating system, include security updates, critical updates, and any important updates provided by your original equipment manufacturer (OEM) or required by non-Microsoft applications. If possible, assign an administrator to regularly update the integrated installation with newly released updates. If various people within your organization will be deploying new computers, do your best to educate them about the importance of installing computers with the integrated installation. To further reduce the risk of new computers being infected, use MBSA and MBSACLI to scan every IP address in your organization for new computers.

4. How will you determine whether clients are being successfully updated?

a. Provide detailed instructions to end users, instructing them to use Add/Remove Programs to identify updates that have been installed and compare that list against the list of available updates on Windows Update.

b. Visit random computers, and view the version numbers of system files to verify that updates have been applied.

c. Use the graphical MBSA console to scan when you have free time available. Configure MBSA to check only the updates that have been approved on SUS servers.

d. Schedule the command-line MBSACLI utility to scan all of Wide World Importers subnets once per week, and examine the reports the following morning. Use the /sus command-line parameter to force MBSACLI to check only those updates approved on your SUS servers.

d. Of these options, the best choice is to schedule the MBSACLI utility. This reduces the burden on you and on end users. It is a less than perfect plan, however, because computers not accessible on the network when the scan runs will not be detected.

Design Activity: Troubleshooting Lab

Page 6-46

1. What is the source of the problem?

   The problem is that the client computer does not have sufficient permissions to request updates from the SUS server. IIS usage logs can be difficult to interpret, but this is an important part of troubleshooting problems related to SUS. The sc-status field contains the Hypertext Transfer Protocol (HTTP) status code that IIS returned to the client. If the request could be successfully filled, the status code would be 200. However, in all of the requests shown in this scenario, the response code is 401. The HTTP status code 401 indicates that the client is unauthorized for the type of request. For more information about HTTP status codes, refer to RFC 2616.

2. How would you troubleshoot the problem?

   You should use IIS Manager to check the permissions for the Web site and the virtual directories used by SUS. Additionally, you should check the file permissions on the Web site root. The root of the Web site, and all SUS content, should be configured to allow anonymous requests.

7 Installing, Configuring, and Managing Certification Services

Exam Objectives in this Chapter:

- Install, manage, and configure Certificate Services.
  - Install and configure root, intermediate, and issuing certification authorities (CAs). Considerations include renewals and hierarchy.
  - Configure certificate templates.
  - Configure, manage, and troubleshoot the publication of certificate revocation lists (CRLs).
  - Configure archival and recovery of keys.
  - Deploy and revoke certificates to users, computers, and CAs.
  - Back up and restore the CA.

Why This Chapter Matters

Encryption is a tremendously powerful security tool, providing authentication and high levels of privacy and data integrity that would otherwise be impossible. For encryption to be useful in an enterprise, you must deploy a public key infrastructure (PKI). Microsoft Windows Server 2003 implements PKI functionality in Certificate Services. As a security administrator, you need to be able to build a PKI infrastructure to suit the needs of organizations ranging from small businesses to enterprises.

Deploying the infrastructure is only the beginning, however. You also need to make the deployment of certificates to end users an easy and straightforward task. Ideally, you will deploy certificates with no user interaction whatsoever. You will also need to be able to save the day when users lose their private keys by recovering the private key and restoring their access to encrypted data.

Lessons in this Chapter:

Before You Begin

If you fulfilled the requirements for the previous chapters, you already have the necessary hardware configured. At a minimum, however, you will need to change the domain membership of Computer2. To do the practices, examples, and lab exercises in this chapter, you must have:

- A private network that is connected to the Internet and protected by a firewall. This network should include only computers that you are using to complete the exercises in this chapter; it specifically must not have any production computers connected to it.

- Two computers. Perform a Windows Server 2003 installation with default settings on both computers. Assign the computer name Computer1 to the first computer. Add the Domain Controller role to the computer using the default settings, and specify the domain name cohowinery.com. Configure the computer to use itself as its own primary Domain Name System (DNS) server. Assign the computer name Computer2 to the second computer. Configure the computer to use Computer1 as its primary DNS server. Then join it to the cohowinery.com domain, and add the Domain Controller role.

Lesson 1: Public Key Infrastructure Fundamentals

Computer networks are no longer closed systems in which a user's mere presence on the network can serve as proof of identity. In this age of information interconnection, an organization's network might consist of intranets, Internet sites, and extranets—all of which are potentially susceptible to access by unauthorized individuals who intend to maliciously view or alter the organization's digital information assets.

There are many potential opportunities for unauthorized access to information stored on networks. A person can attempt to monitor or alter information as it crosses the network, including e-mail messages, electronic commerce transactions, and file transfers. A thief who steals a laptop computer can attempt to access confidential documents stored on the computer. An attacker might attempt to impersonate a legitimate user to gain access to information that would not otherwise be authorized.

A well-planned PKI can reduce the likelihood of each of these common attacks. As a security administrator, you must understand the fundamentals of a PKI, and be able to deploy a Windows Server 2003 Certificate Services infrastructure.

After this lesson, you will be able to

- Describe the significance of public key encryption.
- Explain why a PKI is necessary to enable public key encryption to be used on a large scale.
- List the components of PKIs and the significance of each.
- Deploy Certificate Services on multiple servers.
- Back up and restore important CA data.
- Audit access to CA services.

Estimated lesson time: 50 minutes

Cryptography and Encryption

Cryptography is essential for the secure exchange of information across intranets, extranets, and the Internet. From a technical point of view, cryptography is the science of protecting data by mathematically transforming it into an unreadable format, otherwise known as *encryption*. To a business, cryptography is a means to reduce the likelihood of a costly security compromise by providing authentication, confidentiality, and data integrity.

Network encryption comes in two main varieties: *shared key encryption* and *public key encryption*. Shared key encryption requires both the sender and the recipient of an encrypted message to have a *shared secret*—a password that can be used to encrypt and decrypt the message. Shared key encryption is easy to understand, but it is difficult to implement on a large scale. After all, to allow secure communication between 1,000 employees at a company would require about 1 million passwords to be exchanged, because any two users who wanted to communicate would need to exchange a unique password.

For example, if Sam wants to send an encrypted electronic message to Toby, Sam first walks over to Toby and whispers a password in his ear. Then, when Toby receives the electronic message, Toby decrypts it with the password. As long as nobody else knows the password, Sam can be sure that the contents of the message are private.

The second common network encryption mechanism is public key encryption, also known as *asymmetric key encryption*. Public key encryption uses one key to encrypt a message, and a second, related key to decrypt the message. These two keys form a key pair. One of these keys is kept private, and the other key can be shared publicly (hence the name, public key encryption).

For example, if Sam wants to send an encrypted message to Toby, Sam uses Toby's public key to encrypt the message. When Toby receives the message, Toby uses his private key to decrypt it. Only Toby's private key can be used to decrypt a message encrypted with his public key, so Sam can be sure that nobody else was able to view the contents of the message.

There's another interesting way to use public key encryption: digital signatures. If Sam wants to prove to Toby that Sam, and not somebody else, sent the message, Sam can use Sam's own private key to encrypt the message. After Toby receives it, Toby needs to use Sam's public key to decrypt the message. If it decrypts properly, Toby can be certain that Sam's private key was used to encrypt it and that the message hadn't changed since Sam sent it. Of course, encryption takes a great deal of processing power, so Sam would probably choose to encrypt a short hash of the message instead of the entire message, and append the hash onto the end of the message. That would be sufficient to prove that Sam sent the message and that it hadn't been modified in transit.

Public Key Infrastructure

Public key encryption wouldn't be any easier than shared key encryption if everyone had to manually exchange public keys. That's why we use a PKI—to make the process of managing and exchanging public keys simpler. A PKI is a set of policies, standards, and software that manages certificates and public and private keys. A PKI consists of a set of digital certificates, certification authorities (CAs), and tools that can be used to authenticate users and computers and to verify transactions. In order to place the PKI implementation provided by Windows Server 2003 in the proper context, this section provides a general overview of the components that make up a PKI.

See Also The data formats and network communications used by a PKI are (mostly) standardized. For detailed, but dry, information about PKI standards, refer to RFC 2459.

Certificates

A public key certificate, referred to in this chapter as simply a certificate, is a tool for using public key encryption for authentication and encryption. Certificates are issued and signed by a CA, and any user or application that examines the certificate can safely assume that the CA did indeed issue the certificate. If you trust the CA to do a good job of authenticating users before handing out certificates, and you believe that the CA protects the privacy of its certificates and keys, you can trust that a certificate holder is who he or she claims to be.

Certificates can be issued for a variety of functions, including Web user authentication, Web server authentication, secure e-mail, encryption of network communications, and code signing. CAs even use certificates to identify themselves, create other certificates, and establish a certification hierarchy between other CAs. If the Windows Server 2003 enterprise CA is used in an organization, clients can use certificates to log on to the domain.

Certificates contain some or all of the following information, depending on the purpose of the certificate:

- The user's principal name.
- The user's e-mail address.
- The computer's host name.
- The dates between which the certificate is valid.
- The certificate's serial number, which is guaranteed by the CA to be unique.
- The name of the CA that issued the certificate and the key that was used to sign the certificate.
- A description of the policy that the CA followed to originally authenticate the subject.
- A list of ways the certificate can be used.
- The location of the certificate revocation list (CRL), a document maintained and published by a CA that lists certificates that have been revoked. A CRL is signed with the private key of the CA to ensure its integrity.

Certification authorities

A CA is an entity trusted to issue certificates to an individual, a computer, or a service. A CA accepts a certificate request, verifies the requester's information according to the policies of the CA and the type of certificate being requested, generates a certificate, and then uses its private key to digitally sign the certificate. A CA can be a public third party, such as VeriSign, or it can be internal to an organization. For example, you might choose to use Windows Server 2003 Certificate Services to generate certificates for users and computers in your Active Directory directory service domain. Each CA can have distinct proof-of-identity requirements for certificate requesters, such as a domain account, an employee badge, a driver's license, a notarized request, or a physical address.

Registration is the process by which subjects make themselves known to a CA. Registration can be accomplished automatically during the certificate enrollment process, or it can be accomplished by a trusted entity such as a smart card enrollment station. *Certificate enrollment* is the procedure that a user follows to request a certificate from a CA. The certificate request provides identity information to the CA, and the information the user provides becomes part of the issued certificate.

Certificate life cycle

Certificates cannot be used forever; that would give an attacker too much time to identify the corresponding private key. Certificates have a predefined life cycle and expire at the end of this life cycle. You, as the security administrator, maintain control over the certificate. You can extend the lifetime of a certificate by renewing it, or end the usefulness of a certificate before the expiration date by revoking it.

A number of factors influence the length you will choose for a certificate lifetime, such as the type of certificate, the security requirements of your organization, the standard practices in your industry, and government regulations. In general, longer keys support longer certificate lifetimes and key lifetimes. Longer lifetimes reduce administrative labor, which reduces costs.

When establishing certificate and key lifetimes, you must consider how vulnerable your keys are to compromise and what the potential consequences of compromise are. The following factors influence the lifetimes that you choose for certificates and keys:

- **The length of private keys for certificates.** Because longer keys are more difficult to break, they justify longer safe key lifetimes.
- **The security of the CAs and their private keys.** In general, the more secure the CA and its private key, the longer the safe certificate lifetime. CAs that are operated offline and stored in locked vaults or data centers are the most secure.

- **The strength of the technology used for cryptographic operations.** In general, stronger cryptographic technology supports longer key lifetimes. You can extend key lifetimes if you enhance private key storage by using smart cards and other hardware cryptographic service providers. Some cryptographic technologies provide stronger security, in addition to support for stronger cryptographic algorithms. For example, you might use smart cards for user logon or FIPS 140-1 Crypto Cards for secure mail and secure Web browsers.
- **The vulnerability of the CA certification chain.** In general, the more vulnerable your CA hierarchy is to attack, the longer the CA private keys and the shorter the key lifetimes required.
- **The users of your certificates.** Organizations typically trust their own employees more than they trust employees of other organizations. If you issue certificates to external users, you might want to shorten the lifetimes of those certificates to reduce the time window during which a compromised private key can be abused.
- **The number of certificates that have been signed by a dedicated CA.** The more public the CA public key that is used to sign an issued certificate, the more vulnerable it becomes to attempts to break its key.

An expiration date is defined for each certificate when it is issued. An enterprise CA issues certificates with lifetimes that are based on the certificate template for the requested certificate type.

CA validity periods

Every certificate issued by a CA has a validity period that ends with the certificate's expiration date. Because a CA is really just another entity that has been issued a certificate—either issued by itself (in the case of a root CA) or issued by a parent (in the case of a subordinate CA)—every CA has a built-in expiration date. The expiration date of a CA's certificate is more important than that of other certificates, however.

Although a CA's certificate can be renewed just as easily as any other certificate, a CA cannot issue a certificate with an expiration date valid beyond the expiration date of its own certificate. Therefore, when a CA's certificate reaches the end of its validity period, all certificates it has issued will also expire. Because of this, if you purposely do not renew a CA, you can be assured that all the certificates that the now-expired CA has issued can no longer be used. In other words, there will be no "orphaned" certificates that are still within their validity period but that have been issued by a CA that is no longer valid.

Because a CA that is approaching the end of its own validity period issues certificates valid for shorter and shorter periods of time, you need to have a plan in place to renew the CA well before it expires in order to avoid issuing certificates of a very short validity period. For example, in the case of Windows Server 2003, the root CA's certificate defaults to a validity period of five years. You should renew it every four years, however, to prevent new certificates from being published with lifetimes shorter than a year.

You can reduce the time required to administer a PKI by increasing the validity period of the root CA. As with any certificate, you should choose a validity period shorter than the time required for an attacker to break the root CA key's cryptography. Given the current state of computer technology, one estimate is that a 4096-bit private key would take about 15 to 20 years to crack. While a determined attacker could eventually crack a private key by using the corresponding certificate, the end result would be useless if the certificate had expired by the time the attack completed.

Certificate revocation

A certificate has a specified lifetime, but CAs can reduce this lifetime by the process known as *certificate revocation*. The CA publishes a certificate revocation list (CRL) that lists serial numbers of certificates that it regards as no longer valid. The specified lifetime of CRLs is typically much shorter than that of a certificate. The CA might also include in the CRL the reason the certificate has been revoked. A revocation might occur because a private key has been compromised, because a certificate has been superseded, or because an employee has left the company. The CRL also includes the date the certificate was revoked.

During signature verification, applications can check the CRL to determine whether a given certificate and key pair are still trustworthy. Applications can also determine whether the reason or date of the revocation affects the use of the certificate in question. If the certificate is being used to verify a signature, and the date on the signature precedes the date of the revocation of the certificate by the CA, the signature can still be considered valid.

Off the Record Most applications do not analyze the reason code. If a certificate is revoked, it's revoked. The reason code just isn't that important.

To reduce the number of requests sent to the CA, the CRL is generally cached by the client, which can use it until it expires. If a CA publishes a new CRL, applications that have a valid CRL do not usually use the new CRL until the one they have expires.

Windows Server 2003 Certificate Services

A PKI can be used to dramatically increase the security of an organization's network. To make the task of implementing a PKI simpler, Windows Server 2003 includes Certificate Services to help your organization implement PKI. You can use Certificate Services to create a single CA or an entire hierarchy of CAs. Windows Server 2003 also includes several tools for managing CAs, certificates, and certificate templates. These tools will be discussed in detail in the other lessons in this chapter.

Although you can implement a PKI by using other software, there are distinct advantages to using Windows Server 2003: no additional cost, and tight integration with Active Directory. You can use Group Policy objects to control which users and computers have the rights to issue and manage certificates. You can use standard authorization lists to control the rights of users and computers to request certificates. You can even use certificates issued by your PKI to authenticate users, computers, and domain controllers when they access resources in Active Directory.

See Also This book does not provide information about designing a PKI infrastructure based on Windows Server 2003 because the exam is focused on the tactical installation, configuration, and management tasks. For design information, refer to the Windows Server 2003 Deployment Kit.

Root CAs

The first step in deploying a PKI is to install a CA, and the first CA you install in your organization must be a root CA. You can create two types of root CAs: enterprise and standalone. In a nutshell, enterprise CAs require Active Directory. Because enterprise CAs rely on Active Directory to store and replicate data, all enterprise CAs must also be domain controllers. Enterprise CAs are only capable of issuing certificates to computers and users in the Active Directory forest. Standalone CAs can be used in an Active Directory environment, but they do not require it.

Though there are several requirements and restrictions imposed upon enterprise CAs, they offer some important advantages. You can use autoenrollment with an enterprise CA to dramatically reduce the labor associated with managing certificates. Users performing certificate enrollment with a standalone CA must use Web enrollment, although enterprise CAs provide several other options. Throughout this chapter, differences between enterprise and standalone CAs will be pointed out.

CA hierarchies

CAs can be hierarchical, just as Active Directory forests can be designed in a hierarchy. In a hierarchical CA structure, two or more CAs are organized in a structure with a single root CA and one or more subordinate CAs. The root CA provides a certificate to the subordinate CAs, which in turn can generate certificates for additional subordinate CAs or end users. In Active Directory, trusts are automatically created between domains in a hierarchy. In a CA hierarchy, trust chaining enables certificates issued by subordinate CAs to be trusted by clients who trust the root CA.

Within an organization's certificate hierarchy, some subordinate CAs might be intermediate CAs. In other words, they do not issue certificates to end users or computers; they only issue certificates to other subordinate CAs that are below them in the certification hierarchy. Intermediate CAs are not required. However, using an intermediate CA allows you to take your root CA offline, which greatly increases the security of the root CA. After all, if the root CA is unplugged, it is invulnerable to network attacks.

Subordinate CAs that do issue certificates to end users are known as *issuing CAs*. Of course, root and intermediate CAs are also capable of issuing certificates to end users. Figure 7.1 shows the relationships between root, intermediate, and issuing CAs and the users and computers who use certificates.

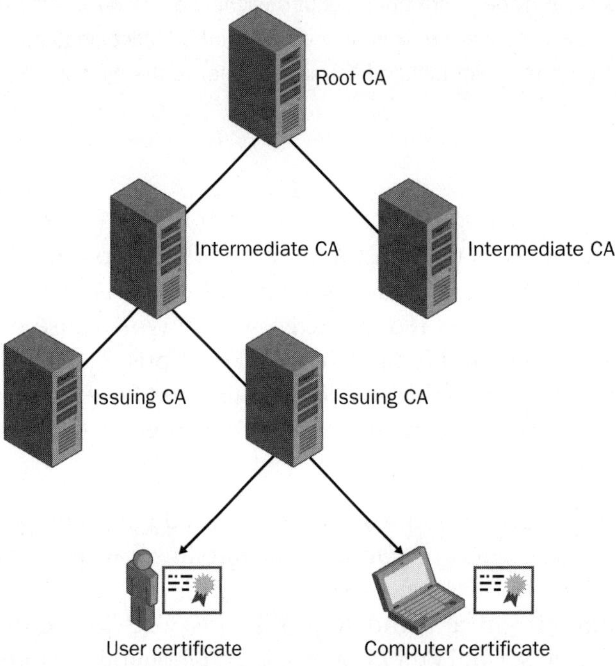

Figure 7.1 A CA hierarchy

You add a subordinate CA to a CA hierarchy by using the same process you use to create a root CA. However, you will need to specify that the computer is an enterprise or standalone subordinate CA, as shown in Figure 7.2. Then you will have to specify the parent CA and provide credentials on the root CA. If you are creating an enterprise subordinate CA, you must provide the user name and password of an account in the Domain Admins group. The entire process of adding a subordinate CA can be accomplished in just a few minutes.

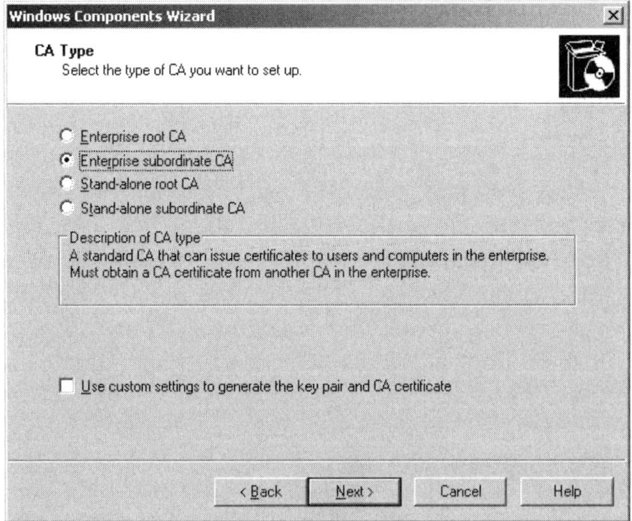

Figure 7.2 Creating a subordinate CA

You will need to spend a few additional minutes if you are using an offline CA, because you must perform an offline certificate request. On the CA Certificate Request page of the subordinate CA installation process, select Save The Request To File instead of Send The Request Directory To A CA. After you complete the installation of the subordinate CA, you will need to transfer the certificate request to the parent CA. On the parent CA, use Web enrollment to perform an advanced certificate request, and select the Submit A Certificate Request By Using A Base-64-Encoded CMC Or PKCS #10 File, Or Submit A Renewal Request By Using A Base-64-Encoded PKCS #7 File option. You will then need to use the Certification Authority console to issue the certificate before transferring it back to the subordinate CA to be installed. Exercise 2 in this lesson will guide you through this process.

You can use qualified subordination to exhibit a great deal of control over what subordinate CAs are allowed to do. For example, you can configure a subordinate CA so that it only issues certificates for a specific namespace, such as partners.cohowinery.com. You can also restrict a subordinate CA to issuing specific types of certificates. This would allow you to create a subordinate CA that issued only smart card certificates. Configuring these options is complex, however, and outside the scope of this book.

See Also For more information about qualified subordination, read the white paper titled "Planning and Implementing Cross-Certification and Qualified Subordination Using Windows Server 2003" at *http://www.microsoft.com/technet/prodtechnol/windowsserver2003/plan/ws03qswp.asp*.

Disaster recovery

Like any other critical service, Certificate Services must be backed up so that they can be restored if a hardware failure or other adverse event occurs. You can back up Certificate Services by using the Certification Authority snap-in, the Backup Utility, or other software.

To manually back up Certificate Services, open the Certification Authority console, right-click the name of your computer, click All Tasks, and then click Back Up CA. The Certification Authority Backup Wizard appears to guide you through the backup process. As shown in Figure 7.3, you can choose to back up the private key and CA certificate, the certificate database, or both. You will be prompted to provide a password that will be used to encrypt the backup file. You will need to have this password to recover the backup.

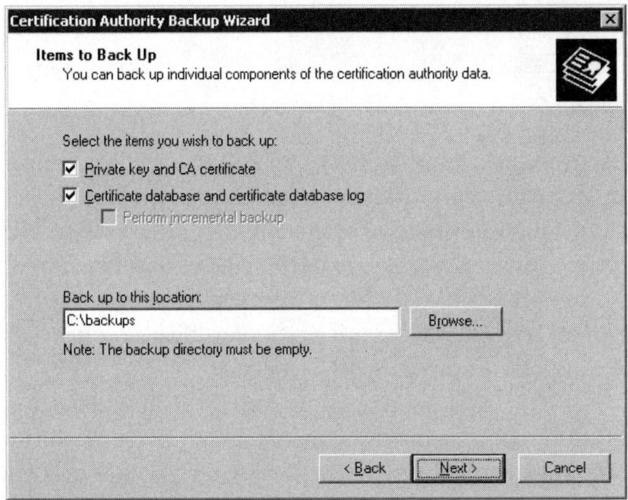

Figure 7.3 Backing up a CA

To restore Certificate Services, open the Certification Authority console, right-click the name of your computer, click All Tasks, and then click Restore CA. You will be prompted to stop Certificate Services. Then the Certification Authority Restore Wizard will appear to guide you through the backup process. During the restore process, you will be prompted for the password you used when creating the backup. After successfully restoring the CA, you will be prompted to restart Certificate Services.

When you use the Backup Utility, Certificate Services is automatically backed up with the system state. If you are using non-Microsoft backup software, and you almost certainly are if your organization has more than one computer, contact the software vendor to make sure that it backs up Certificate Services. Even better, perform a test backup and restore of the server.

Auditing

As with most components of Windows Server 2003, you can and should audit Certificate Services events that might be useful in identifying attacks. To audit Certificate Services events, first enable the Audit Object Access Group Policy setting for the CA. Then open the Certification Authority console, right-click the CA, and click Properties. Click the Auditing tab, and then select the events you want to audit. You can choose from the following self-explanatory events:

- Back up and restore the CA database
- Change CA configuration
- Change CA security settings
- Issue and manage certificate requests
- Revoke certificates and publish CRLs
- Store and retrieve archived keys
- Start and stop Certificate Services

Practice: Configuring a CA Hierarchy

In this practice, you will configure Computer1 as a root CA and Computer2 as a subordinate CA. To complete these exercises, Computer1 and Computer2 must both be domain controllers in the same domain, as described in the "Before You Begin" section of this chapter.

Exercise 1: Creating a Root CA

In this exercise, you will install Certificate Services on Computer1 and configure Computer1 as an enterprise root CA.

1. Log on to the cohowinery.com domain on Computer1 using the Administrator account.
2. Open Add Or Remove Programs in Control Panel.
3. Click Add/Remove Windows Components.
4. In the Windows Components Wizard, select the Certificate Services check box. When prompted, click Yes.
5. Click Next.
6. At the CA Type dialog box, click Enterprise Root CA, and then click Next.

7. In the Common Name For This CA box, type **computer1**. Click Next.

   Note that the default validity period is 5 years, as shown in Figure 7.4.

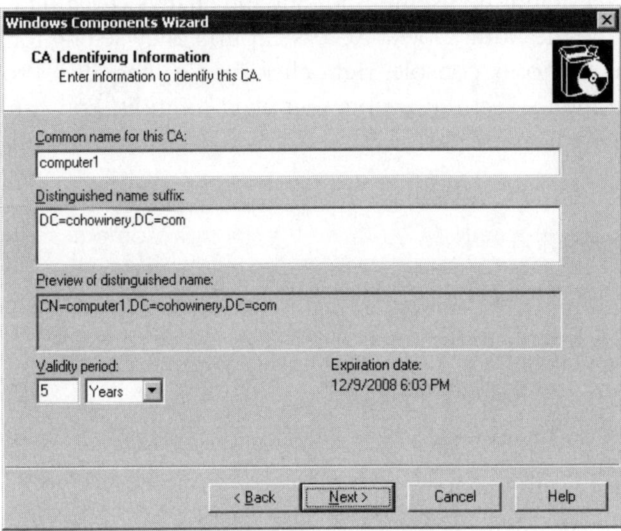

Figure 7.4 Specifying the common name for a CA

8. On the Certificate Database Settings page, accept the defaults by clicking Next. If prompted to stop Internet Information Services (IIS), click Yes.
9. After Certificate Services is installed, click Finish. Close all open windows.

Exercise 2: Creating a Subordinate CA

In this exercise, you will install Certificate Services on Computer2 and configure Computer2 as a subordinate CA to the enterprise root CA, Computer1.

1. Log on to the cohowinery.com domain on Computer2 using the Administrator account.
2. Open Add Or Remove Programs in Control Panel.
3. Click Add/Remove Windows Components.
4. In the Windows Components Wizard, select the Certificate Services check box. When prompted, click Yes.
5. Click Next.
6. In the CA Type dialog box, click Enterprise Root CA, and then click Next.
7. In the Common Name For This CA box, type **computer2**. Click Next.

8. On the Certificate Database Settings page, accept the defaults by clicking Next.
9. On the CA Certificate Request page, click Save The Request To A File. Click Next.

   Note that the default location for the certificate request is C:\computer2.cohowinery.com_computer2.req.
10. If prompted to stop IIS, click Yes.
11. When notified that the Certificate Services installation is incomplete, click OK.
12. After Certificate Services is installed, click Finish. Close all open windows.

   At this point, you have installed Certificate Services on Computer2, but it does not yet have a certificate CA. In the following procedure, you will submit the certificate request to Computer1, which will generate a subordinate CA certificate that you will install on Computer2.
13. Start Microsoft Internet Explorer.

   This exercise demonstrates how to perform an offline certificate request. To simplify the exercise, you will submit the request to Computer1 across the network. This would not be possible if Computer1 were offline. In a production environment, you would need to save the certificate request file to some form of removable media and transfer it to the root CA, and then submit the request from the root CA itself.
14. In the address bar of Internet Explorer, type **http://computer1/certsrv**. Click Go.
15. If you are not automatically authenticated, provide your user name and password when prompted, and then click OK. If you are notified that content from the Web site will be blocked, add Computer1 to the list of trusted computers.
16. Click Request A Certificate.
17. Click Advanced Certificate Request.
18. Click Submit A Certificate Request By Using A Base-64-Encoded CMC Or PKCS #10 File, Or Submit A Renewal Request By Using A Base-64-Encoded PKCS #7 File.
19. Open the certificate request you created in step 9 by clicking Start, clicking Run, typing **Notepad C:\computer2.cohowinery.com_computer2.req**, and then clicking OK.
20. Press CTRL + A to select the entire contents of the file, and then press CTRL + C to copy the contents to the clipboard.
21. Return to Internet Explorer. Click the Saved Request field, and then press CTRL + V to paste the certificate request into the form, as shown in Figure 7.5.

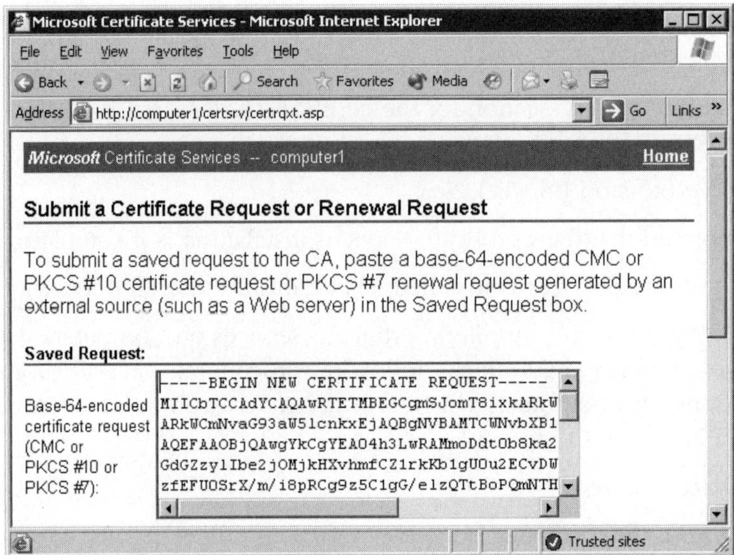

Figure 7.5 Requesting a subordinate CA certificate

22. Click the Certificate Template field, and then click Subordinate Certification Authority. Finally, click Submit.

23. On the Certificate Issued page, click Download Certificate. When prompted, click Save, and save the file on the desktop. Click Close.

    You have submitted the certificate request and it has been approved. The final step is to install the subordinate CA certificate.

24. Start the Certification Authority console.

    Notice that Certificate Services is not started because the subordinate CA certificate has not been installed.

25. Right-click Computer2, click All Tasks, and then click Install CA Certificate. Browse to the desktop. In the Files Of Type box, select X.509 Certificate. Click the new certificate, and then click Open.

26. Right-click Computer2, click All Tasks, and then click Start Service.

    Computer2 will start successfully. This exercise demonstrated the process of configuring a subordinate CA to an offline root CA. If the root CA were online, you could have configured the subordinate CA entirely from the Windows Components Wizard.

Lesson Review

The following questions are intended to reinforce key information presented in this lesson. If you are unable to answer a question, review the lesson materials and try the question again. You can find answers to the questions in the "Questions and Answers" section at the end of this chapter.

1. Which of the following scenarios would use public key encryption to keep a message sent from User A to User B private?
   a. User A encrypts a message with User B's public key.
   b. User A encrypts a message with User A's public key.
   c. User B encrypts a message with User B's private key.
   d. User B encrypts a message with User A's public key.

   ______

2. Which of the following is a feature unique to enterprise CAs?
   a. Web enrollment.
   b. Certificate autoenrollment.
   c. Certificates can be revoked.
   d. Certificates can be renewed prior to their expiration date.

   ______

Lesson Summary

- Public key encryption uses two keys to encrypt and decrypt messages. A message encrypted with one key can be decrypted only with the second key in the key pair, and vice-versa.
- To send a private message by using public key encryption, encrypt the message with the recipient's public key. Only the private key can be used to decrypt the message.
- Public key encryption can be used to digitally sign messages, which proves that the message was sent by the holder of the private key, and that the message was not modified.
- A PKI is used to manage keys and to distribute keys to a large number of users. A PKI consists of many components, including CAs, certificates, and CRLs.
- A CA issues certificates to end users. A certificate is only as trustworthy as the CA that signed it.

- Certificates expire at a time specified when the certificate is generated. CRLs are used to revoke certificates before that specified expiration date.
- Root CAs cannot issue certificates that are valid beyond the CA's certificate's expiration date. Specifying a long lifetime for the root CA reduces labor, but this might increase your vulnerability to brute force attacks.

Lesson 2: Managing Certificate Templates

Large organizations might issue thousands of certificates to users and computers. If you had to provide the configuration settings for each one manually, you could spend all day issuing certificates—and you would probably make a large number of mistakes. Fortunately, you can use certificate templates to simplify the process of creating certificates and to ensure that they are created consistently across an organization.

If you are familiar with certificate templates in Microsoft Windows 2000, you will be pleasantly pleased with the new features available in version 2 certificate templates in Windows Server 2003. Most notably, you now have the ability to combine multiple functions into a single template. You can even remove yourself entirely from the certificate enrollment process and configure templates to install automatically for a computer or user. These capabilities reduce the amount of administration needed to maintain a PKI, and reduce the total number of certificates users and computers need, thereby reducing costs and saving you time.

After this lesson, you will be able to

- Determine the purpose of digital certificates.
- Explain what happens when certificates expire or are revoked and renewed.
- Select digital certificate templates that correspond to the needs of an organization.
- Determine the uses and roles of certificate templates.
- Set appropriate permissions on certificate templates.
- Modify and supersede certificate templates.

Estimated lesson time: 45 minutes

Overview of Certificate Templates

Certificate templates are the sets of rules and settings that define the format and content of a certificate based on the certificate's intended use. Certificate templates also provide the client with instructions on how to create and submit a valid certificate request. In addition, certificate templates define which security principals are allowed to read, enroll, or autoenroll for certificates based on that template. Certificate templates are configured on a CA and are applied against the incoming certificate requests.

When deploying certificates in an organization, you should customize each template for its intended use. For example, there are default certificate templates for users, computers, Encrypting File System (EFS), and code signing. The type of certificate template that you should use in your organization depends on your security requirements and your PKI applications. You can issue multiple types of certificates to meet a variety of security or application requirements and create your own certificates to meet the needs of your organization.

Only enterprise CAs can issue certificates based on certificate templates. When a certificate template is defined, this definition must be available to all CAs in the forest. You can make the definition available by publishing the template in Active Directory and letting the Active Directory replication engine replicate the published template. The replication of the certificate template in the forest depends upon the Active Directory replication schedule, and the certificate template might not be available at all CAs until replication is completed.

To ensure distribution of the certificate template's definition, the certificate template information is stored in Active Directory. Normally, you will use the Certificate Templates snap-in to view and edit templates; however, you can also use the ADSIEdit snap-in to view and modify the Active Directory objects directly. The templates are located in the CN=Certificate Templates,CN=Public Key Services,CN=Services,CN=Configuration,DC=*ForestRootNameDN* container (where *ForestRootNameDN* is the LDAP distinguished name of the forest root domain), as shown in Figure 7.6.

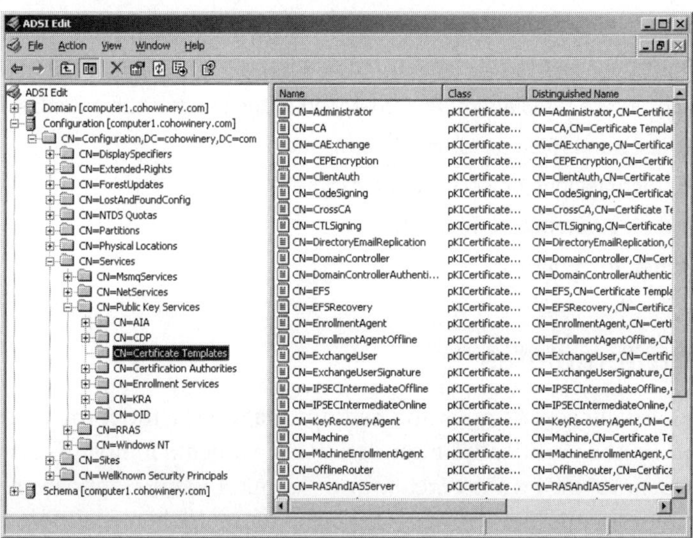

Figure 7.6 Certificate template location

Associated with every certificate template is an access control list (ACL) that defines which security principals have permissions to read, enroll, autoenroll, or modify the certificate template. You can set permissions on the certificate templates by using the Certificate Templates snap-in. Permissions are discussed in more detail later in this lesson.

Certificate Template Versions

Windows Server 2003 supports two types of certificate templates: version 1 and version 2. Version 1 templates provide backward compatibility for servers running Windows 2000 family operating systems. Version 1 templates have a major limitation, however: the information they contain is hard-coded in the certificate. You cannot modify certificate template properties, such as certificate lifetime and key size. Version 2 certificate templates address some of these limitations.

When the first enterprise CA is installed in a forest, version 1 templates are created by default. Unlike version 2 templates, these cannot be modified or removed, but they can be duplicated. When you duplicate a version 1 template, you create a version 2 template. Version 1 templates provide a certificate solution as soon as the CA is installed because they support many general needs for subject certification. For example, there are certificates that allow EFS encryption recovery, client authentication, smart card logon, and server authentication.

Because version 1 certificate templates can be used by both Windows 2000 and Windows XP clients, Windows Server 2003 Certificate Services can work alongside an existing Windows CA infrastructure. Adding a Windows Server 2003 CA does not give computers running Windows 2000 and Windows XP the ability to work with version 2 certificate templates, however. Only Windows Server 2003, Enterprise Edition and Windows Server 2003, Datacenter Edition can issue certificates based on version 2 templates. To enable administration from your desktop, you can create and modify version 2 templates on any computer running Windows XP Professional on which the Windows Server 2003 Administration pack (adminpak.msi) is installed.

Certificate Template Usage

Certificates have the potential to be used by a wide variety of applications. After all, a certificate is simply a piece of data. The operating system and the applications are responsible for using that data to perform functions such as encrypting messages and authenticating connections.

However, there are many different templates designed to be used for various purposes. To specify how a certificate template can be used, you configure the application policies. Application policies, also known as *extended key usage* or *enhanced key usage*, give you the ability to specify which certificates can be used for which purposes. This allows you to issue certificates without being concerned that they will be misused.

For example, a certificate based on the Smartcard User template can be used by a user to send secure e-mail, to perform client authentication, and to logon by using a smart card. By default, it cannot be used to authenticate a server to a client, to recover files, to encrypt files, or to perform many other tasks that rely on a certificate. Further, the certificate can be issued only to a user, not to a computer.

The Smartcard User template, and many other templates, can be used for multiple functions. Using certificate templates with multiple functions is an excellent way to reduce the number of certificates that are needed in an organization. Many certificate templates, however, are single function only. Single-function certificate templates can be highly restricted and used only for a single function. For example, you could issue certificates for a sensitive operation, such as key recovery, with a short certificate lifetime of 2 months. You would not want to combine this certificate function with a function that is not as sensitive, such as an EFS certificate, because an EFS certificate should have a much longer lifetime.

Table 7.1 describes the user certificate templates included with Windows Server 2003. All user certificates included with Windows Server 2003 are version 1.

Table 7.1 Default User Certificate Templates

Name	Description
Administrator	Allows user authentication, EFS encryption, secure e-mail, and certificate trust list signing.
Authenticated Session	Authenticates a user to a Web server. The private key is used to sign the authentication request.
Basic EFS	Encrypts and decrypts data by using EFS. The private key is used to decrypt the file encryption key (FEK) that is used to encrypt and decrypt the EFS-protected data.
Code Signing	Used to digitally sign software.
EFS Recovery Agent	Allows the subject to decrypt files previously encrypted with EFS.
Enrollment Agent	Used to request certificates on behalf of another subject.
Exchange Enrollment Agent (Offline request)	Used to request certificates on behalf of another subject and supply the subject name in the request.
Exchange Signature Only	Used by Exchange Key Management Service to issue certificates to Microsoft Exchange Server users for digitally signing e-mail.
Exchange User	Used by Exchange Key Management Service to issue certificates to Exchange users for encrypting e-mail.
Smartcard Logon	Authenticates a user with the network by using a smart card.
Smartcard User	Identical to the Smartcard Logon template, except that it can also be used to sign and encrypt e-mail.
Trust List Signing	Allows the holder to digitally sign a trust list.
User	Used by users for e-mail, EFS, and client authentication.
User Signature Only	Allows users to digitally sign data.

Table 7.2 describes the computer certificate templates included with Windows Server 2003.

Table 7.2 Default Computer Certificate Templates

Name	Description	Version
CA Exchange	Used to store keys that are configured for private key archival.	2
CEP Encryption	Allows the holder to act as a registration authority (RA) for Simple Certificate Enrollment Protocol (SCEP) requests.	1
Computer	Provides both client and server authentication abilities to a computer account. The default permissions for this template allow enrollment only by computers running Windows 2000 and Windows Server 2003 family operating systems that are not domain controllers.	1
Domain Controller Authentication	Used to authenticate Active Directory computers and users.	2
IPSEC	Provides certificate-based authentication for computers by using IP Security (IPSec) for network communications.	1
IPSEC (Offline request)	Used by IPSec to digitally sign, encrypt, and decrypt network communication when the subject name is supplied in the request.	1
RAS and IAS Server	Enables Remote Access Services (RAS) and Internet Authentication Services (IAS) servers to authenticate their identities to other computers.	2
Router (Offline request)	Used by a router when requested through SCEP from a certification authority that holds a Certificate Enrollment Protocol (CEP) Encryption certificate.	1
Web Server	Authenticates the Web server to connecting clients. The connecting clients use the public key to encrypt the data that is sent to the Web server when using Secure Sockets Layer (SSL) encryption.	1
Workstation Authentication	Enables client computers to authenticate their identities to servers.	2

Finally, there are a handful of service templates that cannot be neatly classified as user or computer certificate templates:

- **Cross-Certification Authority.** Used for cross-certification and qualified subordination.
- **Directory E-mail Replication.** Used to replicate e-mail within Active Directory.
- **Domain Controller.** Provides both client and server authentication abilities to a computer account. Default permissions allow enrollment by only domain controllers.

- **Key Recovery Agent.** Recovers private keys that are archived on the certification authority.
- **Root Certification Authority and Subordinate Certification Authority.** Used to prove the identity of the certification authorities.

Off the Record A certificate template is nothing more than a collection of properties, requirements, and functions. When planning certificate templates, you are not bound to the templates that are included in Windows Server 2003. You can create your own templates to meet the needs of your organization. For example, you could create a template that is used for EFS and e-mail, that is only valid for one year, that archives the keys, and that does not support autoenrollment.

Certificate Template Permissions

Certificate template permissions define the security principals that can read, modify, enroll, or autoenroll for certificates based on certificate templates. You must define the permissions for each certificate template to ensure that only authorized users, computers, or group members can obtain certificates based on a certificate template.

Planning Be sure that you know the members of a group before you issue certificates to that group. Improper planning could lead to a security risk caused by issuing certificates to users who are not required to have those certificates.

The permissions that you can assign to a certificate template include:

- **Full Control.** Allows a security principal to modify all attributes of a certificate template, including the permissions for the certificate template.
- **Read.** Allows a security principal to find the certificate template in Active Directory when enrolling for certificates.
- **Write.** Allows a security principal to modify all the attributes of a certificate template, except for the permissions that are assigned to the certificate template.
- **Enroll.** Allows a security principal to enroll for a certificate based on the certificate template. To enroll for a certificate, the security principal must also have Read permissions for the certificate template.
- **Autoenroll.** Allows a security principal to receive a certificate through the autoenrollment process. Autoenrollment permissions also require that the user have both Read and Enroll permissions.

Security Alert For autoenrollment to function correctly, you must ensure that all three required permissions (Read, Enroll, and Autenroll) are granted to the same user or group. If you assign Read and Enroll to one group and Autoenroll to another group, a user who is a member of both groups will not be allowed to autoenroll for certificates. This is because permissions for a certificate are not additive, like they are NTFS. In this example, because a user is a member of two groups, the CA will treat the group with Read and Enroll permissions separately from the group with Autoenroll permissions. For best results, create a global or universal group for each certificate template. Grant the global or universal group all three permissions, and then add the necessary user groups to this group.

Figure 7.7 shows the permissions you can set on certificate templates.

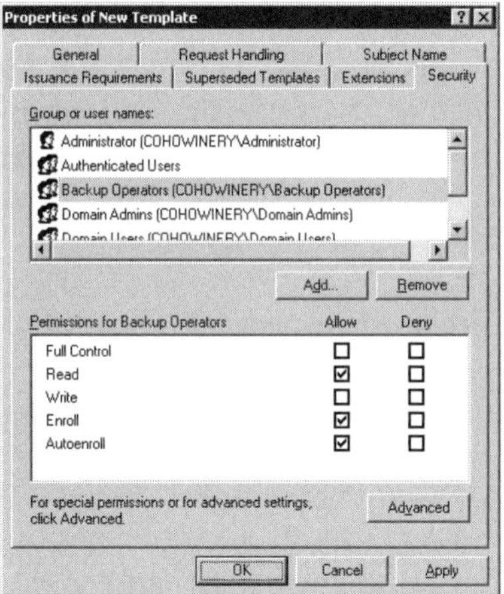

Figure 7.7 Certificate template permissions

Methods for Updating a Certificate Template

In your CA hierarchy, you might have one certificate template for each job function, such as file encryption or code signing, or a few templates that cover functions for most common groups of subjects. You might have to modify an existing certificate template as a result of incorrect settings that were defined in the original certificate template, or you might want to merge multiple existing certificate templates into a single template.

There are two methods for modifying a version 2 certificate template. You either modify the original template, or you create a new one to replace it.

You can modify a version 2 certificate template at any time. After you make the changes, all new certificate enrollees will receive the new settings. To ensure that all clients that have previously been issued certificates based on the template before it was modified receive the new settings, re-issue the certificate by using the Certificates snap-in. This is an excellent way to make sweeping changes to certificates deployed to users and computers in your organization. For example, if you discovered that a certificate could be compromised in less than one year, you could modify the validity period of the certificate to six months and re-enroll all certificate holders.

The second method of modifying a certificate is known as *superseding* a certificate. This method is accomplished by creating a new version 2 certificate template and adding multiple application policies for those certificates that you want to supersede. For example, if multiple certificate templates provide the same or similar functionality, you can supersede the existing certificate templates with a single certificate template. You can accomplish this replacement by designating that a new certificate template supersedes, or replaces, the existing certificate templates. Select the certificates that are to be superseded in the Superseded Templates tab on the new certificate's properties.

When making your decision on whether to modify a certificate template, you should consider the consequences of the modification. For example, if a change is going to affect only a single certificate template, and if the change does not require certificates to be re-issued to all current certificate holders, you can simply modify an existing certificate template. Nice and easy!

Keep in mind that only version 2 certificate templates support modification. If the certificate template that you want to modify is a version 1 certificate template, you must supersede the existing certificate template with a version 2 certificate template.

If the changes you are going to make to the certificate template do not affect previously issued certificates, you do not need to re-issue the certificate to certificate holders. For example, changing the permissions for a certificate template to allow additional groups to enroll the certificate template would not require the re-issuance of all existing certificates.

Certificate management can be time-consuming, especially in an environment that issues a large number of certificates to users and computers. The load on the issuing CA increases, CRLs get bigger, and the end user certificate management can be harrowing. To ease this potential strain on your CAs and end users, consider consolidating multiple existing certificate templates into a single certificate template.

It is not possible to modify a version 1 certificate template, because they do not allow modification. However, by superseding the version 1 certificate template with a version 2 certificate template, you can effectively modify the settings of the template. For example, you could create a new version 2 template that performs the same functions as the original template but that has different settings for the certificate lifetime, key size, or application and issuance policies for a certificate.

In summary, you can update an existing certificate template in two ways. The first way is to modify a version 2 certificate template at any time by making changes to the certificate template. The second way is to supersede an existing certificate template. If the certificate template you want to update is version 1, or if you want to combine multiple certificate templates into a single template, you can supersede the existing certificate template or templates with a version 2 certificate template. After you make the changes, any certificate issued by a CA based on that certificate template will include the modifications you made in the certificate template.

You should modify a template when the changes are minor and affect only a single version 2 certificate template. You should supersede a template when you are consolidating multiple templates, when you are modifying a version 1 certificate template, or when you are changing the lifetime, key size, application policies, or issuance policies.

Security Alert By modifying or superseding templates you affect only those certificates that are issued after you modify the certificate template. Existing certificates are not modified until the user or computer holding the certificate based on the certificate template renews the certificate or enrolls a new certificate based on the modified or superseded certificate template. If autoenrollment is enabled for the updated or superseded certificate template, users or computers will automatically enroll the updated certificates.

Practice: Superseding Certificate Templates

In this practice, you will supersede multiple existing certificate templates.

Exercise: Superseding Multiple Certificates

In this exercise, you will supersede the User certificate template with a new version 2 certificate template.

1. Log on to the cohowinery.com domain on Computer1 using the Administrator account.
2. Click Start, click Run, type **certtmpl.msc** and then click OK.
3. Right-click the User template and then click Duplicate Template.
4. In the Properties Of New Template dialog box, click the General tab and type **Backup Operators** in the Template Display Name box.
5. Specify the validity period as 6 months, as shown in Figure 7.8.

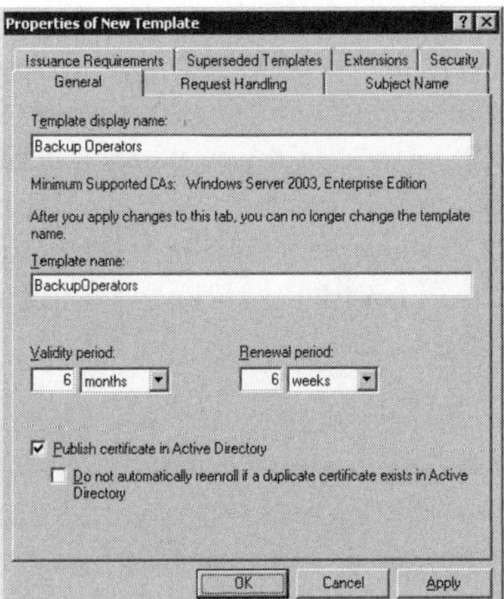

Figure 7.8 Properties of New Template dialog box

6. Click the Extensions tab, click Application Policies, and then click Edit.
7. In the Edit Application Policies Extension dialog box, ensure that Client Authentication, Encrypting File System, and Secure Email are present, and then click Add.
8. In the Add Application Policy dialog box, select Smart Card Logon under Application Policies, and then click OK.
9. In the Edit Application Policies Extension dialog box, verify that Smart Card Logon is now in the list, as shown in Figure 7.9, and then click OK.

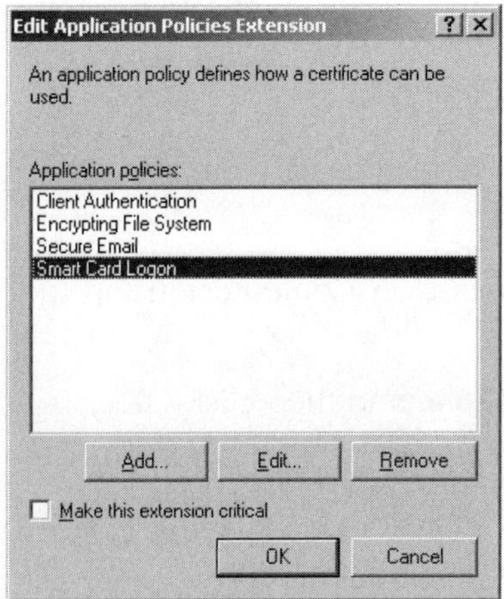

Figure 7.9 Smart Card Logon policy added to the Application Policies list

10. Click the Superseded Templates tab, and then click Add.

11. In the Add Superseded Template dialog box, hold down the CTRL key and click User and Smartcard Logon, and then click OK. Verify that the templates are displayed under Certificate Templates.
12. Click the Security tab, and then click the Add button and add the Backup Operators group. Click OK to return to the Properties Of New Template dialog box.
13. Select Backup Operators and then select the Allow check box for the Read, Enroll, and Autoenroll permissions.
14. Click OK, and then close all open windows.
15. Open the Certification Authority console.
16. Expand Certification Authority. Right-click Certificate Templates, click New, and then click Certificate Template To Issue.
17. In the Enable Certificate Templates dialog box, click Backup Operators, and then click OK.

    Now the Backup Operators certificate template is an available choice for users requesting new certificates. Because of replication latency and template caching in the registry, a certificate authority might not be able to issue a certificate template immediately. The timing of issuance is dependent on replication latency between domain controllers.

Lesson Review

The following questions are intended to reinforce key information presented in this lesson. If you are unable to answer a question, review the lesson materials and try the question again. You can find answers to the questions in the "Questions and Answers" section at the end of this chapter.

1. Which of the following tasks can be performed on version 1 certificate templates? (Choose all that apply.)
   - **a.** Adding a certificate based on the template to a CRL
   - **b.** Changing the expiration date of the template
   - **c.** Superseding the template with a version 2 template
   - **d.** Changing the permissions assigned to the template

---

2. Where in the Active Directory are certificate templates located?

   a. CN=Certificate Templates,CN=Public Key Services,CN=Extended-Rights, CN=Configuration,DC=*ForestRootNameDN*

   b. CN=Certificate Templates,CN=Public Key Services,CN=Services,CN=Configuration,DC=*ForestRootNameDN*

   c. CN=Certificate Templates,CN=Public Key Services,CN=Services,CN=Domain, DC=*ForestRootNameDN*

   d. CN=Certificate Templates,CN=NetServices,CN=Services,CN=Configuration, DC=*ForestRootNameDN*

Lesson Summary

- Certificate templates are the sets of rules that define the content of a certificate based on its intended use.
- Microsoft certification authorities (CAs) support two types of certificate templates: version 1 and version 2. Version 1 templates are provided for backwards compatibility and support many general needs for subject certification. Version 2 templates allow customization of most settings in the template.
- Version 2 templates require Active Directory. They can be created and duplicated by any member of the Windows Server 2003 family; however, certificates based on version 2 templates can be issued only by a CA that is running Windows Server 2003, Enterprise Edition or Windows Server 2003, Datacenter Edition.
- Certificate template permissions define the security principals that can read, modify, enroll, and autoenroll certificates based on certificate templates.
- You can update existing certificate templates by either modifying or superseding them. Only version 2 certificate templates can be modified.

Lesson 3: Deploying and Revoking Certificates

Before you can use the autoenrollment capability of version 2 certificate templates, you will need to enable automatic certificate enrollment for your environment. However, not all certificate management issues can be automated. To maintain a PKI, you will still need to be able to manually issue certificates. Additionally, you will need to revoke certificates when computers are retired, when employees leave, or when security compromises occur. Revoking certificates, and publishing the certificate revocation lists (CRLs), is an important but complicated process.

After this lesson, you will be able to

- Select an appropriate certificate enrollment method.
- Perform manual certificate enrollment.
- Enable autoenrollment of certificates.
- Revoke a certificate.

Estimated lesson time: 45 minutes

Certificate Enrollment Process

Certificate enrollment is the process of requesting and installing certificates for a user, computer, or service. You, as an administrator, define the policies and processes of your CA. Although your options might be restricted by network connectivity or by the use of a standalone CA, the certificate enrollment process involves the same steps at a high level, and occurs as follows:

1. When a user generates a request for a new certificate, the operating system passes the request information to a Cryptographic Service Provider (CSP) that is installed on the user's computer.
2. The CSP generates the private key and the public key—referred to as a *key pair*—for the certificate request. If the CSP is software based, it generates the key pair on the computer on which the request was performed. If the CSP is hardware based, such as a smart card CSP, the CSP instructs the hardware device to generate the key pair.
3. The public key is sent to the CA, along with the certificate requester information. The CSP stores the private key in a secure location. A software CSP encrypts and secures the private key by using the Data Protection API (DPAPI) in the user's profile. A smart card CSP stores the private key on a smart card, which controls access to the key.

4. The CA then either allows or denies the request. If the request is successful, the CA creates and signs the certificate.

5. Finally, the CA issues the completed certificate to the requester, who installs the certificate on the required store on the computer or hardware device.

Certificate Enrollment Methods

A Windows Server 2003 CA provides several methods for certificate enrollment. Your choice of enrollment method for issuing certificates will be dictated by the type of CA that you are requesting the certificate from and whether the client and CA can communicate across a network. For example, a standalone CA does not have the ability to automatically issue a certificate; therefore, autoenrollment is not an option. Additionally, a computer that is not connected to the network cannot automatically enroll for a certificate because autoenrollment requires the client to communicate directly to the enterprise CA. In these circumstances, all certificates will have to be manually submitted by the end user.

When requesting certificates from a standalone CA, you can request certificates by using the Web enrollment pages, the Certificates snap-in, or the Certreq.exe command-line utility. Web-based enrollment is by far the easiest and most intuitive method for end users to enroll for certificates. If users have the ability to use the Certificates snap-in, they have the option of using the console to submit certificate requests directly to the CA. This method will require end users to load and configure a Microsoft Management Console (MMC) snap-in—hardly a user-friendly process. The final method for certificate enrollment is to use the Certreq.exe command directly from the command line. Certreq.exe is primarily used for scripting certificate tasks that cannot be accomplished by using Group Policy settings. Although it can be used to request certificates, it is not intended to be used by end users.

When you use an enterprise CA for certificate enrollment, you can configure enrollment by using the Web enrollment pages, the Certificates snap-in, autoenrollment of certificates by means of Group Policy, or the Certreq.exe command-line utility. The most important advantage of using an enterprise CA with Web enrollment, MMC snap-in, or the command-line utility is the ability of the CA to automatically issue the certificate without a CA administrator approving the certificate. You control whether certificates are autoenrolled or must be manually approved by granting the Autoenroll permission on the certificate template for users and groups that should receive a certificate.

For the ultimate in automation, use Group Policy to cause clients to automatically enroll without prompting the user. There is an important restriction, however. Although computers running Windows 2000 can participate in autoenrollment for computer certificates deployed by means of the Automatic Certificate Request Settings Group Policy setting, autoenrollment of user certificates is not possible for clients running Windows 2000.

Planning When Windows XP and Windows Server 2003 perform autoenrollment, there is a short delay between the time when a user logs on and the time when autoenrollment starts. This delay allows services to start and the user to finish logging on.

In contrast, Windows XP and Windows Server 2003 support autoenrollment for both user and computer certificates by means of Autoenrollment Settings policies and version 2 certificate templates. This solution reduces the number of certificates issued by combining certificate purposes into fewer certificates. It also reduces administration and end user interaction by using autoenrollment. Remember that autoenrollment settings in Group Policy require the use of version 2 certificate templates.

Manual enrollment

If you have client computers running operating systems that are earlier than Windows 2000, you must manually enroll these clients for certificates because the client operating systems do not support Group Policy, and therefore cannot take advantage of autoenrollment. As discussed in the previous section, you can manually enroll for certificates by using a Web-based interface, the Certificates snap-in, or the Certreq.exe utility.

To manually enroll for certificates by using a Web-based interface, ensure that the CA is hosted on a server running Windows Server 2003 Certificate Services that has IIS 6.0 installed. The Web Enrollment application is installed when Certificate Services is installed. It allows users to perform various tasks that are related to requesting certificates from both standalone and enterprise CAs. The Web Enrollment Web site is located at *http://ServerName/certsrv*.

Security Alert By default, SSL is not enabled on the Web-based interface. For increased security, enable SSL on the certsrv virtual directory using a certificate that is trusted by all clients, such as a certificate issued by a public CA.

You can also enroll for certificates by using the Certificate Request Wizard in the Certificates snap-in to request certificates from a computer running Windows Server 2003 that is configured as an enterprise CA. The Certificates snap-in displays the active certificates and other PKI client properties, such as trusted root CAs and existing certificate trust lists. As the administrator of a computer, you can manage certificates that are issued to users, computers, and services. As a user without administrative privileges, you can manage certificates only for your user account.

See Also For more information on how to obtain and install an SSL certificate see *http://msdn.microsoft.com/msdnmag/issues/01/04/ssl/*.

You can use the command-line program Certreq.exe to submit, retrieve, and accept certificate requests. Because it is a command-line program, you have the ability to script the certificate enrollment process. Using Certreq.exe with its primary switches will allow you to perform some common certificate-related tasks. Use the **certreq –submit** command to submit a precreated request file to a CA. Use the **certreq –retrieve** command to retrieve a certificate from a CA. Use the **certreq –accept** command to accept and install certificates from a new request to a CA.

Automatic enrollment

Autoenrollment enables organizations to automatically deploy certificates to both users and computers. The autoenrollment feature allows you to centrally manage all aspects of the certificate lifecycle, including certificate enrollment, certificate renewal, and the modification and superseding of certificates.

Autoenrollment of user certificates provides a quick and simple way to issue certificates to users. It also enables faster deployment of PKI applications, such as smart card logon, EFS, SSL, and Signed Multipurpose Internet Mail Extensions (S/MIME), within an Active Directory environment by eliminating the need for interaction with the end user.

Exam Tip For the exam, know that using autoenrollment minimizes the high cost of PKI deployments and reduces the total cost of ownership for a PKI implementation.

In a Windows Server 2003 PKI, there are two methods of enabling autoenrollment of certificates: Automatic Certificate Request Settings and Autoenrollment Settings. Automatic Certificate Request Settings is a Group Policy setting that enables the deployment of version 1 certificates to computers running Windows 2000, Windows XP, and Windows Server 2003. This type of autoenrollment can be used only to deploy computer certificates, and it occurs each time the computer starts or Group Policy is refreshed. It is most commonly used to deploy certificates to be used for encrypted IPSec connections. This Group Policy setting is located under the Computer Configuration/Windows Settings/Security Settings/Public Key Policies/Automatic Certificate Request Settings node in the Group Policy Object Editor snap-in.

Autoenrollment Settings are based on a combination of Group Policy settings and version 2 certificate templates. This combination allows the client computer running Windows XP Professional or Windows Server 2003 to enroll user or computer certificates automatically when the user logs on. For computer certificates, this Group Policy setting is located under the Computer Configuration/Windows Settings/Security Settings/Public Key Policies node in the Group Policy console. For user certificates, the Group Policy setting is in User Configuration/Windows Settings/Security Settings/Public Key Policies. By default, both user and computer autoenrollment is enabled.

Exam Tip Remember that the Automatic Certificate Request Settings Group Policy setting does not apply to users. It applies only to computers. Because Windows 2000 cannot use Autoenrollment Settings, Windows 2000 can only autoenroll in computer certificates.

Some types of certificates require user interaction to be enrolled. For example, smart card certificates require the user to insert the smart card before the certificate can be generated. In these cases, you can still use autoenrollment by configuring the version 2 certificate template to prompt the user during enrollment. From the certificate's properties dialog box, click the Request Handling tab and then select either Prompt The User During Enrollment or Prompt The User During Enrollment And Require User Input When The Private Key Is Used. When users are autoenrolled, a pop-up window (like those used in update notifications) will prompt the user that interaction is required.

Caution Do not configure computer certificates to prompt the user—it will cause autoenrollment to fail.

Revoking Certificates

You might occasionally need to revoke a certificate because a user has left your organization, because you have decommissioned a computer, or because a private key has been compromised. There are two ways you can revoke certificates: by using the Certification Authority snap-in, and by using the Certutil.exe command-line program.

To revoke a certificate by using the Certification Authority snap-in, select the Issued Certificates node. Then, in the right pane, right-click the certificate you want to revoke, click All Tasks, and then click Revoke Certificate. You will then be prompted to choose the reason for revoking the certificate, which will be included in the CRL. You can choose from the following self-explanatory reason codes:

- Unspecified
- Key Compromise
- CA Compromise
- Change Of Affiliation
- Superseded
- Cease Of Operation
- Certificate Hold

Off the Record The CRL contains the reason code you select for revoking the certificate. Before you select the reason code, think about whether you really want everyone who can access the CRL to know why you revoked it. If you did have a key compromise or a CA compromise, are you ready for that to be public information? If not, just select Unspecified.

Clients discover that a certificate has been revoked by retrieving the certificate revocation list (CRL). There are two kinds of CRLs: full CRLs, which contain a complete list of all of a CA's revoked certificates, and delta CRLs. Delta CRLs are shorter lists of certificates that have been revoked since the last full CRL was published. After a client retrieves a full CRL, the client can download the shorter delta CRL to discover newly revoked certificates.

See Also For detailed information about CRLs, read the white paper "Troubleshooting Certificate Status and Revocation" which is located at *http://www.microsoft.com/technet/prodtechnol/WinXPPro/support/tshtcrl.asp*.

Publishing CRLs

If you need to download a file from a server, you might access the file in several different ways. If you're logged onto the computer locally, you would use Windows Explorer to navigate to the folder containing the file. If you were on a different computer on the same network, you might map a drive to the server and download the file from a shared folder. If the server was behind a firewall and running IIS, you could open a Web browser to retrieve the file.

Having multiple ways to retrieve a file from a server is important, especially when the server will be accessed by a variety of different clients. Certificate Services enables clients to retrieve CRLs by using a wide variety of different protocols: shared folders, Hypertext Transfer Protocol (HTTP), File Transfer Protocol (FTP), and Lightweight Directory Access Protocol (LDAP).

By default, CRLs are published in three different locations. For clients accessing the CRL from a shared folder, they are located in the *Server*\CertEnroll\ share, which is created automatically when Certificate Services is installed. Clients who need to retrieve the CRL by using LDAP can access it from CN=*CAName*,CN=*CAComputerName*,CN=CDP,CN=Public Key Services,CN=Services,CN=Configuration,DC=*ForestRootNameDN*. Web clients can retrieve the CRLs from http://*Server*/certenroll/.

Though the default locations are sufficient for most organizations, you can add locations if you need to. In particular, you must add a location if you are using an offline root CA, since the CA will not be accessible by clients under normal circumstances. Additionally, if certificates are used outside your private network but your CA is behind a firewall, you should publish your CRL to a publicly accessible location. To add a CRL publishing location, go to the Extensions tab of the CA's properties, as shown in Figure 7.10, and then click the Add button.

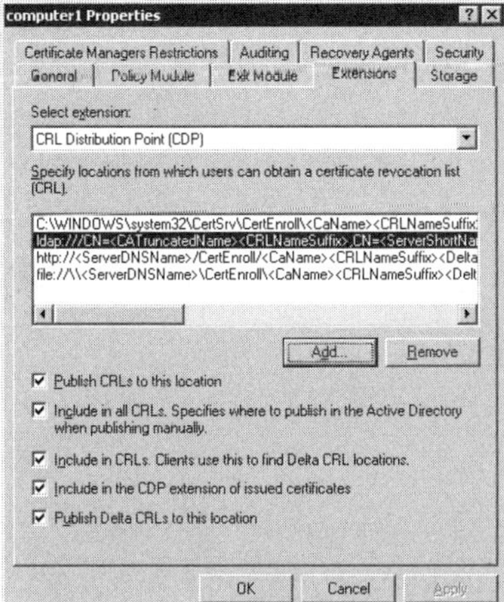

Figure 7.10 CRL publishing list

> **Note** By default, the http:// and file:// CRL publishing locations do not have the Publish CRLs To This Location check box selected. However, CRLs are most definitely available from these locations, because they both map to the C:\WINDOWS\System32\CertSrv\CertEnroll folder by default.

To simplify administration, you can use variable names when entering CRL locations. After you click the Add button, the Add Location dialog box appears and provides a list of variables that you can use, as shown in Figure 7.11. Descriptions for each variable are provided in the Description Of Selected Variable box.

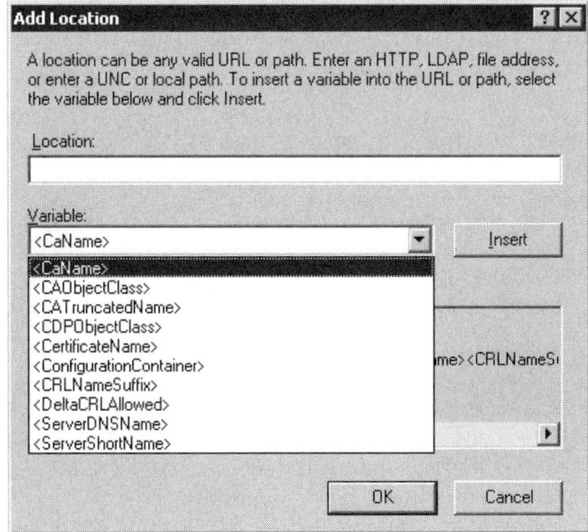

Figure 7.11 Adding a CRL publishing location

After you revoke a certificate, the CRL must be published before clients will discover that the certificate has been revoked. By default, delta CRLs are published daily, and full CRLs are published weekly. You can change these settings by using the Certification Authority snap-in. To do so, right-click the Revoked Certificates node, and then click the CRL Publishing parameters tab. This tab also shows you when the next scheduled updates will occur.

Planning The delta CRL publishing schedule requires careful planning. Increasing the publishing frequency enables clients to identify revoked certificates faster. However, it causes clients to retrieve the CRL more often, which increases network traffic.

Troubleshooting CRL Publishing

You might occasionally discover a client that does not have a published CRL that the client should have retrieved. While publishing and retrieving CRLs is designed to be as automated as possible, you do have the ability to manually publish and retrieve CRLs for troubleshooting purposes. Certutil.exe is a command-line program that is installed along with Certificate Services. It provides a useful interface to a wide variety of Certificate Services functionality.

To manually retrieve the latest CRL from a CA, log on to the CA as an administrator, open a command prompt, and run the command **certutil –GetCRL** *crl-filename*.**crl**. For example, to retrieve the latest CRL and save the CRL with the name latestcrl.crl, you would execute the command certutil –GetCRL latestcrl.crl. To retrieve the latest delta CRL, execute the command **certutil –GetCRL** *crl-delta-filename*.**crl delta**.

You can also use Certutil.exe to retrieve older versions of CRLs. This is useful for pinpointing when a particular certificate was added to a CRL. To retrieve the second CRL, add the parameter **2** to the end of the certutil command line. For example, the command **certutil –GetCRL** *crl-filename*.**crl 2** retrieves the second most recent CRL, and the command **certutil –GetCRL** *crl-filename*.**crl 5** retrieves the fifth most recent CRL. If the older versions of the CRLs are not available, you will receive an error.

Certutil.exe can also be used to verify that a CA is up and running. To determine whether a particular CA is functioning, use the –ping parameter. For example, to determine if Certificate Services is running on the local computer, run the command **certutil –ping**. To check for Certificate Services on a computer with the computer name Computer2 and the CA name Computer2, run the command **certutil –ping –config computer2\computer2**. Use the –pingadmin parameter with the same syntax to verify that the CA administrative functionality is available.

Tip Use the **certutil –dump** command and look for the `Config:` line in the output to identify the computer and CA names of registered CAs.

Practice: Creating and Revoking Certificates

In this practice, you will create two certificates by using two different methods. You will then revoke a certificate and publish a CRL.

Exercise 1: Creating a Certificate Using Web Enrollment

In this exercise, you will create a Basic EFS certificate by using the manual Web enrollment process. To request a certificate by using the Web Enrollment Web site:

1. Log on to the cohowinery.com domain on Computer1 using the Administrator account.
2. Start Internet Explorer.
3. In the address bar of Internet Explorer, type **http://computer1/certsrv**. Click Go.
4. If you are not automatically authenticated, provide your user name and password when prompted, and then click OK.

   The Web interface for manually enrolling for certificates appears, as shown in Figure 7.12.

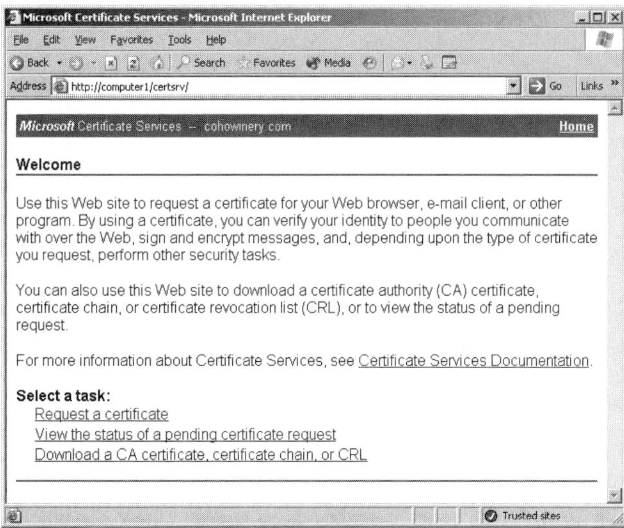

Figure 7.12 Web interface for manual enrollment

5. Click Request A Certificate.

6. Click Advanced Certificate Request.

   The Advanced Certificate Request page appears. Note that you have the option to submit a request based on a previously created certificate request that you have saved. If you click Request A Certificate For A Smart Card On Behalf Of Another User, you will be taken to the Smart Card Enrollment station where you can request a certificate for a smart card on behalf of another user.

7. Click Create And Submit A Request To This CA.

8. On the Advanced Certificate Request page, click the Certificate Template list and then select Basic EFS.

   If you completed the exercise in Lesson 2, you will see Backup Operators available in the Certificate Template list.

9. Select the Enable Strong Private Key Protection check box, as shown in Figure 7.13. Click Submit.

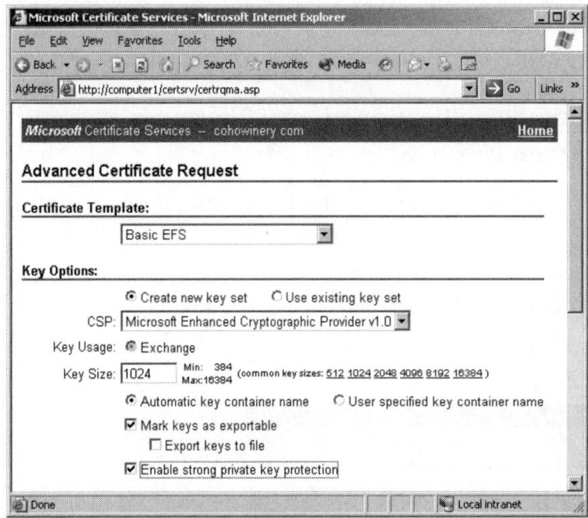

Figure 7.13 Advanced Certificate Request using Web enrollment

10. Click Yes in the Potential Scripting Violation warning dialog box.

11. In the Creating A New RSA Exchange Key dialog box, click Set Security Level.

12. Read the descriptions of the two security level options, and then click High. Click Next.

13. In the Password and Confirm boxes, type a complex password. This does not have to be the same as your domain user password. Click Finish.

14. Click OK.
15. On the Certificate Issued page, click Install This Certificate.
16. Click Yes in the Potential Scripting Violation warning box.
17. Close Internet Explorer.

Exercise 2: Creating a Certificate Using the Certificates Snap-in

In this exercise, you will create a certificate by using the Certificates snap-in. To do so:

1. Log on to the cohowinery.com domain on Computer1 using the Administrator account.
2. Click Start, and then click Run. Type **mmc**, and then click OK.
3. Click File, and then click Add/Remove Snap-In.
4. Click Add. In the Add/Remove Snap-In dialog box, click Certificates, and then click Add.
5. Click My User Account, and then click Finish. Click Close, and then click OK.
6. Expand Certificates, and then expand Personal. Right-click Certificates, click All Tasks, and then click Request New Certificate to start the Certificate Request Wizard.
7. In the Certificate Request Wizard, click Next.
8. On the Certificate Types page, click User. Select the Advanced check box, and then click Next.
9. On the Cryptographic Service Provider page, notice that the Mark This Key As Exportable check box is selected by default, and that Enable Strong Key Protection is disabled by default. Click Next.

   Strong key protection requires the user to provide a password each time the key is used. Lesson 4 discusses the purpose of exporting keys, in addition to the advantages and disadvantages.
10. On the Certificate Authority page, click Next.
11. In the Friendly Name box, type **Personal Certificate**. Click Next.
12. On the Completing The Certificate Request Wizard page, click Finish.
13. After the Certificate Request Wizard has successfully finished, click OK to install the issued certificate with medium security.
14. In the Certificates snap-in, double-click the new certificate. Note that it expires in one year, and that it can be used to encrypt data, protect e-mail, and authenticate you, as shown in Figure 7.14. Click OK.

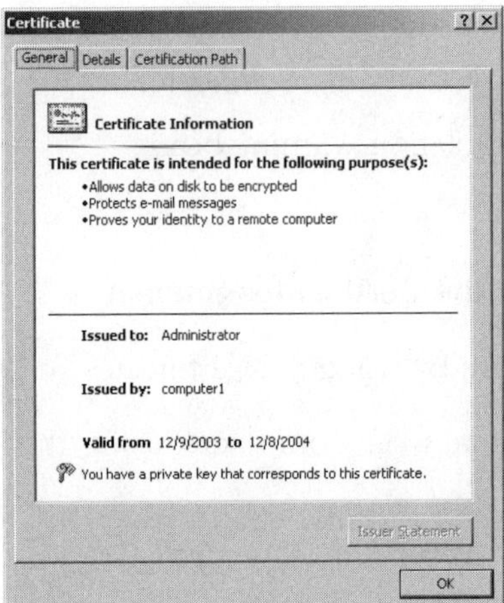

Figure 7.14 Properties for a new certificate

Exercise 3: Revoking a Certificate and Publishing a CRL

In this exercise, you will add a CRL publishing location and then revoke the certificate you just created. To revoke a certificate using the Certification Authority console, perform the following steps:

1. Log on to the cohowinery.com domain on Computer1 using the Administrator account.
2. Open the Certification Authority console from Administrative Tools.
3. Right-click Computer1, and then click Properties. Click the Extensions tab.
4. Click the Add button.
5. In the Location box, type **C:*<CaName><CRLNameSuffix><DeltaCRLAllowed>*.crl**. Click OK.

   Use the Variable list and the Insert button to add the variable names. Review the description of each variable as you add it.
6. In the Computer1 Properties dialog box, select the Publish CRLs To This Location and Publish Delta CRLs To This Location check boxes. Click OK.
7. When prompted to restart Certificate Services, click Yes.
8. Expand Computer1 and then click Issued Certificates. Right-click the COHOWINERY\Administrator certificate, click All Tasks, and then click Revoke Certificate, as shown in Figure 7.15.

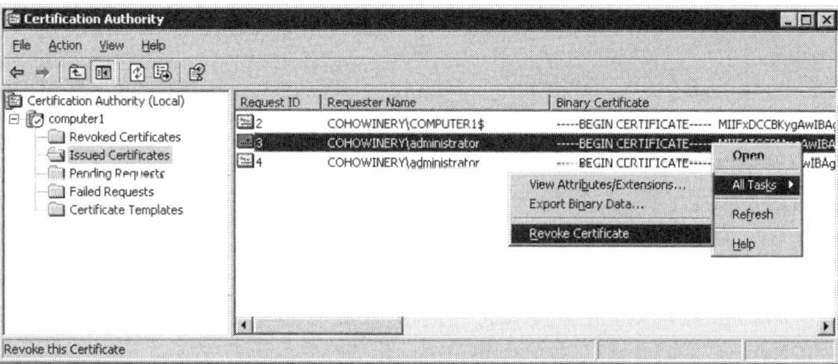

Figure 7.15 Revoking a certificate

9. In the Certificate Revocation dialog box, click the Reason Code list, and then click Key Compromise. Click Yes.
10. Click the Revoked Certificates node in the left pane, and note that the newly revoked certificate appears in the list.
11. Right-click the Revoked Certificates node, click All Tasks, and then click Publish.
12. In the Publish CRL dialog box, click New CRL as shown in Figure 7.16, and then click OK.

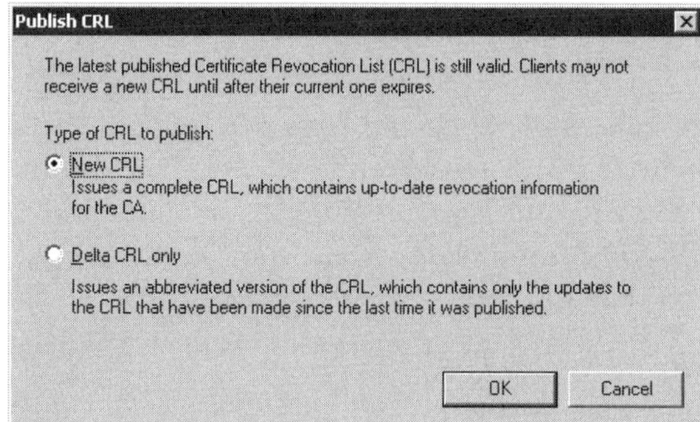

Figure 7.16 Publishing a CRL

13. Start Windows Explorer and navigate to the root of drive C. Notice that two files have been created: Computer1.crl and Computer1+.crl. Double-click each of them, and examine the details of the two certificates. Click the Certificate Revocation List tab to verify that the revoked certificate appears. Click OK.

    Computer1.crl is the full CRL. Computer1+.crl is the delta CRL. Because you have only revoked a single certificate, they both contain the same information.

Lesson Review

The following questions are intended to reinforce key information presented in this lesson. If you are unable to answer a question, review the lesson materials and try the question again. You can find answers to the questions in the "Questions and Answers" section at the end of this chapter.

1. You are a certificate manager for your company's PKI. You are reviewing enrollment methods and have determined that you will implement three methods for certificate enrollment: Web-based enrollment, MMC enrollment by using the Certificate Request Wizard, and autoenrollment. Under what circumstances must you use Web-based enrollment to perform certificate enrollment? (Choose all that apply.)

   a. When enrolling certificates that are issued by an enterprise CA

   b. When performing enrollment from computers running Windows 95 or Windows 98

   c. When enrolling certificates that are issued by a standalone CA

   d. When performing enrollment from computers running Windows 2000

   e. When enrolling for certificates that are issued by a CA on computers running Windows 2000

   ____

2. You are reviewing enrollment methods and have determined that you will implement three methods for certificate enrollment: Web-based enrollment, MMC enrollment by using the Certificate Request Wizard, and autoenrollment. What criteria must you meet if you want a client to use the Certificates console to enroll certificates? (Choose all that apply.)

   a. The issuing CA must be an enterprise CA.

   b. The computer must be a member of an Active Directory domain.

   c. The issuing CA must be a standalone CA.

   d. The client computer must be running Microsoft Windows NT 4.0 or later.

   e. The client computer must be running Windows 2000 or later.

   ____

Lesson Summary

- Certificate enrollment is the process by which a user, computer, or service obtains a certificate from a CA.
- A Windows Server 2003 family CA provides several methods for certificate enrollment: Web-based, the Certificates console, the Certreq.exe command-line utility, and autoenrollment.
- If you have a client using an operating system that is earlier than Windows 2000, you must use manual enrollment because it does not support Active Directory or Group Policy. Windows 2000 supports autoenrollment of computer certificates; Windows XP and Windows Server 2003 support autoenrollment of both user and computer certificates.
- Autoenrollment enables organizations to automatically deploy public key–based certificates to users and computers. It also supports smart card–based certificates.

Lesson 4: Archiving and Recovering Certificates

If your PKI deployment is successful, users and applications will use certificates to protect their private data. Accessing that data, of course, requires the users' private keys. If a user loses access to the private key, or if the user leaves the organization, you will develop a new appreciation for the power of encryption—the data will be inaccessible.

Fortunately, Windows Server 2003 Certificate Services includes the ability to back up private keys and recover lost keys. By using key archival and recovery, you can archive and recover the private key portion of a key pair in the event that a user loses a private key or in the event that an administrator must assume the role of a user to access or recover data.

After this lesson, you will be able to

- Determine the need for key recovery.
- Select appropriate methods to recover keys.
- Export and import keys.
- Perform key archival and recovery.
- Describe how risks associated with key archival are mitigated.

Estimated lesson time: 45 minutes

Overview of Key Recovery

Windows clients store certificates locally on the computer or hardware device that requested the certificate, or, in the case of a user, on the computer or device that the user used to request the certificate. The certificates are stored in a location known as a *certificate store*. There are separate stores known as the *machine store*, used by the computer, and the *user store* (also known as *My store*), used by the currently logged on user. A certificate store will often contain numerous certificates, possibly issued from a number of different certification authorities.

Users will lose their keys occasionally. Often, users lose their keys because of one of the following reasons:

- **The user profile is deleted.** When a CSP encrypts and stores a private key, the encrypted private key is stored in the local file system and registry in the user profile folder. Deleting the profile results in the loss of the private key.
- **The operating system is reinstalled.** When you reinstall the operating system, the previous installation's user profiles are lost, including the private key.

- **The disk is corrupted.** If the hard disk becomes corrupted and the user profile is unavailable, the private key can be lost.
- **The computer is stolen.** If a user's computer is stolen, the user profile containing the private key is also lost.

There are certain PKI tasks that rely on the user having access to a specific certificate. For example, if you encrypt a file by using EFS and then your certificates become unavailable, you must recover the lost certificate to gain access to your file. Creating a new certificate will not allow you to unencrypt the file.

To prevent the potential loss of data that can result from a lost key, Windows Server 2003 provides two methods for backing up and recovering private keys: exporting and importing, and key archival and recovery. Keys can be exported and imported by individual users, without the use of Active Directory. However, exporting and importing keys does not scale well to the volume of keys an enterprise must maintain.

Key archival and recovery allows key recovery agents (KRAs) to retrieve an original certificate, a private key, and a public key from a database stored on the CA. This process is implemented in two phases—key archival and key recovery—and is also referred to as *key escrow*. By using key archival and recovery, you can archive and recover the private key portion of a key pair in the event that a user loses a private key.

Exporting Keys

The simplest method for backing up a key pair is to manually export the key, protect it with a password, and store the export media in a secure location. A PKI uses several formats for importing and exporting certificates, certificate chains, and private keys.

When a user exports a certificate by using the Certificates console, the Certification Authority console, Certutil.exe, or Internet Explorer, the PKCS #7 and PKCS #12 export formats are available. The PKCS #7 format, also known as the *Cryptographic Message Syntax Standard*, should only be used to export certificates without the private key and for certificate chains for a CA. PKCS #7 is not useful for backing up a private key. Instead, use the PKCS #12 format, also known as the *Personal Information Exchange Syntax Standard*. Because the private key is included in the export, the PKCS #12 file requires that a password be used to protect the private key. An exceptionally strong password should be chosen to protect the private key.

Note You can also export keys in the Exchange Protection File (EPF) file format from the Outlook 2000 or Outlook 2002 client.

You can export a certificate by using the Certificates snap-in, the Certification Authority snap-in, or Certutil.exe. You can also use other applications, such as Outlook or Internet Explorer, to export keys for Windows NT 4.0 and earlier operating systems that do not have a snap-in. When you export a certificate by using any of the above utilities, you must enable the certificate template to allow the private key to be exported by selecting the Allow Private Key To Be Exported check box on the certificate template.

The method you should use to export a certificate is dictated by the certificate template upon which the certificate is based. For example, if the certificate contains an application policy for secure e-mail or an extended key usage Object Identifier (OID), you can use either Outlook or the Certificates snap-in. If the certificate does not contain the extended key usage OID, you must use the Certificates snap-in.

Real World

Many security experts debate the issue of exporting private keys. For some, the very fact that you can export a private key is considered a breach of security that weakens trust in the entire PKI system. Others, including myself, argue that you must balance manageability with security. We argue that being able to export a private key can save time and money by enabling the user to move to a new computer or recover files if a private key is lost or corrupt.

Ultimately the choice between security and manageability is yours. However, always remember that encryption is only as secure as the user's private key.

When you export a certificate and the associated keys, you can choose from the following additional options:

- **Include all certificates in the certification path if possible.** This option includes the entire certificate chain of the exported certificate. It allows the import to include all certificates in the certificate chain up to the root certificate. This selection will allow the entire certificate chain to be present on the computer where the certificate is imported, thereby eliminating the possible need to add each individual certificate in the chain. Use this option when exporting a certificate that will be imported on a computer that cannot communicate with the issuing CA, intermediate CAs, or the root CA.
- **Enable strong protection.** This option will store the exported PKCS #12 file with 128-bit encryption. You should still provide a strong password to protect the data. This option requires Internet Explorer 5.0 and Windows NT 4.0 Service Pack 4 or later. You should enable this option as an added security measure to protect the certificate.

- **Delete the private key if the export is successful.** This option deletes the private key that is associated with the certificate from the certificate store. Delete the private key only if you are moving the key to another computer.

After you have successfully exported the private key with a strong password, store the exported file in a physically secure location that cannot be accessed across the network. For example, export the file to a CD-ROM and then store the CD-ROM in a safe location.

Key Archival

Key archival must be performed when the certificate is issued to the user. The version 2 certificate template's configuration, as shown in Figure 7.17, determines whether the CA will archive the key. Version 1 certificate templates cannot be automatically archived by this process.

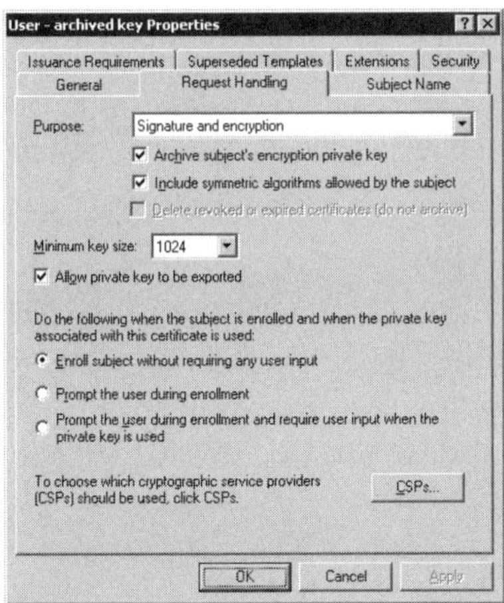

Figure 7.17 Specifying key archival

When an administrator enables key archival by using a version 2 certificate template, the CA encrypts and stores that private key in its database. The key pair is actually generated by the client, and therefore the private key must be transferred back to the CA for archival. The client encrypts the private key with the CA's public key to ensure that the private key is not compromised during transmission. The CA then decrypts and validates the private key, re-encrypts the key by using a random Triple-Data Encryption Standard (3DES) symmetric key, and archives the encrypted private key. The random symmetric key is then encrypted with the public key or keys of the KRAs and stored along with the encrypted private key.

An important aspect of the CA's archival and recovery attributes is that the CA does not hold any information that can be used to decrypt the archived private keys. Decrypting archived private keys requires one of the KRAs' private keys, which is stored in each KRA user's profile. Only public key certificates are used to encrypt the keys needed to gain access to the archived private keys. This ensures that an attacker who compromises the CA cannot compromise the security of the archived keys.

To successfully implement a key archival and recovery strategy in your organization, you must first ensure that the CA meets the following requirements:

- All certificates that require archival are based on version 2 certificate templates.
- The issuing CAs are running Windows Server 2003.
- All clients are using Windows XP or Windows Server 2003.
- You are using enterprise CAs and the Windows Server 2003 schema extensions have been applied to the forest.

Off the Record You can run an enterprise CA running Windows Server 2003 in a Windows 2000 forest without modifying the schema; however, you will not be able to use version 2 certificate templates. When you run `adprep.exe /forestprep` in a Windows 2000 forest, the version 2 templates will be installed the next time you open the certificate templates administration tool.

Additionally, the certificate templates for the certificates you want to archive must be configured for key archival. To configure the template, go to the Request Handling tab on the template's properties and select the Archive Subject's Encryption Private Key check box. Exercise 3 in this lesson prepares the Certificate Services infrastructure for archiving certificates based on a new template.

Key Recovery

After a key is archived, a key recovery agent can use key recovery to recover a corrupted or lost key. At a high level, the certificate manager retrieves the encrypted file that contains the certificate and private key from the CA database. A KRA then decrypts the private key from the encrypted file and returns the certificate and private key to the user.

At a more detailed level, key recovery performs the following process:

1. A certificate manager for the CA that issued the certificate determines the serial number of the certificate. You probably will not have the serial number memorized, so you will need to use the Certificates snap-in to find the certificate relating to the user's private key and retrieve the serial number.
2. A certificate manager extracts the encrypted private key and certificate from the CA database by using the Certutil.exe command-line tool. The export format of the private key and certificate is a PKCS #7 file. The file is encrypted by means of the

KRA's public key. For example, if the certificate manager identified the certificate's serial number as 11593dbc000000000006 in step 1, the following command would recover the key to a file named Recovered.pfx:

```
certutil -getkey 11593dbc000000000006 recovered.pfx
```

Note The encrypted PKCS #7 files in the database, referred to as *blobs*, contain the issuer name and serial number of each Key Recovery Agent certificate for KRA identification purposes during recovery.

3. The certificate manager transfers the PKCS #7 file to the KRA. Because the PKCS #7 file is encrypted so that only the defined KRA can recover the encrypted certificate and private key, no additional security is required for the transfer.
4. The KRA uses the `Certutil -RecoverKey` command to recover the private key and certificate from the encrypted PKCS #7 file. This step should be performed at a secure workstation, also known as a *recovery workstation*. During the recovery process, the KRA will assign a password that the user must provide when importing the certificate. The private key and certificate are stored in an encrypted PKCS #12 file.
5. The KRA then supplies the PKCS #12 file to the user, who provides the KRA-assigned password and imports the certificate and private key into the certificate store by using the Certificates snap-in.

Note If your organization is willing to trust a single person with a great deal of power, you can perform the roles of both the certificate manager and the KRA.

An easier way to perform key recovery is to use the Key Recovery Tool (krt.exe) from the Windows Server 2003 Resource Kit Tools. This graphical tool allows an administrator to:

- Search the CA database for archived keys.
- Display the KRA for a specific archived key.
- Retrieve the encrypted blob.
- Decrypt the blob and set a password on the outputted .pfx file.

You can download the Windows Server 2003 Resource Kit Tools from *http://www.microsoft.com/*.

The private keys of a KRA can be misused to steal other users' private keys from an archive. Guard them carefully by using a dedicated offline computer to store the KRA user profile, and use that computer for all key recovery tasks. You should also remove KRA certificates and private keys from the KRA's user profile. By exporting the keys from the KRA's user profile and importing them only when needed for recovery, you reduce the likelihood of someone misusing the recovery capabilities. Finally, develop a secure method for transporting the recovered private keys to the original owner, and delete the PKCS #12 file to prevent the certificate and private key from being imported in the future.

You must be conscious of the potential for key recovery to be misused. Many companies do not entrust this role to even network administrators, because it would give them the ability to decrypt files created by individuals with higher security clearance, such as managers. Many companies use a dedicated user account as the data recovery agent. This account might require a smart card for logon, or it might even be disabled with the password kept in a secure location, such as a safe. Some companies even break the password in half or into thirds, and entrust two or three different individuals with knowledge of only part of the password. This strategy ensures that no one individual can activate the data recovery agent.

Beyond requiring collusion, you can reduce the likelihood for abuse of the recovery process by revoking the certificate that is associated with the lost private key immediately after you recover the data. For example, if a laptop computer is stolen and the user has encrypted files on a network share, you should recover the private key, decrypt the files, and then revoke the certificate. Then issue the user a new certificate so that the user can re-encrypt the files. After you revoke the certificate, the key pair cannot be used for encryption or digital signing purposes. The private key can still be used to decrypt previously encrypted files, but further attempts to encrypt files by using the public key will fail during the certificate validation process.

Practice: Exporting and Recovering Keys

In this practice, you will create several certificates by using various methods. You will then revoke a certificate and publish a CRL.

Exercise 1: Exporting Keys

In this exercise, you will export a certificate so that you can recover it later.

1. Log on to the cohowinery.com domain on Computer1 using the Administrator account.
2. Click Start, and then click Run.
3. Type **mmc.exe** and then click OK.
4. In the empty MMC console, on the File menu, click Add/Remove Snap-In.
5. In the Add/Remove Snap-In dialog box, click Add.
6. In the Add Standalone Snap-In dialog box, under Available Standalone Snap-Ins, click Certificates, and then click Add.

7. In the Certificates dialog box, click My User Account, click Finish, and then click Close to close the Add Standalone Snap-In dialog box.
8. Expand Certificates, and then expand Personal. Click Certificates. Right-click the last certificate, click All Tasks, and then click Export.
9. On the Welcome To The Certificate Export Wizard page, click Next.
10. On the Export Private Key page, click Yes, Export The Private Key. Click Next.
11. On the Export File Format page, select the Include All Certificates In The Certification Path If Possible check box, ensure that Enable Strong Protection is selected, and then click Next.
12. On the Password page, type a complex password in the Password and Confirm Password boxes. Click Next.
13. On the File To Export page, type **c:\mycert.pfx** and then click Next.

Tip Personal Information Exchange (PFX) is the file format used for exported certificates. It is also known as PKCS #12.

14. The Completing The Certificate Export Wizard page appears, as shown in Figure 7.18. Click Finish, and then, in the Certificate Export Wizard dialog box, click OK to acknowledge that the export was successful.

Figure 7.18 Exporting a certificate

15. Remain logged on to Computer1, and leave the Certificates snap-in open. You will use the console in Exercise 2.

Exercise 2: Recovering Exported Keys

In this exercise, you will delete a certificate and then recover it.

1. In the Certificates snap-in, expand Certificates, and then expand Personal. Click Certificates. Right-click the last certificate and then click Delete.
2. When prompted, click Yes.
3. Right-click Certificates, click All Tasks, and then click Import.
4. On the Welcome To The Certificate Import Wizard page, click Next.
5. In the File Name box, type **c:\mycert.pfx**. Click Next.
6. In the Password box, type the complex password you specified in Exercise 1. Click Next.
7. On the Certificate Store page, click Automatically Select The Certificate Store Based On The Type Of Certificate, as shown in Figure 7.19. Click Next.

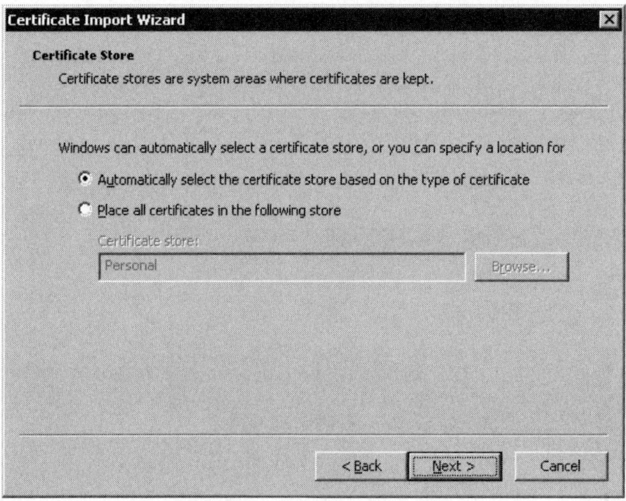

Figure 7.19 Importing a certificate

8. Click Finish. When prompted, click OK.
9. Press F5 to refresh the display of personal certificates. The certificate has been restored.

Exercise 3: Configuring Key Archival

In this exercise, you will create a user account for key recovery, enable key archival on Computer1, and then create a certificate template that automatically archives the private key. In the first procedure, you will create a user account to act as the KRA, and then grant the user the permissions necessary to access the certificate templates.

1. On Computer1, log on to the cohowinery.com domain using the Administrator account.
2. Open Active Directory Users And Computers. Create a new user with the name KeyRecoveryUser. Accept the defaults for the other settings for the user account, and close Active Directory Users And Computers.
3. Open Active Directory Sites And Services. Click Active Directory Sites And Services, and, on the View menu, click Show Services Node.
4. Expand Services, expand Public Key Services, and then click Certificate Templates. Right-click KeyRecoveryAgent, and then click Properties.

Note This exercise uses Active Directory Sites And Services to access certificate templates simply to familiarize you with the tool. It provides the same functionality that you could get by loading the Certificate Templates snap-in directly.

5. Click the Security tab. Allow the KeyRecoveryUser the Read and Enroll permissions, and then click OK.

   Just like any user, the KRA must have Read and Enroll permissions to the Key Recovery Agent certificate template in order to be issued a certificate.

Caution Do not automatically enroll users for KRA certificates because this should be a highly restricted certificate. Using autoenrollment for this certificate might cause confusion for CA Administrators when automatic enrollment is unintentionally initiated, and this could result in additional KRA certificates.

6. Close Active Directory Sites And Services.

At this point, you have created a user to act as the KRA and granted that user the necessary rights to the certificate templates. In the next procedure, you will configure the Key Recovery Agent certificate template so that it can be issued, and then you will request a certificate based on that template.

1. Open the Certification Authority console. Expand Computer1, and then right-click the Certificate Templates node. Click New, and then click Certificate Template To Issue.
2. In the Enable Certificate Templates dialog box, click Key Recovery Agent, and then click OK.
3. Leave the Certification Authority console open, and open Internet Explorer. In the address bar, type **http://computer1/certsrv**. Click Go.

4. In the Connect To Computer1.Cohowinery.Com Authentication dialog box, type the user name **KeyRecoveryUser** and the password you created for the account earlier in this exercise. If Internet Explorer notifies you that content is being blocked, click the Add button and add **http://computer1** to the trusted sites list.
5. On the Welcome page of Certificate Services, click Request A Certificate.
6. On the Request A Certificate Web page, click Advanced Certificate Request.
7. On the Advanced Certificate Request page, click Create And Submit A Request To This CA.
8. In the Certificate Template box, click Key Recovery Agent, and then click Submit.
9. In the Potential Scripting Violation warning box, click Yes. Leave Internet Explorer open.

Because of the high sensitivity of this certificate, the KRA certificate requires CA manager approval. In the following procedure, you will approve the pending KRA certificate and then install it.

1. Return to the Certification Authority console.
2. Expand Computer1, and then click the Pending Requests node. Right-click the pending KRA certificate, click All Tasks, and then click Issue.
3. Leave the Certification Authority console, and return to Internet Explorer. In the address bar, type **http://computer1/certsrv**. Click Go.

Note To perform the above steps, you must use the same computer that was used to generate the request. This is because certificate pending information is stored as a browser cookie.

4. On the Welcome page, select View The Status Of A Pending Certificate Request.
5. On the View The Status Of A Pending Certificate Request page, click Key Recovery Agent Certificate.
6. On the Certificate Issued page, click Install This Certificate.
7. In the Potential Scripting Violation warning box, click Yes.
8. Close Internet Explorer.

The KRA is almost ready. In the final steps of this process, you will configure Certificate Services to use the newly configured KRA certificate, and then create a new certificate template that is configured for key archival.

1. Return to the Certification Authority console.
2. Right-click Computer1, and then click Properties.

3. On the Recovery Agents tab, click Archive The Key, and then click Add.
4. In the Key Recovery Agent Selection dialog box, select the KRA certificate as shown in Figure 7.20, and then click OK.

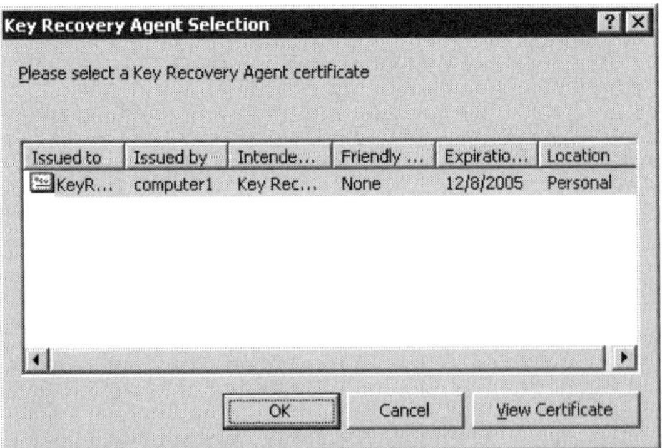

Figure 7.20 Key Recovery Agent Selection dialog box

5. On the Recovery Agents page, click Apply, and then click Yes to restart Certificate Services.

   Notice that the status of the certificate is now Valid.
6. Click OK.
7. In the Certification Authority snap-in, right-click the Certificate Template node, and then click Manage.
8. In the Certificate Templates console, right-click the User certificate template, and then click Duplicate Template.
9. Click the General tab and then type **User–Archived Key** in the Template Display Name box.
10. Click the Request Handling tab, select the Archive Subject's Encryption Private Key check box, and then click OK.
11. Close the Certificate Template console, and open the Certification Authority console.
12. Right-click the Certificate Templates node, click New, and then click Certificate Template To Issue.
13. Click the User–Archived Key template, and then click OK.

All keys associated with certificates issued by using the User–Archived Key certificate template will now be encrypted with the KRA's digital certificate and stored in the CA database. If users lose the private key associated with this certificate, the KRA now has the ability to retrieve their keys from the CA database.

Lesson Review

The following questions are intended to reinforce key information presented in this lesson. If you are unable to answer a question, review the lesson materials and try the question again. You can find answers to the questions in the "Questions and Answers" section at the end of this chapter.

1. The security policy of your organization requires that you implement role separation to ensure the separation of duties in your PKI management strategy. Your organization decides to implement EFS file encryption to protect high-value documents that are stored on network shares. To protect the EFS-encrypted documents, you plan to archive the EFS encryption private keys on the issuing CA. How does role separation secure the key recovery process in the event of a lost EFS encryption key?
   - **a.** Role separation enables the certificate manager to access the PKCS #7 blob in the CA database and enables the KRA to recover the private key.
   - **b.** Role separation enables the KRA to access the PKCS #7 blob in the CA database and enables the certificate manager to recover the private key.
   - **c.** Role separation enables the local administrator to delegate the key recovery process to non-administrators.
   - **d.** Role separation does not add security to the key recovery process.

---

2. You are designated as a certificate manager for the CA that enables private key archival in your CA hierarchy. One of your roles is to determine the KRA for each certificate that has an archived private key. What can you use to determine the KRA for each private key that is archived in the CA database? (Choose all that apply.)
   - **a.** Use **certutil –recoverkey** to determine the KRA.
   - **b.** Use **certutil –getkey** to determine the KRA.
   - **c.** Use the Certification Authority MMC console to determine the KRA.
   - **d.** Use the Certificate MMC console to determine the KRA.
   - **e.** Use the Key Recovery Tool to determine the KRA.

Lesson Summary

- If a user loses access to a private key, the user can lose important data. Specifically, EFS-encrypted files will be inaccessible.
- There are two ways to back up and restore private keys: exporting and importing, and key archival and recovery.
- Key archival and recovery can scale to meet enterprise requirements. However, it requires version 2 certificates, enterprise CAs, and Active Directory.
- You can use either the Certutil.exe command-line utility, included with Windows Server 2003, or the Key Recovery Tool, included with the Windows Server 2003 Resource Kit Tools, to perform key recovery.

Case Scenario Exercise

In this exercise, you will read a scenario about a company's communications privacy challenge, and then answer the questions that follow. The questions are intended to reinforce key information presented in this chapter. If you are unable to answer a question, review the lessons and try the question again. You can find answers to the questions in the "Questions and Answers" section at the end of this chapter.

Scenario

You are a systems administrator for Coho Vineyard. Your organization is planning to conduct a research project with Coho Winery, a partnering firm. This project will involve users in both organizations' research departments. These users will exchange documents and information by means of e-mail messages. Much of this information is considered to be secret, so competitors must not be able to access the information. There are approximately 75 users working in the research department.

Coho Winery has expressed some concern about your ability to ensure that all users in its research department will be able to exchange secure e-mail messages with users in the Coho Vineyard research department. You must present Coho Winery with a plan that illustrates how you will address these concerns. Specifically, they want to know how you will meet the following requirements:

- Users in the Coho Winery research department must be able to send secure e-mail messages.
- Users who leave the Coho Winery research department must no longer be able to send secure e-mail messages.
- Security requirements relating to e-mail might need to change from time to time.

Questions

1. How will you ensure that users in the Coho Winery research department can send secure e-mail messages?

   a. Configure a standalone CA and instruct users to enroll for user certificates by using the Web enrollment tool.

   b. Configure an enterprise CA and use a certificate template to automatically issue certificates that support S/MIME to the domain users group.

   c. Configure an enterprise CA and use a certificate template to issue certificates that support EFS to the research group.

   d. Configure a standalone CA and instruct users to perform advanced certificate requests by using the Web enrollment tool.

---

2. How will you ensure that when users leave the Coho Winery research department they are no longer able to send secure e-mail messages?

   a. Configure a Group Policy setting to delete certificates from the local computer when they are revoked.

   b. Create a group that has been denied the Read permission on the certificate template that the certificates were based on. Add users to this group when they leave the research department.

   c. Place a copy of your certificate revocation list on a public Web server that is accessible by users in Coho Winery.

   d. Provide Coho Winery with a copy of each certificate that belongs to a user who has left the research department. Instruct the administrator to place the certificates in the Untrusted Certificates store.

---

3. How will you reconfigure users in the Coho Winery research department when a new requirement for secure e-mail, such as a longer key, is introduced?

   a. Create a new template with the new parameters. Configure the new template to supersede the old template.

   b. Configure the existing template to contain the longer key length. Configure the template to re-enroll all certificate holders.

   c. Create a second template with the new parameters. Deny research users the right to enroll for certificates based on the old template.

   d. Revoke all certificates. Instruct users to enroll for new certificates based on a new template with the longer key length.

Troubleshooting Lab

In this lab, you will troubleshoot a problem related to certificate enrollment. You will then take the necessary steps to correct the errors that you find. To complete this troubleshooting lab, you must have completed Exercise 3 in Lesson 4.

Read the following scenario and then answer the questions that follow. The questions are intended to reinforce key information presented in this chapter. If you are unable to answer a question, review the lessons and try the question again. You can find answers to the questions in the "Questions and Answers" section at the end of this chapter.

Scenario

A user is attempting to use Web enrollment to install a certificate, using a certificate template that you recently created. After following the instructions you provided for enrollment, the user is receiving the error "Your certificate request was denied," as shown in Figure 7.21.

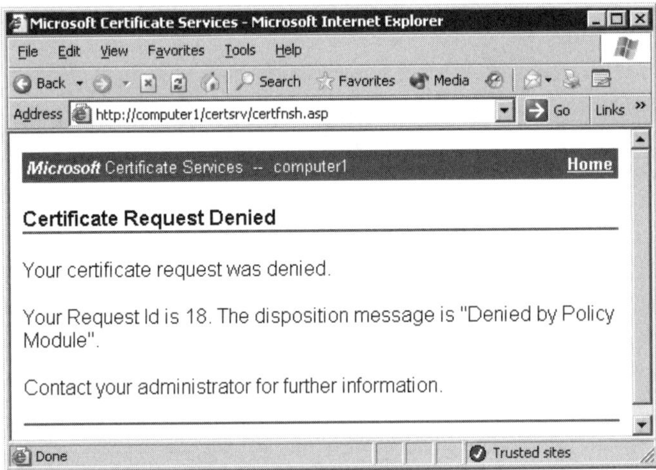

Figure 7.21 Creating a subordinate CA

Exercise 1: Re-Creating the Problem

First, you need to re-create the problem.

1. Log on to the cohowinery.com domain on Computer1 using the Administrator account.
2. Start Internet Explorer.
3. In the address bar of Internet Explorer, type **http://computer1/certsrv**. Click Go.

4. If you are not automatically authenticated, provide your user name and password when prompted, and then click OK. If you are notified that content from the Web site will be blocked, add Computer1 to the list of trusted computers.
5. Click Request A Certificate.
6. Click Advanced Certificate Request.
7. Click Create And Submit A Request To This CA.
8. Click the Certificate Template list, and then select User-Archived Key. Click Submit.
9. Click Yes when prompted.

   You will see the error message that the user described.

Questions

1. What tool can you use to identify the problem?

   ____
   ____
   ____
   ____
   ____
   ____

2. What is the source of the problem?

   ____
   ____
   ____
   ____
   ____
   ____

3. How will you resolve the problem?

   ____
   ____
   ____
   ____
   ____

Chapter Summary

- Public key encryption uses two keys to encrypt and decrypt messages. A message encrypted with one key can only be decrypted with the second key in the key pair, and vice-versa.
- To send a private message using public key encryption, encrypt the message with the recipient's public key. Only the private key can be used to decrypt the message.
- Certificates expire at a time specified when the certificate is generated. CRLs are used to revoke a certificate before that specified time.
- Root CAs cannot issue certificates that are valid beyond the CA's certificate's expiration date. Specifying a long lifetime for the root CA reduces labor, but this might increase your vulnerability to brute force attacks.
- Microsoft certification authorities (CAs) support two types of certificate templates: version 1 and version 2. Version 1 templates are provided for backwards compatibility and support many general needs for subject certification. Version 2 templates allow for the customization of most settings in the template.
- Version 2 templates require Active Directory. They can be created and duplicated by any member of the Windows Server 2003 family: however, certificates based on Version 2 templates can be issued only by a CA that is running Windows Server 2003, Enterprise Edition or Windows server 2003, Datacenter Edition.
- A Windows Server 2003 family CA provides several methods for certificate enrollment: Web-based, the Certificates console, the Certreq.exe command-line utility, and autoenrollment.
- If you have a client running an operating system that is earlier than Windows 2000, you must use manual enrollment because it is not aware of Active Directory and Group Policy. Windows 2000 supports autoenrollment of computer certificates, and Windows XP and Windows Server 2003 support autoenrollment of both user and computer certificates.
- Autoenrollment enables organizations to automatically deploy public key–based certificates to users and computers. It also supports smart card–based certificates.
- If a user loses access to a private key, the user can lose important data. Specifically, EFS-encrypted files will be inaccessible.
- Key archival and recovery can scale to meet enterprise requirements. However, it requires version 2 certificates, enterprise CAs, and Active Directory.

Exam Highlights

Before taking the exam, review the key topics and terms that are presented in this chapter. You need to know this information.

Key Topics

- Understand why PKIs are used and know the various components that make up a PKI.
- Understand how to create and modify certificate templates, and know the functionality of the different versions of templates.
- Understand the restrictions imposed on clients using previous versions of Windows.
- Know the advantages and disadvantages of each enrollment method.
- Be able to describe the purpose of a CRL, how to configure them, and how to troubleshoot them.
- Be able to configure Certificate Services to archive keys, and know how to recover those keys when a private key has been lost.

Key Terms

application policies Application policies, also known as *extended key usage* or *enhanced key usage*, give you the ability to specify which certificates can be used for specific purposes. This allows you to issue certificates widely without being concerned that they will be used for an unintended purpose.

certificate revocation list (CRL) A CRL is a document maintained and published by a CA that lists certificates that have been revoked. A CRL is signed with the private key of the CA to ensure its integrity.

digital certificate A digital certificate provides information about the subject of the certificate, the validity of the certificate, and what applications and services will use the certificate. A digital certificate also provides a way to identify the holder of the certificate.

digital certificate life cycle When a certificate is issued, it passes through various phases and remains valid for a certain period of time. This is called *certificate lifetime.*

certificate templates Certificate templates are the sets of rules and settings that define the format and content of a certificate based on its intended use.

single-function template A single-function template is a certificate template that is highly restricted and can only be used for a single function.

multiple-function template You can use a certificate template for multiple functions. For example, you can use a single user certificate template to encrypt and decrypt files, to authenticate with a server, and to send and receive secure e-mail.

certificate template permissions Certificate template permissions define the security principals that can read, modify, or enroll certificates based on certificate templates.

Questions and Answers

Lesson 1 Review

Page 7-17

1. Which of the following scenarios would use public key encryption to keep a message sent from User A to User B private?

   a. User A encrypts a message with User B's public key.

   b. User A encrypts a message with User A's public key.

   c. User B encrypts a message with User B's private key.

   d. User B encrypts a message with User A's public key.

   a. In this scenario, only User B's private key could decrypt the message.

2. Which of the following is a feature unique to enterprise CAs?

   a. Web enrollment.

   b. Certificate autoenrollment.

   c. Certificates can be revoked.

   d. Certificates can be renewed prior to their expiration date.

   b. Only enterprise CAs can provide certificate autoenrollment.

Lesson 2 Review

Page 7-29

1. Which of the following tasks can be performed on version 1 certificate templates? (Choose all that apply.)

   a. Adding a certificate based on the template to a CRL

   b. Changing the expiration date of the template

   c. Superseding the template with a version 2 template

   d. Changing the permissions assigned to the template

   a, c, and d. While most properties of version 1 certificates cannot be modified, you can change permissions. Version 1 certificate templates can be superseded—in fact, that is the only way to make most types of modifications. Additionally, certificates based on version 1 templates can be added to a CRL.

2. Where in the Active Directory are certificate templates located?

   a. CN=Certificate Templates,CN=Public Key Services,CN=Extended-Rights, CN=Configuration,DC=*ForestRootNameDN*

   b. CN=Certificate Templates,CN=Public Key Services,CN=Services,CN=Configuration,DC=*ForestRootNameDN*

c. CN=Certificate Templates,CN=Public Key Services,CN=Services,CN=Domain, DC=*ForestRootNameDN*

d. CN=Certificate Templates,CN=NetServices,CN=Services,CN=Configuration, DC=*ForestRootNameDN*

b. The certificate templates are contained within the CN=Certificate Templates,CN=Public Key Services,CN=Extended-Rights,CN=Configuration, DC=*ForestRootNameDN* container.

Lesson 3 Review

Page 7-44

1. You are a certificate manager for your company's PKI. You are reviewing enrollment methods and have determined that you will implement three methods for certificate enrollment: Web-based enrollment, MMC enrollment by using the Certificate Request Wizard, and autoenrollment. Under what circumstances must you use Web-based enrollment to perform certificate enrollment? (Choose all that apply.)

   a. When enrolling certificates that are issued by an enterprise CA

   b. When performing enrollment from computers running Windows 95 or Windows 98

   c. When enrolling certificates that are issued by a standalone CA

   d. When performing enrollment from computers running Windows 2000

   e. When enrolling for certificates that are issued by a CA on computers running Windows 2000

   b and c. Web-based enrollment is the only certificate enrollment method that is available for computers running Windows 95 or Windows 98. Also, Web-based enrollment is the only way to enroll certificates from a standalone CA.

2. You are reviewing enrollment methods and have determined that you will implement three methods for certificate enrollment: Web-based enrollment, MMC enrollment by using the Certificate Request Wizard, and autoenrollment. What criteria must you meet if you want a client to use the Certificates console to enroll certificates? (Choose all that apply.)

   a. The issuing CA must be an enterprise CA.

   b. The computer must be a member of an Active Directory domain.

   c. The issuing CA must be a standalone CA.

   d. The client computer must be running Microsoft Windows NT 4.0 or later.

   e. The client computer must be running Windows 2000 or later.

   a, b, and e. You can run the Certificate Request Wizard only on a computer running Windows 2000, Windows XP, or a Windows Server 2003 family operating system. The computer must be a member of a Windows 2000 domain, and you must request the certificate from an enterprise CA.

Lesson 4 Review

Page 7-58

1. The security policy of your organization requires that you implement role separation to ensure the separation of duties in your PKI management strategy. Your organization decides to implement EFS file encryption to protect high-value documents that are stored on network shares. To protect the EFS-encrypted documents, you plan to archive the EFS encryption private keys on the issuing CA. How does role separation secure the key recovery process in the event of a lost EFS encryption key?

   a. Role separation enables the certificate manager to access the PKCS #7 blob in the CA database and enables the KRA to recover the private key.

   b. Role separation enables the KRA to access the PKCS #7 blob in the CA database and enables the certificate manager to recover the private key.

   c. Role separation enables the local administrator to delegate the key recovery process to non-administrators.

   d. Role separation does not add security to the key recovery process.

   a. When you implement role separation, a certificate manager must extract the encrypted private key from the CA database and determine which KRAs can recover the private key. The KRA recovers the private key and distributes it to the original user.

2. You are designated as a certificate manager for the CA that enables private key archival in your CA hierarchy. One of your roles is to determine the KRA for each certificate that has an archived private key. What can you use to determine the KRA for each private key that is archived in the CA database? (Choose all that apply.)

   a. Use **certutil –recoverkey** to determine the KRA.

   b. Use **certutil –getkey** to determine the KRA.

   c. Use the Certification Authority MMC console to determine the KRA.

   d. Use the Certificate MMC console to determine the KRA.

   e. Use the Key Recovery Tool to determine the KRA.

   b and e. Use **certutil –getkey** or the Key Recovery Tool to determine the KRA for an archived private key.

Design Activity: Case Scenario Exercise

Page 7-60

1. How will you ensure that users in the Coho Winery research department can send secure e-mail messages?

   a. Configure a standalone CA and instruct users to enroll for user certificates by using the Web enrollment tool.

   b. Configure an enterprise CA and use a certificate template to automatically issue certificates that support S/MIME to the domain users group.

   c. Configure an enterprise CA and use a certificate template to issue certificates that support EFS to the research group.

   d. Configure a standalone CA and instruct users to perform advanced certificate requests by using the Web enrollment tool.

   b. By using a certificate template that supports secure e-mail (S/MIME) and allowing users to autoenroll for certificates based on the template, you ensure that the required users have a certificate that meets their needs.

2. How will you ensure that when users leave the Coho Winery research department they are no longer able to send secure e-mail messages?

   a. Configure a Group Policy setting to delete certificates from the local computer when they are revoked.

   b. Create a group that has been denied the Read permission on the certificate template that the certificates were based on. Add users to this group when they leave the research department.

   c. Place a copy of your certificate revocation list on a public Web server that is accessible by users in Coho Winery.

   d. Provide Coho Winery with a copy of each certificate that belongs to a user who has left the research department. Instruct the administrator to place the certificates in the Untrusted Certificates store.

   a. To send secure e-mail messages, users must have certificates that support S/MIME on their computers. Even if one of these certificates is revoked, it will remain on the computer unless it is deleted manually. By configuring Group Policy to remove the revoked certificate, the administrator can simply perform the revocation and not worry about manually deleting certificates from client computers.

3. How will you reconfigure users in the Coho Winery research department when a new requirement for secure e-mail, such as a longer key, is introduced?

   a. Create a new template with the new parameters. Configure the new template to supersede the old template.

   b. Configure the existing template to contain the longer key length. Configure the template to re-enroll all certificate holders.

   c. Create a second template with the new parameters. Deny research users the right to enroll for certificates based on the old template.

   d. Revoke all certificates. Instruct users to enroll for new certificates based on a new template with the longer key length.

   b. When certificate requirements change, a certificate template can be modified to include the new requirement. By instructing all users to re-enroll for certificates based on the new template, you ensure that users always have certificates that meet the current requirements.

Design Activity: Troubleshooting Lab

Page 7-62

1. What tool can you use to identify the problem?

   The first tool you should use is Event Viewer. If you have enabled auditing as described in Lesson 1, Event Viewer will show a failure audit in the Security event log on Computer1 with the description "Certificate Services denied a certificate request." That does not help you troubleshoot the problem, but it does verify it. Certificate Services has also added a Warning event to the Application event log. This event provides a more useful description: "Certificate Services denied request 19 because The EMail name is unavailable and cannot be added to the Subject or Subject Alternate name."

2. What is the source of the problem?

   The problem is caused by the Subject Name requirements of the User–Archived Key certificate template. To view these requirements, use the Certificate Templates snap-in to view the User–Archived Key security template properties, and then click the Subject Name tab. The default settings, which specify to build the subject name from Active Directory information, are still selected. By default, this includes the user's e-mail address. Because the users created in this chapter do not have e-mail addresses specified, they cannot enroll for the certificate.

3. How will you resolve the problem?

   If your organization requires all user accounts to have e-mail addresses, you should resolve the problem by assigning an e-mail address to the account. Otherwise, you should change the Subject Name requirements on the certificate template to remove the dependency on the e-mail address. Specifically, you should clear both the E-Mail Name check box and the Include E-Mail Name In Subject Name check box.

8 Planning and Configuring IPSec

Exam Objectives in this Chapter:

- Plan IPSec deployment.
    - Decide which IPSec mode to use.
    - Plan authentication methods for IPSec.
    - Test the functionality of existing applications and services.
- Configure IPSec policies to secure communication between networks and hosts. Hosts include domain controllers, Internet Web servers, databases, e-mail servers, and client computers.
    - Configure IPSec authentication.
    - Configure appropriate encryption levels. Considerations include the selection of perfect forward secrecy (PFS) and key lifetimes.
    - Configure the appropriate IPSec protocol. Protocols include Authentication Header (AH) and Encapsulating Security Payload (ESP).
    - Configure IPSec inbound and outbound filters and filter action.

Why This Chapter Matters

Transmission Control Protocol/Internet Protocol (TCP/IP), the protocol suite used by most private networks and the Internet, was not designed for security. In fact, it is extraordinarily vulnerable. Communications are passed between as many as dozens of different network devices, and in the case of the public Internet, the sender of the message has no control over who owns the network equipment that carries the messages. There is ample opportunity for an attacker to eavesdrop on your private communications.

TCP/IP communications are also easy to impersonate and manipulate. When a computer receives a TPC/IP message, the computer has no way of determining whether the IP address in the message is genuine, or whether the message was modified in transit. This makes TCP/IP vulnerable to such attacks as the man-in-the-middle attack, which an attacker can use to compromise private data and user credentials.

Internet Protocol security (IPSec) is a newer protocol suite that works with TCP/IP to verify the integrity of communications, authenticate computers, and encrypt traffic. When implemented, IPSec dramatically reduces the risk of several common attacks. Microsoft Windows Server 2003, in addition to other recent versions of Microsoft Windows, includes IPSec capabilities. However, understanding, planning, and configuring an IPSec infrastructure is a complex task. This chapter will teach you the fundamentals of IPSec, provide you with information for planning an IPSec deployment, and familiarize you with the tools used to configure IPSec.

Lessons in this Chapter:

Before You Begin

If you fulfilled the requirements for the previous chapters, you already have the necessary hardware and software configured. You can use the computers in the state they were in after completing the previous chapters, or you can install the software from scratch. To perform the practices, examples, and lab exercises in this chapter, you must have:

- A private network that is connected to the Internet and protected by a firewall. This network should not have any production computers connected to it.
- Two computers. Perform a Windows Server 2003 installation with default settings on both computers. On the first computer, assign the computer name Computer1. Add the Domain Controller role to the computer, using the default settings, and specify the domain name cohowinery.com. Configure the computer to use itself as its own primary Domain Name System (DNS) server. On the second computer, assign the computer name Computer2. Configure the computer to use Computer1 as its primary DNS server. Then join it to the cohowinery.com domain as a member server. If you have Computer2 configured as a cohowinery.com domain controller after completing Chapter 7, you can leave the domain controller role intact without affecting the exercises in this chapter.

Lesson 1: IPSec Fundamentals

IPSec in the Windows Server 2003 operating system protects networks from active and passive attacks by securing IP packets through the use of packet filtering, cryptography, and the enforcement of trusted communication. IPSec is useful for improving the privacy and integrity of host-to-host, host-to-network, and network-to-network communications. IPSec can also be used as a host-based firewall to harden clients and servers by using packet filtering.

This lesson will discuss the universal, fundamental aspects of IPSec. The information in this lesson definitely applies to computers running Windows Server 2003 and other Windows-based computers. However, it also accurately represents how UNIX, Linux, and other computers would implement the IPSec standards.

> **See Also** Chapter 9 covers deploying and troubleshooting IPSec.

> **After this lesson, you will be able to**
>
> - Identify common IPSec usage scenarios.
> - Describe the IPSec negotiation process, including the differences between Main Mode and Quick Mode communications.
> - List the two protocols used for protecting IPSec communications.
> - List the improvements in the IPSec implementation included with Windows Server 2003.
>
> **Estimated lesson time: 25 minutes**

IPSec Overview

IPSec is a framework of open standards for helping to ensure private, secure communications over Internet Protocol (IP) networks through the use of cryptographic security services. IPSec supports network-level data integrity, data confidentiality, data origin authentication, and replay protection. Because IPSec is integrated at the Internet layer (layer 3), it provides security for almost all protocols in the TCP/IP suite, and because IPSec is applied transparently to applications, there is no need to configure separate security for each application that uses TCP/IP.

IPSec can be used to provide packet filtering, to encrypt and authenticate traffic between two hosts, and to create a virtual private network (VPN). Using these capabilities of IPSec helps to provide protection against:

- Network-based denial-of-service attacks from untrusted computers.
- Data corruption.

- Data theft.
- User-credential theft.
- Administrative control of servers, other computers, and the network.

Besides simply improving security, IPSec can be used to save money by enabling communications between remote offices and remote access clients across the public Internet, rather than more costly dedicated circuits that offer privacy at the physical level.

See Also This chapter will provide a basic overview of IPSec's functionality. If you want to know the details, and you have the spare time, read the following RFCs: 3457, 3456, 3281, 3193, 2857, 2709, 2451, and approximately 22 more. You can obtain copies at *http://www.ietf.org*.

Securing Host-to-Host Communications

You can use IPSec to encrypt and validate the integrity of communications between two computers. For example, IPSec can protect traffic between domain controllers in different sites, between Web servers and database servers, or between Web clients and Web servers. When an IPSec client attempts to initiate a connection to an IPSec server, the client and server negotiate IPSec integrity and encryption protocols. After the IPSec connection is established, the application's data is transported within the IPSec connection.

For example, consider the common scenario of a user downloading e-mail from a server using Post Office Protocol version 3 (POP3). If IPSec is not enabled, the e-mail client software initiates a connection directly to the e-mail server software. The user name and password will be transmitted in clear text, so that anyone with a protocol analyzer such as Network Monitor can intercept the user's credentials. An attacker who has control of a router can modify the contents of the user's e-mail messages as they are downloaded without being detected.

Now consider the same scenario with IPSec enabled. In this case, when the server receives the POP3 request from the e-mail client, it will send a message back to the client requesting an IPSec connection. The client will agree, and IPSec will negotiate encryption and integrity protocols. Then IPSec on the client computer will intercept the e-mail client's network traffic, store it within encrypted IPSec packets, and send the data to the server using TCP/IP. IPSec on the server will receive the packets, decrypt the contents, and pass the e-mail client's original communication to the e-mail server software.

In this IPSec-enabled scenario, neither the e-mail client nor the e-mail server software is aware that the communications were protected by IPSec. Similarly, routers and firewalls between the client and server cannot modify the communications or extract the user's credentials. In fact, the routers and firewalls cannot even determine that the user is downloading e-mail, because the POP3 protocol is completely hidden within the IPSec packets.

IPSec can operate in two different modes: *transport mode* and *tunnel mode*. Typically, you should use transport mode to protect host-to-host communications. In transport mode, IPSec tunnels traffic starting at the transport layer, also known as layer 4. Therefore, IPSec in transport mode can encrypt the User Datagram Protocol/Transmission Control Protocol (UDP/TCP) protocol header and the original data, but the IP header itself cannot be protected.

IPSec transports an application's data by adding an IPSec header and trailer to outgoing packets. Depending on the IPSec protocol used, the original contents of the outgoing packets will be encrypted. IPSec's position in the packet when functioning in transport mode is shown in Figure 8.1. The diagram shows IPSec using the ESP protocol. ESP is the most common of the two IPSec protocols because it provides both authentication and encryption. IPSec protocols will be described in more detail later in this chapter.

Figure 8.1 Transport mode IPSec

In the past, IPSec traffic could not pass from a privately numbered network to a publicly numbered network through a Network Address Translator (NAT) server, such as a firewall or proxy server. IPSec could not deal with having the NAT server change the source and destination IP address—to IPSec, this translation was tampering with the packet, and the packet would be rejected. IPSec NAT Traversal (NAT-T) allows IPSec traffic to pass through compatible NAT servers. However, both the IPSec hosts and the NAT server must support NAT-T, and the NAT server must be configured to allow traffic on UDP port 4500. Windows Server 2003, Windows XP Professional, and Windows 2000 support NAT-T as IPSec clients. Microsoft Internet Security and Acceleration (ISA) Server and Windows Server 2003 support NAT-T as a firewall.

See Also For more information about NAT-T, refer to RFC 3193.

Planning Planning to use IPSec to authenticate or encrypt communications between a private and public network? Make sure your NAT server supports NAT-T. If not, factor the cost of upgrading into the cost of deploying IPSec.

Securing Host-to-Network Communications

IPSec is often used to authenticate and encrypt traffic sent directly between two hosts. However, IPSec can also protect traffic traveling from a single host to an entire network, as illustrated in Figure 8.2. This is most commonly used in remote access scenarios. In the past, many organizations required users to dial in to remote access servers connected to the organization's private network. Today, organizations can eliminate the cost of maintaining dial-in servers by using IPSec to allow remote users to connect to an organization's private network across the Internet. Most security experts agree that IPSec provides a level of security similar to that of dial-up remote access.

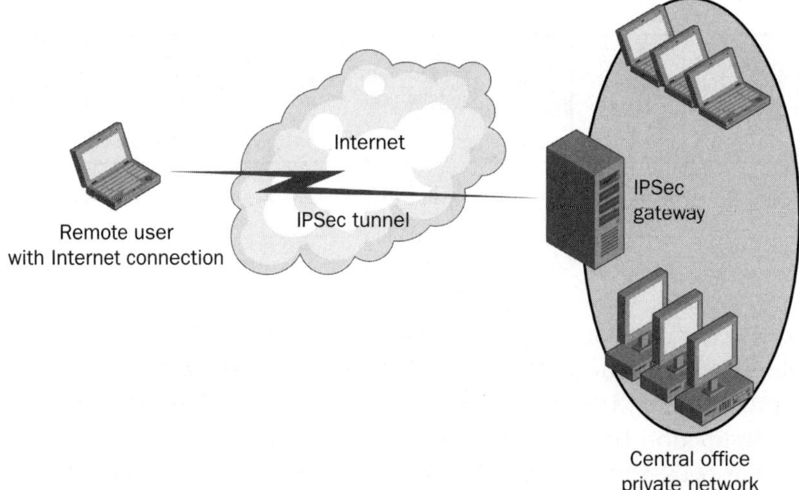

Figure 8.2 Remote access with IPSec

As you recall, when you protect traffic sent directly between two hosts, you will almost always use IPSec transport mode. When you protect traffic between a host and a network, or between two networks, you must use IPSec *tunnel mode*. Although transport mode stores the UDP/TCP header and the application data between an IPSec header and trailer, tunnel mode stores the entire original packet, as shown in Figure 8.3. The IP header, including the source and destination addresses, must be stored within the IPSec packet because the traffic is destined for a computer other than the computer to which the IPSec connection was established.

Exam Tip It's important that you understand when to use tunnel mode and when to use transport mode. It's simple, really. Use transport mode when you communicate with one computer, and use tunnel mode when you communicate with an entire network. If an exam question asks about encapsulating or tunneling the IP header, that's a clue that it's referring to tunnel mode.

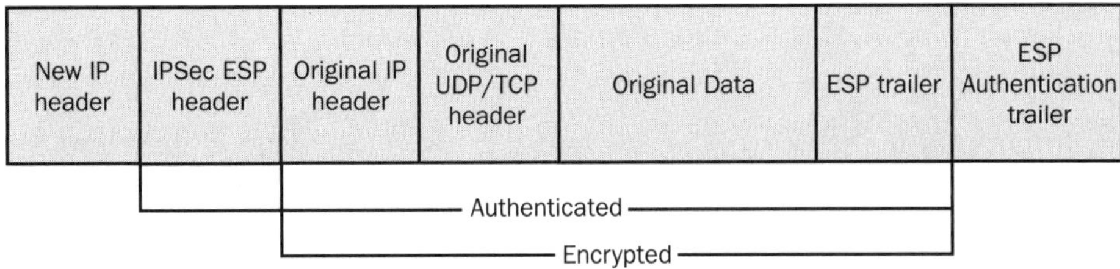

Figure 8.3 Tunnel mode IPSec

Once again, consider the scenario of a remote user retrieving e-mail from a mail server on a private network. When the user's e-mail client attempts to initiate a connection to the mail server's IP address, IPSec on the client computer detects that traffic is being sent to a network that must be accessed by using IPSec tunnel mode. The client's IPSec then establishes an IPSec connection to the IPSec gateway that provides access to the internal network.

IPSec will then encapsulate the entire packet generated by the e-mail client, including the source and destination IP addresses, the TCP header, and the application's data. IPSec adds a new IP header with the destination address of the IPSec gateway. The IPSec gateway will decrypt the packet, restoring the packet to the original condition it was in when sent by the e-mail client. The original IP header is restored too, including the original source and destination IP addresses. Finally, the IPSec gateway forwards the packet to the mail server.

As with transport mode, the e-mail client is not aware that the communications were protected with IPSec. Unlike with transport mode, the mail server's operating system also is unaware that IPSec was in use, because the IPSec gateway removed the IPSec header and trailer before forwarding the packets to the private network.

Real World

If hosts on two networks are communicating across the Internet and all clients are IPSec enabled, transport mode can be used to encrypt traffic between individual hosts, or tunnel mode can be used to encrypt all traffic sent between the two networks. Naturally, tunnel mode is more convenient because it doesn't require every host to have IPSec enabled—but which is more secure?

Tunnel mode is more secure than transport mode, in theory. Remember, VPNs protect against an attacker trying to capture your traffic, analyze it, and use the information gathered to do something malicious. Imagine that an attacker is capturing IPSec-encrypted packets as they travel between the private networks of two competing businesses. If tunnel mode is used, all the attacker can determine is how much traffic is sent between the networks, and when it is being sent. This information might be useful because the attacker might be able to guess that a sudden increase in traffic volume indicates an impending merger between the companies and then use that information to buy some stock and make an illegal profit.

If transport mode is used, attackers can analyze the total volume of traffic being sent, just as they could with tunnel mode. However, they can also analyze the *shape* of traffic sent between hosts within the network. By analyzing the shape, they might be able to determine the internal IP addresses of Web and e-mail servers and build a partial map of the private network. Even though they can't see the encrypted contents of the packets, they can examine the lengths of the packets and the communications patterns. Web traffic, for example, can be recognized even when encrypted because Web browsers send multiple, short requests to a Web server, which returns multiple, much longer responses containing the files that make up a Web page. E-mail servers, backup servers, and Active Directory directory service domain controllers can also be identified by attackers analyzing the shape of traffic.

Now, even if an attacker does manage to capture and analyze your traffic, would this information really be useful? Probably not, but I've talked to a few organizations that use this possibility as a justification to avoid VPNs, so I think it's important to understand the risk. While we're at it, a tin foil hat reduces the risk of aliens reading my mind, but you won't see one on my head.

Securing Network-to-Network Communications

IPSec can also be used to connect two remote networks. Before Internet connectivity was common, remote offices were connected with private links provided by communications companies. These links would typically consist of a circuit (such as a T1 in the United States or an E1 in Europe) from each of the remote offices that connected to a switched frame relay network that would carry the traffic over long distances.

Today, many organizations still use private links to connect offices. Private links offer some distinct advantages, most notably predictability and stability. Although the Internet continues to become more reliable, performance factors such as usable bandwidth, latency, and jitter fluctuate unpredictably. Private links dedicate bandwidth to a communication link and always follow the same path—guaranteeing that performance will always stay the same.

IPSec can connect two remote offices across the Internet, providing the same connectivity as a private link using an existing Internet connection. IPSec uses authentication and encryption to reduce the risk of traffic being intercepted; a private link relies on physical security to reduce the risk of eavesdropping. For many, the security provided by IPSec and private links is similar enough that the additional cost of a private link cannot be justified.

However, IPSec does nothing to stabilize the Internet's available bandwidth or latency, nor to improve the reliability. When IPSec is used to connect two offices across the Internet, both offices lease links to a local Internet service provider (ISP). Then administrators at both offices establish an encrypted IPSec tunnel between an IPSec gateway located at each office, as shown in Figure 8.4. To the clients on both networks, the gateways act like standard routers. The clients do not need to support IPSec to make use of the tunnel.

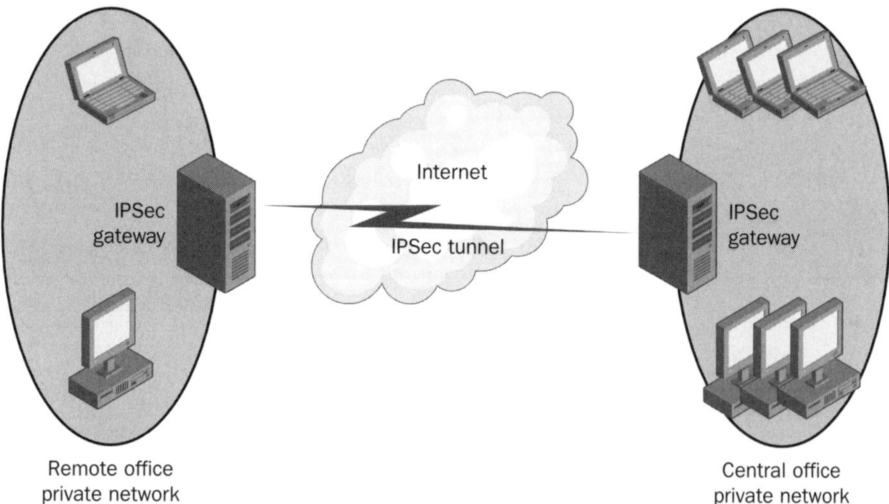

Figure 8.4 A site-to-site IPSec tunnel

> **Real World** **Comparing Security Levels**
>
> During the late 90s, when use of the Internet was skyrocketing, I was working at an ISP that offered a service to connect remote offices using VPNs. At the time, most organizations connected remote offices using leased lines, such as T1s, and frame relay connections. They were comfortable with these "private" connections and extremely wary of allowing their traffic (encrypted or not) to travel across the "public" Internet.

In my opinion, though, private connections are no more secure than public connections. You still rely on a third party to carry traffic between locations. For private connections, you use one or more communications companies. Any of these communications companies could, in theory, tap into your network and watch the unencrypted traffic pass through. For public connections, one or more ISPs carry your traffic. The primary disadvantage of using the public connection is that you don't know who exactly is carrying your traffic. The dynamic nature of the Internet could cause your traffic to be routed to a third-party ISP. In theory, you might not trust this third-party ISP.

However, whether you use public or private networks as the underlying transport, there is probably nobody who has the access, time, and inclination to sniff your traffic. If your traffic does get re-routed to a third-party ISP, they're not going to realize that interesting traffic is passing through their network. Even if they did, they probably don't have the equipment necessary to intercept your encrypted data stream and piece together enough of your data to crack the encryption and find anything useful.

In a nutshell, there is a small theoretical risk that your data could be compromised whether it crosses a public or private network. I think that risk is about the same either way. However, VPNs are much less expensive than private links, which means you have some money left over to spend on other security priorities, like staffing.

Although both ends of the tunnel can be servers running Windows Server 2003, they do not have to be. IPSec is a set of Internet standards that is supported by a wide variety of operating systems and network devices. One or both of the IPSec tunnel endpoints can be non-Microsoft firewalls, network devices, Windows 2000–based servers, or UNIX/Linux servers.

Negotiating IPSec Connections

Unfortunately, IP was not originally designed with authentication or encryption in mind. As the Internet grew and TCP/IP became the network protocol of choice, this unsecured form of communication became the standard. IPSec allows computers to continue using IP, while adding authentication and encryption.

However, most computers on IP networks today do not have IPSec enabled. As a result, computers with IPSec enabled are usually configured to politely ask remote computers to use IPSec to improve the security of the connection. If the two computers determine that they both have IPSec configured, and can agree upon a set of security standards, they can begin to use IPSec. This process is known as *IPSec negotiation*.

Not all IPSec negotiations are successful. Often the negotiations will fail because one of the two computers is not capable of using IPSec. Alternatively, the computers might not have the same security protocols enabled, which would mean that they wouldn't be able to agree on a set of standards. In these cases, the computers will either revert to unprotected IP communications or determine that they will not communicate at all if they cannot use IPSec.

Internet Key Exchange (IKE) is the algorithm by which the first secure Security Association, or SA (a secure channel), is negotiated. IKE is a combination of the Internet Security Association Key Management Protocol (ISAKMP) and the Oakley Key Determination protocol and performs a two-phase negotiation: Main Mode and Quick Mode.

See Also You can read more about IKE negotiation and this process at RFC 2409: *http://www.ietf.org/rfc/rfc2409.txt*.

Main Mode

The initial long form of the IKE negotiation (Main Mode or Phase 1) performs the authentication and generates the master key material to establish an ISAKMP SA between machines. The result is referred to as an *ISAKMP SA* or an *IKE SA*. After the ISAKMP SA is established, it will remain in place for the period of time defined on the host computers—by default, it will last for 8 hours on computers running Windows. If data is actively being transferred at the end of the 8 hours, the Main Mode security association (SA) will be renegotiated automatically.

Main Mode negotiation occurs in three parts:

1. Negotiation of protection suites
2. Diffie-Hellman exchange
3. Authentication

Part 1 of the Main Mode negotiation uses unencrypted communications to identify the protection suites that are available and determines which algorithms will be used during the session. The IPSec client will send the IPSec server a list of protection suites that the client supports. Each proposed protection suite includes attributes for encryption algorithms, hash algorithms, authentication methods, and Diffie-Hellman Oakley groups. The IPSec server then responds to the client with the chosen protection suite. Generally, this will be the first compatible protection suite.

Security Alert A Windows IPSec client will propose protection suites in the order in which they are listed in a filter action. A Windows IPSec server will use the first suitable protection suite listed by the client. Therefore, the Windows client determines the priorities of the protection suites, not the server. You should place this sequence in order from most to least secure. Lesson 3 describes how to configure filter actions.

After a protection suite has been negotiated, part 2 of the Main Mode negotiation generates a Diffie-Hellman public and private key pair based on the negotiated Diffie-Hellman Oakley group. The IPSec hosts exchange public keys and then separately generate the Main Mode master key keying material. This keying material will be used to encrypt the traffic sent between the two hosts, enabling all future communications to be considered private.

Part 3 of the Main Mode negotiation performs authentication. The authentication that occurs for Main Mode negotiation is a computer-based authentication (also known as *machine-based* authentication). The authentication process verifies only the identity of the computers, not the individuals using the computers when the authentication process occurs. The exact messages exchanged during this phase depend on which authentication method is used. Lesson 2 provides more information about the available authentication modes.

Quick Mode

Quick Mode (also known as *Phase 2*) IKE negotiation establishes a secure channel between two computers to protect data. Because this phase involves the establishment of SAs that are negotiated on behalf of the IPSec service, the SAs created during Quick Mode are called the *IPSec SAs*. Two SAs are established, each with its own Security Parameter Index (SPI) label. One IPSec SA is used for inbound traffic, and the other is used for outbound traffic. During Quick Mode, keying material is refreshed or, if necessary, new keys are generated. A protection suite that protects specific IP traffic is also selected.

IPSec hosts will perform IKE Quick Mode negotiation on a regular basis to reduce the risk of an attacker using brute force methods to determine the keys used in the communications. Each renegotiation re-establishes two new IPSec security associations with new keys and SPIs. By default, computers running Windows will perform Quick Mode negotiation every hour (3600 seconds) or after 100 megabytes have been transferred. Either side of the connection can start the renegotiation process. Therefore, the site that first reaches the defined session key limit will initiate renegotiation. Lesson 3 describes how to specify session key limits.

Establishing a handful of IPSec connections is not going to bog your computer down. However, the negotiation process does use a significant amount of processing time. If you have a server that is receiving anywhere from dozens to thousands of incoming IPSec connections per second, monitor the server's processor utilization. If the processor utilization is consistently over 30 percent during peak hours, consider adding a network interface card (NIC) that offloads the IPSec processing. This enables the NIC to handle the negotiations while the server's processor deals with more interesting tasks.

Establishing the IPSec connection is processor-intensive because it uses asymmetric public key cryptography. The data transmitted after the connection is established is encrypted by using symmetric shared key cryptography and does not use a significant (by modern standards) amount of processing capacity. So offloading processor utilization is only going to benefit you if the server is constantly receiving a large number of *new* connections.

Authentication Header and ESP

IPSec can use two protocols: Authentication Header (AH) and ESP. The protocols can be used either separately or together. AH provides data origin authentication, data integrity, and anti-replay protection for the entire packet, including the IP header and the data payload carried in the packet. Naturally, AH does not provide protection for the fields in the IP header that are allowed to change in transit, such as the hop count. AH does not encrypt data, which means it does not provide privacy. Attackers can read the contents of packets if they can intercept them, but the packets cannot be modified.

ESP is more commonly used than AH because it provides data origin authentication, data integrity, anti-replay protection, and the option of privacy. While AH and ESP can be used together, you will use ESP alone in most circumstances. You should choose AH over ESP only when the data and header in the packet need to be protected from modification and authentication but not encrypted. You might do this if you have an intrusion detection system, firewall, or quality of service (QoS) router that needs to inspect the contents of the packet. Otherwise, take advantage of the privacy provided by encryption, and use ESP. If IPSec traffic must traverse a NAT server, you must use ESP, because ESP is the only IPSec protocol that supports NAT-T.

IPSec in Windows

IPSec is natively available and can be used to protect network communications for Windows 2000, Windows XP Professional, and Windows Server 2003. Additionally, a legacy client is available for Microsoft Windows NT 4.0, Windows 98, and Windows Millennium Edition (ME). You can download the legacy client from *http://www.microsoft.com/windows2000/server/evaluation/news/bulletins/l2tpclient.asp.*

Windows Server 2003 improvements

Windows Server 2003 includes several IPSec manageability improvements. The IP Security Monitor snap-in, first introduced with Windows XP Professional, replaces the Ipsecmon.exe tool included with Windows 2000 Server. Now, you can use the Netsh tool to manage IPSec configuration from the command line just as you would other network configuration settings, instead of being required to use dedicated command-line tools. Troubleshooting is easier, too, because you can use the Resultant Set Of Policy (RSoP) snap-in to view existing IPSec policy assignments.

IPSec security is improved, too. Windows 2000 Server was vulnerable to network attacks during startup, even if IPSec had been configured. Now, you can configure computer startup security to manage network traffic during startup. This allows only the outbound traffic that the computer initiates during startup, inbound traffic sent in response to the outbound traffic, and Dynamic Host Configuration Protocol (DHCP) traffic. Previous versions of Windows automatically allowed several types of traffic through IPSec filters. Windows Server 2003, by default, only allows IKE traffic.

Previous versions of Windows could reveal more information than necessary to an attacker when public keys were used to authenticate IPSec connections, but Windows Server 2003 can be configured to exclude the name of the certification authority (CA) to prevent exposure of trust relationships. Now, you can use dynamic addressing to specify the addresses of DHCP servers, DNS servers, WINS servers, and default gateways in IP filters. This allows you to create more restrictive filters than you could with Windows XP or Windows 2000 computers, because you do not have to deploy different filters to different locations just because clients used different network configurations.

Packet filtering

Although the primary purpose of IPSec is to ensure the integrity of hosts and to encrypt traffic, the Windows Server 2003 IPSec implementation also provides limited firewall capabilities for end systems. This was extremely important with versions of Windows released prior to Windows XP. However, Windows XP and Windows Server 2003 include Internet Connection Firewall (ICF), which provides more powerful stateful packet filtering than IPSec.

Although IPSec and ICF functionality overlap, they both have unique features. ICF is stateful, and IPSec provides filtering based on source and destination IP addresses. Fortunately, there's nothing to stop you from using both together on computers running Windows XP Professional and Windows Server 2003.

See Also For more information about ICF and stateful packet filtering, refer to Chapter 4.

You should enable ICF on computers running Windows XP Professional and Windows Server 2003 regardless of whether you use IPSec. However, to ensure proper IKE management of IPSec SAs, you must configure ICF to permit ISAKMP for UDP port 500. If you are using NAT-T, you must also allow traffic on UDP port 4500. ISAKMP is not one of ICF's pre-configured services, however, so you will need to add it. To add ISAKMP, click the Advanced tab in the filtered network interface's properties dialog box. Then click the Settings button. Click the Services tab, and then click Add. Enter settings in the dialog box as shown in Figure 8.5, and then click OK and repeat the process for the second port number.

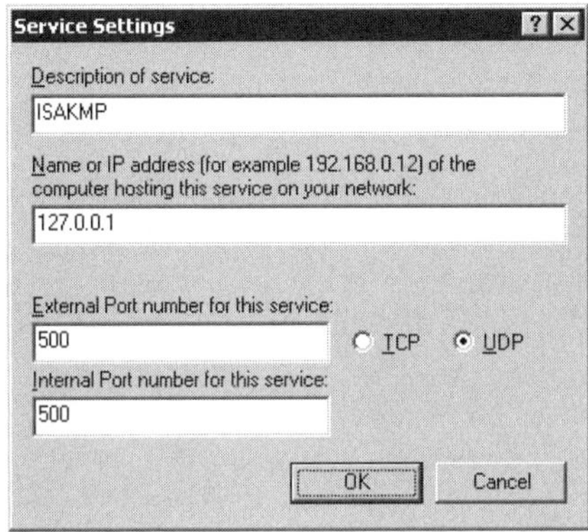

Figure 8.5 Allowing the ISAKMP service through ICF

Lesson 3 provides information on configuring packet filtering by using IPSec.

Lesson Review

The following questions are intended to reinforce key information presented in this lesson. If you are unable to answer a question, review the lesson materials and try the question again. You can find answers to the questions in the "Questions and Answers" section at the end of this chapter.

1. By default, how often does IPSec regenerate Main Mode keys?
   - **a.** Every hour
   - **b.** Every 4 hours
   - **c.** Every 8 hours
   - **d.** Every 24 hours
   - **e.** Weekly

2. Which mode would you use to protect communications between two private networks connected by the Internet?

   a. Transport mode

   b. Tunnel mode

   ____

3. Which mode would you use to protect communications between an IPSec-enabled e-mail client and an e-mail server on a private network?

   a. Transport mode

   b. Tunnel mode

   ____

4. Which of the following IPSec protocols provides encryption for network communications?

   a. AH

   b. ESP

   c. SA

   d. IKE

   e. ISAKMP

   ____

Lesson Summary

- Use IPSec in transport mode to protect communications between two IPSec-enabled computers. Use IPSec in tunnel mode when protecting communications to an entire network.
- Main Mode IKE negotiations occur at the beginning of a session. Quick Mode negotiations occur immediately after Main Mode negotiations complete, and then recur on a regular basis while the session is active.
- You can choose to use either the AH or ESP protocol with IPSec. You will usually use ESP, because ESP provides encryption and is compatible with NAT-T. Use AH only when you specifically do not want to encrypt traffic.
- IPSec can be used to provide packet filtering for computers running Windows, and it compliments ICF by providing filtering based on source or destination IP address.

Lesson 2: Planning an IPSec Infrastructure

You could enable IPSec for your entire domain with a few mouse clicks—but it would not be wise. If configured incorrectly, IPSec can cause minor problems, such as a network application that performs poorly, or major problems, such as total loss of network connectivity. Only careful planning can ensure the success of an IPSec deployment. That planning involves choosing an authentication method, deciding how to manage IPSec's integration with Active Directory, and devising a testing procedure to validate application compatibility with your planned IPSec configuration.

After this lesson, you will be able to

- Describe the considerations for deploying IPSec integrated with an Active Directory domain.
- List the various authentication methods that IPSec in Windows Server 2003 can use, and list the advantages and disadvantages of each.
- Explain the importance of thoroughly testing applications with IPSec, and explain the most critical steps to take during the testing process.

Estimated lesson time: 20 minutes

Active Directory Considerations

For organizations with large numbers of computers that must be managed in a consistent way, it is best to distribute IPSec policies by using Group Policy objects (GPOs). Although you can assign local IPSec policies to computers that are not members of a trusted domain, distributing IPSec policies and managing IPSec policy configuration and trust relationships is much more time-consuming for computers that are not domain members.

Another advantage of using Active Directory–based IPSec policy is that you can delegate permissions on the IP Security Policies On Active Directory container to enable specific administrators to manage IPSec throughout your organization. These administrators do not necessarily need permissions to directly manage the individual computers that will receive the IPSec policy, however. This capability is vital to organizations that divide responsibility for security tasks between various groups.

To delegate permissions on the IP Security Policies container, you must use an Active Directory editing tool, such as ADSI Edit. ADSI Edit is a Windows support tool that uses the Active Directory Service Interfaces (ADSI). The Windows support tools can be installed from the \Support\Tools folder on the Windows 2000 and Windows Server 2003 operating system CDs.

An IPSec policy administrator typically requires Write access to all IPSec policy objects. You should not attempt to assign permissions to individual IPSec policies. If many administrators in your organization want to manage Active Directory–based IPSec policy, you should channel all IPSec changes through existing Domain Admins. The individuals making the changes to IPSec policy can configure local IPSec policy on a computer in a lab environment, and then use IP Security Policy Management to export an IPSec policy file for the domain administrator or another delegated administrator. The Domain Admin can then import the IPSec policy file into the IP Security Policies On Active Directory container. This practice minimizes the number of administrators who can modify IPSec policy, which decreases the risk of human error negatively affecting IPSec policy.

Although an Active Directory–based IPSec policy might be suitable to help secure most communications for a group of servers, you might need to customize an IPSec policy for a specific server. You can do this by using a Windows 2000, Windows XP Professional, or Windows Server 2003 IPSec command-line tool to create a dynamic IPSec policy. Lesson 3 has more information about using command-line tools to configure IPSec policy.

Authentication for IPSec

Peer authentication is the process of ensuring that an IPSec peer is the computer it claims to be. By using peer authentication, IPSec can determine whether to allow communications with another computer before the communication begins. You can choose from three authentication methods: Kerberos v5, public key certificates, and preshared keys.

If you have deployed a Windows 2000 or Windows Server 2003 Active Directory environment, and all hosts that will be using IPSec are part of that domain (or a member of a trusted domain), then you should use Kerberos. If you are communicating with outside organizations, and your partners use a Web-based CA, you can use public key certificates. If neither of these methods is available, you can use a preshared key.

See Also For more information about Kerberos, refer to Chapter 1. For more information about public keys, refer to Chapter 7.

You can mix and match authentication methods as needed. For example, you can configure your public Web server to authenticate internal clients by using Kerberos and external clients by using public key certificates. After you configure IPSec, it will compare the source IP address of the remote host against an IPSec policy rule to determine which authentication method to use.

Kerberos v5 authentication

Kerberos v5 is the default authentication standard in Windows Server 2003 and Windows 2000 domains. This method of authentication can be used by any computer in the domain or a trusted domain. Kerberos is the most natural form of IPSec authentication, and configuration is straightforward and simple. However, there are a couple of important considerations.

First, earlier versions of Windows automatically allowed Kerberos traffic through IPSec filters. However, Windows Server 2003 will drop Kerberos packets if an IPSec rule determines that the traffic should be blocked. If you want to enable Kerberos authentication, you must create filters in the IPSec policy that explicitly allow all traffic to your domain controllers.

Second, for IPSec to use Kerberos authentication across a cross-forest trust, you must use fully-qualified domain names to configure the trusts. In addition, you must configure the IPSec client policy to allow communication to any domain controller in the forest domain hierarchy so that IPSec can obtain a Kerberos ticket from a domain controller in the IPSec peer's domain.

Public key certificates authentication

A public key infrastructure (PKI) can be used to authenticate and encrypt communications for a wide variety of applications, including Web applications, e-mail, and IPSec. Although using public key certificates is not as convenient as using Kerberos, there are specific circumstances for which certificates are the logical choice for authentication in IPSec. Specifically, you should use public key certificates when you need to communicate privately with external business partners or other computers that do not support the Kerberos v5 authentication protocol.

IPSec's use of certificate authentication is compatible with many different PKI architectures, and IPSec places relatively few requirements on the contents of a certificate. Typically, computers that have a common trusted root, or whose certificates can chain through a cross-certification trust relationship, can successfully use IPSec authentication. To use certificates for IPSec authentication, you define an ordered list of acceptable root CA names in the authentication method. This list controls the certificates that IPSec can select and the certificates that IPSec will select.

If IPSec authentication fails, you cannot retry the authentication using a different method. For this reason, before you apply an IPSec policy that can use certificates for authentication, make sure that all target computers have the correct root CA certificates and relevant cross-certificates, in addition to valid computer certificates. Additionally, to ensure that certificate authentication works as intended, test your PKI infrastructure with various IPSec policy configurations before deployment.

In Windows 2000 and Windows Server 2003, you can use Certificate Services to implement the root CA. Certificate Services is integrated with Active Directory and Group Policy, and it simplifies certificate deployment by enabling certificate auto-enrollment and renewal and by providing configurable certificate templates. In addition, by publishing the computer certificate as an attribute of the domain computer account, Certificate Services allows you to use IPSec to restrict access to network services.

See Also Refer to Chapter 7 for information on Certificate Services.

You can also use third-party CAs, which is particularly useful when communicating with external partners. IPSec supports the use of a variety of third-party X.509 PKI systems, in addition to Windows 2000 Server or Windows Server 2003 Certificate Services. Windows Server 2003 IKE has basic compatibility with several certificate systems, including those offered by Microsoft, Entrust, VeriSign, and Netscape. If you are using a third-party PKI system, the PKI system must be able to issue certificates to computers and store their certificates in the Windows Cryptographic Application Programming Interface (CryptoAPI) computer certificate store.

Caution Certificates obtained from Certificate Services with the Enable Strong Private Key Protection option selected cannot be used for IPSec authentication because the user cannot enter a password during IKE negotiation.

Preshared key authentication

If both IPSec peers are not in the same domain and do not have access to a CA, a preshared key can be used. For example, a standalone computer on a network that does not connect to the Internet might need to use a preshared key, because neither Kerberos authentication through the computer's domain account nor access to a CA on the Internet is available. A preshared key is a shared secret key (basically a password) that has been agreed upon by administrators who want to secure the computers' communications by using IPSec. Administrators must manually configure their systems to use the same preshared key.

The preshared key authentication method uses symmetrical encryption to authenticate the hosts, which itself is very secure, but which requires that any two hosts communicating have been configured with a predefined password. Unfortunately, this key is not stored securely on the IPSec hosts. The authentication key is stored in plaintext format in the system registry and hex-encoded in Active Directory–based IPSec policy. If attackers can access your registry, they can find your preshared key, which would allow them to decrypt your traffic or impersonate one of the hosts. Use preshared key authentication only when no stronger method can be used.

If you must use preshared key authentication, use a local IPSec policy, a 25-character or longer random key value, and a different preshared key for each IP address pair. These practices result in different security rules for each destination and ensure that a compromised preshared key compromises only those computers that share the key.

Testing IPSec

As a rule, you should perform extensive testing before making any changes to your infrastructure. This rule certainly holds true when planning to use IPSec. IPSec has the potential to interfere with all network communications and, as a result, can break any network applications that your organization uses.

Begin testing IPSec in a lab environment. Configure computers with the client- and server-side of your critical applications, and verify that the lab is functional and accurately simulating the production environment. Your lab environment should have computers with each of the potential IPSec client operating systems, because different operating systems support different IPSec functionality. Develop performance metrics for each of your applications, and gather baseline performance data that you can use for comparison after IPSec has been implemented. Then implement IPSec policies on the lab computers.

Not all network equipment provides the same IPSec capabilities, and you should use the testing phase to determine which network devices need configuration changes or upgrades. Add firewalls, proxy servers, and routers to the lab environment to simulate the potential for those devices to interfere with IPSec communications in the production environment. If you plan to use IPSec for remote access, be sure to include a remote access client in your lab environment, and have that client connect from a typical remote network. If employees will use IPSec to connect to your internal network from home, test IPSec across a variety of commonly used home routing equipment. Test non-IPSec-enabled clients with IPSec-enabled servers. Even if you plan to deploy IPSec to every computer, there will be a transition period during which some computers will not yet have received the IPSec configuration.

After IPSec clients and network equipment have been configured in the lab environment, test the application functionality. If you identify problems, document the problems and solutions so that they can be quickly resolved if they appear in the production environment. Besides verifying that applications function, verify IPSec functionality. If you allow IPSec clients to use unsecured communications if IPSec negotiations fail, it is possible for applications to appear to be compatible with IPSec when the computers were unable to establish an IPSec session.

See Also Refer to Chapter 9 for information on troubleshooting IPSec problems and monitoring IPSec traffic.

After you verify that all your applications are compatible with IPSec and document the changes required to ensure compatibility, compare the results of your performance tests against the results gathered before IPSec was enabled. If your tests are accurate, they will show a slight degradation in the time required to establish network connections and a slight increase in processor utilization. Make note of the overhead required. Monitor computers in your production environment to ensure that the performance impact will be minimized.

Begin the production IPSec rollout with a pilot deployment. During the pilot phase, you should not require IPSec communications on any computer. All computers should allow non-IPSec communications to support computers that are not part of the pilot. You can only require IPSec communications after all computers have received IPSec configurations. Monitor the pilot computers to verify that IPSec is functioning correctly. When users report problems, identify whether IPSec is the source of the problem, and document a resolution to the problem. Gradually deploying IPSec to your production environment will reduce the problems users experience, which saves your organization money.

Lesson Review

The following questions are intended to reinforce key information presented in this lesson. If you are unable to answer a question, review the lesson materials and try the question again. You can find answers to the questions in the "Questions and Answers" section at the end of this chapter.

1. You are an administrator at an organization that uses Windows Server 2003 Active Directory. Which IPSec authentication method should you recommend for authenticating internal clients to an intranet Web server?

   a. Kerberos authentication

   b. Public key certificates authentication

   c. Preshared key authentication

   ____

2. You need to grant employees at an external partner company access to an application server, but you want to ensure that the communications are authenticated and encrypted. Which IPSec authentication method should you recommend?

   a. Kerberos authentication

   b. Public key certificates authentication

   c. Preshared key authentication

   ____

Lesson Summary

- You should use GPOs to deploy IPSec whenever practical. However, you should limit access to modify the IPSec policies to the smallest number of administrators possible to reduce the opportunity for both human error and abuse.
- Use Kerberos authentication when all IPSec peers are members of a trusted Active Directory forest.
- Use public key certificates for IPSec authentication when Active Directory does not exist or when some computers are external to your organization.
- Use preshared key authentication only when neither Kerberos nor public key certificates can be used to authenticate IPSec connections.

Lesson 3: Configuring IPSec

After IPSec is configured on a computer, IPSec's behavior is determined by the policies that you configure. An IPSec policy consists of IP filter lists, filter actions, and authentication requirements. Combined, these components enable an IPSec policy to identify traffic that should be blocked or permitted, or that requires authentication. Figure 8.6 shows how IP filters, IP filter lists, filter actions, and rules define an IP security policy.

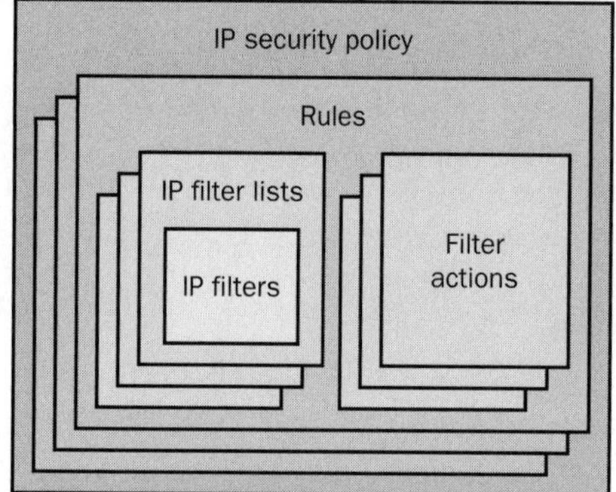

Figure 8.6 IP security policy components

After this lesson, you will be able to

- Describe the components that make up an IPSec policy: IP filters, filter actions, and IP security rules.
- Configure IPSec security policies using graphical or command-line tools.
- Configure CRL checking on Windows 2000–based computers that use IPSec public key certificates authentication.

Estimated lesson time: 60 minutes

IP Filters

IP filters describe network traffic and are used by IPSec policies to determine whether an IP security rule should apply to an individual packet. IP filters can specify traffic to or from a set of IP addresses, WINS servers, DNS servers, DHCP servers, or a default gateway. You can also configure an IP filter to match a packet's source or destination port number, or even a packet's IP protocol number. Each of the following examples can be specified by either a single IPSec IP filter or a combination of multiple filters:

- All traffic to or from IP address 10.4.22.17
- All Internet Control Message Protocol (ICMP) traffic to or from the default gateway

- All traffic sent to TCP port 80, except traffic sent from the internal network
- All outbound connections, except those to specific servers

Multiple IP filters can be combined into an *IP filter list*. In fact, adding an IP filter to an IP filter list is the only thing you can do with an IP filter, because IPSec policies only allow you to specify IP filter lists. If your needs are simple, you can make an IP filter list that consists of a single IP filter. However, most IP filter lists will consist of multiple IP filters.

To add, remove, or modify an IP filter list, right-click the applicable IP Security Policies node in the Group Policy Object Editor or IP Security Policy Management snap-in, and then click Manage IP Filter Lists And Filter Actions. This opens the Manage IP Filter Lists And Filter Actions dialog box. Click the Manage IP Filter Lists tab. You can then click the Add, Edit, or Remove buttons, as shown in Figure 8.7.

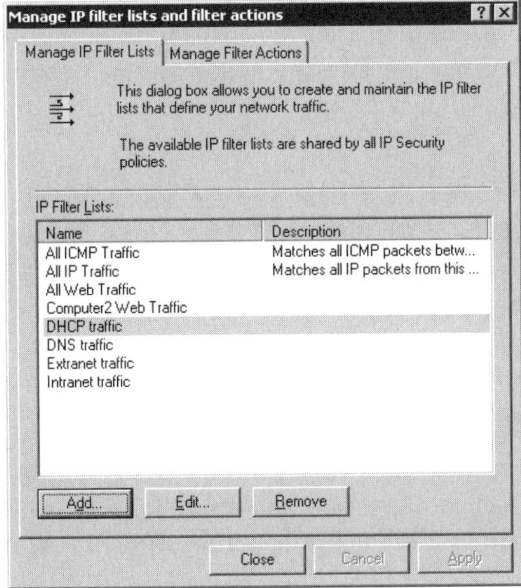

Figure 8.7 The Manage IP Filter Lists And Filter Actions dialog box

Clicking Add in the Manage IP Filter Lists And Filter Actions dialog box opens the IP Filter List dialog box. Clicking Add in this dialog box, in turn, allows you to create IP filters. You have the option of using a wizard to create the IP filter, but the configuration options are so simple that the wizard is not very useful. Regardless of how you configure the filter, the configuration options are the same: Source Address, Destination Address, Mirrored, and Protocol Type.

The source and destination addresses provide identical options. Selecting My IP Address specifies any of the IP addresses configured on the computer. You should use this option in all filters except those for which traffic is passing through the computer. In other words, you should choose My IP Address instead of Any IP Address unless the computer is acting as a firewall, a router, or an IPSec tunnel endpoint. The A Specific IP Subnet and A Specific IP Address options are self-explanatory. They should be used to create IP filters that specify the intranet, the extranet, or specific computers. For example, if you plan to host a Web server that is accessible from the public Internet but requires encryption for traffic originating on the intranet, you should create an IPSec policy with a filter list specifying the IP subnets on your intranet.

If you select the Mirrored check box, it does not matter which addresses you specify for source or destination, because the IP filter will also match traffic where the packet's source IP address matches the filter's destination IP address, and vice versa. You should not select the Mirrored option if creating a filter for an IPSec tunnel, however.

The A Specific DNS Name option is misleading; it does not store the host name in the IP filter. Instead, it looks up the IP address associated with the host name you specify at the time you create the filter and stores the IP address. This is an important distinction because if you create an IP filter that specifies the host name of a computer, and later change that computer's IP address, the IP filter will no longer match traffic from that computer.

In contrast, the DNS Servers, WINS Servers, DHCP Servers, and Default Gateway address options are all built dynamically. Each time an IPSec policy that uses the filter list is used, IPSec will effectively retrieve the list of DNS, WINS, DHCP, or default gateways from the computer's network configuration and attempt to match the traffic to those addresses. This allows you to use these dynamic addresses when deploying IPSec policies to an entire enterprise. If various parts of the organization use different servers, or if server addresses change over time, the dynamic IP filters will still function correctly.

Windows Server 2003 provides two built-in filter lists: All ICMP Traffic and All IP Traffic. You can use All ICMP Traffic to match requests from applications such as Ping and Tracert. As the name indicates, you can use All IP Traffic to match any incoming or outgoing IP traffic.

Filter Actions

You use filter actions, also referred to as *security methods*, to define how an IPSec policy should handle traffic that matches an IP filter. A filter action responds in one of three ways: it drops the traffic, it allows the traffic, or it attempts to negotiate security. If you choose the Permit or Block options for a filter action, there is nothing left to configure. In fact, you never need more than one filter action for each of the Permit and Block options.

There are several additional settings to consider when you configure a filter action to negotiate security. First, you must choose whether the server will allow communications with clients that do not support IPSec by selecting or clearing the Allow Unsecured Communication With Non-IPSec-Aware Computers check box. You can only require IPSec when you have only IPSec-enabled all client computers. Otherwise, clients without IPSec will be denied access to the server. Generally, this setting is enabled only when Active Directory is used to deploy IPSec configuration settings to all networked computers.

You should use the Filter Action Wizard to configure filter actions whenever possible, because configuring integrity and encryption settings can be complicated. The IP Traffic Security page of the wizard enables you to specify the protection suites associated with the filter action. You can choose Integrity And Encryption, Integrity Only, or Custom. If you select Integrity And Encryption, the wizard configures the filter action with ESP-based integrity verification (using Secure Hash Algorithm 1 [SHA1] by default) and encryption (using 3DES by default). If you select Integrity Only, Triple-Data Encryption Standard (3DES) encryption is disabled.

By selecting Custom, you can configure the specific algorithms you want to use for integrity and encryption, including the option to use MD5 for integrity instead of the default SHA1, and standard Data Encryption Standard (DES) for encryption instead of the default 3DES. Selecting Custom also gives you the option to change the default settings for Quick Mode key regeneration by specifying a certain amount of time or a specific amount of data. If you select both of the Generate A New Key Every check boxes, as shown in Figure 8.8, IPSec will use Quick Mode negotiation to generate a new session key after the specified number of bytes have been transferred or after the specified number of seconds has elapsed—whichever comes first. If you do not select either check box, IPSec will automatically initiate Quick Mode negotiation every hour or for every 100 megabytes (MB) of data transferred. The more frequently a session key is regenerated, the harder it is for an attacker to decrypt your traffic. However, regenerating session keys adds performance overhead and decreases network throughput.

Off the Record The default settings will not have a significant negative impact on performance, so don't assume that increasing the session key regeneration interval is going to give you a performance boost. In fact, regenerating session keys will have a noticeable negative impact only if you configure the session keys to be regenerated extremely frequently—say every few seconds.

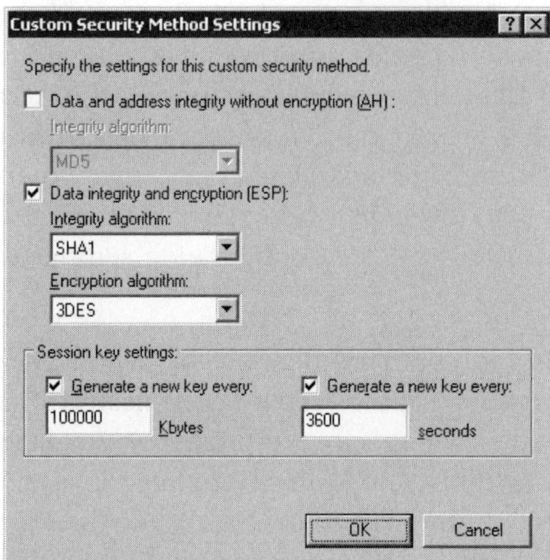

Figure 8.8 Specifying custom data integrity, encryption, and session key settings

You can configure multiple protection suites for a single filter action. If you do, view the filter action's properties, and use the Move Up and Move Down buttons to specify the priority. IPSec will start negotiations with the first security method in the list. If that fails, IPSec will work its way down the list until a connection is successfully negotiated or until the end of the list is reached. You should order the security methods from most secure to least secure. This will ensure that IPSec will negotiate the most secure connection possible with clients and fall back to less secure communications only when negotiations fail.

> **Note** As mentioned in Lesson 1, it is the IPSec client, also referred to as the *initiator*, that determines the order in which the protection suites are evaluated.

Filter actions have one more security option that cannot be configured from the Filter Action Wizard: Use Session Key Perfect Forward Secrecy (PFS). Selecting this check box specifies that you want to renegotiate new master key keying material each time a new session key is required. Basically, this improves the security of the connection by making it more difficult for an attacker to decrypt the communications. However, it requires additional negotiations between the client and server, which reduces performance.

> **Off the Record** Using Session Key PFS discourages only those attackers who use brute-force methods to decrypt traffic, which is an extremely impractical task. Therefore, you should enable PFS only for organizations that have the highest possible security requirements.

To add, remove, or modify a filter action, right-click the applicable IP Security Policies node in the Group Policy Object Editor or IP Security Policy Management snap-in, and then click Manage IP Filter Lists And Filter Actions. This opens the Manage IP Filter Lists And Filter Actions dialog box. Click the Manage Filter Actions tab. You can then click the Add, Edit, or Remove buttons.

Windows Server 2003 provides three built-in filter actions: Permit, Request Security, and Require Security. Permit, obviously, allows traffic to be forwarded. Request Security attempts to negotiate with a client that submits an unsecured connection request. If the client and server cannot agree on a set of IPSec settings, an unsecured connection will be established. Require Security also attempts to negotiate an authenticated and encrypted connection with the client, but it will drop the connection if negotiation fails.

IP Security Rules

An IP security rule consists of an IP filter list, a filter action, and, optionally, a connection type and tunnel endpoint. You can specify only one IP filter list and one filter action per rule. If the rule pertains to traffic traveling between networks across an IPSec tunnel, you should provide the IP address of the tunnel endpoint. This does not conflict with your ability to add IP filter lists; you can configure an endpoint and apply the rule only to traffic on a specific subnet within the destination network accessible through the IPSec tunnel.

The default response rule is used to configure the computer to respond to requests for secure communication when no other rules match the traffic. If an active policy does not have a rule defined for a computer that is requesting secure communication, the default response rule is applied and security is negotiated. For example, when Computer A communicates securely with Computer B, and Computer B does not have an inbound filter defined for Computer A, the default response rule is used.

Note The default response rule cannot be deleted, but it can be deactivated. It is activated by default for all policies.

To avoid the security risks related to unwanted security negotiations, you can disable the default response rule. Attackers can use the IPSec negotiation process enabled by the default response rule to obtain information about the computer through the security negotiation. A skilled Internet attacker can construct specific security negotiation requests to query and obtain the name of the client, trust relationships, and other settings that are configured in the default response rule. For example, if you use Kerberos as the authentication method for the default response rule, an attacker can query the Kerberos identity of the client. The query results will provide the attacker with the computer name and domain hierarchy, such as username@contoso.com. If you use certificate-based authentication as the authentication method for the default response rule, the attacker might be able to obtain the names of the PKI trusted root CAs that are configured for the default response rule.

You must also configure the authentication method. You can only configure a single authentication method by using the IP Security Policy Wizard, but you can later edit the properties of the policy to add additional authentication methods. You have three authentication methods to choose from: Active Directory, certificates, and preshared key. For more information about which authentication method to use, refer to Lesson 2.

Note If you're creating a rule that simply blocks or permits traffic, you will not be prompted to choose an authentication method because authentication is not used or required.

Configuring IP Security Policies with Graphical Tools

IP filters, filter actions, and IP security rules are only useful when added to an IP security policy. When configuring IP security policies on the local computer, you can use the IP Security Policy Management snap-in. You can also use the Group Policy Object Editor snap-in to edit either local or domain GPOs. In the Group Policy Object Editor, expand Computer Configuration, Windows Settings, Security Settings, and then click either IP Security Policies On Local Computer or IP Security Policies On Active Directory. Because this node might have several different labels, this chapter will refer to it as simply IP Security Policies.

To create a new security policy, right-click the applicable IP Security Policies node in the Group Policy Object Editor or IP Security Policy Management snap-in, and then click Create IP Security Policy. This opens the IP Security Policy Wizard, which guides you through the process of creating a security policy.

During the configuration process, you will be prompted to activate the default response rule. In most cases, you should enable the default response rule. If you do, you will be prompted to select an authentication method. For more information about rules, see the section "IP Security Rules" in this lesson.

After you create a policy with the IP Security Policy Wizard, you can edit the policy's properties to add rules or change the name, description, policy change interval, and key exchange settings. The Properties dialog box of the Secure Server (Require Security) IP security policy is shown in Figure 8.9. Use the Rules tab to add, modify, and remove IP security rules. Use the General tab to rename a rule, to modify how often IPSec checks for updates to the policy, and to specify key exchange settings.

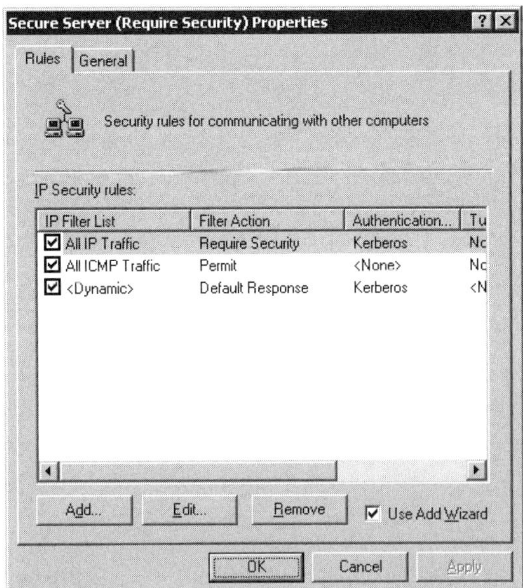

Figure 8.9 Editing IP security policy properties

You can click the Settings button on the General tab of the IP security policy properties dialog box to modify the key exchange settings. When you select the Master Key Perfect Forward Secrecy check box, IPSec will negotiate new master key keying material each time a new session key is required. This makes it more difficult for an attacker to decrypt your communications. However, it also adds performance overhead. If you do not select this check box, which is the default setting, new session keys will be derived from the current master key keying material—a quicker process.

The Methods button on the Key Exchange Settings dialog box opens the Key Exchange Security Methods dialog box, which allows you to control which IKE security methods are used to encrypt credentials during the authentication process. You can add or remove IKE security algorithms and arrange them in the order in which they will be used. IPSec will always attempt to use the first security algorithm before continuing to the remaining algorithms. Unless you have identified unusual security requirements that necessitate changing this list, the default settings should meet your needs.

Windows Server 2003 provides three built-in IP security policies: Client (Respond Only), Server (Request Security), and Secure Server (Require Security). The Client security policy consists only of the default response rule with Kerberos authentication. All computers must have the Client security policy, or another policy with the default response rule, assigned to establish an IPSec connection. If you have servers that will be accessed by clients that might or might not be IPSec-enabled, you should assign the Server (Request Security) built-in policy. If you have servers that should only be accessed by computers that you have configured, you can use Secure Server (Require Security). This policy rejects connection requests from computers that are not IPSec enabled.

Tip If you're managing a computer remotely, be careful about assigning the Secure Server (Require Security) policy, or any other policy that does not allow unsecured communications. You could end up blocking requests from your own computer!

Configuring IP Security Policies with Command-Line Tools

Though you should usually use graphical tools to configure IP security policies, Windows Server 2003 also provides the Netsh command-line tool for scripting IPSec configuration. Netsh is a native Windows Server 2003 command-line scripting tool that you can use to display or modify the local or remote network configuration. The Netsh IPSec commands cannot be used on any other version of Windows.

To use the command line to configure IPSec policies on computers running Windows XP, use Ipseccmd.exe, which is provided on the Windows XP CD, in the \Support\Tools folder. To use the command line to configure IPSec policies on computers running Windows 2000, use Ipsecpol.exe, which is provided with the Windows 2000 Server Resource Kit.

To use Netsh interactively to view or modify IPSec settings, open a command prompt and run the command **Netsh** with no parameters. This starts the Netsh interactive command prompt. Then type **Ipsec static** or **Ipsec dynamic** to set the context for Netsh. For example, the following commands launch Netsh and set the context to Ipsec dynamic:

```
C:\>netsh
netsh>ipsec
netsh ipsec>static
netsh ipsec static>
```

Static mode allows you to create, modify, and assign policies without affecting the active IPSec policy. Dynamic mode allows you to display the active state and immediately implement changes to the active IPSec policy. Dynamic Netsh commands affect the service only when it is running. If it is stopped, dynamic policy settings are discarded.

Dynamic mode can be quite useful, for example, if you need to immediately initiate a change to IPSec processing. Although some IPSec commands require you to stop and start the IPSec service, others do not. However, Dynamic mode can also be a mixed blessing. Should you make a mistake in Dynamic mode, you will have no opportunity to discover it before implementing the change. You could end up creating an incorrect configuration without receiving a warning.

Exam Tip This chapter will not provide detailed documentation for the dozens of Netsh commands relating to configuring and monitoring IPSec policies. For the exam, you should be familiar with the types of things you can use Netsh for. Explore the commands by reviewing the Netsh documentation in Windows Help And Support Center. However, do not feel like you need to memorize the syntax of all the Netsh commands. Even if you use Netsh to create scripts in the real world, you shouldn't waste brain cells memorizing the parameters—just refer to them as needed.

Certificate Revocation List Checking

As you learned in Chapter 7, certificate servers issue Certificate Revocation Lists (CRLs) to update clients when certificates are revoked. For a client computer to validate a certificate completely, it must check the CRL to verify that the certificate has not been revoked by the issuer. Because the standards for checking CRLs were still evolving when Windows 2000 was released, computers running Windows 2000 do not automatically check CRLs for certificates used in IPSec authentication. If you plan to use certificates for IPSec authentication and have computers running Windows 2000 on your network, you should enable CRL checking.

To enable CRL checking on computers running Windows 2000:

1. Under HKEY_LOCAL_MACHINE\System\CurrentControlSet\Services\PolicyAgent\, add a key named Oakley.
2. Inside the new Oakley key, add a DWORD entry named StrongCrlCheck.
3. Assign the StrongCrlCheck entry any value from 0 through 2, where:
   - A value of 0 disables CRL checking (default for Windows 2000).
   - A value of 1 causes CRL checking to be attempted and certificate validation to fail only if the certificate is revoked (default for Windows XP Professional and Windows Server 2003). Other failures that are encountered during CRL checking (such as the revocation URL being unreachable) do not cause certificate validation to fail.
   - A value of 2 enables strong CRL checking, which means that CRL checking is required and that certificate validation fails if any error is encountered during CRL processing. Set this registry value for enhanced security.
4. Open a command prompt, run the command **net stop policyagent**, and then type **net start policyagent** to restart the IPSec-related services.

Windows XP Professional and Windows Server 2003 do automatically check CRLs when authenticating IPSec connections. However, you might want to disable this behavior if you identify CRL checking as the cause of a problem. To disable CRL checking, open a command prompt and run the following command:

netsh ipsec dynamic set config strongcrlcheck 0

Security Alert IPSec CRL checking does not guarantee that certificate validation fails immediately when a certificate is revoked. There is a delay between the time when the revoked certificate is placed on an updated and published CRL and the time when the computer that performs the IPSec CRL checking retrieves this CRL. The computer does not retrieve a new CRL until the current CRL has expired or until the next time the CRL is published. For more information about CRLs, refer to Chapter 7.

Practice: Configuring IP Security Policies

In this practice, you will configure two types of IP security policies: one for packet filtering and one for authentication and data integrity.

Exercise 1: Configure Packet Filtering

In this exercise, you will configure packet filtering on Computer1 to allow all traffic from the 192.168.1.0 network, but to allow only Web requests from other networks. First, you will create two IP filter lists to identify internal traffic and Web traffic from any network.

1. Log on to the cohowinery.com domain on Computer1 using the Administrator account.
2. Open a blank Microsoft Management Console (MMC) console, and then add the IP Security Policy Management snap-in. When prompted to select the computer or domain, select Local Computer.
3. Right-click IP Security Policies On Local Computer, and then click Manage IP Filter Lists And Filter Actions.
4. Click the Manage IP Filter Lists tab, and then click Add.
5. In the Name field, type **External Web Traffic**.
6. Click Add.

   The IP Filter Wizard appears.
7. Click Next, and then click Next again.
8. On the IP Traffic Source page, click the Source Address list, and then click Any IP Address. Click Next.

9. On the IP Traffic Destination page, select My IP Address, and then click Next.
10. On the IP Protocol Type page, click the Select A Protocol Type list, and then click TCP. Click Next.
11. On the IP Protocol Port page, click To This Port, and then type **80**, as shown in Figure 8.10. Click Next.

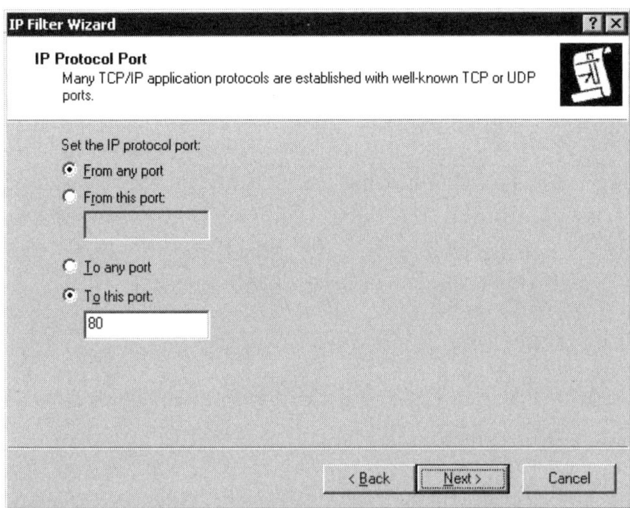

Figure 8.10 Configuring an IP filter list for Web traffic

12. Click Finish, and then click OK.
13. In the Manage IP Filter Lists And Filter Actions dialog box, click Add.
14. In the Name field, type **Internal Traffic**. Click Add.

    The IP Filter Wizard appears.
15. Click Next, and then click Next again.
16. On the IP Traffic Source page, click the Source Address list, and then click A Specific IP Subnet. Type the IP address and subnet mask in the provided fields. For example, if you are using the class C 192.168.1.0 private network, type **192.168.1.0** in the IP Address field, and then type **255.255.255.0** in the Subnet Mask field. Click Next.
17. On the IP Traffic Destination page, select My IP Address, and then click Next.
18. On the IP Protocol Type page, click the Select A Protocol Type list, and then click Any. Click Next.
19. Click Finish, and then click OK.

Next, you will create a filter action to drop traffic:

1. In the Manage IP Filter Lists And Filter Actions dialog box, click the Manage Filter Actions tab. Click Add.

   The IP Security Filter Action Wizard appears.
2. Click Next.
3. On the Filter Action Name page, type **Deny** in the Name field. Click Next.
4. On the Filter Action General Options page, click Block. Click Next.
5. Click Finish, and then click Close.

At this point, you have added an IP filter list and a filter action. However, this does not change the behavior of Computer1. To change the behavior, you must configure an IP security policy. In the IP security policy, you will add three rules to permit internal traffic, to permit external Web traffic, and to block all other traffic.

First, create the security policy:

1. Right-click IP Security Policies On Local Computer, and then click Create IP Security Policy.

   The IP Security Policy Wizard appears.
2. Click Next.
3. On the IP Security Policy Name page, type **Packet Filtering** in the Name field. Click Next.
4. On the Requests For Secure Communication page, clear the Activate The Default Response Rule check box, and then click Next.
5. Leave the Edit Properties check box selected, and then click Finish.

Next, create the first rule to permit all internal traffic:

1. In the Packet Filtering Properties dialog box, click Add.
2. The Create IP Security Rule Wizard appears.
3. Click Next three times.
4. On the IP Filter List page, click Internal Traffic, and then click Next.
5. On the Filter Action page, click Permit. Click Next.
6. Clear the Edit Properties check box, and then click Finish.

Next, create the second rule to permit external Web traffic:

1. In the Packet Filtering Properties dialog box, click Add.

   The Create IP Security Rule Wizard appears.

2. Click Next three times.
3. On the IP Filter List page, click External Web Traffic. Click Next.
4. On the Filter Action page, click Permit. Click Next.
5. Clear the Edit Properties check box, and then click Finish.

Next, add the last rule to block all other traffic. Unlike most firewalls, IPSec doesn't drop traffic by default. Therefore, you needed to explicitly create a rule to drop traffic that was not explicitly permitted.

1. In the Packet Filtering Properties page, click Add.

   The Create IP Security wizard appears.

2. Click Next three times.
3. On the IP Filter List page, click All IP Traffic, and then click Next.
4. On the Filter Action page, click Deny. Click Next.
5. Clear the Edit Properties check box, and then click Finish.
6. Click OK.

There's one last step: assigning the policy. Right-click Packet Filtering in the right pane of the IP Security Policies snap-in, and then click Assign. The policy will immediately take effect, and traffic from external networks not destined for port 80 will be dropped.

Exercise 2: Enable Encryption and Integrity Verification

In this exercise, you will configure Computer1 and Computer2 to use IPSec for encryption and integrity verification, without interfering with communications from other computers.

1. If necessary, log on to the cohowinery.com domain on Computer1 using the Administrator account and open a blank MMC console, and then add the IP Security Policy Management snap-in. When prompted to select the computer or domain, select Local Computer.
2. In the right pane, right-click Server (Request Security), and then click Assign.

3. Log on to the cohowinery.com domain on Computer2 using the Administrator account.
4. Open a blank MMC console, and then add the IP Security Policy Management snap-in. When prompted to select the computer or domain, select Local Computer.
5. Right-click Client (Respond Only), and then click Assign.

   Now all communications between Computer1 and Computer2 will be encrypted and authenticated. Because they are members of the same domain, the default Kerberos authentication protocol configured on the client (Respond Only) and server (Request Security) will successfully authenticate.

Lesson Review

The following questions are intended to reinforce key information presented in this lesson. If you are unable to answer a question, review the lesson materials and try the question again. You can find answers to the questions in the "Questions and Answers" section at the end of this chapter.

1. Which of the following check boxes, when selected, will result in a performance degradation? (Choose all that apply.)
   - **a.** Master Key Perfect Forward Secrecy (PFS)
   - **b.** Use Session Key Perfect Forward Secrecy (PFS)
   - **c.** Accept Unsecured Communication, But Always Respond Using IPSec
   - **d.** Allow Unsecured Communication With Non-IPSec-Aware Computers

   ____

2. Which of the following command-line tools can be used to configure IPSec? (Choose all that apply.)
   - **a.** Netstat
   - **b.** Net
   - **c.** Netsh
   - **d.** Ipseccmd
   - **e.** Ipconfig
   - **f.** Ipsecpol

   ____

Lesson Summary

- IP filters, IP filter lists, filter actions, and rules define an IP security policy.
- Windows Server 2003 IP filters can be dynamic, being defined by IPSec based on the host's network configuration information. Dynamic IP filter lists can be created by using the IP addresses of DNS servers, DHCP servers, WINS servers, and the default gateway.
- IP security policies can be defined on the local computer by using the IP Security Policy Management snap-in. To configure policy for an entire domain, use Group Policy Object Editor.
- IP security policies can also be configured from the command line by using Netsh.
- If you use public key certificates to authenticate IPSec sessions, you should configure Windows 2000 to check CRLs. Windows XP and Windows Server 2003 automatically check CRLs.

Case Scenario Exercise

In this exercise, you will read a scenario about a company's challenge to minimize the risk of confidential data falling into the wrong hands while staying within an extremely limited security budget. The questions are intended to reinforce key information presented in this chapter. If you are unable to answer a question, review the lessons and try the question again. You can find answers to the questions in the "Questions and Answers" section at the end of this chapter.

Scenario

You are an administrator for Contoso, Ltd. Your company is in the mergers and acquisitions business, working closely with public corporations before major business deals. During the process of a merger, Contoso, Ltd., exchanges hundreds of confidential documents with your customer's executive and legal teams. Currently, when confidential documents are exchanged between Contoso, Ltd., and its customers, they must be printed and physically delivered because Contoso, Ltd.'s Chief Information Officer (CIO) is not comfortable allowing your customers to retrieve them from the file servers on which the master copies of the documents are stored. After all, allowing electronic access to your file servers from other networks could open the file server to attack. Many people could profit from advance knowledge of a merger, and profit is a powerful motivator to a skilled attacker.

Unfortunately, the cost of having the paperwork delivered is cutting into your company's profits. Even worse, waiting for the documents to be delivered overnight adds several weeks to the length of the merger process. If you can find a way to provide for secure communications with your external partners and make the CIO comfortable with using electronic communications, you would save your company millions of dollars.

Contoso, Ltd., has offices in New York, Boston, and San Jose. The three offices are networked by means of private links that connect to a switched frame relay network. Additionally, each office has an Internet connection to enable employees to do research by using Internet resources. Many of Contoso, Ltd.'s 300 employees have to travel to customer offices on a regular basis and dial in to Contoso, Ltd.'s bank of modems for access to the internal network. All computers are members of a single Active Directory domain.

Questions

1. Your CIO's main concern is reducing the length of the merger process by allowing customers to retrieve documents electronically from your file servers. How would you propose that this be accomplished?

2. How can you use IPSec to reduce the costs of the private links between the three offices?

3. How can you use IPSec to reduce the costs of maintaining the dial-up modem bank and the long distance costs associated with remote employees dialing in?

____

____

____

____

____

____

4. How can you use IPSec to improve the security of communications on the internal network?

____

____

____

Troubleshooting Lab

In this lab, you will troubleshoot a problem related to monitoring Computer2 by using ICMP. Read the following scenario and then answer the questions that follow. The questions are intended to reinforce key information presented in this chapter. If you are unable to answer a question, review the lessons and try the question again. You can find answers to the questions in the "Questions and Answers" section at the end of this chapter.

Scenario

You use Computer1 to monitor whether Computer2 is available on the network by using ping. You receive a notification that Computer2 is offline. You investigate and discover that Computer2 is definitely online but is not responding to ping requests. Recently, another administrator was using Computer2 to practice for a certification exam. It is possible that the other administrator's configuration changes caused Computer2 to stop responding to ping requests.

To simulate the administrator's changes, run the batch file named ch8-computer2.bat, which is included in this book's companion materials.

Questions

1. Why is Computer2 not responding to ping requests from Computer1?

2. How should you resolve the problem?

3. What else could have caused the problem?

Chapter Summary

- Use IPSec in transport mode to protect communications between two IPSec-enabled computers. Use IPSec in tunnel mode when protecting communications to an entire network.
- Main Mode IKE negotiations occur at the beginning of a session. Quick Mode negotiations occur immediately after Main Mode negotiations complete, and then recur on a regular basis while the session is active.
- You can choose to use either the AH or ESP protocol with IPSec. You will usually use ESP, because ESP provides encryption and is compatible with NAT-T. Use AH only when you specifically do not want to encrypt traffic.
- IPSec can be used to provide packet filtering for Windows systems. It compliments ICF by providing filtering based on source or destination IP addresses.
- You should use GPOs to deploy IPSec whenever practical. However, you should limit access to modify the IPSec policies to the smallest number of administrators possible to reduce the opportunity for both human error and abuse.

- Use Kerberos authentication when all IPSec peers are members of a trusted Active Directory forest. Use public key certificates for IPSec authentication when Active Directory does not exist, or when some computers are external to your organization. Use preshared key authentication only when neither Kerberos nor public key certificates can be used to authenticate IPSec connections.
- Windows Server 2003 IP filters can be dynamic, being defined by IPSec based on the host's network configuration information. Dynamic IP filter lists can be created by using the IP addresses of DNS servers, DHCP servers, WINS servers, and the default gateway.
- IP security policies can be defined on the local computer by using the IP Security Policy Management snap-in. To configure policy for an entire domain, use Group Policy Object Editor. For scripting purposes, IP security policies can also be configured from the command line by using Netsh.
- If you use public key certificates to authenticate IPSec sessions, you should configure Windows 2000 to check CRLs. Windows XP and Windows Server 2003 automatically check CRLs.

Exam Highlights

Before taking the exam, review the key topics and terms that are presented in this chapter. You need to know this information.

Key Topics

- Be able to explain how IPSec determines what traffic to act on, and be able to describe the process IPSec uses when negotiating encryption and authentication protocols.
- List IPSec's various functional modes and the situations in which each mode should be used.
- List the various authentication methods IPSec can use and the situations in which each should be chosen.
- Be able to configure IP security policies on a local computer.
- Understand what planning needs to be done before deploying IPSec to an enterprise, including integrating IPSec management with Active Directory and testing existing applications.

Key Terms

IP filter list A series of IP filters that IP security policies use to identify traffic that should be ignored or acted upon.

filter action Configuration settings that specify the behavior that an IP security policy takes on filtered traffic.

Quick Mode Phase 2 of the IPSec negotiation process. Quick Mode negotiation occurs after Main Mode negotiation to establish a session key to be used for encryption until the next Quick Mode negotiation is scheduled to occur.

Main Mode Phase 1 of the IPSec negotiation process. Main mode negotiation selects a protection suite that both the client and server support, authenticates the computers, and then establishes the master key for the IPSec session.

Transport Mode An IPSec mode wherein only a portion of the packet, including the Transport and Application layer data, is encapsulated by IPSec. Used to provide IPSec protection for communications between two hosts.

Tunnel Mode An IPSec mode wherein IPSec encapsulates entire packets. Used to provide IPSec protection for communications to a network with multiple hosts.

Authentication Header (AH) An IPSec protocol that provides authentication and data integrity but does not provide encryption.

Encapsulating Security Payload (ESP) An IPSec protocol that provides authentication, data integrity, and encryption.

Questions and Answers

Lesson 1 Review

Page 8-15

1. By default, how often does IPSec regenerate Main Mode keys?
   a. Every hour
   b. Every 4 hours
   c. Every 8 hours
   d. Every 24 hours
   e. Weekly

   c. Main Mode generates a new key every 480 minutes by default, which is equal to 8 hours.

2. Which mode would you use to protect communications between two private networks connected by the Internet?
   a. Transport mode
   b. Tunnel mode

   b. You must use tunnel mode to connect two networks.

3. Which mode would you use to protect communications between an IPSec-enabled e-mail client and an e-mail server on a private network?
   a. Transport mode
   b. Tunnel mode

   a. While you could theoretically use tunnel mode, you should always use transport mode to protect communications between two hosts that can directly communicate with IPSec.

4. Which of the following IPSec protocols provides encryption for network communications?
   a. AH
   b. ESP
   c. SA
   d. IKE
   e. ISAKMP

   b. Only ESP provides encryption for IPSec communications.

Lesson 2 Review

Page 8-22

1. You are an administrator at an organization that uses Windows Server 2003 Active Directory. Which IPSec authentication method should you recommend for authenticating internal clients to an intranet Web server?

   a. Kerberos authentication

   b. Public key certificates authentication

   c. Preshared key authentication

   a. Kerberos authentication is the correct choice for authenticating internal computers when Active Directory is used.

2. You need to grant employees at an external partner company access to an application server, but you want to ensure that the communications are authenticated and encrypted. Which IPSec authentication method should you recommend?

   a. Kerberos authentication

   b. Public key certificates authentication

   c. Preshared key authentication

   b. Public key certificates issued from an external root CA enable IPSec to authenticate external computers.

Lesson 3 Review

Page 8-38

1. Which of the following check boxes, when selected, will result in a performance degradation? (Choose all that apply.)

   a. Master Key Perfect Forward Secrecy (PFS)

   b. Use Session Key Perfect Forward Secrecy (PFS)

   c. Accept Unsecured Communication, But Always Respond Using IPSec

   d. Allow Unsecured Communication With Non-IPSec-Aware Computers

   a and b. PFS, whether enabled for the master key or the session key, has the potential to degrade performance. Because session keys are negotiated more frequently, the performance impact is more significant.

2. Which of the following command-line tools can be used to configure IPSec? (Choose all that apply.)

   a. Netstat

   b. Net

   c. Netsh

   d. Ipseccmd

e. Ipconfig

f. Ipsecpol

c, e, and f. Netsh is used to configure IPSec on Windows Server 2003. Ipseccmd configures IPSec on Windows XP, and Ipsecpol can be used to configure Windows 2000.

Design Activity: Case Scenario Exercise

Page 8-40

1. Your CIO's main concern is reducing the length of the merger process by allowing customers to retrieve documents electronically from your file servers. How would you propose that this be accomplished?

   There are several ways to accomplish this. One way would be to connect your file servers to the public Internet and then configure IPSec policies for each of your customers. The IPSec policy could authenticate the customers using public key certificates issued by a third-party CA. If you used the ESP protocol, IPSec would also encrypt all network communications. Additionally, you could use the IPSec policy to implement packet filtering to restrict the file server from processing network traffic not originating from your customer's network or your internal network.

   Other than using IPSec, you could suggest using digital rights management (DRM). Microsoft Office 2003 and the Rights Management Services add-on to Windows Server 2003 encrypt Office documents and enable the document owners to specify granular permissions to documents. DRM would protect documents even after they left your network, restricting whether customers could forward, print, or even copy and paste a document's contents.

2. How can you use IPSec to reduce the costs of the private links between the three offices?

   IPSec in tunnel mode can be used to connect the three offices across the Internet. Ultimately, if testing and a pilot project proved successful, the private links could be eliminated completely. Testing is critical, however, because IPSec tunnels between offices will not perform as well as the existing private links. Additionally, the reliability might not meet Contoso, Ltd.'s needs.

3. How can you use IPSec to reduce the costs of maintaining the dial-up modem bank and the long distance costs associated with remote employees dialing in?

   If you configure an IPSec gateway on your network, you can apply IPSec policy to Contoso, Ltd.'s mobile computers so that they access the private network across an IPSec tunnel mode VPN. This provides a level of privacy that is similar to that of a dial-up link and, depending on the type of Internet access the remote employees have, might actually improve their performance. Employees who do not have access to the Internet through a customer's network can still dial in to a local ISP, eliminating the long distances charges.

4. How can you use IPSec to improve the security of communications on the internal network?

   Most communications on the internal network can be protected with IPSec. This can provide data integrity validation, authentication, and encryption. Because you are using an Active Directory domain, you can use Kerberos authentication.

Design Activity: Troubleshooting Lab

Page 8-42

1. Why is Computer2 not responding to ping requests from Computer1?

   Computer2 has an IPSec policy named TestFilter configured. This policy has a single active rule that uses the built-in IP filter list named All ICMP Traffic and a filter action named DropPacket that the other administrator must have created. This rule results in all ICMP traffic being dropped.

2. How should you resolve the problem?

   The simplest way to resolve the problem is to open the IP Security Policy Management snap-in, right-click the TestFilter policy, and then click Un-Assign. After you do this, Computer1 will immediately begin responding to ping requests.

3. What else could have caused the problem?

   If the same IPSec policy had been applied to Computer1, the results would have been the same because the TestFilter policy would drop ICMP traffic whether it was being sent or received. Also, ICF could have been configured on Computer2 to drop ICMP traffic.

9 Deploying and Troubleshooting IPSec

Exam Objectives in this Chapter:

- Deploy and manage Internet Protocol Security (IPSec) policies.
    - Deploy IPSec policies by using local policy objects or Group Policy objects (GPOs).
    - Deploy IPSec policies by using commands and scripts. Tools include IPSecPol and Netsh.
    - Deploy IPSec certificates. Considerations include deployment of certificates and renewing certificates on managed and unmanaged client computers.
- Troubleshoot IPSec.
    - Monitor IPSec policies by using IP Security Monitor.
    - Configure IPSec logging. Considerations include Oakley logs and IPSec driver logging.
    - Troubleshoot IPSec across networks. Considerations include network address translation, port filters, protocol filters, firewalls, and routers.
    - Troubleshoot IPSec certificates. Considerations include enterprise trust policies and certificate revocation list (CRL) checking.

Why This Chapter Matters

Configuring IPSec on individual computers is straightforward. However, for an IPSec implementation to be successful in a large organization, IPSec policies must be deployed to all computers in the organization. The Active Directory directory service makes deploying IPSec much easier than it would be otherwise, but not all client computers will participate in a trusted domain. To successfully deploy IPSec in the real world, you must understand the various methods used for deploying IPSec and the circumstances in which to use each method.

After IPSec is deployed, you must be able to monitor and troubleshoot IPSec. IPSec requires specialized tools and skills for monitoring and troubleshooting because, by its very nature, it makes network communications next-to-impossible to interpret. Monitoring IPSec is necessary to confirm that IPSec has been successfully deployed and is actively protecting communications. Monitoring is also an important technique for isolating problems that occur during IPSec negotiations.

This chapter describes the various ways to deploy, monitor, and troubleshoot IPSec. The exercises and troubleshooting lab in this chapter will give you the hands-on experience you need to understand IPSec both for the exam and in production environments.

Lessons in this Chapter:

Before You Begin

If you fulfilled the requirements for the previous chapters, you already have the necessary hardware and software configured. You can use the computers in the state they were in after completing the previous chapters, or you can install the software from scratch. To do the practices, examples, and lab exercises in this chapter, you must have:

- A private network that is connected to the Internet and protected by a firewall. This network should not have any production computers connected to it.
- Two computers. Perform a Microsoft Windows Server 2003 installation with default settings, and assign the computer name Computer1. Add the Domain Controller role to the computer, using the default settings, and specify the domain name cohowinery.com. Configure the computer to use itself as its own primary Domain Name System (DNS) server. Then add the Application Server role with the default settings. On the second computer, perform a Windows Server 2003 installation with default settings, and assign the computer name Computer2. Configure the computer to use Computer1 as its primary DNS server. Then join Computer2 to the cohowinery.com domain as a member server.

Lesson 1: Deploying IPSec

Chapter 8 described how to configure IPSec on individual computers. This is sufficient for testing IPSec in your lab environment, but it is impossible to manually configure every computer in a large enterprise. Fortunately, IPSec can be deployed by using Active Directory Group Policy objects (GPOs), much like most other security settings. Alternatively, you can configure IPSec by using batch files and three different IPSec command-line utilities. This provides you with the flexibility to use IPSec on computers that do not participate in a domain or on computers that are members of domains that you do not manage.

Chapter 8 also described how to configure IPSec to use certificates for authentication. While that aspect of configuring certificates-based authentication is simple, actually deploying Windows Server 2003 Certificate Services for IPSec is much more complex. This lesson will list important factors to consider when deploying certificates for IPSec authentication. Additionally, this lesson provides an exercise that guides you through the process of configuring Certificate Services and actually establishing an IPSec session authenticated by certificates to prepare you for deploying such an environment in the real world.

After this lesson, you will be able to

- Describe the various methods for deploying IPSec policies to multiple computers.
- List the steps necessary to deploy IPSec policies by using Active Directory.
- List the tools used for configuring IPSec at the command line and describe the circumstances in which you use each.
- Configure Certificate Services to issue certificates that can be used to authenticate IPSec peers.

Estimated lesson time: 55 minutes

Deploying IPSec by Using Active Directory

If your organization has an Active Directory domain, you should almost always use Active Directory to deploy IPSec. The primary tool for building IPSec policies is the graphical user interface provided by the IP Security Policy Management snap-in. You can use the IP Security Policy Management snap-in to create, modify, and activate IPSec policies, and then assign them to a domain, site, or organizational unit (OU) in Active Directory by using the Group Policy Object Editor snap-in.

Tip To tightly control IPSec policy management, you can dedicate one computer to configure local IPSec policy and then use the IP Security Policy Management Export Policies and Import Policies menu commands to back up and restore IPSec policy. After you create an IPSec policy, use a version control system to track changes to the policy during the development, testing, and deployment phases.

If you decide to deploy IPSec policies by using GPOs, you must understand how IPSec policies differ from other types of security settings. Most settings in a security template can be combined by importing them into a single GPO. If multiple GPOs with overlapping settings are assigned to a single computer, the computer will automatically resolve any conflicting settings. Because multiple security templates and sets of Group Policy settings can be applied to a single computer, role-based security templates work perfectly when a computer serves multiple roles.

Security Alert IPSec policies can be protected just like any other object. Local IPSec policies are stored in the registry under HKEY_LOCAL_MACHINE\Software\Policies\Microsoft\Windows\IPSec\. Active Directory–based IPSec policies are stored in CN=IP Security, CN=System,DC=*domainname*,DC=*topleveldomain*. However, you must keep in mind that local administrators will have Read access to an assigned IPSec policy after it is cached in the local registry. Accordingly, there is no effective way to provide highly restricted Read access to an Active Directory–based IPSec policy.

Only one IPSec policy can be applied to any single computer. If multiple GPOs assign multiple IP security policies to a computer, only the GPO with the highest precedence will be applied. IPSec policy uses the same precedence sequence as other Group Policy settings, which is from lowest to highest: Local GPO, site, domain, OU.

For example, if you create a security policy for Web servers that uses certificates for authentication, and you create another policy for internal servers that uses Kerberos, you cannot assign both policies to a single computer by using multiple GPOs. Instead, one policy will override the other policies. If you attempt to assign an IPSec policy to the local computer and a policy has been assigned to the computer by using a GPO at the domain level, the IP Security Policy Management snap-in will alert you with the message "Policy is assigned, but it is being overridden by Active Directory–assigned policy," as shown in Figure 9.1.

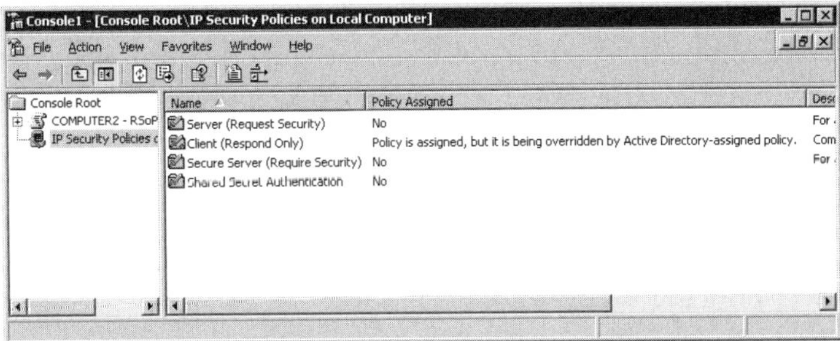

Figure 9.1 Local IPSec policy overridden by a domain policy

See Also As with other GPO settings, you can use Resultant Set of Policy (RSoP) to determine which IPSec policy is effective. For more information about GPOs and RSoP, refer to Chapter 3.

As a result, you should create as few different IPSec policies as possible. Fortunately, you can use IP filters to create complex IP security policies that contain different settings for different computer roles. For example, if your organization requires internal file servers to use Kerberos IPSec authentication and external mail servers to use certificate-based IPSec authentication, you can create a single IPSec policy with rules that negotiate Kerberos authentication for requests from internal clients and certificates authentication for requests from external clients. Alternatively, you could separate the file server and mail server roles onto separate physical computers: apply an IPSec policy requiring Kerberos authentication to the file server, and apply a different IPSec policy requiring certificates-based authentication to the mail server.

Neither of these two solutions is perfect. Separating the roles onto physically separate computers requires additional server hardware and systems administration effort. Using IP filters to create rules that apply different filter actions based on the source IP address does not accommodate the possibility that users can access the file server from an external IP address or attempt to communicate with the mail server from an internal IP address. You could theoretically create IP filters based on the port numbers used by file sharing and messaging protocols, but client computers would only be able to connect to the server as either a file server or a mail server—not as both.

Off the Record There's one way to use multiple security policies on a single computer: by using virtual machines. I use virtual machines extensively to run multiple instances of different operating systems on a single computer simultaneously. Enterprises often use virtual machines in servers to avoid conflicts between server applications, such as the limitation of having a single IPSec policy applied to a computer. I use Microsoft Virtual PC 2004. You can find information about this software at *http://www.microsoft.com/virtualpc/*.

When designing IPSec policies for your organization, follow one guideline before all others: keep it simple. Although you might want to provide different levels of security for different computers, use as few policies as possible to minimize the complexity of your system. A simpler system is less likely to produce problems and is also easier to troubleshoot if it does. You can further simplify the process of deploying IPSec by using the built-in policies: Client, Request Security, and Require Security. These policies have been configured to provide the maximum level of compatibility possible without significantly sacrificing security.

There is a significant limitation to using IPSec to protect communications within a domain: you should not use IPSec and Kerberos authentication between domain members and domain controllers. Establishing an IPSec connection requires sending a request to a domain controller, but if that request requires an IPSec connection to be established, you will never be able to complete the Internet Key Exchange (IKE) negotiation. In addition, no other authenticated connections can be made using other protocols, and no other IPSec policy settings can be applied to that domain member through Group Policy. For these reasons, Microsoft does not support using IPSec for communications between domain members and domain controllers.

There are additional limitations when using IPSec to protect traffic to a cluster. Many clustering and load-balancing services use the same IP address for all nodes in a cluster, which creates incompatibilities with IPSec. Windows Server 2003 IPSec has proprietary extensions that allow it to work with the Windows Server 2003 Network Load Balancing service and Windows Cluster Service. However, support for these extensions does not exist in the current Microsoft Windows 2000 and Windows XP IPSec client implementations, so you will experience some loss of connectivity when you add or remove Windows 2000 cluster nodes.

Deploying IPSec Using Scripts

If a computer is not a member of a Windows 2000 domain or a Windows Server 2003 domain, it cannot retrieve IPSec policy from Active Directory. However, as Chapter 8 described, you can use the Netsh, Ipseccmd.exe, and Ipsecpol.exe command-line tools to create IPSec scripts. You can then include these scripts as startup scripts for each computer on your network. You can use Ipsecpol.exe only on computers running Windows 2000, Ipseccmd.exe only on computers running Windows XP, and the Netsh commands for IPSec only on computers running Windows Server 2003.

Although having three separate scripting tools for the three operating systems makes managing a typical network challenging, the three tools are similar in functionality. Although the exact parameters vary, each tool provides separate static and dynamic configuration modes and the ability to display existing IPSec configuration information. For each tool, the dynamic configuration mode changes the currently running IPSec settings, although static configuration mode changes the persistent configuration. In other words, dynamic configuration changes are lost after you restart your computer, but static configuration changes will remain.

Real World Scripting IPSec Policies

Avoid scripting IPSec policies at all costs. I would make a different recommendation if Microsoft provided a single command-line interface that worked for all Windows operating systems, but, for now, it's just not worth the trouble.

Every organization I've worked with has to support several versions of Windows. So, if you want to script IPSec policies for your entire organization, you'll need to either create separate scripts for Windows Server 2003, Windows XP, and Windows 2000, or create a single complex script that contains commands for each of the scripting tools.

I'm glad Microsoft integrated IPSec functionality into Netsh, but I wish Microsoft would provide a single scripting interface for all supported Windows platforms. Scripting IPSec would be much more practical if the Netsh IPSec extensions were available for previous versions of Windows (perhaps in a feature pack), or if Windows Server 2003 were backwards-compatible with IPSecCmd and IPSecPol. Help, Microsoft!

In the meantime, if you must use IPSec scripting with Active Directory, you'll have to create separate GPOs for each version of Windows and use Windows Management Instrumentation (WMI) filtering to deploy separate logon scripts to different platforms. Or you could create a single script that incorporates each of the three different IPSec scripting tools. That script would look something like this:

```
Netsh IPSec static add …
Netsh IPSec static add …
Netsh IPSec static add …
IPSecCmd …
IPSecPol …
```

Sure, several of the commands won't work on any given version of Windows, but Windows will simply show an error that you can ignore. Besides being sloppy, the biggest drawback to this approach is that it's error prone. You have to know three separate scripting tools, and every time you make a change to IPSec policy, you need to update the commands for each of the tools.

Netsh

To script the creation of IPSec policy on computers running Windows Server 2003, use the Netsh IPSec commands. There are two ways to do this: use the `Netsh ipsec static` add command to add IP filters, rules, and IPSec policies, or use the `Netsh ipsec static importpolicy` command to import a saved IPSec policy.

Note Windows 2000 and Windows XP also include Netsh; however, they lack the IPSec extensions.

The simplest way to populate a list of IP security policies on a computer using a script is, ironically, to use a graphical tool. First, create the policies using the IP Security Policy Management snap-in. Then export the policies to a file. Finally, create a script that imports the policies on the destination Windows Server 2003–based computers by using the Netsh command-line tool. In this way, you can centrally manage the IPSec policies in your organization by exporting policies used by all computers to a central file server. Then distribute startup scripts that import the IP security policies, and assign one of the policies. Exercise 2 at the end of this lesson takes you through the process of exporting an IPSec policy and then importing it by using Netsh.

You can also create IPSec policies directly from the command line, without ever relying on graphical tools. The `Netsh ipsec static add filteraction` command can be used to create new filter actions. The `Netsh ipsec static add filter` and `Netsh ipsec static add filterlist` commands are used to create IP filters and IP filter lists. The `Netsh ipsec static add policy` command creates new policies, which can be immediately assigned. Finally, use the `Netsh ipsec static add rule` command to add rules to a policy by specifying IP filter lists and filter actions.

Tip The Netsh command has a very complicated set of parameters. For a detailed list of parameters, run any of the commands without any parameters. For example, to view the syntax for adding a rule by using Netsh, open a command prompt and run `Netsh ipsec static add rule`.

The following Netsh script creates a new policy. The first line creates and assigns a policy named TestPolicy. Assigning the policy automatically un-assigns any other IPSec policies. The second line adds a filter action named DropPacket with the Block action. The third line adds a rule named NoICMP to the new TestFilter IPSec policy. The NoICMP rule is created by using the built-in IP filter list All ICMP Traffic and the newly created rule named Drop Packet.

```
netsh ipsec static add policy name=TestPolicy assign=yes activatedefaultrule=no
netsh ipsec static add filteraction name=DropPacket action=block
netsh ipsec static add rule name=NoICMP policy=TestPolicy filterlist="All ICMP Traffic
" filteraction=DropPacket
```

IPSecCmd

I used the command `netsh ipsec static add policy` to create the batch file to configure and assign IPSec policy for the troubleshooting lab in Chapter 8. To script the creation of local or Active Directory–based IPSec policy on computers running Windows XP, you can use Ipseccmd.exe, a Windows Support Tool that is included in the Support Tools folder of the Windows XP operating system disc. To install IPSecCmd, you must perform a complete installation of the Support Tools. A normal installation does not install the IPSecCmd tool.

The syntax for IPSecCmd is complex. Creating scripts by using IPSecCmd is challenging even for people experienced with scripting, and the resulting scripts are difficult to maintain. Whenever you create a script, you need to plan for someone else to maintain that script in the event that you leave the organization. Because of IPSecCmd's confusing syntax, administrators who take over the maintenance of your script will certainly have a difficult time updating the scripts. For these reasons, you should avoid using IPSecCmd except when absolutely necessary.

IPSecCmd uses a syntax similar to that of IPSecPol but very different from that of Netsh. While Netsh uses separate commands to create IP filters, rules, filter actions, and policies, IPSecCmd can create each of these components of an IPSec policy with a single command. For example, to create and assign a local policy named TestPolicy, with a rule named SecureTraffic, using a mirrored filter for any traffic to the local computer and a preshared key as the authentication method, run the following command:

```
ipseccmd -f 0+* -a p:"localauth" -w reg -p TestPolicy -r "SecureTraffic" -x
```

Tip For detailed information about using IPSecCmd, open a command prompt and run `Ipseccmd -? | more`.

IPSecPol

To script the creation of local or Active Directory–based IPSec policy on computers running Windows 2000, you can use Ipsecpol.exe, a command-line tool that is provided with the Windows 2000 Server Resource Kit. Ipsecpol.exe is not a full-featured command-line or scripting tool (for example, you cannot use Ipsecpol.exe to delete or rename filter lists or filter actions), nor is it supported under any Microsoft standard support program or service.

IPSecPol, thankfully, uses syntax that is very similar to that of IPSecCmd because IPSecCmd evolved from IPSecPol. In fact, most of the time you only need to change the name of the command when deploying a script to computers running both Windows 2000 and Windows XP. For example, to create and assign a local policy named TestPolicy, with a rule named SecureTraffic, using a mirrored filter for any traffic to the local computer and a preshared key as the authentication method, run the following command:

```
ipsecpol -f 0+* -a p:"localauth" -w reg -p TestPolicy -r "SecureTraffic" -x
```

One notable difference between IPSecCmd and IPSecPol is that IPSecPol cannot be used to display information about the computer's current IPSec configuration. You can download IPSecPol from the Microsoft Web site at *http://www.microsoft.com/windows2000/techinfo/reskit/tools/existing/ipsecpol-o.asp*.

Exam Tip You should know that you must use IPSecCmd for Windows XP, IPSecPol for Windows 2000, and Netsh for Windows Server 2003. It is much more important for you to be familiar with the syntax of Netsh than with the tools used with previous versions of Windows.

Deploying Certificate Services for IPSec

Although Kerberos is the simplest way to authenticate IPSec peers, certificates provide greater flexibility for authenticating non-Windows IPSec peers and other computers that are not members of an Active Directory domain. In Windows 2000 and Windows Server 2003, you can use Certificate Services to automatically manage computer certificates for IPSec authentication. IPSec also supports the use of a variety of non-Microsoft X.509 public key infrastructure (PKI) systems. Windows Server 2003 IKE has basic compatibility with several certificate systems, including those offered by Microsoft, Entrust, VeriSign, and Netscape. If you are using a non-Microsoft PKI system, the PKI system must be able to issue certificates to computers and store their certificates in the Windows Cryptographic Application Programming Interface (CryptoAPI) computer certificate store.

See Also Chapter 7 covered Certificate Services in detail, so this chapter describes only the aspects of Certificate Services that relate directly to deploying certificates for IPSec.

IPSec's use of certificate authentication is compatible with many different PKI architectures, and IKE places relatively few requirements on the contents of a certificate. Typically, computers that have a common trusted root, or whose certificates can chain through a cross-certification trust relationship, can successfully use certificate-based authentication for IPSec. To use certificates for IPSec authentication, you define an ordered list of acceptable root certification authority (CA) names in the authentication method.

Important Certificates obtained from Certificate Services with the advanced option set for Enable strong private key protection do not work for IKE authentication because a personal identification number (PIN) cannot be entered to access the private key during IKE negotiation.

If IKE authentication fails, you cannot retry the authentication using a different method. For this reason, before you apply an IPSec policy that can use certificates for authentication, make sure that all target computers have the correct root CA certificates and valid computer certificates. Additionally, to ensure that certificate authentication works as intended, test your PKI infrastructure with various IPSec policy configurations before deployment.

In Windows Server 2003, you can enable IPSec certificate-to-account mapping, as shown in Figure 9.2. This causes IPSec to look up the peer's computer account in the Active Directory forest during certificate authentication. IPSec allows access from the peer only if the peer has a valid computer account and the account has the Access This Computer From The Network user right. This improves security because it eliminates the possibility that a computer with a valid certificate issued by your CA, but that is not a domain member, can establish an IPSec connection to a server. However, certificate-to-account mapping can only be used when all IPSec connections will come from computers in the same forest.

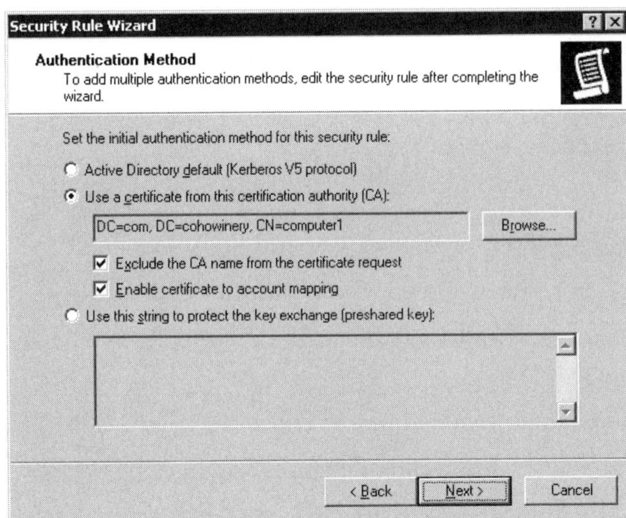

Figure 9.2 Configuring certificate-to-account mapping

If you use certificate authentication to establish trust between IPSec peers, you can configure Windows Server 2003 to exclude CA names from certificate requests. Excluding the CA name prevents a malicious user from learning sensitive information about the trust relationships of a computer, such as the name of the company that owns the computer and the domain membership of the computer (if an internal PKI is being used). Although excluding the CA name from certificate requests enhances security, computers with multiple certificates from different roots might require the CA root names to select the correct certificate. Also, some non-Microsoft IKE implementations might not respond to a certificate request that does not include a CA name. For these reasons, excluding the CA name from certificate requests might cause IKE certificate authentication to fail in certain cases.

Practice: Deploying IPSec Configurations

In this practice, you will deploy IPSec by using two methods: using an Active Directory GPO and importing a policy from the command line.

Exercise 1: Configuring Certificate Services for IPSec Authentication

In this exercise, you will configure Certificate Services to enroll IPSec certificates, enroll Computer1 and Computer2, and then deploy an IPSec policy requiring certificates authentication by using an Active Directory–based GPO.

First, install Certificate Services if it is not yet installed:

1. Log on to the cohowinery.com domain on Computer1 using the Administrator account.
2. Open Add Or Remove Programs in Control Panel.
3. Click Add/Remove Windows Components.
4. On the Windows Components page of the Windows Components Wizard, select the Certificate Services check box. When prompted, click Yes.
5. Click Next.
6. In the CA Type page, click Enterprise Root CA, and then click Next.
7. In the Common Name For This CA box, type **computer1**. Click Next.
8. On the Certificate Database Settings page, accept the defaults by clicking Next. If prompted to stop IIS, click Yes.
9. If prompted, click Yes to enable Active Server Pages.
10. After Certificate Services is installed, click Finish. Close all open windows.

Next, issue the built-in IPSec certificate template:

1. Click Start, point to Administrative Tools, and then click Certification Authority.
2. Expand Computer1. Right-click Certificate Templates, click New, and then click Certificate Template To Issue.

   The Enable Certificate Templates dialog box appears.

3. Click IPSec, and then click OK.

Next, enroll Computer1 and Computer2 by using the IPSec security template. Repeat the following process on both Computer1 and Computer2:

1. Open a blank Microsoft Management Console (MMC) console, and then add the Certificates snap-in. When prompted to select the account, select Computer Account, and then select Local Computer.
2. Expand Certificates. Right-click Personal, click All Tasks, and then click Request New Certificate.

   The Certificate Request Wizard appears.
3. Click Next. On the Certificate Types page, click IPSec.
4. Click Next twice, and then click Finish.

Next, configure an IPSec policy in the Default Domain Policy GPO that uses certificates for authentication:

1. Open a blank MMC console, and then add the Group Policy Object Editor snap-in. When prompted to select the GPO, click Browse and select the Default Domain Policy, click OK, and then click Finish.
2. Expand Default Domain Policy, Computer Configuration, Windows Settings, and Security Settings, and then click IP Security Policies On Active Directory.
3. Right-click IP Security Policies On Active Directory, and then click Create IP Security Policy.

   The IP Security Policy Wizard appears.
4. Click Next. On the IP Security Policy Name page, type **Certificate Authentication**, and then click Next.
5. On the Requests For Secure Communication page, leave Activate The Default Response Rule selected, and then click Next.
6. On the Default Response Rule Authentication Method page, click Use A Certificate From This Certification Authority.
7. Click Browse. If prompted, click Yes. Select Computer1's certificate, and then click OK.
8. Select Enable Certificate To Account Mapping. Click Next.
9. Click Finish.

   The Certification Authentication Properties dialog box appears.
10. Click Add.

    The Security Rule Wizard appears.

11. Click Next three times.
12. On the IP Filter List page, click All IP Traffic. Click Next.
13. On the Filter Action page, click Request Security (Optional). Click Next.
14. On the Authentication Method page, click Use A Certificate From This Certification Authority.
15. Click Browse. If prompted, click Yes. Select Computer1's certificate, and then click OK.
16. Select Enable Certificate To Account Mapping. Click Next.

    You should select Enable Certificate To Account Mapping here because all of the computers that will be authenticating have valid computer accounts in the same forest.
17. Click Finish.
18. On the Certificate Authentication Properties page, click OK.
19. In the Group Policy Object Editor snap-in, right-click Certificate Authentication, and then click Assign.

At this point, you have done everything you need to do to allow Computer1 and Computer2 to communicate by using IPSec authenticated by certificates. To make the new IPSec policy take effect immediately, run the command `Gpupdate /force` on both Computer1 and Computer2. Then verify that Computer1 and Computer2 can successfully establish a connection:

1. On Computer1, start Windows Explorer. On the Tools menu, click Map Network Drive. In the Folder box, type **\\computer2\c$**, and then click Finish. If prompted, provide Administrator credentials for Computer2. Browse the files on Computer2 to generate network traffic.

    The purpose of this step is simply to communicate with Computer2.
2. Open a blank MMC console, and then add the IP Security Monitor snap-in. When prompted to select the computer or domain, select Local Computer, and then click Finish.
3. Expand Computer1, and then expand Main Mode. Click Security Associations.
4. In the right-pane, double-click the Security Association (SA) created between Computer1 and Computer2.

    The Properties dialog box appears. The authentication type is listed as Certificate (RSA Signature), as shown in Figure 9.3. This verifies that IPSec authentication with certificates succeeded.

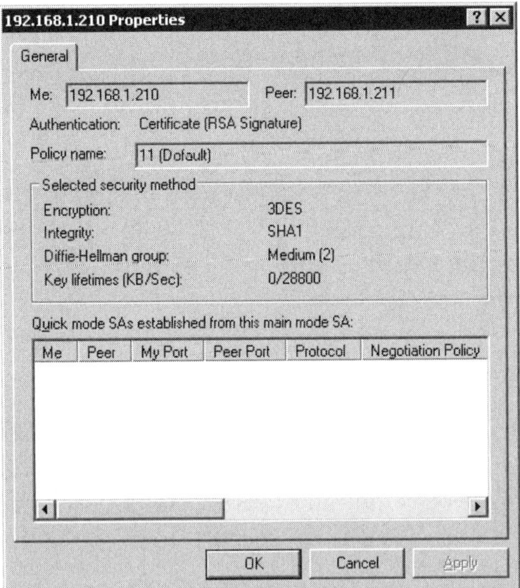

Figure 9.3 Security association authenticated with certificates

5. To prepare the computers for future exercises, return to the IP Security Policies On Active Directory snap-in, right-click Certificate Authentication, and then click Un-Assign.

Exercise 2: Importing IP Security Policies Using Netsh

In this exercise, you will export a security policy from the IP Security Policy Management snap-in. You will then import it by using Netsh to demonstrate how to import security policies by using startup scripts.

1. Log on to the cohowinery.com domain on Computer1 using the Administrator account.
2. Open a blank MMC console, and then add the IP Security Policy Management snap-in. When prompted to select the computer or domain, select Local Computer.
3. In the left pane, right-click IP Security Policies On Local Computer, click All Tasks, and then click Export Policies.
4. In the Save As dialog box, specify **C:\ipsec-policies.ipsec**
5. In the right pane, right-click Server (Request Security), and then click Delete. When prompted, click Yes.

   Deleting this policy allows you to demonstrate that the policies were successfully re-imported later.
6. Leave the MMC console open, and open a command prompt.

7. At the command prompt, run the following command:

   netsh ipsec static importpolicy C:\ipsec-policies.ipsec

8. Switch back to the MMC console, right-click IP Security Policies On Local Computer, and then click Refresh.

   The Server (Request Security) policy will reappear, demonstrating that the policies were successfully exported and then reimported. In a production environment, you would probably locate the exported file on a centralized file server and perform the input from a startup script.

Lesson Review

The following questions are intended to reinforce key information presented in this lesson. If you are unable to answer a question, review the lesson materials and try the question again. You can find answers to the questions in the "Questions and Answers" section at the end of this chapter.

1. Which of the following options ensures that certificates are accepted from only valid computer accounts in the same forest?

   a. Enable Certificate To Account Mapping

   b. Exclude The CA From The Certificate Request

   c. Use Session Key Perfect Forward Secrecy

   d. Use Master Key Perfect Forward Secrecy

   ____

2. Which of the following operating systems could you configure by using the IPSecPol command-line tool?

   a. Windows Server 2003

   b. Windows XP

   c. Windows 2000

   d. Windows 98

   ____

Lesson Summary

- The simplest way to deploy IPSec is to configure IPSec policies by using the Group Policy Object Editor and distribute the GPOs by using Active Directory.
- You can configure IPSec policies on individual computers by using command-line tools. These local policies will be overridden by domain IPSec policies if any exist, however.
- For Windows Server 2003, use Netsh to create IPSec policies from the command line. Use IPSecCmd for computers running Windows XP, and IPSecPol for computers running Windows 2000.
- If all IPSec peers are not in a trusted Active Directory domain, you can use certificates to authenticate computers. Windows Server 2003 includes Certificate Services, which can be used to issue certificates for IPSec.

Lesson 2: Monitoring IPSec

Monitoring IPSec is important for verifying that IPSec is working correctly in your organization. You will also need to closely monitor IPSec if you are having a problem implementing it or if you experience network connectivity problems that might be related to IPSec. This lesson will describe the various tools that you can use to monitor IPSec.

Tip Monitoring IPSec is also the single best way to learn how IPSec functions. If you don't feel like you fully understand IPSec, spend some time establishing IPSec connections and monitoring them by using the various tools described in this lesson.

After this lesson, you will be able to

- Describe the tools available to monitor IPSec.
- List which tools can be used to identify specific IPSec statistics.
- Capture and analyze IPSec network traffic to verify that it is being encrypted.
- Enable auditing of IPSec negotiations and dropped packets to allow for careful analysis of IPSec communications.
- Use the Performance console to gather and analyze IPSec statistics over a period of time.

Estimated lesson time: 45 minutes

IP Security Monitor Snap-In

IP Security Monitor is a Windows XP and Windows Server 2003 snap-in used to monitor and troubleshoot IPSec. If an IPSec policy is active, you can use this console to examine the policy and its operations.

Information in the IP Security Monitor snap-in is divided into three nodes: Active Policy, Main Mode, and Quick Mode. The Active Policy node, as shown in Figure 9.4, displays information about the currently assigned policy. This information includes the policy's name, last modified date, and origin. If you are unsure about how a particular policy was applied to a computer, check this node to identify the GPO that assigned the policy.

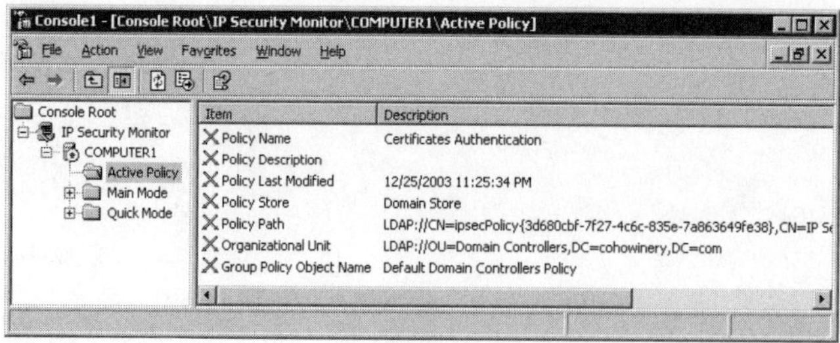

Figure 9.4 The Active Policy node of the IP Security Monitor

See Also For a description of the fundamentals of Main Mode and Quick Mode, refer to Chapter 8.

Main Mode

As you recall from Chapter 8, Main Mode negotiation is the first phase of establishing an IPSec connection. Main Mode establishes common security protocols shared by the two hosts, determines master key keying material that will be used for encrypting communications, and authenticates the computers themselves.

One of the most useful features of the IP Security Monitor snap-in is its ability to quickly view active SAs. To do this, expand Main Mode, and then click Security Associations. The right pane displays a list of active SAs, including the IP address of the IPSec peer. Double-click any SA to view the properties of the SA, as shown in Figure 9.5. The SA properties dialog box shows you the IP addresses of the two peers, the protocols used for encryption and integrity, the key lifetimes, and a list of Quick Mode SAs that were established from that Main Mode SA. The listing of Quick Mode SAs, in turn, reveals the negotiation policy used to establish each Quick Mode SA.

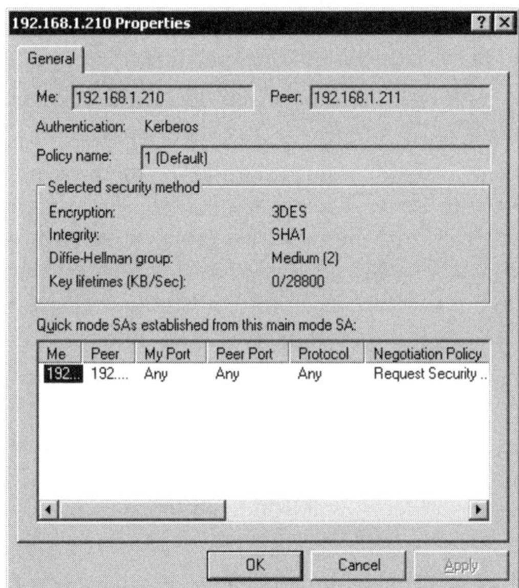

Figure 9.5 Main Mode SA details

The most important node within the Main Mode node of the IP Security Monitor is the Statistics node. The Statistics node will be your primary tool for monitoring IPSec, because it contains statistics about Phase 1 of the IPSec negotiations, including the number of active IKE negotiations and the total number of successful and unsuccessful negotiations and authentications. Table 9.1 lists the most useful Main Mode statistics.

Table 9.1 Descriptions of Main Mode Statistics Parameters

Main Mode statistic	Description
Active Acquire	The number of queued IKE negotiation requests. Typically, the number of active acquires is 1. If IPSec cannot keep pace with the number of incoming requests that require IKE negotiation, this statistic will increase by the number of requests that are queued by IKE for processing. If you are troubleshooting performance problems that occur when clients establish connections to an IPSec-enabled server, monitor this parameter to determine whether Main Mode negotiations are the cause of the problem. If this number stays consistently high, use the Performance snap-in to monitor processor utilization on the server. If processor utilization is also high, consider upgrading the server's processors or using a network card with integrated IPSec processing.
Acquire Failures	The total number of acquire outbound requests that have failed since the IPSec service was last started. It is not unusual to see this counter greater than zero when IPSec is functioning normally. However, if this number climbs, an IPSec peer is having trouble establishing a connection. You can use IKE tracing to identify the peer and the specific problem.
Receive Failures	The total number of errors that have occurred during the process of receiving IKE messages since the IPSec service was last started.
Send Failures	The total number of errors that have occurred during the process of sending IKE messages since the IPSec service was last started. The number of Send Failures typically increases for computers that establish SAs over temporary network connections, such as dial-up connections, virtual private network tunnels, and wireless connections. Therefore, it is not necessarily an indication of a problem that needs to be resolved.
Acquire Heap Size	The Active Acquire statistic measures the number of queued incoming connections; this statistic measures queued outbound connections. This number normally increases under a heavy load and then gradually decreases over time as the acquire heap is cleared. If it remains high, it is an indication that the computer is having problems establishing an IPSec connection to a remote computer.
Authentication Failures	The total number of identity authentication failures that have occurred during Main Mode negotiation since the IPSec service was last started. If you are having difficulty communicating securely, monitor this counter to determine if the problem is caused by a Main Mode negotiation failure. If it is, refer to Lesson 3 for information about troubleshooting authentication problems.

Table 9.1 Descriptions of Main Mode Statistics Parameters

Main Mode statistic	Description
Negotiation Failures	The total number of negotiation failures that have occurred during Main Mode or Quick Mode negotiation since the IPSec service was last started. If this counter increases, check your authentication and security method settings for an unmatched authentication method, an incorrect authentication method configuration, or unmatched security methods or settings.
Total Acquire	The total number of requests that have been submitted to IKE since the IPSec service was last started to establish an SA. This number includes acquires that result in soft SAs that lack encryption.
IKE Main Mode	The total number of successful SAs that have been created during Main Mode negotiations since the IPSec service was last started.
IKE Quick Mode	The total number of successful SAs that have been created during Quick Mode negotiations since the IPSec service was last started.
Soft Associations	The total number of negotiations that resulted in unencrypted soft SAs. This typically reflects the number of associations formed with computers that did not respond to Main Mode negotiation attempts. This can include both non-IPSec-aware computers and IPSec-aware computers that did not have a suitable IPSec policy to successfully complete Main Mode negotiations. Although soft SAs are not the result of Main Mode and Quick Mode negotiations, they are still treated as Quick Mode SAs. Soft SAs are not secured by IPSec.
Invalid Packets Received	The number of received IKE messages that are invalid, including IKE messages with invalid header fields and incorrect payload lengths. Invalid IKE messages are commonly caused by unmatched preshared keys between the IPSec peers. It does not necessarily indicate a problem if this statistic is greater than zero, because invalid packets can be received during normal IPSec communications.

Quick Mode statistics

Quick Mode, also known as Phase 2 of IPSec negotiations, occurs after Main Mode and regularly while an IPSec connection is in use. The IP Security Monitor tool has a Quick Mode node that you can use to view current information about Quick Mode negotiations. The information contained in the Quick Mode node is similar to that of Main Mode, including the listing of active Quick Mode SAs.

The most useful information can be viewed from within the Quick Mode Statistics node. Quick Mode statistics provide more granular information than is available in Main Mode, including the total number of encrypted and authenticated bytes. Table 9.2 lists the most important parameters contained in the Quick Mode Statistics node.

Table 9.2 Descriptions of Quick Mode Statistics Parameters

Quick Mode statistic	Description
Active Security Associations	The number of active Quick Mode SAs.
Offloaded Security Associations	The number of active Quick Mode SAs offloaded to hardware. Certain network adapters can accelerate IPSec processing by performing hardware offload of IPSec cryptographic functions. If you are not using such a network adapter, this value will remain zero.
Pending Key Operations	The number of IPSec key exchange operations that are in progress but are not yet completed.
Key Additions and Key Deletions	The total number of keys for Quick Mode SA negotiations that have been successfully added or deleted since the computer was last started.
Rekeys	The total number of successful rekey operations for Quick Mode SAs since the computer was last started. Rekeying occurs on a regular basis after Main Mode negotiations. If you specify nondefault settings for rekeying, you should monitor this statistic to verify that rekeying is occurring at a realistic rate.
Active Tunnels	The number of active IPSec tunnels.
Bad SPI Packets	The total number of packets for which the Security Parameter Index (SPI) has been incorrect since the computer was last started. If the SPI is incorrect, it might mean that the inbound SA has expired and a packet using the old SPI has recently arrived. This number is likely to increase if rekey intervals are short and there are a large number of SAs. A large number of packets with bad SPIs that are received within a short amount of time might indicate a packet spoofing attack.
Packets Not Decrypted	The total number of packets that could not be decrypted since the computer was last started. A packet might not be decrypted if it fails a validation check.
Packets Not Authenticated	The total number of packets for which data could not be verified (for which the integrity hash verification failed) since the computer was last started. Increases in this number might indicate an IPSec packet spoofing or modification attack or packet corruption by network devices.
Packets With Replay Detection	The total number of packets that have contained an invalid sequence number since the computer was last started. Increases in this number might indicate a network problem or replay attack.
Confidential Bytes Sent and Confidential Bytes Received	The total number of encrypted bytes that have been sent or received by means of the Encapsulating Security Payload (ESP) protocol since the computer was last started.

Table 9.2 Descriptions of Quick Mode Statistics Parameters

Quick Mode statistic	Description
Authenticated Bytes Sent and Authenticated Bytes Received	The total number of authenticated bytes that have been sent or received by means of the Authentication Header (AH) protocol or the ESP protocol since the computer was last started.
Transport Bytes Sent and Transport Bytes Received	The total number of bytes that have been sent or received by means of IPSec Transport Mode since the computer was last started.
Bytes Sent In Tunnels and Bytes Received In Tunnels	The total number of bytes that have been sent or received by means of IPSec Tunnel Mode since the computer was last started.
Offloaded Bytes Sent and Off-loaded Bytes Received	The total number of bytes that have been sent or received by means of IPSec hardware offload since the computer was last started.

Event Viewer

As with many features of Windows Server 2003, you can configure IPSec to add events to the event logs. This is useful for verifying that IPSec is functioning correctly, for troubleshooting problems with IPSec, and for detecting successful or unsuccessful intrusion attempts. IPSec can generate events for two types of actions: successful and unsuccessful negotiations and dropped packets.

Off the Record I'm not a fan of using Event Viewer to troubleshoot IPSec problems. The fact is, the events don't provide nearly enough information to be useful, and you have to weed through far too many events that don't signal a problem condition. I'd rather use the IP Security Monitor snap-in, IKE tracing, and Network Monitor because they provide more detailed, useful troubleshooting information.

Auditing IPSec negotiations

The creation and deletion of IPSec SAs are audited as network logon events. To audit these events, enable success or failure auditing for the Audit Logon Events audit policy for your domain or local computer. IPSec records the success or failure of each Main Mode and Quick Mode negotiation and the establishment and termination of each negotiation as separate events. The IKE event category is also used for auditing user logon events in services other than IPSec, so you won't see just IPSec events.

Planning On a busy server, enabling the auditing of logon events can cause the Security event log to fill with IKE events. Increase the size of the Security event log to prevent losing important information. If you need to enable the Audit Logon Events policy but do not want to see IKE events, create the HKEY_LOCAL_MACHINE\System\CurrentControlSet\Control\Lsa\Audit\DisableIKEAudits registry value and set it to 1. You cannot disable auditing of IKE events on Windows 2000.

To add an event each time a user changes the IPSec policies, enable the Audit Policy Change policy. In Windows 2000, you must enable both the Audit Policy Change and the Audit Process Tracking settings to view the success or failure of IPSec policy change events. In Windows XP and Windows Server 2003, you only need to enable Audit Process Tracking to view the success or failure of IPSec policy change events. After these policies are enabled, the following events will be added to your Security event log:

- **Event ID 541, success audit.** Recorded when IKE successfully negotiates either a Main Mode SA or an IPSec SA. The SA parameters are noted in the description of the event, as shown in Figure 9.6. The information recorded includes the details of the IP filter, security algorithms, and key exchange settings.

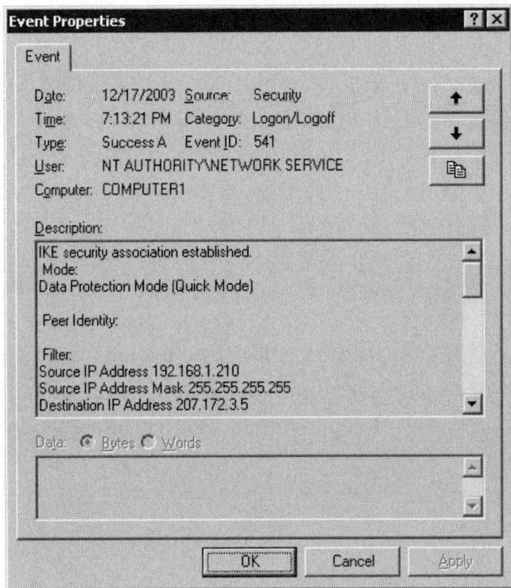

Figure 9.6 Event ID 541 showing a successful IKE SA established

- **Event ID 542, success audit.** Recorded when IKE successfully deletes an IPSec SA. An IPSec SA might be deleted because the SA lifetime expired, because a new SA was generated during Quick Mode rekey, because the IPSec peer sent a delete message, because the IPSec policy changed, or because the IPSec service was stopped.

- **Event ID 543, success audit.** Recorded when IKE successfully deletes a Main Mode SA. An IKE Main Mode SA might be deleted because the SA lifetime expired, because the IPSec peer sent a delete message, because the IPSec policy changed, or because the IPSec service was stopped.
- **Event ID 544, failure audit.** Recorded when the IKE negotiation is terminated because of a certificate trust failure and subsequent authentication failure. This failure might occur because a valid certificate chain could not be found on the IPSec peer, or because the certificate chain that was found could not be sent to a trusted root CA.
- **Event ID 545, failure audit.** Recorded when the IKE negotiation is terminated because of the validation failure of a computer certificate signature. This event is rare because it indicates that the computer certificate on the IPSec peer has a mismatched RSA type public/private key pair.
- **Event ID 546, failure audit.** Recorded when an SA cannot be established because of an invalid IKE proposal from the IPSec peer. This error typically occurs when an IPSec policy is incorrectly configured.
- **Event ID 547, failure audit.** Recorded when the IKE negotiation fails. The causes of the failure are noted in the text of the event. Figure 9.7 shows an event generated when IKE negotiation failed during certificate authentication because a valid machine certificate was not located.

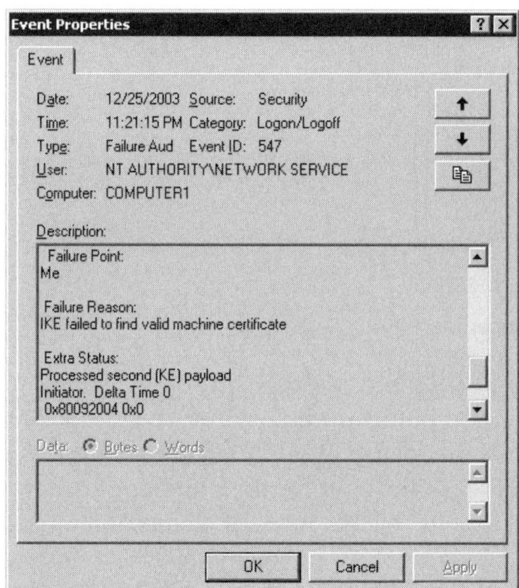

Figure 9.7 Event ID 547 showing an IKE negotiation failure

See Also For information on how to enable auditing, refer to Chapter 3.

Logging dropped packets

IPSec is capable of adding events to the System event log when packets are filtered, as shown in Figure 9.8. The types of packet processing errors that the IPSec driver records in the System event log depend on the level of logging that is provided. IPSec driver logs can record inbound and outbound per-packet drop events during computer startup mode and operational mode. IPSec driver event logging is disabled by default, and it should not be used for extended periods. Depending on the logging level that you set, many events might be generated that will fill the System event log very quickly.

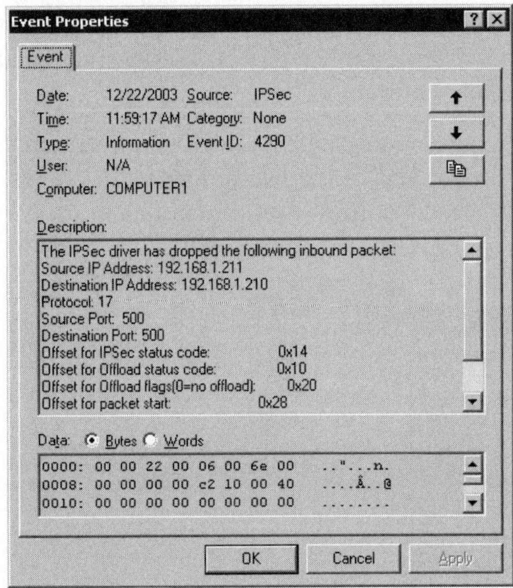

Figure 9.8 Event ID 4290 showing dropped packets

To record all inbound and outbound dropped packets and other packet processing errors in the System event log on a computer running Windows Server 2003, set the IPSec driver event logging level to 7. By default, the IPSec driver writes events to the System event log once an hour or after a threshold for the number of events has been reached. For troubleshooting, you should set this interval to the minimum value, 60 seconds. To enable IPSec diagnostics and set the log interval to 60 seconds, run the following commands at a command prompt, and then restart the computer:

```
netsh ipsec dynamic set config ipsecdiagnostics 7
netsh ipsec dynamic set config ipsecloginterval 60
```

Off the Record The minimum value for the IPSec log interval is 60 seconds, which should cause IPSec to add a group of events for dropped packets once per minute. Exercise 3 in this lesson will demonstrate that it doesn't actually work that way, however. Instead, IPSec will add events once every two minutes. If you set the ipsecloginterval value to something over two minutes, it seems to work correctly. So I guess the actual minimum is 120 seconds. Since the Netsh developers seem to think it's 60 seconds, you should remember that value for the exam, but remember the actual minimum of two minutes for the real world.

The preceding commands cannot be used on a computer running Windows XP, however. To add IPSec driver events to the System event log on a Windows XP computer, set the HKEY_LOCAL_MACHINE\System\CurrentControlSet\Services\IPSec\EnableDiagnostics registry value to 7. To change the diagnostic interval to the minimum of once per minute, set the HKEY_LOCAL_MACHINE\System\CurrentControlSet\Services\IPSec\LogInterval DWORD registry value on the computer running Windows XP to 60, in decimal units.

Note You have to restart your computer after making this change because the IPSec driver reads the diagnostic level only during startup.

By default, packet event logging for the IPSec driver is disabled, which is equivalent to setting the diagnostic level to 0. When you enable packet event logging for the IPSec driver, you can specify any of the following values to enable various levels of logging:

1. Packets with an incorrect Security Parameters Index (SPI), IKE negotiation failures, IPSec processing failures, packets received with invalid packet syntax, and other errors are recorded in the System event log. Unauthenticated hashes (with the exception of the "Clear text received when should have been secured" event) are also logged.
2. Inbound per-packet drop events are recorded in the System event log.
3. Level 1 and level 2 logging are performed. In addition, unexpected clear text events (packets that are sent or received in plaintext) are also recorded.
4. Outbound per-packet drop events are recorded in the System event log.
5. Level 1 and level 4 logging are performed.
6. Level 2 and level 4 logging are performed.
7. All levels of logging are performed.

The IPSec driver records bad SPI events using Event ID 4283 in the System event log when it receives an IPSec-formatted packet that it cannot interpret. These events occur because of the way in which IKE processes the transition of IPSec SAs during rekeys. They can usually be safely ignored.

Note You cannot disable logging for bad SPI events in Windows 2000. By default, Windows XP and Windows Server 2003 do not log these events.

IKE Tracing

Some troubleshooting scenarios require a more detailed analysis than you can do by using Event Viewer. The IKE tracing log is a detailed log intended for troubleshooting IKE interoperability under controlled circumstances. Keep in mind that the details of this tracing log are not well documented and that advanced knowledge of ISAKMP RFC 2408 and IKE RFC 2409 is required to interpret this log. However, experienced IPSec administrators might find it useful. You can enable tracing for IKE negotiations if the audit failure events do not provide enough information.

To enable tracing on a computer running Windows 2000 or Windows XP, create the HKEY_LOCAL_MACHINE\System\CurrentControlSet\Services\PolicyAgent\Oakley\EnableLogging registry value and set it to 1. Then either restart the computer or run the `net stop policyagent` and `net start policyagent` commands at the command prompt.

In Windows Server 2003, you can enable or disable the IKE tracing log dynamically while the IPSec service is running by using the Netsh commands for IPSec. To do this, open a command prompt and run the command `netsh ipsec dynamic set config ikelogging 1`. Alternatively, you can disable IKE tracing by running the command `netsh ipsec dynamic set config ikelogging 0`.

The IKE tracing log appears as the *%systemroot%*\Debug\Oakley.log file. A new Oakley.log file is created each time the IPSec service is started, and the previous version of the Oakley.log file is saved with the file name Oakley.log.sav. The log is limited to 50,000 lines. When the Oakley.log file becomes full, the current file is saved as Oakley.log.bak, and a new Oakley.log file is created.

Because many IKE negotiations can occur simultaneously, you should minimize the number of negotiations and enable the IKE tracing log for as briefly as possible to capture a more easily interpreted log. Use the IP addresses, SPI, timestamps, and SA identifiers to identify messages related to one security negotiation or IPSec SA processing session.

The following is an example of an Oakley log file. At first glance, it looks confusing. However, most of the lines are self-explanatory after careful examination. The first two rows show the date and time, and the remainder of each row is a description of what IPSec is doing at that particular moment.

```
12-22: 16:57:29:383:73c Sending: SA = 0x02B08C60 to 192.168.1.211:Type 2.500
12-22: 16:57:29:383:73c ISAKMP Header: (V1.0), len = 500
12-22: 16:57:29:383:73c   I-COOKIE daa86678465cfcfb
12-22: 16:57:29:383:73c   R-COOKIE 0000000000000000
12-22: 16:57:29:383:73c   exchange: Oakley Main Mode
12-22: 16:57:29:383:73c   flags: 0
12-22: 16:57:29:383:73c   next payload: SA
12-22: 16:57:29:383:73c   message ID: 00000000
12-22: 16:57:29:383:73c Ports S:f401 D:f401
12-22: 16:57:45:406:73c retransmit: sa = 02B08C60 centry 00000000 , count = 5
```

Netsh

Netsh was first introduced in Chapter 8 as a tool for configuring IPSec policies at the command line. It can also be used to monitor and troubleshoot IPSec on computers running Windows Server 2003, however. It provides access to several key pieces of information that are not accessible by means of graphical tools. Monitoring consists of displaying policy information, getting diagnostics and logging IPSec information, or both. By running Netsh, you can find any information that you can find by running the IP Security Monitor snap-in.

To quickly get a detailed snapshot of IPSec information on a computer, run the following commands from a command prompt:

```
Netsh ipsec dynamic show all > ipsec.txt
Notepad ipsec.txt
```

These two commands will output all dynamic IPSec information to a text file and then open it in Notepad. You can, of course, view the information at a command prompt. However, the output from the command is so long that it will quickly scroll off the default command prompt.

Tip I prefer to use the `Netsh ipsec dynamic show all` command so that I don't have to remember each of the various `Netsh ipsec dynamic show` commands. However, if you want more granular control over the information you receive, there are many more specific Netsh parameters. To list them, run the command `Netsh ipsec dynamic show ?` at a command prompt.

Performance Console

The most flexible way to monitor IPSec is to use the Performance console. The Performance console has two snap-ins: System Monitor and Performance Logs And Alerts. System Monitor allows you to monitor the real-time statistics of a wide variety of system counters by using a bar graph, a test report, or a line graph, as shown in Figure 9.9. Performance Logs And Alerts stores specified performance counters in a log file and allows you to later analyze the history of those counters by using the System Monitor snap-in. Performance Logs And Alerts can also send an e-mail message or other kind of alert when a counter reaches a specified threshold.

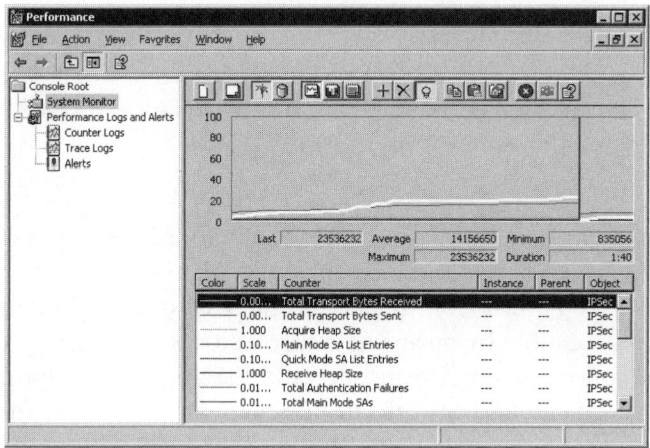

Figure 9.9 Graphing IPSec performance statistics

Both Performance console snap-ins provide the same set of counters. IPSec counters are contained in the IPSec v4 IKE performance object, which contains Main Mode statistics, and the IPSec v4 Driver performance object, which contains Quick Mode statistics. The counters in the performance objects correspond closely to the Statistics parameters provided in the IP Security Monitor snap-in, but the counters are named slightly differently. For example, IP Security Monitor's Transport Bytes Sent parameter in the Quick Mode Statistics node should have the same value as the Total Transport Bytes Sent counter in the IPSec v4 Driver performance object. They can differ slightly, however, because the IP Security Monitor snap-in is updated less frequently.

Exam Tip Oddly, the exam objectives do not mention using the Performance snap-in to monitor IPSec. I think it's much more useful than the IP Security Monitor, but, for the sake of the exam, you should focus your energy on familiarizing yourself with the IP Security Monitor snap-in.

Network Monitor

Network Monitor is a protocol analyzer—a type of tool more commonly referred to as a *sniffer*. Network Monitor is an optional component included with Windows 2000 Server and Windows Server 2003 that can capture and analyze network traffic as it is sent to and from a computer. The version of Network Monitor included for free with the Windows operating systems is a limited version of the Network Monitor tool included with Microsoft Systems Management Server (SMS). The primary limitation is that the version included with Windows will capture only traffic sent directly to and from the computer it runs on. To capture traffic sent to or from other computers, you must use SMS.

The Network Monitor parser in Windows 2000 cannot interpret ESP traffic. In Windows Server 2003, the parser can interpret ESP traffic if an IPSec hardware acceleration adapter performs encryption or decryption of this traffic, or if you use ESP without encryption. Otherwise, as shown in Figure 9.10, you will only be able to see that ESP traffic is being exchanged with a remote computer. You cannot interpret the Application layer data within the ESP header because it is encrypted.

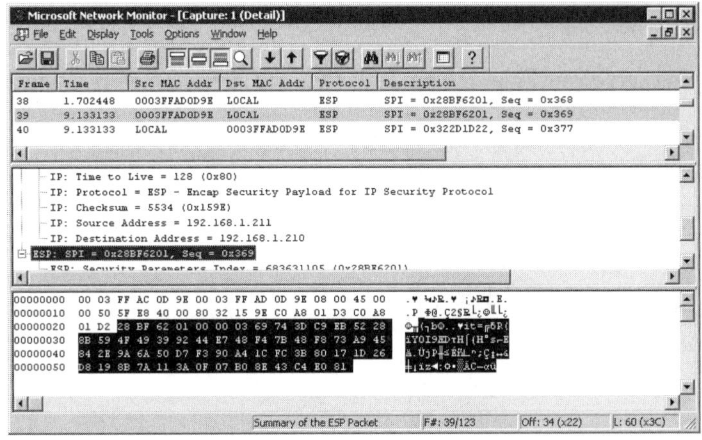

Figure 9.10 Network Monitoring displaying ESP-encrypted packets

To install Network Monitor, open Control Panel, and then open Add Or Remove Programs. Click Add/Remove Windows Components. Click Management And Monitoring Tools, and then click Details. Select the Network Monitor Tools check box, and then click OK. Click Next, and respond to the prompts provided by the wizard. When installation has completed, click Finish.

See Also For information about SMS, see the Systems Management Server Web site at *http://www.microsoft.com/sms/*.

Netcap

Netcap.exe is a command-line utility that you can use to capture network traffic to a capture file. You can then load the file in Network Monitor to view the captured traffic. You do not have to install the Network Monitor tool on the computer running Windows Server 2003 to use Netcap. You can also use Netcap on computers running Windows XP, which makes it an extremely attractive way to capture traffic for later review. The tool is available after the Windows Server 2003 Support Tools have been installed. When you first run the command, the Network Monitor driver is automatically installed.

Ping

The favorite tool for troubleshooting network connectivity, ping, might or might not be useful for troubleshooting IPSec. First, if you use IPSec filters to block Internet Control Message Protocol (ICMP) traffic, neither ping nor Tracert will work because IPSec will filter the incoming requests. Second, ping requests do not initiate a security negotiation if you are using the default security policies. Both Server (Request Security) and Server (Require Security) explicitly permit ICMP traffic, but neither require ICMP traffic to negotiate security, as shown in Figure 9.11.

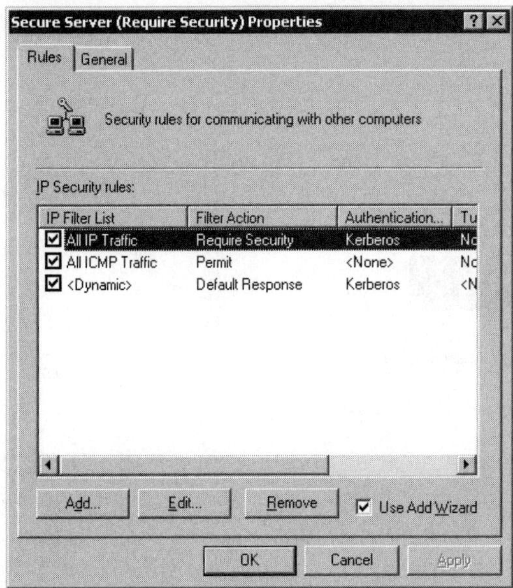

Figure 9.11 Ping permitted, but not secured

If you create an IP security rule with the All ICMP Traffic filter list that uses a filter action set to Negotiate Security, and ICMP traffic is not being blocked by Internet Connection Firewall (ICF) or a firewall, ping can be a useful tool. In these cases, the ping client will show "Negotiating IP Security" during the IKE negotiation process. After negotiation succeeds, you will see the standard ping reply messages, and the successful negotiation will be reflected in the IPSec monitoring tools.

IPSecMon

Computers running Windows 2000 do not include the IP Security Monitor snap-in. Instead, there is a graphical tool named IP Security Monitor. To start this tool on a computer running Windows 2000, click Start, click Run, type **ipsecmon**, and then click OK. The Windows 2000 IP Security Monitor tool shows much of the same information as the IP Security Monitor snap-in, including a list of active SAs, and statistics such as confidential and authenticated bytes sent and the total number of bad SPI packets.

IPSecCmd

As mentioned in Lesson 1, IPSecCmd can be used to display IPSec information at the command line on computers running Windows XP. The syntax used to view all available IPSec information is simply `Ipseccmd show all`. IPSecPol lacks IPSecCmd's query mode, and, as a result, you cannot display IPSec information from the Windows 2000 command line.

Netdiag

Netdiag.exe is a command-line tool that you can use to display IPSec information on computers running Windows 2000 and Windows XP. Netdiag is also available for Windows Server 2003, but the IPSec capabilities of Netdiag have been disabled. For Windows 2000, Netdiag is included with the Windows 2000 Support Tools that you can also download from the Internet. It is also available on the Windows XP Installation CD-ROM. You can install it by running Setup.exe from the Support\Tools folder and choosing the complete installation.

To display information about the current IPSec policy from the command line on a computer running Windows 2000 or Windows XP, run the command `Netdiag /test:ipsec`. The output will resemble the following:

```
IP Security test . . . . . . . . . : Passed
    Service status  is: Started
    Service startup is: Automatic
    Local IPSec Policy Active: 'Client (Respond Only)'

    Description: 'Communicate normally (unsecured). Use the default response rule to
negotiate with servers that request security. Only the requested protocol and port
traffic with that server is secured.'
    Last Change (Timestamp): Thu Dec 25 21:45:33 2003
    Policy Path:

HKLM\SOFTWARE\Policies\Microsoft\Windows\IPSec\Policy\Local\ipsecPolicy
{72385236-70fa-11d1-864c-14a300000000}
    Note: run "ipseccmd /?" for more detailed information
```

Practice: Monitoring IPSec

In this practice, you will use several techniques to monitor IPSec traffic on Computer1 and Computer2.

Exercise 1: Monitor IPSec with the IP Security Monitor

In this exercise, you will monitor IPSec by using the IP Security Monitor snap-in.

1. Log on to the cohowinery.com domain on Computer2 using the Administrator account.
2. Open a blank MMC console, and then add the IP Security Policy Management snap-in. When prompted to select the computer or domain, select Local Computer.
3. In the right pane, right-click Client (Respond Only), and then click Un-Assign.

   This ensures that Computer2 does not have an active SA with Computer1. Later, you will re-assign the Client (Respond Only) policy to demonstrate that you can see the difference by using the IP Security Monitor snap-in.
4. Log on to the cohowinery.com domain on Computer1 using the Administrator account.
5. Open a blank MMC console, and then add the IP Security Monitor snap-in.
6. Expand IP Security Monitor, expand Computer1, and then click Active Policy. In the left pane, verify that the Server (Request Security) policy is listed for the Policy Name item.

   If it is not still active from the exercise in Chapter 8, add the IP Security Policy Management tool and assign the Server (Request Security) policy.
7. In the IP Security Monitor snap-in, expand Main Mode, and then click Statistics.

   Examine the Main Mode statistics, and make note of the Total Acquire, Total Get SPI, Key Additions, Key Updates, IKE Main Mode, IKE Quick Mode, and Soft Associations parameters.
8. In the IP Security Monitor snap-in, expand Quick Mode, and then click Statistics.

   Examine the Quick Mode statistics, and make note of the Active Security Associations, Key Additions, Active Tunnels, Confidential Bytes Sent, Authenticated Bytes Sent, Transport Bytes Sent, and Bytes Sent In Tunnels parameters.
9. Return to Computer2. In the right pane of the IP Security Management snap-in, right-click Client (Respond Only), and then click Assign.
10. Start Windows Explorer. On the Tools menu, click Map Network Drive. In the Folder box, type **\\computer1\c$**, and then click Finish. If prompted, provide Administrator credentials for Computer1. Browse through the files on Computer1 to generate network traffic.

The purpose of this step is simply to communicate with Computer1.

11. Return to Computer1. In the IP Security Monitor snap-in, expand Main Mode, and then click Statistics.

    Examine the Main Mode statistics. As a result of Computer2's incoming connection, all of the parameters you noted in step 7 should have incremented except for the Soft Associations parameter. Soft Associations measures sessions that could not be encrypted, but this session should have been successfully encrypted.

12. In the IP Security Monitor snap-in, expand Quick Mode, and then click Statistics.

    Examine the Quick Mode statistics. As a result of Computer2's incoming connection, all of the parameters you noted in step 8 should have incremented except for the Active Tunnels and Bytes Sent In Tunnels parameters. These parameters measure traffic used with IPSec tunnel mode. However, the connection between Computer1 and Computer2 is using IPSec transport mode.

See Also For more information about tunnel mode and transport mode, refer to Chapter 8.

Exercise 2: Monitor IPSec with Network Monitor

In this exercise, you will use Network Monitor to verify that traffic between Computer1 and Computer2 is encrypted.

1. Log on to the cohowinery.com domain on Computer1 using the Administrator account.
2. Click Start, click Control Panel, and then click Add Or Remove Programs.
3. Click Add/Remove Windows Components.
4. Click Management And Monitoring Tools, and then click Details. Select the Network Monitor Tools check box, and then click OK.
5. Click Next, and then respond to the prompts provided by the wizard. When the installation has completed, click Finish.

   Network Monitor has now been installed. It can be used to monitor traffic on Computer1.

6. Click Start, point to Administrative Tools, and then click Network Monitor.
7. If prompted to select a network connection, expand Local Computer, click Local Area Connection, and then click OK.
8. Click the Capture menu, and then click Start.
9. Log on to the cohowinery.com domain on Computer2 using the Administrator account.

10. Start Windows Explorer. On the Tools menu, click Map Network Drive. In the Folder box, type **\\computer1\c$**, and then click Finish. If prompted, provide Administrator credentials for Computer1. Browse through the files on Computer1 to generate network traffic.

    The purpose of this step is simply to communicate with Computer1. When we later analyze the traffic by using Network Monitor, it will be obvious if the communications are protected by IPSec.

11. Return to Computer1. On the Capture menu, select Stop And View.

    Network Monitor displays a list of all captured frames. If the two computers are connected to a private network with no other hosts, you will see ESP shown in the Protocol box for all frames. This proves that ESP is being used.

12. Double-click one of the frames to view the details of the frame. In the middle pane, expand ESP and examine the information Network Monitor provides about the frame.

    Network Monitor can show you the SPI and the sequence number, but it won't show you anything else of use. The data contained in the packet is encrypted and therefore cannot be analyzed, regardless of whether the capture is performed by a legitimate administrator or an attacker.

Exercise 3: Log dropped packets

In this exercise, you will configure Computer1 to log dropped packets and to filter ICMP packets by using IPSec. You will then ping Computer1 from Computer2 and analyze the events added to the System event log.

1. Log on to the cohowinery.com domain on Computer2 using the Administrator account.

2. Open a command prompt, and run the following command:

    ```
    Ping -t computer1
    ```

    At this point, Computer1 will respond to the ping requests.

3. Log on to the cohowinery.com domain on Computer1 using the Administrator account.

4. Open a command prompt, and run the following commands:

    ```
    netsh ipsec dynamic set config ipsecdiagnostics 7
    netsh ipsec dynamic set config ipsecloginterval 60
    ```

5. Open a blank MMC console, and then add the IP Security Policy Management snap-in. When prompted to select the computer or domain, select Local Computer.

6. Right-click IP Security Policies On Local Computer, and then click Create IP Security Policy.

7. In the IP Security Policy Wizard, click Next.
8. In the Name box, type **Drop ICMP**. Click Next.
9. Clear Activate The Default Response Rule, and then click Next.
10. Click Finish.
11. In the Drop ICMP Properties dialog box, click Add.
12. In the Security Rule Wizard, click Next three times.
13. On the IP Filter List page, click All ICMP Traffic. Click Next.
14. On the Filter Action page, click Deny. Click Next.
15. Clear the Edit Properties check box, and then click Finish.
16. In the Drop IMCP Properties dialog box, click OK.
17. In the IP Security Policies On Local Computer snap-in, right-click Drop ICMP, and then click Assign.

    Within a few seconds, Computer2 will show Request Timed Out because Computer1 is now dropping ICMP traffic.
18. On Computer1, start Event Viewer, and then click the System node in the left pane.
19. In the right pane, double-click an event with the Type value set to Information and a Source of IPSec. If no such events have appeared yet, wait two minutes, and then press F5 to refresh the display.

    The Event Properties dialog box appears, as shown in Figure 9.12. The description shows that an ICMP packet from Computer2's IP address was dropped.

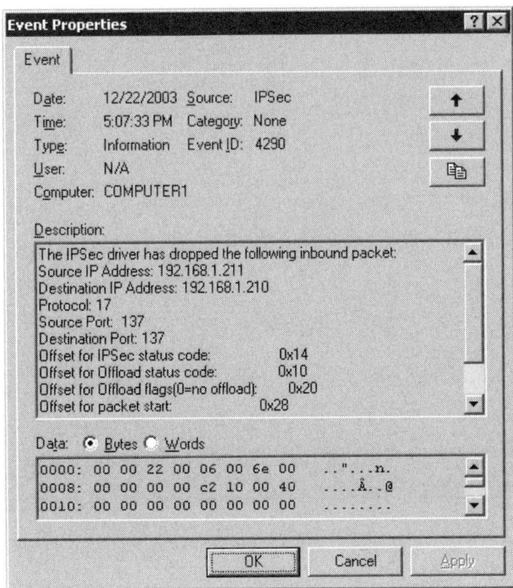

Figure 9.12 Event Viewer details about a dropped ICMP request

20. Click OK. Wait two minutes, and then press F5 to refresh the display. You should see another group of IPSec events added. Note that the event time is two minutes after the last sent events, even though you configured the events to be added every 60 seconds.

21. Close all open windows on both Computer1 and Computer2.

Lesson Review

The following questions are intended to reinforce key information presented in this lesson. If you are unable to answer a question, review the lesson materials and try the question again. You can find answers to the questions in the "Questions and Answers" section at the end of this chapter.

1. Which of the following parameters can be found in IP Security Monitor's Main Mode Statistics? (Choose all that apply.)

   a. IKE Main Mode

   b. Bytes Sent In Tunnels

   c. Transport Bytes Sent

   d. IKE Quick Mode

   e. Total Acquire

   f. Soft Associations

   g. Active Tunnels

---

2. Which of the following tools can be used to verify that network traffic to a specific host is being encrypted on a computer running Windows Server 2003? (Choose all that apply.)

   a. IP Security Monitor

   b. Event Viewer

   c. Netsh

   d. Netdiag

   e. Network Monitor

   f. IPSecMon

   g. Performance console

---

3. Which of the following tools can display the total cumulative number of successful Main Mode negotiations on a computer running Windows Server 2003? (Choose all that apply.)

   a. IP Security Monitor

   b. Event Viewer

   c. Netsh

   d. Netdiag

   e. Network Monitor

   f. IPSecMon

   g. Performance console

Lesson Summary

- Use the IP Security Monitor snap-in to examine Main Mode and Quick Mode IPSec statistics.
- To audit IPSec negotiations, first enable success or failure auditing for Audit Policy Change and possibly for Audit Process Tracking. Then use Event Viewer to examine the Security event log.
- To analyze packets that are dropped, enable IPSec driver event logging by using the Netsh command on Windows Server 2003. (Other versions of Windows require that you add a registry value to enable IPSec driver event logging.) Then use Event Viewer to examine the System event log.
- When you need detailed troubleshooting information, enable IKE tracing by using Netsh. Then examine the *%systemroot%*\Debug\Oakley.log file.

Lesson 3: Troubleshooting IPSec

IPSec has the potential to modify every network communication sent to or from a computer. If that were not intimidating enough, IPSec is extremely complicated to configure. Your standard troubleshooting tools might not work either, since network traffic is usually encrypted. Therefore, you will need specialized skills to effectively troubleshoot problems with IPSec communications. This lesson covers common IPSec troubleshooting scenarios and describes how you should isolate and resolve the problems.

After this lesson, you will be able to

- Describe the first steps to take when isolating a communications problem that might or might not be related to IPSec.
- Describe the overall process you would use to troubleshoot IPSec problems.
- List common problems related to using Kerberos and public key certificate-based authentication.
- Describe how to avoid and resolve problems with firewalls and routers, Network Address Translation (NAT), and computers that do not run Windows.

Estimated lesson time: 25 minutes

General Troubleshooting Guidelines

Regardless of the type of problem you are experiencing, you should first make sure that the necessary services are started and set to automatic on both IPSec peers. On computers running Windows Server 2003, the IPSec Services service must be started. On computers running Windows 2000, the IPSec Policy Agent service must be started.

Sometimes, especially after making significant changes, you might be able to resolve a problem by restarting IPSec services. This completely clears the IKE negotiation state. You can restart IPSec services from a command prompt by running the following commands:

```
net stop policyagent
net start policyagent
```

This is simply a quick way to restart IPSec without restarting the computer. After restarting the IPSec services on both computers, attempt to establish a secure connection. If the problem persists, restart the operating systems on both IPSec peers and try again.

Next, verify that the correct policy has been assigned to each of the IPSec peers by using the IP Security Monitor snap-in. Remember, creating a new policy does not automatically assign it to a computer. Additionally, if you deploy a policy by using a GPO, the settings do not propagate instantly. If the policy is different from the one you were expecting, identify the responsible GPO by using the Resultant Set Of Policy snap-in or the command `Netsh Ipsec Static Show Gpoassignedpolicy`.

Verify that IKE negotiation is succeeding by enabling auditing and checking the Security event log, as described in Lesson 2. If IKE negotiation is not succeeding, verify that authentication, encryption, and key change settings are the same on both IPSec peers. If there is no indication that negotiations are succeeding, use Network Monitor to verify that packets are reaching the correct computer.

If IKE negotiation is succeeding but IPSec communications are still failing, verify that Quick Mode is succeeding by checking the Security event log and the IKE tracing log. If Quick Mode is not succeeding, check to see that all Quick Mode encryption, integrity, key strength, and key change settings are the same on both IPSec peers.

If IPSec negotiations simply do not occur, or if the type of negotiations are different from what you expected, double-check the IPSec filters. If you are specifying source and destination IP addresses in the filter, verify that the filters on each of the IPSec peers are mirrors of each other. Likewise, if you are specifying source and destination port numbers, the remote IPSec peer must have the same port numbers configured, but with the source and destination numbers reversed.

Kerberos Authentication Problems

Kerberos authentication is the default IPSec authentication method. You can quickly identify whether IPSec connectivity problems are caused by authentication by temporarily changing the IPSec authentication method on both IPSec peers to Preshared Key. If IPSec communications succeed with Preshared Key, Kerberos authentication is probably the source of the problem.

For Kerberos authentication to be successful, both IPSec peers must have valid computer accounts in trusted domains, and they must be able to authenticate the remote computers. Each IPSec peer must be able to communicate with domain controllers without having the authentication requests filtered. In earlier versions of Windows, IPSec automatically allowed Kerberos traffic. However, the Kerberos protocol is no longer a default exemption in Windows Server 2003.

To modify the default filtering behavior for Windows Server 2003, use Netsh to set the IPSecExempt value to 0, 1, or 2. By default, the IPSecExempt value is set to 3, which specifies that only Internet Security Association And Key Management Protocol (ISAKMP) traffic is exempt from IPSec filtering. Specifying a value of 2 allows Resource Reservation Setup Protocol (RSVP), Kerberos, and ISAKMP traffic. A value of 1 allows multicast traffic, broadcast traffic, and ISAKMP traffic. Specifying a value of 0 allows multicast, broadcast, RSVP, Kerberos, and ISAKMP traffic. To specify the value, run the following command:

```
netsh ipsec dynamic set config ipsecexempt value={ 0 | 1 | 2 | 3}
```

Both IPSec peers must authenticate to each other; therefore, the problem could be authenticating either of the two computer accounts. On both computers, enable the failure Audit Logon Events audit policy, as described in Lesson 2. Attempt to initiate an IPSec connection, and then review the Security event log on both computers. You should see a failure audit event indicating the nature of the error.

Certificate Authentication Problems

Certificates are a common method for authenticating computers that are not in a trusted domain environment. If you are experiencing problems with IPSec and want to verify that the problem is related to authentication, temporarily change the IPSec authentication method on both IPSec peers to Preshared Key. If IPSec communications succeed with Preshared Key but fail with certificates, the problem is almost certainly related to certificates.

If you have multiple rules in a policy, double-check that those rules will use the same authentication method consistently for any single remote computer. It is acceptable to have a policy that configures Kerberos authentication for hosts on an internal network and uses certificates for hosts on an external network. However, you cannot create one rule that uses Kerberos to authenticate just Transmission Control Protocol (TCP) data and a second rule that authenticates User Datagram Protocol (UDP) traffic by using certificates, for example. The IP Security Policy Management snap-in will not prevent you from creating these rules, but they will not work properly. All rules that apply to a single remote host must use a single authentication method.

Another potential cause of authentication problems is incorrectly obtained certificates. Incorrectly obtained certificates can result in a condition in which the certificate exists and is chosen to be used for IKE authentication, but fails to work because the private key corresponding to the certificate's public key is not present on the local computer. To verify that a certificate you plan to use for IPSec does indeed have a private key:

1. Open a blank MMC console, and then add the Certificates snap-in. When prompted, select Computer Account.
2. Expand Certificates (Local Computer), and then expand Personal.
3. Click the Certificates node.
4. In the right pane, double-click the certificate you want to check. On the General tab, you should see the text "You have a private key that corresponds to this certificate." If you don't see this message, the system won't use this certificate successfully for IPSec.

Depending upon how the certificate was requested and populated into the host's local certificate store, this private key value might not exist, or it might not be available to be used during the IKE negotiation. If the certificate in the personal folder does not have a corresponding private key, certificate enrollment has failed.

If a certificate was obtained from Certificate Services with the option set for Strong Private Key Protection, the user must enter a PIN number to access the private key each time that the private key is used to sign data in the IKE negotiation. Because the IKE negotiation is being done in the background by a system service, there is no window available to the service to prompt the user. So certificates obtained with this option will not work for IKE authentication.

See Also For information about troubleshooting certificate revocation lists, refer to Chapter 8.

Troubleshooting Firewalls, Routers, and Packet Filtering

Packet filtering at firewalls is a common source of IPSec problems because IPSec cannot be permitted or blocked by applying the techniques used for most applications. First, your firewall must allow two-way traffic with a UDP destination port of 500. If the firewall is also a NAT server and you will be using Network Address Translation Traversal (NAT-T), you must also allow UDP traffic with a destination port of 4500. Second, the firewall must allow traffic with an IP protocol ID of 50, which is used by ESP. If you are using AH instead of ESP, you must allow IP protocol 51.

Important The IP protocol ID 50 is not the same as UDP or TCP port 50.

You cannot use conventional packet filters to selectively block traffic that is tunneled or transported within IPSec. Most packet filters block traffic based on TCP or UDP port number, but those numbers are usually encrypted by ESP. Only IPSec filters implemented on the two IPSec peers can perform port-based packet filtering. You can still filter traffic based on source or destination IP address, however.

Network Address Translation Problems

Network Address Translation (NAT) is a common technique for connecting a privately numbered internal network to a public network such as the Internet. As Chapter 8 discussed, earlier implementations of IPSec were not compatible with NAT. This makes sense, because NAT's purpose is to modify the source or destination IP address in a packet without the client or server being aware, and part of IPSec's purpose is to discard packets that have been modified in transit.

Note You won't have problems establishing IPSec connections between two clients on a single private network. It's only when the NAT server performs address translation on IPSec-protected communications that problems can occur.

IPSec NAT Traversal (NAT-T) allows IPSec traffic to pass through compatible NAT servers. However, both the IPSec hosts and the NAT server must support NAT-T, and the NAT server must be configured to allow traffic on UDP port 4500. Windows Server 2003, Windows XP Professional, and Windows 2000 support NAT-T as IPSec clients. Microsoft Internet Security And Acceleration (ISA) Server and Windows Server 2003 support NAT-T as a firewall.

If you are having problems establishing an IPSec connection across a NAT server, first verify that both IPSec clients and the NAT servers support NAT-T. Clients using Windows 2000 or Windows XP must have update 818043 installed. (This update is available from *http://support.microsoft.com/default.aspx?kbid=818043*.) If you are using the built-in NAT capabilities of a computer running Windows XP or Windows 2000, or versions of Windows released prior to Windows 2000, you cannot use IPSec across NAT.

Warning Ensure that you are using ESP. You cannot use AH across a NAT server, because AH is not compatible with NAT-T.

Windows Server 2003 supports IPSec NAT-T as described by version 2 of the IPSec NAT-T Internet drafts, but some applications might not work when their traffic is first protected with IPSec and then passed through a network address translator. Test how your planned implementation of IPSec interacts with network address translators in a lab before deploying IPSec in your environment.

If possible, verify that IPSec works properly between two computers on the same side of the NAT server. If problems persist, the problem might not be related to NAT-T. Verify that the NAT server is not filtering packets required by IPSec, as described in the section "Troubleshooting Firewalls, Routers, and Packet Filtering" in this lesson.

Interoperability Problems

Most problems, particularly problems related to interoperating with non-Windows operating systems, can be resolved by creating the simplest policy possible instead of using the default policies. For example, when you create a new policy, use the IP Security Policy Wizard to clear the default response rule. Then, when you add new rules, choose the default This Rule Does Not Specify A Tunnel option, rather than creating a tunnel.

Next, edit the policy to remove all but a single key exchange security method. To do this, open the policy's property sheet, and then click the General tab. Then click the Settings button, and then click the Methods button. Use the Key Exchange Security Methods dialog box to remove all but the one option that the destination will accept. For example, use the RFC 2049–required IKE security algorithms of DES, SHA1, and the Low (1) Diffie Hellman group, as shown in Figure 9.13.

Figure 9.13 Configuring a policy to use the most common IKE security algorithms

Next, create a filter list with one mirrored filter that specifies the source My IP Address and a destination with the IP address that you are trying to establish IPSec communications with, and then configure the filter list to match only ICMP traffic. Create a new filter action to negotiate security by using only one security method. For example, use the RFC 2049–required set of parameters, such as format ESP using Data Encryption Standard (DES) with SHA1, with no lifetimes specified. Make sure both the Use Session Key Perfect Forward Secrecy and Allow Unsecured Communication With Non-IPSec-Aware Computers check boxes are cleared. Use an authentication method of preshared keys for the rule, and make sure there are no white spaces in the string of characters. The destination must use exactly the same preshared key. Then configure the destination with the same configuration, but reverse the source and destination IP addresses.

Tip If you want to see the traffic in the IPSec-formatted packets with Network Monitor, use Medium Security (AH format).

When you are able to establish an IPSec connection using the lowest possible settings, begin to change the settings one at a time to match your security standards. Test IPSec after each change. When the IPSec connection fails, you will have identified the source of the problem. Then you can choose to either leave that setting at the compatible—but potentially less secure—setting, or you can work with the software vendors to improve interoperability between the IPSec implementations.

Lesson Review

The following question is intended to reinforce key information presented in this lesson. If you are unable to answer a question, review the lesson materials and try the question again. You can find answers to the questions in the "Questions and Answers" section at the end of this chapter.

1. IPSec peers ComputerA and ComputerB, as shown in Figure 9.14, are unable to establish a connection. What is the cause of the problem?

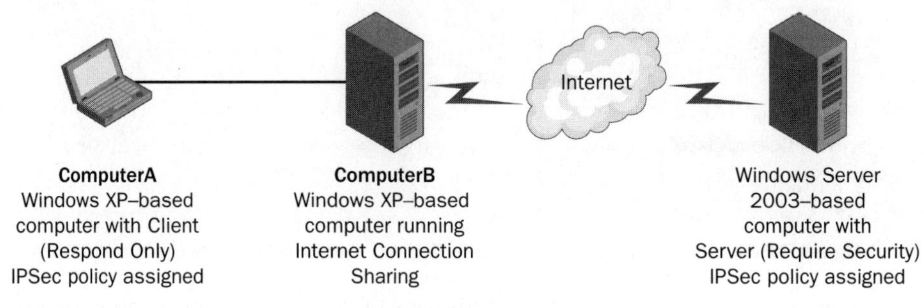

Figure 9.14 Problematic IPSec architecture

____

____

Lesson Summary

- Many IPSec problems can be resolved by simply restarting the IPSec services on the IPSec peers, or by restarting the computers.
- You can isolate IPSec authentication problems by temporarily changing both peers to the Preshared Key authentication method. Authentication problems when using Kerberos are often caused by one of the IPSec peers not being able to reach a domain controller. IPSec authentication using certificates will fail if a private key is not associated with the certificate.
- Firewalls, routers, and other packet-filtering devices must allow traffic on UDP port 4500 and traffic with IP protocol ID 50 for IPSec communications to succeed.
- Both IPSec clients and any firewalls and proxy servers that implement NAT must be compatible with NAT-T for IPSec communications between public and private networks to be successful.

Case Scenario Exercise

In this exercise, you will read a scenario about a company's challenge with protecting e-mail communications and then answer the questions that follow. The questions are intended to reinforce key information presented in this chapter. If you are unable to answer a question, review the lessons and try the question again. You can find answers to the questions in the "Questions and Answers" section at the end of this chapter.

Scenario

A couple of months ago, a systems administrator was fired when he was caught reading one of the executive's e-mail messages. He bought and sold some stock based on the inside information contained in memos within the executive's mailbox, collecting a healthy but illegal profit. He didn't sell enough shares to attract the US Securities and Exchange Commission's attention, and he might have gotten away with it if he hadn't bragged loudly in your company's cafeteria about his antics.

You were asked to explain why he had access to the executive's e-mail, and you determined that it wasn't simply an abuse of administrative privileges. Authorization to your messaging infrastructure had been carefully restricted, and the systems administrator's user account did not have access to the executive's e-mail account.

Fortunately, the team that provides your organization's physical security has had previous experience with questioning employees who have breached the organization's ethical standards. After they explained that they would need to rely on the judicial system if he didn't cooperate, your former coworker quickly confessed that he had gathered the executive's e-mail password by using a sniffer. Specifically, he had run Network Monitor on your mail server and extracted the e-mail password from the captured network communications.

Most of the client computers in your organization are members of an Active Directory domain, though there are a handful of computers that have not joined a domain because they are managed by the users themselves. Microsoft Outlook is your organization's standard mail client, but many users use other mail clients, including non-Microsoft mail clients and some rather obscure clients built into mobile devices, such as two-way pagers. You use Microsoft Exchange Server as your mail server.

Questions

1. How can you prevent internal employees from capturing other employees' passwords in the future?

2. Which of the built-in IPSec policies would you assign to the mail server?

3. Will you use Kerberos, certificates, or a preshared key to authenticate the IPSec connections?

4. Besides IPSec, what measures can you take to reduce the risk of an attacker capturing network communications and misusing that information?

Troubleshooting Lab

In this lab, you will troubleshoot a problem related to a remote client, Computer2, and a local server, Computer1, that cannot establish a secure connection. Read the following scenario and then answer the questions that follow. The questions are intended to reinforce key information presented in this chapter. If you are unable to answer a question, review the lessons and try the question again. You can find answers to the questions in the "Questions and Answers" section at the end of this chapter.

To prepare the computers for this troubleshooting lab, use Windows Explorer to browse through the CD-ROM accompanying this book. On Computer1, log on as an Administrator, open the Labs folder, and then double-click the file named ch9-computer1.bat. On Computer2, log on as an Administrator, open the Labs folder, and then double-click the file named ch9-computer2.bat.

Scenario

You are in the process of deploying IPSec policies to the computers in your domain. You're working with a user at a remote office to verify that his mobile computer is successfully establishing an IPSec connection to an intranet Web server and that all communication is encrypted. Right now, you are simply using IIS' default "Under Construction" Web page to verify that traffic to and from http://computer1 is encrypted. After you verify that communications are encrypted, you plan to deploy the intranet Web application.

Because the client computer is at a remote location, you want to do as much troubleshooting as possible from Computer1.

Questions

1. Which of the following tools can you use to check which IPSec policy is assigned to Computer1? (Choose all that apply.)

   a. IP Security Monitor

   b. Event Viewer

   c. Netsh

   d. Netdiag

   e. Network Monitor

   f. IPSecMon

   g. Performance console

   ____

2. Open Microsoft Internet Explorer on Computer2, type the URL **http://computer1** in the address bar, and then click Go. Is traffic from Computer2 reaching Computer1? How can you tell?

   ____

3. Is the traffic encrypted? How can you tell?

   ____

   ____

   ____

4. Are Main Mode negotiations succeeding? How can you tell?

5. Based on the information you have gathered, what is the likely cause of the problem, and how will you resolve the problem?

6. How will you verify that IPSec negotiations are now successful?

Chapter Summary

- The simplest way to deploy IPSec is to configure IPSec policies by using the Group Policy Object Editor and distributing the GPOs by using Active Directory.
- You can configure IPSec policies on individual computers by using command-line tools. These local policies will be overridden by domain IPSec policies if any exist, however. For Windows Server 2003, use Netsh to create IPSec policies from the command line. Use IPSecCmd for computers running Windows XP; use IPSecPol for computers running Windows 2000.
- If all IPSec peers are not in a trusted Active Directory domain, you can use certificates to authenticate computers. Windows Server 2003 includes Certificate Services, which can be used to issue certificates for IPSec.

- To audit IPSec negotiations, first enable success or failure auditing for Audit Policy Change and possibly for Audit Process Tracking. Then use Event Viewer to examine the Security event log.
- To analyze packets that are dropped, enable IPSec driver event logging by using the Netsh command on Windows Server 2003. (Other versions of Windows require adding a registry value to enable IPSec driver event logging.) Then use Event Viewer to examine the System event log.
- When you need detailed troubleshooting information, enable IKE tracing by using Netsh. Then examine the *%systemroot%*\Debug\Oakley.log file.
- You can isolate IPSec authentication problems by temporarily changing both peers to the Preshared Key authentication method. Authentication problems when using Kerberos are often caused by one of the IPSec peers not being able to reach a domain controller. IPSec authentication using certificates will fail if a private key is not associated with the certificate.
- Firewalls, routers, and other packet-filtering devices must allow traffic on UDP port 4500 and traffic with IP protocol ID 50 for ESP IPSec communications to succeed.

Exam Highlights

Before taking the exam, review the key topics and terms that are presented in this chapter. You need to know this information.

Key Topics

- Understand the various methods for deploying IPSec to large numbers of computers.
- Know how to deploy Certificate Services for the purpose of authenticating IPSec negotiations.
- Be familiar with the various tools available for monitoring IPSec communications. In particular, know how each node of the IP Security Monitor snap-in can be used.
- Know how to troubleshoot common IPSec problems, especially those caused by firewalls and proxy servers.

Key Term

certificate-to-account mapping A feature of Windows Server 2003 that enables IPSec to verify that a certificate matches a valid computer account in the Active Directory forest.

Questions and Answers

Lesson 1 Review

Page 9-16

1. Which of the following options ensures that certificates are accepted from only valid computer accounts in the same forest?

   a. Enable Certificate To Account Mapping

   b. Exclude The CA From The Certificate Request

   c. Use Session Key Perfect Forward Secrecy

   d. Use Master Key Perfect Forward Secrecy

   a. The Enable Certificate To Account Mapping option causes IPSec to look up a valid computer account in the current forest before authenticating a connection from an IPSec peer using a certificate.

2. Which of the following operating systems could you configure by using the IPSecPol command-line tool?

   a. Windows Server 2003

   b. Windows XP

   c. Windows 2000

   d. Windows 98

   c. IPSecPol is a Resource Kit Tool available only for Windows 2000. For Windows XP, you should use IPSecCmd. For Windows Server 2003, use the Netsh tool.

Lesson 2 Review

Page 9-38

1. Which of the following parameters can be found in IP Security Monitor's Main Mode Statistics? (Choose all that apply.)

   a. IKE Main Mode

   b. Bytes Sent In Tunnels

   c. Transport Bytes Sent

   d. IKE Quick Mode

   e. Total Acquire

   f. Soft Associations

   g. Active Tunnels

   a, d, e, and f. These statistics relate to the IKE negotiations, and, as such, are found under Main Mode Statistics. The other answers are found in Quick Mode Statistics because they relate to the IPSec sessions.

2. Which of the following tools can be used to verify that network traffic to a specific host is being encrypted on a computer running Windows Server 2003? (Choose all that apply.)

   a. IP Security Monitor

   b. Event Viewer

   c. Netsh

   d. Netdiag

   e. Network Monitor

   f. IPSecMon

   g. Performance console

   a, c, and e. IP Security Monitor lists active SAs in addition to the methods used for encryption and integrity for any specific connection. Netsh can provide the same information at a command line. Network Monitor captures the entire packets as they are communicated between IPSec-protected computers. If the packets are encrypted, Network Monitor will not be able to interpret the contents of the packets contained within the ESP headers.

3. Which of the following tools can display the total cumulative number of successful Main Mode negotiations on a computer running Windows Server 2003? (Choose all that apply.)

   a. IP Security Monitor

   b. Event Viewer

   c. Netsh

   d. Netdiag

   e. Network Monitor

   f. IPSecMon

   g. Performance console

   a, c, and g. IP Security Monitor displays the IKE Main Mode parameter within the Main Mode Statistics node. Netsh can provide the same information at a command line. The Performance console can display the value for the Total Main Mode SAs counter within the IPSec v4 IKE performance object.

Lesson 3 Review

Page 9-46

1. IPSec peers ComputerA and ComputerB, as shown in Figure 9.15, are unable to establish a connection. What is the cause of the problem?

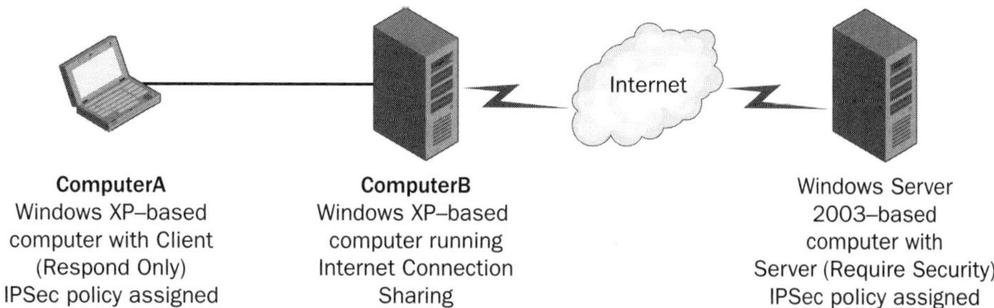

Figure 9.15 Problematic IPSec architecture

Internet Connection Sharing in Windows XP does not support NAT-T, even though Windows XP supports NAT-T as an IPSec client.

Design Activity: Case Scenario Exercise

Page 9-48

1. How can you prevent internal employees from capturing other employees' passwords in the future?

   There are a couple of ways to do this. The simplest way is to configure your e-mail server to use only encrypted protocols. But the choices available for encrypting e-mail transmissions depend on the mail server and client software used. If your environment used Exchange Server and Outlook exclusively, you could choose to encrypt all mail communications and almost entirely eliminate the risk of an attacker gathering passwords by using a sniffer. However, if the organization uses various mail servers or a variety of mail clients, there might not be an encrypted protocol that all the clients can use.

   Given the limitations of using encrypted mail protocols, IPSec is the most attractive choice for encrypting the communications. IPSec provides a way to encrypt network traffic regardless of the server and client applications used.

2. Which of the built-in IPSec policies would you assign to the mail server?

   For the time being, you have no choice but to assign the Request Security IPSec policy. You cannot use the Require Security policy because you have clients that probably don't support IPSec, such as two-way pagers. Even if all clients do support IPSec, it is going to take weeks or months to test and deploy IPSec for all the computers in your organization.

3. Will you use Kerberos, certificates, or a preshared key to authenticate the IPSec connections?

   You should use both Kerberos and certificates. Kerberos is the fastest way to allow IPSec authentication for computers that are members of your domain. You can issue certificates to client computers that are not members of the domain.

4. Besides IPSec, what measures can you take to reduce the risk of an attacker capturing network communications and misusing that information?

   First, you should implement non-technical countermeasures. Create a computer usage agreement that explains what users can and cannot do with the organization's computers, and have all employees sign that agreement. Make it clear that employees can and will be caught if they break the agreement. Employees must understand that when they are caught, they will be punished.

   Second, implement physical security wherever possible. Use network hardware that does not send network communications to all ports. In other words, use Layer 2 switches rather than hubs. Restrict access to your network equipment to prevent a potential attacker from tapping directly into a hub or switch and capturing network traffic.

   Third, use software restrictions to limit the tools users, and even administrators, can run. There are legitimate reasons for running Network Monitor on a server, but the potential for abuse is high. It is difficult to restrict administrators from running applications while allowing them to do their jobs, but it might be worth the effort to reduce the risk of an employee violating another employee's privacy.

Design Activity: Troubleshooting Lab

Page 9-50

1. Which of the following tools can you use to check which IPSec policy is assigned to Computer1? (Choose all that apply.)

   a. IP Security Monitor

   b. Event Viewer

   c. Netsh

   d. Netdiag

   e. Network Monitor

   f. IPSecMon

   g. Performance console

   a and c. IP Security Monitor and Netsh both report the active IPSec policy.

2. Open Microsoft Internet Explorer on Computer2, type the URL **http://computer1** in the address bar, and then click Go. Is traffic from Computer2 reaching Computer1? How can you tell?

   Yes. You can run Network Monitor on Computer1 to verify this.

3. Is the traffic encrypted? How can you tell?

   No. Network Monitor reveals that standard, unencrypted HTTP communications were captured. If the traffic were encrypted, Network Monitor would not have been able to identify the communications as being HTTP.

4. Are Main Mode negotiations succeeding? How can you tell?

   No. There are several ways you can determine this. First, Network Monitor has revealed that traffic is not encrypted, which is a sign that either Main Mode or Quick Mode negotiations have failed. Second, the Main Mode Statistics counters in the IP Security Monitor snap-in are not incrementing in the way they would if Main Mode negotiations were succeeding. You could also review the Oakley.log, which would reveal that Computer1 applied the Server (Request Security) policy to the incoming traffic, but that negotiations with Computer2 failed.

5. Based on the information you have gathered, what is the likely cause of the problem, and how will you resolve the problem?

   Either Computer1 does not have IPSec enabled or Computer1 and Computer2 do not have a compatible set of protocols enabled. You should check the configuration on both computers and assign a policy to Computer2 that would enable IPSec communications with Computer1. The Client (Respond Only) policy would be perfect.

6. How will you verify that IPSec negotiations are now successful?

   You can use Network Monitor to verify that traffic is encrypted and that it is being transferred with ESP. Alternatively, you can use the IP Security Monitor snap-in, the Performance console, or Netsh to verify that the total number of IPSec connections counter has incremented.

10 Planning and Implementing Security for Wireless Networks

Exam Objectives in this Chapter:

- Plan and implement security for wireless networks.
    - Plan the authentication methods for a wireless network.
    - Plan the encryption methods for a wireless network.
    - Plan wireless access policies.
    - Configure wireless encryption.
    - Install and configure wireless support for client computers.

Why This Chapter Matters

In recent years, consumers and businesses have been adopting mobile computing and wireless networks at a breathtaking pace. The benefit to businesses is obvious: employees are more productive because they can work and stay in touch when away from their desks. In an organization that uses a virtual private network (VPN), an employee with a wireless mobile computer can even connect to corporate resources from the airport, the local coffee shop, or thousands of other wireless hot spots.

Unfortunately, wireless networks are also among the most widely exploited consumer and business technologies. If you have a wireless network in place, attackers might be able to access your network without physically entering your building. This can grant them access to your internal network resources, allow them to eavesdrop on your communications, and enable them to impersonate you when attacking other computers on the Internet.

When your wireless network is properly configured, the risks of an attacker compromising it can be dramatically reduced. Microsoft Windows Server 2003 includes several features that allow you to improve the security of your wireless networks and realize their benefits without assuming unnecessary risk. This lesson will describe these features and give you hands-on experience with configuring wireless security.

Lessons in this Chapter:

Before You Begin

If you fulfilled the requirements for the previous chapters, you already have the necessary hardware and software configured. You can use the computers in the state they were in after completing the previous chapters, or you can install the software from scratch. To do the practices, examples, and lab exercises in this chapter, you must have:

- A private network that is not connected to the Internet or any other network. This network should not have any production computers connected to it.
- A wireless access point (WAP) connected to the private network.
- One computer with a wired network connection. On this computer, perform a Windows Server 2003, Enterprise Edition installation with default settings. Assign the name Computer1 to this computer. Add the Domain Controller role to the computer using the default settings, and specify the domain name cohowinery.com. Configure the computer to use itself as its own primary Domain Name System (DNS) server. Then add the Application Server role. Install the Certificate Services service, and configure this computer as an Enterprise Root certification authority (CA).
- One computer with a wireless network connection. On this computer, perform a Microsoft Windows XP Professional or Windows Server 2003 installation with default settings. Assign the name Computer2 to this computer. Add this computer to the cohowinery.com domain as a member computer. Configure this computer to use Computer1 as its primary DNS server. Install a wireless network interface card compatible with the WAP in Computer2, but do not configure it yet.

Lesson 1: Wireless Network Security Fundamentals

For those of us responsible for managing the security of a network, wireless technologies expose severe security weaknesses that we have overlooked for years. Wired networks have relied on physical security to protect the privacy of communications. In other words, the only barrier preventing an attacker from capturing another user's traffic is being unable to physically connect to the user's network. Wired networks almost always rely only on physical security to authorize users to access the network. If you can reach an Ethernet port, you gain complete network access to most companies' intranets.

Wireless networks have these weaknesses too, but they lack the inherent physical security of wired networks. In fact, most corporate wireless networks can be accessed by people with mobile computers in the business' parking lot. To make matters worse, attackers have significant motivation to abuse wireless networks. Accessing a wireless network might grant an attacker access to resources on an organization's internal network. Or it might allow the attacker to access the public Internet while hiding his or her identity, which would allow the intruder to attack hosts on remote networks while disguised with the organization's IP addresses.

The concerns over the abuse of wireless networks are far from theoretical. Intruders have a wide variety of tools available for detecting, connecting to, and abusing wireless networks. As with most aspects of security, there are technologies available that can help you to limit the vulnerabilities presented by wireless networks. Specifically, you can require wireless communications to be authenticated and encrypted. This provides assurance similar to that offered by the physical security of wired networks. The game between security experts and attackers continues, however, and early wireless authentication and encryption technologies can now be easily defeated by an intruder.

After this lesson, you will be able to

- Describe the security risks associated with wireless networks.
- Design a wireless network that minimizes security risks.
- Describe the 802.1X authentication process.
- Choose authentication and encryption methods for a wireless network.

Estimated lesson time: 30 minutes

Security Threats

Because wireless communications are not contained within the physical medium of a wire, wireless networks are more vulnerable to several types of attacks, including:

- **Eavesdropping.** Attackers can capture traffic as it is sent between a wireless computer and the WAP. Depending on the type of antenna used and the transmitting power, an attacker might be able to eavesdrop from hundreds or thousands of feet away.

- **Masquerading.** Attackers might be able to gain access to restricted network resources by impersonating authorized wireless users.
- **Attacks against wireless clients.** Attackers can launch a network-based attack on a wireless computer that is connected to an ad hoc or untrusted wireless network.
- **Denial of service.** Attackers can jam the wireless frequencies by using a transmitter, preventing legitimate users from successfully communicating with a WAP.
- **Data tampering.** Attackers can delete, replay, or modify wireless communications with a man-in-the-middle attack.

To reduce the vulnerability of wireless networks to these types of attacks, you can use Wired Equivalent Privacy (WEP), Wi-Fi Protected Access (WPA), and several other wireless security techniques.

WEP

WEP is a wireless security protocol that helps protect your information by using a security setting, called a *shared secret* or a *shared key*, to encrypt network traffic before transmitting it over the airwaves. This helps prevent unauthorized users from accessing the data as it is being transmitted.

Unfortunately, some smart cryptographers found several theoretical ways to discover WEP's shared secret by analyzing captured traffic. These theoretical weaknesses were quickly implemented in freely available software. The combination of free tools for cracking WEP encryption, the ease of capturing wireless traffic, and the dense proliferation of wireless networks have led WEP to become the most frequently cracked network encryption protocol today.

Security Alert You won't need to understand the details of the WEP standard for the exam, but it is an interesting study on how not to make an encryption protocol. The most easily exploited weakness of WEP is that many of WEP's possible initialization vectors (IVs) are cryptographically weak and can expose individual bytes of the WEP key. WEP changes these IVs over time, and an attacker who captures millions of packets will eventually gather enough packets with weak IVs to crack the entire WEP key. Some wireless network adapters intentionally avoid using weak IVs, which makes it much more time-consuming to expose the WEP key. Ask your network adapter vendor what they've done to make WEP communications more secure. For more detailed information on WEP's weaknesses, search for the paper titled "Weaknesses in the Key Scheduling Algorithm of RC4" on the Internet.

Besides weak cryptography, another factor contributing to WEP's vulnerability is that WEP is difficult to manage because it doesn't provide any mechanism for changing the shared secret. On wireless networks with hundreds of hosts configured to use a WAP, it is practically impossible to regularly change the shared secret on all hosts. As a result, the WEP shared secret tends to stay the same indefinitely. This gives attackers sufficient opportunity to crack the shared secret and all the time they need to abuse their ill-gotten network access.

If you could change the shared secret on a regular basis, however, you would be able to prevent an attacker from gathering enough data to crack the WEP key, and this would significantly improve WEP's privacy. There are techniques for dynamically and automatically changing the shared secret to dramatically reduce WEP's weaknesses. When WEP is used with a dynamic shared secret, it is called *dynamic WEP*. When a static shared key is used with WEP, it is called *static WEP*.

Security Alert Search the Internet for AirSnort and WEPCrack for information on two tools commonly used to break into WEP-protected wireless networks. These tools can derive a WEP key in anywhere from a day to a couple of weeks, depending on how much traffic is transferred across the network, the level of encryption used, and luck. They hardly provide instantaneous access to a wireless network, however.

To put it simply, if you rely only on a static shared secret, you cannot trust WEP to either protect the privacy of your network communications or to prevent uninvited guests from accessing your wireless network. If you are forced to use static WEP to provide compatibility with all of the wireless devices on your network, there are a few things you can do to improve security. First, use the highest level of encryption possible: 128-bit. Short keys might be sufficient in some encryption scenarios, but WEP's 40-bit encryption is very vulnerable. Second, place WAPs in a perimeter network to restrict access to internal resources. If users need access to the internal network from a wireless network, they can use a VPN connection. Third, position your WAPs so that wireless transmissions are limited to locations that you can physically secure, such as the interior of your building.

See Also For more information about perimeter networks, refer to Chapter 4. For more information about VPNs, refer to Chapters 4 and 8.

Real World

WEP gets a lot of criticism for being weak, and the criticism is well deserved...but I think it does accomplish its goal. The name, *Wired Equivalent Privacy*, demonstrates that WEP's ambitions aren't all that high. First, WEP's goal is to provide only privacy, not necessarily data integrity, authentication, or authorization. Second, WEP is only intended to provide privacy similar to that provided by wired networks. In my opinion, traditional wired networks have weak security.

I used to work in a facility that housed one of the Internet's largest datacenters. This datacenter contained hundreds of servers worth millions of dollars, and it stored hundreds of millions of dollars worth of confidential data. Fitting the high value of its contents, the building was constructed with a concrete moat to prevent an attacker from driving a vehicle into the building and to limit access to the primary entrance. At the entrance was a receptionist who was only a phone call away from security guards.

Despite these safeguards, the physical security was almost meaningless. I had a friend who would visit me on a regular basis. She wasn't a trained spy or even an ambitious hacker, but she managed to bypass the security controls almost every time she visited simply by walking past the reception desk with a confident look on her face. If she had been a hacker, she could've connected a mobile computer directly to an available Ethernet port and had access to the network from inside the firewall.

Most buildings aren't that secure. Even if the building has a security guard at the main entrance, the building almost certainly has other entrances. To enter the building, just wait in the parking lot and follow an authorized employee through a side door.

Back to the security of wired networks. At most companies, the only barrier preventing an intruder from accessing the internal network and connecting to many internal resources is being unable to physically plug a wire into an Ethernet jack. The network engineers, therefore, trust the physical security of the facility to protect the privacy of their data. Sure, static WEP can be bypassed by any mildly ambitious intruder, but the same can be said for the physical security of most buildings.

Open and shared network authentication

The initial WEP standards provided for two types of computer authentication: open system and shared secret. Shared secret authentication requires wireless clients to authenticate by using a shared secret; open system authentication allows any client to connect without providing a password.

Fortunately, choosing between open system and shared secret authentication is easy: always use open system authentication. On the surface, this seems illogical because open system authentication merely identifies the wireless client without providing any proof of identity, but shared key authentication requires knowledge of a secret key. However, shared secret authentication actually weakens security because most WEP client implementations, including Windows XP, use the same secret key for both authentication and WEP encryption. A malicious user who captures the keys used for both authentication and encryption can use cryptanalysis methods to determine the shared secret authentication key, and therefore the WEP encryption key.

Once the WEP encryption key is determined, the malicious user has full access to the network, as if WEP encryption were not enabled. Therefore, although shared key authentication is stronger than open system for authentication, it weakens WEP encryption. If you use open system authentication, any computer can easily join your network. However, without the WEP encryption key, the wireless clients cannot send or receive wireless communications, and they will not be able to abuse the wireless network.

802.1X authentication

Although the early implementations of WEP were woefully inadequate, WEP's vulnerability can be significantly reduced by using 802.1X authentication. 802.1X enables WEP to regularly change the encryption keys, which dramatically reduces the likelihood that an attacker will be able to gather enough data to identify the shared secret.

802.1X employs an Internet Engineering Task Force (IETF) standard protocol called Extensible Authentication Protocol (EAP) to carry the authentication conversation between the client, the WAP, and a Remote Access Dial-In User Server (RADIUS) service. As part of the 802.1X secure authentication process, the EAP method generates an encryption key that is unique to each client. RADIUS forces the client to generate a new encryption key on a regular basis, which makes it more difficult for an attacker to capture enough traffic to identify a key. This allows existing WEP-capable hardware to be used while minimizing WEP's vulnerabilities.

See Also For more detailed information on 802.1X authentication, see "IEEE 802.1X Authentication for Wireless Connections" at *http://www.microsoft.com/technet/columns/cableguy/cg0402.asp*.

The process used by a client connecting to a dynamic WEP network with 802.1X authentication, as shown in Figure 10.1, is significantly more complex than the process a client uses to connect to an unsecured wireless network.

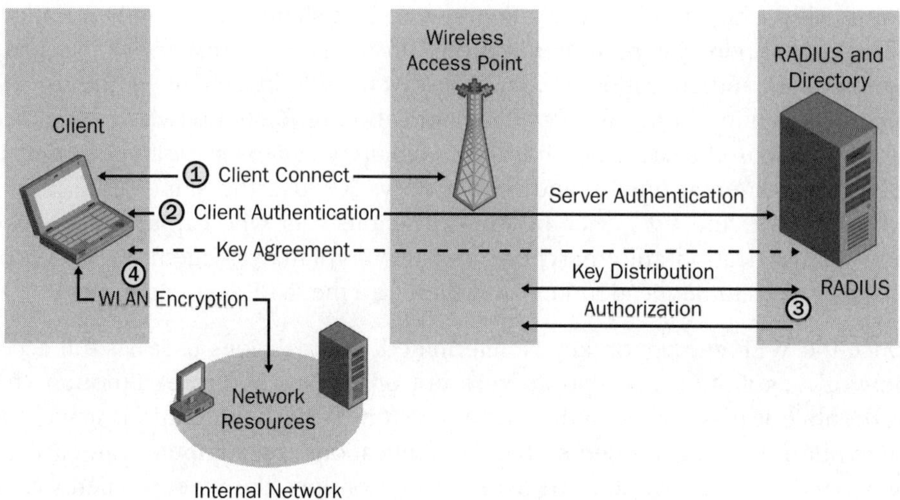

Figure 10.1 Connecting to an 802.1X-authenticated wireless network

Specifically, the client must perform the following steps to connect to an 802.1X-authenticated wireless network:

1. When the client computer is in range of the WAP, it will try to connect to the *Service Set Identifier (SSID)* hosted by the WAP. If the client has been configured with shared network authentication, it will authenticate itself to the WAP by using the network key. Because the WAP is configured to allow only 802.1X-authenticated connections, it issues an authentication challenge to the client. The WAP then sets up a restricted channel that allows the client to communicate only with the RADIUS service.
2. The wireless client examines the RADIUS server's public key certificate to ensure that an attacker is not impersonating the RADIUS server. The client then attempts to authenticate, using 802.1X, to the RADIUS service.
   - If the client and RADIUS service have been configured to use Protected EAP (PEAP) authentication, the client establishes a Transport Layer Security (TLS) session with the RADIUS service and then transmits credentials using the configured authentication protocol.
   - If the client and RADIUS service have been configured to use EAP-TLS authentication, the client authenticates by using public key certificates.

Important There is a third authentication method called EAP-Message Digest 5 Challenge Handshake Authentication Protocol (EAP-MD5 CHAP). However, it is not suitable for authenticating wireless connections, and Windows XP Service Pack 1 removes it as an option. It is not an option in Windows Server 2003.

3. The RADIUS service checks the client credentials against the directory. If it can authenticate the client's credentials and the access policy allows the client to connect, it will grant access to the client. The RADIUS service relays the access decision to the WAP. If the client is granted access, the RADIUS service transmits the dynamic shared secret to the WAP. The client and WAP now share common key material that they can use to encrypt and decrypt the traffic that will pass between them.

Note In Windows environments, the RADIUS service will usually be a Windows Server 2003–based computer running Internet Authentication Service (IAS), and the directory will be an Active Directory directory service domain.

4. The WAP then bridges the client's connection to the internal network, completing the 802.1X authentication process. If the client is configured to use Dynamic Host Configuration Protocol (DHCP), it can now request a lease.

The sections that follow describe the authentication methods and the role of the RAIDUS service in more detail.

PEAP PEAP is typically used to authenticate wireless clients by using a user name and password; EAP-TLS is used to authenticate wireless clients by using public key certificates. Although using a user name and password is not as strong as using public key certificates, because passwords can be stolen or guessed, the resulting encryption is still very strong. When PEAP authentication is used with a RADIUS service that forces encryption keys to change regularly, the resulting WEP encryption is not likely to be compromised in a reasonable amount of time. PEAP's primary advantage over EAP-TLS is that it is easier to deploy because it does not require you to implement a Public Key Infrastructure (PKI).

The PEAP authentication method has two phases. Phase 1 authenticates the RADIUS server by using the RADIUS server's public key certificate and then establishes a TLS session to the RADIUS server. Phase 2 requires a second EAP method tunneled inside the PEAP session to authenticate the client to the RADIUS service. This allows PEAP to use a variety of client authentication methods.

This is an important point: PEAP uses two separate types of authentication, one in each authentication phase. The first authentication is handled by PEAP without requiring administrative configuration. You must configure the second authentication protocol, however. Although wireless standards could theoretically support any authentication method, Windows Server 2003 and Windows XP support two by default: Microsoft Challenge Handshake Authentication Protocol version 2 (MS-CHAP v2) and certificates using EAP-TLS tunneled inside PEAP. You will almost always use MS-CHAP v2 with PEAP, however, because you should use EAP-TLS for certificate-based authentication. Certificate-based authentication does not require the additional layer of encryption provided by PEAP.

Security Alert It's a good thing the MS-CHAP v2 authentication is protected by TLS encryption, because MS-CHAP v2 is indeed susceptible to an offline dictionary attack. An attacker who can capture a successful MS-CHAP v2 exchange can methodically guess passwords until the correct one is determined. It would take a while, but the attacker will eventually get the password.

After the user is successfully authenticated, the authentication server supplies dynamically generated keying material to the WAP. From this keying material, the WAP creates new encryption keys for data protection.

Exam Tip If you have a hard time remembering the difference between PEAP and EAP-TLS, you can think of the P in PEAP as standing for *password*, because you usually use PEAP for password-based authentication, and you use EAP-TLS when client certificates are available.

EAP-TLS EAP-TLS performs the same functions as PEAP by authenticating the client computer and generating keying material that will be used for encrypting the wireless communications. However, EAP-TLS uses public key certificates to authenticate both the client and the RADIUS service. EAP-TLS was designed by Microsoft and is based on an authentication protocol that is nearly identical to the protocol used in the Secure Sockets Layer (SSL) protocol for securing Web transactions. While public key certificates provide strong authentication and encryption, you should only use EAP-TLS if you already have a PKI in place for another application or your organization's security requirements do not allow simple password authentication.

See Also For more information about EAP-TLS, refer to RFC 2716.

RADIUS RADIUS is a standardized service used primarily to authenticate dial-up users. Windows Server 2003 includes a RADIUS service and proxy named IAS. The traditional use for IAS on Windows networks is to allow an Internet Service Provider (ISP) to authenticate an organization's users based on the Active Directory domain credentials stored on the organization's private network.

Because RADIUS is designed to allow network hardware to authenticate against an external user database, WAPs also can use RADIUS to authenticate wireless users as they join the network. Authenticating to a RADIUS service allows user authentication for wireless networks to be centralized, rather than forcing administrators to store user credentials on each WAP.

See Also Chapter 4 describes the fundamentals of RADIUS and specific instructions for installing IAS.

The RADIUS service receives a user-connection request from the WAP and authenticates the client against its authentication database. A RADIUS service can also maintain a central storage database of other relevant user properties. In addition to the simple yes or no response to an authentication request, RADIUS can provide other applicable connection parameters for the user, including static IP address assignment and maximum session time.

The ability to specify a maximum session time enables the RADIUS service to force the client to reauthenticate on a regular basis. This reauthentication automatically generates a new shared secret, which upgrades static WEP to dynamic WEP. Each time the shared secret is changed, an attacker must restart the process of cracking the encryption key. If the maximum session time is low enough, it will be practically impossible for an attacker to capture enough data to crack the shared secret key. As a result, dynamic WEP can be considered adequately secure for most environments.

Wi-Fi Protected Access

Although WEP with dynamic re-keying is secure enough to meet the needs of most organizations, WEP still has security weaknesses. WEP still uses a separate static key for broadcast packets. An attacker can analyze these broadcast packets to build a map of private IP addresses and computer names. WEP keys have to be renewed frequently, which places an additional burden on RADIUS services.

Off the Record Dynamic WEP is very secure. Its biggest weakness might be its bad reputation. Often, executives at a company won't allow a wireless deployment because they've heard about the ability for attackers to break through WEP security. Even though standard WEP is not at all easy to exploit, and almost impossible to exploit when dynamic re-keying is used, the publicity WEP's vulnerabilities have received makes WPA even more attractive.

To address these lingering weaknesses with WEP, the Wi-Fi Alliance, a consortium of the leading wireless network equipment vendors, developed Wi-Fi Protected Access (WPA). WPA can use the same authentication mechanisms and encryption algorithms as WEP. This compatibility allows support for WPA to be added to WAPs with a simple firmware upgrade. However, WPA virtually eliminates WEP's most exploited vulnerability by using a unique encryption key for each packet.

Real World

As with any bleeding-edge technology, you're going to run into problems implementing wireless security on heterogeneous networks. Here's how every wireless network I've deployed has gone:

1. I configure a WAP that supports the latest security standard. Today, I look for WPA compatibility. A couple of years ago, I used WEP with 128-bit encryption.
2. I configure the clients, typically computers running Windows XP or Windows 2000, to connect as securely as possible to the WAP.
3. A week or two later, I get a call that some new computer or device can't connect to the network. Usually, this is a Windows XP–based computer with a different vendor's wireless network adapter driver, a Linux computer with an open source driver, or some wireless appliance.
4. After some troubleshooting, I determine that the new wireless device isn't currently compatible with the security I've configured. Faced with the option of waiting for updated drivers or lowering the wireless security level, the client chooses to lower the security to a compatible level.

As a result, even wireless networks that start their lives with strong security end up vulnerable. The moral of this story is that you might be forced to restrict the devices that connect to your network to maintain strong security. Over time, this should get better.

There are two encryption options for WPA: Temporal Key Integrity Protocol (TKIP) and Advanced Encryption System (AES). TKIP is the encryption algorithm used by WEP, and it will be used in the vast majority of WPA implementations. WPA improves upon WEP's implementation of TKIP, however. WPA with TKIP reuses initialization vectors (IVs) less frequently than WEP with TKIP, and, as a result, significantly reduces the likelihood that an attacker will collect enough traffic to compromise the encryption. Additionally, WPA with TKIP creates a unique encryption key for every frame, whereas WEP can use the same key for weeks or months. Finally, WPA with TKIP implements the message integrity code (MIC), often referred to as *Michael*, to guard against forgery attacks.

WPA can also use AES, a more secure encryption algorithm than TKIP. Unfortunately, although most existing wireless equipment can be upgraded to support WPA, most equipment cannot be upgraded to support AES. As a result, you will probably not be able to use AES unless you specifically choose equipment that supports it.

When you enable WPA, you establish a passphrase that is automatically associated with the dynamically generated security settings. This passphrase is stored with your other network settings on the base station and on each of your networked computers. Only wireless devices with the WPA passphrase can join your network and decrypt network transmissions.

WPA provides better security than WEP. However, WEP data protection, when combined with strong authentication and rapidly changing encryption keys, can meet the security requirements of most organizations. This is fortunate because many organizations will be forced to continue using WEP. Not all wireless network hardware supports WPA, but WEP is universally supported. Windows 2000 and earlier versions of Windows do not have built-in support for WPA, though you might be able to download an update from the vendor of your wireless network adapter. Finally, WPA must be configured manually on Windows XP clients because WPA configuration settings cannot be defined by using Group Policy objects (GPOs) with the built-in Active Directory functionality included with Windows Server 2003. For these reasons, you might be forced to choose WEP over WPA, even though you will sacrifice some degree of security.

Other Wireless Security Techniques

WEP and WPA are the most important wireless network security techniques. However, there are several secondary security techniques that you should be familiar with: media access control (MAC) address filtering, disabling SSID broadcasts, and VPNs.

MAC address filtering

One common technique used to make it more difficult for a casual user to connect to your wireless network is to configure your WAPs to allow only a predefined set of MAC addresses. Just like wired Ethernet cards, every wireless network card is assigned a unique MAC address by the manufacturer.

When a WAP is configured to use MAC address filtering, it will ignore any messages from wireless cards that use a MAC address not on the approved list. While this does improve security, it has significant manageability drawbacks. First, you must manually maintain the list of MAC addresses on your WAP, which would be impossible to do if you managed more than a dozen computers or multiple WAPs. Second, WAPs typically have limited memory and might not be able to store your organization's complete list of MAC addresses. Third, if an attacker is knowledgeable and determined enough to circumvent your WEP or WPA encryption, the attacker will also be able to identify and spoof an approved MAC address.

> **Exam Tip** It's important to be familiar with MAC address filtering, but, in the real world, the security gains are so minimal that it's not worth the trouble to set up.

Disabling SSID broadcasts

WAPs provide the option of disabling SSID broadcasts, but this should not be treated as a security feature. SSID broadcasts allow wireless clients to detect an available wireless network. In fact, Windows XP displays a notification to the user when it first receives a SSID broadcast from a wireless network. This is convenient; if you want users to be actively notified of the presence of the wireless client, you should enable SSID broadcasts.

Disabling SSID broadcasts will prevent the casual computer user from discovering your network, but it does nothing to prevent a skilled attacker from detecting your network. For example, a user with the free Network Stumbler tool installed can quickly identify the SSID of a wireless network that has SSID broadcasts disabled, because 802.11 association/disassociation messages are always sent unencrypted and contain the SSID that the client wants to associate to or disassociate from.

See Also You can download Network Stumbler from *http://www.stumbler.net*.

VPNs

While a VPN is an excellent solution for securely traversing a public network such as the Internet, VPNs are not the best solution for securing wireless networks. For this kind of application, a VPN is unnecessarily complex and costly. It adds little additional security to dynamic WEP, but it significantly increases costs, reduces usability, and removes important pieces of the functionality.

VPN clients usually require the user to initiate a connection to the VPN server; therefore, the connection will never be as transparent as a wired network connection. Non-Microsoft VPN clients might also prompt for logon credentials, in addition to the standard network or domain logon, when the connection is established. If the VPN disconnects because of a poor wireless signal or because the user is roaming between WAPs, the user has to repeat the connection process.

Because the VPN connection is only user-initiated, an idle, logged-off computer will not be connected to the internal network. Therefore, a computer cannot be remotely managed or monitored unless a user is logged on. Certain computer GPO settings, such as startup scripts and computer-assigned software, might never be applied. Finally, mobile computers often go into standby or hibernation mode. However, resuming from standby or hibernation does not automatically re-establish the VPN connection; the user has to do this manually.

Lesson Review

The following questions are intended to reinforce key information presented in this lesson. If you are unable to answer a question, review the lesson materials and try the question again. You can find answers to the questions in the "Questions and Answers" section at the end of this chapter.

1. Which of the following authentication methods would you use to protect a wireless network for an organization that has an existing PKI and in which all computers and users have been issued certificates with private keys? (Choose all that apply.)
   a. Open network authentication
   b. Shared network authentication
   c. 802.1X PEAP authentication
   d. 802.1X EAP-TLS authentication
   e. 802.1X EAP-MD5 CHAP authentication

   ____

   ____

2. Which of the following authentication methods would you use to protect a wireless network for an organization that prefers using user names and passwords for authentication? (Choose all that apply.)
   a. Open network authentication
   b. Shared network authentication
   c. 802.1X PEAP authentication
   d. 802.1X EAP-TLS authentication
   e. 802.1X EAP-MD5 CHAP authentication

   ____

   ____

Lesson Summary

- Wireless networks have a high potential for abuse because potential attackers can access the network without physically entering a building.
- WEP provides authentication and encryption. However, because of a weakness in the way static WEP uses encryption keys, it is vulnerable to attacks that can compromise the privacy and integrity of network communications.

- 802.1X authentication can be used to overcome static WEP's most significant security vulnerability by forcing wireless clients to reauthenticate to a RADIUS service on a regular basis, thereby generating a new shared secret. When WEP is forced to automatically generate a new shared secret on a regular basis, it is called dynamic WEP.
- To authenticate wireless users by using a user name and password pair, use PEAP authentication. To authenticate users with public key certificates, use EAP-TLS.
- WPA provides stronger encryption than WEP, but it is not as widely supported.

Lesson 2: Configuring Wireless Security

Although almost anyone can set up a wireless network in a few minutes, configuring a wireless network with security features is significantly more complex. Fortunately, Windows Server 2003 provides all of the software you need to deploy a wireless infrastructure with authentication, encryption, message integrity, and dynamically changing WEP shared secrets. At a high level, you will follow these steps to configure a wireless network infrastructure:

1. Plan wireless access policies.
2. Create a structure for authorizing users and computers to access the wireless network.
3. Plan the certificate infrastructure, and optionally deploy a PKI.
4. Configure IAS servers, including assigning a certificate and creating remote access policies (RAPs).
5. Update and configure wireless clients with the SSID and security settings.
6. Configure WAPs with security settings and the IP addresses of the IAS servers.

After this lesson, you will be able to

- Design an authorization strategy to assign wireless network privileges to users and computers.
- Configure a certificate infrastructure to authenticate wireless clients.
- Configure IAS to authenticate wireless users.
- Configure wireless clients manually and by using GPOs.
- Identify the information required to configure a WAP.

Estimated lesson time: 45 minutes

Planning Wireless Access Policies

There are several aspects to planning wireless access policies. First, it is important to plan wireless access policies to help prevent WAPs from being installed in your organization with insufficient security. You should draft a policy that, at a minimum, defines the following requirements for new WAPs:

- **Authentication requirements.** Generally, you should require that all wireless users are authenticated and specify whether PEAP or EAP-TLS will be used. If you plan to allow guests to access your wireless network, you should make provisions for creating WAPs providing limited access to your internal network that will be used only by guests.

Security Alert If you allow wireless access to guests and do not force guests to use a different IP subnet, add a policy stating that no application shall rely on the IP source address for authorization.

- **Encryption.** Some level of encryption should always be required. Unless you have wireless devices that do not support it, your policy should mandate the highest level of encryption available.
- **Physical security.** Just like any other piece of network equipment, WAPs should be protected by lock and key to prevent attackers from tampering with the hardware.
- **SSID broadcast and naming conventions.** Your policy should specify whether WAPs are configured to broadcast the SSID, and it should detail naming conventions for SSIDs.
- **Actively maintained list of WAPs.** You must maintain a list of all WAPs on your network that at a minimum includes the SSID, the security settings, the administrator's name, and patching requirements.
- **Auditing requirements.** You should specify how usage information is gathered and how logs are archived.

Besides documenting requirements for the configuration of new WAPs, you should define how users can and cannot use wireless access. Consider restricting the times of day when wireless access is available and physically shutting down WAPs after business hours. To reduce the likelihood of wireless-capable computers being attacked while connected to untrusted wireless networks, consider forbidding users to connect to wireless networks other than your own or restricting access to a list of approved networks.

See Also SANS provides a template for a wireless communications policy at *http://www.sans.org/resources/policies/Wireless_Communication_Policy.pdf*.

Another way to use policy to control the risks associated with wireless networks is to specifically state that WAPs managed by end users are not allowed in your organization's computer usage policy. Existing employees should be notified that the computer usage agreement has been updated and that they are not allowed to connect a WAP to your organization's network. If you decide not to use wireless networks in your organization, you need to pursue this strategy in an active rather than a passive way. You should back up this decision with a clear, published policy and ensure that all employees are aware of it and of the consequences of violating it. Consider using scanning equipment and network packet monitors to detect the use of unauthorized wireless equipment on your network.

Planning The single most effective way to prevent users from adding their own WAPs is to proactively provide wireless access and make it easy for users to connect.

Designing the Authorization Strategy

Although many organizations choose to allow all computers and users in the organization to access the wireless network, other organizations choose to restrict access. On Windows networks, you will restrict access to wireless networks by using domain security groups. Although it is possible to use the dial-in properties of domain user objects to allow and deny access to individuals, this is tedious to administer for more than a few users.

One method for implementing this is to create a three-tiered structure for assigning permissions. At the top level, create a universal group, and grant this universal group access by using a remote access policy in IAS. At the second level, create domain global groups for users and computers that will be granted wireless access. Add to these security groups users and groups that should be granted wireless access. An example of such a hierarchy is shown in Figure 10.2.

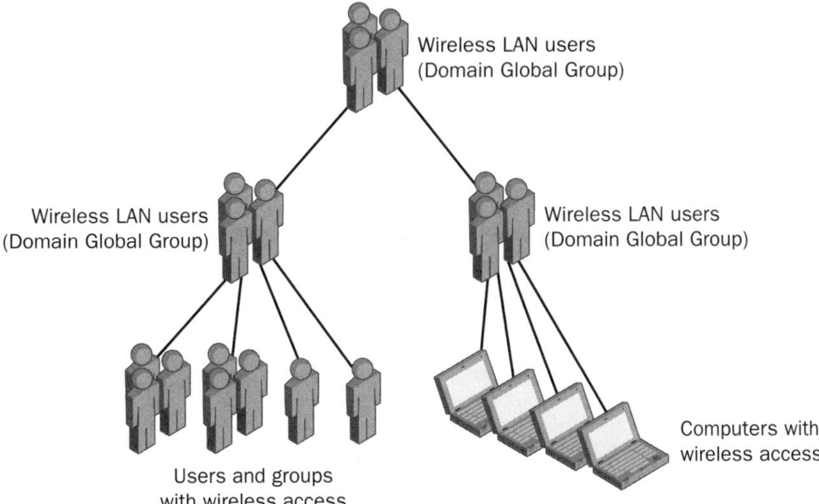

Figure 10.2 Sample user and group hierarchy for controlling wireless network authorization

You should strive to have all wireless computers joined to the same domain as your IAS computers. You can have wireless clients that are not members of a domain, but you will have to configure the wireless network client settings manually because GPOs are not applicable. If the user does not log on to the domain, user authentication to the wireless network will require a separate user name and password prompt.

Configuring the Certificate Infrastructure

Regardless of which authentication method you choose, you will need at least one computer certificate to use 802.1X authentication. This certificate must be installed on the IAS servers that will perform RADIUS services. For computer authentication with EAP-TLS, you must also install a computer certificate on the wireless client computers. A computer certificate installed on a wireless client computer is used to authenticate the wireless client computer so that the computer can obtain network connectivity to the enterprise intranet and download computer Group Policy settings prior to user logon. For user authentication with EAP-TLS after a network connection is made and the user logs on, you must use a user certificate on the wireless client computer.

Table 10.1 summarizes the certificates that need to be installed or enrolled for the two types of supported wireless authentication.

Table 10.1 Authentication Types and Certificates

Authentication type	Certificates on each wireless client	Certificates on each IAS computer
EAP-TLS	One computer certificate, one or more user certificates, and the root CA certificates for issuers of IAS server computer certificates	One computer certificate and the root CA certificates for issuers of wireless client computer and user certificates
PEAP with MS-CHAP v2	The root CA certificates for issuers of IAS server computer certificates	One computer certificate

If the certificate of the root CA that issued the IAS servers' certificates is already installed as a root CA certificate on your wireless clients, no other configuration is necessary. If your issuing CA is a Windows 2000 Server or Windows Server 2003 online root enterprise CA, the root CA certificate is automatically installed on each domain member through computer configuration GPO settings. If it is not, you must install the root CA certificates of the issuers of the computer certificates of the IAS servers on each wireless client.

Generally, you should configure Windows Server 2003 Certificate Services to issue the IAS server certificate—even if the only reason you create the CA is to issue a single certificate for the IAS server. Alternatively, you can purchase a certificate from a public CA. Regardless of whether you deploy your own PKI or buy a certificate, the root CA certificate of the CA that issued the IAS server certificate must be installed on each wireless client.

Windows XP includes the root CA certificates of many public CAs. If you purchase your IAS server certificates from a public CA that corresponds to an included root CA certificate, no additional wireless client configuration is required. If you purchase your IAS server certificates from a public CA for which Windows XP does not include a corresponding root CA certificate, you must install the root CA certificate on each wireless client.

See Also For more information about Certificate Services, refer to Chapter 7.

If you are using a Windows Server 2003 or Windows 2000 Certificate Services enterprise CA as an issuing CA, you can install a computer certificate on the IAS server by configuring a GPO for the autoenrollment of computer certificates. If you plan to use the EAP-TLS authentication method, you should also configure autoenrollment for computer and user certificates for computers and users that will be accessing the wireless network. User certificate autoenrollment is supported only by Windows XP and Windows Server 2003 wireless clients.

Tip When enrolling user certificates, consider creating a duplicate of the User certificate template specifically for wireless users.

A client computer configured to use EAP-TLS authentication can obtain certificates for the authentication of wireless connections in three ways: autoenrollment, Web enrollment, and importing a certificate file. If you choose to import the certificates, you can either create and distribute certificates individually for each user or distribute a single certificate file to all users. A single certificate used for a group of users is known as a *group certificate*, which is the least secure certificate deployment, because anyone who obtains the certificate file could use it to successfully authenticate a wireless connection.

Important Pocket PCs do not support GPOs, and, as a result, you will have to manually enroll them. Pocket PCs can use only user certificates because they do not support computer certificates.

Configuring IAS

IAS is a component of Windows Server 2003 that provides RADIUS services capable of authenticating users based on information contained within Active Directory. When configuring the security of a wireless network, you must configure the IAS server to use specific authentication methods and to grant access to authorized users. This configuration is done by using two types of policies: Remote Access Policies (RAP) and Connection Request Policy (CRP).

See Also For more information about IAS, including how to harden IAS servers, refer to Chapter 4.

The RAP controls how or whether a connection is authorized to the network. A RAP contains a set of policy conditions that determine whether that policy applies to a given connection request. When configuring a RAP for wireless network access, you can create policy conditions that specify the Active Directory security group that a client must be a member of, the time of day, or the connection type of the requesting client, as shown in Figure 10.3. A RAP is also configured to allow or deny the connection request. If there are multiple RAPs on an IAS server, each connection request is evaluated against them according to the priority until a matching RAP either allows or denies the request.

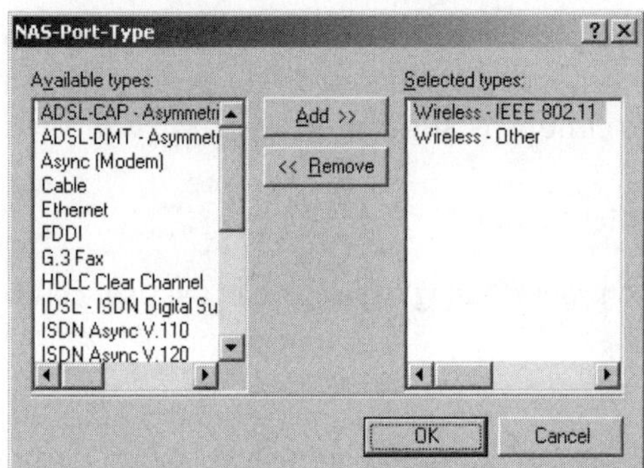

Figure 10.3 Configuring policy conditions to apply the policy to wireless connections

A RAP also contains a profile that applies to new connections. When creating a RAP for wireless access, the most important profile settings are the authentication methods and the session timeout. Clicking the Authentication tab on the Edit Dial-In Profile dialog box, as shown in Figure 10.4, allows you to configure the authentication method. Click the EAP Methods button to specify the EAP types that will be available: Protected EAP or Smart Card Or Other Certificate.

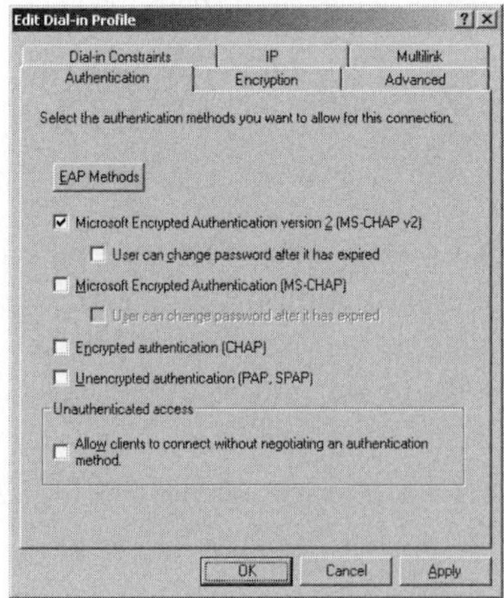

Figure 10.4 Configuring authentication methods for a RAP

Regardless of the EAP type you choose, you can select a computer certificate that the IAS server will present to the wireless client. If the IAS server has only one computer certificate, this certificate will automatically be selected. If you choose the PEAP authentication method, you also have the option to enable fast reconnects. Generally, you should select the Enable Fast Reconnect check box on the Protected EAP Properties dialog box to improve performance when wireless clients switch from one WAP to another.

Click the Dial-In Constraints tab to specify the session timeout, which is necessary to enable dynamic WEP. The Minutes Client Can Be Connected (Session-Timeout) value controls the frequency with which WEP encryption keys are regenerated. You should specify a value of 10 minutes for WEP, as shown in Figure 10.5. For WPA, specify a value of 8 hours (480 minutes). Exercise 2 of this lesson guides you step by step through the process of configuring a RAP.

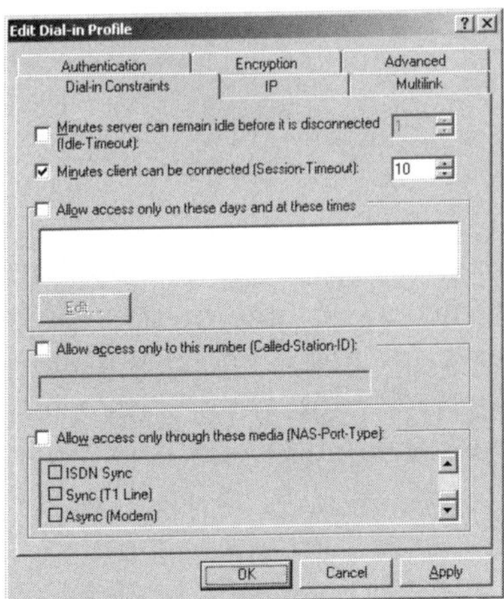

Figure 10.5 Configuring session timeout for WEP

RAPs are not used exclusively for controlling wireless access. As a result, there are several configuration options that you can safely ignore. Specifically, the multilink settings are not useful for wireless connections, and they should always be disabled. Additionally, specifying the Called-Station-ID value is only useful when you are creating a RAP for dial-up users.

Successful and rejected authentication events generated from wireless network devices and users will be recorded in the System event log of the IAS server if you select Rejected Authentication Requests and Successful Authentication Requests in the Internet Authentication Service Properties dialog box, as shown in Figure 10.6. Authentication information is most useful for troubleshooting authentication issues, although this information might also be used for security auditing and alerting purposes.

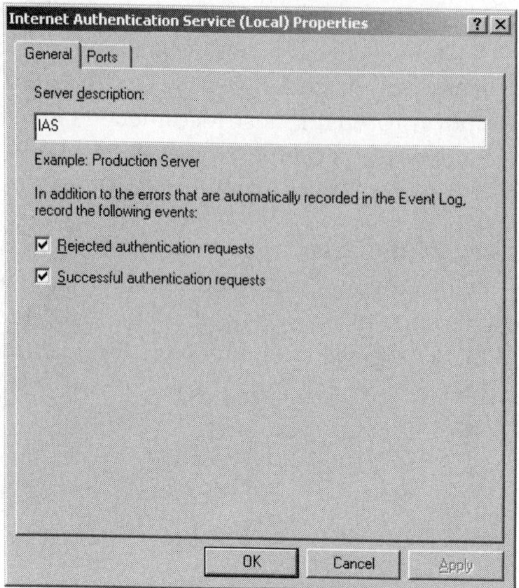

Figure 10.6 Enabling IAS authentication auditing

Initially, you should keep event logging enabled so that you can verify that authentication is working properly. Unless your organization's security policy requires you to maintain auditing information, you should disable auditing of successful authentication requests after the system has stabilized. IAS events have IAS as the source and an Event ID of 2. In the text of the event message, look for the remote access policy name next to the Policy-Name box.

Configuring Wireless Clients

The first step to configure a wireless client is to ensure that the computer has the software required to authenticate and connect to your wireless network. Computers running Windows 2000 require the Microsoft 802.1X Authentication Client, available from *http://support.microsoft.com/?kbid=313664*. Additionally, you must start the Wireless Zero Configuration service and set its startup type to Automatic. If you plan to use WPA with any Windows client, including Windows XP and Windows Server 2003, you must install the Windows WPA client update on all clients. You can download the client from *http://support.microsoft.com/?kbid=815485*.

Windows XP and Windows Server 2003 wireless clients have an Authentication tab in the properties dialog box for a wireless connection, as shown in Figure 10.7. On this tab, you can enable 802.1X authentication, specify and configure the EAP type, and choose the sets of credentials that the computer will use for the authentication.

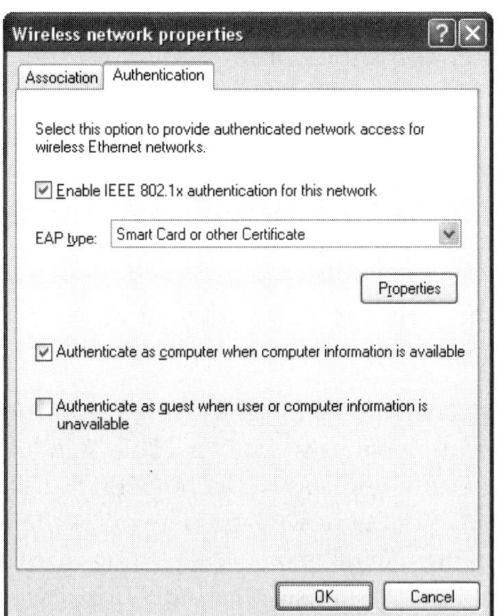

Figure 10.7 Windows XP wireless network authentication configuration

Select the Enable Network Access Control Using IEEE 802.1X check box to use 802.1X authentication for the network connection. You can leave this option selected even if you have not yet configured 802.1X. If the check box is selected, the computer will attempt to perform an 802.1X authentication when the network interface is initialized. If the computer does not receive a response to its authentication requests, the computer will behave as though the connection does not require authentication. Therefore, it is always okay to leave this check box selected.

Use the EAP Type list to specify the EAP type to use for IEEE 802.1X authentication. By default, you can choose from Protected EAP (PEAP) and Smart Card Or Other Certificate. However, other options will be listed if an application has installed additional EAP libraries.

If you select Smart Card Or Other Certificate, click the Properties button to configure whether the client certificate is located on a smart card or the client's certificate store. If there is more than one user certificate installed, the user will be prompted to choose a certificate. You can also choose whether the client will authenticate the RADIUS service by validating that the server's certificate has not expired, and which root CAs to trust. If the RADIUS service's root CA is not trusted when the client validates the server's certificate, the user will automatically be prompted to trust the certificate. You do not need to select the Use A Different User Name For The Connection check box; its only effect is to cause the user to be prompted to select a certificate even if the user has only one certificate installed.

If you select Protect EAP (PEAP) from the EAP Type list, you have the same option to validate the RADIUS service's certificate. You should also specify the authentication method that you will use—either Secured Password (EAP-MSCHAP v2) or Smart Card Or Other Certificate. If you choose to use EAP-MSCHAP v2, click the Configure button to choose whether to automatically use the current logon credentials or to prompt the user for other credentials. You should usually select the Enable Fast Reconnect check box to allow the RADIUS service to immediately authenticate the client if the computer moves from one WAP to another. If the Enable Fast Reconnect check box is cleared, the client computer will have to perform the complete PEAP authentication process each time it connects to a WAP.

To automate the configuration of wireless network settings for wireless clients running Windows XP (Service Pack 1 and later) and Windows Server 2003, Windows Server 2003 Active Directory domains support a new Wireless Network (IEEE 802.11) Policies Group Policy extension that allows you to configure wireless network settings that are part of Computer Configuration GPO settings. Wireless network settings in the Wireless Network (IEEE 802.11) Policies Group Policy extension include global wireless settings, the list of preferred networks, WEP settings, and IEEE 802.1X settings. These settings encompass all of the items on the Association and Authentication tabs in the properties dialog box for a wireless network on a Windows XP or Windows Server 2003 wireless client, and they also include some additional settings.

To configure wireless network security by using a GPO, follow this procedure:

1. Open a blank Microsoft Management Console (MMC) console, and add the Group Policy Object Editor snap-in. Open the GPO you will use to apply the wireless network configuration settings.
2. Expand the GPO, Computer Configuration, Windows Settings, and then Security Settings. Click Wireless Network (IEEE 802.11) Policies.
3. By default, there are no policies. Right-click Wireless Network (IEEE 802.11) Policies, and then click Create Wireless Network Policy.

   The Wireless Network Policy Wizard appears.
4. Click Next.
5. Type a name for the policy, and then click Next.
6. Select the Edit Properties check box, and then click Finish.

   The properties dialog box appears.

7. Click the General tab, as shown in Figure 10.8. The security-related settings are Networks To Access, which specifies whether the client is allowed to connect to ad hoc networks, and Automatically Connect To Non-Preferred Networks, which you might want to disable to prevent clients from connecting to potentially dangerous, untrusted wireless networks.

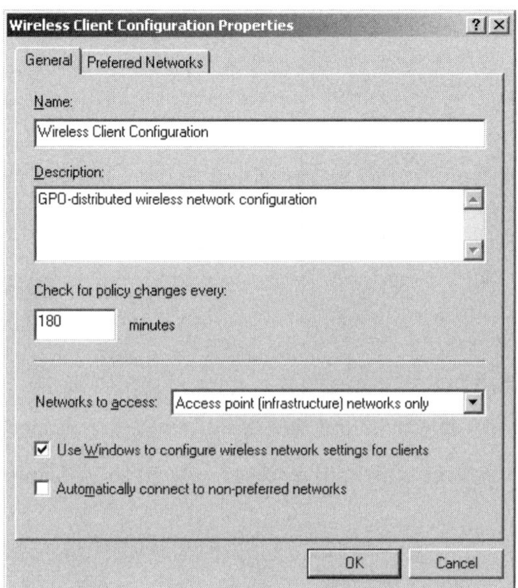

Figure 10.8 The General tab of the wireless network policy properties dialog box

8. Click the Preferred Networks tab.

   This tab lists preferred networks, which are networks that Windows XP will automatically connect to. There are no preferred networks by default.

9. Click Add.

   The New Preferred Setting Properties dialog box appears, as shown in Figure 10.9. The Network Properties tab allows you to specify whether WEP encryption will be used. Generally, you should select the Data Encryption and The Key Is Provided Automatically check boxes. Leave the Network Authentication check box cleared to use open network authentication.

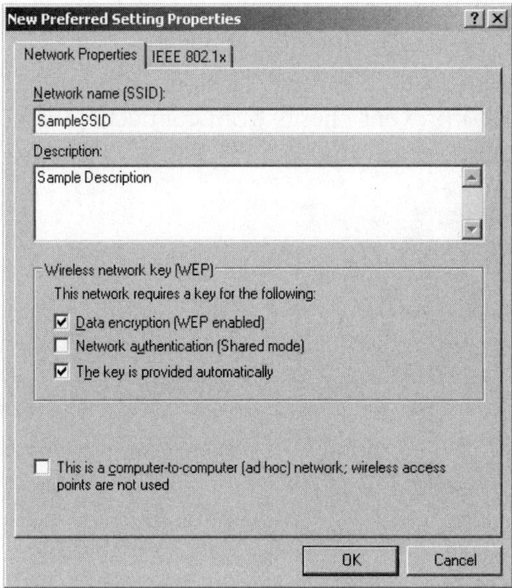

Figure 10.9 The Network Properties tab of the New Preferred Setting Properties dialog box

10. Click the IEEE 802.1X tab. Select the Enable Network Access Control Using IEEE 802.1X check box.
11. If you want to be able to manage the computer across a wireless network when no user is logged on, select the Authenticate As Computer When Computer Information Is Available check box.
12. Click the EAP Type list to select either Smart Card Or Other Certificate or Protected EAP. This setting must correspond to the setting specified on the IAS server.
13. Click the Settings button to configure the selected EAP type. This dialog box is exactly the same as the dialog box used to configure wireless clients locally.
14. Click OK three times to return to the MMC console.

Note that you can only create a single wireless network policy for each GPO.

To obtain detailed information about the EAP authentication process for Windows XP, you must enable tracing for the EAPOL and RASTLS components by using the following commands at a command prompt:

```
netsh ras set tracing eapol enabled
netsh ras set tracing rastls enabled
```

After these commands are issued, the information about the authentication process will be logged in the Eapol.log and Rastls.log files in the *SystemRoot*\Tracing folder.

Configuring WAPs

The final step of the wireless network configuration process is to configure and enable your WAPs. Unfortunately, the user interface varies for each WAP. At a minimum, you will need to configure the following settings:

- Select WEP or WPA encryption and the encryption level.
- Specify 802.1X authentication and the authentication method.
- Specify the SSID.
- Specify the IP address of the IAS RADIUS servers.
- Specify a shared key corresponding to the shared secret specified during the IAS configuration.

Figure 10.10 shows the wireless security settings of a common inexpensive WAP.

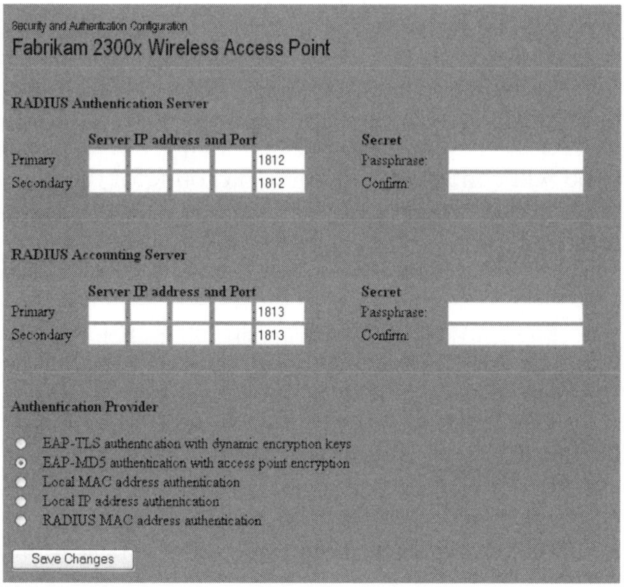

Figure 10.10 Configuring security on a WAP

Practice: Deploying WEP Encryption with PEAP Authentication

In this practice, you will configure a wireless network environment using PEAP authentication. This practice requires that Computer1 has Windows Server 2003, Enterprise Edition installed, that it has been configured as a domain controller, and that it has Certificate Services installed as an Enterprise Root CA. For more information about how to configure the computer, refer to the "Before You Begin" section of this chapter.

Exercise 1: Configure the Active Directory infrastructure

In this exercise, you will configure the cohowinery.com domain with user, computer, and group accounts that you can use to control access to the wireless network. In the first procedure, you will create groups to contain the wireless users and computers.

1. Log on to the cohowinery.com domain on Computer1 using the Administrator account.
2. Open the Active Directory Users And Computers console.
3. In the console tree, expand cohowinery.com.
4. In the Active Directory Users And Computers console, right-click Users, click New, and then click Group.
5. In the New Object – Group dialog box, type **GGWirelessUsers** in the Group Name box. Click OK.
6. In the Active Directory Users And Computers console, right-click Users, click New, and then click Group.
7. In the New Object – Group dialog box, type **GGWirelessComputers** in the Group Name box. Click OK.

In the second procedure, you will configure a computer account for the wireless computer and allow dial-in access. The computer will not literally dial-in, but this permission is required for wireless access. You will then add the account to the GGWirelessUsers group.

1. In the Active Directory Users And Computers console, right-click Computer2, and then click Properties.
2. Click the Dial-In tab.
3. Click Allow Access.
4. Click the Member Of tab, and then click the Add button. In the Enter The Object Names To Select box, type **GGWirelessComputers**, and then click OK twice.

In the third procedure, you will configure a user account for the wireless user and allow dial-in access. You will then add the account to the GGWirelessComputers group.

1. In the Active Directory Users And Computers console, right-click Users, click New, and then click User.
2. In the New Object – User dialog box, type **WirelessUser** in the First Name box, and then type **WirelessUser** in the User Logon Name box.

3. Click Next. Type a password of your choice in the Password and Confirm Password boxes. Clear the User Must Change Password At Next Logon check box.
4. Click Next, and then click Finish.
5. In the Active Directory Users And Computers console, click the Users node. Right-click WirelessUser, and then click Properties.
6. Click the Dial-In tab.
7. Click Allow Access.
8. Click the Member Of tab, and then click the Add button. In the Enter The Object Names To Select box, type **GGWirelessUsers**, and then click OK twice.

Exercise 2: Configure IAS

In this exercise, you will install IAS and configure RADIUS for authentication of wireless users and computers.

1. Log on to the cohowinery.com domain on Computer1 using the Administrator account.
2. Install IAS by using Add Or Remove Programs in Control Panel. Click Add/Remove Windows Components. In the Windows Components Wizard, click Networking Services, and then click Details. Select Internet Authentication Service, click OK, and then click Next. After IAS is installed, click Finish.
3. Open the Internet Authentication Service console from the Administrative Tools program group.
4. Right-click Internet Authentication Service, and then click Register Server In Active Directory.

   This ensures that IAS has sufficient permissions to Active Directory to authenticate users.
5. Click OK twice.
6. Expand the Internet Authentication Service tree, right-click RADIUS Clients, and then click New RADIUS Client.

   The New RADIUS Client Wizard appears.
7. In the Friendly Name box, type **WirelessAP**. In the Client Address box, type the IP address of your WAP. Click Next.
8. On the Additional Information page, type a complex shared secret in both the Shared Secret and Confirm Shared Secret boxes. Click Finish.
9. Right-click Remote Access Policies, and then click New Remote Access Policy.

   The New Remote Access Policy Wizard appears.

10. Click Next. In the Policy Name box, type **Wireless Network Access**, and then click Next.
11. On the Access Method page, click Wireless, and then click Next.
12. On the User Or Group Access page, click Group, and then click Add. Add both the GGWirelessComputers and GGWirelessUsers groups, and then click OK to return to the wizard.

Tip In the Select Groups dialog box, just type **GGWireless**. The Multiple Names Found dialog box will appear, and you can select both groups by using the CTRL key and the mouse button.

13. Click Next. On the Authentication Methods page, notice that Protected EAP is selected by default. Click Configure, and then select the Enable Fast Reconnect check box. Notice that the EAP Types list contains the Secured Password (EAP-MSCHAP v2) EAP type by default, as shown in Figure 10.11. Click OK.

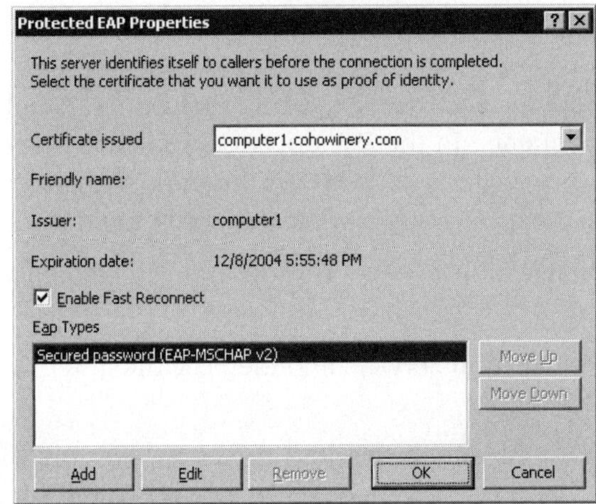

Figure 10.11 Default IAS PEAP properties

14. Click Next. On the Completing The New Remote Access Policy Wizard page, review the conditions that the wizard generated. It should read

```
Conditions: NAS-Port-Type matches "Wireless - Other OR Wireless - IEEE 802.11"
AND Windows-Groups matches "COHOWINERY\GGWirelessComputers;COHOWINERY
\GGWirelessUsers"
```

You should understand this syntax so that you can manually update the remote access policy to make changes in the future.

15. Click Finish.
16. Right-click Wireless Network Access, and then click Properties.
17. Click Edit Profile.

18. Select the Minutes Client Can Be Connected (Session-Timeout) check box, and then set the value to **8** minutes.
19. Click the Authentication tab, and then click the EAP Methods button.
20. Click Protected EAP, and then click Edit.

    The Protected EAP Properties dialog box appears. Notice that the Certificate Issued list already has a computer certificate registered because Computer1 is an enterprise CA. Also notice that Secured Password (EAP-MSCHAP v2) is selected in the EAP Types list.
21. Click OK four times to return to the Internet Authentication Service console.

Exercise 3: Configure the WAP

In this exercise, you will configure your WAP to use 802.1X authentication by sending requests to the IAS service on Computer1. Unfortunately, each vendor's WAP has a different interface for configuring it. Refer to the documentation of the WAPs.

Configure the WAP with the following settings:

- WEP/RADIUS security mode
- An SSID of WEP_TEST
- A RADIUS service address corresponding to Computer1's IP address
- A shared key corresponding to the shared secret specified during the IAS configuration
- The highest available form of WEP encryption

Exercise 4: Configure the client computer

In this exercise, you will configure the client computer to connect to the wireless network.

1. Log on to the cohowinery.com domain on Computer2 using the WirelessUser account.
2. Open the Network Connections window.
3. Right-click Wireless Network Connection, and then click Properties.
4. Click the Wireless Networks tab. In the Available Networks box, click WEP_TEST, and then click Configure.
5. Click the Association tab. Click the Data Encryption (WEP Enabled) option. Verify that The Key Is Provided For Me Automatically check box is selected.
6. Click the Authentication tab. Select the Enable IEEE 802.1X Authentication For This Network check box. In the EAP Type list, click Protected EAP.

7. Verify that the Authenticate As Computer When Computer Information Is Available check box is selected. This ensures the computer can be managed while connected to the wireless network when a user is not logged on.
8. Click Properties. In the Protected EAP Properties dialog box, select the Connect To These Servers check box, and then select the Enable Fast Reconnect check box, as shown in Figure 10.12.

   Notice that Secure Password (EAP-MSCHAP v2) is the selected authentication method by default.

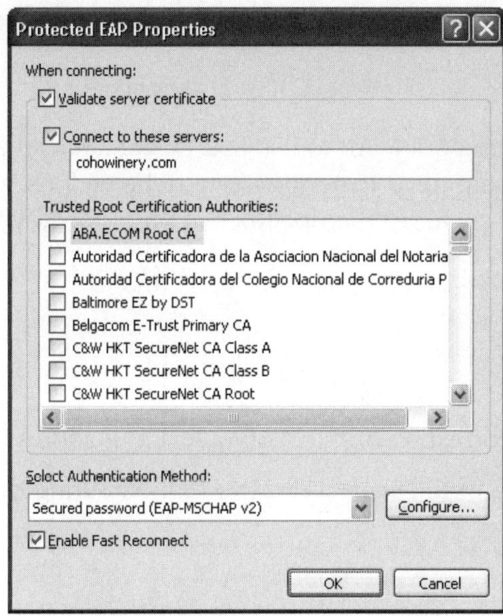

Figure 10.12 The Protected EAP Properties dialog box

9. Click OK three times.

   Computer2 should now authenticate to the wireless network.
10. Start Internet Explorer. In the Address box, type **http://computer1/certsrv/**, and then click Go.

    The Microsoft Certificate Services Web page should appear, verifying that Computer2 is connected to the wireless network.

Lesson Review

The following questions are intended to reinforce key information presented in this lesson. If you are unable to answer a question, review the lesson materials and try the question again. You can find answers to the questions in the "Questions and Answers" section at the end of this chapter.

1. Which of the following can be configured by using a GPO?
   - **a.** A Windows XP Service Pack 1 wireless client with WEP encryption
   - **b.** A Windows XP Service Pack 1 wireless client with WPA encryption
   - **c.** A Windows 98 wireless client with WEP encryption
   - **d.** A Microsoft Windows Mobile 2003 wireless client with WEP encryption

   ____

   ____

2. Which setting must be enabled to initiate dynamically rekeyed WEP?
   - **a.** Minutes Server Can Remain Idle Before It Is Disconnected
   - **b.** Minutes Client Can Be Connected
   - **c.** Allow Access Only On These Days And At These Times
   - **d.** Allow Access Only To This Number
   - **e.** Allow Access Only Through These Media

   ____

   ____

3. Which of the following pieces of information is *not* required when configuring the WPA?
   - **a.** The IP addresses of the wireless clients
   - **b.** The IP address of the RADIUS server
   - **c.** The SSID
   - **d.** The shared key
   - **e.** The encryption level
   - **f.** The authentication method

   ____

   ____

Lesson Summary

- You should publish policies defining how wireless networks can be used and should be configured in your organization.
- The most efficient way to assign authorization rights for wireless clients is to create groups specifically for wireless users and computers in Active Directory.

- You can use Certificate Services to enroll certificates for the IAS server and, if you use EAP-TLS authentication, for the wireless clients.
- If you use WEP encryption, you can configure Windows XP and Windows Server 2003 wireless clients by using a GPO.

Case Scenario Exercise

In this exercise, you will read a scenario about a company's wireless networking security challenge and then answer the questions that follow. The questions are intended to reinforce key information presented in this chapter. If you are unable to answer a question, review the lessons and try the question again. You can find answers to the questions in the "Questions and Answers" section at the end of this chapter.

Scenario

You are the lead systems administrator at a large law firm. Law firms are among the slowest adopters of new technologies, and your employer is no exception. Your organization has, to date, not deployed a wireless network. After bringing up the benefits of wireless networks at a recent meeting with the senior partners, you learned that you will not be deploying a wireless network for several years, if ever.

The lack of an IT-configured wireless network has not entirely stopped their adoption, however. Yesterday, you noticed a junior attorney accessing the Web from the firm's library—without an Ethernet cable. When you asked the attorney how he was connected to the network, he confessed that he plugged a consumer WAP into the network port in his office.

You need to explain to the senior partners why your organization needs a wireless network security policy even if they do not want to sponsor a wireless network.

Questions

1. Which of the following risks are posed to your organization by the presence of a rogue wireless network? (Choose all that apply.)
   - **a.** An attacker could use a wireless network card to capture traffic between two wired network hosts.
   - **b.** An attacker could access hosts on your internal network from the lobby of your building with a wireless-enabled mobile computer.
   - **c.** An attacker could use your Internet connection from the lobby of your building with a wireless-enabled mobile computer.

d. An attacker could capture an attorney's e-mail credentials as the attorney downloads his messages across the wireless link.

e. An attacker with a wireless network card could join your Active Directory domain.

____

____

____

2. Which of the following would reduce the risk of a security compromise resulting from a vulnerable rogue wireless network? (Choose all that apply.)

a. Publishing a wireless network security policy allowing employee-managed WAPs that have authentication and encryption enabled.

b. Publishing a wireless network security policy forbidding employee-managed WAPs.

c. Publishing instructions for other employees to access the current employee-managed WAP.

d. Deploying an IT-managed WAP using open network authentication without encryption.

e. Deploying an IT-managed WAP with WEP encryption and 802.1X authentication.

f. Educating internal employees about the risks associated with wireless networks.

____

____

____

____

Troubleshooting Lab

In this lab, you will troubleshoot a problem related to connecting a new computer to a wireless network. Read the following scenario and then answer the question that follows. The question is intended to reinforce key information presented in this chapter. If you are unable to answer the question, review the lessons and try the question again. You can find answer to the question in the "Questions and Answers" section at the end of this chapter.

Scenario

You are a systems administrator responsible for managing your organization's wireless network. Currently, you use four WAPs to provide wireless connectivity across your company's entire facility. You have two IAS servers acting as RADIUS servers, as shown in Figure 10.13. You manage your own PKI, and you issued the certificates for your two IAS servers. All connections use WEP encryption and PEAP authentication using domain user names and passwords. You manage the client configurations by specifying policy settings in the Default Domain GPO.

Figure 10.13 Wireless network architecture

An employee calls you because he is having a problem connecting to the wireless network with a new laptop computer running Windows XP that he brought from home. Though this computer is not a member of the domain, the employee copied the wireless network settings from a computer with a working wireless network connection. You double-check the configuration settings, and they seem to be correct.

Question

1. Which of the following is the likely cause of the problem?
   a. The mobile computer is not a member of the domain.
   b. The wireless network configuration was not applied by a GPO.
   c. The laptop computer does not support WPA.
   d. SSID broadcasts are disabled.
   e. The laptop computer does not trust your root CA.
   f. MAC address filtering is enabled and does not have the laptop computer's MAC address listed.

____

____

____

____

____

Chapter Summary

- Wireless networks have a high potential for abuse because potential attackers can access the network without physically entering a building.
- WEP provides authentication and encryption. However, because of a weakness in the way static WEP uses encryption keys, it is vulnerable to attacks that can compromise the privacy and integrity of network communications.
- 802.1X authentication can be used to overcome static WEP's most significant security vulnerability by forcing wireless clients to reauthenticate to a RADIUS service on a regular basis, thereby generating a new shared secret. When WEP is forced to automatically generate a new shared secret on a regular basis, it is called *dynamic WEP*.
- To authenticate wireless users by using a user name and password pair, use PEAP authentication. To authenticate users with public key certificates, use EAP-TLS.
- WPA provides stronger encryption than WEP but is not as widely supported.
- You should publish policies defining how wireless networks can be used and how they should be configured in your organization.
- The most efficient way to assign authorization rights for wireless clients is to create groups specifically for wireless users and computers in Active Directory.
- You can use Certificate Services to enroll certificates for the IAS server and, if you use EAP-TLS authentication, the wireless clients.
- If you use WEP encryption, you can configure Windows XP and Windows Server 2003 wireless clients by using a GPO.

Exam Highlights

Before taking the exam, review the key topics and terms that are presented in this chapter. You need to know this information.

Key Topics

- Be able to list the risks associated with wireless networks, and be able to assess the ability for an organization to mitigate those risks.
- Know the various authentication and encryption protocols available to protect wireless networks.
- Be able to explain the significance of a RADIUS sever for improving the security of wireless networks.
- Know how to configure Certificate Services to issue certificates for wireless clients.

- Know how to configure an IAS server to act as a RADIUS server for a WAP.
- Be able to configure one or many wireless clients to use authentication and encryption.

Key Terms

dynamic WEP A term used to describe WEP when it has been configured to automatically change the shared secret in order to limit the amount of encrypted data an attacker can capture for cryptanalysis.

Extensible Authentication Protocol-Transport Layer Security (EAP-TLS) An authentication method that enables clients to authenticate by using a public key certificate.

Protected Extensible Authentication Protocol (PEAP) A two-phase authentication method that protects the privacy of user authentication by using TLS.

Remote Access Dial-In User Server (RADIUS) A standardized service that network equipment, such as a WAP, can use to authenticate users.

Service Set Identifier (SSID) The name of the wireless network that is used by the client to identify the correct settings and credential type to use for this wireless network.

shared secret The password that the wireless clients, the WAP, and often the RADIUS server have access to. The shared secret is used to build the encryption key.

static WEP A term used to describe the traditional implementation of WEP, in which a shared secret is manually configured and does not change on a regular basis.

Transport Layer Security (TLS) A method for encrypting tunneled traffic to protect the privacy of communications.

Wi-Fi Protected Access (WPA) A method for encrypting wireless communications that improves upon the privacy provided by WEP.

Wired Equivalent Privacy (WEP) A method for encrypting wireless communications that is standardized and widely deployed, but that suffers from serious well-exploited vulnerabilities.

Questions and Answers

Page 10-15

Lesson 1 Review

1. Which of the following authentication methods would you use to protect a wireless network for an organization that has an existing PKI and in which all computers and users have been issued certificates with private keys? (Choose all that apply.)

   a. Open network authentication

   b. Shared network authentication

   c. 802.1X PEAP authentication

   d. 802.1X EAP-TLS authentication

   e. 802.1X EAP-MD5 CHAP authentication

   a and d. To authenticate users and computers with certificates, you should use open network authentication and 802.1X EAP-TLS authentication.

2. Which of the following authentication methods would you use to protect a wireless network for an organization that prefers using user names and passwords for authentication? (Choose all that apply.)

   a. Open network authentication

   b. Shared network authentication

   c. 802.1X PEAP authentication

   d. 802.1X EAP-TLS authentication

   e. 802.1X EAP-MD5 CHAP authentication

   a and c. To authenticate users by using a user name and password, you should use open network authentication and 802.1X PEAP authentication.

Lesson 2 Review

Page 10-34

1. Which of the following can be configured by using a GPO?

   a. A Windows XP Service Pack 1 wireless client with WEP encryption

   b. A Windows XP Service Pack 1 wireless client with WPA encryption

   c. A Windows 98 wireless client with WEP encryption

   d. A Microsoft Windows Mobile 2003 wireless client with WEP encryption

   a. Windows XP clients can be configured with WEP encryption. The other clients cannot be configured by using a GPO.

2. Which setting must be enabled to initiate dynamically rekeyed WEP?
   a. Minutes Server Can Remain Idle Before It Is Disconnected
   b. Minutes Client Can Be Connected
   c. Allow Access Only On These Days And At These Times
   d. Allow Access Only To This Number
   e. Allow Access Only Through These Media

   b. When editing a RAP, you should specify a number of minutes in the Minutes Client Can Be Connected box to cause WEP to generate a new encryption key on a regular basis.

3. Which of the following pieces of information is *not* required when configuring the WPA?
   a. The IP addresses of the wireless clients
   b. The IP address of the RADIUS server
   c. The SSID
   d. The shared key
   e. The encryption level
   f. The authentication method

   a. You do not have to configure the IP addresses of the wireless clients. In fact, wireless clients do not receive an IP address until after authenticating.

Design Activity: Case Scenario Exercise

Page 10-36

1. Which of the following risks are posed to your organization by the presence of a rogue wireless network? (Choose all that apply.)
   a. An attacker could use a wireless network card to capture traffic between two wired network hosts.
   b. An attacker could access hosts on your internal network from the lobby of your building with a wireless-enabled mobile computer.
   c. An attacker could use your Internet connection from the lobby of your building with a wireless-enabled mobile computer.
   d. An attacker could capture an attorney's e-mail credentials as the attorney downloads his messages across the wireless link.
   e. An attacker with a wireless network card could join your Active Directory domain.

   b, c, and d. Attackers can use a rogue WAP that is poorly secured to access your internal network, capture wireless traffic, and use your Internet connection, but they cannot capture wired traffic or gain access to internal resources that require authentication.

2. Which of the following would reduce the risk of a security compromise resulting from a vulnerable rogue wireless network? (Choose all that apply.)

   a. Publishing a wireless network security policy allowing employee-managed WAPs that have authentication and encryption enabled.

   b. Publishing a wireless network security policy forbidding employee-managed WAPs.

   c. Publishing instructions for other employees to access the current employee-managed WAP.

   d. Deploying an IT-managed WAP using open network authentication without encryption.

   e. Deploying an IT-managed WAP with WEP encryption and 802.1X authentication.

   f. Educating internal employees about the risks associated with wireless networks.

   a, b, e, and f. Deploying an IT-managed WAP would be ideal because it would allow employees to take advantage of the benefits of wireless networks while minimizing the risks by allowing IT to configure authentication and encryption. Additionally, educating employees and publishing a security policy reduces the risk that an employee will configure an unprotected WAP.

Design Activity: Troubleshooting Lab

Page 10-38

1. Which of the following is the likely cause of the problem?

   a. The mobile computer is not a member of the domain.

   b. The wireless network configuration was not applied by a GPO.

   c. The laptop computer does not support WPA.

   d. SSID broadcasts are disabled.

   e. The laptop computer does not trust your root CA.

   f. MAC address filtering is enabled and does not have the laptop computer's MAC address listed.

   e. The laptop computer must be configured to trust your root CA before it can establish a connection to the RADIUS server. The other possible causes would not prevent the computer from connecting, with the exception of MAC address filtering. MAC address filtering could cause this problem, because the laptop computer's MAC address would not be on the approved list on the WAP. However, MAC address filtering is rarely used on networks with multiple WAPs.

11 Deploying, Configuring, and Managing SSL Certificates

Exam Objectives in this Chapter:

- Deploy, manage, and configure Secure Sockets Layer (SSL) certificates, including uses for Hypertext Transfer Protocol Secure (HTTPS), Lightweight Directory Access Protocol (LDAP) over SSL (LDAPS), and wireless networks. Considerations include renewing certificates and obtaining self-issued certificates instead of publicly issued certificates.
  - Obtain self-issued certificates and publicly issued certificates.
  - Install certificates for SSL.
  - Renew certificates.
  - Configure SSL to secure communication channels. Communication channels include client computer to Web server, Web server to Microsoft SQL Server computer, client computer to Active Directory domain controller, and e-mail server to client computer.

Why This Chapter Matters

Secure Sockets Layer (SSL) protects the most important transactions on the Internet. Millions of people have relied on SSL to validate servers and keep their personal information private. As a security administrator, it is extremely likely that you will have to deploy and manage SSL certificates on a Microsoft Windows Server 2003 network. Even if you do not need SSL to protect Web communications, you can use the protocol to protect Active Directory directory service domain controller communications, database queries, and e-mail messages. This chapter will give you the knowledge and experience you need to use SSL to provide communications encryption and integrity for Windows Server 2003 network applications.

Lessons in this Chapter:

Before You Begin

If you fulfilled the requirements for the previous chapters, you already have the necessary hardware and software configured. You can use the computers in the state they were in after completing the previous chapters, or you can install the software from scratch. To do the practices, examples, and lab exercises in this chapter, you must have:

- A private network that is connected to the Internet and protected by a firewall. This network should not have any production computers connected to it.
- One computer. Perform a Windows Server 2003 installation with default settings, and assign the computer name Computer1. Add the Domain Controller role to the computer using the default settings, and specify the domain name cohowinery.com. Configure the computer to use itself as its own primary DNS server. Then add the Application Server role with the default settings. Finally, add Certificate Services and configure the computer as an Enterprise CA.

Additionally, this chapter contains examples that use SQL Server 2000, Microsoft Exchange Server 2003, and Microsoft Office Outlook 2003. To fully understand the examples, you should have these applications available.

Lesson 1: Overview of Secure Sockets Layer (SSL)

SSL was developed by Netscape Communications Corporation in 1994 to secure transactions over the World Wide Web. Soon after, the Internet Engineering Task Force (IETF) began work to develop a standard protocol to provide the same functionality. SSL 3.0 was used as the basis for that work, which is known as the Transport Layer Security (TLS) protocol. The implementation of the SSL/TLS protocol in Windows Server 2003 closely follows the specification defined in RFC 2246, "The TLS Protocol Version 1.0."

SSL is widely used because it provides strong authentication, message privacy, and data integrity. Unlike other proprietary techniques for improving communication security, SSL is an open standard that is widely deployed and supported by a variety of servers and clients. As a result of the wide adoption, the security community has carefully examined the SSL standards and popular SSL implementations. This close examination, combined with the relative maturity of the SSL standards, has resulted in a highly secure method for authenticating clients and servers and protecting the privacy of communications.

After this lesson, you will be able to

- Describe how an SSL session is established.
- Identify scenarios in which SSL should be used.
- Understand the differences between IP Security (IPSec) and SSL.
- List the changes required to allow SSL-protected communications through a firewall.

Estimated lesson time: 25 minutes

How SSL Works

SSL provides encryption, authentication, and data integrity by using a public key certificate. When the SSL session is established, the server's public key certificate is used to encrypt and exchange a shared secret between the client and server. This shared secret is then used to encrypt communications for the rest of the session. The following describes the step-by-step procedures for establishing an SSL session:

1. The client requests the public key from the server.
2. The server sends the public key to the client.
3. The client sends the server a session key, encrypting it with the public key.
4. The server decrypts the session key received from the client by using the server's private key.

The session key can then be used as a shared secret to encrypt and decrypt data exchanged between the client and server.

Exam Tip Remember that SSL uses both public key encryption and shared key encryption. Public keys are used for authentication and to transmit the shared key. The shared key is then used to encrypt the data, because encrypting and decrypting data with a shared key uses less processing time than public key encryption.

Comparing SSL with IPSec

IPSec is commonly used to provide the same services as SSL: authentication, privacy, and message integrity. However, the approach IPSec takes is different from that of SSL. IPSec is implemented by the operating system and is completely transparent to the applications that use IPSec. As a result, IPSec can be used to protect almost any type of network communication. IPSec also provides a flexible authentication scheme. The Microsoft Windows implementation of IPSec allows clients and servers to authenticate each other by using either public key certificates or a shared secret.

SSL, on the other hand, must be implemented by individual applications. Therefore, you cannot use SSL to encrypt all communications between two hosts. Additionally, SSL is less flexible than IPSec because it only supports authentication by means of public key certificates. SSL does provide several distinct advantages, however. Most significantly, SSL is supported by a wide variety of servers and clients, and the maturity of the standard has practically eliminated interoperability problems.

Additionally, SSL allows one-way authentication, while IPSec requires both sides of a connection to authenticate. One-way authentication allows SSL to be used to authenticate the server without placing the burden of registering for a public key certificate on the client. This enables SSL to be used to encrypt communications with public Web sites while protecting the privacy of the end user by not revealing the details of a user certificate to the Web server. Table 11.1 summarizes the differences between SSL and IPSec.

Table 11.1 Comparison of IPSec with SSL

IPSec	SSL
Requires authentication for both the client and the server	Requires either the client or the server, or both, to be authenticated
Authenticates by using either public key certificates or a shared secret	Requires public key certificate–based authentication
Can be used to authenticate and encrypt communications for any application	Can be used only to authenticate and encrypt communications for applications that specifically support SSL
Is capable of tunneling communications between entire networks	Can be used only to encrypt traffic between two hosts

Table 11.1 Comparison of IPSec with SSL

IPSec	SSL
Is a relatively new technology that is not yet widely adopted	Is a mature technology that is widely adopted
Used primarily for intranet communications	Used primarily for Internet communications

Obtaining SSL Certificates

To use SSL, the server must have a suitable public key certificate. Additionally, some SSL scenarios allow or require the client to use a public key certificate. SSL is one of the most common uses for public key certificates, and, as a result, you can obtain SSL certificates from a wide variety of places.

Any organization with a computer running Windows Server 2003 can deploy Certificate Services to issue SSL certificates without any additional cost. These certificates are suitable for intranet scenarios, in which both the servers and the clients are controlled by a single organization. These certificates should not be used for communications that cross organizations, however.

As with any public key infrastructure (PKI), SSL certificates can only be trusted if the root certification authority (CA) is trusted. You can use Group Policy objects (GPOs) to add your CA to the list of trusted root CAs on clients on an intranet, but it is much more difficult to configure clients on the public Internet. For this reason, if you do not control the client computers, you should obtain an SSL certificate from a public CA that is trusted by the client applications that will be establishing a connection to your server. If the server is a Web server, your clients will be Web browsers. As shown in Figure 11.1, Microsoft Internet Explorer is configured by default to trust a large number of public CAs.

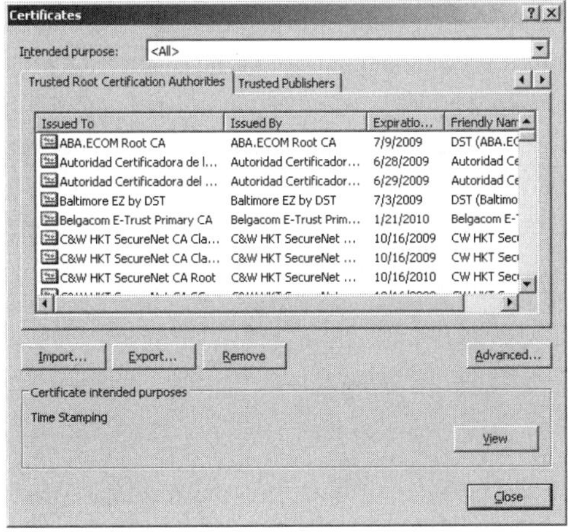

Figure 11.1 Internet Explorer's trusted root CAs

Exam Tip Some CAs, including Verisign, offer free certificates for testing purposes. These certificates are generally not issued by the CA's trusted root certificate and, as a result, will not be automatically trusted by client browsers. However, these testing certificates are a perfect way to gain experience with publicly issued certificates to prepare for the exam.

If the client does not trust the CA that issued your certificate, the client will usually show a warning to the end user, as shown in Figure 11.2. This warning does not prevent the user from establishing an SSL-encrypted session with your server. However, the warning might cause the user to cancel the connection. Although establishing a connection to a server with an untrusted CA still provides encryption and message integrity, using an SSL certificate issued by an untrusted CA defeats the purpose of the authentication provided by SSL.

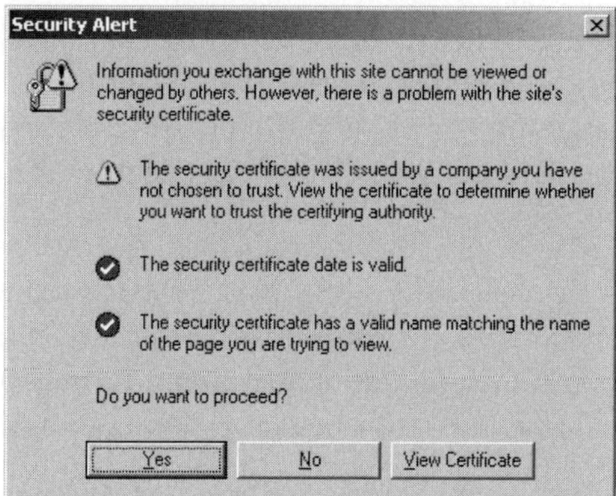

Figure 11.2 Internet Explorer warning regarding an untrusted CA

Planning If you decide to use public certificates for SSL, take some time to choose your CA carefully. The prices charged for certificates vary widely, from free to several thousands of dollars. More expensive CAs offer warranties providing coverage in the event that your certificate is cracked, seals that you can display on your Web site, certificate management services, and security services. Additionally, you should be sure that the CA will continue to actively pursue being trusted by common Web browsers. If you are curious about what a CA needs to go through to become trusted, read about the WebTrust for Certification Authorities program sponsored by The American Institute for Certified Public Accountants (AICPA) at *http://www.webtrust.org/certauth.htm*.

Renewing SSL Certificates

Like any other public key certificate, each SSL certificate has a lifetime. At some point in the future, the certificate will expire. You should plan to renew the certificate three to six months prior to the expiration to ensure that there is no period during which the certificate is invalid.

The specific process you use for renewing the certificate will vary. If you are using a certificate issued by a public CA, the CA will provide a renewal process. If you are using a certificate issued by Certificate Services, you can renew the certificate by using Web enrollment, the Certificates snap-in, or the Web Server Certificate Wizard. The Web Server Certificate Wizard is described in Lesson 2.

See Also For more information about Web enrollment and the Certificates snap-in, refer to Chapter 7.

Configuring Firewalls

Applications use a unique port number for SSL-protected communications. As a result, you must change your firewall configuration to allow the encrypted traffic.

There are two approaches to allowing SSL traffic through a firewall. The first approach is to open the firewall to allow all traffic with a designated port. The typical ports that various applications use for SSL are listed in Table 11.2. Although this will allow SSL sessions to be established through the firewall, the firewall will not be able to analyze the contents of the SSL-encrypted packets. As a result, the firewall will be able to use only the origin and destination of the packet to determine whether to let packets through.

Table 11.2 Port Numbers Used by Standard and SSL-Encrypted Protocols

Protocol	Standard port	SSL port
Hypertext Transfer Protocol (HTTP)	80	443
Simple Mail Transfer Protocol (SMTP)	25	465
Post Office Protocol version 3 (POP3)	110	995
Internet Message Access Protocol (IMAP)	143	993
Network News Transfer Protocol (NNTP)	119	563
Lightweight Directory Access Protocol (LDAP)	389	636
Global catalog queries	3268	3269

The second approach is to configure the firewall as a proxy server. In this case, the client actually establishes an SSL session with the firewall. The firewall, in turn, establishes an SSL session with the destination server. Although the client must trust the firewall to perform authentication and to protect the privacy of the communication, this is the only way to use SSL for encryption while allowing the firewall to examine the contents of the communications.

Lesson Review

The following questions are intended to reinforce key information presented in this lesson. If you are unable to answer a question, review the lesson materials and try the question again. You can find answers to the questions in the "Questions and Answers" section at the end of this chapter.

1. Which of the following is an advantage that SSL has over IPSec?
   - **a.** It can use a shared secret for authentication.
   - **b.** It can tunnel traffic between two networks.
   - **c.** It does not require the client to be authenticated.
   - **d.** It is transparent to the application.

2. Which of the following is an advantage of using an SSL certificate issued by a public CA?
   - **a.** You can use the certificate for free.
   - **b.** Browsers will trust the CA by default and will not warn the user.
   - **c.** It takes less time to obtain a certificate from a public CA.
   - **d.** You do not have to reveal personal information to the CA.

3. Which port should you open on a firewall to allow HTTP traffic protected by SSL?
   - **a.** 80
   - **b.** 110
   - **c.** 443
   - **d.** 995

4. Which port will you open on a firewall to allow POP3 traffic protected by SSL?
   - **a.** 80
   - **b.** 110
   - **c.** 443
   - **d.** 995

Lesson Summary

- Applications can use SSL to provide authentication, data integrity, and encryption for network communications.
- When an SSL session is established, the client retrieves the server's public key and uses it to encrypt a shared secret. The shared secret is then used to encrypt the rest of the session.
- SSL and IPSec provide similar functionality. However, SSL is more commonly used on the Internet because it does not require the client to have a public key certificate.
- You can obtain SSL certificates from public CAs or issue them yourself by using Windows Server 2003 Certificate Services.
- When SSL is used to protect a session, the communications use a different TCP port number. You will have to reconfigure your firewall to allow traffic on the different port number.

Lesson 2: Configuring SSL for IIS

The most common use of SSL is to authenticate Web servers and to encrypt communications between Web browsers and Web servers. SSL, when used to protect HTTP, is referred to as *Hypertext Transfer Protocol Secure (HTTPS).* HTTPS is used by virtually every e-commerce Web site on the Internet to protect private information about end users and to protect end users from submitting private information to a rogue server impersonating another server.

Internet Information Services (IIS) 6.0, included with Windows Server 2003, supports both server and client SSL certificates. Configuring these certificates is simple when you are managing a single Web site with a single server certificate. However, managing certificates can be complicated when a server has multiple certificates or when you are using client certificates for authentication.

After this lesson, you will be able to

- Describe how to use SSL to protect Web communications.
- Create, assign, and renew SSL Web server certificates.
- Use client certificates to control access to a Web site.
- Troubleshoot problems with SSL certificates.

Estimated lesson time: 45 minutes

Using SSL Certificates with a Web Site

You can use SSL certificates to allow users to verify the identity of your Web site and to encrypt traffic sent between the client and the Web site. It is important to understand that an SSL certificate identifies a *Web site*, and not a *Web server.* A single Web server can host multiple Web sites. Alternatively, a single Web site can be hosted on multiple Web servers to provide redundancy and scalability.

For example, an Internet service provider (ISP) that hosts Web sites for 20 customers on a single Web server needs 20 SSL certificates to allow each site to use encryption. Alternatively, if an ISP stores a copy of a Web site on 10 different servers to allow the Web site to remain online in the event of a hardware failure, the same certificate can be installed on all 10 servers.

SSL certificates use the *fully qualified domain name (FQDN)* to identify the Web site. When the client retrieves the site's SSL certificate, the client checks the FQDN of the Web site against the *subject name*, also known as the *common name*, listed in the certificate. Checking the name used to identify the site against the name listed in the certificate prevents a rogue Web site from intercepting traffic destined for a different site.

Security Alert SSL certificates help reduce the risk of attacks against Domain Name System (DNS). For example, an attacker could compromise your DNS server and add a DNS record for the FQDN *www.microsoft.com* so that it resolved to the IP address of a rogue Web site. When you went to visit *http://www.microsoft.com*, your requests would actually be sent to the rogue Web site. The rogue Web site could then collect any information you intended to send to *www.microsoft.com*, which might include personal information or credit card numbers.

However, if you visited *https://www.microsoft.com*, the rogue Web site would have to return an SSL certificate to your Web browser. The rogue Web site could return a certificate with the common name *www.microsoft.com*, but no trusted CA would issue such a certificate. Therefore, your Web browser would warn you that the CA was untrusted. Alternatively, the rogue Web site could perform a true man-in-the-middle attack and forward your Web browser *www.microsoft.com*'s actual certificate. However, the rogue Web site would not be able to establish an SSL session with your browser, because it would not have the private key associated with the public key in the certificate.

Though you assign SSL certificates to individual Web sites, you can configure SSL to help protect confidential data on a URL-by-URL basis. One part of the Web site might require encryption of data transmissions with SSL (by specifying HTTPS in the URL), and another part of the Web site might allow unencrypted data transmission (by specifying HTTP in the URL). This flexibility in security configuration allows you to provide encryption of confidential data as required, while not incurring the performance penalty inherent in encryption and decryption.

To better understand how this is used, visit your favorite e-commerce Web site. While browsing the catalog, you will notice that the URL uses the http:// protocol. Next, attempt to purchase an item. At some point during the purchase process, you will begin to use SSL, and the URL will show that the https:// protocol is being used. E-commerce sites typically use HTTPS only when exchanging private information, because this reduces the burden of public key cryptography and encryption on their Web servers.

Real World

One way you can reduce the processing overhead of using SSL is to use a hardware SSL accelerator. A hardware SSL accelerator is a fast, hardware-based encryption/decryption mechanism that outperforms software-based implementations. If you don't have a hardware SSL accelerator, your server will use its main processor to perform the SSL calculations required for authentication and encryption. As a result, the computer will have less processing power available for serving Web pages. Accelerators offload all encryption/decryption work to the on-board CPU, similar to the way 3-D video cards take on complex graphic computations to save the main CPU for other tasks.

Although hardware SSL accelerators do outperform software SSL accelerators, you might never see the benefit. Unfortunately, you wouldn't know that from examining the vendor's marketing material. Their marketing material will show you dramatic improvements in performance, which in theory will lead to improved scalability and a better end-user experience.

However, these statistics are misleading. Every piece of marketing material I've seen shows the performance gains in terms of new SSL sessions established, but new SSL sessions are usually established only when a new user connects to the Web site. As mentioned in Lesson 1, establishing an SSL session involves using public key cryptography, which is extremely processor-intensive. However, maintaining an SSL session involves only shared key encryption, which is not nearly as processor-intensive. Therefore, highlighting the benefits of hardware SSL accelerators by showing a large number of new SSL sessions does not reflect real world benefits.

You should investigate hardware SSL accelerators only if your Web site is currently processor limited. Specifically, if the processor time averages greater than 30 percent utilization during peak times. Even then, you should compare the cost of hardware SSL accelerators against the cost of upgrading the processor, adding an additional Web server, or optimizing your code. These other methods of adding processing capability allow all aspects of your Web site to benefit—not just SSL session establishment. When accounting for the cost of the hardware SSL accelerators, be sure to factor in the cost of managing an additional device, and the risk associated with adding an additional point of failure to your Web site.

The Web Server Certificate Wizard

Using HTTPS on an IIS Web server requires the server to have a certificate installed and configured. The exact process you will use to configure the certificate varies depending on the source of the certificate; however, you will always use the Web Server Certificate Wizard to perform the configuration.

To launch the Web Server Certificate Wizard:

1. Click Start, click Administrative Tools, and then click Internet Information Services (IIS) Manager.
2. Expand the computer name, and then expand Web Sites. Right-click the Web site for which you want to configure an SSL certificate, and then click Properties.

> **Tip** You can configure an SSL certificate only for a Web site, not for an entire Web server or for individual virtual directories. However, you can configure individual virtual directories to require SSL.

3. Click the Directory Security tab, and then click the Server Certificate button.

   The Web Server Certificate Wizard appears.

You can use the Web Server Certificate Wizard to request a new certificate, assign an existing certificate, renew a certificate, and delete a certificate, as described in the following sections.

Requesting a new certificate

To request a new certificate by using the Web Server Certificate Wizard, follow these steps:

1. On the first page of the Web Server Certificate Wizard, click Next.

   The Server Certificate page appears.

2. Click Create A New Certificate, and then click Next.
3. If you need to send the certificate request to an offline CA, click Prepare The Request Now, But Send It Later. If you want to enroll by using an enterprise CA and there is one present in your domain, click Send The Request Immediately To An Online Certification Authority. Click Next.
4. On the Name And Security Settings page, type a name for the new certificate that will help you remember its purpose. Generally, you should leave the Bit Length setting at its default unless you have determined specifically that a greater bit length is required. Click Next.
5. On the Organization Information page, type a description in the Organization and Organizational Unit boxes. Click Next.
6. On the Your Site's Common Name page, type the common name for the computer. This should be the name that other computers will use to find the server on the intranet or Internet. Click Next.
7. On the Geographical Information page, select your Country/Region, State/Province, and City/Locality. Click Next.
8. If you chose Prepare The Request Now, But Send It Later in step 3, type a name for the file. If you chose Send The Request Immediately To An Online Certification Authority in step 3, select the CA from the Certification Authorities list.
9. Click Next twice, and then click Finish.

If you chose Prepare The Request Now, But Send It Later in step 3, submit the certificate request to a CA. You can use a public CA, in which case, they will provide a process for you to submit the certificate request. If you are submitting the request by using Web-based enrollment on a Windows Server 2003 CA, follow these steps:

1. Start Internet Explorer.
2. In the address bar of Internet Explorer, type **http://*ca-name*/certsrv**. Click Go.
3. If you are not automatically authenticated, provide your user name and password when prompted, and then click OK.
4. Click Request A Certificate.
5. Click Advanced Certificate Request.
6. Click Submit A Certificate Request By Using A Base-64-Encoded CMC Or PKCS #10 File, Or Submit A Renewal Request By Using A Base-64-Encoded PKCS #7 File.
7. Open the certificate request file that you saved earlier in Notepad. Copy the contents of the certificate request file and paste it into the Saved Request box in Internet Explorer.
8. Click the Certificate Template list, and then click Web Server. Click Submit.
9. Click DER Encoded, and then click Download Certificate. Save the file to your local computer.
10. Start the Web Server Certificate Wizard again.
11. On the Welcome To The Web Server Certificate Wizard page, click Next.
12. On the Pending Certificate Request page, click Process The Pending Request And Install The Certificate. Click Next.
13. On the Process A Pending Request page, select the certificate file, and then click Next.
14. On the SSL Port page, leave the default port of 443 selected, and then click Next.
15. Click Next again, and then click Finish.

By default, IIS will accept both unencrypted HTTP and encrypted HTTPS requests after a certificate is configured. If you do not want to allow unencrypted requests, open the Web site properties dialog box, click the Directory Security tab, click the Edit button, and then select the Require Secure Channel check box, as shown in Figure 11.3. Optionally, you can select the Require 128-Bit Encryption check box. Today, most clients will support 128-bit encryption, which is very difficult for an attacker to break. If you do not select the Require 128-Bit Encryption check box, clients that support 128-bit encryption will still use 128-bit encryption.

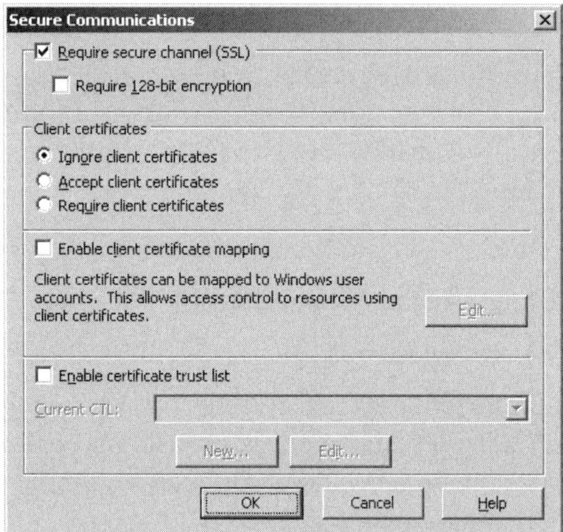

Figure 11.3 Requiring HTTPS for a Web server

Off the Record Requiring HTTPS encryption isn't all that useful because browsers don't automatically try to connect by using HTTPS. So if a user types just your Web server's domain name into a browser, as most users will do, the browser will attempt to connect with unencrypted HTTP. If you don't allow unencrypted HTTP, IIS returns a fairly complicated error message. Some users will read the message and follow the instructions to connect to the Web site by using https:// in the URL, but others will simply think the Web server is down.

A better way to require HTTPS is to set up a separate Web site in IIS to redirect standard HTTP requests to HTTPS. That way, when a user types just your domain name in a Web browser, your Web server will automatically redirect them to your Web site using HTTPS.

Assigning an existing certificate

If a suitable certificate is already present on the local machine authority on the server because you have created a certificate by using Web enrollment, the Certificates snap-in, or through a public CA, follow these steps:

1. On the first page of the Web Server Certificate Wizard, click Next.

   The Server Certificate page appears.

2. Click Assign An Existing Certificate. Click Next.
3. On the Available Certificates page, click a certificate, and then click Next.
4. On the SSL Port page, leave the default port of 443 selected, and then click Next.
5. Click Next again, and then click Finish.

Renewing a certificate

You can also use the Web Server Certificate Wizard to renew certificates. You can renew at any time; you do not need to wait for the certificate to expire or even approach expiration. To renew a certificate, make sure you have a certificate installed, and then follow these steps:

1. On the first page of the Web Server Certificate Wizard, click Next.

   The Modify The Current Certificate Assignment page appears.

2. Click Renew The Current Certificate. Click Next.
3. If you need to send the certificate request to an offline CA, click Prepare The Request Now, But Send It Later. If you want to enroll by using an enterprise CA and there is one present in your domain, click Send The Request Immediately To An Online Certification Authority. Click Next.
4. If you chose Prepare The Request Now, But Send It Later in step 3, type a name for the file. If you chose Send The Request Immediately To An Online Certification Authority in step 3, select the CA from the Certification Authorities list.
5. Click Next twice, and then click Finish.

If you chose Prepare The Request Now, But Send It Later in step 3, submit the renewal request to a CA. If you are using a public CA, they will provide a process for you to use to submit the renewal request. You will then return to the Web Server Certificate Wizard to install the renewed certificate.

Client Certificates

Although Basic, Digest, and Integrated Windows authentication are the most common ways to authenticate users, you can also authenticate users with certificates. In anonymous environments, where many requests go unauthenticated, client certificates are not a good solution. Client certificates require an administrator to have access to the IIS server and to each client that will be connecting to it. This is not feasible in many Internet solutions, in which clients from just about anywhere can be used to attempt a connection. On the other hand, client certificates are the only way to connect to IIS when all other authentication methods—Anonymous, Basic, Integrated, Digest, and Passport—are disabled on the server.

Although the simplest way to authenticate users with certificates is to allow any user with a valid certificate to access the site, this does little to provide security for your organization. By default, your IIS server will trust certificates issued by any trusted root CA, including public CAs that issue user certificates to people you might not want accessing your site.

> **Important** IIS cannot process client certificates unless you have previously installed a server certificate and enabled HTTPS.

There are two ways to improve the security of client certificates. First, you can use client certificate mapping to restrict access to users with specific certificates. (You can also use client certificate mapping to control authorization by mapping the certificates to existing user accounts.) Second, you can configure a certificate trust list (CTL) to reduce the number of root CAs that can issue certificates to your users.

One-to-one client certificate mapping

Client certificate mapping has two modes: one-to-one and many-to-one. One-to-one certificate mapping relates a single exported certificate to an Active Directory user account, as shown in Figure 11.4. When Web users present the certificate, they will be authenticated as if they had presented a valid user name and password.

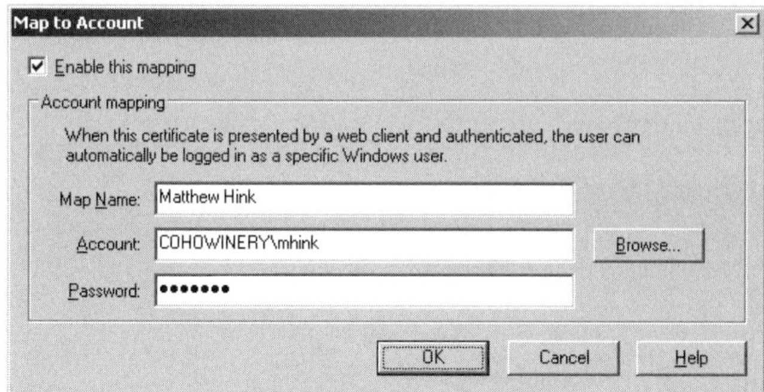

Figure 11.4 Configuring one-to-one certificate mapping

To add one-to-one certificate mappings, first export the user's certificate. Then perform these steps:

1. View the properties for the Web site, click the Directory Security tab, and click the Edit button in the Secure Communications box.
2. Select the Enable Client Certificate Mapping check box, and then click the Edit button.
3. Click the 1-1 tab, and then click the Add button.
4. Select the exported certificate, and then click Open.
5. Complete the Map Name, Account, and Password boxes, and then click OK.
6. Confirm the password when prompted, and then click OK again.

Many-to-one client certificate mapping

Many-to-one certificate mapping uses wildcard matching rules that verify whether a client certificate contains specific information, such as the issuer or subject. This mapping does not identify individual client certificates; it accepts all client certificates fulfilling the specific criteria. If a client gets another certificate containing all the same user information, the existing mapping will still work. Certificates do not need to be exported for use in many-to-one mappings.

To add many-to-one certificate mappings, follow this procedure:

1. View the properties for the Web site, and then click the Directory Security tab.
2. Click the Edit button in the Secure Communications box.
3. Select the Enable Client Certificate Mapping check box, and then click the Edit button.
4. Click the Many-1 tab, and then click the Add button.
5. On the General page, type a name for the rule in the Description box. Click Next.
6. On the Rules page, click New to add a rule.

   The Edit Rule Element dialog box appears, as shown in Figure 11.5.

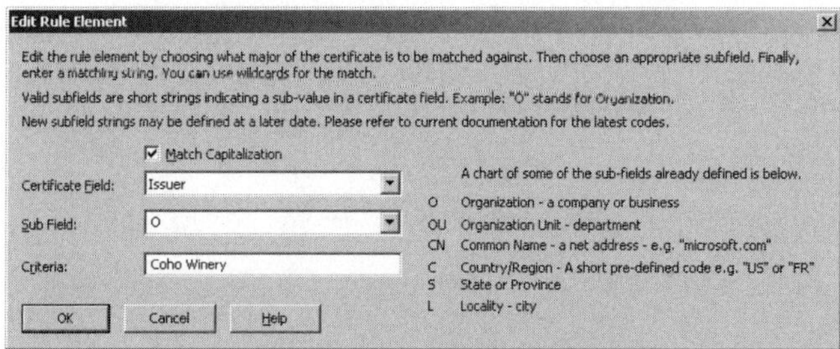

Figure 11.5 Editing rule properties for many-to-one client certificate mappings

7. In the Edit Rule Element dialog box, click the Certificate Field list to choose either Issuer or Subject. Select Issuer to filter based on the CA that issued the certificate. Choose Subject to filter based on who the certificate was issued to. After completing the rule element, click OK.

Security Alert When creating certificate mapping rules, keep in mind how easy it is to create your own root CA. Attackers could easily create their own root CA using your domain names. To prevent this type of impersonation, use certificate mapping along with a certificate trust list.

8. To add an additional rule, return to step 6.

9. Click Next.
10. On the Mapping page, click Refuse Access to reject logons that match the criteria, or click Accept This Certificate For Logon Authentication to map matching certificates to a user account. If you choose to accept the certificate, complete the Account and Password boxes. Click Finish. If prompted, confirm the password and then click OK.

Before you can authenticate users with client certificates, you must issue client certificates. If the users are members of an Active Directory domain and you are using an enterprise CA, autoenrollment is the most efficient way to enroll users. Web servers are often used to communicate with users outside of your organization, however. For these users, you should use Web enrollment. The exercise at the end of this lesson demonstrates the process of enrolling a user certificate by using Web enrollment and then authenticating that user to IIS.

See Also For more information about autoenrollment, refer to Chapter 7.

Certificate trust lists

You can use the Certificate Trust List Wizard to obtain and manage CTLs. A CTL is a list of trusted CAs for a particular Web site. By configuring your CTL, you can allow client certificates issued by a specific CA but deny client certificates issued from other CAs. CTLs are available only at the Web-site level and are not available for File Transfer Protocol (FTP) sites.

To use the Certificate Trust List Wizard, perform the following steps:

1. View the properties for the Web site, click the Directory Security tab, and then click the Edit button in the Secure Communications box.
2. Select the Enable Certificate Trust List check box.
3. Click the New button to open the Certificate Trust List Wizard, which allows you to select CAs from the local machine authority or an exported certificate file.

Troubleshooting SSL

Troubleshooting SSL-encrypted connections is difficult because, like IPSec connections, the traffic is encrypted. In some ways, troubleshooting SSL is even more difficult than troubleshooting IPSec because of the wide variety of Web browser clients that need to be able to analyze your public key certificate and establish an HTTPS connection to your Web server. Though the problems are much less frequent than they were in the late 1990s when the use of HTTPS was only beginning to gain popularity, you can run into problems when using a non-Microsoft browser that you would not experience when using Internet Explorer. Because you often have no control over what browser end users use, you might have to isolate the source of the problem to determine which component is not compliant with standards.

The SSL Diagnostic Utility for IIS, available from *http://www.microsoft.com/technet/prodtechnol/windowsserver2003/downloads/ssldiags.asp*, is helpful for isolating SSL-related problems. As shown in Figure 11.6, it provides a much more detailed analysis of HTTPS traffic than is possible by capturing SSL traffic by using Network Monitor.

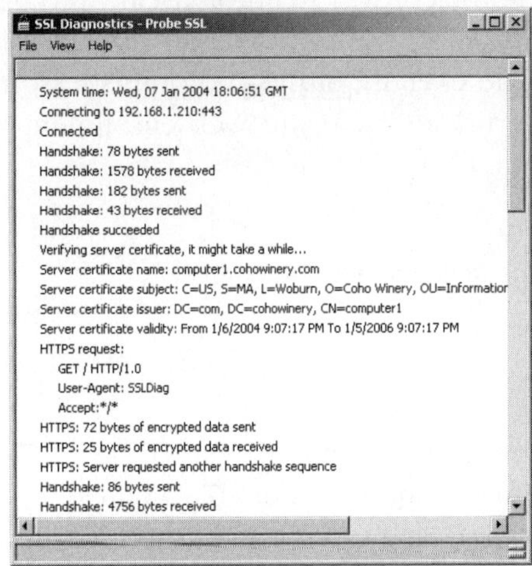

Figure 11.6 The SSL Diagnostic Utility probing IIS

The SSL Diagnostic Utility has the capability to quickly create a self-signed SSL certificate. If you are experiencing problems with a certificate, you can create a self-signed certificate to determine whether the problem occurs with a different certificate. If the problem occurs with your original certificate but not with the certificate generated by the SSL Diagnostic Utility, you know the problem you are experiencing is related to a unique aspect of the original certificate. You can then quickly restore the original certificate to continue troubleshooting.

As shown in Figure 11.7, you can also use the SSL Diagnostic Utility to monitor client certificate–based authentication. If a user is experiencing problems authenticating with a client certificate, this tool will verify that the client's browser submitted a certificate, show you the certificate's subject and issuer, and report whether the authentication was successful.

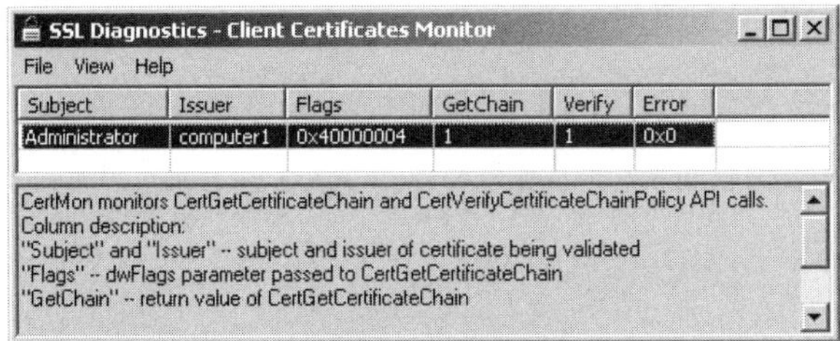

Figure 11.7 The SSL Diagnostic Utility monitoring client certificates

Practice: Using Certificates for SSL

In this practice, you will use certificates to enable SSL encryption for Web communications. Additionally, you will learn how to use client certificates to authenticate Web users.

Exercise: Configure SSL for an IIS Server and Client

In this exercise, you will configure an IIS server to provide the communication security possible by requiring HTTPS and client certificates. After you complete this exercise, the only clients that will be allowed to access the Web site will be those with valid certificates. In the first process, you will configure the Web server with a server certificate and require HTTPS.

1. Log on to the cohowinery.com domain on Computer1 using the Administrator account.
2. Click Start, click Administrative Tools, and then click Internet Information Services (IIS) Manager.
3. Expand Computer1, and then expand Web Sites.
4. Right-click Default Web Site, and then click Properties.
5. Click the Directory Security tab.
6. Click the Server Certificate button.

   The Web Server Certificate Wizard appears.
7. Click Next.
8. Click Create A New Certificate, and then click Next.
9. Click Send The Request Immediately To An Online Certification Authority. Click Next.
10. Click Next again to accept the default settings for the certificate.
11. In the Organization box, type **Coho Winery**. In the Organizational Unit box, type **Information Technology**. Figure 11.8 shows this dialog box completed. Click Next.

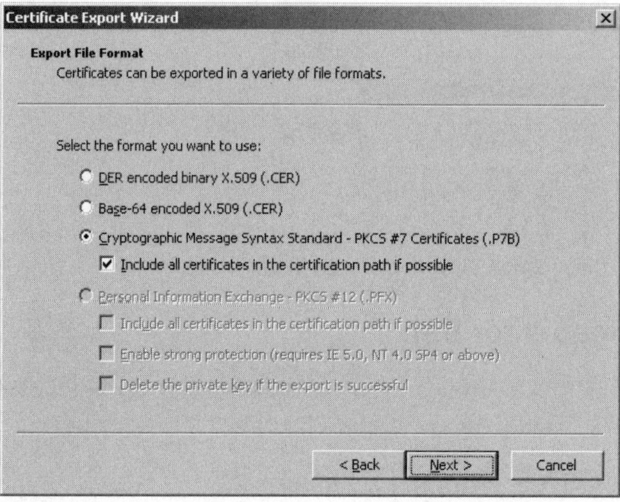

Figure 11.8 Exporting a SQL Server certificate

12. On the Your Site's Common Name page, in the Common Name box, type **computer1.cohowinery.com**. Click Next.

Note If the common name doesn't match what appears in the user's browser, the browser will report an error. On the Internet, users will need to type a fully qualified domain name (FQDN). On your intranet, they can usually use either an FQDN or simply a host name.

13. On the Geographical Information page, type **MA** in the State/Province box, and then type **Woburn** in the City/Locality box. Click Next.
14. On the SSL Port page, click Next.
15. On the Choose A Certification Authority page, click the Certification Authorities list, and then click Computer1.cohowinery.com\Computer1. Click Next.
16. Click Next, and then click Finish.
17. In the Secure Communications box, click Edit.
18. Select Require Secure Channel (SSL), and then click Require Client Certificates.
19. Select the Enable Certificate Trust List check box, and then click the New button.

    The Certificate Trust List Wizard appears.
20. Click Next. On the Certificates In The CTL page, click Add From Store. Click the certificate for Computer1, and then click OK.
21. Click Next. In the Friendly Name box, type **Coho Winery CAs**. Click Next, and then click Finish.
22. Click OK three times to return to the Internet Information Services (IIS) Manager.

23. Expand Default Web Site. Right-click CertSrv, and then click Properties.
24. Click the Directory Security tab. In the Secure Communications box, click the Edit button.
25. Clear the Require Secure Channel (SSL) check box, and then click OK twice.

    You must disable this requirement for the CertSrv virtual directory to allow users to enroll for certificates.

Exercise: Enroll for a client certificate access

At this point in the exercise, you have configured IIS to require client certificates to access the default Web page. In the next process, you will enroll for a client certificate and access the Web site by using HTTPS.

1. Start Internet Explorer. In the Address box, type **http://computer1/certsrv**. Click Go.
2. When prompted, type the Administrator user name and password.
3. Click Request A Certificate.
4. Click User Certificate.
5. Click the Submit button, and then click Yes.
6. Click Install This Certificate, and then click Yes.
7. In the Address box, type **http://computer1**. Click Go.

   Internet Explorer shows a description of the HTTP 403.4 error message that IIS returned, as shown in Figure 11.9.

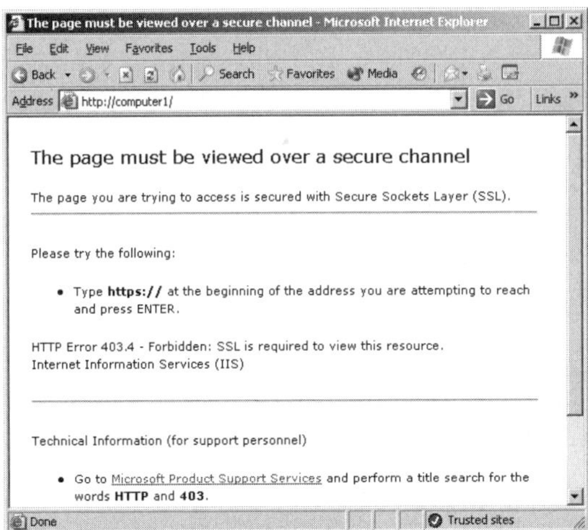

Figure 11.9 IIS configured to require SSL

8. In the Address box, type **https://computer1**. Click Go. When warned, click OK.
9. The Security Alert dialog box appears, as shown in Figure 11.10, warning you that although the CA is valid and the certificate has not expired, the name on the security certificate is not valid. This error message appears because you entered Computer1 in the Address box but entered Computer1.Cohowinery.com in the Common Name box when requesting the certificate. Click No.

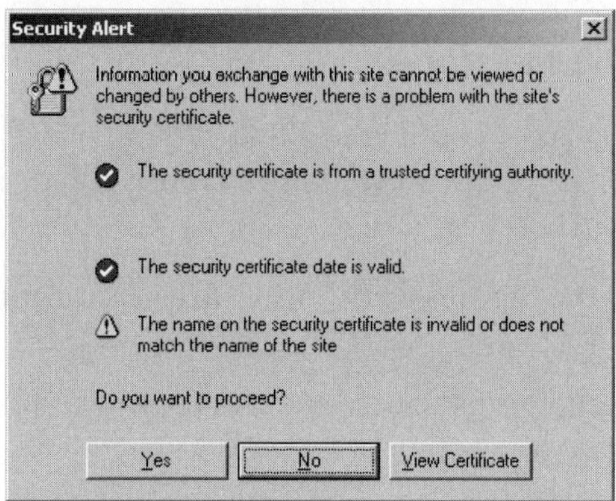

Figure 11.10 The requested host name does not match the common name in the certificate

10. In the Address box, type **https://computer1.cohowinery.com**. Click Go. When warned, click OK.
11. The Client Authentication dialog box appears. Click Users, and then click OK.

    Internet Explorer displays the default Under Construction page, which proves that IIS successfully authenticated the user certificate.

Lesson Review

The following questions are intended to reinforce key information presented in this lesson. If you are unable to answer a question, review the lesson materials and try the question again. You can find answers to the questions in the "Questions and Answers" section at the end of this chapter.

1. Which of the following scenarios are appropriate for using client certificates? (Choose all that apply.)
   - **a.** To authenticate users returning to a public e-commerce site.
   - **b.** To authenticate and authorize users at a partnering company that manages its own CA.
   - **c.** To gather demographic information about the users who visit your Web site.
   - **d.** To authenticate users on an intranet when an enterprise CA is present.

___

2. A user is having a problem authenticating with a client certificate. Which of the following is the best tool to troubleshoot this problem?
   a. Network Monitor
   b. IIS Manager
   c. Certificates snap-in
   d. SSL Diagnostics Utility

Lesson Summary

- You can use the Web Server Certificate Wizard to request, assign, renew, and delete SSL certificates.
- Although only the server requires an SSL certificate to establish an HTTPS session, you can use client certificates to authenticate users.
- The best tool for troubleshooting problems with SSL certificates is the SSL Diagnostics Utility.

Lesson 3: Other SSL Applications

The vast majority of SSL certificates are installed on Web servers. However, Windows networks can use SSL certificates to protect several other protocols: LDAP, SMTP, POP3, NNTP, and SQL. This section will describe how to use SSL certificates to encrypt these communications protocols.

> **After this lesson, you will be able to**
>
> - Use SSL certificates to encrypt LDAP and global catalog queries.
> - Use SSL certificates to encrypt database queries.
> - Use SSL certificates to protect messaging communications.
>
> **Estimated lesson time: 45 minutes**

Enabling SSL on Active Directory Domain Controllers

Applications use LDAP to query Active Directory domain controllers for information contained in the directory, such as the IP addresses of registered services or the contact information for users. LDAP queries can reveal a tremendous amount of confidential information, including user names, personal details about users, and locations of services on the network. As shown in Figure 11.11, a protocol analyzer can be used to capture and read LDAP traffic when an SSL certificate is not used.

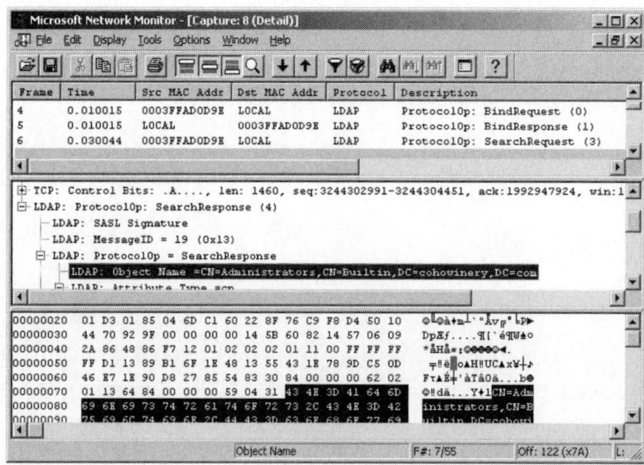

Figure 11.11 Network Monitor displaying the results of an unencrypted LDAP query

Fortunately, you can install a computer certificate on a domain controller to enable SSL/TLS communications to encrypt LDAP queries and responses, in addition to global catalog traffic, by using LDAP over SSL (LDAPS). If you configure a domain controller as an enterprise CA, this happens automatically. In fact, after configuring a single enterprise CA, all domain controllers in the forest will automatically enroll for and install the appropriate certificate.

You can also use a certificate from a non-Microsoft CA. As long as the Enhanced Key Usage extension includes the Server Authentication object identifier, Active Directory will accept LDAPS queries. As with other types of certificates-based encryption, the client and server must both trust the root CA that issued the certificate. Additionally, the common name of the domain controller must appear in either the Subject or Subject Alternative Name field of the certificate, as shown in Figure 11.12.

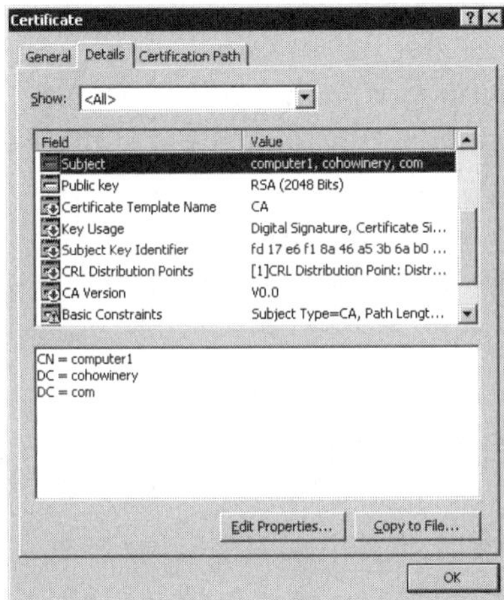

Figure 11.12 The subject field of a certificate containing the domain controller's common name

Normal unencrypted LDAP traffic uses TCP port 389. When SSL is used to encrypt LDAP queries and responses, it uses TCP port 636. When SSL is used to encrypt global catalog queries, clients will connect to TCP port 3269 instead of the standard global catalog port of 3268.

Unlike IPSec, LDAPS is not transparent to the application. Additionally, LDAPS does not provide clients and servers the opportunity to negotiate a level of encryption. Even after SSL is enabled, clients can send queries to TCP port 389, and 3268 will be allowed to send and receive unencrypted communications. You might have to configure applications that query Active Directory specifically to use SSL. The exercise at the end of this lesson demonstrates this phenomenon.

Enabling SSL on Computers Running SQL Server

SQL Server queries and results often contain confidential data. For example, an accounting front-end application might send financial information to a computer running SQL Server. An e-commerce Web server will send private end-user account information to a computer running SQL Server. By default, these communications are not encrypted and are vulnerable to eavesdropping. However, they can be encrypted by using an SSL certificate.

SQL Server SSL encryption can be enabled on either the SQL Server–based computer itself or on individual SQL Server–based clients. If you want to encrypt all communications to a particular server running SQL Server, and that server will not have any clients that do not support SSL encryption, you should require encryption on the computer running SQL Server. If some clients can connect to a SQL Server–based computer by using SSL encryption, but other clients must use an unencrypted connection, enable encryption on a client-by-client basis.

To enable encryption on a server running SQL Server 2000 for all clients connecting to that server, first install a server authentication certificate and store it in the local machine authority on the server, and then configure all clients to trust that certificate's root CA. The client computer does not require a computer certificate itself, but it must trust the CA that issued the server certificate. If the computer is a member of an Active Directory domain and the certificate was issued by the domain's enterprise CA, this trust will be automatically configured.

> **Note** The SetCert tool, included with the SQL Server Resource Kit, permits you to control the certificate used for SQL Server. The tool is only available by purchasing the SQL Server Resource Kit or with a TechNet subscription.

Configuring clients to trust the root CA

If the clients do not automatically trust the root CA, you should manually configure the trust on each of the clients that will use encryption by following these steps:

1. Log on as an administrator to the computer running SQL Server.
2. Open the Internet Properties dialog box on the client computer, either by clicking Internet Options in Control Panel or by starting Internet Explorer, clicking Tools, and then clicking Internet Options.
3. Click the Content tab.
4. Click the Certificates button.
5. Click the Trusted Root Certification Authorities tab.
6. Click the certification authority that issued the certificate of the computer running SQL Server, and then click Export.

   The Certificate Export Wizard appears.
7. Click Next.

8. On the Export File Format page, click Cryptographic Message Syntax Standard - PKCS #7 Certificates (.P7B).
9. Select the Include All The Certificates In The Certification Path If Possible check box. Click Next.
10. On the File To Export page, type the name of a file in which to store the exported certificate, and then click Next.
11. On the final page, click Finish, and then click Close.

At this point, you have exported the SQL Server certificate. Now you need to transfer the exported certificates to each of the clients and then import the certificate into each client's trusted root CAs by following this procedure:

12. Log on as an administrator on the client computer running SQL Server.
13. Open the Internet Properties dialog box on the client computer, either by clicking Internet Options in Control Panel or by launching Internet Explorer, clicking Tools, and then clicking Internet Options.
14. Click the Content tab.
15. Click the Certificates button.
16. Click the Trusted Root Certification Authorities tab.
17. Click the Import button.

    The Certificate Import Wizard appears.
18. Click Next.
19. On the File To Import page, select the certificate that you exported from the computer running SQL Server. Click Next.
20. Click Automatically Select The Certificate Store Based On The Type Of Certificate.
21. Click Next, and then click Finish.
22. When prompted to verify the addition to the root store, click Yes, and then click OK. Finally, click Close.

Requiring encryption at the SQL Server computer

Although encryption is enabled when SQL Server initializes and an appropriate SSL certificate is found, you can choose to require encryption to eliminate the possibility of clients connecting to the computer running SQL Server by using an unencrypted session. To require encryption on the computer running SQL Server, follow these steps:

1. Click Start, click All Programs, click Microsoft SQL Server, and then click Enterprise Manager.

2. Expand Microsoft SQL Servers and locate the computer running SQL Server for which you want to enable SSL.
3. Right-click the server's node, and then click Properties.
4. Click the General tab, and then click Network Configuration.
5. Select the Force Protocol Encryption check box.
6. Click OK. When notified that the SQL Server service must be restarted, click OK. Click OK again to return to the SQL Server Enterprise Manager.
7. Right-click the server's node, and then click Stop. When prompted, click Yes.
8. Right-click the server's node, and then click Start.

Enabling encryption for individual clients

To enable encryption on a computer running SQL Server 2000 for only specific clients, first verify that the client has Microsoft Data Access Components (MDAC) version 2.6 or later installed. You can download the latest version of MDAC from *http://www.microsoft.com/*. After the computer running SQL Server has a certificate that is trusted by the client, you must configure encryption for either individual database applications or for all database connections initiated by the client.

If you choose to enable encryption individually for each application, the specific steps you follow will vary depending on the client application that accesses the computer running SQL Server. If the application uses an Open Database Connectivity (ODBC) connection string, add a semicolon and the phrase `Encrypt=Yes` to the end of the string. For example, the following is an ODBC connection string that will attempt to use SSL encryption when connecting to a computer running SQL Server:

```
Driver=SQLServer;Server=ServerName;UID=UserId;
PWD=Password;Network=DBNETLIB.DLL;Encrypt=YES
```

If the application uses an OLE DB connection string, add a semicolon and the phrase `Use Encryption for Data=True` to the end of the string. For example, the following is an OLE DB connection string that will attempt to use SSL encryption when connecting to a computer running SQL Server:

```
Provider=SQLOLEDB.1;Integrated Security=SSPI
;Persist Security Info=False;Initial Catalog=dbName;Data
Source=ServerName;Use Encryption for Data=True
```

You can configure encryption for all database connections initiated from the client by using the SQL Server Client Network utility if the SQL Server Client Tools are installed. However, this requires encryption for all SQL connections initiated by the client, and it does not allow the client to connect to SQL Server 7.0 or earlier databases. Therefore, you should enable encryption on a per-application basis by editing the connection string whenever possible.

> **Note** To install the SQL Server Client tools, launch setup.bat from the root of the SQL Server 2000 CD-ROM, and follow the prompts.

To enable encryption by using the SQL Server Client Network utility, perform these steps:

1. Click Start, click All Programs, click Microsoft SQL Server, and then click Client Network Utility.
2. Click the General tab, and then select the Force Protocol Encryption check box.
3. Click OK.

Unfortunately, there is no easy way to verify that a particular database connection is encrypted. The best way to verify encryption is to use Network Monitor to capture and analyze the network traffic.

Enabling SSL on Mail Servers

Although there is currently no widely supported standard for encrypting communications between mail servers on the Internet, it is possible to encrypt messages transmitted from a client to a server, or between mail servers within an organization, by using SSL and TLS.

> **See Also** Microsoft Exchange uses both SSL and TLS, for different purposes. For instructions on requiring TLS encryption for a virtual server in Exchange, refer to Chapter 4.

Differences Between SSL and TLS

SSL and TLS are often referred to as *SSL/TLS*. Though the two protocols are similar, they are indeed different and cannot interoperate. One important difference is that TLS 1.0 applies a Keyed-Hashing for Message Authentication Code (HMAC) algorithm, whereas SSL 3.0 applies the Message Authentication Code (MAC) algorithm. HMAC produces an integrity check value as MAC does, but it uses a hash function construction that makes the hash much harder to break.

SMTP and POP3 services are built into Windows Server 2003 and can be installed by adding the Mail Server (POP3, SMTP) server role. However, only the SMTP service can be configured with an SSL certificate. To configure an SSL certificate to allow SMTP encryption, follow these steps:

1. Click Start, click Administrative Tools, and then click Internet Information Services (IIS) Manager.
2. In the left pane, expand the computer node. Right-click Default SMTP Virtual Server, and then click Properties.
3. Click the Access tab, and then click the Certificate button.

   The Web Server Certificate Wizard appears. This enables you to configure an SSL certificate exactly as you would for a Web site, as described in Lesson 2.

Clients downloading messages by using POP3, IMAP4, or NNTP from a server running Exchange can use SSL to encrypt the communications if the server running Exchange is configured with a certificate. To configure a certificate for a server running Exchange Server 2003, begin by opening the Web Server Certificate Wizard by following these steps (the sequence of steps will be slightly different for Exchange Server 2000):

1. Click Start, click All Programs, click Microsoft Exchange, and then click System Manager.
2. In the left pane, locate the Servers node. Then expand Servers, expand the computer node you are configuring, expand Protocols, and expand SMTP.
3. Right-click the SMTP, POP3, IMAP4, or NNTP virtual server, and then click Properties.
4. Click the Access tab, and then click the Certificate button.

   The Web Server Certificate Wizard appears. Notice that it is called the *Web Server* Certificate Wizard because SMTP, POP3, IMAP4, and NNTP are components of IIS, not Exchange. However, the certificate you assign or create will be used for messaging.

After a certificate has been installed on the virtual server, encryption is automatically enabled for clients that request it. However, by default, the server running Exchange will still accept unencrypted communications. You can require that all clients use encryption by performing the following steps:

1. Click Start, click All Programs, click Microsoft Exchange, and then click System Manager.
2. In the left pane, locate the Servers node. Expand Servers, expand the computer node you are configuring, expand Protocols, and then expand SMTP.
3. Right-click the SMTP, POP3, or IMAP4 virtual server, and then click Properties.
4. Click the Access tab, and then click the Communication button.

5. Select the Require Secure Channel check box, as shown in Figure 11.13. Optionally, select the Require 128-Bit Encryption check box.

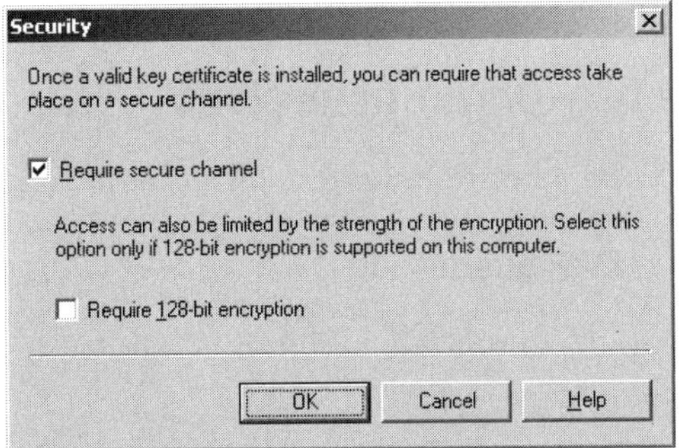

Figure 11.13 Requiring messaging encryption

6. Click OK twice.

Security Alert If your organization allows users to retrieve e-mail by using a Web server interface, such as with Outlook Web Access (OWA), configure the Web server with an SSL certificate to encrypt the communications and authenticate the server.

Enabling SSL on Microsoft Outlook

After a server running Exchange, or another messaging server, has had a certificate installed and has been configured to enable encrypted communications, the messaging client must be configured to use encryption. Unlike IPSec, messaging encryption will not automatically negotiate authentication and encryption protocols.

Although every messaging client is different, the following procedure enables SSL encryption for the otherwise unsecured POP3, IMAP4, or SMTP protocols for an existing e-mail account on an Outlook 2003 client:

1. Open Control Panel, and then double-click Mail.
2. Click the E-Mail Accounts button.
3. The E-Mail Accounts Wizard appears.
4. Click View Or Change Existing E-Mail Accounts, and then click Next.
5. Click the account for which you want to enable encryption, and then click Change.
6. On the Internet E-Mail Settings page, click the More Settings button.
7. Click the Advanced tab.

8. Select the This Server Requires An Encrypted Connection (SSL) check box for the protocols you want to enable encryption for. Click OK.
9. Click Next, and then click Finish.

Practice: Protecting Active Directory Communications

In this practice, you will use SSL certificates to encrypt LDAP queries.

Exercise 1: Analyze unencrypted LDAP queries

In this exercise, you will generate and analyze unencrypted LDAP queries by using the Address Book accessory.

1. Log on to the cohowinery.com domain on Computer1 using the Administrator account.
2. Click Start, click Control Panel, and then click Add Or Remove Programs.
3. Click Add/Remove Windows Components.
4. Click Management And Monitoring Tools, and then click Details. Select the Network Monitor Tools check box, and then click OK.
5. Click Next, and then respond to the prompts provided by the wizard. When installation has completed, click Finish.

   Network Monitor has now been installed and can be used to monitor traffic on Computer1.
6. Click Start, click Administrative Tools, and then click Network Monitor.
7. If prompted to select a network connection, expand Local Computer, click Local Area Connection, and then click OK.

   If you have other computers on your subnet, or if other computers are communicating with Computer1, you might want to create a capture filter to restrict captured traffic to the packets exchanged with Computer2.
8. Click the Capture menu, and then click Start.

At this point in the exercise, Network Monitor is running on Computer1. In the next process, you will use the Address Book accessory to generate unencrypted LDAP queries. You will then examine them in Network Monitor.

1. Log on to the cohowinery.com domain on Computer2 using the Administrator account.
2. Click Start, click All Programs, click Accessories, and then click Address Book.
3. Click the Find People button.

4. Click the Look In list, and then click Active Directory.
5. In the Name box, type the letter **a**, as shown in Figure 11.14. Click Find Now.

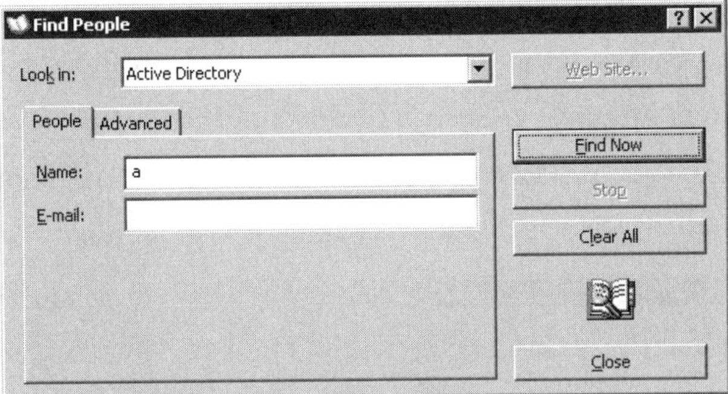

Figure 11.14 Creating an Address Book query

6. Address Book will return three results: Account Operators, Administrator, and Administrators.
7. Return to Computer1. On the Capture menu, click Stop And View.
8. Click the first frame with a Src MAC Addr of LOCAL and a Description of ProtocolOp: SearchResponse (4). In the middle pane, expand LDAP, and then expand each LDAP: ProtocolOp = SearchResponse node.

   Notice that Network Monitor's analysis of the frame shows three results with the following object names:

   - CN=Administrators,CN=Builtin,DC=cohowinery,DC=com
   - CN=Account Operators,CN=Builtin,DC=cohowinery,DC=com
   - CN=Administrator,CN=Users,DC=cohowinery,DC=com

Network Monitor would only be able to analyze the frame and determine the results of the query if the LDAP queries were transmitted without encryption. As you can see, configuring the Active Directory domain controller with a certificate is not sufficient to force encrypted communications; the client application must also be configured. Leave Network Monitor open, because you will use it in the next exercise.

Exercise 2: Encrypt LDAP queries

In this exercise, you will configure an LDAP client—the Address Book accessory—to submit encrypted LDAP queries. You will then use Network Monitor to examine the encrypted traffic.

1. On Computer1, in Network Monitor, click the File menu, and then click Close.
2. On the Capture menu, click Start. When prompted, click No.

3. On Computer2, in the Find People dialog box, click Close.
4. On the Tools menu, click Accounts.
5. Click Active Directory, and then click Properties.
6. In the Active Directory Properties dialog box, click the Advanced tab.
7. Select the This Server Requires A Secure Connection (SSL) check box.
8. In the Search Base box, type **DC=cohowinery,DC=com**, as shown in Figure 11.15.

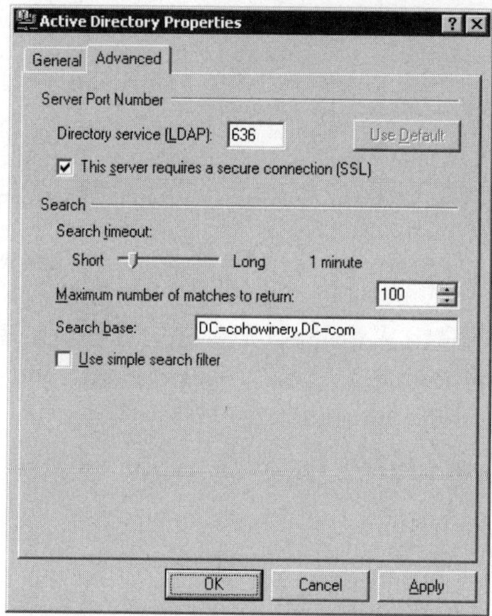

Figure 11.15 Configuring Address Book for encryption

9. Click OK, and then click Close.
10. Click the Find People button.
11. In the Look In list, click Active Directory.
12. In the Name box, type the letter **a**. Click Find Now.

    Address Book will return three results: Account Operators, Administrator, and Administrators.

13. Return to Computer1. On the Capture menu, click Stop And View.
14. Examine the captured frames.

    The majority of the frames will have the protocol listed as TCP. This indicates that Network Monitor was not able to perform an Application layer analysis on the frame. These frames have a TCP port of 636, which Network Monitor describes as

LDAP Protocol Over TLS/SSL. However, as shown in Figure 11.16, the contents of the packets do not reveal the LDAP query or the response.

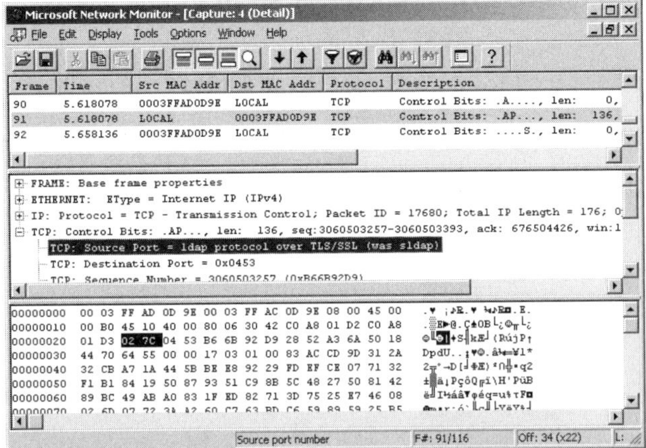

Figure 11.16 Network Monitor attempting to analyze SSL-encrypted LDAP queries

You will also notice LDAP queries that were transmitted unencrypted. These queries were used by Computer2 to locate a domain controller. They do not contain the LDAP query created by Address Book to find user names that start with the letter A.

Lesson Review

The following questions are intended to reinforce key information presented in this lesson. If you are unable to answer a question, review the lesson materials and try the question again. You can find answers to the questions in the "Questions and Answers" section at the end of this chapter.

1. When a certificate is installed on a domain controller, which of the following types of communications can be protected with SSL? (Choose all that apply.)

   a. Kerberos authentication

   b. Global catalog traffic

   c. DNS queries

   d. LDAP queries

   e. File replication

2. After installing an SSL certificate on a computer running SQL Server, how can you protect database communications by using SSL? (Choose all that apply.)

   a. Select the Force Protocol Encryption check box on the computer running SQL Server.

   b. Add `Encrypt=YES` to the ODBC connection string.

   c. Add `Use Encryption for Data=True` to the ODBC connection string.

   d. Add `Encrypt=YES` to the OLE DB connection string.

   e. Add `Use Encryption for Data=True` to the OLE DB connection string.

Lesson Summary

- Allowing LDAP queries to be encrypted requires only enrolling the domain controllers with a computer certificate. No manual configuration is required.
- SSL certificates can be used to encrypt SQL queries. However, encryption must be either required on the computer running SQL Server or enabled in the SQL client application configuration.
- The best way to encrypt messaging communications is to install a computer certificate on the mail server and then configure the mail clients to use SSL encryption.

Case Scenario Exercise

In this exercise, you will read a scenario about a company's challenge with providing security for communications to and from its public Web site, and then answer the questions that follow. The questions are intended to reinforce key information presented in this chapter. If you are unable to answer a question, review the lessons and try the question again. You can find answers to the questions in the "Questions and Answers" section at the end of this chapter.

Scenario

You are a systems engineer at Adventure Works, a publicly owned company that manages hundreds of sporting goods stores throughout the United States. Your management is under pressure to continually increase sales, but the company's capital budget is too low to build new stores. Lacking the funds to expand reach by using traditional retail outlets, Adventure Works management has decided to sell sporting goods directly to consumers by using a public Web site.

At the request of your management, you acquired the domain name adventure-works.com. After talking to the Web developers, you have determined that you will need to configure two Web servers (for redundancy and performance) and a single database server. For at least the first six months, you plan to host the Web servers on the perimeter network at your company's headquarters, which is connected to the public Internet by a 45-megabits-per-second (Mbps) T3 connection. The planned systems architecture is shown in Figure 11.17.

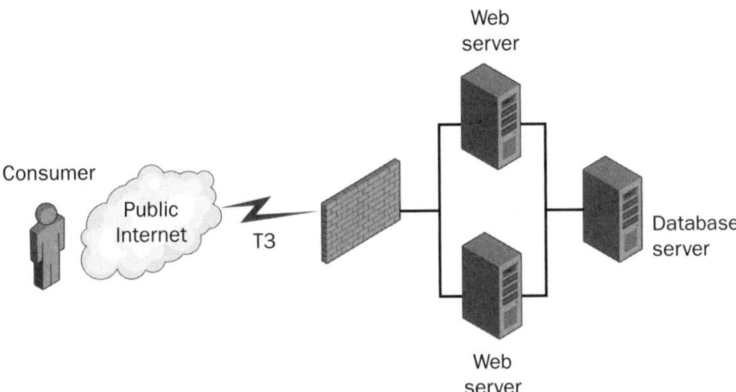

Figure 11.17 Systems architecture for www.adventure-works.com

Questions

1. How should you protect the personal information and credit card numbers of consumers purchasing products from your Web site?

   a. IPSec

   b. S/MIME

   c. PKI

   d. SSL

   e. Physical security

2. You want to purchase SSL certificates created by a trusted public CA for your Web servers so that users will not be prompted about the certificate. How many SSL certificates do you need to purchase?

   a. 1

   b. 2

   c. 3

   d. 4

   ---

3. How can you protect the communications between the Web servers and the database servers? (Choose all that apply.)

   a. IPSec

   b. S/MIME

   c. PKI

   d. SSL

   e. Physical security

Troubleshooting Lab

In this lab, you will troubleshoot a problem related to a browser error while establishing an SSL session. Read the following scenario and then answer the questions that follow. The questions are intended to reinforce key information presented in this chapter. If you are unable to answer a question, review the lessons and try the question again. You can find answers to the questions in the "Questions and Answers" section at the end of this chapter.

To prepare the computer for this troubleshooting lab, perform these steps:

1. Log on to the cohowinery.com domain on Computer1 using the Administrator account.
2. Use Windows Explorer to open the CD-ROM included with this book. Double-click the Addhosts.bat file.
3. Open the Internet Information Services (IIS) Manager.
4. Expand Web Sites. Right-click Default Web Site, and then click Properties.
5. Click the Directory Security tab.

6. In the Secure Communications box, click Server Certificate.

   The Web Server Certificate Wizard appears.

7. Click Next.
8. Click Import A Certificate From A .PFX File, and then click Next.
9. Click the Browse button and then select the Www.Adventure-Works.Com.pfx file on the CD-ROM included with this book. Click Next.
10. In the Password box, type **password**.
11. Click Next three times, and then click Finish.
12. Click OK.

Scenario

You are a systems engineer at Adventure Works, a publicly owned company that manages hundreds of sporting goods stores throughout the United States. You are in the process of deploying a Web site with the name www.adventure-works.com. To protect communications that include credit card numbers and personal information, you have installed an SSL certificate on your Web servers.

One of the members of your Quality Assurance (QA) team discovered a problem, however. SSL works fine when she accesses the site by using the URL *https://www.adventure-works.com*. However, her browser reports an error when she uses the URL *https://adventure-works.com*.

Questions

1. First, reproduce the error by using Internet Explorer on Computer1. What is the exact error message?

   ____

   ____

   ____

2. Examine the certificate. What is the cause of the problem?

   ____

   ____

   ____

3. How can you resolve the problem? (Choose all that apply.)

   a. Add the adventure-works.com common name to the certificate.

   b. Install a second SSL certificate with the name adventure-works.com on the same Web site.

   c. Create a second Web site using the IIS Manager, and configure that Web site with the host header adventure-works.com. Configure that Web site to redirect requests to *http://www.adventure-works.com.*

   d. Configure adventure-works.com to use a second IP address, and add that IP address to your Web server. Create a second SSL certificate with the name adventure-works.com, and associate that certificate with the second IP address.

   e. Add a redirection directive to the certificate to instruct the browser to send requests to *https://www.adventure-works.com.*

Chapter Summary

- Applications can use SSL to provide authentication, data integrity, and encryption for network communications.
- When an SSL session is established, the client retrieves the server's public key and uses it to encrypt a shared secret. The shared secret is then used to encrypt the rest of the session.
- SSL and IPSec provide similar functionality. However, SSL is more commonly used on the Internet because it does not require the client to have a public key certificate.
- You can obtain SSL certificates from public CAs or issue them yourself by using Windows Server 2003 Certificate Services.
- When SSL is used to protect a session, the communications use a different TCP port number. You will have to reconfigure your firewall to allow traffic on the different port number.
- Although only the server requires an SSL certificate to establish an HTTPS session, you can use client certificates to authenticate users.
- Allowing LDAP queries to be encrypted requires only enrolling the domain controllers with a computer certificate. No manual configuration is required.

- SSL certificates can be used to encrypt SQL queries. However, encryption must either be required on the computer running SQL Server or enabled in the SQL client application configuration.
- The best way to encrypt messaging communications is to install a computer certificate on the mail server and then configure the mail clients to use SSL encryption.

Exam Highlights

Before taking the exam, review the key topics and terms that are presented in this chapter. You need to know this information.

Key Topics

- Understand when it is appropriate to use SSL certificates to protect communications.
- Know the advantages and disadvantages of publicly and privately issued certificates.
- Explain how client certificates can be used to authenticate users.
- Be able to configure SSL certificates to encrypt Web, LDAP, SQL, and e-mail communications.

Key Terms

fully qualified domain name (FQDN) The host name and domain used to uniquely identify a computer on the Internet, such as www.microsoft.com.

Secure Sockets Layer (SSL) An open standard for encrypting network communications and authenticating clients or servers.

subject name The subject name listed in an SSL certificate. If the subject name in the certificate does not exactly match the name in the user's browser, the browser will display a warning message.

Questions and Answers

Lesson 1 Review

Page 11-8

1. Which of the following is an advantage that SSL has over IPSec?

   a. It can use a shared secret for authentication.

   b. It can tunnel traffic between two networks.

   c. It does not require the client to be authenticated.

   d. It is transparent to the application.

   c. SSL's primary advantage over IPSec is that it does not require the client to be authenticated. This allows users on the Internet to access the Web server without providing personally identifiable information.

2. Which of the following is an advantage of using an SSL certificate issued by a public CA?

   a. You can use the certificate for free.

   b. Browsers will trust the CA by default and will not warn the user.

   c. It takes less time to obtain a certificate from a public CA.

   d. You do not have to reveal personal information to the CA.

   b. The primary advantage of using a certificate issued by a public CA is that browsers and other applications will trust the CA by default, without requiring the user to add the root CA to the application's list of trusted CAs.

3. Which port should you open on a firewall to allow HTTP traffic protected by SSL?

   a. 80

   b. 110

   c. 443

   d. 995

   c. HTTP protected by SSL uses TCP port 443.

4. Which port will you open on a firewall to allow POP3 traffic protected by SSL?

   a. 80

   b. 110

   c. 443

   d. 995

   d. POP3 protected by SSL uses TCP port 995.

Lesson 2 Review

Page 11-24

1. Which of the following scenarios are appropriate for using client certificates? (Choose all that apply.)

   a. To authenticate users returning to a public e-commerce site.

   b. To authenticate and authorize users at a partnering company that manages its own CA.

   c. To gather demographic information about the users who visit your Web site.

   d. To authenticate users on an intranet when an enterprise CA is present.

   b and d. Client certificates are ideal for authenticating users at partnering companies that manage their own CAs. You can use many-to-one mapping to allow access to users who have valid certificates, thereby delegating responsibility for managing user access to the partner company. Client certificates can also be used on an intranet when users have been issued user certificates.

2. A user is having a problem authenticating with a client certificate. Which of the following is the best tool to troubleshoot this problem?

   a. Network Monitor

   b. IIS Manager

   c. Certificates snap-in

   d. SSL Diagnostics Utility

   d. Although you can capture and analyze client certificate authentication traffic by using Network Monitor, the best tool to use is the SSL Diagnostics Utility.

Lesson 3 Review

Page 11-37

1. When a certificate is installed on a domain controller, which of the following types of communications can be protected with SSL? (Choose all that apply.)

   a. Kerberos authentication

   b. Global catalog traffic

   c. DNS queries

   d. LDAP queries

   e. File replication

   b and d. Only global catalog traffic and LDAP queries can be protected with SSL. However, Kerberos authentication is always encrypted, and file replication might be encrypted by means of different mechanisms, such as IPSec.

2. After installing an SSL certificate on a computer running SQL Server, how can you protect database communications by using SSL? (Choose all that apply.)

    a. Select the Force Protocol Encryption check box on the computer running SQL Server.

    b. Add `Encrypt=YES` to the ODBC connection string.

    c. Add `Use Encryption for Data=True` to the ODBC connection string.

    d. Add `Encrypt=YES` to the OLE DB connection string.

    e. Add `Use Encryption for Data=True` to the OLE DB connection string.

    a, b, and e. If you want to require encryption for all incoming connections to the computer running SQL Server, select the Force Protocol Encryption check box on the computer running SQL Server. Otherwise, add the appropriate string to the ODBC or OLE DB connection strings.

Design Activity: Case Scenario Exercise

Page 11-39

1. How should you protect the personal information and credit card numbers of consumers purchasing products from your Web site?

    a. IPSec

    b. S/MIME

    c. PKI

    d. SSL

    e. Physical security

    d. You should use SSL to authenticate your Web servers to the consumer to prevent man-in-the-middle attacks and to encrypt the communications to prevent eavesdropping. SSL only provides protection for the information in transit, however. The private information can still be exposed if your Web servers, or any other servers that have access to the information, are compromised by an attacker.

2. You want to purchase SSL certificates created by a trusted public CA for your Web servers so that users will not be prompted about the certificate. How many SSL certificates do you need to purchase?

    a. 1

    b. 2

    c. 3

    d. 4

    a. You only need a single certificate for both Web servers because they are hosting a single Web site. The two servers will have an identical common name: www.adventure-works.com. As a result, you can install the same certificate on both servers. However, the CA you use to issue the certificates might require you to purchase a certificate for each physical Web server as part of the service agreement.

3. How can you protect the communications between the Web servers and the database servers? (Choose all that apply.)

   a. IPSec

   b. S/MIME

   c. PKI

   d. SSL

   e. Physical security

   a, d, and e. You can use either IPSec or SSL to authenticate your database server and encrypt the communications between the Web servers and the database servers. Additionally, you can physically secure the network hardware connecting the computers to reduce the opportunity that attackers have for eavesdropping. You can choose to use one, two, or all three of these mechanisms.

Design Activity: Troubleshooting Lab

Page 11-41

1. First, reproduce the error by using Internet Explorer on Computer1. What is the exact error message?

   A Security Alert message box appears when you attempt to access the page https://adventure-works.com. The message box shows a warning symbol and the message "The name on the security certificate is invalid or does not match the name of the site."

2. Examine the certificate. What is the cause of the problem?

   The common name shown on the certificate is www.adventure-works.com. This is sufficient to allow users to access the site by using that name in the URL. However, if users leave off the www portion of the FQDN, they will receive the error message you saw because the URL does not exactly match the name on the certificate.

3. How can you resolve the problem? (Choose all that apply.)

   a. Add the adventure-works.com common name to the certificate.

   b. Install a second SSL certificate with the name adventure-works.com on the same Web site.

   c. Create a second Web site using the IIS Manager, and configure that Web site with the host header adventure-works.com. Configure that Web site to redirect requests to *http://www.adventure-works.com*.

d. Configure adventure-works.com to use a second IP address, and add that IP address to your Web server. Create a second SSL certificate with the name adventure-works.com, and associate that certificate with the second IP address.

e. Add a redirection directive to the certificate to instruct the browser to send requests to *https://www.adventure-works.com.*

c and d. Only one SSL certificate can be associated with a given IP address/port number combination. Therefore, you cannot use separate SSL certificates with host headers. However, you can configure a Web site with host headers that redirects all non-SSL requests to *http://www.adventure-works.com*. Users will still receive a warning if they type *https://adventure-works.com* directly into the address bar, however. To avoid this potential problem, you can add a second IP address to the Web server and associate a second SSL certificate with that IP address.

12 Securing Remote Access

Exam Objectives in this Chapter:

- Configure security for remote access users.
    - Configure authentication for secure remote access. Authentication types include PAP, CHAP, MS-CHAP v1, MS-CHAP v2, EAP-MD5, EAP-TLS, and multifactor authentication that combines smart cards and EAP.
    - Configure and troubleshoot virtual private network (VPN) protocols. Considerations include Internet service provider (ISP), client operating system, network address translation devices, Routing And Remote Access servers, and firewall servers.
    - Manage client configuration for remote access security. Tools include remote access policy and the Connection Manager Administration Kit.

Why This Chapter Matters

Your organization's private network provides employees access to many important resources, including file servers, application servers, and intranet Web servers. These resources contain a great deal of confidential information, and you probably have taken steps to keep people outside your network from accessing them. There are many times, however, when your organization's employees will be outside your offices and need access to these resources.

Microsoft Windows Server 2003 and previous versions of Windows server operating systems have included a component called Routing And Remote Access. Routing And Remote Access enables a server to act as a remote access server capable of connecting remote workers to your organization's private networks. Allowing legitimate users remote access poses a risk, however, because an attacker could potentially use the remote access server to access your confidential data remotely. To minimize the risk of uninvited guests using remote access, you must first choose between dial-up and VPN remote access and then configure appropriate authentication and encryption protocols.

Lessons in this Chapter:

Before You Begin

If you fulfilled the requirements for the previous chapters, you already have the necessary hardware and software configured. You can use the computers in the state they were in after completing the previous chapters, or your can install the software from scratch. To do the practices, examples, and lab exercises in this chapter, you must have:

- A private network that is not connected to any other networks. This network should not have any production computers connected to it.
- One computer with two network interface cards (NICs). On this computer, perform a Windows Server 2003, Enterprise Edition installation with default settings, and assign the computer name Computer1. Configure one NIC with the IP address 192.168.3.1, configure the other NIC with the IP address 192.168.4.1, and use the subnet mask 255.255.255.0 for both.
- Add the Domain Controller role to the computer with the default settings, and specify the domain name cohowinery.com. Configure the computer to use itself as its own primary Domain Name System (DNS) server. Add the Application Server role. Raise the domain functional level to Windows Server 2003.
- One computer with a single network interface card. On this computer, perform a Microsoft Windows XP Professional or Windows Server 2003 installation with default settings, and assign the name Computer2. Configure the NIC with the IP address 192.168.3.2, and connect that NIC to Computer1's NIC with the IP address 192.168.3.1 by using a hub, switch, or crossover cable. Add the computer to the cohowinery.com domain as a member computer. Configure the computer to use Computer1 as its primary DNS server.

Lesson 1: Remote Access Fundamentals

Windows Server 2003 provides two main types of remote access methods: dial-up and VPN. For each remote access type, there are several authentication and encryption protocols to choose from. You will have to choose the remote access type and security protocols based on the clients that will be connecting to your internal network and based on your existing infrastructure. This lesson will describe the two remote access methods and the various encryption and authentication protocols to allow you to make educated recommendations.

After this lesson, you will be able to

- Describe the advantages and disadvantages of dial-up and VPN remote access methods.
- Choose between Point-to-Point Tunneling Protocol (PPTP) and Layer Two Tunneling Protocol (L2TP), given an organization's requirements.
- List the various methods for authenticating remote access users, and describe scenarios in which each authentication method should be used.

Estimated lesson time: 20 minutes

Remote Access Methods

There are two primary methods for connecting remote users to a private network: *dial-up networking* and *virtual private networking*. Dial-up networking enables a remote access client to establish a temporary dial-up connection to a physical port on a remote access server by using the service of a telecommunications provider, such as analog phone lines, Integrated Services Digital Network (ISDN), or X.25. The most common use of dial-up networking is that of a dial-up networking client that dials the phone number of a modem attached to the remote access server. This establishes a circuit between the two devices.

Off the Record A dial-up connection was once a dedicated circuit on the Public Switched Telephone Network (PSTN). There would literally be a pair of copper wires, connected by a series of analog switches, that connected the dial-up client to the server. Telephone companies are constantly striving to become more efficient, and today telephone communications are carried digitally. In fact, it's entirely possible that the only points in which your dial-up connection will actually be a dedicated circuit are between the two modems and the telephone company. After it reaches the telephone company, your traffic might be carried in Internet Protocol (IP) packets, and it might cross the public Internet!

Virtual private networking is the creation of an encrypted, authenticated point-to-point connection across a public network such as the Internet. A VPN client uses special network protocols called *tunneling protocols* to make a virtual call to a virtual port on a VPN server.

> **See Also** IPSec-based VPNs are thoroughly described in Chapter 8.

A common example of virtual private networking is that of a VPN client who makes a VPN connection to a remote access server that is connected to the Internet. The remote access server answers the virtual call, authenticates the caller, and transfers data between the VPN client and the corporate network. In contrast to dial-up networking, virtual private networking is always a logical, indirect connection between the VPN client and the VPN server over a public network such as the Internet.

Real World

There are many factors to consider when choosing between using dial-up and VPN remote access. Obviously, you need to compare upfront and ongoing costs. VPN access has a significant cost advantage because providing dial-up access requires purchasing modem equipment and leasing circuits from your telecommunications provider, whereas providing VPN access uses an existing Internet connection. Though the Internet connection might need to be upgraded to provide the additional bandwidth needed by the VPN clients, the costs will almost certainly be lower than building a dial-up infrastructure.

You should also compare the security level provided by the two access methods. Many people immediately assume that dial-up access provides greater security than a VPN. After all, allowing people on the public Internet access to your entire intranet sounds very risky. However, if you analyze the security risks point-by-point, dial-up and VPN access have similar risks:

- Attackers can methodically identify both dial-up and VPN ports. If attackers want to find your dial-up ports, they'll use a war dialer. If attackers want to find your VPN ports, they'll use an IP scanner.
- Once the ports are identified, the attacker will need to authenticate to the remote access server. Both dial-up and VPN remote access servers use exactly the same authentication protocols. However, attackers can send requests to a VPN server faster than they can to a dial-up server. Therefore, dial-up servers have a bit of an advantage here because the long connection time makes them less vulnerable to brute-force attacks.

- Regardless of whether a dial-up or VPN connection is used, it will be difficult for an attacker to eavesdrop on a user's traffic. Gaining access either to an ISP or a public telephone provider would be difficult for the attacker. It would be much simpler for the attacker to eavesdrop on traffic on either end of the remote access connection by installing a sniffer on the remote access client or server.

Add it all up, and VPN servers are slightly less secure than dial-up servers, but significantly less expensive. In the real world, you'll be better off using a VPN and spending the money you save on other security initiatives—like an intrusion detection system to detect brute-force attacks against your VPN server.

VPN Protocols

Windows Server 2003 supports two VPN protocols: PPTP and L2TP. In most circumstances, either protocol will work equally well. They both provide similar levels of privacy and data integrity because they support the same authentication and encryption standards. They primarily differ in stability and compatibility. PPTP is more mature, but it is not an Internet standard. L2TP is relatively new, but it might be supported by a wider variety of non-Microsoft clients because it is an Internet standard.

Planning The number of incoming connections supported is one of the factors that differentiate the various editions of Windows Server 2003. Windows Server 2003, Web Edition and Windows Server 2003, Standard Edition can support up to 1,000 incoming PPTP connections and 1,000 incoming L2TP VPN connections. Windows Server 2003, Enterprise Edition and Windows Server 2003, Datacenter Edition each support 16,384 PPTP and L2TP connections. However, Windows Server 2003, Web Edition can accept only one VPN connection at a time, which should be used to manage the server remotely.

PPTP

PPTP is a VPN protocol that takes advantage of the authentication, compression, and encryption mechanisms of Point-to-Point Protocol (PPP), the most common standard used for dial-up remote access. PPTP first stores the IP datagram being transmitted inside a PPP frame. PPTP tunnels the PPP frame within a Generic Routing Encapsulation (GRE) header using IP protocol 47 and a Transmission Control Protocol (TCP) header using port 1723, as illustrated in Figure 12.1.

Data-link header	IP header	GRE header	PPP header	Encrypted IP datagram	Data-link trailer

Figure 12.1 PPTP-tunneled data packet structure

PPTP relies on PPP's encryption to protect the privacy of the tunneled data. The PPP frame is encrypted with Microsoft Point-to-Point Encryption (MPPE) by using encryption keys generated from the Microsoft Challenge Handshake Authentication Protocol version 1 (MS-CHAP v1), Microsoft Challenge Handshake Authentication Protocol version 2 (MS-CHAP v2), or Extensible Authentication Protocol (EAP) authentication process. VPN clients must use the MS-CHAP v1, MS-CHAP v2, or EAP authentication protocol in order for the payloads of PPP frames to be encrypted. PPTP does not do the encryption itself; rather, it takes advantage of the underlying PPP encryption by encapsulating a previously encrypted PPP frame.

PPTP requires additional configuration to allow it to traverse a Network Address Translation (NAT) server or a firewall. To allow PPTP traffic through a firewall, the firewall must allow TCP port 1723 and IP protocol 47. Many NAT servers are capable of allowing a client on the internal network to connect to a PPTP server on the public network. The NAT server must specifically support PPTP, however. Although every NAT server is capable of translating standard IP traffic, the GRE protocol requires special consideration. The NAT server built into Routing And Remote Access is one example of a NAT server that supports PPTP.

PPTP has been supported in every version of Windows that has been released since Microsoft Windows NT 4.0 and Windows 98, and it is still the default VPN protocol in Windows Server 2003. Earlier versions of Windows do not support either PPTP or L2TP when initially installed, but you can add support by installing additional software that can be downloaded for free from Microsoft. To use a computer running Windows 95 or Windows 98 as a PPTP client, you must install the Windows Dial-Up Networking version 1.4 Upgrade, available at *http://support.microsoft.com/?kbid=285189*. Microsoft does not support either PPTP or L2TP on Windows NT version 3.5*x*, even with a software upgrade.

L2TP/IPSec

L2TP is a standardized RFC-based tunneling protocol. While PPTP uses MPPE to encrypt PPP datagrams, L2TP relies on IP Security (IPSec) for encryption services. The combination of L2TP and IPSec is known as *L2TP/IPSec*. To establish a VPN connection, both L2TP and IPSec must be supported by both the VPN client and the VPN server. Because L2TP is an industry standard, it is supported on a wider variety of non-Microsoft operating systems than PPTP. In fact, you should always choose L2TP over PPTP when designing a VPN solution for heterogeneous client operating systems.

For many years, one of PPTP's advantages over L2TP/IPSec was that PPTP could work through a NAT server. L2TP/IPSec used the source and destination IP addresses for authentication and embedded this information inside the encrypted portion of the packet. Therefore, NAT servers were incapable of changing the source and destination IP addresses. NAT Traversal (NAT-T), a new capability of L2TP/IPSec, enables you to use L2TP to connect to an L2TP server when the client is located behind a NAT server. However, the client, the server, and the NAT server must all support NAT-T.

See Also For more information on IPSec and NAT-T, refer to Chapters 8 and 9.

Encapsulation for L2TP/IPSec packets consists of two layers: L2TP encapsulation and IPSec encapsulation. L2TP wraps an L2TP header and a User Datagram Protocol (UDP) header around a PPP frame containing the tunneled data, which is similar to the way PPTP performs tunneling. The resulting L2TP message is then wrapped with an IPSec Encapsulating Security Payload (ESP) header and trailer, an IPSec Authentication trailer that provides message integrity and authentication, and a final IP header, as illustrated in Figure 12.2. IPSec encrypts the message by using Data Encryption Standard (DES) or Triple DES (3DES) by using encryption keys generated from IPSec's Internet Key Exchange (IKE) negotiation process.

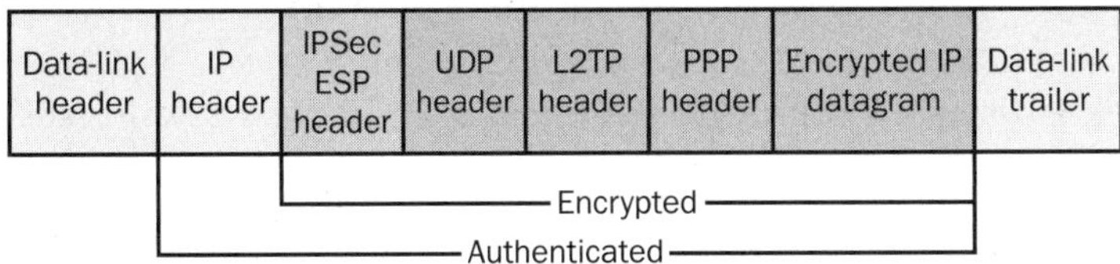

Figure 12.2 L2TP-tunneled data packet structure

Like most IPSec connections, L2TP/IPSec is generally used with public key certificates. Unless you are using a preshared key for authentication (which should be used only for testing purposes), you must configure public key certificates on both the VPN server and the client. Additionally, both the client and the server must trust the root CA that issued the other's certificate.

Client support for L2TP is built in to the Windows Server 2003, Windows XP, and Windows 2000 remote access client, and VPN server support for L2TP is built in to Windows 2000 and Windows Server 2003. However, L2TP is not supported out-of-the-box on versions of Windows released prior to Windows 2000. To use computers running Windows 98, Windows ME, or Windows NT Workstation 4.0 as L2TP clients, you must install the Microsoft L2TP/IPSec VPN client, which is available at *http://www.microsoft.com/windows2000/server/evaluation/news/bulletins/l2tpclient.asp*.

Before you can install the Microsoft L2TP/IPSec VPN client on computers running Windows 95 or Windows 98, you must have Microsoft Internet Explorer 5.01 or later installed, in addition to the Dial-Up Networking version 1.4 upgrade. You can download the Dial-Up Networking upgrade from *http://support.microsoft.com/?kbid=285189*.

Exam Tip How do you choose between PPTP and L2TP on the exam? Pick PPTP unless something in the question requires L2TP, such as a reference to UNIX, Linux, or another non-Microsoft operating system.

Authentication Methods

Because dial-up, PPTP, and L2TP all use PPP for authentication, they all support the same authentication methods. There are several authentication methods available. Some you will already be familiar with because they are the same methods used for wireless networks or IPSec. Others are used primarily for authenticating remote access users.

When choosing a remote access authentication method, you must first choose between authenticating users against a Remote Authentication Dial-In User Service (RADIUS) server or authenticating them against the local user database or Active Directory domain. If you choose to authenticate users against a RADIUS server, you will have configuration options similar to those used when configuring a RADIUS server to authenticate wireless users. Specifically, you must specify the IP addresses and port numbers of one or more RADIUS servers.

See Also For information about hardening Internet Authentication Service (IAS) servers, refer to Chapter 4. For information about using RADIUS servers for authentication, refer to Chapter 10.

Regardless of whether you choose Windows or RADIUS as the authentication provider, you can choose from several authentication methods: EAP, MS-CHAP v2, MS-CHAP v1, Challenge Handshake Authentication Protocol (CHAP), Shiva Password Authentication Protocol (SPAP), Password Authentication Protocol (PAP), preshared key, and unauthenticated access. You should choose the most secure authentication method that all remote access clients support. All Windows operating systems can be updated to support every standard authentication method except for EAP. Only Windows Server 2003, Windows XP, and Windows 2000 support EAP. Non-Windows operating systems might have different restrictions.

Exam Tip Expect to see more than one exam question for which you need to know the features and limitations of various authentication protocols. At a minimum, you should be able to answer the following:

- Which protocol is required for smart cards?
- Which protocol is required for public key certificates?
- What are the special configuration requirements for CHAP?
- When is MS-CHAP v2 the best choice of authentication methods?
- What is the difference between authentication encryption and data encryption, and which protocols support each?
- Which protocols support mutual authentication?

Table 12.1 shows the supported client operating systems and key features of the various authentication methods.

Table 12.1 Authentication Methods Supported by Versions of Windows

	EAP	MS-CHAP v2	MS-CHAP v1	CHAP	SPAP	PAP	Pre-shared key
Supported by Windows Server 2003, Windows XP, and Windows 2000 clients		√	√	√	√	√	√
Supported on updated versions of Windows prior to Windows 2000		√*	√	√	√	√	√
Supported by default on a computer running Windows Server 2003 and Routing And Remote Access	√	√	√				
Provides authentication encryption	√	√	√	√	√		√
Provides data encryption	√	√					√
Provides mutual authentication	√	√					√

Table 12.1 Authentication Methods Supported by Versions of Windows

	EAP	MS-CHAP v2	MS-CHAP v1	CHAP	SPAP	PAP	Pre-shared key
Allows changing of passwords during authentication process		√	√				
Requires passwords to be stored with reversible encryption			√	√			
Vulnerable to Replay attacks					√	√	

* Windows 95 does not support MS-CHAP v2 over dial-up connections.

As when controlling wireless access, you can use a RADIUS server to authenticate dial-up and VPN users. Any standard RADIUS server will work, including Internet Authentication Service (IAS). If you do choose to use IAS, you can use IAS to further restrict authentication, encryption, group access, and other aspects of a remote access policy (RAP).

See Also For information on hardening an IAS server, refer to Chapter 4. For information on configuring an IAS server to authenticate users, refer to Chapter 10.

As shown in Figure 12.3, configuring Routing And Remote Access to connect to a RADIUS server involves the same information used to configure wireless users to authenticate to a RADIUS server: the primary RADIUS server's IP address, optionally an IP address for a secondary RADIUS server, and a shared secret. After completing the initial configuration, you can use the Routing And Remote Access console to add additional RADIUS servers if necessary. Additionally, you must configure the RADIUS servers to accept the Routing And Remote Access server as a client and to use the same shared secret.

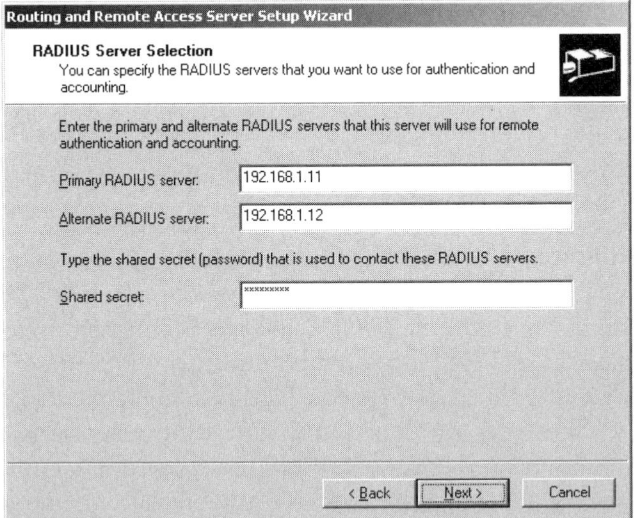

Figure 12.3 Configuring Routing And Remote Access to authenticate to a RADIUS server

You can use the same authentication methods whether you choose RADIUS or Windows authentication, as described in the following sections.

EAP

EAP, the protocol itself, enables an arbitrary authentication mechanism to authenticate a remote access connection. Routing And Remote Access includes support for Protected EAP (PEAP), Message Digest 5 Challenge (MD5-Challenge), and Smart Card Or Other Certificate by default, though other authentication methods could be added to EAP by non-Microsoft applications.

> **See Also** For more information on EAP, refer to Chapter 10.

MD5-Challenge MD5-Challenge is a supported EAP type that uses the same challenge handshake protocol as PPP-based CHAP, but the challenges and responses are sent as EAP messages. A typical use for MD5-Challenge is to authenticate non-Microsoft remote access clients, such as those running Mac OSX. You can also use MD5-

Challenge to test EAP interoperability. EAP with MD5-Challenge does not support encryption of connection data.

PEAP PEAP is primarily used to authenticate wireless users with a user name and password. MS-CHAP v2 is the preferred method for authenticating dial-up or VPN users with user name and password credentials; therefore, you should never configure PEAP for use with a VPN.

Smart Card Or Other Certificate This authentication method, also known as EAP-Transport Layer Security (EAP-TLS), is used to enable remote access authentication with a smart card or a public key certificate. Only Windows Server 2003, Windows XP, and Windows 2000 remote access clients support this authentication method. The computer certificate that you assign to the L2TP/IPSec client must contain either the Client Authentication purpose or the IPSec purpose in the certificate extensions. The VPN server certificate must contain the Server Authentication purpose if it is deployed as a remote access server, or it must contain both the Server Authentication purpose and the Client Authentication purpose if it is deployed in a router-to-router VPN.

See Also For more information about public key certificates, refer to Chapter 7.

You must install a user certificate on all VPN clients, and if the authenticating server is a RADIUS server, you must also install a Server Authentication computer certificate on the RADIUS server. When two or more purposes are required, they must be included in the extensions of the same certificate.

Exam Tip Remember that only Windows 2000, Windows XP, and Windows Server 2003 support EAP. Windows NT version 4.0, Windows 98, and Windows 95 do not support EAP. Also remember that you will always use EAP if smart cards or public key certificates are used for authentication.

MS-CHAP v1

The Windows Server 2003 family includes support for MS-CHAP v1. MS-CHAP v1 is a one-way authentication method offering both authentication encryption and data encryption. However, this encryption is relatively weak because MS-CHAP v1 bases the cryptographic key on the user's password and will use the same cryptographic key as long as the user has the same password. This gives an attacker more data with which to crack the encryption, making the cryptography weak.

MS-CHAP v1's sole advantage is that it is supported by earlier Windows clients, such as Windows 95 and Windows 98, without additional software upgrades. By default, Windows Server 2003 Routing And Remote Access will accept MS-CHAP v1 authentication if the client requests it, enabling clients that haven't been upgraded to connect successfully. You can choose to disable this authentication method if all clients can use MS-CHAP v2.

MS-CHAP v2

The Windows Server 2003 family includes support for MS-CHAP v2, the preferred method for authenticating remote access connections that do not use smart cards or public key certificates. Unlike MS-CHAP v1, MS-CHAP v2 authenticates both the client and the server. Additionally, MS-CHAP v2 uses much stronger cryptography than MS-CHAP v1, including the use of a new cryptographic key for each connection and each direction of transmission.

If you do not change any of the default settings, Windows VPN remote access clients will use MS-CHAP v2 to authenticate. Windows 95 with the Windows Dial-Up Networking Performance & Security Upgrade supports MS-CHAP v2, but only for VPN connections, not for dial-up connections. MS-CHAP (version 1 and version 2) is the only authentication protocol provided with the Windows Server 2003 family that supports password change during the authentication process. If you use a different authentication method, the user will have to connect to a domain controller through a mechanism other than a VPN to change the password.

Tip If you have users who always work remotely, not being able to change a password during authentication can be a real problem because they cannot simply change the password the next time they are in the office. One way to allow remote users to change their passwords is to set up a computer with Terminal Services. Have the users connect to the Terminal Services server when a password change is required. When they log in, they will be prompted to change their passwords.

CHAP

CHAP is a challenge-response authentication protocol that uses the industry-standard MD5 hashing scheme to encrypt the response. CHAP is used by various vendors of network access servers and clients. A computer running Windows Server 2003 and Routing And Remote Access does not allow CHAP authentication by default. However, you can enable CHAP authentication so that remote access clients that support CHAP but do not support MS-CHAP can be authenticated.

CHAP does not support encryption of connection data. Because CHAP requires the use of reversibly encrypted passwords, you should avoid using it whenever possible. Enabling reversibly encrypted passwords makes it easier for an attacker to identify users' passwords if the attacker gains access to your user database. If a remote access user uses CHAP for authentication and his or her password expires, the user cannot change the password during the remote access authentication process. The user will need to authenticate by using MS-CHAP or connect to your internal network directly.

SPAP

The Shiva Password Authentication Protocol (SPAP) is a reversible encryption mechanism employed by Shiva. A computer running Windows XP Professional, when connecting to a Shiva LAN Rover, uses SPAP, as does a Shiva client that connects to a server running Routing And Remote Access. This form of authentication is more secure than plaintext but less secure than CHAP or MS-CHAP. SPAP is not enabled by default on computers running Windows Server 2003 and Routing And Remote Access, and it should not be enabled unless specifically required.

> **Security Alert** When you enable SPAP as an authentication protocol, any particular user password is always sent in the same reversibly-encrypted form. This makes SPAP authentication susceptible to replay attacks, in which an attacker captures the packets of the authentication process and replays the responses to gain authenticated access to your intranet. Don't use SPAP unless absolutely necessary.

PAP

Password Authentication Protocol (PAP) uses plaintext passwords and is the least secure authentication protocol. Anyone capturing the packets of the authentication process can easily read the password and use it to gain unauthorized access to your intranet. The use of PAP is highly discouraged, especially for VPN connections. It is disabled by default, and it should only be used if the remote access client and the remote access server cannot negotiate a more secure form of validation.

Unauthenticated access

The Windows Server 2003 family supports unauthenticated access, which means that user credentials (a user name and password) are not required. There are some situations in which unauthenticated access is useful. Specifically, if you are using a RAP to control access by another means, such as callback or caller ID, you might decide that additional authentication is not required. Alternatively, you might encounter a scenario in which you want to allow guests to connect to a remote access server without requiring any form of authentication.

Preshared keys

Preshared key authentication is the only way to use L2TP/IPSec without installing a computer certificate on the remote access server. Preshared keys are never the preferred authentication method for enterprises because managing preshared keys on large numbers of computers is time consuming. If the preshared key on a remote access server is changed, a client with a manually configured preshared key will be unable to connect to that server until the preshared key on the client is changed. If the preshared key was distributed to the client within a Connection Manager profile, that profile must be reissued with the new preshared key and reinstalled on the client computer.

Additionally, because the same preshared key must be distributed to all clients, the likelihood of the preshared key being discovered by an attacker is very high. Unless you distribute the preshared key within a Connection Manager profile, each user must manually type the preshared key. This limitation further reduces security and increases the probability of error. Preshared keys are unlike certificates in that the origin and history of a preshared key cannot be determined. For these reasons, the use of preshared keys to authenticate L2TP/IPSec connections is considered a relatively weak authentication method.

Finally, the use of preshared keys is supported with only Windows Server 2003 and Windows XP clients. While preshared key authentication is useful for testing purposes, if you want a long-term, strong authentication method for L2TP/IPSec, you should use public key certificates.

Lesson Review

The following questions are intended to reinforce key information presented in this lesson. If you are unable to answer a question, review the lesson materials and try the question again. You can find answers to the questions in the "Questions and Answers" section at the end of this chapter.

1. Which of the following authentication protocols can be used by fully updated Windows 98 VPN clients? (Choose all that apply.)

   a. EAP

   b. MS-CHAP v2

   c. MS-CHAP v1

   d. CHAP

   e. SPAP

   f. PAP

---

2. Your organization's security policy has a requirement that passwords not be stored with reversible encryption. Which of the following authentication protocols can you use? (Choose all that apply.)

   a. EAP

   b. MS-CHAP v2

   c. MS-CHAP v1

   d. CHAP

   e. SPAP

   f. PAP

---

3. Your organization still has clients running Windows 95. Which of the following protocols can you use to authenticate dial-up clients? (Choose all that apply.)

   a. EAP

   b. MS-CHAP v2

   c. MS-CHAP v1

   d. CHAP

   e. SPAP

   f. PAP

Lesson Summary

- Windows Server 2003 supports two VPN protocols: PPTP and L2TP/IPSec. PPTP was developed by Microsoft and is the default protocol. L2TP/IPSec is an Internet standard that provides interoperability with a greater number of clients.
- Windows Server 2003 supports eight methods for authenticating users: EAP, MS-CHAP v2, MS-CHAP v1, CHAP, SPAP, PAP, preshared keys, and unauthenticated access.
- Use EAP to authenticate users with a public key certificate or a smart card. Only Windows Server 2003, Windows XP, and Windows 2000 clients support EAP.

Lesson 2: Configuring Remote Access Servers

On remote access clients, you specify the minimum authentication and encryption levels that the client will accept. On the server, you specify the authentication and encryption levels that it will offer to the client. The client and server will then negotiate and choose the authentication and encryption levels with the highest level of security that both are compatible with. If the server doesn't allow authentication or encryption levels that meet the client's requirements, or if the client doesn't support the server's minimum authentication and encryption levels, the remote access will fail.

This lesson covers remote access server security configuration, and Lesson 3 will cover configuring the remote access client.

After this lesson, you will be able to

- Configure a remote access server with acceptable authentication methods.
- Configure user dial-up properties to control which users can connect to a remote access server.
- Use remote access policies to further restrict the circumstances under which users can and cannot connect.

Estimated lesson time: 25 minutes

Configuring Authentication

You create a remote access server by using the Routing And Remote Access Server Setup Wizard, as described in Exercise 1 of this lesson. This wizard does not provide the opportunity to configure authentication and encryption settings, however. To view or modify remote access server security settings after the initial configuration, open the properties dialog box for the server from the Routing And Remote Access console, and then click the Security tab.

As shown in Figure 12.4, the default settings for a dial-up or VPN server use Windows Authentication and Windows Accounting. These settings are compatible with the client's default settings, which allows administrators who are not concerned with fine-tuning remote access security to bring the service online quickly. If you have decided to use a preshared key to authenticate L2TP/IPSec VPN connections, select the Allow Custom IPSec Policy For L2TP Connection check box, and then type a preshared key.

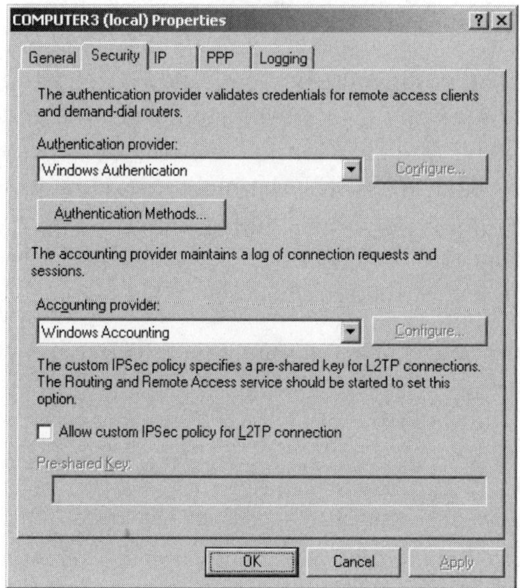

Figure 12.4 Default server authentication and accounting settings

If you plan to use a RADIUS server, such as an IAS server, to authenticate users, click the Authentication Provider list and then click RADIUS Authentication. Then click the Configure button to create a list of RADIUS servers. Along with the IP address, shared secret, port number, and time out configuration of each server, you will specify an Initial Score. The remote access server will attempt to contact RADIUS servers with a higher initial score. As time goes on, the RADIUS server will keep track of the responsiveness of each RADIUS server and adjust that server's score. Ultimately, this will lead to efficient load-balancing between multiple RADIUS servers, even if the servers have different processing capabilities.

Whether you use Windows or RADIUS authentication, you can click the Authentication Methods button to control which authentication protocols the server will accept from the client. By default, the server accepts EAP, MS-CHAP v2, and MS-CHAP v1, as shown in Figure 12.5.

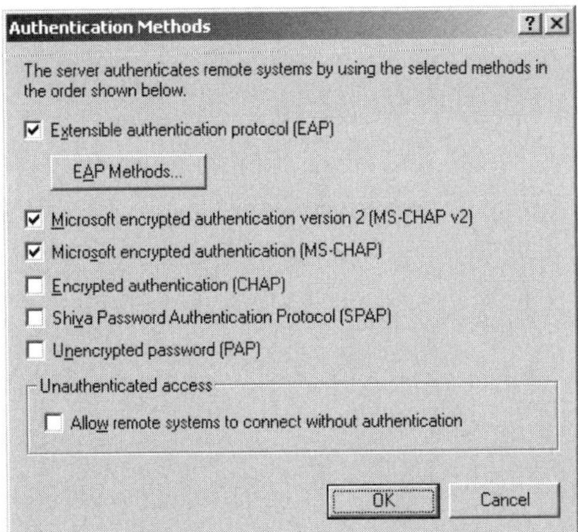

Figure 12.5 Default server authentication methods

You cannot configure encryption levels by using the server's properties dialog box. Instead, you use RAPs. RAPs also allow you to restrict authentication and encryption based on other factors, such as the client's phone number and group memberships.

Configuring Authorization

After the credentials submitted with the remote access connection are authenticated, the connection must be authorized. Remote access authorization consists of two steps: first, verification of the dial-in properties of the user account submitted by the dial-up connection, and second, application of the first matching RAP.

User account properties

Dial-in properties, which apply to both direct dial-up and VPN connections, are configured on the Dial-In tab of the domain or local user account properties dialog box, as shown in Figure 12.6. If a user is authenticating with a domain account, a user account corresponding to the name sent through the dial-up connection must already exist in the domain. Dial-in properties for this account can thus be configured in the Active Directory Users And Computers console. If the user is dialing in to a standalone server, however, the account must already exist as a user account in the answering server's local user database. Dial-in properties for this account can thus be configured in the Local Users And Groups snap-in within the Computer Management console.

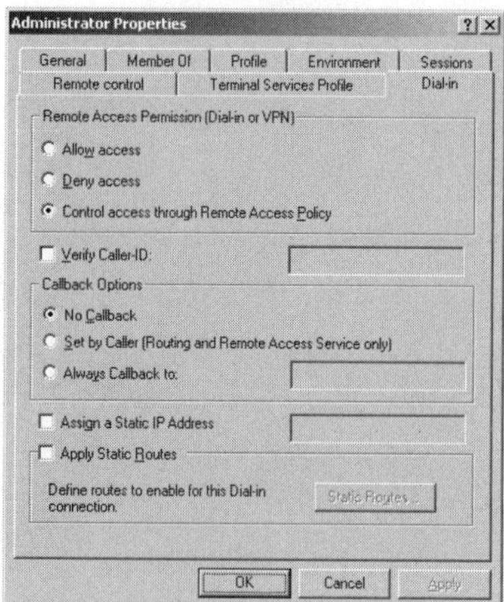

Figure 12.6 Editing user dial-in properties

The most important security setting on this tab is Remote Access Permission. Setting this to Allow Access or Deny Access controls whether the user will be allowed to connect remotely when no RAPs are specified. Selecting Control Access Through Remote Access Policy, the default for standalone computers and computers in a Windows Server 2003 domain, allows the Routing And Remote Access service or the RADIUS server to determine whether the user is allowed to connect. By default, RAPs block all remote access connections. The Control Access Through Remote Access Policy radio button is not available on domain user accounts unless the domain is at a Windows Server 2003 domain functional level.

When you use the Allow Access and Deny Access settings along with RAPs, Deny Access will always override the RAP. In other words, a user with the Deny Access setting selected will never be able to connect. A user with Allow Access can connect if no RAP denies the user access. For example, dial-up hours specified in a RAP profile might prevent a user account from connecting in the evening hours even when the Allow Access option has been set for the dial-in properties of the user account. However, the Allow Access option specifies that the Deny Remote Access Permission setting in RAPs is ignored.

If the Verify Caller ID check box is selected, the server verifies the caller's phone number for dial-up access or the source IP address for VPN access. If the Verify Caller ID value does not match the user's phone number or source IP address, the connection attempt is denied. For dial-up users, caller ID must be supported by the caller, the phone system between the caller and the remote access server, and the remote access server. You should only use this feature for VPN users that always connect by using a single statically assigned IP address.

Tip The fact that you can use the Verify Caller ID setting to specify a source IP address is not clear from the user interface. As a result, it's underused. However, it's a great way to reduce the risk of an attacker misusing a user's credentials if that user always connects from a single IP address.

To use callback to improve dial-up security by having the remote access server call the user at a specified phone number, click Always Callback To and type the user's phone number. Generally, you should use this only when the user consistently calls from the same number and you do not have the option of verifying caller ID. This slows connection time considerably because the remote access server must authenticate the user, disconnect the session, and then establish a new session.

Security Alert Selecting Set By Caller for a user's callback options does not improve your security. In fact, attackers who could successfully authenticate could abuse this. For example, they could configure the user account to have your server dial a long distance phone number that would incur unnecessary charges. An attacker could even profit directly by having the server dial a 1-900 number owned by the attacker!

Remote access policies

RAPs control how or whether a connection is authorized to the network. A RAP contains a set of policy conditions that determine whether that policy applies to a given connection request. If you are using IAS as a RADIUS server, you should create the RAPs by using the Internet Authentication Service console on the IAS server. Otherwise, create the RAPs by using the Routing And Remote Access console on the remote access server.

See Also Chapter 10 covered creating RAPs for wireless users by using the Internet Authentication Service. The procedures and concepts are exactly the same for remote access connections, whether you add the RAPs to IAS or the Routing And Remote Access service. Therefore, they will not be repeated here.

A typical use of a dial-up or VPN RAP is to create policy conditions that specify the Active Directory security group that a client must be a member of, the time of day, or the connection type of the requesting client. A RAP is also configured to allow or deny the connection request. If there are multiple RAPs on a server, each connection request is evaluated against them according to the priority until a matching RAP either allows or denies the request.

The process of configuring a RAP for wireless users and remote access users is very similar; however, there is a significant difference. You typically restrict encryption for wireless users at the wireless access point (WAP). However, you must use a RAP to specify whether a remote access client uses 48-bit, 56-bit, or 128-bit encryption. To specify the encryption levels, view the RAP properties, and then click the Edit Profile button. In the Edit Dial-In Profile dialog box, click the Encryption tab. As shown in Figure 12.7, you can then select from Basic Encryption (MPPE 40 bit), Strong Encryption (MPPE 56 bit), Strongest Encryption (MPPE 128 bit), or No Encryption.

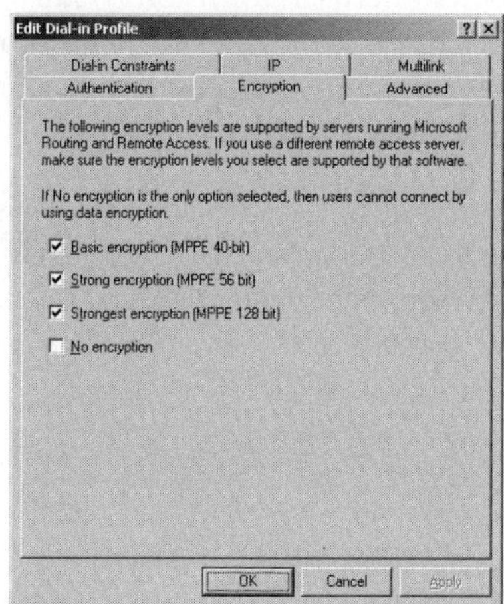

Figure 12.7 Configuring RAP encryption levels

By default, two RAPs are preconfigured in Windows Server 2003. The first built-in policy is Connections To Microsoft Routing And Remote Access Server. As the name suggests, this policy is configured to match every remote access connection to the Routing And Remote Access service. When Routing And Remote Access is reading this policy, the policy naturally matches every incoming connection. However, when the policy is being read by an IAS server, network access might be provided by a non-Microsoft vendor; consequently, this policy will not match those connections.

The second built-in RAP is Connections To Other Access Servers. This policy is configured to match every incoming connection regardless of network access server type. However, because the first policy matches all connections to Routing And Remote Access, only connections to other remote access servers read and match the policy when the default policy order is not changed. Unless the first policy is deleted or the default policy order is rearranged, this second policy can be read only by IAS servers.

Generally, you should not edit the built-in RAPs. Editing the built-in RAPs can cause confusion for other administrators, which can lead to security vulnerabilities. For example, if you choose to edit the profile of the Connections To Microsoft Routing And Remote Access Server RAP to allow unencrypted communication, another administrator might assume that the policy still requires encryption without double-checking the settings. Instead of modifying the built-in RAPs, add additional RAPs that have higher priority ratings.

Configuring Authentication with Certificates or Smart Cards

Enabling EAP authentication might or might not be enough to allow your users to authenticate with a smart card or public key certificate. If you are using an enterprise CA and your Routing And Remote Access servers are members of the same domain, they will be automatically configured to allow EAP authentication for certificates signed by the enterprise CA. To verify that certificate or smart card authentication is enabled for a remote access policy, follow this procedure:

1. Open the Routing And Remote Access console.
2. In the left pane, expand the server node, and then click Remote Access Policies.
3. In the right pane, right-click the RAP that applies to the users who will authenticate with certificates, and then click Properties. If the RAP does not yet exist, create one.
4. Click Edit Profile, and then click the Authentication tab.
5. Click the EAP Methods button.

   The Select EAP Providers list appears.
6. If Smart Card Or Other Certificate is not listed in the EAP Types list, click Add. Click Smart Card Or Other Certificate, and then click OK.
7. Click Smart Card Or Other Certificate, and then click Edit.
8. Click the Certificate Issued To list, and then click the certificate you will use to identify the Routing And Remote Access server. Click OK four times.

If your certificates are not issued by an enterprise CA, or if your computer has more than one certificate, you should add a remote access policy specifically for authenticating users with a smart card or other certificate. To do so, follow this procedure:

1. Open the Routing And Remote Access console.
2. In the left pane, expand the server node. Right-click Remote Access Policies, and then click New Remote Access Policy.

   The New Remote Access Policy Wizard appears.
3. Click Next.
4. On the Policy Configuration Method page, in the Policy Name box, type a name for the policy. Click Next.
5. On the Access Method page, click either VPN or Dial-Up. Click Next.

6. On the User Or Group Access page, select your preferred authorization method. Click Next.
7. On the Authentication Methods page, select Extensible Authentication Protocol (EAP). Click the Type list, and then click Smart Card Or Other Certificate.
8. Click the Configure button. Click the Certificate Issued list, and then click the certificate you will use to identify the Routing And Remote Access server. Click OK.
9. Clear Microsoft Encrypted Authentication Version 2 (MS-CHAPv2). Click Next.
10. On the Policy Encryption Level page, select the encryption levels you want to allow. Click Next, and then click Finish.
11. In the left pane, click Remote Access Policies. In the right pane, right-click the new policy, and then click Properties.
12. Click Grant Remote Access Permission, and then click OK.

Practice: Configuring a VPN Server and Client

In this practice, you will connect two computers by using a VPN. First, make sure that the computers are connected and configured as shown in Figure 12.8. Computer1 must have two network interface cards, each connected to a different computer, for this practice to be successful.

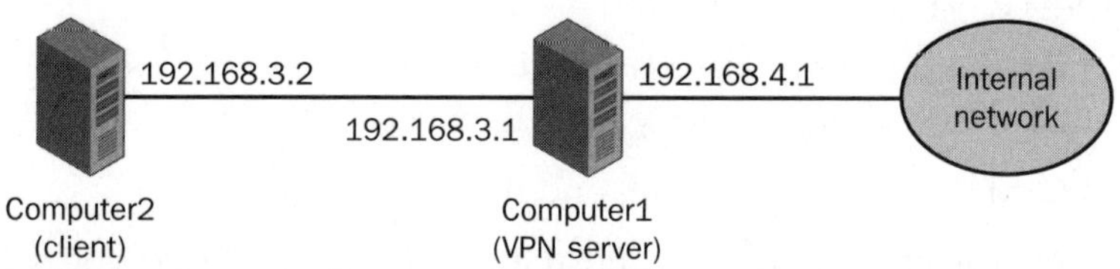

Figure 12.8 Network architecture for testing VPN connectivity

Exercise 1: Configuring a VPN server

In this exercise, you will configure Computer1 as a VPN server. First, create a user and group to assign remote access to.

1. Log on to the cohowinery.com domain on Computer1 by using the Administrator account.
2. Click Start, point to Administrative Tools, and then click Active Directory Users And Computers.
3. Expand cohowinery.com. Right-click Users, point to New, and then click Group.
4. In the Group Name box, type **Remote Access Users**. Click OK.
5. Right-click Users, point to New, and then click User.

6. In the User Logon Name box, type **User1**. In the Full Name box, type **User1**. Click Next.
7. In the Password and Confirm Password boxes, type a complex password. Clear the User Must Change Password At Next Logon check box. Click Next, and then click Finish.
8. Double-click User1. Click the Member Of tab. Click the Add button.
9. In the Enter The Object Names To Select box, type **Remote Access Users**. Click OK.
10. Click the Dial-In tab, and then click Allow Access.
11. Select the Verify Caller-ID check box, and then type **192.168.3.2** in the box. Click OK.

    Configuring the Verify Caller-ID box with the client's IP address reduces the risk that the account will be used to authenticate from a different location on the Internet. This option is available only for user accounts located on a standalone server or on an Active Directory domain with a Windows Server 2003 functional level.

In this part of the exercise, you will configure Routing And Remote Access.

1. Click Start, point to Administrative Tools, and then click Routing And Remote Access.
2. Right-click Computer1 (Local), and then click Configure And Enable Routing And Remote Access.

   The Routing And Remote Access Server Setup Wizard appears.
3. Click Next.
4. On the Configuration page, click Remote Access (Dial-Up Or VPN), and then click Next.
5. On the Remote Access page, click VPN, and then click Next.
6. On the VPN Connection page, click 192.168.3.1, and then click Next.

   The 192.168.3.1 interface connects to Computer2, which will simulate the VPN client connecting across the Internet. Notice that the Enable Security On The Selected Interface By Setting Up Static Packet Filters check box is selected by default. If you were to leave this check box selected on a production system, all non-VPN services would become unavailable across the public network interface.
7. On the IP Address Assignment page, click From A Specified Range Of Addresses. Click Next.
8. On the Address Range Assignment page, click New.

9. In the Start IP Address box, type **192.168.4.10**. In the Number Of Addresses box, type **10**. Click OK.

   Notice that the addresses are on the destination network.

10. Click Next. On the Managing Multiple Remote Access Servers page, accept the default setting to not use a RADIUS server by clicking Next.

11. Click Finish.

12. You can disregard the Routing And Remote Access warning box that appears because you are not using DHCP to assign addresses. Click OK.

Exercise 2: Configuring a VPN client

In this exercise, you will configure Computer2 as a VPN client configured to use Computer1 as the VPN server. You will then test connectivity by communicating with Computer1.

1. Log on to Computer2 by using the Administrator account.

2. Open Control Panel, open Network Connections, and then open New Connection Wizard.

   The Welcome To New Connection Wizard page appears.

3. Click Next.

4. On the Network Connection Type page, click Connect To The Network At My Workplace. Click Next.

5. On the Network Connection page, click Virtual Private Network Connection. Click Next.

6. On the Company Name page, type **Test VPN** in the Company Name box. Click Next.

7. On the Public Network page, click Do Not Dial The Initial Connection. Click Next.

   You would use this page if users were connecting to the private network across the public Internet. Having users dial in to an ISP before establishing a VPN connection is a common, economical way to provide dial-up access to your users.

8. On the VPN Server Selection page, type **192.168.3.1** in the Host Name Or IP Address box. Click Next twice, and then click Finish.

   The Connect Test VPN dialog box appears.

9. In the User Name box, type **User1**. In the Password box, type the complex password you assigned to User1.

10. Select the Save This User Name And Password For The Following Users check box, as shown in Figure 12.9.

Figure 12.9 Creating a new test VPN connection

> **Security Alert** Saving the password is convenient for users. However, if a mobile computer is compromised—for example, if it's stolen—an attacker can connect directly to your internal network.

11. Click Connect.

    The computer establishes a VPN connection to Computer1.

12. Open a command prompt. Run the command `Ipconfig`.

    Notice that Computer2 now has two network interfaces listed. The Local Area Connection will have the IP address 192.168.3.2, and the test VPN connection will have the IP address 192.168.4.11. Numbering for the private networks started at 192.168.4.10, but Computer1 claimed 192.168.4.10 for itself to act as the default gateway.

13. Run the command `ping 192.168.4.1`.

    Ping will receive responses from the private interface of Computer1.

Lesson Review

The following questions are intended to reinforce key information presented in this lesson. If you are unable to answer a question, review the lesson materials and try the question again. You can find answers to the questions in the "Questions and Answers" section at the end of this chapter.

1. Your organization has multiple dial-up servers configured to authenticate to an IAS RADIUS server. Which tool should you use to restrict the hours during which users can dial up?
   - **a.** Active Directory Users And Computers
   - **b.** Computer Management
   - **c.** Routing And Remote Access
   - **d.** Internet Authentication Service

   ___

2. Your organization uses Windows authentication to verify the credentials of remote VPN clients. Which tool should you use to restrict the groups that can connect to the VPN server?
   - **a.** Active Directory Users And Computers
   - **b.** Computer Management
   - **c.** Routing And Remote Access
   - **d.** Internet Authentication Service

   ___

3. In an Active Directory domain environment, which of the following conditions must be met in order to use RAPs to control which remote access users are allowed to connect?
   - **a.** The domain functional level must be Windows 2000 Mixed.
   - **b.** The domain functional level must be Windows Server 2003.
   - **c.** You must use MS-CHAP v1 or MS-CHAP v2 authentication.
   - **d.** You must use an IAS RADIUS server.

   ___

Lesson Summary

- You can configure a remote access server and clients without changing the default settings. By default, encryption is required, and MS-CHAP v2 or MS-CHAP v1 authentication will be used.
- Edit the remote access server's properties to expand or restrict the available authentication protocols. Select EAP authentication to enable authentication with public key certificates or smart cards.
- User authorization can be controlled in three places: the user's dial-up properties, a RAP configured on the remote access server, or a RAP configured on the IAS RADIUS server.

Lesson 3: Configuring Remote Access Clients

You can configure clients to connect to a remote access server in one of two ways: by using the network connection properties or by using the Connection Manager Administration Kit (CMAK). Manually configuring a connection by using network connection properties is convenient when you are using the default security settings or when you need to configure fewer than ten clients. However, it would not be possible to configure and maintain VPN or dial-up network connection configurations on hundreds or thousands of client computers.

The CMAK allows you to easily configure large numbers of clients by creating an executable file that you can distribute to your users. When your users run the file, it creates a dial-up or VPN connection with your customized security settings. If you later change authentication or encryption methods, you can re-run the CMAK and distribute a new executable file to overwrite the previous configuration. You can even automate the distribution of the CMAK executable file by distributing it with a Group Policy object.

After this lesson, you will be able to

- Manually create a dial-up or VPN connection.
- Customize the authentication and encryption protocols accepted by a client for a remote access connection.
- Use the CMAK wizard to create an executable file that a user can use to automatically create a remote access connection with customized security settings.

Estimated lesson time: 30 minutes

Configuring Client-Side Authentication Protocols

You create a remote access connection by using the New Connection Wizard, as described in Lesson 2, Exercise 2. However, the New Connection Wizard does not allow you to configure the acceptable authentication or encryption settings for the connection. To view or modify the authentication protocols enabled for a remote access connection on the client, open the properties dialog box of the dial-up or VPN connection on the client, and then click the Security tab.

Note This lesson describes the configuration of Windows XP and Windows Server 2003 clients, which use identical user interfaces. Other remote access clients might use a different user interface.

Figure 12.10 shows the default settings on the Security tab. The Typical option is selected, and a secured password and data encryption are required. Automatically Use My Windows Logon Name And Password is not selected. This default setting is the more secure choice. If you choose to automatically use the current credentials, an intruder who takes over the active desktop of the client can successfully authenticate and connect to your internal network, potentially compromising far more than a single computer. When the option is cleared, the user must provide credentials each time a connection is made.

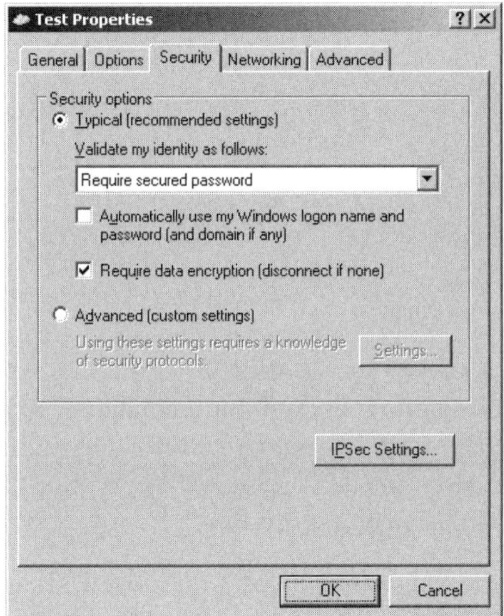

Figure 12.10 Default client authentication settings

To enable authentication with a smart card, in the Validate My Identity As Follows list, click Use Smart Card. When the user attempts to connect, the user will be prompted to insert a smart card. Once the smart card is detected, the certificate on the smart card will be used to authenticate the user to the remote access server.

The Typical setting, by default, requires a secured password and data encryption, but it does not give you any control over which specific protocols are used. To control these, click Advanced, and then click the Settings button. The Advanced Security Settings dialog box appears, as shown in Figure 12.11.

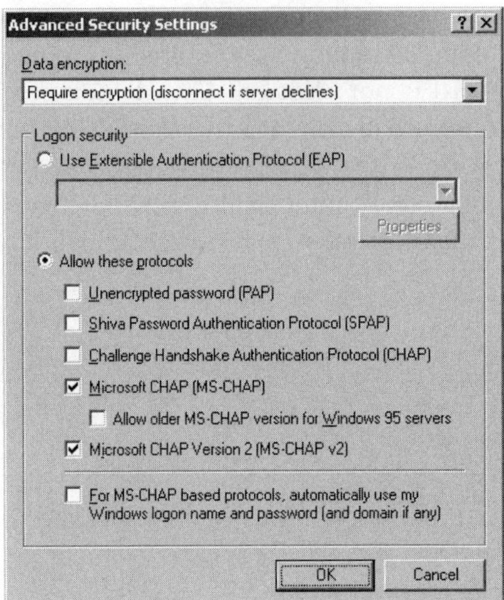

Figure 12.11 Advanced client authentication settings

This dialog box enables you to specify a minimum allowable encryption level by using the Data Encryption list. You can choose to allow encryption if available, require it, or require the highest encryption level. If the server is not capable of providing encryption, the VPN session will fail. You can also choose to disallow encryption. However, you should only use this setting for troubleshooting purposes.

The Advanced Security Settings dialog box also allows you to choose EAP authentication, which you will use when authenticating with a smart card or a public key certificate. Clicking the Properties button enables you to configure server validation and trusted root CAs. Alternatively, you can click Allow These Protocols and then select the acceptable authentication protocols.

There is one other configuration option on the network: the preshared key for L2TP/IPsec VPN connections. To specify this preshared key, click the IPSec Settings button on the Security tab of the Network Connection Properties dialog box. Then select the Use Preshared Key For Authentication check box and type the preshared key.

CMAK Wizard

Manually configuring remote access connections on clients is straightforward, but configuring hundreds or thousands of clients would be impossible. Unfortunately, you cannot use Group Policy objects to directly control a user's available network connections. However, you can use the CMAK to create an executable file that you can deploy to users. When users run this file, the CMAK adds a connection by using the settings you specified with the CMAK wizard.

Though most of the pages of the wizard do not involve security settings, there are several important pages that you can use to control the security settings on the resulting network connection. Specifically, the VPN Entries and Dial-Up Networking Entries pages allow you to restrict authentication and encryption on the client. The VPN Entries and Dial-Up Networking Entries pages are identical, except that the VPN settings allow you to choose between PPTP and L2TP.

Use the VPN Entries page, as shown in Figure 12.12, to add configuration information for your remote access servers. First, click the New button. On the General tab, in the Name box, type a name to identify the VPN server. Then click the Security tab to edit the authentication and encryption settings.

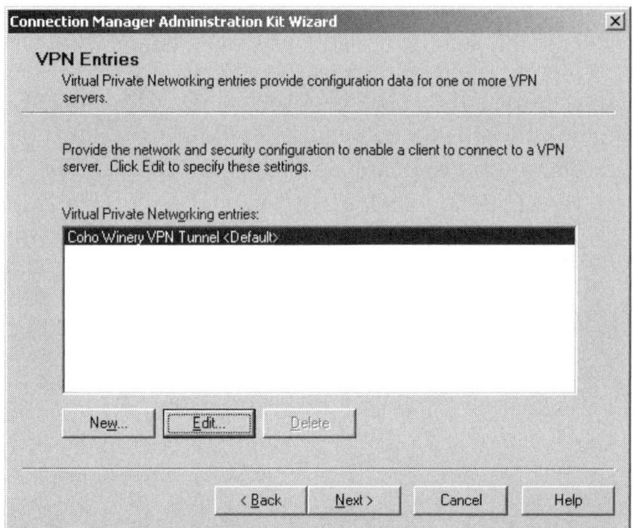

Figure 12.12 Configuring VPN servers and security settings

The Security tab allows you to configure either basic or advanced security settings. Basic settings are supported by any client, but advanced settings are supported only by Windows 2000, Windows XP, and Windows Server 2003 clients. If all remote access clients are using Windows 2000 or later, you should click the Security Settings list and then select Use Advanced Security Settings. Otherwise, leave the default setting of Use Both Basic And Advanced selected.

To configure the basic security settings for all clients, click the basic security settings Configure button. The Basic Security Settings dialog box appears, as shown in Figure 12.13. Selecting Require A Microsoft Secured Password causes the client to disconnect if the server does not support MS-CHAP v1 or MS-CHAP v2, and selecting the Require Data Encryption check box causes the client to disconnect if encryption is not available. By default, the client will always use PPTP. If you prefer L2TP/IPSec, click Use L2TP/IPSec If Available, and optionally specify that a preshared key should be used.

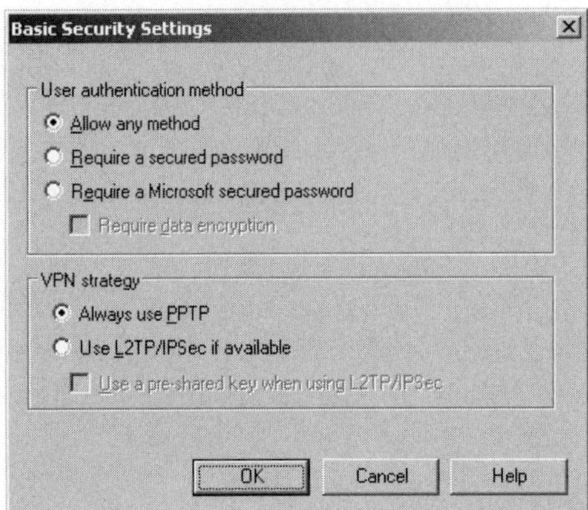

Figure 12.13 Editing basic VPN security settings by using the CMAK wizard

To configure the advanced security settings for Windows 2000, Windows XP, and Windows Server 2003 clients, click the advanced security settings Configure button. The Advanced Security Settings dialog box appears, as shown in Figure 12.14. By default, encryption is required and MS-CHAP v1 or MS-CHAP v2 authentication is used. Click the VPN Strategy list to choose whether the client prefers PPTP or L2TP connections.

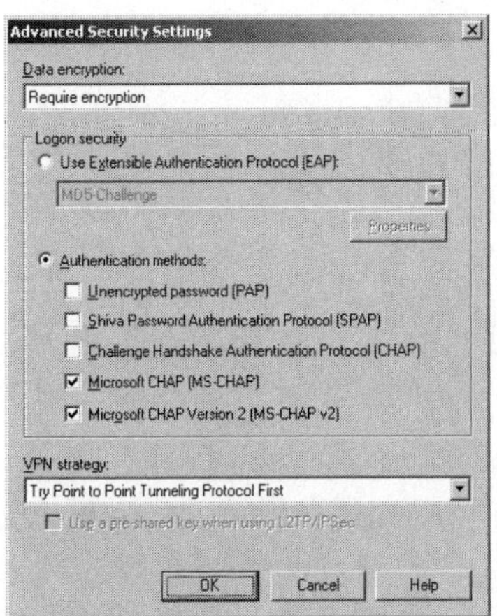

Figure 12.14 Editing advanced VPN security settings by using the CMAK wizard

If you are using public key certificates or smart cards for authentication, click Use Extensible Authentication Protocol (EAP), and then select Smart Card Or Other Certificate. You can then click the Properties button to open the Smart Card Or Other Certificate Properties dialog box, as shown in Figure 12.15. This dialog box enables you to choose between smart cards and public key certificates and to configure server verification and trusted root CAs.

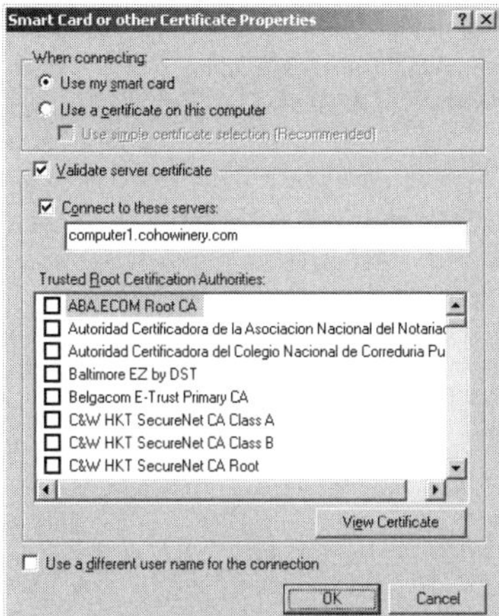

Figure 12.15 Editing EAP configuration settings

> **Exam Tip** The CMAK wizard allows you to configure a large number of settings. The exam, and this lesson, focus only on the security settings. Specifically, you should familiarize yourself with how to configure the authentication and encryption settings by using the CMAK wizard. The practice at the end of this lesson will give you the necessary hands-on experience.

Additionally, the License Agreement page enables you to prompt the user to agree to a license agreement before connecting. Work with your organization's legal team to create a license agreement that you can use to make it easier to enforce your organization's remote access usage policies. This license agreement appears when the user clicks OK to begin the initial installation of your network connection profile. If the user accepts the license agreement, installation continues. If not, installation is cancelled. Although the license agreement probably won't prevent users from misusing your network, it can be helpful when disciplining users after they are identified. Use a text-editor program such as Notepad to create your license agreement as a text (.txt) file. To avoid formatting problems, do not use hard returns (forced line breaks) at the end of lines. Line-wrapping for the license agreement is done automatically when the service profile is built.

Practice: Using the CMAK

In this practice, you will use the CMAK on Computer1 to configure a remote access network connection with minimal effort on Computer2.

Exercise 1: Creating a VPN file

In this exercise, you will create a VPN file containing the IP names and IP addresses of imaginary VPN servers on your network.

1. Log on to the cohowinery.com domain on Computer1 by using the Administrator account.
2. Click Start and then click Run. In the Open box, type **Notepad**. Click OK.
3. In the Untitled – Notepad window, type the following:

```
[Settings]
default=Coho Winery - Woburn
UpdateURL=http://computer1.cohowinery.com/VPNfile.txt
Message=Please select a server from the following list. Choose a server closest to
 your location or to your data.

[VPN Servers]
Coho Winery - Woburn=computer1.cohowinery.com
Coho Winery - Redmond=computer4.cohowinery.com
Coho Winery - Pflugerville=computer5.cohowinery.com
Coho Winery - San Francisco=computer6.cohowinery.com
```

4. On the File menu, click Save.
5. In the File Name box, type **C:\Inetpub\Wwwroot\VPNfile.txt**. Click Save.

   Notice that the `UpdateURL` line in the file is set to http://computer1.cohowinery.com/VPNfile.txt. This URL relates to C:\Inetpub\Wwwroot\VPNfile.txt. Therefore, you can later update the VPN file and clients will automatically receive the updates.
6. Close Notepad.

Exercise 2: Installing the Connection Manager Administration Kit

In this exercise, you will install the CMAK.

1. Log on to the cohowinery.com domain on Computer1 by using the Administrator account.
2. Click Start, point to Control Panel, and then click Add Or Remove Programs.
3. Click Add/Remove Windows Components.
4. Click Management And Monitoring Tools, and then click the Details button.
5. Select the Connection Manager Administration Kit and Connection Point Services check boxes. Click OK.
6. Click Next. When the Optional Network Components dialog box appears, click Yes. Click Finish.

Exercise 3: Creating a service profile

In this exercise, you will create a service profile with the CMAK.

1. Start the CMAK Wizard by clicking Start, pointing to Administrative Tools, and then clicking Connection Manager Administration Kit.

   The CMAK Wizard appears.

2. Click Next. On the Service Profile Selection page, click New Profile, and then click Next.

3. On the Service And File Names page, type **Coho Winery VPN** in the Service Name box.

   The service name will appear in several places, including in the title bar of the logon dialog box, in the Connection Manager installation dialog boxes, and as the name of the network connection.

4. Type **Coho-VPN** in the File Name box. Click Next.

5. On the Realm Name page, accept the default setting of Do Not Add A Realm Name To The User Name, and then click Next.

   You only need to specify a realm name for dial-up access. This would be useful, for example, if users were connecting through an ISP but were being authenticated by your RADIUS server.

6. On the Merging Profile Information page, click Next.

7. On the VPN Support page, select the Phone Book From This Profile check box. Click Allow The User To Choose A VPN Server Before Connecting. Click the Browse button. In the File Name box, type **C:\Inetpub\Wwwroot\VPNfile.txt**. Click Open, and then click Next.

8. On the VPN Entries page, click Coho Winery VPN Tunnel, and then click Edit. Click the TCP/IP Settings tab.

   Notice that, by default, the Make This Connection The Client's Default Gateway check box is selected. This causes clients to route all traffic through your VPN server to your private network, even if the traffic is destined for the public Internet. In other words, when this check box is selected, traffic destined for the public Internet will travel through the VPN tunnel to your VPN server and then through your private network and back onto the Internet. This causes Internet access to seem very slow for the end user but allows you to route the client's traffic through your firewall, which might reduce the likelihood of the client being infected by a worm or virus on the Internet and then spreading that worm or virus to your internal network.

9. Click the Security tab. In the Security Settings list, click Use Advanced Security Settings.

   In this exercise, there are no Windows NT 4.0, Windows 95, Windows 98, or Windows ME clients. Therefore, you can choose to use only the advanced security settings without causing problems for any previous versions of Windows.

10. Click the Advanced Security Settings Configure button. Verify that Require Encryption is selected in the Data Encryption list.

    Note that you can choose to not use encryption. This would reduce the processing time required to maintain the VPN connection, but your data could be subject to eavesdropping.

11. Verify that Authentication Methods is selected.

    If you wanted to authenticate by using a smart card or a public key certificate, you would select Use Extensible Authentication Protocol (EAP) and then select Smart Card Or Other Certificate. You could then click the Properties button to configure a user certificate, in a manner similar to the way you configure certificates for authenticating wireless connections.

    Notice that MS-CHAP and MS-CHAP v2 are enabled by default. If you know that all your clients will use a single authentication method, you should clear the other check boxes. If you have non-Microsoft clients that must use PAP, SPAP, or CHAP, you will need to enable those authentication methods in this dialog box.

See Also For information on using certificates to authenticate wireless connections, refer to Chapter 10.

12. In the VPN Strategy list, click Try Layer Two Tunneling Protocol First. Click OK twice, and then click Next.

    Notice that, by default, PPTP will be tried first. You can improve the security of your VPN servers by limiting the VPN strategy to either L2TP or PPTP. This practice reduces the potential attack surface. In other words, if a vulnerability is later discovered in either the L2TP or PPTP services, you will not be vulnerable if you do not allow incoming connections with that protocol.

13. On the Phone Book page, clear the Automatically Download Phone Book Updates check box, and then click Next.

14. On the Dial-Up Networking Entries page, click Next. On the Routing Table Update page, click Next.

    Notice that you have the option of manually configuring routing updates that will be applied when a client connects. Earlier in this exercise, you left the Make This Connection The Client's Default Gateway check box selected. If you had cleared this check box, you would need to specify a route file that contained a list of internal networks so that the client would direct traffic destined for those networks across the VPN instead of to the public Internet.

15. Click Next to accept the default settings on the Automatic Proxy Configuration, Custom Actions, Logon Bitmap, and Help File pages.
16. On the Support Information page, in the Support Information box, type **For technical support, contact IT at 555-0199**. Click Next.
17. On the Connection Manager Software page, click Next. On the License Agreement page, click Next. On the Additional Files page, click Next. On the Ready To Build The Service Profile page, click Next.

    The CMAK Wizard creates your service profile.
18. Note the location of your service profile, which should be C:\Program Files\Cmak\Profiles\Coho-VPN\Coho-VPN.exe. Click Finish.

Exercise 4: Installing the service profile

In this exercise, you will install the service profile on Computer2 and verify that Computer2 can connect to the VPN.

1. Log on to the cohowinery.com domain on Computer2 by using the Administrator account.
2. Copy the Coho-VPN.exe file from Computer1 to C:\Coho-VPN.exe on Computer2.
3. Click Start, and then click Run. In the Open box, type **C:\Coho-VPN.exe**. Click OK.
4. In the Coho Winery VPN dialog box, click Yes.

   Notice that the name of the dialog box is the name you specified in Exercise 3.
5. Click My Use Only, and then click OK.
6. The logon dialog box appears. Click the Properties button.

   Notice that the message For technical support, contact IT at 555-0199, which was specified in Exercise 3, appears on the dialog box.
7. In the Coho Winery VPN Properties dialog box, click VPN.
8. Click the VPN Destination list.

   As shown in Figure 12.16, the listing of destinations provided in the VPN file created in Exercise 1 appears. Coho Winery – Woburn appears as the default because it is specified by the default key in the [Settings] section of the VPN file.

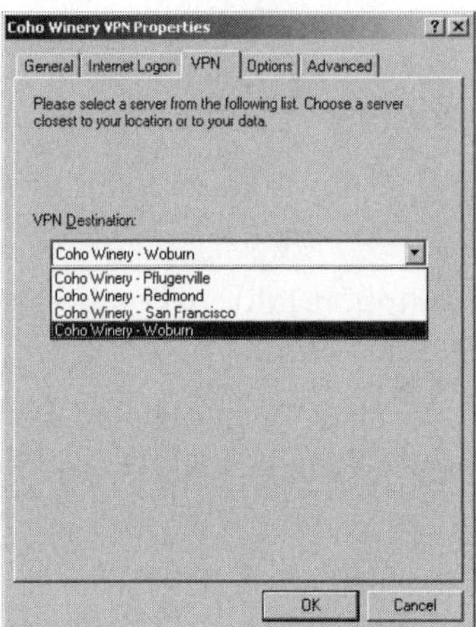

Figure 12.16 VPN destinations as specified in the VPN file

9. Click OK.

10. In the User Name box, type **User1**. In the Password box, type the complex password you created in the exercise in Lesson 2. Click Connect.

    The connection establishes successfully. Notice how simple the process of configuring the client is after you create the service profile by using the CMAK.

11. Right-click the Coho Winery VPN icon for the network connection in the notification area on the taskbar, and then click Status.

12. Click the Details tab. As shown in Figure 12.17, the connection was established by using L2TP, authenticated by using MS-CHAP v2, and encrypted by using IPSec ESP 3DES. Click Close.

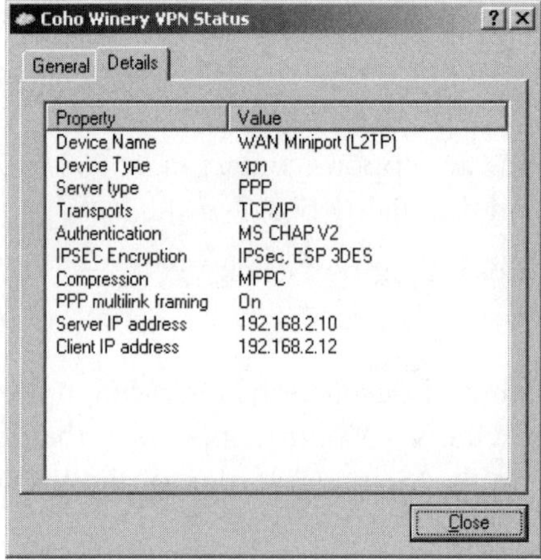

Figure 12.17 VPN connection details confirming security configuration

13. Open a command prompt, and run the command `ping 192.168.4.1`. Computer1 will respond, indicating that the VPN connection is successful.

Lesson Review

The following question is intended to reinforce key information presented in this lesson. If you are unable to answer the question, review the lesson materials and try the question again. You can find answers to the question in the "Questions and Answers" section at the end of this chapter.

1. Which tools can you use to configure authentication and encryption methods for remote access connections on clients? (Choose all that apply.)

   a. The Group Policy Object Editor snap-in

   b. The CMAK Wizard

   c. The network connections properties dialog box

   d. The remote desktops console

Lesson Summary

- You can manually configure remote access authentication and encryption settings on individual client computers by editing the properties of the network connection.
- Use the CMAK Wizard to create executable files that create preconfigured remote access connections on client computers.

Case Scenario Exercise

In this exercise, you will read a scenario about a company's remote access challenge and then answer the questions that follow. The questions are intended to reinforce key information presented in this chapter. If you are unable to answer a question, review the lessons and try the question again. You can find answers to the questions in the "Questions and Answers" section at the end of this chapter.

Scenario

You are an administrator at Fabrikam, Inc., an enterprise services company with approximately 2,000 employees. Approximately 250 of those employees are consultants who are required to travel almost constantly with mobile computers running Windows XP. They need to stay in touch with the rest of Fabrikam, Inc., while they travel, so your management decided to forward POP3 requests at the NAT server that separates the public and private networks in order to allow consultants to retrieve their e-mail from the computer that runs Microsoft Exchange Server.

There's a problem, though. The consultants have asked to access other resources on the internal network: file servers, intranet servers, and databases. You can't forward all of this traffic through your Windows Server 2003–based NAT server. Even if you could, you would not want to allow the communications to travel across the Internet unencrypted. In fact, your IT group has done everything they can to reduce unencrypted communications on the internal network, and they have deployed IPSec with a public key infrastructure (PKI) to provide authentication.

Your manager has asked you to provide a way to allow traveling consultants to access the resources on the internal network while minimizing the risks.

Questions

1. Which of the following solutions will you recommend?
   a. Deploy dial-up servers running Windows Server 2003. Configure the clients to dial directly in to the Fabrikam, Inc., headquarters and authenticate to the remote access servers by using MS-CHAP v2 authentication.
   b. Deploy dial-up servers running Windows Server 2003. Configure the clients to dial directly in to the Fabrikam, Inc., headquarters and authenticate to the remote access servers by using EAP authentication with public key certificates.
   c. Configure the Windows Server 2003–based NAT server with VPN services. Configure the clients to connect directly to the VPN server and authenticate by using MS-CHAP v2 authentication.
   d. Configure the Windows Server 2003–based NAT server with VPN services. Configure the clients to connect directly to the VPN server and authenticate by using EAP authentication with public key certificates.

   ____

2. Will you recommend using a PPTP or L2TP/IPSec VPN?

   ____

   ____

3. How will you configure the network connections on the client computers?

   ____

   ____

4. Should you recommend using a RADIUS server?

____

____

Troubleshooting Lab

In this lab, you will troubleshoot a problem related to a user who cannot connect to a newly added VPN server. Read the following scenario and then answer the questions that follow. The questions are intended to reinforce key information presented in this chapter. If you are unable to answer a question, review the lessons and try the question again. You can find answers to the questions in the "Questions and Answers" section at the end of this chapter.

Scenario

As part of an effort to reduce costs, you are migrating users from dial-up access to using a VPN to access the internal network. One user, Jo Berry, is unable to connect to the VPN server. However, she is still able to dial in to the remote access server.

You are able to duplicate the problem, so you examine the user's dial-in properties, as shown in Figure 12.18.

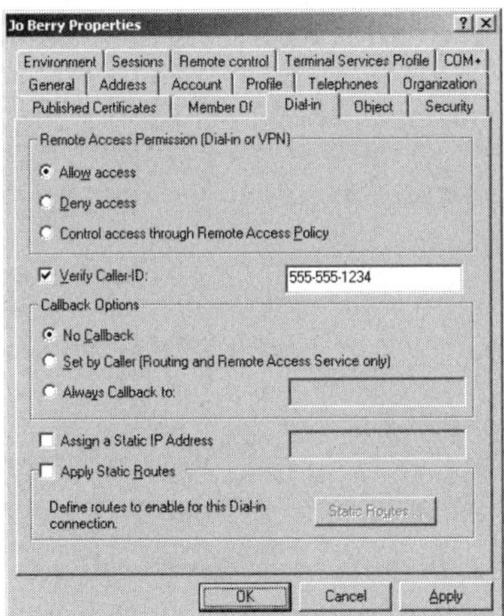

Figure 12.18 Dial-in properties of problematic user account

Questions

1. What is the source of the problem?

____

____

2. How will you resolve the problem?

____

____

Chapter Summary

- Windows Server 2003 supports two VPN protocols: PPTP and L2TP/IPSec. PPTP was developed by Microsoft, and it is the default protocol. L2TP/IPSec is an Internet standard that provides interoperability with a greater number of clients.
- Windows Server 2003 supports eight methods for authenticating users: EAP, MS-CHAP v2, MS-CHAP v1, CHAP, SPAP, PAP, preshared keys, and unauthenticated access.
- Use EAP to authenticate users with a public key certificate or smart card. Only Windows Server 2003, Windows XP, and Windows 2000 clients support EAP.
- You can configure a remote access server and clients without changing the default settings. By default, encryption is required, and MS-CHAP v2 or MS-CHAP v1 authentication will be used.
- Edit the remote access server's properties to increase or restrict the available authentication protocols. Select EAP authentication to enable authentication with public key certificates or smart cards.
- User authorization can be controlled from three places: the user's dial-up properties, a RAP configured on the remote access server, and a RAP configured on the IAS RADIUS server.
- You can manually configure remote access authentication and encryption settings on individual client computers by editing the properties of the network connection.
- Use the CMAK Wizard to create executable files that create preconfigured remote access connections on client computers.

Exam Highlights

Before taking the exam, review the key topics and terms that are presented in this chapter. You need to know this information.

Key Topics

- Understand the advantages and disadvantages of dial-up and VPN access.
- Be able to list the various authentication methods, the operating systems that support each, and their advantages and disadvantages.
- Be able to describe scenarios in which you would choose to use either PPTP or L2TP/IPSec VPN protocols.
- Know the factors that determine whether a user is authorized to establish a dial-up or VPN connection.
- Know how to configure both remote access clients and remote access servers, and know how to use the CMAK.

Key Terms

Challenge Handshake Authentication Protocol (CHAP) A challenge-response authentication protocol for PPP connections, documented in RFC 1994, that uses the industry-standard MD5 one-way encryption scheme to hash the response to a challenge issued by the remote access server.

Extensible Authentication Protocol (EAP) An authentication method primarily used to provide authentication based on smart cards or public key certificates. EAP is supported by Windows Server 2003, Windows XP, and Windows 2000.

Layer Two Tunneling Protocol (L2TP) A standardized RFC-based tunneling VPN protocol. L2TP relies on IPSec for encryption services.

Microsoft Challenge Handshake Authentication Protocol (MS-CHAP) An encrypted authentication mechanism for PPP connections. MS-CHAP is similar to CHAP. The remote access server sends to the remote access client a challenge that consists of a session ID and an arbitrary challenge string. The remote access client must return the user name and a Message Digest 4 (MD4) hash of the challenge string, the session ID, and the MD4-hashed password. MS-CHAP v2 improves on MS-CHAP v1 by offering mutual authentication for both the client and the server.

Password Authentication Protocol (PAP) A simple plaintext authentication scheme for authenticating PPP connections. The user name and password are requested by the remote access server and returned by the remote access client in plaintext.

Point-to-Point Protocol (PPP) An industry-standard suite of protocols for the use of point-to-point links to transport multiprotocol datagrams. PPP is primarily used to connect dial-up users to a remote access server. PPP is documented in RFC 1661.

Point-to-Point Tunneling Protocol (PPTP) A VPN protocol designed by Microsoft and based on PPP. PPTP relies on MPPE for encryption services.

Shiva Password Authentication Protocol (SPAP) A two-way, reversible encryption mechanism for authenticating PPP connections employed by Shiva remote access servers.

Questions and Answers

Lesson 1 Review

Page 12-15

1. Which of the following authentication protocols can be used by fully updated Windows 98 VPN clients? (Choose all that apply.)

   a. EAP

   b. MS-CHAP v2

   c. MS-CHAP v1

   d. CHAP

   e. SPAP

   f. PAP

   b, c, d, e, and f. After appropriate updates have been applied, Windows 98 supports all authentication protocols except EAP.

2. Your organization's security policy has a requirement that passwords not be stored with reversible encryption. Which of the following authentication protocols can you use? (Choose all that apply.)

   a. EAP

   b. MS-CHAP v2

   c. MS-CHAP v1

   d. CHAP

   e. SPAP

   f. PAP

   a, b, e, and f. Only MS-CHAP v1 and CHAP require passwords to be stored with reversible encryption.

3. Your organization still has clients running Windows 95. Which of the following protocols can you use to authenticate dial-up clients? (Choose all that apply.)

   a. EAP

   b. MS-CHAP v2

   c. MS-CHAP v1

  d. CHAP

  e. SPAP

  f. PAP

c, d, e, and f. Windows 95 does not support EAP. It does support MS-CHAP v2 for VPN connections but not for dial-up connections.

Lesson 2 Review

Page 12-28

1. Your organization has multiple dial-up servers configured to authenticate to an IAS RADIUS server. Which tool should you use to restrict the hours during which users can dial up?

   a. Active Directory Users And Computers

   b. Computer Management

   c. Routing And Remote Access

   d. Internet Authentication Service

   d. You should create a RAP on the IAS server by using the Internet Authentication Service console.

2. Your organization uses Windows authentication to verify the credentials of remote VPN clients. Which tool should you use to restrict the groups that can connect to the VPN server?

   a. Active Directory Users And Computers

   b. Computer Management

   c. Routing And Remote Access

   d. Internet Authentication Service

   c. You should create a RAP on the remote access server by using the Routing And Remote Access console.

3. In an Active Directory domain environment, which of the following conditions must be met in order to use RAPs to control which remote access users are allowed to connect?

   a. The domain functional level must be Windows 2000 Mixed.

   b. The domain functional level must be Windows Server 2003.

   c. You must use MS-CHAP v1 or MS-CHAP v2 authentication.

   d. You must use an IAS RADIUS server.

   b. The only requirement is that the domain functional level must be Windows Server 2003.

Lesson 3 Review

Page 12-41

1. Which tools can you use to configure authentication and encryption methods for remote access connections on clients? (Choose all that apply.)

   a. The Group Policy Object Editor snap-in

   b. The CMAK Wizard

   c. The network connections properties dialog box

   d. The remote desktops console

   b and c. Use the CMAK Wizard to create an executable file that you can distribute to clients to create the preconfigured connections, and use the network connections properties dialog box to manually configure authentication and encryption for remote access connections.

Design Activity: Case Scenario Exercise

Page 12-42

1. Which of the following solutions will you recommend?

   a. Deploy dial-up servers running Windows Server 2003. Configure the clients to dial directly in to the Fabrikam, Inc., headquarters and authenticate to the remote access servers by using MS-CHAP v2 authentication.

   b. Deploy dial-up servers running Windows Server 2003. Configure the clients to dial directly in to the Fabrikam, Inc., headquarters and authenticate to the remote access servers by using EAP authentication with public key certificates.

   c. Configure the Windows Server 2003–based NAT server with VPN services. Configure the clients to connect directly to the VPN server and authenticate by using MS-CHAP v2 authentication.

   d. Configure the Windows Server 2003–based NAT server with VPN services. Configure the clients to connect directly to the VPN server and authenticate by using EAP authentication with public key certificates.

   d. Though any of these solutions would work, using a VPN is more cost-effective than configuring dial-up servers because it does not require the purchase of additional hardware or software. You should recommend EAP authentication with public key certificates because you already have a PKI deployed and all clients are running Windows XP, Windows 2000, or Windows Server 2003. If you did not already have a PKI in place, MS-CHAP v2 authentication would be preferable.

2. Will you recommend using a PPTP or L2TP/IPSec VPN?

   Either PPTP or L2TP/IPSec will allow the consultants to access the internal network by using both authentication and encryption. However, you are already using IPSec on the internal network, so L2TP/IPSec would be the logical choice.

3. How will you configure the network connections on the client computers?

You could configure them manually or provide instructions to the consultants to configure the connections. However, the most efficient way to configure the connections is to use the CMAK Wizard to create an executable file and then distribute this executable file to the consultants.

4. Should you recommend using a RADIUS server?

There is no need for the addition of a RADIUS server because there will only be a single VPN server, and that server is already running Windows Server 2003. You can use Windows authentication and remote access policies on the remote access server itself.

Design Activity: Troubleshooting Lab

Page 12-44

1. What is the source of the problem?

The user has the Verify Caller-ID check box selected. This is an excellent way to improve security; however, the value specified is a phone number that was left over from when the user connected by using a dial-up connection.

2. How will you resolve the problem?

When a user connects to a VPN, the Verify Caller-ID value is used to validate the user's source IP address, not the user's phone number. You should either clear the Verify Caller-ID check box or change the value to the user's IP address.

Part II
Prepare for the Exam

13 Implementing, Managing, and Troubleshooting Security Policies (1.0)

The vast majority of security configuration on a Microsoft Windows Server 2003 network is carried out by applying security policies either through Active Directory directory service or by means of local Group Policy objects. Group Policy controls almost every aspect of the operation of a computer running Windows Server 2003, from the software installed to disk quotas and the appearance of the desktop. Of interest to the candidate for this exam is the Security Settings node located under Windows Settings in the Computer Configuration section of Group Policy Objects. The security settings node hosts almost all of the Windows Server 2003 security policies. Event logs, restricted groups, system services, and file system and registry permissions can be configured from this node.

How these policies are configured depends on the types of services the server to which they are applied is hosting. Although a domain controller and an Internet Information Services system will have many policy settings in common, there will be several policies, unique to the role of the server, that must be configured differently. Understanding the differences between the needs of each server is a critical part of performing well on this particular exam objective.

Security templates are text files that store configurations for all of the policies found under the security settings node. Security templates are the recommended way to make changes to Group Policy security settings. This is because templates are easily stored and provide a built-in record of the changes that have been made to Group Policy. Security templates can be created and edited in several ways. The easiest way to create and edit security templates is to use the Security Templates snap-in that can be added to any custom Microsoft Management Console (MMC). Performing this task by using the Security Templates snap-in enables you to use a simple visual interface to configure security. Creating and editing templates can also be performed by using a text editor such as Notepad.

After the security templates have been created, they need to be deployed. Deployment is generally done by putting the servers that will be the targets of the Group Policy object (GPO) into a separate organizational unit (OU), creating a new GPO, importing the template to the GPO, and then applying the GPO to the newly created OU. Security templates can also be imported and applied individually to servers at the local policy level.

Security templates are not the complete security solution for Windows Server 2003 or Microsoft Windows XP Professional. There are many Group Policy options that cannot be configured by using security templates. When a situation arises for which a policy must be set, and that cannot be done by using a template, these changes have to either be configured manually, if the system to which they are being applied does not fall under the influence of Group Policy, or have an appropriate policy applied if they do.

Testing Skills and Suggested Practices

The skills that you need to successfully master the Managing and Implementing Disaster Recovery objective domain on Exam 70-299: *Implementing and Administering Security in a Microsoft Windows Server 2003 Network* include:

- Prepare to use security templates.
  - Practice 1: Create an OU structure for the member servers in your organization. Name the parent OU Member Servers. Under Member Servers, create child OUs for File and Print, Web, and Infrastructure servers. Move each specific category of member server into its appropriate OU container. Edit the properties of the OU and add a new GPO. Edit the GPO. Select the Security Settings node under Computer Configuration\Windows Settings. Right-click and note the import command. This is used to import security templates into a Group Policy object.
  - Practice 2: Create a custom MMC for editing security templates by following these steps: on the Start menu, click Run and then type MMC. On the File menu, click Add/Remove Snap-in. Select ADD and select the Security Templates snap-in. Save this console to the desktop as SecurityConsole.msc. You will use this security console in later exercises.
- Edit and apply security templates.
  - Practice 1: Use the security console that you created in a previous exercise to create a new security template that sets the maximum application log size to 16,384 kilobytes and sets the retention method for the application log to "Do not overwrite events (clear log manually)."
  - Practice 2: Create a new universal group named test-restrict in the domain. Create four new user accounts named alpha, beta, gamma, and delta. Create a new security template. Configure the restricted groups option and restrict the membership of the test-restrict group to accounts alpha, beta, and gamma. Save the template. Create a new GPO and apply it to the domain. Import the newly created security template into the new GPO. Run GPUPDATE /FORCE from the command line. Use the NET GROUP TEST-RESTRICT command from the command line to note the membership of the group. Use Active Directory Users and Computers to add the delta user account to the

test-restrict group. From the command line, use the NET GROUP TEST-RESTRICT command again to check group membership. Note the group membership. Now force a policy update by typing GPUPDATE /FORCE from the command line. Perform a final check of the group's membership by running a NET GROUP TEST-RESTRICT.

- Analyze and roll back templates.
  - Practice 1: Use the SECEDIT command to create a rollback policy for the hisecws security template named hsrollbk.inf. Learn the syntax of this command by issuing the SECEDIT /? command from a command prompt.
  - Practice 2: Create a new MMC, and add the Security Configuration and Analysis snap-in. Open several of the built-in policies and analyze them to gain a greater understanding of the functionality of this tool.

Further Reading

This section lists supplemental readings by objective. We recommend that you study these sources thoroughly before taking this exam.

Objective 1.1 Chapter 4, "Hardening Computers for Specific Roles"

Microsoft Corporation. Windows Server 2003 Help and Support Center. Review "Predefined Security Templates."

Microsoft Corporation. Windows Server 2003 Help and Support Center. Review "Security Templates Overview."

Microsoft Corporation. Windows Server 2003 Security Guide, Chapter 4, "Hardening Domain Controllers." *http://go.microsoft.com/fwlink/?LinkId=14845*

Microsoft Corporation. Windows Server 2003 Security Guide, Chapter 5, "Hardening Infrastructure Servers." *http://go.microsoft.com/fwlink/?LinkId=14845*

Microsoft Corporation. Windows Server 2003 Security Guide, Chapter 6, "Hardening File Servers." *http://go.microsoft.com/fwlink/?LinkId=14845*

Microsoft Corporation. Windows Server 2003 Security Guide, Chapter 7, "Hardening Print Servers." *http://go.microsoft.com/fwlink/?LinkId=14845*

Microsoft Corporation. Windows Server 2003 Security Guide, Chapter 8, "Hardening IIS Servers." *http://go.microsoft.com/fwlink/?LinkId=14845*

Microsoft Corporation. Windows Server 2003 Security Guide, Chapter 9, "Hardening IAS Servers." *http://go.microsoft.com/fwlink/?LinkId=14845*

Microsoft Corporation. Exchange Server 2003 Deployment Guide. *http://www.microsoft.com/technet/treeview/default.asp?url=/technet/prodtechnol/exchange/Exchange2003/proddocs/library/DepGuide.asp*

Objective 1.2 Review Chapter 3, "Hardening Computers for Specific Roles"

Objective 1.3 Microsoft Corporation. Windows Server 2003 Help and Support Center. Review "Checklist: Securing Computers Using Security Configuration Manager: Security Templates."

Microsoft Corporation. Windows Server 2003 Help and Support Center. Review "Security Templates Overview."

Microsoft Corporation. Windows Server 2003 Security Guide. *http://go.microsoft.com/fwlink/?LinkId=14845*

Objective 1.4 Microsoft Corporation. Windows Server 2003 Help and Support Center. Review "Secedit."

Microsoft Corporation. Windows Server 2003 Help and Support Center. Review "Gpupdate."

Microsoft Corporation. Windows Server 2003 Security Guide. *http://go.microsoft.com/fwlink/?LinkId=14845*

Objective 1.5 Review Chapter 6, "Planning, Configuring, and Deploying a Secure Member Server Baseline."

Review Chapter 7, "Planning, Configuring, and Implementing Secure Baselines for Server Roles."

Review Chapter 8, "Planning, Configuring, and Implementing and Deploying a Client Computer Baseline."

Microsoft Corporation. Windows Server 2003 Security Guide. *http://go.microsoft.com/fwlink/?LinkId=14845*

Objective 1.1

Plan Security Templates Based on Computer Role

The type of security that a computer running Windows Server 2003 requires is highly dependent on the role that the server performs. Each type of server has a different set of security requirements specific to its role. The requirements for a domain controller are significantly different from those of an Internet Authentication Server. Similarly, the security requirements of a computer running Microsoft Exchange Server 2003 are very different from those of a server running Internet Information Services. Objective 1.1 in the 70-299 exam involves planning security templates based on the role a server has. The server roles that can be tested in the exam include Exchange Server 2003, domain controllers, Internet Authentication Service, and Internet Information Services servers. You may be asked in the exam to differentiate which type of template is appropriate for a particular server, so knowing the security needs of each of these systems is a vital step in your exam preparation. These security needs are highly dependent on the services provided.

Objective 1.1 Questions

1. You are in the process of planning the development of a security template that will be applied to the 35 domain controllers that are used to support your organization's nationwide domain. All domain controllers run Windows Server 2003, Standard Edition. Your company has 15 branch sites, each with two domain controllers for the purpose of redundancy. Your headquarters site hosts five domain controllers to cope with the increased load in addition to roles such as schema master and global catalog server. Out of the 15 branch sites, the largest eight also have one of their domain controllers serving the global catalog server role. Each of the domain controllers is also able to respond to host name lookup requests in addition to processing host name updates.

   Which of the following system services can be disabled in the security template to be applied to the organization's 35 domain controllers?

   A. distributed file system (DFS)

   B. Domain Name System (DNS) Server service

   C. Kerberos Key Distribution Center (KDC)

   D. Distributed Transaction Coordinator

   E. intersite messaging

2. You are planning a security template that is to be applied to an organizational unit that hosts a group of computers running Windows Server 2003 on which Exchange Server 2003 is to be installed. Your domain is running at the Windows Server 2003 functional level. You need to ensure that Exchange Server 2003 can be installed when the security template is imported to a GPO that is applied to the OU that holds the member systems running Windows Server 2003. Which of the following services do you need to enable in the security template? (Select all that apply.)

   A. World Wide Web publishing service

   B. Simple Mail Transfer Protocol (SMTP) service

   C. Terminal Services

   D. Telnet service

   E. Network News Transfer Protocol (NTTP) service

3. Rooslan is planning a security template for several domain controllers in his organization, Tailspin Toys. Rooslan has a set of goals that the security template he is planning must meet. These goals are divided into primary and secondary goals, and are as follows:

Primary Goal: Allow members of the Backup Operators group to log on by means of Terminal Services to restore files and directories on the domain controllers.

Secondary Goal 1: Allow only members of the Administrators and Server Operators groups to shut down the domain controller.

Secondary Goal 2: Ensure that the next time a user changes his or her password, the domain controller does not store the LAN Manager hash value for the new password.

Using the Security Templates add-in on a custom MMC, Rooslan configures the following policies in a new security template called RooslanDC:

Allow log on through Terminal Services: Administrators, Backup Operators

Enable computer and user accounts to be trusted for delegation: Administrators

Restore files and directories: Administrators, Server Operators

Shut down the system: Administrators, Server Operators, Backup Operators

Network security: Do not store LAN Manager hash value on next password change

When the RooslanDC template is imported into the default domain controllers GPO, which of Rooslan's primary and secondary goals will be met?

A. Rooslan's primary goal and both secondary goals will be met.

B. Rooslan's primary goal and one secondary goal will be met.

C. Rooslan's primary goal will be met, but no secondary goals will be met.

D. Rooslan's primary goal will not be met, but both secondary goals will be met.

E. Rooslan will only meet one secondary goal.

4. You are planning a security template for an Internet Authentication Service (IAS) server that is to be located on your company's perimeter network (also known as DMZ, demilitarized zone, and screened subnet) LAN. Users will authenticate against the server with their domain accounts. The internal firewall has been configured to allow necessary traffic between the IAS server and the organization's domain controllers. At present, you are considering which services the template should start automatically. The template will be configured so that all services that are not critical to the function of the IAS server will be disabled. Which of the following services is critical for the function of an IAS server? (Select all that apply.)

A. Certificate Services

B. Background Intelligent Transfer Service

C. Distributed Link Tracking Server

D. Netlogon

E. IAS service

5. You are configuring a baseline security policy for two computers running Windows Server 2003 that run Internet Information Services (IIS). The servers are used to display sensitive information to authenticated users via a secure HTTP connection. You are deciding which services should be disabled on the server in the security template that will eventually be imported into the Group Policy that is applied to the OU in which the servers reside. Which of the following services should not be disabled on these two particular servers? (Select all that apply.)

A. HTTP Secure Sockets Layer (SSL)

B. IIS Admin Service

C. IAS service

D. Certificate Services

E. World Wide Web publishing service

Objective 1.1 Answers

1. Correct Answers: D

A. Incorrect: The Active Directory System Volume (Sysvol) requires that the DFS service be running.

B. Incorrect: The question text indicates that all of the domain controllers are functioning in Active Directory integrated mode. This means that DNS duties are distributed across the domain with any domain controller server being able to respond to requests or process updates.

C. Incorrect: The KDC service is required to allow security accounts to log on to the network. A non-functional KDC service means that logon authentication cannot complete.

D. Correct: This service is not used by domain controllers. It is used on servers such as database servers for coordinating transactions that are distributed across multiple systems.

E. Incorrect: Intersite messaging is used by the Active Directory replication processes and is hence a service that must be active on a domain controller.

2. Correct Answers: A, B, and E

A. Correct: To install Exchange Server 2003, the World Wide Web publishing service, the NNTP service, and the SMTP service must be installed and enabled. If these services are not enabled, Exchange Server 2003 will not install.

B. Correct: To install Exchange Server 2003, the World Wide Web publishing service, the NNTP service, and the SMTP service must be installed and enabled. If these services are not enabled, Exchange Server 2003 will not install.

C. Incorrect: Terminal Services does not need to be installed for the Exchange Server 2003 setup program to function correctly. To install Exchange Server 2003, the World Wide Web publishing service, the NNTP service, and the SMTP service must be installed and enabled. If these services are not enabled, Exchange Server 2003 will not install.

D. Incorrect: The Telnet service does not need to be functional for the Exchange Server 2003 setup program to execute. To install Exchange Server 2003, the World Wide Web publishing service, the NNTP service, and the SMTP service must be installed and enabled. If these services are not enabled, Exchange Server 2003 will not install.

E. Correct: To install Exchange Server 2003, the World Wide Web publishing service, the NNTP service, and the SMTP service must be installed and enabled. If these services are not enabled, Exchange Server 2003 will not install.

3. **Correct Answers: E**

A. **Incorrect:** Rooslan's primary goal is not met because the Backup Operators group, while being able to log on to each domain controller via Terminal Services, does not have the right to restore files. The first secondary goal is not met because members of the Backup Operators group do have the right to shut down the server, and this right should be limited only to Administrators and Server Operators. The second secondary goal is met because the next time a user changes his or her password, the LAN Manager hash value will not be stored.

B. **Incorrect:** Rooslan's primary goal is not met because the Backup Operators group, while being able to log on to each domain controller via Terminal Services, does not have the right to restore files. The first secondary goal is not met because members of the Backup Operators group do have the right to shut down the server, and this right should be limited only to Administrators and Server Operators. The second secondary goal is met because the next time a user changes his or her password, the LAN Manager hash value will not be stored.

C. **Incorrect:** Rooslan's primary goal is not met because the Backup Operators group, while being able to log on to each domain controller via Terminal Services, does not have the right to restore files. The first secondary goal is not met because members of the Backup Operators group do have the right to shut down the server, and this right should be limited only to Administrators and Server Operators. The second secondary goal is met because the next time a user changes his or her password, the LAN Manager hash value will not be stored.

D. **Incorrect:** Rooslan's primary goal is not met because the Backup Operators group, while being able to log on to each domain controller via Terminal Services, does not have the right to restore files. The first secondary goal is not met because members of the Backup Operators group do have the right to shut down the server, and this right should be limited only to Administrators and Server Operators. The second secondary goal is met because the next time a user changes his or her password, the LAN Manager hash value will not be stored.

E. **Correct:** Rooslan's primary goal is not met because the Backup Operators group, while being able to log on to each domain controller via Terminal Services, does not have the right to restore files. The first secondary goal is not met because members of the Backup Operators group do have the right to shut down the server, and this right should be limited only to Administrators and Server Operators. The second secondary goal is met because the next time a user changes his or her password, the LAN Manager hash value will not be stored.

4. **Correct Answers: D and E**

   A. **Incorrect:** Certificate Services is critical for the function of a Certificate Server, but not for an IAS server.

   B. **Incorrect:** The Background Intelligent Transfer Service is not used by an IAS server.

   C. **Incorrect:** Distributed Link Tracking Server is used for tracking linked files across NTFS drives and has nothing to do with running an IAS server.

   D. **Correct:** Netlogon maintains a secure channel between the IAS server and a domain controller so that authentication can occur against domain accounts.

   E. **Correct:** The IAS Service forms the core of an IAS server's functions, and hence is mandatory in any security template supporting the IAS server role.

5. **Correct Answers: A, B, and E**

   A. **Correct:** HTTP SSL allows Windows Server 2003 systems running IIS to respond to SSL traffic. Given that the servers are used to display sensitive information to authenticated users via secure HTTP, this service must not be disabled.

   B. **Correct:** The IIS Admin Service allows the administration of all areas of IIS. If this service is disabled, Web requests will fail.

   C. **Incorrect:** The IAS service is used for Remote Authentication Dial-in User Service (RADIUS) servers, not for IIS servers authenticating clients.

   D. **Incorrect:** This service is used by Windows when it is installed as a certification authority (CA). Although authentication can be carried out with a certificate, this service is not necessary on a system running Windows Server 2003 that is working as described in the scenario.

   E. **Correct:** This service must be running for Web pages to be served up by the systems running Windows Server 2003.

Objective 1.2

Configure Security Templates

Security templates are text files that store policy settings from the Security node in an Active Directory Group Policy. These text files can be imported and applied to GPOs, altering the settings in the GPO to conform to a particular security standard. Because they are text files, security templates are often far easier to manipulate than GPOs.

Security templates can be edited in two ways. The first is by using the Security Template snap-in of the Microsoft Management Console. This method is the simplest way to edit the templates because it displays them in a form that is similar to that of the Group Policy Editor. Because security templates are stored in text file format, you can also edit security templates by using a text editor such as Notepad. This method is far more complicated and requires detailed knowledge of the security template syntax. Unless there is a compelling reason to do so, use the Security Template snap-in, because editing by using Notepad might lead to inadvertent errors in a template which, when applied, could make a system insecure.

Objective 1.2 Questions

1. You are configuring a new security template for a computer running Windows Server 2003. The computer will be running IIS. The server will be accessed only by users who have specific log on names and passwords. The new security template is called IIS-SERVERS. You have configured the Audit Policy section so that the "Audit account logon events" and "Audit logon events" sections will audit success and failure.

   You are currently editing the Event Log settings of the template. The editing window is displayed in the figure below. You want to ensure that the log that records the user's name and the location that they are coming from remains recorded until the relevant log is manually cleared. You also want to set the maximum log size of the relevant log to 16,385 KB. Which policies from this figure should you configure by using the security template? (Select two.)

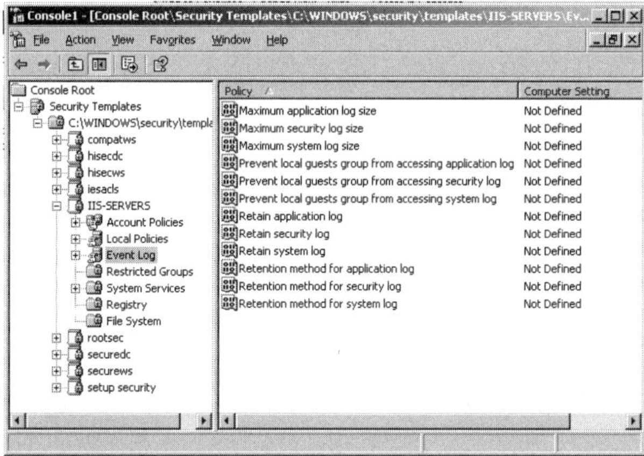

   A. maximum application log size

   B. maximum security log size

   C. maximum system log size

   D. retention method for application log

   E. retention method for security log

   F. retention method for system log

2. You have created a domain local security group named IISADMINS in the single domain that is used at your organization. This group will be assigned special permissions and rights on your organization's Web servers. You want to limit the membership of that group to four users: Orin, Oksana, Kasia, and Shan. The computers running Windows Server 2003 that host the organization's Web Servers have all been placed in

an organizational unit named IISSERV. IISSERV is a child OU of the MEMBERSERV OU. There are three sites at your company: HQ, Branch One, and Branch Two. Two IIS servers are located at Branch One, three are located at HQ, and one is located at Branch Two. You have configured the restricted groups node of a security template as shown in the figure below. The IISADMINS group has been assigned permissions only on the servers that are located within the IISSERV OU. Which of the following methods represents the best way of using this security template to meet your goal of limiting the membership of the IISADMINS group to the specified users?

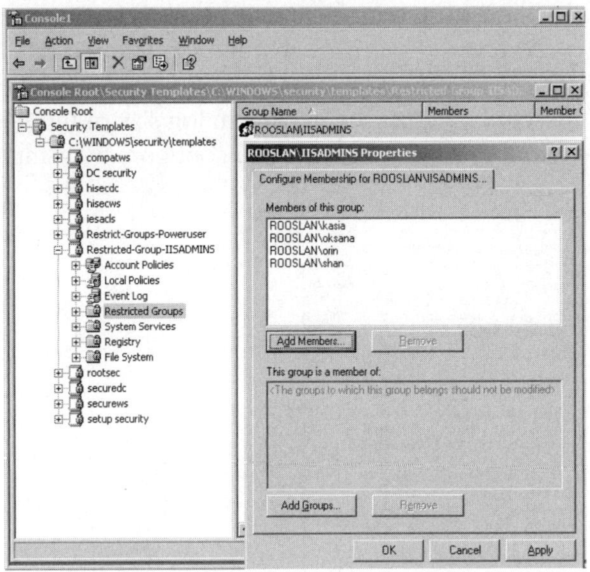

A. Import the Restricted-Group-IISADMINS security template into the Default Domain GPO.

B. Import the Restricted-Group-IISADMINS security template into a GPO which you then apply to the IISSERV OU.

C. Create a GPO, import the Restricted-Group-IISADMINS security template, and apply the GPO to the IISADMINS group.

D. Log on to each IIS server locally and import the Restricted-Group-IISADMINS security template into the local Group Policy object.

3. Rooslan is the senior systems administrator at Tailspin Toys. There is a group of developers at the company who need to be given access to modify the HKEY_LOCAL_MACHINE hive on member systems running Microsoft Windows XP

Professional and Windows Server 2003. These member systems are located within the EASTDEV organizational unit. All of the developers' user accounts are also located in the EASTDEV organizational unit. Which of the following courses of action should Rooslan take to ensure that only the developers get the required access to the HKEY_LOCAL_MACHINE hive, and that they get access only to the specified computers?

A. Rooslan should create a security template and add the registry key MACHINE. In the Database Security dialog box, he should change the security setting of the USERS group to Full Control: Allow. He should then select the permissions to Propagate Inheritable Permissions To All Subkeys. He should save the security template as TST-DEV. He should create a GPO and import the security template. He should then apply the GPO to the EASTDEV OU.

B. Rooslan should create a security template and add the registry key MACHINE. In the Database Security dialog box, he should change the security setting of the USERS group to Full Control: Allow. He should then select the permissions to Propagate Inheritable Permissions To All Subkeys. He should save the security template as TST-DEV. He should create a GPO and import the security template. He should then apply the GPO to the Domain that hosts the EASTDEV OU.

C. Rooslan should create a security template and add the registry key MACHINE. He should add the user accounts of all of the developers that require this access to a universal security group named DEVREG. In the Database Security dialog box, he should add the DEVREG group and set its security setting to Full Control: Allow. He should then select the permissions to Propagate Inheritable Permissions To All Subkeys. He should save the security template as TST-DEV. He should create a GPO and import the security template. He should then apply the GPO to the EASTDEV OU.

D. Rooslan should create a security template and add the registry key MACHINE. He should add the user accounts of all of the developers that require this access to a universal security group named DEVREG. In the Database Security dialog box, he should add the DEVREG group and set its security setting to Full Control: Allow. He should then select the permissions to Propagate Inheritable Permissions to All Subkeys. He should save the security template as TST-DEV. He should create a GPO and import the security template. He should then apply the GPO to the domain that hosts the EASTDEV OU.

E. Rooslan should create a security template and add the registry key CLASSES_ROOT. He should add the user accounts of all of the developers that require this access to a universal security group named DEVREG. In the Database Security dialog box, he should add the DEVREG group and set its security setting to Full Control: Allow. He should then select the permissions to Propagate Inheritable Permissions To All Subkeys. He should save the security template as TST-DEV. He should create a GPO and import the security template. He should then apply the GPO to the EASTDEV OU.

4. Rooslan works for a medium-sized enterprise that has a single Windows Server 2003 functional level domain. Rooslan has the following goals for the security configuration of a group of workstations running Windows XP Professional that belong to members of the DEVELOPERS security group.

Primary Goal: That the IPSEC Services, the Error Reporting Service, the Indexing Service, and the Smart Card service can all be started, stopped, and paused by members of the DEVELOPERS security group.

First Secondary Goal: That members of the DEVELOPERS group be given full control over the HKEY_LOCAL_MACHINE\HARDWARE, HKEY_LOCAL_MACHINE\SOFTWARE, and HKEY_LOCAL_MACHINE\SYSTEM hives of the registry on their workstations running Windows XP Professional.

Second Secondary Goal: That the right to debug programs, adjust memory quotas for a process, and increase scheduling priority be assigned to members of the DEVELOPERS group.

Which of these goals can Rooslan achieve by configuring a security template and importing it into a GPO that is applied to an organizational unit in which the workstations running Windows XP Professional belonging to members of the DEVELOPERS security group reside? (Select one.)

A. The primary and both secondary goals can be accomplished by configuring a security template and importing it into the GPO applied to the OU housing the workstations running Windows XP Professional.

B. The primary and one secondary goal can be accomplished by configuring a security template and importing it into the GPO applied to the OU housing the workstations running Windows XP Professional.

C. The primary goal, but no secondary goals, can be accomplished by configuring a security template and importing it into the GPO applied to the OU housing the workstations running Windows XP Professional.

D. Both secondary goals can be accomplished by configuring a security template and importing it into the GPO applied to the OU housing the workstations running Windows XP Professional. The primary goal cannot be accomplished by this method.

E. One secondary goal can be accomplished by configuring a security template and importing it into the GPO applied to the OU housing the workstations running Windows XP Professional. The primary goal cannot be accomplished by this method.

5. Part of understanding the benefits of security templates is understanding what the limitations of those templates are. Which of the following policies can be configured by importing a security template? (Select all that apply.)

   A. registry permissions

   B. wireless network (IEEE 802.11) policies

   C. disk quotas

   D. folder redirection

   E. event log policies

6. Which tool would you use to configure policy files for clients running Windows NT Workstation 4.0 that are located in a Windows Server 2003 mixed mode domain?

   A. POLEDIT.EXE

   B. REGEDIT.EXE

   C. REGEDT32.EXE

   D. Security Templates snap-in for the MMC

Objective 1.2 Answers

1. **Correct Answers: B and E**

   A. **Incorrect:** The application log does not store this information. The security log stores the information that you are interested in.

   B. **Correct:** The security log stores the relevant information. By setting the maximum log size of the security log to 16,385 KB and ensuring that the log must be cleared manually, you will meet the goal of this scenario.

   C. **Incorrect:** The system log does not store this information. The security log stores the information that you are interested in.

   D. **Incorrect:** The security log, rather than the application log, is the log of interest in this scenario.

   E. **Correct:** This policy will need to be set to "Do not overwrite events (clear log manually)" to meet the conditions of the scenario.

   F. **Incorrect:** The security log, rather than the system log, is the log of interest in this scenario.

2. **Correct Answers: B**

   A. **Incorrect:** Unless there is good reason to do otherwise, try to be as specific as possible when importing security templates. Because this template influences only servers in the IISSERV OU, this OU is the best place to apply a GPO that has had this template imported.

   B. **Correct:** This answer follows the principle of applying Group Policy objects as specifically as possible. Rather than all computers in the domain having to process this policy when it isn't relevant, only member systems in the IISSERV OU will have to process it.

   C. **Incorrect:** Group Policy objects cannot be applied to groups. They can be applied only to organizational units, sites, and domains.

   D. **Incorrect:** The Restricted Groups node is not available in local Group Policy objects. This security template can only be used on policies applied at the site, domain, or organizational unit level.

3. **Correct Answers: C**

   A. **Incorrect:** Performing these steps will give all users, not just the developers, full control permission to the HKEY_LOCAL_MACHINE hive of computer objects within the EASTDEV OU.

B. Incorrect: Performing these steps will give all users in the domain full control permission to the HKEY_LOCAL_MACHINE hive of the registry on every computer object within the domain.

C. Correct: Performing this set of steps will provide Rooslan with the desired outcome. He has limited the permissions to only those developers that require them. He has applied the GPO with the requisite security settings to the correct OU, meaning that only computer objects within that OU will fall under its influence.

D. Incorrect: This particular sequence gives the developers access to the HKEY_LOCAL_MACHINE hive of the registry to all computer objects in the domain.

E. Incorrect: Performing these steps will give the required permissions to the wrong hive of the registry. This sequence will grant allow full control to HKEY_CLASSES_ROOT rather than HKEY_LOCAL_MACHINE.

4. **Correct Answers: A**

A. Correct: All of Rooslan's goals with respect to security policy can be configured by importing a properly configured security template.

B. Incorrect: All of Rooslan's goals with respect to security policy can be configured by importing a properly configured security template.

C. Incorrect: All of Rooslan's goals with respect to security policy can be configured by importing a properly configured security template.

D. Incorrect: All of Rooslan's goals with respect to security policy can be configured by importing a properly configured security template.

E. Incorrect: All of Rooslan's goals with respect to security policy can be configured by importing a properly configured security template.

5. **Correct Answers: A and E**

A. Correct: Registry permissions are located under the Windows Components | Security Settings node of the Computer Configuration section of Group Policy. Registry permissions can be configured by importing a security template.

B. Incorrect: Although wireless network policies are located under the Windows Components | Security Settings node of the Computer Configuration section of Group Policy, wireless network policies cannot be configured by importing a security template.

C. Incorrect: Disk quota policies are not located within the Security Settings node and hence cannot be configured by importing a security template.

D. **Incorrect:** Folder redirection policies are not located within the Security Settings node and hence cannot be configured by importing a security template.

E. **Correct:** Event log policies are located under the Windows Components | Security Settings node of the Computer Configuration section of Group Policy. Event log policies can be configured by importing a security template.

6. **Correct Answers: A**

A. **Correct:** POLEDIT.EXE is used to configure policies for computers running Windows NT Workstation 4.0 and Windows NT Server 4.0. Policies are used to secure computers running Windows NT Workstation 4.0 and Windows NT Server 4.0 because they are not able to be fully configured using Active Directory technology, which made its debut with Windows 2000.

B. **Incorrect:** REGEDIT.EXE is used to edit the registry of computers running Windows. Although many settings can be configured in the registry, it is not used to configure policy files for clients running Windows NT Workstation 4.0.

C. **Incorrect:** REGEDT32.EXE is used to edit the registry of computers running Windows. Although many settings can be configured in the registry, it is not used to configure policy files for clients running Windows NT Workstation 4.0.

D. **Incorrect:** The Security Templates snap-in interfaces with Group Policy objects. It cannot be used to configure policy files for clients running Windows NT Workstation 4.0 in a Windows Server 2003 mixed mode domain.

Objective 1.3

Deploy Security Templates

After a security template is created, it must be deployed before it can have any influence on the security configuration of a system. Security templates are generally deployed by importing them into a Group Policy object. Once they have been imported into a Group Policy object, that Group Policy object can then be applied to sites, domains, and organizational units. Security templates can also be deployed by importing them into local Group Policy objects on standalone systems that are not a part of the domain. This can be done by editing the local Group Policy object (gpedit.msc) or by importing the template using the secedit command.

The principles involved in deploying a security template across a domain are similar to the principles involved in deploying Group Policy objects. In general, deployment should be as specific as possible. Grouping target systems into organizational units or sites is far preferable to deploying GPOs with security templates applied at the domain level. This way only the systems that are the targets of these policies will have to process them, and systems for which the policies are not relevant will not be delayed. The more Group Policy settings that are applied within a domain to all machines, the longer those machines take during startup and logon to process all of the policies to reach a final configuration.

Objective 1.3 Questions

1. You have received a security template from your organization's security administrator. It defines a password policy and an account lockout policy for all users in the domain. The password policy enforces a maximum password age of 21 days and a minimum password age of 7 days, and the password complexity requirements are enforced. The account lockout duration is set to 60 minutes, and the account lockout threshold is set to 5 invalid logon attempts. Which of the following methods describes the best way to deploy this security template?

   A. Edit the Default Domain Controller Policy and import the new security template.

   B. Create a new GPO. Import the new security template. Apply the GPO to the Users container in Active Directory Users and Computers.

   C. Create a new GPO. Import the new security template. Apply the GPO to the EVERYONE group in Active Directory Users and Computers.

   D. Create a new GPO. Import the new security template. Apply the GPO to the Computers container in Active Directory Users and Computers.

2. Tailspin Toys has a forest made up of the following six domains:

   tailspintoys.com

   tonga.tailspintoys.com

   djibouti.tailspintoys.com

   suriname.tailspintoys.com

   botswana.tailspintoys.com

   bhutan.tailspintoys.com

   Tailspintoys.com is the root domain. Each of the other five domains is a child domain of the root domain. The administrative team that oversees security for Tailspin Toys has created a security template for the organization's 30 computers that run Exchange Server 2003. There are five computers that run Exchange Server 2003 in each domain. Which of the following represents a method of deploying these security templates to each computer running Exchange Server 2003 in the forest while not assigning the security template to computers that do not run Exchange?

   A. Import the security template into the default domain GPO in the forest root domain.

B. Create a universal group named EXCH2K3 and add the computer accounts of all 30 computers running Exchange Server 2003 to this group. Import the security template into the default domain GPO in the forest root domain, and edit the security options of the GPO so that only the EXCH2K3 group is within the GPO's scope.

C. In the forest root domain, create an organizational unit called EXSRV2003. Create a copy of each of the computer accounts for the 30 computers running Exchange Server 2003, and place them in this OU. Create a GPO and link it to the EXSRV2003 OU. Import the security template for the computers running Exchange Server 2003 into this GPO.

D. In each domain, create an organizational unit called EXSRV2003. Place the computer accounts of each domain's computers that run Exchange Server 2003 in the EXCHSRV2003 OU for that domain. Create a GPO in the forest root domain and import the settings from the security template. Apply the GPO in the forest root domain to the EXSRV2003 organizational units in each of the domains.

3. Site A has a GPO applied that has had a security template with the following settings imported:

Maximum system log size: 16,384 kilobytes

Retain system log: 7 days

Retention method for system log: Overwrite events as needed

Site B has a GPO applied that has had a security template with the following settings imported:

Maximum system log size: 32,768 kilobytes

Retain system log: 14 days

Retention method for system log: Overwrite events by days

Site A includes computers on the following subnet: 10.10.10.64 /26

Site B includes computers on the following subnet: 10.10.10.0 /26

Which of the following statements are true, assuming that no other Group Policy objects have been applied throughout the organization? (Select all that apply.)

A. A computer that has the IP address 10.10.10.31 will retain its system log for 7 days.

B. A computer that has the IP address 10.10.10.70 will retain its system log for 7 days.

C. A computer that has the IP address 10.10.10.24 will have a maximum system log size of 16,384 kilobytes.

D. A computer that has the IP address 10.10.10.93 will have a maximum system log size of 32,768 kilobytes.

E. A computer that has the IP address 10.10.10.11 will have the retention method for system log set as "Overwrite events by days."

4. You are the systems administrator for Tailspin Toys. Your company has five branch locations and a main office location. You have three separate security templates that need to be applied. The first template needs to be applied to half of the computers at the main office and all of the computers at the first branch office. The second template needs to be applied to the second, third, and fourth branch offices. The third template needs to be applied to computers at the fifth branch office and to the other half of the computers at the main office (the ones that do not have the first template applied). Tailspin Toys has a single domain running at the Windows Server 2003 functional level. At present, there are no Group Policy objects applied in the domain other than the Default Domain Group Policy, which has default settings. Which of the following methods will allow you to deploy these security templates throughout the Tailspin Toys organization? (Select two answers. Each forms a part of the solution.)

A. Create two organizational units, and put the computers that require the first template to be applied into the first main office OU and the computers that require the third template to be applied into the second main office OU. Edit the properties of each OU and create a new GPO. Edit each of these GPOs, import the first security template into the GPO applied to the first main office OU, and import the third security template into the GPO applied to the second main office OU.

B. Create two organizational units, and put the computers that require the first template to be applied into the first main office OU and the computers that require the third template to be applied into the second main office OU. Edit the properties of each OU and create a new GPO. Edit each of these GPOs, import the first security template into the GPO applied to the first main office OU, and import the second security template into the GPO applied to the second main office OU.

C. Create a GPO, import the third security template, and apply it to the site that represents the first branch office. Create a second GPO, import the second security template, and apply it to the sites that represent the second, third, and fourth branch offices. Create a third GPO, import the first security template, and apply it to the site that represents the fifth branch office.

D. Create a GPO, import the second security template, and apply it to the site that represents the first branch office. Create a second GPO, import the first security template, and apply it to the sites that represent the second, third, and fourth branch offices. Create a third GPO, import the third security template, and apply it to the site that represents the fifth branch office.

E. Create a GPO, import the first security template, and apply it to the site that represents the first branch office. Create a second GPO, import the second security template, and apply it to the sites that represent the second, third, and fourth branch offices. Create a third GPO, import the third security template, and apply it to the site that represents the fifth branch office.

5. You have three security templates with the following settings:

Template One:

Audit process tracking: Success

Audit system events: Success

Audit policy change: Success

Template Two:

Audit account logon events: Success

Audit account management: Success

Audit directory service access: Success

Template Three:

Audit privilege use: Success

Audit logon events: Success

Audit object access: Success

In your Windows Server 2003 domain, you have an organizational unit named DEVELOPERS. There are also three sites: Headquarters, Waverley, and Volgograd. You have the following goals:

Primary Goal: Audit account logon events for all computers in the domain.

First Secondary Goal: Audit object access and account management at the Waverley site.

Second Secondary Goal: Audit privilege use and directory service access at the Volgograd site.

You perform the following actions:

Create a GPO, import the Template Two security template, and apply this GPO to the domain. Create a second GPO, import the Template One security template, and apply this GPO to the Waverley site. Finally, create a third GPO, import the Template Three security template, and apply this GPO to the Volgograd site. No other GPOs influence the computers on the network. Which of your goals have you achieved?

A. The primary and both secondary goals have been achieved.

B. The primary goal and one secondary goal have been achieved.

C. The primary goal has been achieved. No secondary goals have been achieved.

D. The primary goal has not been achieved. Both secondary goals have been achieved.

E. None of the goals have been achieved.

Objective 1.3 Answers

1. **Correct Answers: A**

   A. **Correct:** Account lockout and password policies must be applied at the domain level. This is best done by importing the security template into the Default Domain GPO. Importing this template into the Default Domain Controller policy will have no influence on the password and account lockout policies for users in the domain.

   B. **Incorrect:** Group Policy objects cannot be applied to the Users container in Active Directory Users and Computers. Account lockout and password policies must be applied at the domain level. This is best done by importing the security template into the Default Domain GPO.

   C. **Incorrect:** Group Policy objects cannot be applied to security groups.

   D. **Incorrect:** Group Policy objects cannot be applied to the Computers container in Active Directory Users and Computers. Account lockout and password policies must be applied at the domain level. This is best done by importing the security template into the Default Domain GPO.

2. **Correct Answers: D**

   A. **Incorrect:** This will apply the security template settings to all computers in the forest root domain. It will not discriminate between computers running Exchange Server 2003 and other computers. The Exchange Servers in the child domains will not receive the security settings.

   B. **Incorrect:** This will apply the security settings only to the computers running Exchange Server 2003 that are located in the forest root domain.

   C. **Incorrect:** This will not achieve the goal of ensuring that all computers running Exchange Server 2003 in the domain have the requisite security settings.

   D. **Correct:** Although it might be simpler to create a GPO in each domain, import the settings from the security template, and then apply that GPO to an OU containing the computers in that domain that run Exchange Server 2003, GPOs that are located in one domain in a Windows Server 2003 functional level forest can be applied to organizational units in another domain.

3. **Correct Answers: B and E**

   A. **Incorrect:** Computers at site B will retain their system logs for 14 days.

   B. **Correct:** Computers at site A will retain their system logs for 7 days.

C. **Incorrect:** Computers at site B will have a maximum system log size of 32,768 kilobytes.

D. **Incorrect:** Computers at site A will have a maximum system log size of 16,384 kilobytes.

E. **Correct:** Computers at site B will have the retention method for system log set to "Overwrite events by days."

4. **Correct Answers: A and E**

A. **Correct:** This forms the first part of the solution. If you perform these steps, all of the computers located at the main office will have the correct security settings applied.

B. **Incorrect:** This answer is incorrect because the second main office OU has the security settings from the second security template rather those of than the third security template, as specified in the question statement.

C. **Incorrect:** This answer applies the wrong security template to the first and fifth branch offices.

D. **Incorrect:** This answer applies the wrong security templates to the wrong site. The second, third, and fourth branch offices need the second security template and the first branch office needs the first security template.

E. **Correct:** This forms the second part of the answer and takes care of all of the branch office sites. It would also be possible to apply the GPO already applied to the first main office OU to computers in the first branch site rather than creating a new GPO. The same applies for the GPO already applied to the second main office OU and the fifth branch office.

5. **Correct Answers: B**

A. **Incorrect:** The first secondary goal has not been achieved.

B. **Correct:** The primary goal is achieved by importing the Template Two security template and applying this template to the domain. Part of the second secondary goal is achieved by importing the Template Three security template and applying this GPO to the Volgograd site. Because directory service access is already being audited across the domain (because of Template Two) the second part of the second secondary goal is also achieved. The first secondary goal has not been achieved.

C. **Incorrect:** The primary goal is achieved by importing the Template Two security template and applying this template to the domain. Part of the second secondary goal is achieved by importing the Template Three security template and applying this GPO to the Volgograd site. Because directory service access is already being audited across the domain (because of Template Two) the second part of the second secondary goal is also achieved. The first secondary goal has not been achieved.

D. **Incorrect:** The primary goal is achieved by importing the Template Two security template and applying this template to the domain. Part of the second secondary goal is achieved by importing the Template Three security template and applying this GPO to the Volgograd site. Because directory service access is already being audited across the domain (because of Template Two) the second part of the second secondary goal is also achieved. The first secondary goal has not been achieved.

E. **Incorrect:** The primary goal is achieved by importing the Template Two security template and applying this template to the domain. Part of the second secondary goal is achieved by importing the Template Three security template and applying this GPO to the Volgograd site. Because directory service access is being audited already across the domain (because of Template Two) the second part of the second secondary goal is also achieved. The first secondary goal has not been achieved.

Objective 1.4

Troubleshoot Security Template Problems

One of the advantages to using security templates to configure the security settings in Group Policy objects is that they provide a documented point of reference for determining what went wrong when unexpected results appear. The security configuration and analysis tool can be used to look into the expected results. An administrator can also diagnose where what was planned diverged from what actually happened. One of the most common problems that occurs when security settings are applied is that the rules of Group Policy inheritance are forgotten. Policies applied at the organizational unit level override those applied at the domain level, which in turn override those applied at the site level, which finally override those that are applied locally. This gets even more complicated when policies are applied with the "no override" and "block inheritance" settings. Understanding how these options work is the key to diagnosing problems that occur in the application of security templates.

Objective 1.4 Questions

1. In your Windows Server 2003 functional level domain CONTOSO.COM, you have a domain global group named SUPERUSERS. A security template has been configured that specifies the membership of the SUPERUSERS group as Rooslan, Oksana, Kasia, Shan, and Mick. This security template also assigns the SUPERUSERS group a large number of administrative rights. This security template has been imported into a GPO that is applied at the domain level and has been running perfectly for the past week. Today you get a call from your junior administrator who believes that he might have accidentally added the user accounts of Orin and Laherty to the SUPERUSERS group through the Active Directory Users and Computers console on the domain controller. You log on to the domain controller to check, and indeed these accounts have been added to the SUPERUSERS group. Which of the following steps should you take to most easily return the membership of the SUPERUSERS group to the original five users listed in the restricted groups policy as quickly as possible?

- **A.** From the command prompt on the domain controller, issue the GPUPDATE /FORCE command.
- **B.** Delete Orin, Laherty, and Mick's user accounts from the membership of the SUPERUSERS group.
- **C.** Remove the GPO that is applied to the domain. Import the new security template into the Default Domain Policy GPO.
- **D.** Import the new security template back into the GPO that is applied to the domain.
- **E.** From the command prompt on the domain controller, issue the SECEDIT /REFRESHPOLICY command.

2. Which of the following could be used to generate a rollback security template named ROLLBKIIS.INF to undo the effects of the application of a security configuration template named IISLOCK.INF?

- **A.** Create a new GPO in the Group Policy Object Editor. Right-click the security node and select Export. In the dialog box, type ROLLBKIIS.INF as the name of the exported security template.
- **B.** Create a new GPO in the Group Policy Object Editor. Right-click the security node, select Import, and then select the IISLOCK.INF security template. Right-click the security node again and select Export. Save the security template file with the name ROLLBKIIS.INF.

C. Create a new GPO in the Group Policy Object Editor. Right-click the security node, select Import, and then select the IISLOCK.INF security template. Right-click the security node again and select Rollback. Save the security template file with the name ROLLBKIIS.INF.

D. SECEDIT /GENERATEROLLBACK /CFG IISLOCK.INF /RBK ROLLBKIIS.INF

3. You configure a security template with the following settings:

Network Security: Do not store LAN Manager hash value on next password change (enabled).

Network Security: LAN Manager authentication level: Send NTLMv2 response only\refuse LM & NTLM.

Your network environment includes clients running Windows 98. You import the security template into a new GPO and apply the new GPO to the domain controllers container in Active Directory Users and Computers. Soon after you apply this policy, you receive reports that your Windows 98 users are having problems accessing resources on the network. Which of the following should you do to enable Windows 98 users to log on to the domain? (Select two answers.)

A. Install and configure the DSClient software on the Windows 98 clients.

B. Edit the security template so that the "Do not store LAN Manager hash value on next password change" policy is set to disabled.

C. Install the IPSec client on the clients running Windows 98.

D. Edit the security template so that the "LAN Manager authentication level" is set to "Send NTLMv2 responses only."

4. You are the network administrator at Contoso, Ltd. There is a single domain named CONTOSO.COM. There is an OU named DEVELOPERS that hosts the developer's computers and user accounts. This OU is a child OU of the ITSTAFF OU. There are two sites: Headquarters and Melbourne.

Security template Alpha has the following settings:

Shut down the system: CONTOSO\Administrators; CONTOSO\IISADMINS

Security template Beta has the following settings:

Shut down the system: CONTOSO\Administrators; CONTOSO\SUPERUSERS

Security template Gamma has the following settings:

Shut down the system: CONTOSO\Administrators; CONTOSO\DEVELOPERS

Security template Alpha has been imported into a GPO that is applied to the Melbourne site. Security template Beta has been imported into a GPO that is applied to the ITSTAFF OU. Security template Gamma has been imported into a GPO that is applied to the DEVELOPERS OU. You get a call from a user who is located at the Melbourne site. He complains that he is unable to shut down his computer. You look at his computer's account and find that it is located in the DEVELOPERS OU. You ascertain that his user account is a member of the IISADMINS and DEVELOPERS security groups. Given that no other GPOs are in operation besides those listed here, which of the following might explain why this user is unable to shut down his computer?

- **A.** The Group Policy applied to the Melbourne site is set to "block inheritance."
- **B.** The Group Policy applied to the DEVELOPERS OU is set to "block inheritance."
- **C.** The Group Policy applied to the ITSTAFF OU is set to "block inheritance."
- **D.** The Group Policy applied to the Melbourne site is set to "no override."
- **E.** The Group Policy applied to the ITSTAFF OU is set to "no override."

5. You have just installed Windows XP Professional for an organization that runs many customized applications that were originally written to run on Windows 98. Since the installation of Windows XP, you have received complaints that some of the applications don't work. You've diagnosed this problem and found that in some cases ordinary users require higher levels of permissions than those that you've allowed in your security policy. You've placed all of the computer accounts for this group within a separate OU. You create a Group Policy object and apply it to this new OU. Which of the following preconfigured templates should you import to this OU to ensure that the users are able to run their customized Windows 98–based applications on their workstations that run Windows XP Professional?

- **A.** security.inf
- **B.** notssid.inf
- **C.** rootsec.inf
- **D.** hisecws.inf
- **E.** compatws.inf

Objective 1.4 Answers

1. **Correct Answers: A**

   A. **Correct:** When the membership of a restricted group is altered manually by someone adding new members to the group, those members will remain until a policy update is forced. You can accomplish this instantly by running a GPUPDATE /FORCE from the command prompt. After this is done, the group membership will be returned to its proper state.

   B. **Incorrect:** This will not solve the problem. Mick's user account is also supposed to be a part of the SUPERUSERS group.

   C. **Incorrect:** This step is not necessary; on the next Group Policy update the membership of the group will be returned to its proper state.

   D. **Incorrect:** This will not change anything; the GPO already has the correct security settings. The membership of the group will be returned properly when the next Group Policy update occurs.

   E. **Incorrect:** Although this technique would have worked with Windows 2000, in Windows Server 2003 SECEDIT /REFRESHPOLICY has been replaced by the GPUPDATE command.

2. **Correct Answers: D**

   A. **Incorrect:** The export command cannot be used on new Group Policy objects.

   B. **Incorrect:** All that this will do is generate a security template that is identical to the original one.

   C. **Incorrect:** The Group Policy Object Editor does not have this functionality.

   D. **Correct:** The SECEDIT command can be used to generate a rollback template for a specific security template. Although it is not important to remember every switch involved in commands such as SECEDIT and GPUPDATE for the exam, having knowledge of what can be accomplished with the command lines is important.

3. **Correct Answers: A and D**

   A. **Correct:** If the DSClient software is installed on the Windows 98 clients, they will be able to handle the increased security level of the LAN Manager authentication.

   B. **Incorrect:** Only clients running operating systems much earlier than Windows 98, and the occasional earlier application, require the LAN Manager hash value. Windows 98 is able to interact with the domain if the LAN Manager hash value is not stored.

C. **Incorrect:** IPSec has nothing to do with the problems currently being experienced by the clients running Windows 98.

D. **Correct:** This approach will also work because this is the maximum LAN Manager authentication level that clients running Windows 98 can handle without the installation of the DSClient software.

4. **Correct Answers: E**

A. **Incorrect:** This behavior cannot be explained by the GPO applied to the Melbourne site being set to "block inheritance."

B. **Incorrect:** This behavior cannot be explained by the GPO applied to the DEVELOPERS OU being set to "block inheritance."

C. **Incorrect:** This behavior cannot be explained by the GPO applied to the ITSTAFF OU being set to "block inheritance."

D. **Incorrect:** If this were the case, because the user is a member of the IISADMINS group, he would be able to shut down his computer.

E. **Correct:** The only explanation for this behavior is that the policy being applied to the ITSTAFF OU is overriding the policy being applied to the DEVELOPERS OU.

5. **Correct Answers: E**

A. **Incorrect:** This is the default security template; it is created on each computer during the installation of Windows. It will not provide the required compatibility.

B. **Incorrect:** This particular security policy is used with terminal servers running in application compatibility mode. It will not help users run customized Windows 98–based applications on workstations running Windows XP Professional.

C. **Incorrect:** Rootsec.inf is used to specify permissions for the root directory of the system drive. It is used to set the NTFS permissions of the root directory. It is not used to ensure compatibility with applications customized for Windows 98.

D. **Incorrect:** This is the high security template for workstations. Of the preconfigured security templates that ship with Windows XP and Windows Server 2003, this is the strictest. Because of its strictness, it will not allow programs that require unusual access to the registry, such as those that are customized to run under Windows 98, to execute.

E. **Correct:** The compatws.inf security template is designed to allow normal users to have a greater level of permissions than they would normally have under Windows XP Professional. The compatibility template alters the file and registry permissions that are granted to normal users. This alteration allows many applications that were written for Windows 98, rather than Windows 2000 or Windows XP, to run.

Objective 1.5

Configure Additional Security Based on Computer Roles

The security that can be provided by deploying security templates does not represent the end point of hardening a system. There are many aspects to securing a system that cannot be controlled by the settings located within the security node of a Group Policy object. How these extra options and services are configured is highly dependent on the role that the computer is assigned. Aspects of security configuration that might be appropriate for a particular role may include hiding desktop icons and Start menu items on a computer that is used as an information kiosk device. Other aspects of security configuration could include port blocking with IPSec filters or renaming the Administrator account. For the most part, these changes can be made by deploying Group Policy. Remember that many areas of policy useful for securing a computer cannot be configured by using security templates. This must be done by manually editing Group Policy objects. Some security measures can also involve editing the registry to disable specific options that cannot be configured by Group Policy.

Objective 1.5 Questions

1. You are configuring a workstation running Windows XP Professional to work as an information kiosk at the local shopping mall. You want to limit the functionality so that teenagers who regularly visit the mall cannot hijack the system and use it for purposes other than for providing information to mall patrons about the services available. The information is provided by means of a custom Web application that runs off a computer running Windows Server 2003 and IIS that is located in the shopping mall's administrative section. Which of the following lockdown options cannot be applied by means of the Windows XP Professional local GPO?

   A. Security Zones: Do not allow users to add/delete sites.

   B. Security Zones: Do not allow users to change policies.

   C. Enable/Disable image caching.

   D. Make proxy settings per machine (rather than per user).

2. You want to lock down Microsoft Internet Explorer as much as possible for computers located in a student laboratory at the local college. You have the following goals:

   Primary Goal: The students are allowed to run only specific applications, such as Microsoft Word, Microsoft Excel, and Microsoft PowerPoint. This is to stop the students from running unauthorized programs such as network games.

   First Secondary Goal: The students are prevented from accessing the command prompt. Students should also be prevented locking the computer by using Ctrl+Alt+Del. This is so that students do not lock the screen when they leave the laboratory, denying access to other students.

   Second Secondary Goal: The students are prevented from accessing the registry editing tools. The students are also restricted from running the programs chat.exe and strategy.exe from Windows Help. This is because some enterprising students found a way to create Help files to launch these particular applications.

   You perform the following tasks:

   Create an organizational unit called LAB MACHINES and move all of the computer accounts into this organizational unit. Create another organizational unit called LAB STUDENTS and move all of the user accounts of students that use the lab into this organizational unit. Create a Group Policy object with the following settings:

   User Configuration\Administrative Templates\System

   \Ctrl+Alt+Del Options\Remove Change Password: Configured

\Ctrl+Alt+Del Options\Remove Task Manager: Configured

\Run only allowed Windows applications

\Prevent access to the command prompt: Configured

\Restrict these programs from being launched from help: Configured

\Prevent access to the command prompt: Configured

\Prevent access to registry editing tools: Configured

You edit the "Restrict these programs from being launched from help" policy and add chat.exe and strategy.exe. After you have performed all of the listed tasks, which of your goals have you achieved?

- **A.** The primary goal and both secondary goals are achieved.
- **B.** The primary goal and one secondary goal are achieved.
- **C.** The primary goal is achieved. No secondary goals are achieved.
- **D.** The primary goal is not achieved. Both secondary goals are achieved.
- **E.** The primary goal is not achieved. One secondary goal is achieved.

3. You are configuring an IIS system that runs on Windows Server 2003. For the purposes of security, you want to limit the installed components to only those that are critical for the operation of the system. The system only serves up static Web pages in HTML format. It provides no dynamic Web pages, nor does it provide any type of Web application or Web service. The server will be patched manually and will not use the Windows Update or Software Update Service. Given this information, which of the following components in the Application Server dialog box or the Internet Information Services dialog box, located in the Add/Remove Windows Components section of Add/Remove Programs, do not need to be installed on this server for it to be able to complete its function? (Select all that apply.)

- **A.** Enable network COM+ access.
- **B.** Message Queuing
- **C.** Background Intelligent Transfer Service (BITS) server extension
- **D.** Microsoft FrontPage 2002 Server Extensions
- **E.** common files

4. Recently, your security audits have shown repeated brute force dictionary attacks occurring against the local administrator accounts on computers running Windows XP Professional, Windows NT 4.0 Workstation, and Windows Server 2003 on your network. Your network is made up of a forest of three domains. The root domain, tailspintoys.com, is made up entirely of computers running Windows Server 2003. The child domain, structured.tailspintoys.com, is made up of computers running Windows Server 2003 and Windows XP Professional. The child domain, legacy.tailspintoys.com, is made up of computers running Windows Server 2003 and Windows NT 4.0 Workstation. The attack appears unsophisticated in that it only targets the Administrator account and does not try to gain access to other accounts. With this in mind, you decide to change the name of the Administrator account on all computers in your forest to Sysmanager. Because the attack is singling out the Administrator account specifically, it will not have any chance of success after the name is changed to Sysmanager. Which of the following represents a method of changing the name of the Administrator account to Sysmanager on all computers in the forest?

A. Create a new GPO and apply it to the tailspintoys.com domain. In this GPO, configure the Accounts: Rename Administrator Account policy to rename the administrator account to Sysmanager. Run GPUPDATE /FORCE on the schema master to propagate this change throughout the forest.

B. Create a new GPO and apply it to the tailspintoys.com domain. In this GPO, configure the Accounts: Rename Administrator Account policy to rename the administrator account to Sysmanager. Perform the same action on the two child domains. Run GPUPDATE /FORCE in all three domains to propagate this change.

C. Create a new GPO and apply it to the tailspintoys.com domain. In this GPO, configure the Accounts: Rename Administrator Account policy to rename the administrator account to Sysmanager. Perform the same action on the structured.tailspintoys.com child domain. Run GPUPDATE /FORCE in both domains to propagate this change. In the legacy.tailspintoys.com domain, manually rename the local administrator account to Sysmanager on each of the computers running Windows NT 4.0 Workstation and Windows Server 2003.

D. Create a new GPO and apply it to the tailspintoys.com domain. In this GPO, configure the Accounts: Rename Administrator Account policy to rename the administrator account to Sysmanager. Perform the same action on the legacy.tailspintoys.com child domain. Run GPUPDATE /FORCE in both domains to propagate this change. In the structured.tailspintoys.com domain, manually rename the local administrator account to Sysmanager on each of the computers running Windows NT 4.0 Workstation and Windows Server 2003.

Objective 1.5 Answers

1. **Correct Answers: C**

   A. **Incorrect:** This policy can be applied at the local GPO level. This policy is found in the Computer Configuration\Administrative Templates\Internet Explorer node of the local GPO.

   B. **Incorrect:** This policy can be applied at the local GPO level. This policy is found in the Computer Configuration\Administrative Templates\Internet Explorer node of the local GPO.

   C. **Correct:** This option is configured by editing the registry; it cannot be configured by means of the local GPO. This key can be found at HKEY_LOCAL_MACHINE\SOFTWARE\MICROSOFT\INTERNET EXPLORER\IMAGE CACHING. Although you are not expected to be familiar with the Windows registry for the security exam, you are expected to be knowledgeable about the policies that can be applied by means of local and non-local Group Policy objects. The other settings in this question are all reasonably obvious policies; this one should be the only one that stands out as unusual.

   D. **Incorrect:** This policy can be applied at the local GPO level. This policy is found in the Computer Configuration\Administrative Templates\Internet Explorer node of the local GPO.

2. **Correct Answers: E**

   A. **Incorrect:** The primary goal is not achieved because, although the "Run only allowed Windows applications" policy was configured, the specific programs Word, Excel, and PowerPoint were not added. A hint to the fact that this had not occurred was given in that the specific programs that were restricted from running by means of Help were added. The first secondary goal is not achieved because the lock workstation option was not configured in Group Policy. The second secondary goal is achieved.

   B. **Incorrect:** The primary goal is not achieved because, although the "Run only allowed Windows applications" policy was configured, the specific programs Word, Excel, and PowerPoint were not added. A hint to the fact that this had not occurred was given in that the specific programs that were restricted from running by means of Help were added. The first secondary goal is not achieved because the lock workstation option was not configured in Group Policy. The second secondary goal is achieved.

   C. **Incorrect:** The primary goal is not achieved because, although the "Run only allowed Windows applications" policy was configured, the specific programs Word, Excel, and PowerPoint were not added. A hint to the fact that this had not occurred was given in that the specific programs that were restricted from running by means of Help were added. The first secondary goal is not achieved because the lock workstation option was not configured in Group Policy. The second secondary goal is achieved.

D. Incorrect: The primary goal is not achieved because, although the "Run only allowed Windows applications" policy was configured, the specific programs Word, Excel, and PowerPoint were not added. A hint to the fact that this had not occurred was given in that the specific programs that were restricted from running by means of Help were added. The first secondary goal is not achieved because the lock workstation option was not configured in Group Policy. The second secondary goal is achieved.

E. Incorrect: The primary goal is not achieved because, although the "Run only allowed Windows applications" policy was configured, the specific programs Word, Excel, and PowerPoint were not added. A hint to the fact that this had not occurred was given in that the specific programs that were restricted from running by means of Help were added. The first secondary goal is not achieved because the lock workstation option was not configured in Group Policy. The second secondary goal is achieved.

3. Correct Answers: B, C, and D

A. Incorrect: This component is required for the World Wide Web Service and IIS Manager to function.

B. Correct: This particular service does not need to be enabled for the functions described in the question to be performed.

C. Correct: This service is required if the computer running Windows Server 2003 will be automatically updated with patches and hotfixes. Because this is to be done manually in this case, this component does not need to be installed.

D. Correct: FrontPage 2002 Server Extensions need to be enabled only if they are actually used. Because the question makes no mention of FrontPage 2002 Extensions, it is safe to assume that this component does not need to be installed.

E. Incorrect: IIS requires the common files to run. Without them, IIS is unable to function.

4. Correct Answers: C

A. Incorrect: This will only rename the administrator account in the root domain. The two child domains will retain their original settings.

B. Incorrect: Although this will rename the administrator account on all of the computers running Windows Server 2003 and Windows XP Professional, it will not rename the administrator account on the computers running Windows NT 4.0 Workstation.

C. **Correct:** Performing these actions will achieve your goals. Workstations running Windows NT 4.0 cannot have their administrator accounts renamed by means of Group Policy as they are not Group Policy aware.

D. **Incorrect:** This solution will not work because the workstations running Windows NT 4.0 are located in the legacy.tailspintoys.com domain, not the structured.tailspintoys.com domain.

14 Implementing, Managing, and Troubleshooting Patch Management Infrastructure (2.0)

It's commonly known among developers that no software product is released without bugs. Millions of lines of code compiled into different programs that interact in a complex and unique way can result in problems that were unseen by Microsoft at the time of a product's release. To paraphrase a quote from a NASA engineer during the development of the lunar module for the Apollo project, writing and running such complex software is similar to coordinating a room full of dancers, each moving to a song that only they can hear. Problems are inevitable. To deal with problems that appear after a product's release, Microsoft has an aggressive strategy of releasing hotfixes and service packs. Vital skills for systems administrators are knowing how to trial deploy these updates, how to assess their relevance to your existing network environment, how to check whether or not a system is as patched as it should be, and finally, knowing the different options in rolling out those updates.

Testing Skills and Suggested Practices

The skills that you need to successfully master the Managing and Implementing Disaster Recovery objective domain on Exam 70-299: *Implementing and Administering Security in a Microsoft Windows Server 2003 Network* include:

- Manual installation of hotfixes.
  - Practice 1: Use Windows Update to locate a hotfix that your Microsoft Windows Server 2003 system requires but is not yet installed. Manually download this hotfix to the c:\temp folder. From the command prompt run `hotfix.exe /help` (where hotfix.exe is the hotfix name) to bring up all of the installation options.
  - Practice 2: Manually install the hotfix that you downloaded in Practice 1. Reboot your server if necessary. Check in the Add/Remove programs control panel that the hotfix has installed. From the command prompt, use the appropriate switches (discover them by using the Help switch) to uninstall this hotfix. Do not uninstall using Add/Remove programs. Reboot the server if necessary. Return to Add/Remove programs to verify that the hotfix has been removed.

- Using the Microsoft Baseline Security Analyzer (MBSA) tool.
  - ❑ Practice 1: Download and install the MBSA tool from the Microsoft Web site. Using the GUI, run a single scan against each of the computers on your local network. Locate computers that have security patches that must be applied using the MBSA tool. Download the relevant patches from the Microsoft Web site. Install the patches on the systems that require them.
  - ❑ Practice 2: From the command prompt, use the MBSA command-line tool to scan the range of IP addresses on your LAN that you scanned individually in Practice 1. If you have installed the patches correctly you should now see a text-based report informing you that these patches have been successfully applied.
- Working with service packs.
  - ❑ Practice 1: Download Microsoft Windows XP Service Pack 1a from the Microsoft Web site. Use the command xpsp1a_en_x86.exe –x to extract the service pack to a suitable location. Locate the file update.msi.
  - ❑ Practice 2: Use the update.msi file to create a software installation package in a Group Policy object (GPO) that will deploy Windows XP Service Pack 1a to a new organizational unit (OU). Take note of extra installation options such as Uninstall This Application When It Falls Out Of The Scope Of Management found in the Deployment tab of the service pack software deployment properties.

Further Reading

This section lists supplemental readings by objective. We recommend that you study these sources thoroughly before taking this exam.

Objective 2.1 Best Practices for using UPDATE.MSI to deploy service packs. *http://support.microsoft.com/default.aspx?scid=kb;en-us;278503*

Managing Security Hotfixes. *http://www.microsoft.com/technet/security/tips/sechotfx.asp*

Microsoft Windows XP Hotfix Installation and Deployment Guide. *http://www.microsoft.com/windowsxp/pro/downloads/servicepacks/sp1/hfdeploy.asp*

Objective 2.2 Microsoft Baseline Security Analyzer Home Page. *http://www.microsoft.com/technet/security/tools/mbsahome.asp*

MBSA Q&A. *http://www.microsoft.com/technet/security/tools/mbsaqa.asp*

MBSA Support Webcast.

http://support.microsoft.com/default.aspx?scid=/servicedesks/webcasts/wcd011003/wcdblurb011003.asp

MBSA White Paper. *http://www.microsoft.com/technet/security/tools/mbsawp.asp*

Objective 2.3 Software Update Services: *http://www.microsoft.com/windowsserversystem/sus/default.mspx*

Managing Security Hotfixes. *http://www.microsoft.com/technet/security/tips/sechotfx.asp*

Best Practices for using UPDATE.MSI to deploy service packs. *http://support.microsoft.com/default.aspx?scid=kb;en-us;278503*

Microsoft Windows XP Hotfix Installation and Deployment Guide. *http://www.microsoft.com/windowsxp/pro/downloads/servicepacks/sp1/hfdeploy.asp*

Objective 2.1

Plan the Deployment of Service Packs and Hotfixes

When it comes to managing the security for the systems on a network, many administrators are tempted to install service packs and hotfixes the moment that they are released. Although such a strategy can keep you on the cutting edge of security, following the strategy blindly will eventually lead to cutting yourself. Although Microsoft has excellent processes in place for testing its service packs and hotfixes, from time to time an update is withdrawn because it has unintended consequences that severely impact upon some customer's systems. It is also possible that you may work in an environment that has a unique mix of applications. Microsoft cannot test for all eventualities and it is possible that a released hotfix or service pack may disable an important customized business application that your organization is dependent on. An ounce of prevention is worth a pound of cure, and a strategy of thoroughly testing hotfixes and service packs before you roll them out to your organization can save you hours, perhaps days, of mopping up operations if something goes wrong. It is also worth remembering that even though a hotfix may be able to be installed on a system, this does not mean that the hotfix should be installed on a system. Careful judgments should be made as to whether or not the hotfix is applicable and relevant for the environment that it might be deployed in. Finally, it is important to know how to get back from a position once you have arrived there. Even with thorough testing something can be missed, and having an effective rollback strategy before a service pack or hotfix is rolled out is much better than attempting to develop such a strategy once a hotfix is installed on production systems and is causing unforeseen problems.

Objective 2.1 Questions

1. You are the systems administrator for five servers on a network of Windows Server 2003 systems. Server one runs Windows Server 2003 Web Edition. Server two runs Windows Server 2003 with SQL Server 2000. Server three runs Windows Server 2003 with ISA Server 2000 and has been upgraded from Windows 2000 Server. Server four runs Windows Server 2003 with Microsoft Exchange Server 2003 installed. Server five is a Windows Server 2003 domain controller that has been upgraded from Windows 2000 Server.

You are reviewing some of the latest security updates. The bulletin number, KB (Knowledge Base) article number, and products affected by the update are listed in the following table:

Bulletin	KB	Products Affected
MS03-039	824146	Windows NT 4.0, Windows 2000, Windows XP, Windows Server 2003.
MS03-037	822715	Microsoft Visual Basic for Applications SDK 5.0, 6.0, 6.2, and 6.3. Office 97, Windows 2000, and Windows XP. Visio 2000 and Office Visio 2003. Project 2000 and 2002. Publisher 2002.
MS03-031	815495	Microsoft SQL Server 7.0, Microsoft Data Engine 1.0 (MSDE 1.0), Microsoft SQL Server 2000, Microsoft Desktop Engine 2000 (MSDE 2000), Microsoft SQL Server 2000 Desktop Engine (Windows).
MS03-028	816456	Microsoft Internet Security and Acceleration Server 2000 (ISA Server).
MS03-025	822679	Windows 2000.

You are planning to deploy the relevant updates to the five servers you are responsible for. Which of the following correctly lists the security updates, by KB number, that need to be applied to each Windows Server 2003 system? (Select all that apply.)

A. Server one: 824146

B. Server two: 824146, 822715, and 815495

C. Server three: 824146, 816456, and 822679

D. Server four: 824146

E. Server five: 824146 and 822679

2. Foley is planning the phased deployment of a new service pack for Windows XP Professional across the A. Datum Corporation organization. A. Datum Corporation has 700 users whose accounts are all contained within the default Users container of Active Directory directory service. The 700 computer accounts of the systems that these users use are located in the default Computers container. The users are divided into four domain global security groups. The Engineers group has 400 members, the Sales group has 150 members, the Secretarial group has 100 members, and the Management group has 50 members. Employees at A. Datum Corporation use their own workstations. In consultation with management, Foley has decided to split the deployment of the service pack into four phases. These phases are as follows:

- Phase One: 200 members of the Engineers group
- Phase Two: The rest of the Engineers group
- Phase Three: Sales group and Secretarial group
- Phase Four: Management group

Which of the following plans would allow Foley to carry out this phased deployment plan with the minimum of administrative effort?

A. Create two new global security groups: ENG-PH1 and ENG-PH2. Create a GPO that assigns the service pack in the Computer Configuration\Software Settings\Software Installation node. For Phase One, apply this GPO to the ENG-PH1 group. For Phase Two, apply this GPO to the ENG-PH2 group. For Phase Three, apply this GPO to the Sales and Secretarial groups. For Phase Four, apply this GPO to the Managers group.

B. Create two new global security groups: ENG-PH1 and ENG-PH2. Create a GPO that assigns the service pack in the User Configuration\Software Settings\Software Installation node. For Phase One, apply this GPO to the ENG-PH1 group. For Phase Two, apply this GPO to the ENG-PH2 group. For Phase Three, apply this GPO to the Sales and Secretarial groups. For Phase Four, apply this GPO to the Managers group.

C. Create four new global security groups: Phase1, Phase2, Phase3, and Phase4. Add the computer accounts for the systems that the first 200 groups of engineers use to the Phase1 group. Add the computer accounts for the rest of the engineers' systems to the Phase2 group. Add the computer accounts for the systems that the sales and secretarial groups use to the Phase3 group. Add the computer accounts for the systems that the managers use to the Phase4 group. Create a GPO that assigns the service pack in the User Configuration\Software Settings\Software Installation node. Assign this GPO to the default Users container, but in the Group Policy properties make sure that the Authenticated Users group does not have the Read and Apply Group Policy Allow check boxes checked. For each phase, add a security group and assign the Read and Apply Group Policy (allow) permission.

D. Create four new global security groups; Phase1, Phase2, Phase3, and Phase4. Add the computer accounts for the systems that the first 200 groups of engineers use to the Phase1 group. Add the computer accounts for the rest of the engineers' systems to the Phase2 group. Add the computer accounts for the systems that the sales and secretarial groups use to the Phase3 group. Add the computer accounts for the systems that the managers use to the Phase4 group. Create a GPO that assigns the service pack in the Computer Configuration\Software Settings\Software Installation node. Assign this GPO to the default Users container, but in the Group Policy properties make sure that the Authenticated Users group does not have the Read and Apply Group Policy Allow check boxes checked. For each phase, add a security group and assign the Read and Apply Group Policy (allow) permission.

E. Create four new organizational units called Phase1, Phase2, Phase3, and Phase4. Move the computer accounts for the systems that the first 200 engineers use to the Phase1 OU. Move the rest of the engineers' computer accounts to the Phase2 OU. Move all the computer accounts for the systems that the Sales and Secretarial group use to the Phase3 OU. Move all of the computer accounts for the systems that the managers use to the Phase4 OU. Create a new GPO named XPSP_DEPLOY. Configure the GPO so that it assigns the Windows XP service pack in the Computer Configuration\Software Settings\Software Installation node. For phase one, assign the XPSP_DEPLOY GPO to the Phase1 OU. For phase two of the deployment, assign the XPSP_DEPLOY GPO to the Phase2 OU. For phase three, assign the XPSP_DEPLOY GPO to the Phase3 OU. To finalize the deployment, assign the XPSP_DEPLOY GPO to the Phase4 OU.

3. Rooslan is planning on installing a new Windows Server 2003 system that will run Microsoft SQL Server 2000. At the time he is performing the installation, Windows Server 2003 has one service pack released and six relevant hotfixes. SQL Server 2000 is up to Service Pack 3 and has five relevant hotfixes. Of the options listed, which represents the best way for Rooslan to install the server software, the service packs, and the hotfixes?

A. Rooslan should install in the following order: Windows Server 2003; Windows Server 2003 Service Pack 1; all six relevant Windows Server 2003 hotfixes; the five relevant SQL Server 2000 hotfixes; SQL Server 2000.

B. Rooslan should install in the following order: Windows Server 2003; SQL Server 2000; Windows Server 2003 Service Pack 1; SQL Server 2000 Service Pack 1; SQL Sever 2000 Service Pack 2; SQL Server 2000 Service Pack 3; the five SQL Server 2000 hotfixes; the six Windows Server 2003 hotfixes.

C. Rooslan should install in the following order: Windows Server 2003; SQL Server 2000; Windows Server 2003 Service Pack 1; SQL Server 2000 Service Pack 1; SQL Sever 2000 Service Pack 2; SQL Server 2000 Service Pack 3; five SQL Server 2000 hotfixes; six Windows Server 2003 hotfixes.

D. Rooslan should install in the following order: Windows Server 2003; Windows Server 2003 Service Pack 1; the six Windows Server 2003 hotfixes; SQL Server 2000; SQL Server 2000 Service Pack 3.

E. Rooslan should install in the following order: Windows Server 2003; Windows Server 2003 Service Pack 1; the six Windows Server 2003 hotfixes; SQL Server 2000; SQL Server 2000 Service Pack 3; the five SQL Server 2000 hotfixes.

4. You are considering a pilot program for the rollout of the first service pack for Office 2003 in your organization. All of the workstations in your organization are running Windows XP Professional. Your organization has five departments. There is also a small IT unit with five staff members. Each department has its own OU within the Active Directory structure. Approximately 100 user accounts reside in each OU. Because the requirements for each department are different, each department's OU has an individualized Group Policy Object applied. You want the pilot program to run for a month before you deploy Office 2003 Service Pack 1 across the rest of your organization. You want to make sure that all applications currently used in the organization are compatible with the service pack. Which of the following is the best suggestion for membership of the pilot program?

A. Create a lab with five different workstations running Windows XP. Add each of these workstations to the OU that corresponds to each department.

B. Select one user from each department to be a member of the pilot program.

C. Select five users from each department to be members of the pilot program.

D. Have each member of IT join a corresponding departmental OU. Deploy the service pack to each IT staff member's system.

5. You have three hotfixes that you need to apply to the workstations running Windows XP Professional in your domain. Each hotfix requires the system to be rebooted. Rather than force your users to endure three reboots in a row, you want to configure a script that will install these hotfixes, which were released in early 2004:

```
WindowsXP-KB812345-x86-ENU.exe
WindowsXP-KB812346-x86-ENU.exe
WindowsXP-KB812347-x86-ENU.exe
```

You then want the computer to reboot. Which of the following scripts will perform this function?

A.

```
@echo off
setlocal
set PATHTOFIXES=E:\hotfix

%PATHTOFIXES%\WindowsXP-KB812345-x86-ENU.exe /Z /Q
%PATHTOFIXES%\WindowsXP-KB812346-x86-ENU.exe /Z /Q
%PATHTOFIXES%\WindowsXP-KB812347-x86-ENU.exe /Z /Q
shutdown -r
```

B.
```
@echo off
setlocal
set PATHTOFIXES=E:\hotfix

%PATHTOFIXES%\WindowsXP-KB812345-x86-ENU.exe
%PATHTOFIXES%\WindowsXP-KB812346-x86-ENU.exe
%PATHTOFIXES%\WindowsXP-KB812347-x86-ENU.exe
```

C.
```
@echo off
setlocal
set PATHTOFIXES=E:\hotfix

QCHAIN.EXE %PATHTOFIXES%\WindowsXP-KB812345-x86-ENU.exe
QCHAIN.EXE %PATHTOFIXES%\WindowsXP-KB812346-x86-ENU.exe
QCHAIN.EXE %PATHTOFIXES%\WindowsXP-KB812347-x86-ENU.exe
```

D. This cannot be done. The changes for each hotfix must be processed before the next hotfix can be installed.

6. Oksana works as the systems administrator in the contoso.com domain. At present, service packs on the network are rolled out by assigning the appropriate file to a specific set of computers in the software installation and maintenance area of Group Policy. Which of the following options must Oksana set so that the service pack can be uninstalled by using Group Policy settings at a later date?

A. This is not possible. Service packs can only be uninstalled manually.

B. Oksana needs to make sure that she publishes the service pack rather than assigning it.

C. Oksana needs to make sure that she assigns the service pack rather than publishing it.

D. Oksana needs to ensure that, in the Deployment tab of the service pack software deployment properties, the option Uninstall This Application When It Falls Out Of The Scope Of Management is enabled.

7. Which of the following methods will allow you to roll back a hotfix that has been installed on 500 workstations running Windows XP Professional that are located in three domains of a single Windows Server 2003 functional level forest?

A. Write a script that calls the spuninst.exe utility from the particular service pack uninstall directory located under the %systemroot% directory of each workstation running Windows XP. Assign this script to run during startup on each system.

B. Place the hotfix on an accessible network share in each domain. Write a script that calls the hotfix on the network share with the /uninstall and /quiet switches. Assign this script to run during startup on each system.

C. Revoke the publication of the hotfix.exe in the Active Directory software deployment for the OU hosting all 500 computers running Windows XP.

D. Write a script that manually deletes all files and folders that the hotfix updated. Restore these from a pre-hotfix backup.

E. Use the driver rollback facility of Windows XP to roll back to the pre-hotfix system state.

8. You have recently deployed a hotfix named WindowsServer2003-KB828035-x86-ENU.exe by means of a startup script to 40 computers running Windows Server 2003 in a domain. There have been several problems and you want to remove this particular hotfix from all computers running Windows Server 2003. Your login script works by means of a batch file. All hotfixes are located on a network share assigned to the Z: drive of each computer running Windows Server 2003. Which command should you add to the startup script applied by a GPO to the OU containing all 40 computers running Windows Server 2003 to remove this hotfix without requiring any administrator interaction? (Select two.)

A. Z:\WindowsServer2003-KB828035-x86-ENU.exe /uninstall /quiet

B. Z:\WindowsServer2003-KB828035-x86-ENU.exe –m –y

C. %systemroot%\$NtUninstallkb828035$\spuninst\spuninst.exe /u

D. %systemroot%\$NtUninstallkb828035$\WindowsServer2003-KB828035-x86-ENU.exe –m –y

Objective 2.1 Answers

1. Correct Answers: A and D

- A. **Correct:** Of the updates listed above, only 824146 is relevant to Windows Server 2003 Web Edition.
- B. **Incorrect:** This particular server only requires update 824145 and update 815495. Update 824146 is required for Windows Server 2003. Update 815495 is required for SQL Server 2000. Update 822715 is designed for systems running Microsoft Office, Visio, Project, and Publisher.
- C. **Incorrect:** This particular server only requires updates 824146 and 816456. Update 824146 is required for Windows Server 2003. Update 816456 is required for ISA Server 2000. Although this server was upgraded from Windows 2000 Server, it no longer requires hotfixes for that product, hence update 822679 is not necessary.
- D. **Correct:** Only the Windows Server 2003 hotfix, 824146, is relevant to server four. None of the security updates mention Exchange Server 2003.
- E. **Incorrect:** Only the Windows Server 2003 hotfix, 824146, is relevant to server four. Although the server has been upgraded from Windows 2000 Server, this does not mean that hotfixes relevant to only Windows 2000 should be installed on this type of machine.

2. Correct Answers: E

- A. **Incorrect:** Group Policy objects cannot be assigned to global security groups. GPOs can only be assigned to sites, domains, and organizational units.
- B. **Incorrect:** Group Policy objects cannot be assigned to global security groups. GPOs can only be assigned to sites, domains, and organizational units.
- C. **Incorrect:** Group Policy Objects cannot be assigned to the default Users container in Active Directory. Also, GPOs cannot be assigned to the default Computers container, to the Builtin container, or to the ForeignSecurityPrinciples container.
- D. **Incorrect:** Group Policy Objects cannot be assigned to the default Users container in Active Directory. Also, GPOs cannot be assigned to the default Computers container, to the Builtin container, or to the ForeignSecurityPrinciples container.
- E. **Correct:** As the computer accounts were all in the Computers container, there was existing infrastructure where GPOs were being applied to computers at the OU level. This leaves open the option of shifting the computer accounts into specific computer OUs and then assigning service packs via GPO. The same GPO can be applied to multiple OUs within a domain.

3. Correct Answers: E

A. **Incorrect:** SQL Server hotfixes should be installed after SQL Server 2000 is installed.

B. **Incorrect:** If he installs SQL Server Service Pack 3, there is no need to install Service Pack 1 or Service Pack 2 because Service Pack 3 is cumulative and contains all of the fixes from the first two service packs. Also, in this answer he does not install all of the necessary hotfixes for Windows Server 2003.

C. **Incorrect:** Although this will bring the system up to date, it is not necessary to install SQL Server 2000 Service Pack 1 and Service Pack 2 because Service Pack 3 is cumulative and contains all of the fixes from the first two service packs.

D. **Incorrect:** This will not install the five relevant SQL Server 2000 hotfixes.

E. **Correct:** This installs all relevant service packs and hotfixes in a logical way, without the redundancy of installing prior service packs. Before you install software it is wise to check if there is any special install order. Generally with Microsoft this is not a problem, though with some other vendors problems can arise if you do not follow a specific checklist (installing the application before applying the Windows service pack, and then patching the application).

4. Correct Answers: C

A. **Incorrect:** Although you have added a computer to each OU, a pilot program should test the change in a normal everyday environment under normal usage conditions.

B. **Incorrect:** Although this is a good start, pilot programs should include more than one user from a particular environment. It may be that the user you have chosen from a particular environment uses a computer in an unusual way.

C. **Correct:** This will create a pilot program of 25 users. By having five users participate from each department, you will avoid the problem of perhaps selecting a single user with unique habits.

D. **Incorrect:** Members of IT staff rarely make good members of pilot programs, unless the rollout is specifically targeted at them. IT staff use their computers and applications differently from the way workers in other departments do. When running a pilot program you want to simulate day-to-day usage patterns; you don't want people guessing how day-to-day usage occurs.

5. Correct Answers: A

A. Correct: Hotfixes released after mid-2001 have the qchain.exe functionality used on Windows 2000 and Microsoft Windows NT 4.0 built into them. This means that you can install multiple hotfixes as long as you remember to append them with the Do Not Reboot switch (/z). To initiate a reboot, issue the shutdown –r command.

B. Incorrect: This script will not work as directed by the question because each hotfix will reboot the computer.

C. Incorrect: Qchain functionality was included in all hotfixes released after mid-2001. This script will not execute properly.

D. Incorrect: Hotfixes released after mid-2001 have built-in qchain functionality, which means that they process updates in an orderly manner that does not require a reboot after each hotfix has been installed.

6. Correct Answers: D

A. Incorrect: This is not true, as long as you deploy the service pack with the Uninstall This Application When It Falls Out Of The Scope Of Management option enabled. This option can be found in the Deployment tab of the service pack software deployment properties.

B. Incorrect: This makes no difference. Whether published or assigned, service packs can be removed as long as the Uninstall This Application When It Falls Out Of The Scope Of Management option is enabled upon deployment.

C. Incorrect: This makes no difference. Whether published or assigned, service packs can be removed as long as the Uninstall This Application When It Falls Out Of The Scope Of Management option is enabled upon deployment.

D. Correct: If this option is enabled, the service pack can be uninstalled by means of Group Policy settings at a later date.

7. Correct Answers: A and B

A. Correct: When a hotfix is installed, a corresponding uninstallation directory is created off the %systemroot% directory. This directory is called $NtUninstallkbhotfixnumber$, where hotfixnumber is the KB hotfix number. KB can also be replaced by Q, which refers to a QFE (Quick Fix Engineering). Within this directory is an uninstallation directory that hosts a utility that will remove the hotfix if executed by a script.

B. Correct: Hotfixes can be uninstalled by executing the hotfix by a script and using the /uninstall and /quiet switches.

C. **Incorrect:** Hotfixes (unlike service packs) are not installed by using the software deployment options of Active Directory. Active Directory can be used to assign a script that will uninstall the hotfix.

D. **Incorrect:** This would most likely break a lot of systems. It is also unlikely to work reliably. Finally, performing a software restore on each of 500 workstations running Windows XP would be somewhat tedious.

E. **Incorrect:** The driver rollback facility cannot be used in this way. Hotfixes tend to have little to do with drivers. The driver rollback facility is used when a new driver creates problems on your computer, not when you want to uninstall a troublesome hotfix.

8. **Correct Answers: A and C**

A. **Correct:** Running this command will remove the hotfix and reboot the server if required. On the next startup, the command will be ignored because the hotfix has been removed. Newer Windows Server 2003 hotfixes have different syntax from those used on Windows 2000 and Windows NT 4.0.

B. **Incorrect:** This procedure would work with a Windows 2000 or Windows NT 4.0 hotfix, but it does not work with a Windows Server 2003 hotfix because the syntax has changed. To find the correct syntax, use the /help switch after the hotfix name.

C. **Correct:** Although from the outset this may seem difficult, every hotfix that is installed on a system can be uninstalled by running the spuninst.exe utility located in an individual directory off %systemroot%. This directory is called **$NtUninstallkb*hotfixnumber*$**, where ***hotfixnumber*** is the KB hotfix number. *KB* can also be replaced by *Q*, which refers to a QFE. Hotfixes can also be uninstalled by using Add/Remove Programs in Control Panel, though only on a per-system basis.

D. **Incorrect:** Unlike prior versions of Windows, Windows Server 2003 does not store the hotfix in the uninstallation directory. It stores a program called spuninst.exe, which can be used to remove any installed hotfix.

Objective 2.2

Assess the Current Status of Service Packs and Hotfixes

The Microsoft Baseline Security Analyzer (MBSA) is a tool that is not included on the Windows Server 2003 installation media, but that must be downloaded from the Microsoft Web site. The URL for this tool is located in the "Further Reading" section earlier in this chapter. This URL will provide you with the latest version of this tool, though the exam is written based on version 1.1.1. The MBSA tool is used for the identification of common security problems that occur on Windows Server 2003. The tool can be installed on computers running Windows 2000, Windows XP, and Windows Server 2003. The MBSA tool is able to analyze the following products for misconfiguration: Windows NT 4.0, Windows 2000, Windows XP, Windows Server 2003, Internet Information Server (IIS) 4.0 and IIS 5.0, SQL Server 7.0 and 2000, Microsoft Internet Explorer 5.01 or later, and Office 2000, 2002, and 2003.

The MBSA tool will also scan for missing security updates for the following Microsoft products: Windows NT 4.0, Windows 2000, Windows XP, Windows Server 2003, IIS 4.0 and IIS 5.0, SQL Server 7.0 and 2000, Internet Explorer 5.01 or later, Exchange Server 5.5 and 2000 (version 1.1.1 does not support Exchange Server 2003, though later versions will), and Windows Media Player 6.4 or later.

Objective 2.2 Questions

1. You are in charge of application and server support at a large multinational company named Contoso, Ltd., which is made up of two divisions. Within those divisions are two distinct network environments that you need to deal with. Division one is made up of a Windows 2000 Server native mode domain. Clients in division two all use Windows 2000 Professional and Microsoft Office 2000. Division two is made up of a Windows 2000 mixed-mode domain, with workstations running Windows NT 4.0 and Office 97. The workstations running Windows NT 4.0 have Internet Explorer 5.01 installed. Division two also hosts a server running Exchange 5.5 and computer running SQL Server 6.5. Each division has its own Systems Management Server (SMS). The SMS 2.0 servers have the MBSA-enabled Software Update Services Feature Pack installed. The feature pack is used to automatically scan each division's workstations and servers to generate a report from which you can deploy appropriate updates to each division's systems. Which of the following Microsoft products on your network is not supported by the MBSA-enabled SMS 2.0 Software Update Services Feature Pack? (Select all that apply.)

   A. Exchange 5.5

   B. Office 2000

   C. Windows NT 4.0 Workstation

   D. Office 97

   E. Internet Explorer 5.01

   F. SQL Server 6.5

2. Leo is preparing to run the MBSA 1.1.1 command-line tool against six computers running Windows Server 2003 on his network. The network can be seen in the figure below.

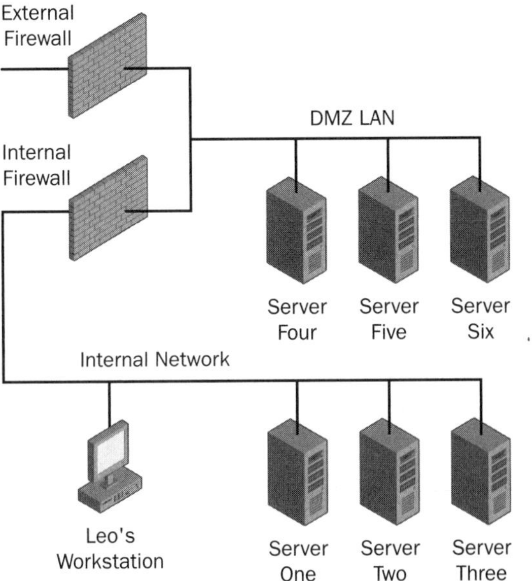

Leo's workstation, which runs Windows XP, is a member of the contoso.com domain. Servers One, Two, and Four are members of the contoso.com domain. Servers Three, Five, and Six are standalone servers. Leo's account is a member of the Domain Administrators group for the contoso.com domain. Ports 80, 139, and 445 are open between the internal LAN and the perimeter network (also known as DMZ) LAN. Port 80 is open between the perimeter network LAN and the Internet. HTTP traffic can traverse both firewalls without passing through a proxy from Leo's workstation. Which of the computers running Windows Server 2003 will Leo be able to successfully check with the MBSA command-line tool? (Select all that apply.)

A. Server One

B. Server Two

C. Server Three

D. Server Four

E. Server Five

F. Server Six

3. Rooslan is the systems administrator of the Tailspintoys.com network. Tailspin Toys has a single network with two firewalls and a perimeter network LAN. Located on the perimeter network LAN is a proxy server that users authenticate against with their domain accounts to gain access to the World Wide Web. Located on the internal LAN is a Windows Server 2003 member server running Software Update Services (SUS). The figure below provides a view of the network.

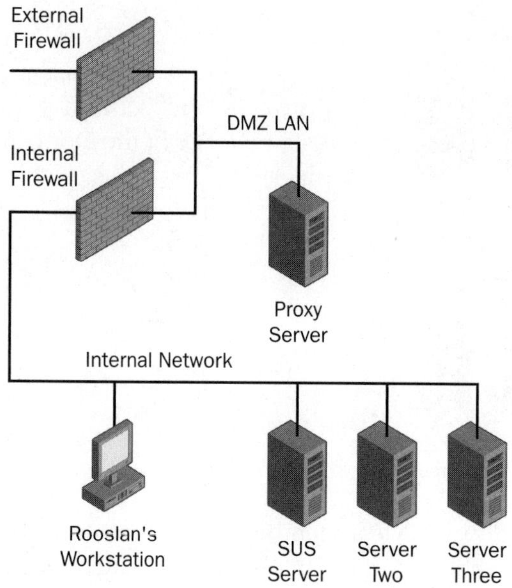

Rooslan wants to scan all of the computers running Windows Server 2003, including server two and server three on his network. Both server two and server three are members of the domain, but they are not currently configured to use the SUS server also located on the internal network. Rooslan's user account is a member of the domain administrators group. Which of the following statements about this situation is true? (Select all that apply.)

A. Rooslan will be able to run the MBSA tool, using the Windows Update servers to provide him with the hotfix checklist, against both server two and server three without any extra configuration.

B. Rooslan will be able to run the MBSA tool and have it use the list of approved hotfixes stored on the SUS server against both server two and server three.

C. Rooslan can run the MBSA tool locally on server two and server three using the Windows Update servers to provide the hotfix checklist.

D. Rooslan can run the MBSA tool locally on server two and server three using the SUS server to provide the hotfix checklist.

E. Rooslan can configure both server two and server three to be clients of the SUS server. He can then run the MBSA tool against these two servers from his workstation.

4. You have a single Windows Server 2003 domain running in native mode. You are responsible for making sure that 500 computers running Windows XP Professional and 20 computers running Windows Server 2003 are kept up to date with the latest security hotfixes from Microsoft. All of these systems are members of the domain. Currently all HTTP traffic at your company must go through a proxy server. All non-proxy HTTP traffic is blocked at the firewall. Your user account is a member of the Domain Administrators group. You want to use the MBSA tool to check which systems on the network require that hotfixes be installed. Which of the following actions could you take to allow this to happen? (Select all that apply.)

A. No extra action needs to be taken to get the MBSA tool to work.

B. Download and install the mssecure.cab file from the Microsoft Web site on the workstation in which you have installed MBSA.

C. Download the mssecure.cab file from the Microsoft Web site. Use Group Policy to deploy this file to each of the systems that you will be scanning remotely.

D. Configure a Windows Server 2003 member system on the network as an SUS server. Approve a list of hotfixes and then run the MBSA tool on your workstation, pointing it at the new SUS server to get its hotfix checklist.

5. You are configuring a security template for a group of computers running Windows Server 2003 that are located in the MemberServer OU on your network. You will be regularly using the MBSA tool to remotely check which hotfixes, if any, are to be installed on these servers. Which of the following services must you not disable in the security template on the computers running Windows Server 2003 if they are to be remotely checked by using the MBSA? (Select all that apply.)

A. Server service

B. Workstation service

C. Remote Registry service

D. File and Print Sharing

E. Client for Microsoft Networks

6. You have a computer running Windows XP Professional on which you have installed the MBSA tool. You want to run the MBSA tool against a four-node active/passive cluster of computers running Windows Server 2003 and IIS on your company's perimeter network LAN. Which of the following conditions need to be met before you will be able to check which hotfixes need to be installed on the servers making up the cluster? (Select all that apply.)

   A. You must install the cluster service on the computer running Windows XP Professional.

   B. You must install the IIS common files on the computer running Windows XP Professional.

   C. That the Windows Server 2003 cluster running IIS be a member of the domain in which your user account can be assigned local administrator privileges, or a domain that is trusted by that domain.

   D. That your workstation have direct HTTP access to an SUS server, that your workstation have direct HTTP access to the Windows Update servers, or that the mssecure.cab file be downloaded and installed on your workstation.

   E. That your user account be a member of the power users group on the Active nodes of the Windows Server 2003 IIS cluster.

7. You are scanning a computer running Windows XP Professional that is connected to the Internet by a cable modem. The system is currently configured with two network cards. This allows you to implement Internet Connection Sharing so that other computers on your home network are able to access the Internet through the computer running Windows XP Professional. You have configured the Internet Connection Firewall on the network card connected to the firewall. You have downloaded and installed the MBSA tool. You are logged on with an account with local administrator access. You run a scan against your local computer with the default options. Which of the following checks will be made against your system? (Select all that apply.)

   A. Local Account Password Test

   B. Restrict Anonymous

   C. Internet Connection Firewall

   D. Remote Desktop

   E. ICS Authentication

8. Parsons is responsible for performing a security audit on four computers running Windows Server. Parsons' account is a member of the Domain Administrators group. The first system is a Windows Server 2003 domain controller. The second is a Windows Server 2003 member server running SQL Server 2000. The third system is a standalone computer running Windows Server 2003 Web Server Edition. This server is located on the company perimeter network. The fourth system is a standalone server running Windows 2000, Host Integration Server, and Services for Unix 3.0, and is located on the internal LAN. All traffic to the Internet must go through a proxy server on the perimeter network that requires authentication. Parsons also has access to an SUS server running on a standalone computer that runs Windows Server 2003.

Parsons has the following goals:

Primary Goal: Develop a customized list of approved and tested patches that can be rolled out to all four computers running Windows Server 2003.

Secondary Goal 1: Ensure that a list is generated for patches that need to be applied to each specific computer that runs Windows Server 2003.

Secondary Goal 2: Patch all computers running Windows Server 2003 so that they are up to date.

Parsons does the following:

He generates a list of approved patches and updates on the SUS server. From a computer running Windows XP Professional, he runs a remote scan with the default options on the first and second Windows Server 2003–based computers. He uses the SUS server to provide mssecure.cab. Using the Remote Desktop client, he logs in to the third server with an Administrator account, downloads the MBSA tool, and runs it from the command line with the default options on the local server. Which of the goals has Parsons met? (Select one.)

- **A.** Parsons has met his primary and all of his secondary goals.
- **B.** Parsons has met his primary goal and one of his secondary goals.
- **C.** Parsons has met his primary goal but none of his secondary goals.
- **D.** Parsons has not met his primary goal but has achieved both of his secondary goals.
- **E.** Parsons has not achieved any of his goals.

Objective 2.2 Answers

1. **Correct Answers: D and F**

   A. **Incorrect:** Exchange Server 5.5 is supported by the MBSA technology in the Software Update Services Feature pack. Appropriate updates can be deployed by using SMS.

   B. **Incorrect:** Office 2000 is supported by the MBSA technology in the Software Update Services Feature pack. Appropriate updates can be deployed by using SMS.

   C. **Incorrect:** Windows NT 4.0 is supported by the MBSA technology in the Software Update Services Feature pack. Appropriate updates can be deployed by using SMS.

   D. **Correct:** Office 97 is not supported by the MBSA tool and in turn is not supported by the Software Update Services Feature Pack for SMS 2.0. The best option in this case would to be to upgrade Office 97 to Office 2000, which can still be run on a workstation running Windows NT 4.0.

   E. **Incorrect:** Internet Explorer 5.01 is supported by the MBSA technology in the Software Update Services Feature pack. Appropriate updates can be deployed by using SMS.

   F. **Correct:** SQL Server 6.5 is not supported by the MBSA tool and in turn is not supported by the Software Update Services Feature Pack for SMS 2.0. Although it would perhaps be somewhat arduous, migrating to SQL Server 7.0, or even SQL Server 2000, should be open to consideration for security reasons.

2. **Correct Answers: A, B, and D**

   A. **Correct:** Server One is a member of the domain, which means that Leo's account has local administrator access. Local administrator access is required for the MBSA tool to work. HTTP access to the Internet means that the Windows Update servers can be contacted by the tool.

   B. **Correct:** Server Two is a member of the domain, which means that Leo's account has local administrator access. Local administrator access is required for the MBSA tool to work. HTTP access to the Internet means that the Windows Update servers can be contacted by the tool.

   C. **Incorrect:** Server Three is a standalone system. The MBSA command-line tool has no provision to authenticate against a remotely scanned system that is not a member of the domain. Because no remote authentication against a standalone system can occur, this system cannot be scanned. The MBSA tool must be run locally on this system by an account that has local administrator rights.

D. **Correct:** Server Four is a member of the domain, which means that Leo's account has local administrator access. Local administrator access is required for the MBSA tool to work. The correct ports are open on the internal firewall for this check to occur. HTTP access to the Internet means that the Windows Update servers can be contacted by the tool.

E. **Incorrect:** Server Five is a standalone system. The MBSA command-line tool has no provision to authenticate against a remotely scanned system that is not a member of the domain. Because no remote authentication against a standalone system can occur, this system cannot be scanned. The MBSA tool must be run locally on this system by an account that has local administrator rights.

F. **Incorrect:** Server Six is a standalone system. The MBSA command-line tool has no provision to authenticate against a remotely scanned system that is not a member of the domain. Because no remote authentication against a standalone system can occur, this system cannot be scanned. The MBSA tool must be run locally on this system by an account that has local administrator rights.

3. **Correct Answers: B, D, and E**

A. **Incorrect:** The MBSA tool cannot authenticate against a proxy server. The MBSA tool either requires direct HTTP access to the Internet or for the administrator to download and install the mssecure.cab file from the Microsoft Web site.

B. **Correct:** Even though server two and server three are not currently configured as clients of the SUS server, the MBSA tool can be configured to run against the SUS server. It is beneficial that a proxy server is in use in this situation because SUS can be configured to communicate by a proxy, whereas the MBSA tool cannot authenticate against a proxy and hence cannot contact the Windows Update servers.

C. **Incorrect:** The MBSA tool cannot authenticate against a proxy server. The MBSA tool either requires direct HTTP access to the Internet or for the administrator to download and install the mssecure.cab file from the Microsoft Web site.

D. **Correct:** Even though server two and server three are not currently configured as clients of the SUS server, the MBSA tool can be configured to run against the SUS server. It is beneficial that a proxy server is in use in this situation because SUS can be configured to communicate by a proxy, whereas the MBSA tool cannot authenticate against a proxy and hence cannot contact the Windows Update servers.

E. **Correct:** When the MBSA tool is run against a remote server, and that remote server is an SUS client, the MBSA tool retrieves the location of the SUS server and uses the checklist located there rather than downloading it from the Windows Update servers.

4. Correct Answers: B and D

A. **Incorrect:** In the current network's configuration, there is no way for the MBSA tool to get access to a hotfix checklist. To get access to such a checklist, either HTTP access needs to be granted through the firewall to your workstation, an SUS server that can generate its own hotfix file needs to be set up, or the mssecure.cab file needs to be downloaded from the Microsoft Web site and installed manually.

B. **Correct:** The mssecure.cab file can be downloaded manually and used as a hotfix checklist. The hotfix checklist is necessary for the MBSA to run and to generate a list of patches that need to be installed.

C. **Incorrect:** Although access to the mssecure.cab file is necessary, because it contains the hotfix checklist, it needs to only be installed on the scanning computer. Installing it on the remotely scanned computer will not help in any way.

D. **Correct:** Although the MBSA tool cannot authenticate against a proxy, at least as of version 1.1.1, which is the version in use when the 70-299 exam was written, SUS can. This means that SUS can be used to build a hotfix checklist that the MBSA tool can then use to check other systems on the network.

5. Correct Answers: A, C, and D

A. **Correct:** The Server service must be enabled on the target system for the MBSA tool to be able to check which hotfixes need to be installed.

B. **Incorrect:** The Workstation service does not need to be installed on the target system, though it does need to be installed on the system running the MBSA scan.

C. **Correct:** The Remote Registry service must be enabled on the target system for the MBSA tool to be able to check which hotfixes need to be installed.

D. **Correct:** The File and Print Sharing service must be enabled on the target system for the MBSA tool to be able to check which hotfixes need to be installed.

E. **Incorrect:** Client for Microsoft Networks is only required on the scanning computer. This service is not required on the target computer.

6. Correct Answers: B, C, and D

A. **Incorrect:** The cluster service cannot be installed on a computer running Windows XP Professional, nor is the cluster service required to successfully run the MBSA tool against a remote Windows Server 2003 IIS Cluster.

B. **Correct:** If you are going to be using the MBSA tool to analyze a system running IIS, the scanning system must have the IIS common files installed so that it can work with the remote system's metabase.

C. **Correct:** The MBSA tool has no ability to authenticate against systems that are not members of the domain or trusted domains. Your user account must have local administrator privileges on both the scanning and the scanned systems.

D. **Correct:** Your workstation must be able to locate the hotfix checklist. This can be done in one of three ways: downloading the checklist manually from Microsoft, using a generated checklist on a local SUS server, or by a direct HTTP connection from your workstation to the Windows Update servers.

E. **Incorrect:** To run MBSA correctly, your user account will need to be a member of the local administrators group on the Windows Server 2003 IIS cluster. Being a member of the power users group is irrelevant as to whether or not the MBSA tool will be able to scan a remote system.

7. **Correct Answers: A and B**

A. **Correct:** Local Account Password Test will check if any accounts on the local system have simple or blank passwords.

B. **Correct:** Restrict Anonymous checks that the workstation is correctly locked down against anonymous access.

C. **Incorrect:** This check is not performed by the MBSA tool.

D. **Incorrect:** There is no test to ascertain whether the remote desktop will accept connections.

E. **Incorrect:** ICS doesn't authenticate. There is also no ICS Authentication test in the MBSA tool.

8. **Correct Answers: B**

A. **Incorrect:** Parsons has met his primary goal by generating a list of approved patches on the SUS server. Creating this list will generate a custom mssecure.cab file that will be used to check against the other servers that Parsons is responsible for. Parsons has met his first secondary goal: the scan will generate the requisite reports. He can remote scan the member servers, but he must locally scan the standalone system. Parsons does not meet his second secondary goal. At no point are the computers running Windows Server 2003 patched. This can be done by forcing them to use the SUS server or by deploying patches by the SUS server.

B. **Correct:** Parsons has met his primary goal by generating a list of approved patches on the SUS server. Creating this list will generate a custom mssecure.cab file which will be used to check against the other servers that Parsons is responsible for. Parsons has met his first secondary goal: the scan will generate the requisite reports. He can remote scan the member servers, but he must locally scan the standalone system. Parsons does not meet his second secondary goal. At no point are the Windows Server 2003 systems patched. This can be done by forcing them to use the SUS server or by deploying patches by the SUS server.

C. **Incorrect:** Parsons has met his primary goal by generating a list of approved patches on the SUS server. Creating this list will generate a custom mssecure.cab file that will be used to check against the other servers that Parsons is responsible for. The fourth server runs Windows 2000 and hence is not included in any goal listed in the question. Parsons has met his first secondary goal: the scan will generate the requisite reports. He can remote scan the member servers, but he must locally scan the standalone system. Parsons does not meet his second secondary goal. At no point are the computers running Windows Server 2003 patched. This can be done by forcing them to use the SUS server or by deploying patches by the SUS server.

D. **Incorrect:** Parsons has met his primary goal by generating a list of approved patches on the SUS server. Creating this list will generate a custom mssecure.cab file that will be used to check against the other servers that Parsons is responsible for. The fourth server runs Windows 2000 and hence is not included in any goal listed in the question. Parsons has met his first secondary goal: the scan will generate the requisite reports. He can remote scan the member servers, but he must locally scan the standalone system. Parsons does not meet his second secondary goal. At no point are the computers running Windows Server 2003 patched. This can be done by forcing them to use the SUS server or by deploying patches by the SUS server.

E. **Incorrect:** Parsons has met his primary goal by generating a list of approved patches on the SUS server. Creating this list will generate a custom mssecure.cab file that will be used to check against the other servers that Parsons is responsible for. The fourth server runs Windows 2000 and hence is not included in any goal listed in the question. Parsons has met his first secondary goal: the scan will generate the requisite reports. He can remote scan the member servers, but he must locally scan the standalone system. Parsons does not meet his second secondary goal. At no point are the computers running Windows Server 2003 patched. This can be done by forcing them to use the SUS server or by deploying patches by the SUS server.

Objective 2.3

Deploy Service Packs and Hotfixes

Utilities like the MBSA tool, covered in the previous section, can generate a list for the systems administrator of the service packs and hotfixes which need to be applied to the system. Once this list exists, and the hotfixes or service packs have been tested, it is time for the systems administrator to patch systems running on a production network. Even when you have extensively tested patches and hotfixes in a non-production lab, coming to the point where you apply them to a mission critical server can be nerve-wracking. In the back of every systems administrator's mind is the thought, "What if something goes wrong?" In Objective 2.1 we covered how you can plan for that eventuality. Objective 2.3 deals with the practicalities of getting service packs and hotfixes out onto the systems that are being used by people in your organization. The traditional method of installing such patches is to burn them onto a CD-ROM or copy them to a convenient network share and send members of the support team out to manually update each system by hand.

Objective 2.3 Questions

1. You are the systems administrator responsible for maintaining 20 computers running Windows Server 2003, Web Edition, at a large Web-hosting company named A. Datum Corporation. You administer each system remotely by means of the Remote Desktop client. Each computer running Windows Server 2003, Web Edition, has a separate partition named drive Z that hosts the \i386 installation files. This is so that as components are added or removed you do not have to go down to the server cage and manually insert the installation media. Last month Microsoft released the first service pack for Windows Server 2003. After testing this in the lab on development computers, you are ready to install it on the 20 production systems. You log on to the first system using the Remote Desktop client and download the service pack from the FTP server where you keep it. You create a directory called z:\w2k3sp1 and copy the file there. You then run a command prompt on the Web Edition server and from the z:\w2k3sp1 directory issue the

```
w2k3sp1.exe -x
```

command and specify the z:\w2k3sp1 directory when the routine asks you where you want to place the files. When this is done you use Windows Explorer to navigate to the z:\w2k3sp1\i386\update directory and run the update.exe command, installing Windows Server 2003 Service Pack 1 on the Web server. After the service pack is installed, you reboot the server and log back on by the Remote Desktop connection. At this point you want to update the files in the z:\i386 directory so that if you install new components you will not have to re-apply Service Pack 1. Which of the commands listed below, if issued from the command line in the z:\w2k3sp1\i386\update directory on the computer running Windows Server 2003, Web Edition, will update the z:\i386 files? (Select one.)

   A. slipstream.exe –s:z:\i386

   B. update.exe –s:c:\windows\system32

   C. slipstream.exe –s:c:\windows\system32

   D. upgrade.exe –s:z:\i386

   E. update.exe –s:z:\i386

2. Oksana is responsible for administering five Windows Server 2003 member servers for the A. Datum Corporation. Each computer running Windows Server 2003 has been patched to Service Pack 1 and is up to date with the most recent hotfixes from the Microsoft Web site. The role of two of the servers has recently changed. Rather than providing basic file and print services, the first server will now be deployed as a Web server on the Internet. Similarly, the second server will move from providing file and print services to working as an SUS server. To retask the servers, Oksana uses the Add/Remove Windows Components section of Add/Remove programs to install Internet Information Services. On the first server she configures the new Web site and imports the relevant data. On the second server she installs and configures SUS. When she is asked to provide a location for the files, she inserts her original installation media into the CD-ROM drive. Which of the following steps should Oksana take next to ensure that both servers are up to date with hotfixes and service packs? (Select one.)

   A. Oksana should run the IIS lockdown tool on each server.

   B. Oksana should reinstall Service Pack 1 and then reinstall all hotfixes.

   C. Oksana should reinstall all hotfixes.

   D. Oksana should reinstall Service Pack 1.

   E. Oksana doesn't have to do anything. Her system will be up to date.

3. Rooslan is the systems administrator of a Windows Server 2003 functional level domain that encompasses two locations separated by an ISDN BRI link. The name of the domain is adatum.com. All servers on the A. Datum Corporation network run Windows Server 2003, and all clients run Windows XP Professional patched to Service Pack 1. Presently, each system on the network independently contacts the Microsoft Windows Update service to obtain all hotfixes and service packs. This has led to two problems for your organization. The first problem is that any update Microsoft flags as relevant is being downloaded and installed onto systems in the organization. Some updates have caused problems with preexisting custom applications used for the organization's front line business. Another problem has been an increased bill for Internet traffic as 500 computers running Windows XP all successfully download the exact same file individually from the Windows Update Servers. Rooslan has the following goals:

   Primary Goal: To put in place a system where only approved updates are deployed to all of the organization's computers running Windows XP Professional and Windows Server 2003.

   Secondary Goal One: To ensure that each individual update is only downloaded once to the organization.

   Secondary Goal Two: To ensure that updates are installed automatically at 7:00 P.M. every Thursday.

Rooslan takes the following steps. On the network of one of the computers running Windows Server 2003, he installs Software Update Services. This server is renamed susupdates.adatum.com. He synchronizes this with Microsoft Windows Update services and then selects a set of approved service packs and hotfixes. On a domain controller he creates a new GPO. In the Computer Configuration\Administrative Templates\Windows Components\Windows Update node he configures the following policies:

Configure Automatic Updates: Enabled. Auto Download and schedule the install. Install Day Thursday. Install time 19:00.

Specify intranet Microsoft update service location: Enabled. Set the intranet update service for detecting updates: http://susupdates.adatum.com. Set the intranet statistics server: http://susupdates.adatum.com.

Rooslan then applies the GPO to the default site in Active Directory. When Rooslan has completed this step, how many of his goals has he achieved? (Select one.)

- **A.** Rooslan has achieved his primary goal and both secondary goals.
- **B.** Rooslan has achieved his primary goal and one secondary goal.
- **C.** Rooslan has achieved only his primary goal.
- **D.** Rooslan has not achieved his primary goal, but he has achieved both secondary goals.
- **E.** Rooslan has achieved none of his goals.

4. You are the systems administrator of an organization that has a mix of Windows Server 2003–based systems, some Windows 2000 member servers running Exchange 2000, and clients running Windows XP Professional and Windows 2000. All are members of a Windows Server 2003 functional level domain. Microsoft has recently released a hotfix that applies to Windows Server 2003, Windows XP, Windows 2000 Server, and Windows 2000 Professional. The names of the hotfix files are as follows:

Windows2000-KB823182-x86-ENU.exe

WindowsXP-KB823182-x86-ENU.exe

WindowsServer2003-KB823182-x86-ENU.exe

Which of the following methods should you use to deploy the relevant hotfix to the correct computers in the domain? (Select one.)

A. Create three security groups: 2000hotfix, Xphotfix, and 2003hotfix. Add the computer accounts of all of the systems to the relevant group. Place the hotfixes on a globally accessible network share. Write a unique script for each group that installs the hotfix. Edit the group properties and assign the relevant unique script to the appropriate group.

B. Write a unique script for each operating system group that installs the hotfix. Using the new multiple select feature of Active Directory Users and Computers, select all of the computer accounts from a particular group. From the Profile tab, assign the appropriate unique logon script to its appropriate group.

C. Create three security groups; 2000hotfix, Xphotfix, and 2003hotfix. Add the computer accounts of all of the systems to the relevant group. Place the hotfixes on a globally accessible network share. Write a unique script for each group that installs the corresponding hotfix. Create three GPOs. Call the first 2000hotfix_deploy. In the Computer Configuration\Windows Settings\Scripts node, add the unique Windows 2000 hotfix installation script to the startup policy. Call the second GPO XPhotfix_deploy. In the Computer Configuration\Windows Settings\Scripts node, add the unique Windows XP hotfix installation script to the startup policy. Call the final GPO 2003hotfix_deploy. In the Computer Configuration\Windows Settings\Scripts node, add the unique Windows Server 2003 hotfix installation script to the startup policy. Apply each of these GPOs to the Builtin Computers group. Remove the authenticated users group from the Read and Apply Group Policy (allow) permission on all GPOs. On each GPO, assign the Read and Apply Group Policy (allow) permission to the corresponding security group. For example, for the 2000hotfix_deploy GPO, set the permission for the 2000hotfix group to Read and Apply Group Policy (allow).

D. Create three security groups: 2000hotfix, Xphotfix, and 2003hotfix. Add the computer accounts of all of the systems to the relevant group. Place the hotfixes on a globally accessible network share. Write a unique script for each group that installs the corresponding hotfix. Create three GPOs. Call the first 2000hotfix_deploy. In the Computer Configuration\Windows Settings\Scripts node, add the unique Windows 2000 hotfix installation script to the startup policy. Call the second GPO XPhotfix_deploy. In the Computer Configuration\Windows Settings\Scripts node, add the unique Windows XP hotfix installation script to the startup policy. Call the final GPO 2003hotfix_deploy. In the Computer Configuration\Windows Settings\Scripts node, add the unique Windows Server 2003 hotfix installation script to the startup policy. Apply each of these GPOs to the domain. Remove the authenticated users group from the Read and Apply Group Policy (allow) permission on all GPOs. On each GPO, assign the Read and Apply Group Policy (allow) permission to the corresponding security group. For example, for the 2000hotfix_deploy GPO, set the permission for the 2000hotfix group to Read and Apply Group Policy (allow).

5. Your Windows Server 2003 domain is made up of five computers running Windows Server 2003, 70 computers running Windows 2000 Professional, and 30 computers running Windows XP Professional. Your organization has a policy that no one staff member is assigned a particular office or desk. When workers arrive each morning they are assigned a desk automatically. Depending on when they arrive in the morning, a user could be using a computer running Windows XP Professional or a computer running Windows 2000 Professional. Your company has three different locations spread out across the city. Last week the fifth service pack for Windows 2000 was released. You want to roll out this service pack only to the computers that run Windows 2000 Professional in your organization. Which of the following methods will allow you to do this? (Select all that apply.)

   A. Extract the Windows 2000 service pack to a shared folder and locate the update.msi file. Create a new OU named 2KPRO. Move all of the computer accounts for the 2KPRO systems into this OU. Create a new GPO and assign it to the 2KPRO OU. In the Computer Configuration\Software Settings\Software Installation node, add the update.msi file from the service pack as software to be installed. Ensure that, on the Deployment tab of the service pack software deployment properties, the option Uninstall This Application When It Falls Out Of The Scope Of Management is enabled.

   B. Extract the Windows 2000 service pack to a shared folder and locate the update.msi file. Create a new GPO and assign it to the domain. In the Computer Configuration\Software Settings\Software Installation node, add the update.msi file from the service pack as software to be installed. Ensure that, on the Deployment tab of the service pack software deployment properties, the option Uninstall This Application When It Falls Out Of The Scope Of Management is enabled.

   C. Copy the Windows 2000 service pack to a shared folder on the network. Create a new OU named 2KPRO. Move all of the computer accounts for the 2KPRO systems into this OU. Create a script that installs the service pack without the requirement of intervention from the user. Create a new GPO and assign it to the 2KPRO OU. In the Computer Configuration\Windows Settings\scripts node, add the new script as a startup script.

   D. Copy the Windows 2000 service pack to a shared folder on the network. Create a new OU named 2KPRO. Move all of the computer accounts for the 2KPRO systems into this OU. Create a script that installs the service pack without the requirement of intervention from the user. Create a new GPO and assign it to the domain. In the Computer Configuration\Windows Settings\scripts node, add the new script as a startup script.

E. Extract the Windows 2000 service pack to a shared folder and locate the update.msi file. Create a new GPO and assign it to the head office site. In the Computer Configuration\Software Settings\Software Installation node, add the update.msi file from the service pack as software to be installed. Ensure that, on the Deployment tab of the service pack software deployment properties, the option Uninstall This Application When It Falls Out Of The Scope Of Management is enabled.

6. After he left the company, you learned that one of your junior administrators manually installed Windows XP Service Pack 3 on at least 30 computers in the domain. This was done before any systematic pilot program had assessed what effects, if any, deployment of the service pack would have on the organization. You want to uninstall this service pack until you've had time to perform a proper trial and assess the impact of the service pack. The problem is that you do not know which of the computers running Windows XP Professional have been affected by the junior administrator's actions. Checking the job log, you find that since the release of the service pack several months ago the junior administrator worked on at least 80 computers. Although your company spans five different locations, it appears that the last time the junior administrator went out to one of them was two weeks before the service pack was released by Microsoft. Which of the following methods could you use to uninstall the service pack with the least administrative effort? (Select one.)

A. Create a Group Policy object and apply it to the site where the junior administrator worked. In this Group Policy object, assign a software deletion policy and add Windows XP Service Pack 3.

B. Create a Group Policy object and apply it to the site where the junior administrator worked. In this software policy object, assign a software installation policy and install Windows XP Service Pack 3. After all computers running Windows XP have installed Service Pack 3, remove the service pack from the software installation policy.

C. Write a script that calls the program.

%systemroot%\$ntservicepackuninstall$\spuninst\spuninst.exe –u –q

Create a Group Policy object and apply it to the site where the junior administrator worked. In this Group Policy object, in the Computer Configuration\Windows Settings\Scripts node, add the newly created script that calls spuninst.exe.

D. Place the service pack on a network share that is accessible to all users in the domain. Write a script that calls the program.

xpsp3_en_x86.exe –x

from the network share location. Create a Group Policy object and apply it to the site where the junior administrator worked. In this Group Policy Object, in the Computer Configuration\Windows Settings\Scripts node, add the newly created script that calls xpsp3_en_x86.exe –x

Objective 2.3 Answers

1. **Correct Answers: E**

   A. **Incorrect:** Although this process is known as slipstreaming, this is not the command used to update the files in the z:\i386 directory. The correct command is update.exe –s:z:\i386.

   B. **Incorrect:** Although the switch applied to the update command is correct, the target folder in this case is the c:\windows\system32 directory rather than the z:\i386 directory. The correct command is update.exe –s:z:\i386.

   C. **Incorrect:** Although this process is known as slipstreaming, this is not the command used to update the files in the z:\i386 directory. The correct command is update.exe –s:z:\i386.

   D. **Incorrect:** This command is quite close, but uses upgrade, which does not exist, rather than the required update. The correct command is update.exe –s:z:\i386.

   E. **Correct:** This is the correct command. The –s switch indicates that the service pack is to be slipstreamed into the current installation files, updating them so that they reflect the changes issued in the new service pack. This is a useful systems administrator trick because it ensures that if components need to be added or removed from the system at a later stage, the service pack will not need to be reapplied; the files will already be up to date.

2. **Correct Answers: B**

   A. **Incorrect:** Although it is good practice after a new installation of Internet Information Server to run the IIS lockdown tool, this will do nothing to ensure that Oksana's server is up to date with hotfixes and service packs By installing from the original installation media, you could reintroduce to the system a fault that has since been repaired by the application of a hotfix or service pack. This is why the service pack should be reapplied, unless the installation media has had the service pack slipstreamed into it.

   B. **Correct:** After new components have been added to a Windows Server 2003 system, you should always go back and reapply any service packs or hotfixes that you have applied previously. By installing from the original installation media, you could reintroduce to the system a fault that has since been repaired by the application of a hotfix or service pack. The reinstallation of the service pack can be avoided if the service pack has been slipstreamed into the installation files.

C. **Incorrect:** Oksana will need to reinstall Service Pack 1 and all hotfixes. By installing from the original installation media, you could reintroduce to the system a fault that has since been repaired by the application of a hotfix or service pack. The reinstallation of the service pack can be avoided if the service pack has been slipstreamed into the installation files.

D. **Incorrect:** Oksana will need to reinstall Service Pack 1 and all hotfixes. By installing from the original installation media, you could reintroduce to the system a fault that has since been repaired by the application of a hotfix or service pack. The reinstallation of the service pack can be avoided if the service pack has been slipstreamed into the installation files.

E. **Incorrect:** Oksana will need to reinstall Service Pack 1 and all hotfixes. By installing from the original installation media, you could reintroduce to the system a fault that has since been repaired by the application of a hotfix or service pack. The reinstallation of the service pack can be avoided if the service pack has been slipstreamed into the installation files.

3. **Correct Answers: E**

A. **Incorrect:** Although he did everything correctly, because he applied the Group Policy to the default site rather than the domain, only computers at the default site are influenced by this policy. This means that computers at the second site will still be downloading their updates from Microsoft; they will ignore any list of approved updates and will install updates on an unscheduled basis. On the other hand, all of the computers at the default site will download only approved updates from the SUS server and install them on Thursday evening at 7:00 P.M., and they will not contact the Windows Update servers at all.

B. **Incorrect:** Although he did everything correctly, because he applied the Group Policy to the default site rather than the domain, only computers at the default site are influenced by this policy. This means that computers at the second site will still be downloading their updates from Microsoft; they will ignore any list of approved updates and will install updates on an unscheduled basis. On the other hand, all of the computers at the default site will download only approved updates from the SUS server and install them on Thursday evening at 7:00 P.M., and they will not contact the Windows Update servers at all.

C. **Incorrect:** Although he did everything correctly, because he applied the Group Policy to the default site rather than the domain, only computers at the default site are influenced by this policy. This means that computers at the second site will still be downloading their updates from Microsoft; they will ignore any list of approved updates and will install updates on an unscheduled basis. On the other hand, all of the computers at the default site will download only approved updates from the SUS server and install them on Thursday evening at 7:00 P.M., and they will not contact the Windows Update servers at all.

D. **Incorrect:** Although he did everything correctly, because he applied the Group Policy to the default site rather than the domain, only computers at the default site are influenced by this policy. This means that computers at the second site will still be downloading their updates from Microsoft; they will ignore any list of approved updates and will install updates on an unscheduled basis. On the other hand, all of the computers at the default site will download only approved updates from the SUS server and install them on Thursday evening at 7:00 P.M., and they will not contact the Windows Update servers at all.

E. **Correct:** Although he did everything correctly, because he applied the Group Policy to the default site rather than the domain, only computers at the default site are influenced by this policy. This means that computers at the second site will still be downloading their updates from Microsoft; they will ignore any list of approved updates and will install updates on an unscheduled basis. On the other hand, all of the computers at the default site will download only approved updates from the SUS server and install them on Thursday evening at 7:00 P.M., and they will not contact the Windows Update servers at all.

4. **Correct Answers: D**

A. **Incorrect:** Login scripts cannot be assigned by editing group properties.

B. **Incorrect:** Although user account objects have a Profile tab where logon scripts can be assigned, this is not true for computer account objects.

C. **Incorrect:** Group Policy objects cannot be applied to the Builtin Computers group.

D. **Correct:** To make sure that every computer in the domain gets the relevant hotfix, you'll need to apply Group Policy at the domain level. Use security group membership to limit the scope of the Group Policy to only those systems that are appropriate. This way only the computers running Windows 2000 will be influenced by the 2000hotfix_deploy GPO, and only the computers running Windows XP will be influenced by the XPhotfix_deploy GPO.

5. **Correct Answers: A and C**

A. **Correct:** This will deploy the service pack by the Active Directory software deployment settings to the computers running Windows 2000 Professional. This will not deploy the software to other systems within the domain. Note that if a system is removed from the OU, the service pack will be uninstalled.

B. **Incorrect:** This will attempt to install the service pack on all systems within the domain, not just the computers running Windows 2000 Professional.

C. **Correct:** This method of installing the service pack will also work. The downside to using this method is that it does not give you the fine level of control that installing by deployment of the update.msi would.

D. **Incorrect:** This will attempt to install the service pack on all computers within the domain. It will not limit itself to computers running Windows 2000.

E. **Incorrect:** This will apply the service pack to all computers within the head office site. It will not limit itself to the computers running Windows 2000.

6. **Correct Answers: C**

A. **Incorrect:** Software can only be removed by means of the software installation node of Group Policy if it was installed by that method. Because the junior administrator installed the software manually, this method cannot be used to uninstall it.

B. **Incorrect:** This method certainly does not involve the minimum amount of administrative effort. It is also unlikely that it will work properly because those systems that already have Service Pack 3 installed will ignore the policy.

C. **Correct:** When applied, the script will call spuninst.exe, which in turn will uninstall the service pack.

D. **Incorrect:** This will merely extract Service Pack 3; running this particular command will do nothing to uninstall Service Pack 3 from the systems where it was installed.

15 Implementing, Managing, and Troubleshooting Security for Network Communications (3.0)

IP Security (IPSec) is a network layer technology that is used to secure communications. IPSec encrypts the information carried by Internet Protocol (IP) datagrams. This means that even if these packets are captured, the data contained within the packets exists only in an encrypted form and cannot be read by the interceptor. IPSec has been supported natively since Microsoft Windows 2000. Microsoft Windows Server 2003 ships with three default IPSec policies that can be applied by means of Group Policy objects (GPOs) or local policy. These policies are as follows:

- Client (Respond Only). When this policy is configured, the computer will use IPSec only if its communication partner requests that such a connection be established. The client itself will not request that IPSec be used.
- Server (Request Security). When this policy is configured, the computer will request that its communication partner use IPSec. If the communication partner is unable to service this request, communication will continue in an insecure manner.
- Secure Server (Require Security). When this policy is configured, the computer will communicate only with partners that support IPSec.

On top of this set of IPSec policies, specific policies can be created that are more specific. These policies can be restricted to specific hosts, subnets, and protocols. Custom policies can also be deployed by means of GPOs or local policy.

IPSec is considered by many to be the future of communication. Without IPSec, transmissions across a network are unencrypted. Such transmissions can be intercepted by packet sniffing utilities. This could potentially lead to valuable information falling into the hands of unauthorized parties. With IPSec, even if communication is intercepted, it cannot be read because the content is encrypted.

Testing Skills and Suggested Practices

The skills that you need to successfully master the Implementing, Managing, and Troubleshooting Security for Network Communications objective domain on Exam 70-299: *Implementing and Administering Security in a Microsoft Windows Server 2003 Network* include:

- Apply IPSec policies.
  - Practice 1: Requires two computers, both members of the same domain. Configure one computer with the Server (Request Security) local policy. Install a File Transfer Protocol (FTP) server by means of Internet Information Server (IIS) on this computer. Test that it works by connecting to the server from the local host. Configure a second computer without an IPSec security policy. Attempt to connect to the FTP server. You will be able to, although the connection will not be encrypted by IPSec.
  - Practice 2: Requires two computers, both members of the same domain. Configure one computer with the Secure Server (Require Security) local policy. Install an FTP server by means of IIS on this computer. Test that it works by connecting to the server from the local host. Configure a second computer without an IPSec security policy. Attempt to connect to the FTP server. When this does not work, edit the local policy on the second computer, and set the IPSec policy to Client (Respond Only). Attempt to connect to the FTP server from the second computer. This time the connection will work and traffic passing between the two systems will be encrypted.
- Create individual IPSec policies.
  - Practice 1: Requires two computers, both members of the same domain. On the first computer, edit the local policy object. In the Computer Configuration\Windows Settings\Security Settings\IP Security policies node, create a new IPSec policy by using the wizard. Activate the default response rule, which uses Active Directory default authentication. Add a new security rule. Do not specify a tunnel. Then Set Network Type as All Network Connections. Set Authentication to Active Directory default. Set the rule for all IP traffic. Set the filter action to Require Security. Ensure that the second computer has no IPSec policy set. Try to ping the first computer. Now configure a Client (Respond Only) policy on the second computer. Try to ping the first computer again. You should meet with success.
  - Practice 2: Requires two computers. The two computers do not need to be members of the same domain. On the first computer, edit the local policy object. In the Computer Configuration\Windows Settings\Security Settings\IP Security policies node, create a new IPSec policy by using the wizard. When asked for the Default Response Rule Authentication Method, select Preshared

Key. Enter a key with the value "Quis Custodiet Custodes". Add a new security rule. Do not specify a tunnel. Set Network Type as All Network Connections. Set Authentication to Select Preshared Key. Enter a key with the value "Quis Custodiet Custodes". Set the rule for all IP traffic. Set the filter action to Require Security. Configure a Client (Respond Only) policy on the second computer. Try to ping the first computer. Because the Client (Respond Only) defaults to Active Directory authentication, no authentication will be able to be negotiated. On the second computer, edit the properties of the Client (Respond Only) IPSec policy. Edit the <Dynamic> rule. On the Authentication Methods tab, select Add, and then add the preshared key "Quis Custodiet Custodes". Apply the policy. Try to ping the first computer again. Now that both computers have the same shared key, you should meet with success.

- Use the netsh ipsec utility.
  - Practice 1: Run a command prompt on a single computer running Windows Server 2003. Investigate the properties of the Secure Server (Require Security) policy by issuing the following commands:
    - `netsh`
    - `ipsec`
    - `static`
    - `show policy "Secure Server (Require Security)" verbose`
  - Practice 2: Assign one of the default IPSec policies to the local policy by using the command line. Examine the default local policy and ensure that no IPSec policies are set. Assign the Secure Server (Require Security) policy by issuing the following command sequence at the command prompt:
    - `netsh`
    - `ipsec`
    - `static`
    - `set policy name="Secure Server (Require Security)" assign=yes`
  - Verify that this procedure has worked by using the default local policy Microsoft Management Console (MMC) and checking that the Secure Server (Require Security) policy has been set.
- Troubleshoot IPSec.
  - Practice 1: Open a Microsoft Management Console (MMC). Using the Add/Remove snap-in feature, add the IP Security Monitor console. Configure an IPSec policy on the server on which you are running the console. Configure a similar policy on another computer within your test domain. In the IP Security Monitor console, view the Security Associations node under the Main

Mode node. Enable some Transmission Control Protocol/Internet Protocol (TCP/IP) traffic to pass between the two computers within your test domain (and ensure that both are not using client-only policies). View information about the connections in the Security Associations node.

- ❑ Practice 2: Run `netsh` from the command line on a computer running Windows Server 2003 and set the computer to the `ipsec dynamic` context. After you have done this, run the `show config` command to display config behavior. Run the `show mmsas` command to view the security associations.

- Implement security for wireless networks.
  - ❑ Practice 1: Log on to a domain controller and create a new GPO. Navigate to the Computer Configuration\Windows Settings\Security Settings\Wireless Network (IEEE 802.11) Policies node. Right-click the node and then click Create A New Wireless Policy. This will launch the Welcome To The Wireless Network Policy Wizard. Continue to click Next until you reach the Properties tab. Set the Networks To Access to Access Point (Infrastructure) Networks Only.
  - ❑ Practice 2: Edit the properties of the wireless network policy you created in practice 1. Click the Preferred Networks tab. Click Add. View the WEP properties. Select the IEEE 802.1x key. View the different Extensible Authentication Protocol (EAP) types available by clicking the Settings button. It does not matter if you don't actually have access to a wireless network; the purpose of this practice is to familiarize yourself with the options available in the policies.
- Install and reenroll SSL certificates.
  - ❑ Practice 1: Install an enterprise root certification authority (CA) in your test domain. Log on to the CA by using the Web browser on another computer running Windows Server 2003. Use the URL *http://enterprisecaname.domain/certsrv*. Once you have logged on, select the Request A Certificate option. Then submit an Advanced Certificate Request. Next, select Create And Submit A Request To This CA. In the Advanced Certificate Request form, note the various types of certificates available. In this case, request a Server Authentication certificate.
  - ❑ Practice 2: On the enterprise root CA in your test domain, run the Certificate Templates console. This can be done by clicking Start, clicking Run, and then typing certtmpl.msc. After you have run the Certificate Templates console, right-click the Domain Controller Authentication certificate template and click Reenroll All Certificate Holders.
- Configure remote access security.
  - ❑ Practice 1: Install Routing and Remote Access (RRAS) on one of your test computers running Windows Server 2003. This can be done from the Administrative Tools menu by running the Routing and Remote Access MMC. Right-

click the server and then click Configure Routing and Remote Access to run the Routing And Remote Access Server Setup Wizard. Set up the RRAS server for remote access (dial-up or VPN); it doesn't matter if you don't have a modem installed on the server. Select the Dial-up check box. Set IP addresses to be assigned from a range, and choose a range of five free IP addresses on your network. Click Next. Let Routing and Remote Access authenticate connection requests. Click Finish. Once the server is configured, right-click the Remote Access Policies node in the Routing and Remote Access console and then click New Remote Access Policy. Select the Use The Wizard To Set Up A Typical Policy For A Common Scenario option, and give the policy the name TEST2. Click Next. Use dial-up as the access method for which the policy is created. Grant access based on permissions specified in the user account. Set the Authentication Methods to MS-CHAP v2 Only. Set the Policy Encryption Level to Strongest Encryption Only. Click Finish.

- Practice 2: Install and run the Connection Manager Administration Kit (CMAK). The kit can be installed by running the Add/Remove Windows Components Wizard in Management And Monitoring tools. After the kit is installed, run it from the Administrative Tools menu. Create a new profile, click Next, and then give the profile the service name and file name test1. Click Next. Do not add a realm name. Click Next. Click Next again when you get to the Merging Profile Information page. Click Next on the VPN Support page. Clear the Automatically Download Phonebook Updates check box, and then click Next. On the Dial-up Networking Entries page, edit the test1<default> profile. On the Security tab, set the security setting to Use Advanced Security Settings. Configure the advanced security settings to require encryption. Clear the CHAP check box. Click OK. Click OK again to return to the Dial-up Networking Entries page. Continue to click Next until the service profile is built, taking note of the different options available.

Further Reading

This section lists supplemental readings by objective. We recommend that you study these sources thoroughly before taking this exam.

Objective 3.1 Review Chapter 9, "Deploying and Troubleshooting IPSec"

Microsoft Corporation. Windows Server 2003 Help and Support Center. Review "Internet Protocol Security."

Microsoft Corporation. Windows Server 2003 Help and Support Center. Review "Internet Protocol Security Overview."

Microsoft Corporation. *Microsoft Windows Server 2003 Deployment Kit.* Volume: Deploying Network Services. Redmond, Washington. Microsoft Press, 2003.

Microsoft Corporation. *Microsoft Windows 2000 Server Resource Kit.* Volume: Windows 2000 Server TCP/IP Core Networking Guide. Redmond, Washington. Microsoft Press, 2000.

Objective 3.2 Review Chapter 9, "Deploying and Troubleshooting IPSec."

Microsoft Corporation. Windows Server 2003 Help and Support Center. Review "Internet Protocol Security."

Microsoft Corporation. Windows Server 2003 Help and Support Center. Review "Internet Protocol Security Overview."

Microsoft Corporation. *Microsoft Windows Server 2003 Deployment Kit.* Volume: Deploying Network Services. Redmond, Washington. Microsoft Press, 2003.

Microsoft Corporation. *Microsoft Windows 2000 Server Resource Kit.* Volume: Windows 2000 Server TCP/IP Core Networking Guide. Redmond, Washington. Microsoft Press, 2000.

Objective 3.3 Review Chapter 9, "Deploying and Troubleshooting IPSec."

Microsoft Corporation. Windows Server 2003 Help and Support Center. Review "Managing IPSec from the Command Line."

Microsoft Corporation. Windows Server 2003 Help and Support Center. Review "Netsh Commands for Internet Protocol Security (IPSec)."

Microsoft Corporation. *Microsoft Windows Server 2003 Deployment Kit.* Volume: Deploying Network Services. Redmond, Washington. Microsoft Press, 2003.

Microsoft Corporation. *Microsoft Windows 2000 Server Resource Kit.* Volume: Windows 2000 Server TCP/IP Core Networking Guide. Redmond, Washington. Microsoft Press, 2000.

Objective 3.4 Review Chapter 9, "Deploying and Troubleshooting IPSec."

Microsoft Corporation. Windows Server 2003 Help and Support Center. Review "Internet Protocol Security."

Microsoft Corporation. Windows Server 2003 Help and Support Center. Review "Internet Protocol Security Overview."

Review IPSec troubleshooting tools on Microsoft TechNet: *http://www.microsoft.com/technet/prodtechnol/windowsserver2003/proddocs/standard/sag_ipsec_tools.asp*

Objective 3.5 Review Chapter 10, "Planning and Implementing Security for Wireless Networks."

Microsoft Corporation. Windows Server 2003 Help and Support Center. Review "Security Information for Wireless Networks."

Microsoft Corporation. Windows Server 2003 Help and Support Center. Review "Understanding 802.1X Authentication for Wireless Networks."

Microsoft Corporation. Windows Server 2003 Help and Support Center. Review "Define Preferred Wireless Networks in Group Policy."

Objective 3.6 Review Chapter 2, "Planning and Configuring an Authorization Strategy."

Review Chapter 3, "Deploying and Troubleshooting Security Templates."

Review configuring SSL on Microsoft SQL Server 2000 on Microsoft TechNet: *http://support.microsoft.com/default.aspx?scid=kb;en-us;276553&sd=tech*

Review certificate autoenrollment in Windows XP on Microsoft TechNet: *http://www.microsoft.com/technet/treeview/default.asp?url=/technet/prodtechnol/winxppro /maintain/certenrl.asp?frame=true*

Objective 3.7 Review Chapter 12, "Securing Remote Access."

Review the Connection Manager Administration Kit on Microsoft TechNet: *http://www.microsoft.com/technet/treeview/default.asp?url=/technet/prodtechnol/windowsserver2003/proddocs/standard/cmak_ops_03.asp*

Microsoft Corporation. Windows Server 2003 Help and Support Center. Review "Security Information for Remote Access: Routing and Remote Access."

Microsoft Corporation. Windows Server 2003 Help and Support Center. Review "Virtual Private Networking with IPSec."

Microsoft Corporation. Windows Server 2003 Help and Support Center. Review "Tunneling Protocols: Routing and Remote Access."

Objective 3.1

Plan IPSec Deployment

IPSec is a complex technology that can effectively secure the network communications of an organization. Understanding the functionality of IPSec and the roles of various policy options is important to ensure that communications are secure. An administrator who applies the Server (Request Security) policy may believe that this will lead to secure communications on the network, but this will only be the case if all other clients on the network have an appropriate IPSec policy applied. If, for example, there is a computer on the network running Windows XP Professional that does not have an IPSec policy applied, and the Server (Request Security) policy is in general use, transmissions between this computer and any other computer in the domain will be insecure. Because the only way to test whether communications are encrypted is to capture traffic and analyze it, it is better to ensure that the right policies are applied. This is much better than attempting to debug policies by capturing traffic to determine which of the clients on the network is transmitting in an insecure fashion.

Objective 3.1 Questions

1. You are the security administrator for a medium-sized financial consulting firm, and you are investigating ways to keep the company documents secure. Currently, all documents stored on the server are encrypted by means of Encrypting File System (EFS). These documents contain extremely sensitive financial information about clients of your firm. These documents are also copied from the servers to portable computers so that they can be worked on after business hours. Sometimes documents are copied between portable computers. All of the servers at your company are running Windows Server 2003. All of the portable computers at your company are running Windows XP Professional. Documents stored on portable computers are also encrypted. You want to ensure that all documents transmitted across the network are also encrypted, so that if somehow the building's internal wirings were tapped, no useful information could be retrieved. Which IPSec policy should you deploy to all computers at your organization to meet this goal? (Select all that apply.)

   A. No policy is required.

   B. Client (Respond Only)

   C. Server (Request Security)

   D. Secure Server (Require Security)

2. Rooslan is the security administrator for A. Datum Corporation. He is responsible for five computers running Windows Server 2003 that host file shares and printers and a mix of 200 workstations running Windows XP Professional and Windows 2000 Professional. Some of the workstations running Windows 2000 Professional share color inkjet printers on the network. Within A. Datum, there is a group of 50 users who encrypt all of the documents that they use by using EFS. These documents contain confidential information and are located in a shared folder on the third computer running Windows Server 2003. Twenty of these users have workstations running Windows 2000 Professional. Fifteen of these users share inkjet printers that the others in this group use from time to time. Of these 15 users, five are running Windows 2000 Professional. Rooslan's manager Alex has come to him and asked that he develop a plan so that whenever any of these 50 users copy an encrypted document to one of their workstations, or send one of them to a shared printer, the document remain in an encrypted state during its transmission across the network. All other users on the network should remain unaffected, and their network transmissions should remain unsecured. The 50 users also occasionally access files on the first and second computers running Windows Server 2003, and they must be able to do so in the future. Similarly, 20 users who are not members of this group of 50 also access files on the third computer running Windows Server 2003 and must be able to do so in the future. Which of the following plans could Rooslan implement to meet Alex's goal?

A. Rooslan does not need to make any modifications. When a document is encrypted by EFS, it remains encrypted when transmitted across the network.

B. Rooslan should configure the default domain GPO with the Client (Respond Only) IPSec policy.

C. Rooslan should configure the local IPSec policy on the third computer running Windows Server 2003 to Secure Server (Require Security). He should place the workstations running Windows 2000 Professional and Windows XP Professional in a new OU and apply a Group Policy object to the OU that has the Client (Respond Only) IPSec policy set.

D. Rooslan should create a new OU. He should then move the computer accounts for the third computer running Windows Server 2003, and the computer accounts for the 50 workstations used by the users who require encryption, into this OU. He should then create a GPO with the IPSec policy Server (Request Security) and apply it to this OU.

E. Rooslan cannot meet Alex's goals without upgrading all of the computers running Windows 2000 Professional to Windows XP.

3. Oksana is the security administrator at Tailspin Toys. At the head office, there are three computers running Windows Server 2003, each of which hosts files for different departments within the company. The first computer running Windows Server 2003 hosts plans for future toys. All of the files on this server are confidential and are encrypted by EFS. Only the Managers and Architects groups have permission to access the files on this server. The second computer running Windows Server 2003 hosts the company financial records. All of these files are also confidential, though they are not encrypted by EFS. They are locked down with NTFS permissions and are only accessible to the Accountants and Managers groups. The third computer running Windows Server 2003 hosts the human resources department files, which include some confidential documents that are encrypted by EFS, but it also hosts company policy documents that should be accessible to all users within the Tailspin Toys organization. Oksana has the following goals:

Primary goal: Ensure that all data transmitted to and received from the first computer running Windows Server 2003 is encrypted.

First secondary goal: Ensure that data transmitted from the third Windows Server 2003–based computer to the human resources department computers is encrypted.

Second secondary goal: Ensure that all data transmitted to and received from the second computer running Windows Server 2003 is encrypted.

Oksana takes the following steps:

- Creates an organizational unit (OU) named SecureServer

- Moves the computer accounts of the first, second, and third computers running Windows Server 2003 into this OU
- Creates a GPO with the IPSec policy Secure Server (Require Security) set and applies it to the SecureServer OU
- Edits the Default Domain GPO and sets the IPSec policy to Client (Respond Only)

How many of her goals did Oksana achieve?

A. Oksana has achieved her primary goal and both secondary goals.

B. Oksana has achieved her primary goal and one secondary goal.

C. Oksana has achieved only her primary goal.

D. Oksana did not achieve her primary goal; she did, however, achieve one of her secondary goals.

E. Oksana achieved none of her goals.

4. Your organization has a single standalone server running Windows Server 2003 that is located on a screened subnet. Files are regularly uploaded and downloaded to and from this server from your internal local area network (LAN) and from hosts around the world connected through the Internet by means of the FTP protocol. The only ports open on the internal and external firewalls to this host are those used by the FTP protocol. You only want hosts that have a particular digital certificate installed from a certification authority (CA) to be able to establish secured IPSec connections to the FTP server on the screened subnet. All data transmissions to the FTP server must be secured using IPSec. How can you configure the local GPO on the standalone server running Windows Server 2003 to meet these objectives?

A. Edit the local GPO on the standalone server running Windows Server 2003, and set the IPSec policy to Client (Respond Only).

B. Edit the local GPO on the standalone server running Windows Server 2003, and set the IPSec policy to Server (Request Security).

C. Edit the local GPO on the standalone server running Windows Server 2003, and set the IPSec policy to Secure Server (Require Security).

D. Create a new custom IPSec policy on the standalone server running Windows Server 2003. Set the default response rule to require Kerberos as an authentication method. Ensure that all TCP traffic on the FTP data and control ports requires security using Kerberos as an authentication method.

E. Create a new custom IPSec policy on the standalone server running Windows Server 2003. Set the default response rule to require the certificate as an authentication method. Ensure that all IP traffic requires security using the certificate as an authentication method.

5. You are the network administrator for A. Datum Corporation. Your network environment consists of a single domain with 20 computers running Windows Server 2003, 400 workstations running Windows XP Professional, and 200 workstations running Windows 2000 Professional. You want to ensure that all communication between the workstations running Windows XP Professional and 10 of the computers running Windows Server 2003 is encrypted by IPSec. Furthermore, you do not want the workstations running Windows 2000 Professional making encrypted transmissions. The workstations running Windows 2000 Professional must be able to communicate with each other, the workstations running Windows XP, and the computers running Windows Server 2003 without using IPSec transmissions. Which of the following actions do you need to perform to achieve these goals? (Select two. Each forms a part of the solution.)

A. Create an OU and place the computer accounts of all workstations running Windows XP Professional in it. Create a GPO with the Server (Request Security) IPSec policy.

B. Create an OU and place the computer accounts of all workstations running Windows XP Professional in it. Create a GPO with the Secure Server (Require Security) IPSec policy.

C. Create an OU and place the computer accounts of the 10 computers running Windows Server 2003 in it. Create a GPO with the Server (Request Security) IPSec policy.

D. Create an OU and place the computer accounts of the 10 computers running Windows Server 2003 in it. Create a GPO with the Secure Server (Require Security) IPSec policy.

E. Edit the default domain GPO and set the IPSec policy to Server (Request Security).

6. Rooslan is the administrator of Litware, Inc. Litware, Inc., has a single Windows Server 2003 domain that contains three separate sites. The computers at each site are as follows:

Site A: 500 computers running Windows XP Professional, 10 computers running Windows 2000 Server, 5 computers running Windows Server 2003

Site B: 300 computers running Windows 2000 Professional, 10 computers running Windows Server 2003

Site C: 200 computers running Windows XP Professional, 5 computers running Windows NT Server 4.0, 5 computers running Windows Server 2003

Rooslan has been asked by his manager to develop a plan by which all transmissions between computers on the Litware, Inc., network are encrypted by using IPSec. Rooslan's manager has formalized his request by providing Rooslan with a list of goals. This list is as follows:

Primary goal: All transmissions between computers on the network are encrypted.

1st secondary goal: All transmissions between computers at Site A and Site B are encrypted.

2nd secondary goal: All transmissions between computers at Site A and Site C are encrypted.

Rooslan performs the following steps: He creates a new security template that sets the IPSec policy to Server (Request Security). He creates a new GPO and imports the security template. He applies the GPO to Site A, Site B, and Site C.

Which of the manager's goals has Rooslan accomplished?

A. Rooslan has accomplished the primary goal and both secondary goals.

B. Rooslan has accomplished the primary goal and one secondary goal.

C. Rooslan has accomplished both secondary goals.

D. Rooslan has accomplished one secondary goal only.

E. Rooslan has accomplished none of his manager's goals.

7. You have a domain running at the Windows Server 2003 Interim level. This domain has 10 computers running Windows Server 2003, 150 computers running Windows XP Professional, and 60 computers running Windows NT Workstation 4.0. There are three sites. Site A hosts 8 computers running Windows Server 2003 and 100 computers running Windows XP Professional. Site B hosts one computer running Windows Server 2003 that acts as a domain controller, a global catalog server, and a file and print server, in addition to 50 computers running Windows XP Professional. Site C hosts one computer running Windows Server 2003 that acts as a domain controller, a global catalog server, and a file and print server, in addition to 60 computers running Windows NT Workstation 4.0. Network transmissions between computers in the domain are unencrypted and insecure. Transmissions in the domain only occur between workstations and servers—there is no workstation to workstation communication. You have been asked to rectify this situation and to ensure that all transmissions that occur between computers in your domain are encrypted by IPSec. Which of the following plans will meet this objective with the least administrative effort?

A. Create a single GPO with the IPSec policy set to Client (Respond Only). Apply this GPO to Site A, Site B, and Site C.

B. Create a single GPO with the IPSec policy set to Server (Request Security). Apply this GPO to Site A, Site B, and Site C.

C. Create a single GPO with the IPSec policy set to Secure Server (Require Security). Apply this GPO to Site A, Site B, and Site C.

D. Upgrade all computers in the domain running Windows NT Workstation 4.0 to Windows XP Professional. Create a security template that sets the IPSec policy to Secure Server (Require Security), and apply this template to the local GPO on each computer running Windows Server 2003. Create a new GPO with the IPSec policy set to Client (Respond Only). Apply this GPO to Site A, Site B, and Site C.

E. Upgrade all computers in the domain running Windows NT Workstation 4.0 to Windows XP Professional. Create a security template that sets the IPSec policy to Secure Server (Require Security). Create a new GPO, and import this template. Apply this GPO to Site A, Site B, and Site C.

Objective 3.1 Answers

1. **Correct Answers: C and D**

   A. Incorrect: Although the documents are encrypted by means of EFS, when transmitted over the network they are decrypted by the sender. If the document is copied to an NTFS drive, it will be re-encrypted by the receiver. If it is copied to a file allocation table (FAT) drive it will not be re-encrypted. The important thing to note is that the document is unencrypted and vulnerable to interception while it is in transit.

   B. Incorrect: This policy only encrypts traffic if the partner that the system is communicating with requests it. If no request is made, the documents will pass across the network unencrypted. If all computers are configured with this policy, none will request encrypted transmission.

   C. Correct: Under this scheme, when transmission begins, a computer will request that IPSec be used. If the partner supports IPSec, encrypted transmission will commence; otherwise unsecured IP communication will occur. Because all computers in the organization will be configured with this policy, all will be able to service a request for IPSec communication. Portable computers running Windows XP can be assigned a server IPSec policy.

   D. Correct: This policy is the best option because transmission will not occur until security is negotiated.

2. **Correct Answers: D**

   A. Incorrect: Documents encrypted by EFS do not remain encrypted as they pass across the network, unless IPSec is used.

   B. Incorrect: When all clients are configured with the Client (Respond Only) IPSec policy, there will be no encrypted transmissions across the network. This is because encrypted transmissions will only occur if they are specifically requested, and the Client (Respond Only) IPSec policy does not do this.

   C. Incorrect: Although this will ensure that the communication between the 50 users and the server is encrypted by IPSec, when documents are sent between their workstations they will be unencrypted because no security will be negotiated. Furthermore, the 20 users who are connecting to the third computer running Windows Server 2003, but who are not members of the group of 50, will be unable to communicate with that server because their systems are not configured to negotiate IPSec communications.

D. **Correct:** If Rooslan implements this plan, it will meet the goals outlined by Alex. The Server (Request Security) policy requests IPSec communication. If the partner supports IPSec, communication occurs by means of IPSec; if the partner does not support IPsec, communication occurs by means of an unsecured method. If all of the computers in question have this policy applied, communication between them will be encrypted. Communication with computers outside this group of 51 (one server, 50 workstations) will be insecure—which is what was stated in Alex's plan.

E. **Incorrect:** Windows 2000 Professional supports IPSec, as do Windows 2000 Server, Windows XP Professional, and Windows Server 2003.

3. **Correct Answers: A**

A. **Correct:** Policies applied at the OU level override those applied at the domain level; hence, the three servers in the SecureServer OU will retain the Secure Server (Require Security) IPSec policy. All other computers in the domain will have the Client (Respond Only) policy. The impact of this will be that all communication between the three computers running Windows Server 2003 and the computers in the rest of the domain will be encrypted. This meets the conditions of the primary goal and both secondary goals.

B. **Incorrect:** Policies applied at the OU level override those applied at the domain level; hence, the three servers in the SecureServer OU will retain the Secure Server (Require Security) IPSec policy. All other computers in the domain will have the Client (Respond Only) policy. The impact of this will be that all communication between the three computers running Windows Server 2003 and the computers in the rest of the domain will be encrypted. This meets the conditions of the primary goal and both secondary goals.

C. **Incorrect:** Policies applied at the OU level override those applied at the domain level; hence, the three servers in the SecureServer OU will retain the Secure Server (Require Security) IPSec policy. All other computers in the domain will have the Client (Respond Only) policy. The impact of this will be that all communication between the three computers running Windows Server 2003 and the computers in the rest of the domain will be encrypted. This meets the conditions of the primary goal and both secondary goals.

D. **Incorrect:** Policies applied at the OU level override those applied at the domain level; hence, the three servers in the SecureServer OU will retain the Secure Server (Require Security) IPSec policy. All other computers in the domain will have the Client (Respond Only) policy. The impact of this will be that all communication between the three computers running Windows Server 2003 and the computers in the rest of the domain will be encrypted. This meets the conditions of the primary goal and both secondary goals.

E. **Incorrect:** Policies applied at the OU level override those applied at the domain level; hence, the three servers in the SecureServer OU will retain the Secure Server (Require Security) IPSec policy. All other computers in the domain will have the Client (Respond Only) policy. The impact of this will be that all communication between the three computers running Windows Server 2003 and the computers in the rest of the domain will be encrypted. This meets the conditions of the primary goal and both secondary goals.

4. Correct Answers: E

A. **Incorrect:** This will not meet the objectives outlined in the question. This will not force IPSec communication, nor will that communication be authenticated by digital certificate.

B. **Incorrect:** This will not meet the objectives outlined in the question. This will not force IPSec communication, nor will that communication be authenticated by digital certificate.

C. **Incorrect:** This will not meet the objective in the question that communication must be authenticated by digital certificate.

D. **Incorrect:** This particular custom IPSec policy uses Kerberos, rather than a specific digital certificate, as an authentication method.

E. **Correct:** Although a more specific custom IPSec policy can be created using the actual ports used by the FTP protocol, this particular policy will meet the goals outlined in the question statement.

5. Correct Answers: A and C

A. **Correct:** If you use this policy, when transmissions are made to other hosts that use this policy, they will be encrypted. When transmissions are made to other hosts that do not use this policy, they will be unencrypted.

B. **Incorrect:** If you perform this action, the workstations running Windows XP Professional will not be able to communicate with the workstations running Windows 2000 Professional in an insecure manner, which is one of your stated goals.

C. **Correct:** With this policy applied, communication between the set of 10 computers running Windows Server 2003 and the computers running Windows XP Professional (assuming they have the policy applied as described in answer A) will be encrypted. Communication with the computers running Windows 2000 Professional will remain unencrypted.

D. **Incorrect:** If this action were taken, the computers running Windows 2000 Professional would not be able to communicate with the Windows Server 2003 computers unless IPSec was used.

E. Incorrect: Performing this action would force all computers within the organization to send encrypted transmissions. While this is fine for the computers running Windows XP, the question specified that the computers running Windows 2000 Professional should not be using encrypted transmissions.

6. Correct Answers: D

A. Incorrect: Computers running Windows NT Server 4.0 and Windows NT Workstation 4.0 cannot communicate with the version of IPSec that ships with Windows 2000, Windows XP, and Windows Server 2003. This means that any transmissions from computers running Windows NT Server 4.0 at Site C to any other computer on the Litware, Inc., network will be insecure. This means that the primary goal will not be accomplished, and neither will the second secondary goal. The first secondary goal does not involve any computers running Windows NT 4.0, and hence can be achieved.

B. Incorrect: Computers running Windows NT Server 4.0 and Windows NT Workstation 4.0 cannot communicate with the version of IPSec that ships with Windows 2000, Windows XP, and Windows Server 2003. This means that any transmissions from computers running Windows NT Server 4.0 at Site C to any other computer on the Litware, Inc., network will be insecure. This means that the primary goal will not be accomplished, and neither will the second secondary goal. The first secondary goal does not involve any computers running Windows NT 4.0, and hence can be achieved.

C. Incorrect: Computers running Windows NT Server 4.0 and Windows NT Workstation 4.0 cannot communicate with the version of IPSec that ships with Windows 2000, Windows XP, and Windows Server 2003. This means that any transmissions from computers running Windows NT Server 4.0 at Site C to any other computer on the Litware, Inc., network will be insecure. This means that the primary goal will not be accomplished, and neither will the second secondary goal. The first secondary goal does not involve any computers running Windows NT 4.0, and hence can be achieved.

D. Correct: Computers running Windows NT Server 4.0 and Windows NT Workstation 4.0 cannot communicate with the version of IPSec that ships with Windows 2000, Windows XP, and Windows Server 2003. This means that any transmissions from computers running Windows NT Server 4.0 at Site C to any other computer on the Litware, Inc., network will be insecure. This means that the primary goal will not be accomplished, and neither will the second secondary goal. The first secondary goal does not involve any computers running Windows NT 4.0, and hence can be achieved.

E. Incorrect: Computers running Windows NT Server 4.0 and Windows NT Workstation 4.0 cannot communicate with the version of IPSec that ships with Windows 2000, Windows XP, and Windows Server 2003. This means that any transmissions from computers running Windows NT Server 4.0 at Site C to any other computer on the Litware, Inc., network will be insecure. This means that the primary goal will not be accomplished, and neither will the second secondary goal. The first secondary goal does not involve any computers running Windows NT 4.0, and hence can be achieved.

7. Correct Answers: E

A. **Incorrect:** This will not work for two reasons. The first reason is that this policy only encrypts IPSec transmissions when a request is made. If all computers have this policy applied, no request will be made. The second reason this will not work is that computers running Windows NT Workstation 4.0 cannot use IPSec without resorting to a non-Microsoft IPSec solution.

B. **Incorrect:** Computers running Windows NT Workstation 4.0 cannot use IPSec without resorting to a non-Microsoft IPSec solution. Although the computers running Windows XP and Windows Server 2003 will use IPSec, all transmissions to and from the computers running Windows NT Workstation 4.0 will be insecure.

C. **Incorrect:** Computers running Windows NT Workstation 4.0 cannot use IPSec without resorting to a non-Microsoft IPSec solution. Although the computers running Windows XP and Windows Server 2003 will use IPSec, no transmission will be able to be made from these computers to the computers running Windows NT Workstation 4.0.

D. **Incorrect:** The local policy will be overridden by the site policy, so the policy on all computers throughout the domain will be Client (Respond Only). The Client (Respond Only) will only encrypt traffic if requested. If all computers have this policy, none will request IPSec transmissions.

E. **Correct:** Only Windows 2000, Windows XP, and Windows Server 2003 natively support IPSec. Windows NT Workstation 4.0 and Windows NT Server 4.0 do not support IPSec. The Secure Server (Require Security) policy will ensure that all transmissions that occur within the domain will be encrypted.

Objective 3.2

Configure IPSec Policies to Secure Communication between Networks and Hosts

IPSec filters are a powerful way of securing communications between hosts and servers on a network. Using IPSec filters, hosts sending and receiving e-mail can do so via an encrypted connection rather than transmitting in an insecure manner. Most e-mail is textual information that, if not encrypted via IPSec, could be easily intercepted and read by a nefarious user with a packet sniffer. Using IPSec filters to secure this communication lessens the need for users to manually encrypt messages before they are sent or decrypt others when they arrive. Similarly, IPSec can be used to encrypt communications between a Web server on a screened subnet and a computer running Microsoft SQL Server on the internal network. This is especially useful if the computer running SQL Server hosts confidential data about customers of your company. IPSec filters can use three forms of authentication. The default method is Kerberos, which is used for computers that reside within the same domain or forest. The second method is to use a shared certificate from a trusted certificate authority. Finally, a preshared key can be used. IPSec policies are not limited to one single authentication method, and another method can be used as a fallback if the first one fails.

Objective 3.2 Questions

1. You have a computer running Windows Server 2003 and IIS 6.0 located on a screened subnet. This computer runs a Web server that is used to provide product information to potential customers around the country. The computer is a member of your company's domain. You want to configure the server so that all communication, except that accessing the Web site, must be encrypted by IPSec. This IPSec communication must be authenticated by Kerberos. Which of the following components would you include in the configuration of a custom IPSec policy that would be applied to the computer running Windows Server 2003? (Each correct answer forms part of the solution.)

A. Default Response Rule. Active Directory Default Authentication.

B. New Rule. No Tunnel Specified. All Network Connections. IP Filter List with the following properties. Source: Any IP Address. Destination: My IP Address. Protocol Type: TCP. From Any Port to Port 80. Permit Unsecured IP Packets.

C. New Rule. No Tunnel Specified. All Network Connections. Require Security. Active Directory Default Authentication.

D. New Rule. No Tunnel Specified. All Network Connections. IP Filter List with the following properties. Source: Any IP Address. Destination: My IP Address. Protocol Type: TCP. From Any Port to Port 25. Permit Unsecured IP Packets.

E. New Rule. No Tunnel Specified. All Network Connections. Request Security. Active Directory Default Authentication.

2. You are configuring an IPSec policy to allow only computers that have a specific digital certificate installed to send and receive e-mail by means of the Post Office Protocol 3 (POP3) service on Windows Server 2003. Which ports should you configure rules for? (Select all that apply.)

A. Port 23

B. Port 25

C. Port 80

D. Port 110

E. Port 143

3. You are configuring an IPSec filter for a computer running Windows Server 2003, and you have constructed a filter list as shown in the following figure.

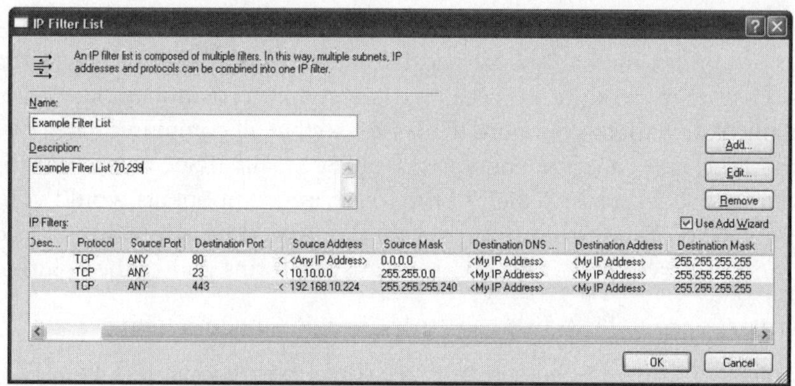

If the Filter Action for this list were set to permit, and there were a filter list also configured to require security for all other IP traffic, which of the following statements would be true? (Select all that apply.)

A. Any host would be able to access any Web content hosted on the computer running Windows Server 2003.

B. A host with IP address 10.11.21.22 would be able to initiate a Telnet session to the computer running Windows Server 2003.

C. A host with IP address 10.10.5.6 would be able to initiate a Telnet session to the computer running Windows Server 2003.

D. A host with IP address 192.168.10.230 will be able to access the Secure Sockets Layer (SSL) Web site on the computer running Windows Server 2003.

E. A host with IP address 192.168.10.245 will be able to access the SSL Web site on the computer running Windows Server 2003.

4. You are in the process of configuring a set of IPSec filters for a Windows Server 2003 domain controller on your network. You want to make sure that you permit traffic to the Lightweight Directory Access Protocol (LDAP), Kerberos, and global catalog server ports. Given your requirements, which of the following ports should you permit traffic to? (Select all that apply.)

A. Port 3268

B. Port 3389

C. Port 53

D. Port 389

E. Port 80

5. You have a set of five servers running Windows Server 2003, Web Edition that are located on a screened subnet. These Web servers are each running a Web application that needs to access data on a computer running SQL Server 2000 that is located on your internal network. The IP addresses of the Web servers on the screened subnet are:

Server 1: 192.168.1.130

Server 2: 192.168.1.140

Server 3: 192.168.1.150

Server 4: 192.168.1.160

Server 5: 192.168.1.170

The IP address of the computer running Windows Server 2003 that is located on the internal network is 10.10.1.100. You want to ensure that data transmissions between the Web servers on the screened subnet and the computer running SQL Server on the internal network are encrypted by IPSec. You don't need other traffic between the Web servers and the computer running SQL Server to be encrypted because such traffic is already blocked by the internal firewall, and the encryption and decryption process would just add to processor overhead. Which of the following custom rules would achieve this goal if it was set to Require Security? (Select all that apply.)

A. Protocol: TCP; Source Port: Any; Destination Port: 1433; Source Address: 192.168.1.128; Source Mask: 255.255.255.128; Destination Address: 10.10.1.100; Destination Mask: 255.255.255.255

B. Protocol: TCP; Source Port: Any; Destination Port: 1433; Source Address: 192.168.1.128; Source Mask: 255.255.255.192; Destination Address: 10.10.1.100; Destination Mask: 255.255.255.255

C. Protocol: TCP; Source Port: 1433; Destination Port: Any; Source Address: 10.10.1.100; Source Mask: 255.255.255.192; Destination Address: 192.168.1.128; Destination Mask: 255.255.255.255

D. Protocol: TCP; Source Port: Any; Destination Port: 1433; Source Address: 192.168.1.128; Source Mask: 255.255.255.224; Destination Address: 10.10.1.100; Destination Mask: 255.255.255.255

E. Protocol: TCP; Source Port: Any; Destination Port: 1433; Source Address: 192.168.1.128; Source Mask: 255.255.255.240; Destination Address: 10.10.1.100; Destination Mask: 255.255.255.255

Objective 3.2 Answers

1. **Correct Answers: A, B, and C**

   A. Correct: Configuring the Default Response Rule will allow IPSec connections to be negotiated with this server if requested by the client.

   B. Correct: Port 80 is the port used by the HTTP protocol. Creating this filter means that Web site traffic can be received and transmitted without requiring secured IPSec packets. Without this connection, Web site traffic would be encrypted via IPSec, limiting it to authorized users and locking out the potential customers.

   C. Correct: This rule in combination with the rule articulated in answer B will lock out all other forms of traffic unless it is secured via IPSec authenticated via Kerberos. This rule is required to meet the specification outlined in the question

   D. Incorrect: This component of an IPSec policy would allow insecure access to port 25. Port 25 is not the Web server port, and hence should only allow secure access.

   E. Incorrect: This rule only requests security. If none is forthcoming, the connection will be insecure.

2. **Correct Answers: B and D**

   A. Incorrect: Port 23 is used for Telnet. Port 23 has nothing to do with the POP3 service.

   B. Correct: Port 25 is the SMTP port. It is used by POP3 clients to send e-mail. A rule should be configured for this port so that only clients with a specific digital certificate can use it to send e-mail. In real life this could cause a problem because outside mail servers use port 25 to send e-mail from remote networks to the server. If such a policy were implemented, those hosts would be unable to make connections on port 25.

   C. Incorrect: Port 80 is the HTTP port. It doesn't have anything to do with the POP3 service, but is used by IIS for HTTP traffic.

   D. Correct: Port 110 is the POP3 port. POP3 clients connect to this port to retrieve e-mail from a POP3 server. A rule should be configured for this port so that only clients with a specific digital certificate can use it to retrieve e-mail.

   E. Incorrect: Port 143 is used by the IMAP service. Although the IMAP service is used for e-mail, it is not used by the POP3 service in Windows Server 2003.

3. **Correct Answers: A, C, and D**

A. **Correct:** The first line of the filter allows this to occur.

B. **Incorrect:** Only hosts with IP addresses 10.10.0.0 through 10.10.255.255 will be able to access a Telnet server on the computer running Windows Server 2003.

C. **Correct:** Only hosts with IP addresses 10.10.0.0 through 10.10.255.255 will be able to access a Telnet server on the computer running Windows Server 2003.

D. **Correct:** Only hosts with IP addresses 192.168.10.225 through 192.168.10.238 will be able to access the SSL Web site on the computer running Windows Server 2003.

E. **Incorrect:** Only hosts with IP addresses 192.168.10.225 through 192.168.10.238 will be able to access the SSL Web site on the computer running Windows Server 2003.

4. **Correct Answers: A and D**

A. **Correct:** This port is used by the global catalog server.

B. **Incorrect:** This port is used by Terminal Services servers. It is not relevant to the task at hand.

C. **Incorrect:** Port 53 is the DNS server port. Nothing has been mentioned about this particular computer running a DNS server.

D. **Correct:** This port is used by LDAP, an integral component of Active Directory.

E. **Incorrect:** This port is used by the HTTP protocol. Nothing has been mentioned about this particular computer running a Web server.

5. **Correct Answers: A and B**

A. **Correct:** This rule will allow data transmissions from the Web servers to the computers running SQL Server to be encrypted by IPSec. This answer includes all IP addresses in the range 192.168.1.129 through 192.168.1.254. Port 1433 is used for computers running SQL Server.

B. **Correct:** This rule will allow data transmissions from the Web servers to the computers running SQL Server to be encrypted by IPSec. This answer includes all IP addresses in the range 192.168.1.129 through 192.168.1.190. Port 1433 is used for computers running SQL Server.

C. **Incorrect:** This particular filter specifies an incorrect source address and source port.

D. **Incorrect:** The source mask in this answer will only allow hosts from IP addresses 192.168.1.129 through 192.168.1.158. This will exclude Web servers 4 and 5.

E. **Incorrect:** The source mask in this answer will only allow hosts from IP addresses 192.168.1.129 through 192.168.1.142. This will exclude Web servers 3, 4, and 5.

Objective 3.3

Deploy and Manage IPSec Policies

IPSec policies can be deployed in two ways. The first way is to use Group Policy objects or local policy objects with IPSec policy set within. Group Policy objects can be applied at the site, domain, and organizational unit levels with the usual rules of inheritance. Local Group Policy only applies to a specific computer and is overridden by any Group Policy object applied at a higher level.

The second way that IPSec policies can be deployed is by means of scripting by using the `netsh` command. The `netsh` command can be used to automatically generate complex IPSec policies. This technique is useful to administrators of standalone Windows Server 2003–based computers who cannot deploy IPSec policy by means of GPOs. The IPSec context of the `netsh` command can be entered by performing the following steps:

- Run a command prompt.
- Enter thc `netsh` command.
- Enter the IPSec context by entering `ipsec`.

IPSec policies can be managed by using the `netsh` command in the IPSec context or the IPSec Monitor snap-in for the Microsoft Management Console. Both tools provide information such as how traffic is being authenticated and which hosts have security associations. Both tools also display which IPSec policy is currently in effect. It is important to remember that only one IPSec policy can be applied at a time and that they are not cumulative. When multiple policies are deployed by means of Active Directory, only the policy applied last will have influence over a computer.

Objective 3.3 Questions

1. Which of the following commands, when issued from the `ipsec static>` prompt when `netsh ipsec` is run on the command line, will add a filter to the secureweb filterlist that will deal traffic coming from network 10.10.2.32 /27 to the Web server located on the local host?

   A. `ipsec static>add filter filterlist=secureweb srcaddr=10.10.2.32 dstaddr=Me protocol=TCP mirrored=yes srcmask=255.255.255.224 dstmask=255.255.255.0 srcport=0 dstport=80`

   B. `ipsec static>add filter filterlist=secureweb srcaddr=10.10.2.32 dstaddr=Me protocol=ICMP mirrored=yes srcmask=255.255.255.240 dstmask=255.255.255.0 srcport=0 dstport=80`

   C. `ipsec static>add filter filterlist=secureweb srcaddr=192.168.0.32 dstaddr=Me protocol=TCP mirrored=yes srcmask=255.255.255.224 dstmask=255.255.255.0 srcport=80 dstport=0`

   D. `ipsec static>add filter filterlist=secureweb srcaddr=192.168.0.32 dstaddr=Me protocol=TCP mirrored=yes srcmask=255.255.255.0 dstmask=255.255.255.0 srcport=80 dstport=0`

2. Which of the following are limitations on the authentication methods that can be used by a standalone computer running Windows Server 2003 that is using IPSec to ensure that its network communications are encrypted?

   A. There are no limitations on the authentication methods that can be used by a standalone computer running Windows Server 2003.

   B. Standalone computers running Windows Server 2003 cannot use the Kerberos authentication method for IPSec. They are limited to using digital certificates or preshared keys.

   C. Standalone computers running Windows Server 2003 cannot use a digital certificate as an authentication method for IPSec.

   D. Standalone computers running Windows Server 2003 cannot use preshared keys as an authentication method for IPSec.

3. Rooslan has created an IPSec policy on a computer running Windows Server 2003 by entering the following list of commands from the `netsh ipsec static>` context command prompt:

```
add filterlist name=testlist

add filteraction name=testaction inpass=no soft=no action=negotiate
```

```
add filter filterlist=testlist srcaddr=any dstaddr=Me protocol=TCP mir-
rored=YES srcmask=0.0.0.0 dstmask=255.255.255.255 srcport=0 dstport=110

add filter filterlist=testlist srcaddr=any dstaddr=Me protocol=TCP mir-
rored=YES srcmask=0.0.0.0 dstmask=255.255.255.255 srcport=0 dstport=25

add policy name=testpolicy activatedefaultrule=no assign=no

add rule name=testrule policy=testpolicy filterlist=testlist filterac-
tion=testaction psk="Quis Custodiet Custodes"
```

The computer running Windows Server 2003 is running the POP3 service. Which of the following statements about Rooslan's IPSec policy are true, given the configuration listed above? (Select all that apply.)

A. The testpolicy IPSec policy will not be assigned when it is created.

B. This policy deals with all traffic being sent to the local Windows Server 2003–based computer on which the testpolicy IPSec policy is applied.

C. This policy uses Kerberos 5 authentication to negotiate the IPSec connection.

D. If computers checking e-mail on the POP3 service hosted on the local Windows Server 2003–based computer are unable to negotiate IPSec security, insecure transmission will be allowed.

E. The default response rule is not activated in this policy.

4. You are the security administrator for the Tailspin Toys forest. The forest is running at the Windows Server 2003 functional level. There are three domains in this forest: root.tailspintoys.com, melbourne.tailspintoys.com, and redmond.tailspintoys.com. There is a group of 500 workstations running Windows XP Professional that are members of the melbourne.tailspintoys.com domain. There are 10 file and print servers running Windows 2000 Server that are members of the melbourne.tailspintoys.com domain. The 500 computers running Windows XP Professional are members of an organizational unit named WORKSTATION. The 10 file and print servers running Windows 2000 Server are members of the organizational unit named MEMBERSERV. The 10 file and print servers running Windows 2000 Server and the 500 computers running Windows XP Professional are all located at Site B within the domain. Several GPOs have been created, each of which has a different IPSec policy. These GPOs and their corresponding IPSec policies are listed below:

GPO one: No IPSec policy set

GPO two: Client (Respond Only) IPSec policy set

GPO three: Server (Request Security) IPSec policy set

GPO four: Secure Server (Require Security) IPSec policy set

GPO one is applied to the WORKSTATION OU. GPO two is applied to the melbourne.tailspintoys.com domain. GPO three is applied to the root.tailspintoys.com domain. GPO four is applied to Site B. Assume that no other IPSec policies are applied in the forest. Given this information, which of the following statements is correct?

A. If a computer running Windows NT Workstation 4.0 at Site B attempted to copy a file from one of the 10 file and print servers running Windows 2000 Server in the MEMBERSERV OU, the file transmission would be encrypted by IPSec.

B. Data transmissions between the 500 workstations running Windows XP Professional in the WORKSTATION OU and the 10 file and print servers running Windows 2000 Server in the MEMBERSERV OU will be encrypted by IPSec.

C. Data transmission between one of the 500 workstations running Windows XP Professional that is located in the WORKSTATION OU and a computer running Windows Server 2003 that is located in the root.tailspintoys.com domain will be encrypted by IPSec.

D. All data transmissions between computers located at Site B will be encrypted by IPSec.

5. Several users in your domain are attempting to use the FTP protocol to upload files to a computer running Windows Server 2003 on your organization's screened subnet. The computer running Windows Server 2003 on the screened subnet has an IPSec policy set that requires security. Because it is a standalone computer, it does not use the default Active Directory/Kerberos IPSec authentication. Instead it uses a preshared key with the phrase "qua partis tutis". All computers running Windows XP Professional in the domain are subject to a GPO at the domain level with the IPSec policy set Server (Request Security). What step or steps can you take to ensure that the users within your domain who require FTP access to the computer running Windows Server 2003 on the screened subnet can make encrypted connections to this computer?

A. Alter the IPSec policy in the GPO applied at the domain level to Client (Respond Only).

B. Alter the IPSec policy in the GPO applied at the domain level to Secure Server (Require Security).

C. Alter the local policy object on the computer running Windows Server 2003 on the screened subnet to allow Kerberos authentication of IPSec connections.

D. Edit the Server (Request Security) IPSec policy properties in the GPO applied at the domain level. Edit the properties of the <Dynamic> and ALL IP Traffic Rules. On the Authentication Methods tab, add a new authentication method of preshared key, and enter "qua partis tutis" as the string.

Objective 3.3 Answers

1. **Correct Answers: A**

   A. **Correct:** This command provides all of the correct source addresses, masks, and ports, in addition to destination addresses, mask, and ports. A srcport or dstport set to 0 is equivalant to "any".

   B. **Incorrect:** This answer has the incorrect protocol (ICMP rather than TCP) and the incorrect source mask (which for /27 should be 255.255.255.224).

   C. **Incorrect:** This answer has the incorrect source address (192.168.0.32 rather than 10.10.2.32) in addition to the incorrect source port (which should be 0, which is understood as "any") and destination port.

   D. **Incorrect:** This answer has the incorrect source address (192.168.0.32 rather than 10.10.2.32) in addition to the incorrect source port (which should be 0, which is understood as "any") and destination port. It also has the incorrect source mask, which should be 255.255.255.224 rather than 255.255.255.0.

2. **Correct Answers: B**

   A. **Incorrect:** Standalone computers running Windows Server 2003 cannot use the Kerberos authentication method.

   B. **Correct:** Because they are not members of the domain, standalone computers running Windows Server 2003 cannot use the Kerberos authentication method for IPSec. They are limited to using digital certificates or preshared keys.

   C. **Incorrect:** Because they are not members of the domain, standalone computers running Windows Server 2003 cannot use the Kerberos authentication method for IPSec. They are limited to using digital certificates or preshared keys.

   D. **Incorrect:** Because they are not members of the domain, standalone computers running Windows Server 2003 cannot use the Kerberos authentication method for IPSec. They are limited to using digital certificates or preshared keys.

3. **Correct Answers: A and E**

   A. **Correct:** The assign=no switch of the add policy command ensures that the testpolicy IPSec policy will not be assigned.

   B. **Incorrect:** This policy deals with all traffic to ports 25 and 110 from all hosts to the local Windows Server 2003–based computer on which the policy is applied.

   C. **Incorrect:** This policy uses the preshared key "Quis Custodiet Custodes" to negotiate the IPSec connection.

   D. **Incorrect:** The soft=no switch of the add filteraction command specifies that only secure transmission will be allowed on these ports.

E. **Correct:** The activatedefaultrule=no switch of the add policy command specifies that the default response rule is not activated in this policy.

4. **Correct Answers: C**

A. **Incorrect:** The policy that has influence over the 10 file and print servers running Windows 2000 Server is the Client (Respond Only) policy. Windows NT Workstation 4.0 does not natively support IPSec, hence any file transmission between a computer running Windows NT 4.0 and one of the 10 computers running Windows 2000 Servers will be insecure.

B. **Incorrect:** The policy that influences computers in both OUs is the Client (Respond Only) IPSec policy. Only one IPSec policy can be active at one time. Although OU policies do have precedence over domain policies, the fact that no policy is set in GPO one means that GPO two will remain dominant.

C. **Correct:** The root.tailspintoys.com domain has the Secure Server (Require Security) policy set. This means that all transmissions between computers in this domain and any other host will be encrypted by IPSec.

D. **Incorrect:** Downstream GPOs applied at the domain level enforce the Client (Respond Only) IPSec policy. As no policy specifies that IPSec should be requested, data transmission between clients in the melbourne.tailspintoys.com domain will be insecure.

5. **Correct Answers: D**

A. **Incorrect:** Performing this step will not enable secure communication between computers on your network running Windows XP Professional and the Windows Server 2003–based computer running FTP on the screened subnet. By default, this policy uses Kerberos 5 authentication rather than the required preshared key.

B. **Incorrect:** Performing this step will not enable secure communication between computers on your network running Windows XP Professional and the Windows Server 2003–based computer running FTP on the screened subnet. By default, this policy uses Kerberos 5 authentication rather than the required preshared key.

C. **Incorrect:** This cannot be done because the computer running Windows Server 2003 on the screened subnet is not a member of the domain, and hence cannot use Kerberos authentication methods.

D. **Correct:** Performing these steps will enable computers in your domain to initiate IPSec connections to the standalone computer running Windows Server 2003 on the screened subnet. After it has been determined that the Kerberos method of authentication does not work, the preshared-key method will be tried. Because the same preshared key exists on both source and destination computers, an IPSec connection will be able to be established.

Objective 3.4

Troubleshoot IPSec

Several tools can be used to troubleshoot IPSec. One tool that has been improved significantly in Windows Server 2003 is the IP Security Monitor Console. From this console, you are able to view security associations and determine which clients are connecting securely to the computer on which you are running the console. You are also able to determine the authentication method that they are using. Similar functionality is found by running `netsh ipsec dynamic show mmsas` from the command line. The `netsh` command, in the ipsec dynamic context, can provide a wealth of information that cannot be gained from the GUI. The `netsh` command can also be used to configure many aspects of IPSec that cannot be configured from the GUI, such as how to treat certificate revocation list (CRL) revocations and the configuration of IPSec logging.

Objective 3.4 Questions

1. Rooslan is configuring all of the workstations in his organization to use IPSec with a digital certificate for authentication. Until digital certificates can be installed on all workstations, they will be using preshared keys for authentication. There are two file servers that all workstations within the domain access. Both of these file servers run Windows Server 2003 and are configured with the Secure Server (Require Security) IPSec policy. This policy has been modified so that it accepts both certificate and preshared key authentication methods. Rooslan's assistant Alex has been keeping, on his Handheld PC, a list of computers by location and IP address that have had certificates installed. Unfortunately the Handheld PC has been misplaced, and now Rooslan needs to know which workstations are still using a preshared key for IPSec authentication and which are using certificates. Which of the following actions will enable Rooslan to get a list of IP addresses for computers that are still using preshared keys? (Select two.)

A. Check the \Main Mode\Security Associations node in IP Security Monitor on both of the file servers running Windows Server 2003.

B. On both of the file servers running Windows Server 2003, run a command prompt. From the `netsh ipsec static` prompt type `show all`

C. On both of the file servers running Windows Server 2003, run a command prompt. From the `netsh ipsec dynamic` prompt type `show mmsas`

D. On both of the file servers running Windows Server 2003, check the Active Policy node of the IP Security Monitor.

E. On both of the file servers running Windows Server 2003, use the Security Configuration and Analysis MMC to list the IPSec security associations.

2. There are three standalone computers running Windows XP Professional on your network. Each has an IPSec policy set that requires security. Rather than use the default Active Directory authentication, each standalone workstation running Windows XP Professional uses preshared key authentication.

Host 1 uses a preshared key of Quis Custodiet Custodes and has an IP address of 10.10.10.22.

Host 2 uses a preshared key of Ita Erat Quando Hic Adveni and has an IP address of 10.10.10.30.

Host 3 uses a preshared key of Nullo Metro Compositum Est and has an IP address of 10.10.10.36.

Each of these hosts needs to be able to securely communicate with a computer running Windows Server 2003 that has the IP address 10.10.10.230, but currently only host 1 is able to communicate with the server. The computer running Windows Server 2003 is configured with a Secure Server (Require Security) policy, the properties of which are displayed in the following figure.

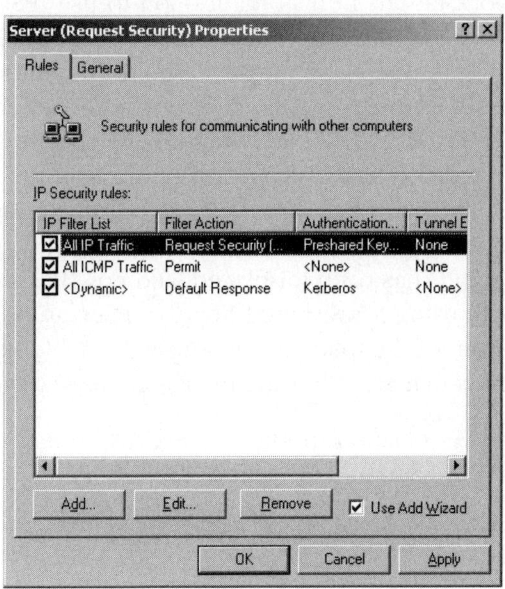

Which of the following correctly describes how the computer running Windows Server 2003 can be configured so that hosts 2 and 3 can communicate with it and with host 1? (You do not need to worry about other hosts on the network.)

A. Reconfigure the IPSec policies on host 2 and 3 to use the preshared key Nullo Metro Compositum Est.

B. Reconfigure the IPSec policies on hosts 2 and 3 to use the preshared key Ita Erat Quando Hic Adveni.

C. On the computer running Windows Server 2003, edit the properties of the Secure Server (Require Security) IPSec policy. From this computer, edit the All IP Traffic Filter list. From the Authentication Methods tab, add two new authentication methods that use the preshared key. The first authentication method should use the preshared key Nullo Metro Compositum Est. The second authentication method should use the preshared key Ita Erat Quando Hic Adveni.

D. On the computer running Windows Server 2003, edit the properties of the Secure Server (Require Security) IPSec policy. Create two new filters. The first filter should be named 10.10.10.30 and should deal with TCP traffic from host 10.10.10.30 to My IP Address. The second filter should be named 10.10.10.36 and should deal with TCP traffic from host 10.10.10.36 to My IP Address. Create two new rules. The first rule should use the filter named 10.10.10.30 and should require security. The authentication method should be set to Preshared Key, and the key should be set to Nullo Metro Compositum Est. The second rule should use the filter named 10.10.10.36 and should require security. The authentication method should be set to Preshared Key, and the key should be set to Ita Erat Quando Hic Adveni.

E. On the computer running Windows Server 2003, edit the properties of the Secure Server (Require Security) IPSec policy. Create two new filters. The first filter should be named 10.10.10.30 and should deal with TCP traffic from host 10.10.10.30 to My IP Address. The second filter should be named 10.10.10.36 and should deal with TCP traffic from host 10.10.10.36 to My IP Address. Create two new rules. The first rule should use the filter named 10.10.10.36 and should require security. The authentication method should be set to Preshared Key, and the key should be set to Nullo Metro Compositum Est. The second rule should use the filter named 10.10.10.30 and should require security. The authentication method should be set to Preshared Key, and the key should be set to Ita Erat Quando Hic Adveni.

3. Darren is having some problems with IPSec on a member server running Windows Server 2003. It appears that some of the Internet Key Exchange (IKE) main mode and quick mode negotiations are failing, but it is not clear why this is happening. Darren wants to log IKE exchanges on this server. Which of the following methods could Darren use to enable this form of logging?

A. He needs to edit the properties of the enabled IPSec policy on the computer running Windows Server 2003. He should select the Enable IKE Logging check box on the General tab.

B. He needs to run regedit on the member server running Windows Server 2003. He then needs to set the value of the `HKEY_LOCAL_MACHINE\System\CurrentControlSet\Services\PolicyAgent\Oakley\EnableLogging` DWORD to 0. He should then restart the IPSec service.

C. He needs to run the `netsh` command on the member server running Windows Server 2003. He should type `set config ikelogging 1` at the `netsh ipsec dynamic` prompt.

D. He needs to run the `netsh` command on the member server running Windows Server 2003. He should type `set config ikelogging 0` at the `netsh ipsec dynamic` prompt.

E. He needs to run regedit on the member server running Windows Server 2003. He then needs to set the value of the `HKEY_LOCAL_MACHINE\System\CurrentControlSet\Services\PolicyAgent\Oakley\EnableLogging` DWORD to 1. He should then restart the IPSec service.

4. Oksana wants to ensure that authentication will fail if any problems occur during the Certificate Revocation List (CRL) check during IKE certificate authentication on several computers running Windows Server 2003 in her domain. These computers are all members of the same OU. Which of the following methods will allow Oksana to achieve this goal?

   A. Create a GPO and assign it to the OU. Edit the IPSec policy properties. Edit the rule that enforces security by certificate. Select the Perform CRL Check check box.

   B. Create a GPO and assign it to the site. Edit the IPSec policy properties. Edit the rule that enforces security by certificate. Select the Perform CRL Check check box.

   C. Type `netsh ipsec dynamic set config strongcrlcheck 2` from the command prompt.

   D. Type `netsh ipsec dynamic set config strongcrlcheck 0` from the command prompt.

5. Rooslan has the following goals for a member server running Windows Server 2003 in his domain:

   Primary goal: Enable IPSec driver event logging.

   First secondary goal: Disable CRL checks during IKE certificate authentication.

   Second secondary goal: Exempt all broadcast, multicast, and Kerberos traffic from IPSec filtering.

   Rooslan performs the following actions:

   He logs directly on to the computer running Windows Server 2003 by using Remote Desktop. He types the following from a command prompt:

```
netsh ipsec dynamic set config ipsecdiagnostics 7

netsh ipsec dynamic set config strongcrlcheck 2

netsh ipsec dynamic set config ipsecexempt 0
```

   Rooslan then exits the command prompt and restarts the member server.

   Which of the goals has Rooslan accomplished?

   A. The primary goal and both secondary goals have been accomplished.

   B. The primary goal and one secondary goal have been accomplished.

   C. The primary goal has been accomplished, but no secondary goals have been accomplished.

   D. The primary goal has not been accomplished. Both secondary goals have been accomplished.

   E. No goals have been accomplished.

Objective 3.4 Answers

1. **Correct Answers: A and C**

   A. Correct: The \Main Mode\Security Associations node lists all of the computers that connect by means of IPSec to the hosts. It also lists the authentication method. In this case, the authentication method will list whether a preshared key or a certificate was used.

   B. Incorrect: This will display configuration information on IPSec policies, rules, and filter lists; it will not list which authentication method was used for individual clients.

   C. Correct: This will output a list of IP addresses and the authentication modes that they used to connect.

   D. Incorrect: This node lists policy information, such as policy name, description, and modification date. It will not show a list of associations.

   E. Incorrect: The Security Configuration and Analysis MMC does not have this functionality.

2. **Correct Answers: E**

   A. Incorrect: The question asks how the computer running Windows Server 2003 can be reconfigured, not how the host workstations running Windows XP can be reconfigured. Furthermore, Nullo Metro Compositum Est is the preshared key for host 3. In the scenario, the computer running Windows Server 2003 can only communicate with host 1, indicating that it is set to use the preshared key Quis Custodiet Custodes.

   B. Incorrect: The question asks how the computer running Windows Server 2003 can be reconfigured, not how the host workstations running Windows XP can be reconfigured. Furthermore, Ita Erat Quando Hic Adveni is the preshared key for host 2. In the scenario, the computer running Windows Server 2003 can only communicate with host 1, indicating that it is set to use the preshared key Quis Custodiet Custodes.

   C. Incorrect: For any given filter, there can only be a single preshared key.

   D. Incorrect: The first rule should use the filter named 10.10.10.36, and the second rule should use the filter named 10.10.10.30. In this answer, the preshared keys are switched around.

   E. Correct: This answer assigns the correct preshared keys to the correct IP addresses. Because there is a rule governing all traffic that has a preshared key that allows communication with host 1, host 1 will remain in communication after these new rules and filters are added. When security is negotiated, the authentication essentially works its way down the list until it either finds a rule it matches or until it runs out of rules.

3. **Correct Answers: C**

   A. **Incorrect:** Logging IKE exchanges cannot be enabled from the GUI. It must be enabled from the command line by using the netsh command in the ipsec context.

   B. **Incorrect:** This registry entry describes how logging of IKE exchanges is enabled in Windows 2000 or Windows XP. This method will not work in Windows Server 2003. Furthermore, setting the EnableLogging DWORD to 0 will disable logging of IKE exchanges on these operating systems.

   C. **Correct:** This will enable logging of IKE exchanges on the member server running Windows Server 2003.

   D. **Incorrect:** This command sequence will disable logging of IKE exchanges on the member server running Windows Server 2003.

   E. **Incorrect:** This will enable logging of IKE exchanges in Windows 2000 and Windows XP, but not in Windows Server 2003.

4. **Correct Answers: C**

   A. **Incorrect:** The CRL behavior cannot be modified by using the GUI. It must be modified by means of the netsh ipsec dynamic set config strongcrlcheck command.

   B. **Incorrect:** The CRL behavior cannot be modified by using the GUI. It must be modified by means of the netsh ipsec dynamic set config strongcrlcheck command.

   C. **Correct:** By default, Windows Server 2003 does perform CRL checks, though in some cases this will not stop the IKE certificate authentication. CRL checks can be modified by using the netsh ipsec dynamic set config strongcrlcheck [0/1/2] command. A setting of 2 will cause authentication to fail if any error occurs. A setting of 0 will disable the CRL check.

   D. **Incorrect:** By default, Windows Server 2003 does perform CRL checks, though in some cases this will not stop the IKE certificate authentication. CRL checks can be modified by using the netsh ipsec dynamic set config strongcrlcheck [0/1/2] command. A setting of 2 will cause authentication to fail if any error occurs. A setting of 0 will disable the CRL check.

5. Correct Answers: B

A. **Incorrect:** The commands that Rooslan has issued will enable IPSec driver logging (the first command), will set strong CRL checks during IKE certificate authentication (the second command), and will exempt all broadcast, multicast, and Kerberos traffic from IPSec filtering (the final command). Because the second command does not disable CRL checks during IKE certificate authentication, the first secondary goal is not accomplished. The primary goal and the second secondary goal are accomplished.

B. **Correct:** The commands that Rooslan has issued will enable IPSec driver logging (the first command), will set strong CRL checks during IKE certificate authentication (the second command), and will exempt all broadcast, multicast, and Kerberos traffic from IPSec filtering (the final command). Because the second command does not disable CRL checks during IKE certificate authentication, the first secondary goal is not accomplished. The primary goal and the second secondary goal are accomplished.

C. **Incorrect:** The commands that Rooslan has issued will enable IPSec driver logging (the first command), will set strong CRL checks during IKE certificate authentication (the second command), and will exempt all broadcast, multicast, and Kerberos traffic from IPSec filtering (the final command). Because the second command does not disable CRL checks during IKE certificate authentication, the first secondary goal is not accomplished. The primary goal and the second secondary goal are accomplished.

D. **Incorrect:** The commands that Rooslan has issued will enable IPSec driver logging (the first command), will set strong CRL checks during IKE certificate authentication (the second command), and will exempt all broadcast, multicast, and Kerberos traffic from IPSec filtering (the final command). Because the second command does not disable CRL checks during IKE certificate authentication, the first secondary goal is not accomplished. The primary goal and the second secondary goal are accomplished.

E. **Incorrect:** The commands that Rooslan has issued will enable IPSec driver logging (the first command), will set strong CRL checks during IKE certificate authentication (the second command), and will exempt all broadcast, multicast, and Kerberos traffic from IPSec filtering (the final command). Because the second command does not disable CRL checks during IKE certificate authentication, the first secondary goal is not accomplished. The primary goal and the second secondary goal are accomplished.

Objective 3.5

Plan and Implement Security for Wireless Networks

War driving is a hacker term for driving around with a Global Positioning System (GPS) device and a wireless LAN card taking note of locations with wireless access points. These wireless access points are locations where a wireless LAN has been implemented by an organization, but because the transmission area of the wireless LAN is greater than the boundaries of the organization's building, the wireless LAN spills out into public areas such as streets and sidewalks. War drivers compile lists of such locations and post them on the Internet.

Without adequate security, a wireless network can be accessed by anyone with a wireless Ethernet card. People who download locations compiled by war drivers might just be looking for free access to the Internet to browse sites that might attract the attention of their Internet service provider (ISP) or other authorities, or they might be trying to gain access to a mail server to send junk e-mail messages, or even trying to access data stored on an organization's network. An insecure wireless LAN is an easy target. If a wireless LAN is necessary at an organization, it needs to be secured. With the release of Windows XP Service Pack 1 and Windows Server 2003, Microsoft has included technology that can be used to secure wireless LANs. This technology can be used to secure wireless LANs so that they are inaccessible to unauthorized clients. If this technology is properly implemented, your organization's wireless network will not end up listed somewhere on the Internet as a place where anyone can stroll up and gain access.

Objective 3.5 Questions

1. Rooslan is in the process of planning security for a wireless network. His company will be installing the wireless network in a converted aircraft hanger. There are 10 access points located throughout the hanger to ensure that there is an unbroken field of coverage. Workers who are using Tablet PCs with wireless network adapters must be able to communicate securely. Workers will frequently be changing location and must be able to retain network connectivity when they do so. Which of the following things should Rooslan take into account during the design of the wireless network policy? (Select all that apply.)

- **A.** Plan the preferred networks list to include all access points in the converted aircraft hanger.
- **B.** Plan the preferred networks list to specify only the native access point.
- **C.** Plan to use shared key authentication on the network.
- **D.** Plan to use IEEE 802.1X authentication on the network.

2. You are the systems administrator at a private school that provides students with laptop computers that they use for school work. These laptop computers are equipped with wireless Ethernet cards that are used to connect to access points located in classrooms, in the library, and in special study areas. When in class, the library, or the study areas, students log on to the PVTSCHOOL domain. Recently, the administration has become aware that students are playing networked games with each other over peer-to-peer wireless networks. The administration has asked you to ensure that students can only connect to a network by means of an access point, and that they cannot create peer-to-peer networks with the wireless network cards. All student laptop computers are members of the LAPTOP OU, which is a child OU of the STUDENT OU. All computers and users at the school are members of the PVTSCHOOL domain. Which of the following sets of steps will enable you to implement the administration's goals?

- **A.** Create a new GPO and assign it to the PVTSCHOOL domain. In this GPO, create a wireless network policy, and configure the policy so that the Networks To Access setting is set to Any Available Network.
- **B.** Create a new GPO and assign it to the LAPTOP OU. In this GPO, create a wireless network policy, and configure the policy to allow infrastructure networking only.
- **C.** Create a new GPO and assign it to the LAPTOP OU. In this GPO, create a wireless network policy, and configure the policy to allow ad hoc networking only.
- **D.** Create a new GPO and assign it to the LAPTOP OU. In this GPO, create a wireless network policy, configure that policy to use IEEE 802.1X, and set the Extensible Authentication Protocol (EAP) type to Protected EAP.

3. Rooslan is the security administrator of an organization. Employees of the organization have been issued laptop computers with wireless network cards. This allows them to access the company network from any conference room or from their offices. Logon to all computers is done by means of smart cards, and the laptop computers come equipped with built-in smart card readers. Because company communication is often of a sensitive nature, wireless transmissions are to be secured by means of Wireless Encryption Protocol (WEP) in addition to 802.1X. Rooslan is currently configuring the authentication protocols that will be used with the company's wireless network. Which authentication protocols can he use in his solution?

   A. Extensible Authentication Protocol-Transport Level Security (EAP-TLS)

   B. Protected EAP-Microsoft Encrypted Authentication Version 2 (PEAP-MS-CHAP v2)

   C. Password Authentication Protocol (PAP)

   D. Shared Key

4. You are the systems administrator at a private school that provides students with laptop computers that they use for school work. These laptop computers are equipped with wireless network cards that are used to connect to access points located in classrooms, in the library, and in special study areas. When in class, the library, or the study areas, students log on to the PVTSCHOOL domain. Students log in by using a user name and password combination. The wireless network has been configured with WEP in addition to 802.1x. Which of the following extensible authentication protocol types will provide the best level of security for the kind of authentication used at the private school?

   A. EAP-TLS

   B. MD5

   C. PEAP

   D. PAP

Objective 3.5 Answers

1. **Correct Answers: A and D**

   A. **Correct:** This will allow users to roam between access points without losing their connection to the network.

   B. **Incorrect:** If Rooslan only specifies the native access point, when workers with Tablet PCs move beyond these points they will be unable to access the network without restarting their Tablet PCs.

   C. **Incorrect:** Shared keys are generated between the native access point and the client. If the client moves beyond the initial access point, a new shared key would need to be generated. This could cause problems for users roaming between access points with Tablet PCs.

   D. **Correct:** If you use IEEE 802.1X authentication on the network, new keys will not be required when users with Tablet PCs roam between access points. New keys would be required for these roaming users if you were to use shared key authentication.

2. **Correct Answers: B**

   A. **Incorrect:** This will allow students to join peer-to-peer networks.

   B. **Correct:** The Allow Infrastructure Networking Only setting forces wireless connections to go through access points.

   C. **Incorrect:** This GPO will allow only ad hoc networks to be used; this is the type of network type that you're trying to restrict.

   D. **Incorrect:** This will do nothing to curb the problem of having students use ad hoc networks.

3. **Correct Answers: A**

   A. **Correct:** EAP-TLS is the only Windows Server 2003 authentication protocol that supports smart cards.

   B. **Incorrect:** PEAP-MS-CHAP v2 does not support smart cards, and hence cannot be used as the authentication protocol in this particular solution.

   C. **Incorrect:** PAP does not support smart cards, and hence cannot be used as the authentication protocol in this particular solution.

   D. **Incorrect:** Shared Key authentication does not support smart cards, and hence cannot be used as the authentication protocol in this particular solution.

4. **Correct Answers: C**

   A. **Incorrect:** This protocol is used for authentication with certificates, generally smart cards. This protocol is not suited for password-based authentication.

   B. **Incorrect:** Although MD5 can be used for password authentication, it is not as strong as PEAP, which provides the strongest password-based authentication for WEP with 802.1X.

   C. **Correct:** PEAP provides the strongest password-based authentication for a WEP solution with 802.1X.

   D. **Incorrect:** PAP cannot be used for authentication with a WEP solution with 802.1X.

Objective 3.6

Deploy, Manage, and Configure SSL Certificates

SSL is primarily used to secure data sent over networks. The Hypertext Transfer Protocol Secure (HTTPS) protocol, used for securing Web traffic, encrypts all headers, URLs, cookies, and of course data submitted to the Web site. Any Web application that requests the transmission of confidential data, such as credit card information, over the Internet, needs to use SSL to make sure that intercepted transmissions are not easily read by malicious users.

SSL can also be used to secure traffic between a Web server on a perimeter network (also known as DMZ, demilitarized zone, and screened subnet) and a Microsoft SQL Server computer located on an internal LAN. Similarly, SSL can be used to secure traffic from a client workstation to an Active Directory server in addition to e-mail traffic between Microsoft Office Outlook 2003 and a Microsoft Exchange Server computer.

Certificate reenrollment can be configured through Active Directory or by using the Certificate Templates MMC on the certification authority (CA). It is important to note that a CA cannot issue a certificate that expires after its own certificate does. If the renewal request specifies an interval that ends after the CA's issuing certificate, the request will be truncated to the same date as the issuing certificate's expiration.

Objective 3.6 Questions

1. Rooslan is currently configuring communication between a computer running Windows Server 2003, Web Edition that is located on the company perimeter network and a computer running Windows Server 2003, Standard Edition that hosts a SQL Server 2000 installation on the internal LAN. The internal LAN also hosts a standalone root CA that is installed on a separate standalone computer that is running Windows Server 2003. The SQL Server computer stores confidential information that will be displayed to authorized clients of a Web application running on the computer running Windows Server 2003, Web Edition. Rooslan wants to configure an SSL connection between the server running SQL Server 2000 and the computer on the perimeter network that runs Windows Server 2003, Web Edition. When logged on to the SQL Server computer's console, Rooslan runs Microsoft Internet Explorer and connects to the standalone root CA. He submits an advanced certificate request, selecting to create and submit a request to this particular CA. When he is presented with the Advanced Certificate Request form, he is asked what type of certificate is needed. Which type of certificate should Rooslan choose to install on the SQL Server computer on the internal LAN?

   A. E-mail Protection Certificate

   B. Code Signing Certificate

   C. Time Stamp Signing Certificate

   D. IPSec Certificate

   E. Server Authentication Certificate

2. You are configuring the domain controllers in your domain to use SSL to encrypt Lightweight Directory Access Protocol (LDAP) traffic. This will mean that domain controller communication, in addition to communication from global catalog servers, will be secure. Your domain has a single enterprise root CA installed. It is the only domain in the forest. To proceed with this configuration, you are editing the Default Domain Controllers Policy. In the Computer Configuration\Windows Settings\Public Keys Policies node, you are configuring the Automatic Certificate Request Settings. For which of the following certificate templates should you configure automatic certificate requests to use SSL to encrypt Active Directory traffic? (Select all that apply.)

   A. Computer

   B. Domain Controller

   C. Enrollment Agent (Computer)

   D. IPSec

3. Tailspin Toys has a CA infrastructure represented by the information in the following table.

CA name	CA role	Certificate end date
entrootca.tailspintoys.com	Enterprise root CA	May 12, 2005
ausca.tailspintoys.com	Australia intermediate CA	December 28, 2004
nzca.tailspintoys.com	New Zealand intermediate CA	November 03, 2004
melbca.tailspintoys.com	Melbourne issuing CA	July 27, 2004
auckca.tailspintoys.com	Auckland issuing CA	May 12, 2004

The CA hierarchy is displayed in the following figure.

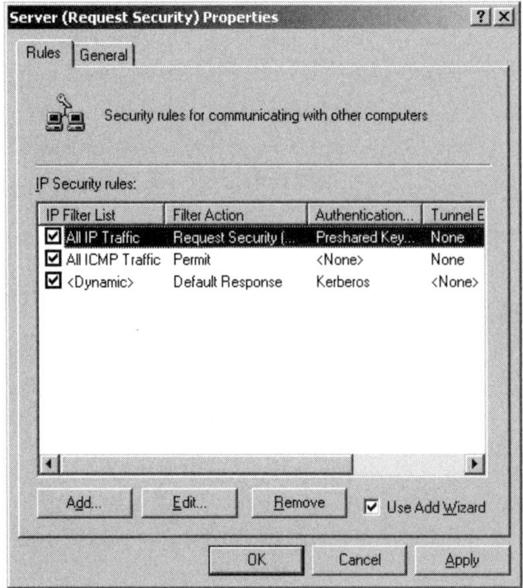

Today's date is January 26, 2004. Which of the following statements about certificate renewal is true?

A. A computer running Windows XP Professional that requests a one-year certificate renewal from melbca.tailspintoys.com will receive a certificate with an end date of January 26, 2005.

B. If the melbca.tailspintoys.com issuing CA attempts to renew its certificate for one year, it will receive a certificate with an end date of December 28, 2004.

C. If the nzca.tailspintoys.com issuing CA attempts to renew its certificate for one year, it will receive a certificate with an end date of May 12, 2005.

D. A computer running Windows XP Professional that attempts to renew a certificate from the auckca.tailspintoys.com CA will be issued a certificate that expires on January 26, 2005.

4. Which of the following represents the fastest way to reenroll all certificate holders of the Workstation Authentication certificate in a single-domain forest with an enterprise root CA running on a Windows Server 2003 domain controller?

A. Log on to the enterprise root CA. Run the Certificate Templates MMC. Right-click the Workstation Authentication certificate. Select the Reenroll All Certificate Holders option.

B. Create a GPO and apply it to the domain. In the \Computer Configuration\Windows Settings\Security Settings\Public Key Policies node, right-click the Automatic Certificate Request settings and run the Automatic Certificate Request Setup Wizard. Select the Workstation Authentication Certificate.

C. From the command prompt, run the `netsh certificates reenroll wrkstnauth` command.

D. Create a logon script and deploy it to each computer in the domain. In the logon script, include the command-line command `certificates reenroll /auto`.

Objective 3.6 Answers

1. **Correct Answers: E**

   A. **Incorrect:** This sort of certificate, when installed on the SQL Server computer, will not allow SQL traffic between the server and the computer on the perimeter network that runs Windows Server 2003, Web Edition to be encrypted by SSL.

   B. **Incorrect:** This sort of certificate, when installed on the SQL Server computer, will not allow SQL traffic between the server and the computer on the perimeter network that runs Windows Server 2003, Web Edition to be encrypted by SSL. This type of certificate is generally used to prove that a particular organization authored specific software that you might download and install on your computer.

   C. **Incorrect:** This sort of certificate, when installed on the SQL Server computer, will not allow SQL traffic between the server and the computer on the perimeter network that runs Windows Server 2003, Web Edition to be encrypted by SSL.

   D. **Incorrect:** This question discusses SSL rather than IPSec. Although it is possible to encrypt communication between the computer running Windows Server 2003, Web Edition and the SQL Server computer using shared certificates, that is not the method of secure communication discussed in the question text.

   E. **Correct:** A Server Authentication Certificate is the appropriate type of certificate to request and install on the SQL Server computer. SQL Server can then be configured to force protocol encryption. As long as the server running Windows Server 2003, Web Edition is configured to trust certificates issued by the standalone root CA on the internal LAN, communication between it and the SQL Server will not be encrypted by SSL.

2. **Correct Answers: A and B**

   A. **Correct:** Both the Computer and the Domain Controller certificate templates are required to encrypt all LDAP traffic transmitted to and from domain controllers by SSL.

   B. **Correct:** Both the Computer and the Domain Controller certificate templates are required to encrypt all LDAP traffic transmitted to and from domain controllers by SSL.

   C. **Incorrect:** The Enrollment Agent (Computer) certificate template is not required to encrypt all LDAP traffic transmitted to and from domain controllers by SSL.

   D. **Incorrect:** An IPSec certificate template is not required to encrypt all LDAP traffic transmitted to and from domain controllers by SSL, though it could be used if data were to be encrypted by IPSec.

3. Correct Answers: B

A. Incorrect: A CA will truncate any request to the date in which its own certificate expires. In this case, any certificate issued from the melbca.tailspintoys.com issuing CA will expire on or before July 27, 2004.

B. Correct: The melbca.tailspintoys.com issuing CA is below the ausca.tailspintoys.com intermediate CA in the hierarchy. The ausca.tailspintoys.com CA cannot issue a certificate dated later than the expiration of its own certificate, which in this case is December 28, 2004.

C. Incorrect: If the nzca.tailspintoys.com issuing CA attempts to renew its certificate for one year, that renewal will be granted. The new certificate will expire on January, 26 2005, rather than May 12, 2005.

D. Incorrect: The auckca.tailspintoys.com CA will be unable to issue a certificate dated later than May 12, 2004.

4. Correct Answers: A

A. Correct: This represents the fastest way to reenroll all certificate holders of the Workstation Authentication certificate.

B. Incorrect: This is used for the automatic request of certificates, not for the reenrollment of certificates. To reenroll all certificate holders, run the Certificate Templates MMC on the CA. Right-click the certificate template you want to have reenrolled, and then click Reenroll All Certificate Holders.

C. Incorrect: The netsh command cannot be used to reenroll certificates. To reenroll all certificate holders, run the Certificate Templates MMC on the CA. Right-click the certificate template you want to have reenrolled, and then click Reenroll All Certificate Holders.

D. Incorrect: There is no certificates reenroll /auto command. To reenroll all certificate holders, run the Certificate Templates MMC on the CA. Right-click the certificate template you want to have reenrolled and then click Reenroll All Certificate Holders.

Objective 3.7

Configure Security for Remote Access Users

Security does not end at the perimeter network firewall. Almost all networks have users that access them remotely. A network that is secured internally is still vulnerable if remote access connections are not properly configured. The two most popular ways to remotely access a network are by dial-up analog modem connection and by a virtual private network (VPN) tunnel through the Internet. Both of these methods of remote access are secured by setting remote access policies on a Routing and Remote Access (RRAS) server.

It is important to understand the various authentication methods. Certain authentication methods can be used with encrypted connections, and other authentication methods cannot. Some authentication methods are only compatible with Windows 2000, with Windows XP, or with Windows Server 2003, and others can be used by almost any client that can connect by modem. Similarly, it is important to understand the difference between tunneling protocols available to Windows XP–based and Windows Server 2003–based VPN clients.

Administrators in the position of needing to roll out a substantial number of connections to computers in an organization can use the Connection Manager Administration Kit. This will create an executable file to completely configure a remote access connection to a network.

Objective 3.7 Questions

1. Tailspin Toys has 50 sales representatives who go to various toy fairs and conventions across the country. Each of these sales representatives is equipped with a Tablet PC running Windows XP that has a built-in analog modem. Currently, when at these locations, sales representatives dial long distance to a remote access server equipped with modems at the Tailspin Toys headquarters site. Using this connection, they are able to access the company network. Rather than maintain this arrangement, the company has decided to give the 50 sales representatives a Point-to-Point Protocol (PPP) dialup account with a national Internet service provider (ISP). After they have connected to a local point of presence, they will connect by means of a VPN to the Tailspin Toys headquarters network. You are preparing for a meeting to decide whether or not this solution should implement Layer Two Tunneling Protocol (L2TP) or Point-to-Point Tunneling Protocol (PPTP). Your manager has the following preferences for the solution:

   - Authentication of tunnels can occur without the use of IPSec.
   - Headers should be compressed as much as possible.
   - The solution must support transmission over PPP dialup connection and IP networks.
   - The solution must be compatible with Windows XP and Windows Server 2003.
   - The solution must provide proof that data was not modified in transit.

   A VPN using PPTP is proposed by another attendee at the meeting. Your manager asks you to comment on this proposal based upon her preferences. Which of your manager's preferences does this proposal fail to meet? (Select all that apply.)

   A. The solution must be compatible with Windows XP and Windows Server 2003.

   B. The solution must support transmission over PPP dialup connection and IP networks.

   C. Authentication of tunnels can occur without the use of IPSec.

   D. Headers should be compressed as much as possible.

   E. The solution must provide proof that data was not modified in transit.

2. You are attempting to troubleshoot the VPN connections that are made between laptop computers running Windows XP Professional that are connected to 100BaseT LANs at airport terminals and your company's Windows Server 2003–based VPN server, which is located at the main office. You want to know which type of tunnel and encryption

combination the VPN server running Windows Server 2003 will attempt to negotiate with connecting clients running Windows XP. Which of the following will the VPN server running Windows Server 2003 attempt to negotiate first?

A. Microsoft Point-to-Point Encryption with IPSec

B. PPTP with IPSec

C. L2TP with Microsoft Point-to-Point Encryption

D. PPTP with Microsoft Point-to-Point Encryption

E. L2TP with IPSec

3. You are configuring a computer running Windows Server 2003 to host several modems so that employees at your company are able to dial into the organization's network. One of your concerns is that the security of employees' home telephone connections cannot be guaranteed. Your specific concern is that they might have been tapped and that information transmitted over the telephone lines might be intercepted. To deal with this concern, you want to disable all authentication protocols on the dial-up server running Windows Server 2003 that do not support data encryption. The dialog box that will enable you to do this is presented in the following figure:

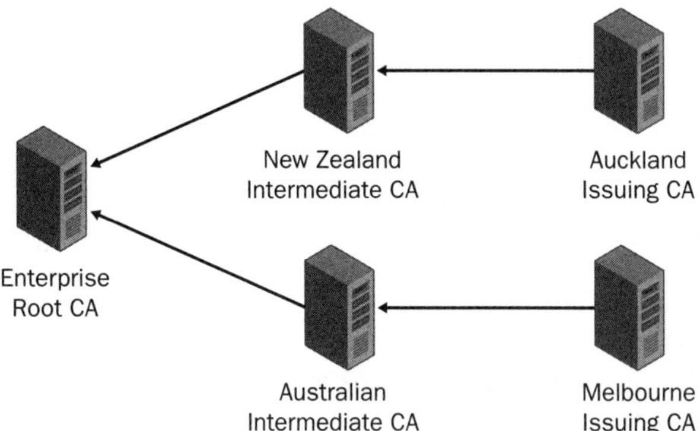

Which of the following protocols should you disable? (Select all that apply.)

A. EAP

B. MS-CHAP v2

C. MS-CHAP

D. CHAP

E. Shiva Password Authentication Protocol (SPAP)

4. Rooslan is editing a dial-up networking entry for Fourth Coffee in the Connection Manager Administration Kit Wizard, as shown in the following figure:

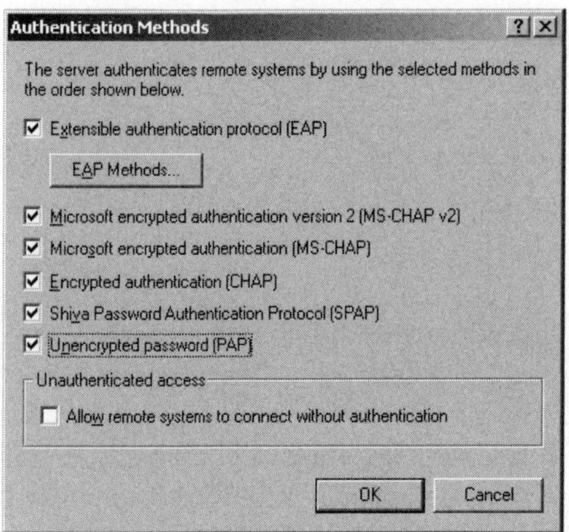

Rooslan wants to ensure that only smart cards can be used for logon authentication and that all data transmitted over the connection is encrypted. Which of the following settings should Rooslan configure to meet these goals?

A. Rooslan should set the Security settings to Use Basic Security Settings. He should configure the Basic Security Settings to Require A Microsoft Secured Password and Require Data Encryption.

B. Rooslan should set the Security settings to Use Both Basic And Advanced. He should leave the default values in place for both the Basic and Advanced security settings.

C. Rooslan should set the Security settings to Use Advanced Security Settings. He should configure the Advanced Security Settings to Use Extensible Authentication Protocol (EAP): MD5-Challenge and set the Data Encryption to Require Encryption.

D. Rooslan should set the Security settings to Use Advanced Security Settings. He should configure the Advanced Security Settings to Use Extensible Authentication Protocol (EAP): Smart Card Or Other Certificate (Encryption Enabled) and set the Data Encryption to Require Encryption.

5. You have configured a member server that runs Windows Server 2003 in your domain as a Routing and Remote Access server. This member server has two analog modems attached to it and is to be used by technical support staff to access the network remotely if the company's normal Internet link fails. You want MS-CHAP v2 to be the only authentication method available. Furthermore, you want to set the encryption level to Microsoft Point to Point Encryption (MPPE) 128 bit and to disallow multilink connections. All staff members who should have access to this service have accounts located in the Techie organizational unit (OU). Which of the following methods can you use to achieve your goals?

A. Create a new GPO and apply it to the Techie OU. In the \User Configuration\Windows Settings\Security Settings\Remote Access node, create a new remote access policy. Configure the remote access policy to limit the available authentication methods to EAP-TLS. Set the only allowable encryption level to Strongest, and disallow multilink connections.

B. Create a new GPO and apply it to the Techie OU. In the \User Configuration\Windows Settings\Security Settings\Remote Access node, create a new remote access policy. Configure the remote access policy to limit the available authentication methods to MS-CHAP v2. Set the only allowable encryption level to Strong, and disallow multilink connections.

C. On the Routing and Remote Access server running Windows Server 2003, create a new remote access policy for dial-up connections by using the wizard. Have this policy apply to the Techras OU. On the Authentication Methods page of the wizard, make sure that only the check box for MS-CHAP v2 is checked. On the Policy Encryption Level page, ensure that only the Strong Encryption check box is checked. After the wizard has finished, edit the properties of the new policy, and then edit the profile. On the Multilink tab, click Do Not Allow Multilink Connections.

D. Add all staff members who should be granted this remote access to a domain global group named Techras. On the Routing and Remote Access server running Windows Server 2003, create a new remote access policy for dial-up connections by using the wizard. Have this policy apply to the Techras group. On the Authentication Methods page of the wizard, make sure that only the check box for MS-CHAP v2 is checked. On the Policy Encryption level page, ensure that only the Strongest Encryption check box is checked. After the wizard has finished, edit the properties of the new policy, and then edit the profile. On the Multilink tab, click Do not Allow Multilink Connections.

Objective 3.7 Answers

1. **Correct Answers: C, D, and E**

   A. **Incorrect:** The proposal is compatible with Windows XP and Windows Server 2003, and hence meets your manager's preference.

   B. **Incorrect:** The proposal will work over PPP dialup connections and IP networks, and hence meets your manager's preference.

   C. **Correct:** PPTP does not provide tunnel authentication unless IPSec is used. L2TP provides tunnel authentication independently of IPSec. The proposal would need to use L2TP to meet your manager's preferences.

   D. **Correct:** L2TP provides better header compression than PPTP (4 bytes versus 6 bytes). The proposal to use PPTP does not meet your manager's preference that maximum header compression should occur.

   E. **Correct:** PPTP does not provide data integrity (proof that data was not modified in transit) or data origin authentication (proof that the data was sent by the authorized user). Only solutions using L2TP with IPSec provide data integrity and data origin authentication. Hence the PPTP proposal does not meet your manager's preference that proof must be shown that data was not modified in transit.

2. **Correct Answers: E**

   A. **Incorrect:** Both of these are encryption protocols, and neither is used to generate a VPN tunnel to a VPN server running Windows Server 2003.

   B. **Incorrect:** A VPN server running Windows Server 2003 will first attempt to negotiate an L2TP with IPSec connection before moving on to other tunneling protocol and encryption combinations. L2TP with IPSec is the most secure VPN method available to Windows Server 2003.

   C. **Incorrect:** A VPN server running Windows Server 2003 will first attempt to negotiate an L2TP with IPSec connection before moving on to other tunneling protocol and encryption combinations. L2TP with IPSec is the most secure VPN method available to Windows Server 2003.

   D. **Incorrect:** A VPN server running Windows Server 2003 will first attempt to negotiate an L2TP with IPSec connection before moving on to other tunneling protocol and encryption combinations. L2TP with IPSec is the most secure VPN method available to Windows Server 2003.

   E. **Correct:** A VPN server running Windows Server 2003 will first attempt to negotiate an L2TP with IPSec connection before moving on to other tunneling protocol and encryption combinations. L2TP with IPSec is the most secure VPN method available to Windows Server 2003.

3. Correct Answers: D and E

A. Incorrect: Data transmissions can only be encrypted if MS-CHAP, MS-CHAP v2, or EAP (TLS or MD5) authentication is used. These protocols generate their own encryption keys that are then used to encrypt data transmission.

B. Incorrect: Data transmissions can only be encrypted if MS-CHAP, MS-CHAP v2, or EAP (TLS or MD5) authentication is used. These protocols generate their own encryption keys that are then used to encrypt data transmission.

C. Incorrect: Data transmissions can only be encrypted if MS-CHAP, MS-CHAP v2, or EAP (TLS or MD5) authentication is used. These protocols generate their own encryption keys that are then used to encrypt data transmission.

D. Correct: Although the authentication in CHAP is encrypted, which means that user names and passwords are not transmitted in plaintext, no encryption key is generated that can be used to encrypt the transmission after authentication occurs. So, although passwords that are intercepted cannot be instantly read, any data transmitted after authentication that is intercepted will pass unencrypted across the telephone line to the modem.

E. Correct: Although the authentication in SPAP is encrypted, which means that user names and passwords are not transmitted in plaintext, no encryption key is generated that can be used to encrypt the transmission after authentication occurs. So, although passwords that are intercepted cannot be instantly read, any data transmitted after authentication that is intercepted will pass unencrypted across the telephone line to the modem.

4. Correct Answers: D

A. Incorrect: Although this will ensure that data encryption is used, the basic security settings do not allow for the use of smart cards. This will not meet Rooslan's goals.

B. Incorrect: The default values require a secure password (not a smart card) and allow encryption to remain optional. This will not meet Rooslan's goals.

C. Incorrect: Although this will ensure that data is encrypted, MD5-Challenge configures password authentication, rather than smart card/certificate authentication, to be used. This will not meet Rooslan's goals.

D. Correct: This will ensure that data is encrypted and that a smart card is used. The default setting for Smart Card Or Other Certificate is My Smart Card. It is also possible to use a digital certificate installed on the connecting computer.

5. **Correct Answers: D**

A. **Incorrect:** Remote access policies are not configured by GPO. They are configured on a Routing and Remote Access server and applied to groups or to individual users.

B. **Incorrect:** Remote access policies are not configured by GPO. They are configured on a Routing and Remote Access server and applied to groups or to individual users.

C. **Incorrect:** This particular remote access policy does not set the encryption level to MPPE 128, but to MPPE 56. Remote access policies can only apply to individual users and groups, not to OUs.

D. **Correct:** Remote access policies are configured on the Routing and Remote Access server, not by means of Group Policy. Remote access policies are applied to groups or users, not to Group Policy objects or domains. Strongest Encryption sets the encryption to MPPE 128. If this method is followed, the goals described in the question will be achieved.

16 Planning, Configuring, and Troubleshooting Authentication, Authorization, and PKI (4.0)

If you don't have the ability to correctly verify the identity of users on a network, there is no way to ensure that users get the specific type of access that they are entitled to. This is why authentication and authorization are some of the most important steps in the security process. The authorization process starts with the authorization protocol. By default, Microsoft Windows Server 2003 uses the Kerberos v5 authentication protocol. This protocol is supported by Windows 2000 Server and clients running Microsoft Windows 2000 Professional and Windows XP Professional. Windows Server 2003 also supports both versions of NTLM, which is the authentication protocol used by Microsoft Windows NT 4.0 and earlier, in addition to Windows 95, Windows 98, and Windows Millennium Edition. The authentication protocol that is used is negotiated: Kerberos is attempted first, and NTLMv2 is attempted if that fails.

Windows Server 2003 brings a large improvement to the configuration of trust relationships by introducing the forest trust. In Windows Server 2003, with the configuration of a single trust, all domains in one forest can be configured to trust all domains in another forest. This is vastly easier than it was in Windows NT 4.0 or Windows 2000, in which trusts were configured on a domain-by-domain basis.

Now that cross-forest trusts are easier to configure, understanding group scopes is of greater importance. Domain local groups are used to assign permissions to resources within a domain. They are also used to assign rights. Assigning permissions and rights to groups rather than individual users simplifies the administration process. Global groups can be used throughout the forest, but they can only contain members from a single domain. Universal groups can contain members from any domain in the forest, including global groups and other universal groups. When trust relationships exist, however, the only group type that can have member groups from other forests is the domain local group.

Certification authorities (CAs) form the core of public key infrastructure. Windows Server 2003 supports four types of CAs. For close integration of certificates with Active Directory directory service, there are enterprise CAs. These are available in the root and subordinate versions. When integration with Active Directory is not required, CAs can be configured as standalone. Like the enterprise CA, the standalone also is also available in the root and subordinate versions. Best practice is to issue certificates from the subordinate and only use the root to issue certificates to subordinate CAs. Understanding how all of these technologies interact forms a fundamental part of the knowledge required to pass the 70-299 exam.

Testing Skills and Suggested Practices

The skills that you need to successfully master the Managing and Implementing Disaster Recovery objective domain on Exam 70-299, Implementing and Administering Security in a Microsoft Windows Server 2003 Network, include:

- Configuring trust relationships.
  - Practice 1: Configure four computers running Windows Server 2003 in the following way: Configure the first computer as the root domain controller in a new forest. Call this computer rootdc1. Configure the second computer as a domain controller in a child domain of the first computer. Call this computer childdc1. Configure the third computer as a domain controller in root domain in a new forest. Call this computer rootdc2. Configure the fourth computer as the domain controller of a child domain of the third computer's root domain. Call this computer childdc2. After this is done, you should have two separate forests, each containing a single tree with two domains per forest. Create some test accounts in each of the four domains. Each test account should have a unique name. Consider creating account names that contain the domain name the account is created in so that it's easy to tell from the name alone where the account resides. Configure an external trust relationship between rootdc1 and rootdc2. Do this by using the Active Directory Domains and Trust console, which is located on the Administrative Tools menu. Ensure that the trust relationship goes both ways. Use Active Directory Users and Computers to add users from the first computer's domain to local groups from the third computer's domain. Note that you will be unable to add users from any of the child domains.
  - Practice 2: Using the setup from Practice 1, remove the external trust relationship. Ensure that all forests are running at the Windows Server 2003 forest functional level. This will involve using the Active Directory Domains and Trust console, which is located on the Administrative Tools menu, to raise the domain functional level and forest functional levels from the default. Once the requisite functional level has been achieved, establish a forest trust relationship between the two forests. To test this trust relationship, create a shared folder on childdc1. Set permissions for users in the first, third, and fourth domains. Because the forest trust relationship ensures that all domains now trust each other, you will be able to assign permissions for resources to objects in all domains in both forests.

- Configuring the nesting of groups.
  - Practice 1: On a Windows Server 2003–based computer that is a member of a domain running at the Windows Server 2003 functional level, and that is also a member of a forest that contains at least another domain, create a new universal group. Try to add the following types of groups to the universal group, and note which ones you can and cannot add. (Some of these objects cannot be nested into a universal group.)
    —A domain local group from the local domain
    —A domain local group from another domain in the forest
    —Some users from the local domain
    —Some users from another domain in the forest
    —A global group from another domain in the forest
    —A universal group from another domain in the forest
  - Practice 2: On a Windows Server 2003—based computer that is a member of a domain running at the Windows Server 2003 functional level, and that is also a member of a forest that contains at least one other domain, create a new domain local group. Try to add the following types of groups to the domain local group, and note which ones you can and cannot add. (Some of these objects cannot be nested into a domain local group.)
    —A domain local group from the local domain
    —A domain local group from another domain in the forest
    —Users from the local domain
    —Users from another domain in the forest
    —A global group from another domain in the forest
    —A universal group from another domain in the forest
- Configuring permissions and rights.
  - Practice 1: On a computer running Windows Server 2003, create four different local groups. Add a single test user account to all of these groups. Create a temporary folder. Configure the NTFS permissions for this folder so that each of the newly created local groups has a different level of permissions. After this is done, click the Advanced button, and then use the Effective Permissions tab to calculate the effective permissions for the test user that you added to these four groups at the start of this exercise.
  - Practice 2: On a member server running Windows Server 2003, create a nonprivileged local user account with no special rights. Verify that this user can log on to the member server. Log the user off, and then log back on with Administrator credentials. Edit the local Group Policy settings for a computer running Windows Server 2003 by running gpedit.msc. In the Computer Configuration\Windows Settings\Security Settings\User Rights Assignment node of the local computer policy, remove the users group from the Allow Log on

Locally policy. Log off from the administrator account and try again to log on with the newly created normal local user account.

- Installing and configuring certificate services.
  - Practice 1: Install an enterprise root certificate server on a computer in a Windows Server 2003 domain. Run the CA Microsoft Management Console (MMC) from the Administrative Tools menu, and examine the certificate templates that are available.
  - Practice 2: Install and configure an enterprise subordinate server on a computer in a Windows Server 2003 domain using the enterprise root CA as a parent. After the server is installed, open the CA MMC from the Administrative Tools menu. Right-click the enterprise subordinate CA. On the General tab, view the certificate. Examine the Certification Path tab to view the certificate hierarchy.

Further Reading

This section lists supplemental readings by objective. We recommend that you study these sources thoroughly before taking this exam.

Objective 4.1 Review Chapter 1, "Planning and Configuring an Authentication Strategy."

Microsoft Corporation. Windows Server 2003 Help and Support Center. Review "Authentication."

Microsoft Corporation. Windows Server 2003 Help and Support Center. Review "Trusts."

Enabling Delegated Authentication. *http://www.microsoft.com/technet/treeview/default.asp?url=/technet/prodtechnol/windowsserver2003/proddocs/deployguide/dsscc_aut_vwcs.asp*

How to configure IIS Web Site Authentication in Windows Server 2003. *http://support.microsoft.com/default.aspx?kbid=324274*

Objective 4.2 Review Chapter 1, "Planning and Configuring an Authentication Strategy."

Review Chapter 2, "Planning and Configuring an Authorization Strategy."

Microsoft Corporation. Windows Server 2003 Help and Support Center. Review "Universal Groups."

Microsoft Corporation. Windows Server 2003 Help and Support Center. Review "Domain Local Groups."

Microsoft Corporation. Windows Server 2003 Help and Support Center. Review "Global Groups."

Understanding Groups. *http://www.microsoft.com/technet/treeview/default.asp?url=/technet/prodtechnol/windowsserver2003/proddocs/standard/sag_AdunderstandGroups.asp*

Objective 4.3 Review Chapter 2, "Planning and Configuring an Authorization Strategy."

Microsoft Corporation. Windows Server 2003 Help and Support Center. Review "Access Control."

Microsoft Corporation. Windows Server 2003 Help and Support Center. Review "Effective Permissions."

Microsoft Corporation. Windows Server 2003 Help and Support Center. Review "User Rights."

User Rights Assignment. *http://www.microsoft.com/technet/treeview/default.asp?url=/technet/prodtechnol/windowsserver2003/proddocs/standard/URAtopnode.asp*

Objective 4.4 Review Chapter 7, "Installing, Configuring, and Managing Certification Services."

Review Chapter 3, "Deploying and Troubleshooting Security Templates."

Microsoft Corporation. Windows Server 2003 Help and Support Center. Review "Installing and Configuring a Certification Authority."

Microsoft Corporation. Windows Server 2003 Help and Support Center. Review "Backing up and Restoring a Certification Authority."

Public Key Infrastructure. *http://www.microsoft.com/technet/treeview/default.asp?url=/technet/prodtechnol/windowsserver2003/proddocs/entserver/SE_PKI.asp*

Objective 4.1

Plan and Configure Authentication

Authentication is the process by which credentials are validated. Windows Server 2003 uses several different authentication protocols, including NTLM and NTLMv2, Kerberos v5, Secure Sockets Layer/Transport Layer Security SSL/TLS, Digest authentication, and .NET Passport, to authenticate access to Web services. Some of these protocols can also be used to validate logons. Windows Server 2003 can be configured with several types of trust relationships. Like Windows 2000 Server, Windows Server 2003 can be configured with two-way external trusts between domains. This means that objects in one domain can be given permission to resources in another domain. Windows Server 2003 also introduces the forest trust. Unlike an external trust, a forest trust ensures that every domain in one forest trusts every domain in another forest. This greatly simplifies the administration of trust relationships because in the past individual external trusts needed to be set up between all domains in different forests to achieve a similar result. All members of a Windows Server 2003 forest have an automatic trust relationship that does not need to be configured, because it is created when a child domain domain controller is installed in a forest.

Objective 4.1 Questions

1. You are the administrator of the Active Directory forest for the science department at the local university. You want to create a forest trust relationship with the Active Directory forest for the arts department. All domain controllers in both forests are running Windows Server 2003. All domains in each forest are running at the Windows Server 2003 functional level. When you attempt to create the forest trust relationship, you are only given the option to create an external trust relationship. What do you need to do to create a forest trust relationship between the forests of the arts department and the science department?

A. Forest trust relationships are only available in Windows 2000 forests.

B. You need to install an enterprise root CA in each forest.

C. The first forest needs an enterprise root CA. The second forest needs an enterprise subordinate CA that trusts the enterprise root CA from the first forest.

D. You must raise the forest functional level of both forests to Windows Server 2003.

2. You are responsible for coordinating the forest trust relationships at the local university. There are seven departments, each of which has its own Windows Server 2003 Active Directory infrastructure. The Medicine, Science and Engineering forests are running at the Windows Server 2003 forest functional level. The Arts, Economics, Law, and Education forests are running at the Windows 2000 functional level. Forest trust relationships exist between Medicine and Science, and between Science and Engineering. External trust relationships exist between the root domains of the following forests: between Arts and Science, between Arts and Economics, between Law and Medicine, between Law and Education, and between Education and Engineering.

You have received a telephone call from the Administrator of the Science forest. She asks the following question: If she creates a domain local group in one of the child domains for the Science forest, from which of the other department forests will she be able to add universal groups? How should you answer her question?

A. Arts

B. Medicine

C. Engineering

D. Economics

E. Law

F. Education

3. There are five accounts that are members of the Domain Admins group in your domain. Because these accounts are sensitive, you want to restrict delegated authentication for these accounts. Which of the following methods could you use to do this?

   A. On the General tab of the properties of the Domain Admins group, ensure that the Account Is Sensitive And Cannot Be Delegated check box is checked.

   B. Configure the membership of the Domain Admins group by using the restricted groups node of the default domain Group Policy object (GPO).

   C. In the Account Policies node of the default domain GPO, add the Domain Admins group to the Restrict Delegated Authentication policy.

   D. Use Active Directory Users And Computers to select the user accounts for all five members of the Domain Admins group. Edit the properties of these accounts. On the Account tab in the Account Options section, ensure that the Account Is Sensitive And Cannot Be Delegated check box is selected.

4. Parsons is the administrator for an Internet Web site that is run by an accounting company. There are particular areas of the Web site that Parsons wants to secure from unauthorized access. Because much of the information stored on the site is confidential, a strong form of authentication is required. The root domain of the accounting company's forest is adatum.com. The Web server is located on the perimeter network in a special child domain named pn.adatum.com. Each user that is to be given access to the confidential area of the site will have a special account created for him within a special child domain called clients.adatum.com. Parsons has the following requirements for the Web site's authentication strategy:

   - Authentication must occur without reference to any third party.
   - Authentication between client and server must not transmit credentials over the Internet without encryption.
   - Authentication must be able to occur through proxy servers and firewalls.
   - Authentication must be as secure as possible, given the constraints of the other conditions.

   Parsons has made sure that anonymous access has been disabled. Which of the following authentication methods should Parsons use for the accounting company's Web site?

   A. .NET Passport authentication

   B. Basic authentication

   C. Integrated Windows authentication

   D. Digest authentication for Windows domain servers

5. You are planning the rollout of Windows Server 2003 to an environment with a mixed set of clients. The company for which you will be installing Windows Server 2003 has a mixture of computers running Windows NT 4.0 Workstation, notebook computers running Windows Millennium Edition, and computers running Windows 2000 Professional. Which of the following authentication protocols will be used by the computers running Windows NT 4.0 Workstation when they authenticate against a domain controller running Windows Server 2003?

A. NTLM/NTLMv2

B. SSL/TLS

C. Digest authentication

D. .NET Passport authentication

E. Kerberos v5 authentication

Objective 4.1 Answers

1. **Correct Answers: D**

   A. **Incorrect:** Forest trust relationships can only be created if both forests are running at the Windows Server 2003 functional level. Although all of the domains in the example are running at the Windows Server 2003 functional level, and this would enable the forest to be running at this level, unless the level of the forest is explicitly raised, it will stay at the default Windows 2000 functional level.

   B. **Incorrect:** Forest trust relationships can exist irrespective of the presence of an enterprise root CA. Forest trust relationships can only be created if both forests are running at the Windows Server 2003 functional level. Although all of the domains in the example are running at the Windows Server 2003 functional level, and this would enable the forest to be running at this level, unless the level of the forest is explicitly raised, it will stay at the default Windows 2000 functional level.

   C. **Incorrect:** Forest trust relationships can exist irrespective of the presence of an enterprise root CA. Forest trust relationships can only be created if both forests are running at the Windows Server 2003 functional level. Although all of the domains in the example are running at the Windows Server 2003 functional level, and this would enable the forest to be running at this level, unless the level of the forest is explicitly raised, it will stay at the default Windows 2000 functional level.

   D. **Correct:** Forest trust relationships can only be created if both forests are running at the Windows Server 2003 functional level. Although all of the domains in the example are running at the Windows Server 2003 functional level, and this would enable the forest to be running at this level, unless the level of the forest is explicitly raised, it will stay at the default Windows 2000 functional level.

2. **Correct Answers: B and C**

   A. **Incorrect:** Forest trust relationships are nontransitive. In other words, just because Forest A trusts Forest B, and Forest B trusts Forest C, it does not automatically mean that Forest A trusts Forest C. The difference between a forest trust and an external trust is that an external trust is on a domain-to-domain basis. So a child domain of the Science forest will not be able to use an external trust relationship configured between the root domain of the Science forest and the root domain of another forest.

   B. **Correct:** Forest trust relationships are nontransitive. In other words, just because Forest A trusts Forest B, and Forest B trusts Forest C, it does not automatically mean that Forest A trusts Forest C. The difference between a forest trust and an external trust is that an external trust occurs on a domain-to-domain basis. So a child domain of the Science forest will not be able to use an external trust relationship configured between the root domain of the Science forest and the root domain of another forest.

C. Correct: Forest trust relationships are nontransitive. In other words, just because Forest A trusts Forest B, and Forest B trusts Forest C, it does not automatically mean that Forest A trusts Forest C. The difference between a forest trust and an external trust is that an external trust occurs on a domain-to-domain basis. So a child domain of the Science forest will not be able to use an external trust relationship configured between the root domain of the Science forest and the root domain of another forest.

D. Incorrect: Forest trust relationships are nontransitive. In other words, just because Forest A trusts Forest B, and Forest B trusts Forest C, it does not automatically mean that Forest A trusts Forest C. The difference between a forest trust and an external trust is that an external trust occurs on a domain-to-domain basis. So a child domain of the Science forest will not be able to use an external trust relationship configured between the root domain of the Science forest and the root domain of another forest.

E. Incorrect: Forest trust relationships are nontransitive. In other words, just because Forest A trusts Forest B, and Forest B trusts Forest C, it does not automatically mean that Forest A trusts Forest C. The difference between a forest trust and an external trust is that an external trust occurs on a domain-to-domain basis. So a child domain of the Science forest will not be able to use an external trust relationship configured between the root domain of the Science forest and the root domain of another forest.

F. Incorrect: Forest trust relationships are nontransitive. In other words, just because Forest A trusts Forest B, and Forest B trusts Forest C, it does not automatically mean that Forest A trusts Forest C. The difference between a forest trust and an external trust is that an external trust occurs on a domain-to-domain basis. So a child domain of the Science forest will not be able to use an external trust relationship configured between the root domain of the Science forest and the root domain of another forest.

3. Correct Answers: D

A. Incorrect: This option must be set on an account-by-account basis. This is done by editing the account properties, clicking the Accounts tab, and, in the Account Options section, selecting the Account Is Sensitive And Cannot Be Delegated check box.

B. Incorrect: This option must be set on an account-by-account basis. This is done by editing the account properties, clicking the Accounts tab, and, in the Account Options section, selecting the Account Is Sensitive And Cannot Be Delegated check box. This cannot be done by using restricted groups.

C. **Incorrect:** This option must be set on an account-by-account basis. There is no Restrict Delegated Authentication policy. To restrict delegated authentication, edit the account properties, click the Accounts tab, and, in the Account Options section, select the Account Is Sensitive And Cannot Be Delegated check box.

D. **Correct:** This option must be set on an account-by-account basis. This is done by editing the account properties, clicking the Accounts tab, and, in the Account Options section, selecting the Account Is Sensitive And Cannot Be Delegated check box.

4. **Correct Answers: D**

A. **Incorrect:** .NET Passport authentication occurs with reference to a third party, and hence does not meet Parson's requirements.

B. **Incorrect:** Basic authentication transmits authentication credentials across the network in plaintext format, and hence does not meet Parson's requirements.

C. **Incorrect:** Although Integrated Windows authentication does provide the most secure authentication solution (aside from using digital certificates), it cannot be used over most proxy servers or firewalls.

D. **Correct:** Digest authentication for Windows domain servers transmits credentials by means of an encrypted MD5 hash. It works for trusted domains. Given that pn.adatum.com and clients.adatum.com are members of the same forest, there will be a trust relationship between them. Digest authentication for Windows domain servers also works over proxies and firewalls.

5. **Correct Answers: A**

A. **Correct:** Computers running Windows NT 4.0 Workstation do not support the default Kerberos v5 authentication that would be used between a computer running Windows 2000 Professional or Windows XP Professional and a domain controller running Windows Server 2003.

B. **Incorrect:** This authentication protocol is used to authenticate against a Web server running Internet Information Services. It is not used to authenticate domain logons.

C. **Incorrect:** This authentication protocol is used to authenticate against a Web server running Internet Information Services. It is not used to authenticate domain logons.

D. **Incorrect:** This authentication protocol is used to authenticate against a Web server running Internet Information Services. It is not used to authenticate domain logons.

E. **Incorrect:** Computers running Windows NT 4.0 Workstation do not support the default Kerberos v5 authentication that would be used between a computer running Windows 2000 Professional or Windows XP Professional and a domain controller running Windows Server 2003.

Objective 4.2

Plan Group Structure

The manner in which groups are used in an Active Directory forest depends on the functional level of each domain. At some functional levels, such as Windows 2000 Mixed and Windows Server 2003 Interim, universal groups are not supported. Similarly, the functionality of global groups varies depending on the functional level of the domain. At the Windows Server 2003 functional level, global groups can contain other global groups from the same domain. Whenever possible, permissions should be assigned to groups rather than to individual users. The recommended technique for assigning permissions in forests is to add users in domains to global groups, add those global groups to forest-wide universal groups, and then add universal groups to domain local groups in which permissions should be applied. This makes the management of groups simpler and also reduces global catalog server replication traffic.

Objective 4.2 Questions

1. Tailspin Toys is migrating from a Windows NT 4.0 network to a Windows Server 2003 network. Windows NT 4.0 backup domain controllers (BDCs) are gradually being replaced by Windows Server 2003 domain controllers on a site-by-site basis. There are three domains in the Tailspin Toys forest. These domains are named west.tailspintoys.com, east.tailspintoys.com, and central.tailspintoys.com. The west.tailspintoys.com domain is the forest root domain. There are no servers running Windows 2000 in the Tailspin Toys forest. Only users from one domain—west.tailspintoys.com—authenticate completely against computers running Windows Server 2003. The other domains still have some Windows NT 4.0 BDCs. Each domain is running at its highest possible functional level. You are configuring a group strategy for the Tailspin Toys forest. Which of the following statements are true?

   A. All domains in the forest can use domain local groups.

   B. All domains in the forest can use global groups.

   C. All domains in the forest can use universal groups.

   D. A global group in the central.tailspintoys.com domain can have a global group in the east.tailspintoys.com as a member.

   E. A universal group running in the west.tailspintoys.com domain can have members from the central.tailspintoys.com and east.tailspintoys.com domains.

2. A forest trust relationship exists between the science.internal and the arts.internal forests. The administrator of the philosophy.arts.internal domain wants to give certain users from the mathematics.science.internal and the physics.science.internal domains access to certain domain resources. This access will be mediated through membership of groups. Which of the following methods could the administrator of the philosophy.arts.internal domain use to configure this access while using the least possible number of groups?

   A. Create a global group in the philosophy.arts.internal domain. Then add the individual accounts that should be given access from the mathematics.science.internal and physics.science.internal domains to this global group. Finally, use this global group to apply the required permissions to the appropriate domain resources.

   B. Create a universal group in the philosophy.arts.internal domain. Ask the administrators of the mathematics.science.internal and physics.science.internal domains to add the required user accounts to universal groups in each respective science.internal domain. Add the universal groups from the mathematics.science.internal and physics.science.internal domains to the universal group created in the philosophy.arts.internal domain. Apply the required permissions for the resource to this universal group.

C. Create a global group in the mathematics.science.internal domain. Add the appropriate users from this domain to this group. Create a global group in the physics.science.internal domain. Add the appropriate users from this domain to this group. Create a domain local group in the philosophy.arts.internal domain. Add the global groups that you created to the domain local group in the philosophy.arts.internal domain. Apply the required permissions for the resource to this domain local group.

D. Create a domain local group in the philosophy.arts.internal domain. Ask the administrators of the mathematics.science.internal and physics.science.internal domains to add the required user accounts from each respective science.internal domain to a universal group located in the mathematics.science.internal domain. Add the universal group from the mathematics.science.internal domain to the domain local group created in the philosophy.arts.internal domain. Apply the required permissions for the resource to this domain local group.

3. You are the network administrator at a university. The university has a disparate set of departments, each of which has instituted its own Active Directory infrastructure. Three departments—law, science, and arts—have configured trust relationships between their domains. The Law forest is at Windows Server 2003 functional level. The Science forest is at Windows 2000 native functional level. The Arts forest is at Windows 2000 mixed functional level. External trusts exist between the root domain of the Law forest and the root domain of the Science forest, between the root domain of the Science forest and the root domain of the Arts forest, and between the root domain of the Arts forest and the root domain of the Law forest. You are configuring a domain local group in the root domain of the Law forest. Which of the following groups can you add to this group?

A. A universal group from a child domain of the Law forest

B. A global group from the root domain of the Arts forest

C. A universal group from a child domain of the Science forest

D. A domain local group from a child domain of the Arts forest

E. A domain local group from a child domain of the Law forest

4. A. Datum Corporation has an Active Directory forest that contains three trees. The root of the first tree is adatum.com, the root of the second tree is proseware.com, and the root of the third tree is contoso.com. Each domain in the forest uses a combination of Windows Server 2003 and Windows 2000 Server domain controllers. There are no Windows NT 4.0 domain controllers present. If the domains and the forest are configured to the highest functional level possible while maintaining the Windows 2000 Server domain controllers, which of the following statements would be correct? (Select all that apply.)

A. A domain local group created in the western.adatum.com domain can include a universal group from the southern.contoso.com domain in its membership.

B. A universal group created in the northern.proseware.com domain can include domain local groups from the southern.proseware.com and western.proseware.com domains in its membership.

C. A global group created in the southern.contoso.com domain can include global groups from the northern.proseware.com and eastern.adatum.com domains in its membership.

D. A global group created in the eastern.adatum.com domain can include a universal group from the proseware.com domain in its membership.

E. A universal group created in the western.proseware.com domain can include universal groups from the southern.adatum.com and northern.contoso.com domains in its membership.

5. Rooslan is the systems administrator for A. Datum Corporation. The company's network infrastructure has a forest configured at the Windows Server 2003 functional level. The forest has two separate domain trees. The root domain of the first domain tree and the forest is adatum.com. The root domain of the second domain tree is proseware.com. The adatum.com tree contains five domains and the proseware.com tree contains three domains.

There are several users in the A. Datum Corporation organization who have exceptional systems administration skills. Unfortunately, the accounts of these users are located in different domains. The users and their domains are listed in the following table.

User	Domain
Rooslan	adatum.com
Oksana	western.adatum.com
Mick	eastern.adatum.com
Agim	western.proseware.com
Kasia	northern.proseware.com
Shan	southern.adatum.com

Rooslan is in the process of configuring a strategy for the implementation of groups.

He has the following goals:

Primary goal: Create a single group whose membership includes all of these users.

First secondary goal: Grant administrator permissions to these users on all member servers in all domains, except for the root domains adatum.com and proseware.com.

Second secondary goal: No other users, except for the ones in this list, should be able to become members of the sysadmins group.

Rooslan plans to do the following:

- Add each of the users in the list to a universal group in the adatum.com domain named sysadmins.
- Add the sysadmins group to the local administrator group on each member server in all domains, except for the adatum.com and proseware.com domains.

Which goals will Rooslan accomplish with this plan?

A. Rooslan's plan accomplishes the primary goal and both secondary goals.

B. Rooslan's plan accomplishes the primary goal and one secondary goal.

C. Rooslan's plan accomplishes only the primary goal.

D. Rooslan's plan does not accomplish the primary goal; however, it does accomplish both secondary goals.

E. Rooslan's plan accomplishes only one of the secondary goals. It does not accomplish the primary goal.

F. Rooslan's plan accomplishes none of his goals.

Objective 4.2 Answers

1. **Correct Answers: A, B, and E**

   A. **Correct:** Of the listed domains, only west.tailspintoys.com domain will be running at the Windows Server 2003 functional level. The east.tailspintoys.com and central.tailspintoys.com domains are most likely running in either Windows Server 2003 interim or Windows 2000 mixed mode, because both of these modes support Windows NT 4.0 BDCs. Domain local groups can be used in all domain functional levels.

   B. **Correct:** Of the listed domains, only west.tailspintoys.com domain will be running at the Windows Server 2003 functional level. The east.tailspintoys.com and central.tailspintoys.com domains are most likely running in either Windows Server 2003 interim or Windows 2000 mixed mode, because both of these modes support Windows NT 4.0 BDCs. Global groups can be used at all domain functional levels.

   C. **Incorrect:** Of the listed domains, only west.tailspintoys.com domain will be running at the Windows Server 2003 functional level. The east.tailspintoys.com and central.tailspintoys.com domains are most likely running in either Windows Server 2003 interim or Windows 2000 mixed mode, because both of these modes support Windows NT 4.0 BDCs. Universal groups can only be used at the Windows 2000 native or Windows Server 2003 functional level, so only the west.tailspintoys.com domain can use such a group.

   D. **Incorrect:** Of the listed domains, only west.tailspintoys.com domain will be running at the Windows Server 2003 functional level. The east.tailspintoys.com and central.tailspintoys.com domains are most likely running in either Windows Server 2003 interim or Windows 2000 mixed mode, because both of these modes support Windows NT 4.0 BDCs. Global groups can only contain other global groups as members if the domain is running at the Windows 2000 native or Windows Server 2003 functional level.

   E. **Correct:** Of the listed domains, only west.tailspintoys.com domain will be running at the Windows Server 2003 functional level. The east.tailspintoys.com and central.tailspintoys.com domains are most likely running in either Windows Server 2003 interim or Windows 2000 mixed mode, because both of these modes support Windows NT 4.0 BDCs. Global groups can only contain other global groups as members if the domain is running at the Windows 2000 native or Windows Server 2003 functional level. Even though the east.tailspintoys.com and central.tailspintoys.com domains are not running at the Windows Server 2003 functional level, user accounts from these domains can be added to a universal group in the west.tailspintoys.com domain.

2. **Correct Answers: D**

   A. **Incorrect:** Global groups cannot have users from trusted domains as members. Only users, computers, and global groups from the domain in which the global group is created can be added to a global group.

   B. **Incorrect:** Universal groups from one forest cannot include universal groups from another forest as members.

   C. **Incorrect:** Although this method would work, it does not use the least possible number of groups. A universal group could be created in the physics.science.internal or mathematics.science.internal domain, and the requisite users from the science.internal forest could be added to this universal group. This universal group could in turn be added to a domain local group in the philosophy.arts.internal domain. After this was done, the appropriate permissions could be applied.

   D. **Correct:** This method achieves the goals and uses the least possible number of groups.

3. **Correct Answers: A and B**

   A. **Correct:** Universal groups from the same domain can be added to domain local groups.

   B. **Correct:** A global group from the root domain of a trusted domain can be added to a domain local group in the root domain of the Law forest.

   C. **Incorrect:** Because forest trusts have not been configured, universal groups from child domains in the Science forest will not be visible to the root domain of the Law forest.

   D. **Incorrect:** Even if a forest trust were configured, under no circumstances can domain local groups from remote domains be added to domain local groups.

   E. **Incorrect:** Under no circumstances can domain local groups from remote domains be added to domain local groups.

4. **Correct Answers: A and E**

   A. **Correct:** Domain local groups can include universal groups from the same forest.

   B. **Incorrect:** Domain local groups cannot be members of universal groups.

   C. **Incorrect:** Global groups can only have global groups, users, and computers from the same domain as members. Global and universal groups from other domains in a forest cannot be members of a global group.

   D. **Incorrect:** Global groups can only have global groups, users, and computers from the same domain as members. Global and universal groups from other domains in a forest cannot be members of a global group.

   E. **Correct:** Universal groups can have other universal groups from within the forest as members.

5. **Correct Answers: B**

A. **Incorrect:** Universal groups are visible in all domains in a forest configured at the Windows Server 2003 functional level. Universal groups can be added to computer local groups, such as the administrators groups on member servers. Universal groups can have members from any domain in the forest. Rooslan's first action accomplishes the primary goal. Rooslan's second action accomplishes the first secondary goal. Because Rooslan institutes no restricted Group Policy, the second secondary goal is not accomplished.

B. **Correct:** Universal groups are visible in all domains in a forest configured at the Windows Server 2003 functional level. Universal groups can be added to computer local groups, such as the administrators groups on member servers. Universal groups can have members from any domain in the forest. Rooslan's first action accomplishes the primary goal. Rooslan's second action accomplishes the first secondary goal. Because Rooslan institutes no restricted Group Policy, the second secondary goal is not accomplished.

C. **Incorrect:** Universal groups are visible in all domains in a forest configured at the Windows Server 2003 functional level. Universal groups can be added to computer local groups, such as the administrators groups on member servers. Universal groups can have members from any domain in the forest. Rooslan's first action accomplishes the primary goal. Rooslan's second action accomplishes the first secondary goal. Because Rooslan institutes no restricted Group Policy, the second secondary goal is not accomplished.

D. **Incorrect:** Universal groups are visible in all domains in a forest configured at the Windows Server 2003 functional level. Universal groups can be added to computer local groups, such as the administrators groups on member servers. Universal groups can have members from any domain in the forest. Rooslan's first action accomplishes the primary goal. Rooslan's second action accomplishes the first secondary goal. Because Rooslan institutes no restricted Group Policy, the second secondary goal is not accomplished.

E. **Incorrect:** Universal groups are visible in all domains in a forest configured at the Windows Server 2003 functional level. Universal groups can be added to computer local groups, such as the administrators groups on member servers. Universal groups can have members from any domain in the forest. Rooslan's first action accomplishes the primary goal. Rooslan's second action accomplishes the first secondary goal. Because Rooslan institutes no restricted Group Policy, the second secondary goal is not accomplished.

F. **Incorrect:** Universal groups are visible in all domains in a forest configured at the Windows Server 2003 functional level. Universal groups can be added to computer local groups, such as the administrators groups on member servers. Universal groups can have members from any domain in the forest. Rooslan's first action accomplishes the primary goal. Rooslan's second action accomplishes the first secondary goal. Because Rooslan institutes no restricted Group Policy, the second secondary goal is not accomplished.

Objective 4.3

Plan and Configure Authorization

Permissions allow users and groups to access resources. Permissions are configured though access control lists (ACLs). ACLs can be configured for user or group objects. Often a user will be a member of more than one group that is assigned permissions to a resource. Working out the permissions for a user in such a situation can be accomplished by using the effective permissions tools. Permissions can be assigned at a share level, in addition to NTFS permissions. Share level permissions are not as detailed as file and folder permissions. When users access a resource by means of a share, they are assigned whichever of the share and the NTFS permissions are more restrictive.

Rights allow users to perform tasks. Rights are configured by means of local policy or Group Policy objects applied at the domain, site, or organizational unit (OU) level. Rights enable users to perform actions, such as logging on locally to a computer. By using Group Policy settings, you can prevent a particular group of users from logging on to a particular set of computers. Because there are many rights, the actions that different groups of users can and cannot perform on a network can be controlled with precision.

Objective 4.3 Questions

1. Your organization consists of three Active Directory forests running Windows Server 2003. The forests are all configured at the Windows Server 2003 functional level. Each of the three forests has a single domain tree. The first forest's root domain is adatum.com. The first forest hosts the child domains western.adatum.com and northern.adatum.com. The second forest's root domain is proseware.com. The second forest hosts the child domains sydney.proseware.com, adelaide.proseware.com, and melbourne.proseware.com. The third forest's root domain is contoso.com. The third forest hosts only a single child domain, node.contoso.com. Forest trust relationships exist between the first and the second forests and between the second and third forests. A two-way external trust relationship exists between northern.adatum.com and contoso.com.

   You are configuring the folder permissions for a file server located in the node.contoso.com domain. Which of the following users and groups will you be able to assign permissions to? (Select all that apply.)

   A. Global groups created in the contoso.com domain

   B. Global groups created in the northern.adatum.com domain

   C. Universal groups created in the melbourne.proseware.com domain

   D. Global groups created in the adelaide.proseware.com domain

   E. Universal groups created in the western.adatum.com domain

2. You are configuring permissions for an important file share on a member server running Windows Server 2003 in the resources.proseware.com domain. The resources.proseware.com domain is a member of the forest that has proseware.com as its root domain. The adatum.com and contoso.com domain trees are also members of the same forest as the proseware.com tree. The proseware.com forest is running at the Windows Server 2003 functional level.

   The user principal names (UPNs) of specific users are as follows:

   Rooslan rooslan@core.adatum.com

   Foley foley@users.proseware.com

   Mick mick@cheltenham.contoso.com

   Laherty laherty@blackburn.contoso.com

Rooslan is a member of the Easternsub universal group that was created in the eastern.adatum.com domain. Foley and Mick are members of the Bayside universal group that was created in the core.proseware.com domain. Laherty is a member of the Northsub universal group that was created in the core.contoso.com domain. Two domain local groups have been created in the resources.proseware.com domain. The first domain local group, which is named Chatter, includes in its membership the Easternsub universal group. The second domain local group, which is named Redux, includes in its membership the Northsub and Bayside universal groups.

Share and folder permissions for the important file share are as follows:

User or Group	Permission
Chatter	Read (Allow)
Redux	Change (Allow)
Easternsub	Full Control (Allow)
Bayside	Modify (Allow)
Northsub	Write (Allow)
mick@cheltenham.contoso.com	Full Control (Deny)

Given this set of permissions, which of the users will be able to delete a file named test.xls that is located in this file share and subject to the permissions listed above?

A. Rooslan

B. Foley

C. Mick

D. Laherty

E. None of the above

3. Agim is the systems administrator for the department of arts at the local University. He has spoken with his manager James about problems that the department has been having with students accessing computers that they are not supposed to access. Some students have been attempting to access staff files on the three departmental file servers. It has also been noted that some academic staff members allow their postgraduate students to log on to their computers when they are not in the office. Finally, some undergraduate students are using the postgraduate computer lab for network access when there are no available computers in the undergraduate lab.

The faculty has a single Windows Server 2003 forest that contains only one domain. All departmental file servers are located in the Memberserv OU. The user accounts of all students, both undergraduate and postgraduate, are stored in the Students OU. All staff computer accounts are stored in the Staffwkstn OU. All computer accounts for the postgraduate lab are in the Postgradlab OU, and all computer accounts for the undergraduate lab are in the Undergradlab OU. All postgraduate students are members of the Postgrad domain global group. All undergraduate students are members of the Undergrad domain global group.

To address his concerns, James creates the following list of goals for Agim to implement:

Primary goal: Deny network access to the three departmental file servers to all user accounts in the Students OU.

First secondary goal: Deny all postgraduate students the ability to log on locally to a staff member's computer.

Second secondary goal: Deny all undergraduate students the ability to log on locally to computers in the postgraduate laboratory.

Agim performs the following actions:

He creates a GPO and applies it to the Staffwkstn OU. In the \Computer Configuration\Windows Settings\Security Settings\Local Policies\User Rights Assignment node, he configures the Deny Log On Locally policy to include the Postgrad and Undergrad groups.

He creates a GPO and applies it to the Postgradlab OU. In the \Computer Configuration\Windows Settings\Security Settings\Local Policies\User Rights Assignment node, he configures the Deny Log On Locally policy to include the Undergrad group.

He creates a GPO and applies it to the Memberserv OU. In the \Computer Configuration\Windows Settings\Security Settings\Local Policies\User Rights Assignment node, he configures the Deny Log On Locally policy to include the Undergrad and Postgrad groups.

After Agim has performed these actions, which of James' goals has he achieved?

- **A.** Agim has achieved the primary goal and both secondary goals.
- **B.** Agim has achieved the primary goal and one secondary goal.
- **C.** Agim has achieved the primary goal only.
- **D.** Agim has achieved both secondary goals. Agim has not achieved the primary goal.
- **E.** Agim has achieved one of the secondary goals. Agim has not achieved the primary goal.

4. You are responsible for training a group of interns in the art of systems administration. All of the interns are members of the Interns group. This week you want them to be able to log on to the member servers in your domain and make a backup. They don't need to be able to restore any files. They should log on to each member server by using Remote Desktop. They should be restricted from logging on to each server locally.

   You don't want to add them to the Backup Operators group. Rather, you want to alter the rights assigned to the Interns group. You want to do this by editing a GPO applied to the OU that hosts the member servers in your domain and applying policies located in the \Computer Configuration\Windows Settings\Security Settings\User Rights Assignment node. Which of the following are the minimum rights that you should assign to the Interns group by editing policies in this node? (Select all that apply.)

   A. Back Up Files And Directories

   B. Bypass Traverse Checking

   C. Deny Log on Locally

   D. Allow Log On Through Terminal Services

   E. Impersonate A Client After Authentication

   F. Load And Unload Device Drivers

5. You want to calculate a user's permissions with the least possible administrative effort. The user is a member of several groups that are assigned permissions to a particular folder. What should you do?

   A. Calculate the permissions manually.

   B. Use the Effective Permissions tool.

   C. From the command line, run the `cacls` tool with the `/showperms` user@domain-name switch.

   D. Use the Security Configuration And Analysis tool.

Objective 4.3 Answers

1. **Correct Answers: C and D**

   A. **Incorrect:** The fact that all forests are configured at the Windows Server 2003 functional level implies that all domains in the forest are also configured at the Windows Server 2003 functional level. At this level, global groups from domains in the same forest can be assigned permissions to shared folders.

   B. **Incorrect:** Although a two-way external trust relationship exists between northern.adatum.com and contoso.com, that trust doesn't filter down to the child domain node.contoso.com. There is no forest trust relationship between the adatum.com and contoso.com forests. Even though there are trust relationships between both adatum.com and contoso.com with the proseware.com forest, forest trusts are not transitive.

   C. **Correct:** Because a forest trust relationship exists between the contoso.com forest and the proseware.com forest, universal groups created in the proseware.com domain can be assigned permissions to local resources.

   D. **Correct:** Global groups from trusted forests can be assigned permissions to local resources.

   E. **Incorrect:** Although a two-way external trust relationship exists between northern.adatum.com and contoso.com, that trust doesn't filter down to the node.contoso.com child domain or to the western.adatum.com domain. There is no forest trust relationship between the adatum.com and contoso.com forests. Even though there are trust relationships between both adatum.com and contoso.com with the proseware.com forest, forest trusts are not transitive.

2. **Correct Answers: B**

   A. **Incorrect:** Rooslan is a member of the Easternsub and Chatter groups. At the share level, his permission will be Read (Allow). At the NTFS level, his permission will be Full Control (Allow). The effective overall permission is the most restrictive of the share and NTFS permissions, which leaves his permission at Read.

   B. **Correct:** Foley is a member of the Bayside and Redux groups. At the share level, his permission will be Change (Allow). At the NTFS level, his permission will be Modify (Allow). Both of these permissions allow for the deletion of files, hence Foley will be able to delete the file named test.xls.

   C. **Incorrect:** Mick is a member of the Bayside and Redux groups. At the share level, his permission will be Change (Allow). At the NTFS level, his permission will be Full Control (Deny) because a permission is set explicitly for his account. A deny permission overrides other set permissions. Mick will be unable to delete the test.xls file.

D. Incorrect: Laherty is a member of the Northsub and Redux groups. At the share level, his permission will be Change (Allow). At the NTFS level, his permission will be Write (Allow). Of these permissions, Write (Allow) is more restrictive. Laherty will be unable to delete the test.xls file.

E. Incorrect: Foley has access, hence this answer is incorrect.

3. Correct Answers: D

A. Incorrect: Agim correctly restricts postgraduate students from logging on locally to computers in the Staffwkstn OU. This meets the first secondary goal. He also restricts undergraduate students, but this is irrelevant to the question. Agim correctly restricts undergraduate students from logging on to computers in the Postgradlab OU. This meets the second secondary goal. Agim does not restrict network access to the departmental file servers to the students; he merely denies them the ability to log on locally. This means that he has not met the primary goal.

B. Incorrect: Agim correctly restricts postgraduate students from logging on locally to computers in the Staffwkstn OU. This meets the first secondary goal. He also restricts undergraduate students, but this is irrelevant to the question. Agim correctly restricts undergraduate students from logging on to computers in the Postgradlab OU. This meets the second secondary goal. Agim does not restrict network access to the departmental file servers to the students; he merely denies them the ability to log on locally. This means that he has not met the primary goal.

C. Incorrect: Agim correctly restricts postgraduate students from logging on locally to computers in the Staffwkstn OU. This meets the first secondary goal. He also restricts undergraduate students, but this is irrelevant to the question. Agim correctly restricts undergraduate students from logging on to computers in the Postgradlab OU. This meets the second secondary goal. Agim does not restrict network access to the departmental file servers to the students; he merely denies them the ability to log on locally. This means that he has not met the primary goal.

D. Correct: Agim correctly restricts postgraduate students from logging on locally to computers in the Staffwkstn OU. This meets the first secondary goal. He also restricts undergraduate students, but this is irrelevant to the question. Agim correctly restricts undergraduate students from logging on to computers in the Postgradlab OU. This meets the second secondary goal. Agim does not restrict network access to the departmental file servers to the students; he merely denies them the ability to log on locally. This means that he has not met the primary goal.

E. Incorrect: Agim correctly restricts postgraduate students from logging on locally to computers in the Staffwkstn OU. This meets the first secondary goal. He also restricts undergraduate students, but this is irrelevant to the question. Agim correctly restricts undergraduate students from logging on to computers in the Postgradlab OU. This meets the second secondary goal. Agim does not restrict network access to the departmental file servers to the students; he merely denies them the ability to log on locally. This means that he has not met the primary goal.

4. Correct Answers: A, C, and D

A. Correct: This policy will allow the members of the Interns group to back up files and folders.

B. Incorrect: This policy is not required to achieve your goals for the Interns group. The abilities granted in this policy are already built into the Back Up Files And Directories policy.

C. Correct: This will meet the requirement that members of the Interns group should not be able to log on locally to the member servers in your domain.

D. Correct: This policy is required if members of the Interns group are to be able to log on by using the Remote Desktop protocol.

E. Incorrect: This policy is not required to achieve your goals for the Interns group.

F. Incorrect: This policy is not required to achieve your goals for the Interns group.

5. Correct Answers: B

A. Incorrect: The Effective Permissions tool, which you can access by clicking the Advanced button on the Security tab of the folder's properties dialog box, can calculate the effective permissions of a user.

B. Correct: The Effective Permissions tool, which you can access by clicking the Advanced button on the Security tab of the folder's properties dialog box, can calculate the effective permissions of a user.

C. Incorrect: The cacls tool does not have this functionality.

D. Incorrect: The Security Configuration And Analysis tool does not have this functionality.

Objective 4.4

Install, Manage, and Configure Certificate Services

Certificate Services form the basis of a public key infrastructure. A computer running Windows Server 2003 that has certificate services installed is known as a certification authority (CA). Windows Server 2003 supports four types of CAs. Enterprise root CAs are the first CAs installed in a forest. They can issue certificates directly, though it is a better practice to allow the second type of CA—the enterprise subordinate CA—to issue certificates in the root's place. Enterprise CAs are heavily integrated with Active Directory and cannot be installed on standalone computers running Windows Server 2003 that are not members of the domain. The other two types of CA are the standalone root and the standalone subordinate CAs. These CAs can exist independently of Active Directory. If they are installed in an Active Directory environment, they can make use of Active Directory; however, they will not be able to automatically issue certificates to Active Directory users in the way that an enterprise root CA can. Because CAs play such a fundamental role in the public key infrastructure (PKI) infrastructure, they must be backed up periodically. If a root CA is lost and no backup exists, all certificates that it has issued, in addition to those issued by subordinate CAs, will become invalid.

Objective 4.4 Questions

1. Which of the following restrictions apply to the installation of an enterprise root CA? (Select all that apply.)

   A. Must be installed in the root domain of a forest.

   B. Must be installed on a domain controller.

   C. Requires that a certificate be obtained from a commercial CA.

   D. Requires that Active Directory be present.

   E. The server running the enterprise root CA cannot change its name or domain membership.

   F. Should not be installed on any node in a server cluster.

2. Rooslan is the systems administrator for the local university's department of arts. The department has an Active Directory forest that has a child domain for each department. The department of arts forest has a forest trust relationship with the university administration's Active Directory forest. The root domain of the university administration's forest has an enterprise root CA and two enterprise subordinate CAs. The science department wants Rooslan to install a CA that is integrated with Active Directory so that certificates can be issued automatically. In this situation, which of the following statements is true?

   A. Rooslan can install an enterprise subordinate CA on a member server in the science domain by using the forest trust relationship with the administration's forest to obtain a certificate from the administration enterprise root CA.

   B. Rooslan can install an enterprise subordinate CA on a member server in the science domain by using the forest trust relationship with the administration's forest to obtain a certificate from the administration enterprise subordinate CA.

   C. Rooslan can install an enterprise root CA in the science department's child domain.

   D. Rooslan can install a standalone root CA on a standalone server located on the same subnet as the science child domain.

   E. Rooslan can install a standalone root CA on a member server in the science child domain.

3. You are the certificate administrator for the proseware.com forest. The proseware.com forest has a forest trust configured with the adatum.com forest. The certificate administrator of the adatum.com forest wants to set up an enterprise subordinate CA based on a certificate issued by the enterprise root CA in the proseware.com forest. The adatum.com certificate administrator has given you a disk containing a certificate request file named subca.adatum.com.req.

   Which of the following methods do you need to use to provide the certificate administrator of the adatum.com forest with a certificate that the administrator can use for his or her enterprise subordinate CA?

   A. Run the Certificate Approval Wizard, and select the subca.adatum.com.req file on the disk. Store the approved certificate on the disk.

   B. The certificate request file is unnecessary because a forest trust relationship exists between the proseware.com forest and the adatum.com forest.

   C. On the enterprise root CA, right-click the server, select All Tasks, and then select Submit New Request. Load the subca.adatum.com.req file. Save the approved certificate back to the disk.

   D. Insert the disk into the drive on the enterprise root CA. In Windows Explorer, right-click the certificate and then select Approve.

4. Which of the following methods can you use to back up a CA's private key, CA certificate, certificate database, and certificate database log? (Select all that apply.)

   A. In the Certificate Authority MMC, right-click the CA and, on the All Tasks menu, click Back Up CA. When the wizard runs, ensure that the Private Key and CA Certificate check boxes, in addition to the Certificate Database and Certificate Database Log check boxes, are selected. When prompted, enter a backup password.

   B. Run the `certutil -backup backupdirectory` command from the command line, and enter the backup password when prompted.

   C. Copy the contents of the C:\%systemroot%\system32\certsrv and certlog directories to a network share.

   D. In the Certificate Authority MMC, right-click the CA and then click Export List.

5. You are the systems administrator of the contoso.internal domain. You have just installed an enterprise root CA on a member server running Windows Server 2003. You want to enable key recovery by means of an account you've created with the UPN keymaster@contoso.internal. Which of the following steps will you need to take to allow this to occur? (Select all that apply.)

A. Use the Run As command to run an MMC with the UPN keymaster@contoso.internal. Add the Certificates snap-in with the focus on the current user. From the Personal node, run the Certificate Request Wizard and request a Key Recovery Agent certificate.

B. Use the Run As command to run an MMC with the UPN keymaster@contoso.internal. Add the Certificates snap-in with the focus on the current user. From the Personal node, run the Certificate Request Wizard and request an Administrator certificate.

C. In the Certification Authority MMC, right-click the Certificate Templates node and then select New Certificate Template To Issue. Select the EFS Recovery Agent certificate template.

D. Edit the properties of the Key Recovery Agent certificate template in the Certificate Templates MMC. On the Security tab, add the keymaster@contoso.internal account, and ensure that it has the Read and Enroll permissions. On the Issuance Requirements tab, clear the CA Certificate Manager Approval check box.

E. In the Certification Authority MMC, right-click the Certificate Templates node and then select New Certificate Template To Issue. Select the Key Recovery Agent certificate template.

F. In the Certification Authority MMC, right-click the CA. Click the Recovery Agents tab. Click Archive The Key, leaving the number of recovery agents to use as 1. Click Add, and then select the keymaster@contoso.internal account. Install the certificate. Click OK and allow Certificate Services to restart.

Objective 4.4 Answers

1. Correct Answers: D, E, and F

A. **Incorrect:** An enterprise root CA must be installed by a user with enterprise administrator privileges. This does not, however, restrict an enterprise root CA from being installed in a child domain within a forest.

B. **Incorrect:** An enterprise root CA can be installed on a member server. An enterprise root CA cannot be installed on a standalone server because there would be no access to Active Directory.

C. **Incorrect:** An enterprise root CA generates its own root certificate. It does not require a root certificate from another organization, such as a commercial CA.

D. **Correct:** An enterprise root CA requires that Active Directory be present.

E. **Correct:** When an enterprise root CA is installed, the computer name and domain membership cannot be changed because this information is bound to Active Directory. Changing the name would invalidate the certificates issued by the CA.

F. **Correct:** Microsoft recommends against installing Certificate Services on any node in a server cluster because this will prevent the service from running correctly.

2. Correct Answers: C

A. **Incorrect:** A forest trust relationship will not allow a certificate to be automatically issued to a subordinate CA in a separate forest. The trust relationship between domains in the same forest will allow an enterprise root CA to issue a certificate to an enterprise subordinate CA located in a child domain.

B. **Incorrect:** A forest trust relationship will not allow a certificate to be automatically issued to a subordinate CA in a separate forest.

C. **Correct:** Enterprise root CAs can be installed in child domains and in root domains. You can have an enterprise root CA in a child domain and have a subordinate and issuing CA in the root domain of a forest.

D. **Incorrect:** A standalone root CA installed on a standalone server will not integrate with Active Directory.

E. **Incorrect:** A standalone root CA installed on a member server will not automatically issue certificates based on information located in Active Directory.

3. **Correct Answers: C**

   A. **Incorrect:** There is no Certificate Approval Wizard.

   B. **Incorrect:** Although you can request a certificate from an enterprise root CA in a trusted forest when you are setting up an enterprise subordinate CA, this request will automatically be denied by the policy module on the enterprise root CA. If a certificate is issued, it must be issued manually.

   C. **Correct:** Although it might seem counter-intuitive to use Submit New Request to approve a request, this is the method by which request files can be approved as certificates. This certificate can now be imported into the enterprise subordinate CA, though during the process the enterprise root CA from the other forest must be explicitly trusted.

   D. **Incorrect:** This method cannot be used to approve a certificate.

4. **Correct Answers: A and B**

   A. **Correct:** This is one method that can be used to back up the CA's private key, CA certificate, certificate database, and certificate database log.

   B. **Correct:** This method will also work. It can also be scripted to occur at regular intervals.

   C. **Incorrect:** This will not correctly back up the private key, CA certificate, certificate database, and certificate database log.

   D. **Incorrect:** This will not correctly back up the private key, CA certificate, certificate database, and certificate database log.

5. **Correct Answers: A, D, E, and F**

   A. **Correct:** This will force the enterprise root CA to issue a Key Recovery Agent certificate to the keymaster@contoso.internal account.

   B. **Incorrect:** This step is not required. The keymaster@contoso.internal account requires a Key Recovery Agent certificate rather than an Administrator certificate.

   C. **Incorrect:** By default, Windows Server 2003 CAs are already able to issue EFS Recovery Agent certificates. An EFS Recovery Agent certificate cannot be used as a Key Recovery Agent on a Windows Server 2003 enterprise root CA.

   D. **Correct:** This allows the keymaster@contoso.internal account to request and enroll itself in this particular type of certificate without the intervention of the CA certificate manager.

   E. **Correct:** This allows key recovery agent certificates to be issued by the enterprise root CA.

   F. **Correct:** This is the final step in setting up a recovery agent: selecting an account that has the correct Key Recovery Agent certificate installed, installing that certificate, and then restarting Certificate Services.

Glossary

access control entry (ACE) An entry in an object's access control list that grants permissions to a user or group.

access control list (ACL) A collection of access control entries that collectively defines the access that all users and groups have to an object.

application policies Also known as *extended key usage* or *enhanced key usage*. Application policies give you the ability to specify which certificates can be used for specific purposes. This allows you to issue certificates widely without being concerned that they will be used for an unintended purpose.

authentication The process of verifying the identity of something or someone. Authentication usually involves a user name and a password, but it can include any method of demonstrating identity, such as smart cards, retinal scans, voice recognition, or fingerprinting.

Authentication Header (AH) An IP Security (IPSec) protocol that provides authentication and data integrity but does not provide encryption.

authorization The process of determining whether an identified user or process is permitted access to a resource, and determining the appropriate level of access for the user. The owner of a resource, or someone who has been granted permission, determines whether a user is in a predetermined group or has a certain level of security clearance. By setting the permissions on a resource, the owner controls which users and groups on the network can access the resource.

Background Intelligent Transfer Service (BITS) A service that transfers data from the Software Update Services or Windows Update server to the Automatic Updates client with minimal impact to other network services.

certificate revocation list (CRL) A document maintained and published by a certification authority (CA) that lists certificates that have been revoked. A CRL is signed with the private key of the CA to ensure its integrity.

certificate template permissions Permissions that define the security principals that can read, modify, or enroll certificates based on certificate templates.

certificate templates The sets of rules and settings that define the format and content of a certificate, based on its intended use.

certificate-to-account mapping A feature of Microsoft Windows Server 2003 that enables IP Security (IPSec) to verify that a certificate matches a valid computer account in the Active Directory forest.

Challenge Handshake Authentication Protocol (CHAP) A challenge-response authentication protocol for Point to Point Protocol (PPP) connections, documented in Request for Comments (RFC) 1994, that uses the industry-standard Message Digest (MD5) one-way encryption scheme to hash the response to a challenge issued by the remote access server.

critical update A broadly released fix addressing a critical non-security-related bug for a specific problem.

denial-of-service attack An attack that prevents users from using network resources.

digital certificate A certificate that provides information about the subject of the certificate, the validity of the certificate, and the applications and services that will use the certificate. A digital certificate also provides a way to identify the holder of the certificate.

digital certificate life cycle When a certificate is issued, it passes through various phases and remains valid for a certain period of time. This is called *certificate lifetime.*

dynamic WEP A term used to describe Wired Equivalent Privacy (WEP) when it has been configured to automatically change the shared secret in order to limit the amount of encrypted data an attacker can capture for cryptoanalysis.

Encapsulating Security Payload (ESP) An IPSec protocol that provides authentication, data integrity, and encryption.

exploit A worm, virus, Trojan horse, or other tool that can be used by an attacker to compromise a vulnerable computer.

Extensible Authentication Protocol (EAP) An authentication method primarily used to provide authentication based on smart cards or public key certificates. EAP is supported by Microsoft Windows Server 2003, Microsoft Windows XP, and Windows 2000.

Extensible Authentication Protocol-Transport Layer Security (EAP-TLS) An authentication method that enables clients to authenticate by using a public key certificate.

filter action Configuration settings that specify the behavior that an IP security policy takes on filtered traffic.

firewall A system that creates a boundary between a public and a private network.

fully qualified domain name (FQDN) The host name and domain used to uniquely identify a computer on the Internet, such as www.microsoft.com.

Group Policy A mechanism for storing many types of policy data, for example, file deployment, application deployment, logon/logoff scripts and startup/shutdown scripts, domain security, and Internet Protocol security. The collections of policies are referred to as Group Policy objects (GPOs).

Group Policy object (GPO) The Group Policy settings that administrators create are contained in GPOs, which are in turn associated with selected Active Directory containers: sites, domains, and organizational units (OUs).

hotfix A single package composed of one or more files used to address a problem in a product. Hotfixes address a specific customer situation and are only available through a support relationship with Microsoft. They cannot be distributed outside the customer organization without written legal consent from Microsoft. The terms *QFE* (Quick Fix Engineering update), *patch*, and *update* have been used in the past as synonyms for *hotfix*.

IP filter list A series of IP filters that IP security policies use to identify traffic that should be ignored or acted upon.

Kerberos The default authentication protocol for Windows 2000 and Windows XP Professional. The Kerberos protocol is designed to be more secure and scalable across large, diverse networks.

Layer Two Tunneling Protocol (L2TP) A standardized RFC-based tunneling Virutal Private Network (VPN) protocol. L2TP relies on IP Security (IPSec) for encryption services.

least privilege A fundamental security principal wherein the administrator makes an effort to grant users only the minimal permissions they need to do their job.

Main Mode Phase 1 of the IP Security (IPSec) negotiation process. Main Mode negotiation selects a protection suite that both the client and server support, authenticates the computers, and then establishes the master key for the IPSec session.

man-in-the-middle attack A security attack in which an attacker intercepts and possibly modifies data that is transmitted between two users. To each user, the attacker pretends to be the other user. During a successful man-in-the-middle attack, the users are unaware that there is an attacker between them who is intercepting and modifying their data. Also referred to as a *bucket brigade attack*.

Microsoft Challenge Handshake Authentication Protocol (MS-CHAP) An encrypted authentication mechanism for Point to Point Protocol (PPP) connections. MS-CHAP is similar to CHAP. The remote access server sends to the remote access client a challenge that consists of a session ID and an arbitrary challenge string. The remote access client must return the user name and a Message Digest 4 (MD4) hash of the challenge string, the session ID, and the MD4-hashed password. MS-CHAP v2 improves on MS-CHAP v1 by offering mutual authentication for both the client and the server.

multiple-function template A certificate template that is used for multiple functions. For example, you can use a single user certificate template to encrypt and decrypt files, to authenticate with a server, and to send and receive secure e-mail.

NTLM protocol A service that uses a challenge-response mechanism to authenticate users and computers running Windows ME and earlier, or computers running Windows 2000 and later that are not part of a domain.

packet filter A basic function of firewalls that examines incoming and outgoing packets and drops packets based on predefined criteria, such as port numbers, source IP address, and destination IP address.

Password Authentication Protocol (PAP) A simple plaintext authentication scheme for authenticating Point to Point Protocol (PPP) connections. The user name and password are requested by the remote access server and returned by the remote access client in plaintext.

perimeter network A small network that is set up separately from an organization's private network and the Internet. A perimeter network provides a layer of protection for internal systems in the event that a system offering services to the Internet is compromised. Also known as a *demilitarized zone (DMZ)* or a *screened subnet.*

Point-to-Point Protocol (PPP) An industry-standard suite of protocols for the use of point-to-point links to transport multiprotocol datagrams. PPP is primarily used to connect dial-up users to a remote access server. PPP is documented in Request for Comments (RFC) 1661.

Point-to-Point Tunneling Protocol (PPTP) A virtual private network (VPN) protocol designed by Microsoft and based on Point to Point Protocol (PPP). PPTP relies on Microsoft Point-to-Point Encryption (MPPE) for encryption services.

Protected Extensible Authentication Protocol (PEAP) A two-phase authentication method that protects the privacy of user authentication by using Transporter Level Security (TLS).

Quick Mode Phase 2 of the IP Security (IPSec) negotiation process. Quick Mode negotiation occurs after Main Mode negotiation to establish a session key to be used for encryption until the next Quick Mode negotiation is scheduled to occur.

Remote Access Dial-In User Server (RADIUS) A standardized service that network equipment, such as a Wireless Access Protocol (WAP), can use to authenticate users.

Secure Sockets Layer (SSL) An open standard for encrypting network communications and authenticating clients or servers.

security rollup package A collection of security patches, critical updates, other updates, and hotfixes released as a cumulative offering or targeted at a single product component, such as Internet Information Services (IIS) or Microsoft Internet Explorer. Allows for easier deployment of multiple software updates.

security template A physical file representation of a security configuration that can be applied to a local computer or imported to a Group Policy Object (GPO) in Active Directory. When you import a security template to a GPO, Group Policy processes the template and makes the corresponding changes to the members of that GPO, which can be users or computers.

security update A broadly released fix that addresses a security vulnerability for a specific product. A security patch is often described as having a *severity*, which actually refers to the Microsoft Security Response Center (MSRC) severity rating of the vulnerability that the security patch addresses.

service pack A cumulative set of hotfixes, security patches, critical updates, and other updates that have been released since the release of the product, including many resolved problems that have not been made available through any other software updates. Service packs might also contain a limited number of customer-requested design changes or features. Service packs are broadly distributed and are more thoroughly tested by Microsoft than any other software updates.

Service Set Identifier (SSID) The name of the wireless network that is used by the client to identify the correct settings and credential type to use for the wireless network.

shared secret The password that the wireless clients, the Wireless Access Protocol (WAP), and often the RADIUS server have access to. The shared secret is used to build the encryption key.

Shiva Password Authentication Protocol (SPAP) A two-way, reversible encryption mechanism for authenticating Point to Point Protocol (PPP) connections employed by Shiva remote access servers.

single-function template A certificate template that is highly restricted and can only be used for a single function.

slipstreaming The process of integrating a service pack into operating system setup files so that new computers immediately have the service pack installed.

special groups Groups created by Windows Server 2003 whose membership is dynamic and determined by the way a user interacts with the system.

static WEP A term used to describe the traditional implementation of Wired Equivalent Privacy (WEP), in which a shared secret is manually configured and does not change on a regular basis.

subject name The subject name listed in an Secure Socket Layer (SSL) certificate. If the subject name in the certificate does not exactly match the name in the user's browser, the browser will display a warning message.

system policy Used by system administrators to control user and computer configurations for operating systems prior to Windows 2000 from a single location on a network. System policies propagate registry settings to a large number of computers without requiring the administrator to have detailed knowledge of the registry.

Transport Layer Security (TLS) A method for encrypting tunneled traffic to protect the privacy of communications.

transport mode An IP Security (IPSec) mode wherein only a portion of the packet, including the Transport and Application layer data, is encapsulated by IPSec. Used to provide IPSec protection for communications between two hosts.

trusts The mechanisms that ensure that users who are authenticated in their own domains can access resources in any trusted domain.

tunnel mode An IP Security (IPSec) mode wherein IPSec encapsulates entire packets. Used to provide IPSec protection for communications to a network with multiple hosts.

update A broadly released fix for a specific problem. Addresses a non-critical, non-security-related bug.

Wi-Fi Protected Access (WPA) A method for encrypting wireless communications that improves upon the privacy provided by Wired Equivalent Privacy (WEP).

Wired Equivalent Privacy (WEP) A method for encrypting wireless communications that is standardized and widely deployed, but that suffers from serious well-exploited vulnerabilities.

Index

Numeric

A

B

C

D

F

G

H

K

N

O

P

S

W

Z

Hardware Requirements

Each computer must have the following minimum configuration. All hardware should be on the Microsoft Windows Server 2003 Hardware Compatibility List.

- Computer with 550 MHz or higher processor recommended; 133 MHz minimum required in the Intel Pentium/Celeron family or the AMD K6/Athlon/Duron family
- 256 MB RAM or higher recommended; 128 MB minimum required memory
- 1.25 to 2 GB free hard disk space
- CD-ROM drive or DVD-ROM drive
- Super VGA (800x600) or higher-resolution monitor recommended; VGA or hardware that supports console redirection required
- Keyboard and Microsoft Mouse or compatible pointing device or hardware that supports console redirection

Additionally, one of the chapters requires you to have a wireless access point available.

Software Requirements

- Microsoft Windows Server 2003

For some exercises, you will need the following:

- Microsoft Windows XP to simulate a network client operating system
- Microsoft Exchange Server 2000 or later
- Microsoft SQL Server 2000 or later

MCSA and MCSE for Microsoft Windows Server 200

The Microsoft Certified Systems Engineer (MCSE) credential is the premier certification for professionals who analyze the business requirements and design and implement the infras ture for business solutions based on the Microsoft® Windows Server™ 2003 platform and Microsoft Windows Server System. Implementation responsibilities include installing, co uring, and troubleshooting network systems.

The Microsoft Certified Systems Administrator (MCSA) credential proves that you have the skills to successfully implement, manage, and troubleshoot the ongoing needs of Windo Server 2003–based operating environments.

For information on study materials, training, and certification for Microsoft Windows Server 2003, please visit: **www.microsoft.com/traincert**.

MCSA/MCSE Core Requirements

MCSA

Three core exams, including:

- Two Networking System exams
- One Client Operating System exam

MCSE

Six core exams, including:

- Four Networking System exams
- One Client Operating System exam
- One Design exam

Networking System Exams

MCSA (Two Exams Required)	MCSE (Four Exams Required)	Core Exams: Networking System	Microsoft Press® Study Materials	ISBN
✓	✓	Exam 70-290: Managing and Maintaining a Microsoft Windows Server 2003 Environment	MCSA/MCSE Self-Paced Training Kit (Exam 70-290): Managing and Maintaining a Microsoft Windows Server 2003 Environment	0-7356-1437-7
			MCSE Self-Paced Training Kit: Microsoft Windows Server 2003 Core Requirements, Exams 70-290, 70-291, 70-293, 70-294	0-7356-1953-0
✓	✓	Exam 70-291: Implementing, Managing, and Maintaining a Microsoft Windows Server 2003 Network Infrastructure	MCSA/MCSE Self-Paced Training Kit (Exam 70-291): Implementing, Managing and Maintaining a Microsoft Windows Server 2003 Network Infrastructure	0-7356-1439-3
			MCSE Self-Paced Training Kit: Microsoft Windows Server 2003 Core Requirements, Exams 70-290, 70-291, 70-293, 70-294	0-7356-1953-0
N/A	✓	Exam 70-293: Planning and Maintaining a Microsoft Windows Server 2003 Network Infrastructure	MCSE Self-Paced Training Kit (Exam 70-293): Planning and Maintaining a Microsoft Windows Server 2003 Network Infrastructure	0-7356-1893-3
			MCSE Self-Paced Training Kit: Microsoft Windows Server 2003 Core Requirements, Exams 70-290, 70-291, 70-293, 70-294	0-7356-1953-0
N/A	✓	Exam 70-294: Planning, Implementing, and Maintaining a Microsoft Windows Server 2003 Active Directory® Infrastructure	MCSE Self-Paced Training Kit (Exam 70-294): Planning, Implementing, and Maintaining a Microsoft Windows Server 2003 Active Directory Infrastructure	0-7356-1438-5
			MCSE Self-Paced Training Kit: Microsoft Windows Server 2003 Core Requirements, Exams 70-290, 70-291, 70-293, 70-294	0-7356-1953-0

Client Operating System Exams

MCSA (Choose One)	MCSE (Choose One)	Core Exams: Client Operating System	Microsoft Press Study Materials	ISBN
✓	✓	Exam 70-270: Installing, Configuring, and Administering Microsoft Windows® XP Professional	MCSE Training Kit (Exam 70-270): Windows XP Professional	0-7356-1429-6
✓	✓	Exam 70-210[1]: Installing, Configuring, and Administering Microsoft Windows 2000 Professional	MCSA/MCSE Self-Paced Training Kit (Exam 70-210): Microsoft Windows 2000 Professional, Second Edition	0-7356-1766-X

Design Exams

MCSA (Not Applicable)	MCSE (Choose One)	Core Exams: Design	Microsoft Press Study Materials	ISBN
N/A	✓	Exam 70-297[2]: Designing a Microsoft Windows Server 2003 Active Directory and Network Infrastructure	MCSE Self-Paced Training Kit (Exam 70-297): Designing a Microsoft Windows Server 2003 Active Directory and Network Infrastructure	0-7356-1970-0
N/A	✓	Exam 70-298[2]: Designing Security for a Microsoft Windows Server 2003 Network	MCSE Self-Paced Training Kit (Exam 70-298): Designing Security for a Microsoft Windows Server 2003 Network	0-7356-1969-7

1 Candidates who passed Windows NT 4.0 Exams 70-067, 70-068, and 70-073 had the option to take the comprehensive Exam 70-240: Microsoft Windows 2000 Accelerated Ex for MCPs Certified on Microsoft Windows NT 4.0. By passing this exam, candidates met the MCSE exam requirement for 70-210. Exam 70-240 is no longer available.

2 Exams 70-297 and 70-298 may each count once as either one core design exam or one elective exam.